THE ACTIVE ROLE OF COURTS IN CONSUMER LITIGATION

AF775474

# THE ACTIVE ROLE OF COURTS IN CONSUMER LITIGATION

## Applying EU Law of the National Courts' Own Motion

Anthi BEKA

intersentia
Cambridge – Antwerp – Chicago

Intersentia Ltd
Sheraton House | Castle Park
Cambridge | CB3 0AX | United Kingdom
Tel.: +44 1223 370 170 | Fax: +44 1223 370 169
Email: mail@intersentia.co.uk
www.intersentia.com | www.intersentia.co.uk

*Distribution for the UK and Ireland:*
NBN International
Airport Business Centre, 10 Thornbury Road
Plymouth, PL6 7PP
United Kingdom
Tel.: +44 1752 202 301 | Fax: +44 1752 202 331
Email: orders@nbninternational.com

*Distribution for Europe and all other countries:*
Intersentia Publishing nv
Groenstraat 31
2640 Mortsel
Belgium
Tel.: +32 3 680 15 50 | Fax: +32 3 658 71 21
Email: mail@intersentia.be

*Distribution for the USA and Canada:*
Independent Publishers Group
Order Department
814 North Franklin Street
Chicago, IL 60610
USA
Tel.: +1 800 888 4741 (toll free) | Fax: + 1312 337 5985
Email: orders@ipgbook.com

The Active Role of Courts in Consumer Litigation. Applying EU Law of the National Courts' Own Motion
© Anthi Beka 2018

The author has asserted the right under the Copyright, Designs and Patents Act 1988, to be identified as author of this work.

No part of this book may be reproduced, stored in a retrieval system, or transmitted, in any form, or by any means, without prior written permission from Intersentia, or as expressly permitted by law or under the terms agreed with the appropriate reprographic rights organisation. Enquiries concerning reproduction which may not be covered by the above should be addressed to Intersentia at the address above.

Artwork on cover: Franz Marc, Abstrakte Formen II © bpk / LWL-Museum für Kunst und Kultur, Münster / Sabine Ahlbrand-Dornseif und Rudolf Wakonigg

ISBN 978-1-78068-617-2
D/2018/7849/63
NUR 822

British Library Cataloguing in Publication Data. A catalogue record for this book is available from the British Library.

*To Judge José María Fernández Seijo*
*for the "courage of law"*

*I'm fine with a world where people have the right to break the law. But I also want, as a judge, the right to make people respect it. Isn't that what liberalism is?*

Emmanuel Carrère, *Other lives but mine* (translated by Linda Coverdale)

London, Serpent's Tail, 2012

# FOREWORD BY PROFESSOR ELISE POILLOT

For me, it is a real pleasure to present Dr. Anthi Beka's monograph devoted to *The Active Role of Courts in Consumer Litigation – Applying EU Law of the National Courts' Own Motion*, as it was a pleasure for me to supervize her doctoral research during her four years at the University of Luxembourg. The book, published today, is a revised version of her PhD thesis which revealed her outstanding research qualities. It was presented to, and discussed, by a prestigious European committee composed of: Prof. Dr. Vassilios Skouris, then-President of the Court of Justice of the European Union (CJEU); Prof. Dr. Norbert Reich, University of Bremen, who is considered the father of German consumer law; Prof. Dr. Eleftheria Neframi, University of Luxembourg, a renowned expert on EU law; Prof. Dr. Christian Twigg-Flesner, University of Warwick, a consultant on the UK's Consumer Rights Act; and Dr. José María Fernández Seijo, Judge at the Commercial Court of Appeal, Barcelona, who made the very first CJEU reference for preliminary ruling on the matter of the role of the courts in consumer proceedings, followed by other such important requests in connection with Spanish consumer law. Since then, Dr. Anthi Beka has worked as a legal administrator in the chambers of a Member of the Court of Justice. Dr. Beka did not, however, abandon the world of legal research as confirmed by her most recent publications.*

Her monograph on the "Active Role of Courts in Consumer Litigation" is more evidence of the excellence of her scientific production. It transforms a young researcher's work, already quite remarkable by reason of its scientific quality, into a mature work that describes, analyzes and provides a critical appraisal of the complexity of the relationship which exists between national legal orders and the EU legal framework. Beyond the extremely valuable

* A. Beka, "The Protection of the Primary Residence of Mortgage Debtors: Embedding the 'Basic Needs' Principle in Mortgage Repossession Proceedings" in L. Ratti (ed.), *Embedding the Principles of Life Time Contracts, A Research Agenda for Contract Law* (The Hague, Eleven Publishing, 2018), 247–276; G. Cuniberti and A. Beka, "National Report – Luxembourg" in B. Hess et al. (eds.), *Evaluation Study of National Procedural Law and Practices in Terms of their Impact on the Free Circulation of Judgments and on the Equivalence and Effectiveness of the Procedural Protection of Consumers under EU Consumer Law*, MPI Luxembourg for Procedural Law as commissioned by the Directorate-General for Justice and Consumers, European Commission (Nomos/Hart forthcoming 2018).

contribution of Dr. Beka's study to the doctrine of active courts in consumer litigation, her book brings to light the very essence of the relationship which exists between judges – whether they operate at a national level or at a regional level – and citizens. It is more than a legal study; it is a social study. It is the narrative of human and judicial bondage.

The book reflects Dr. Beka's original, innovative, and remarkably insightful look into the *ex officio* power of European judges in the context of consumer law. While conducting her extensive research of this doctrine from a theoretical (i.e., legislative and doctrinal) perspective, Dr. Beka went further, by examining the practical application of the *ex officio* power by first-instance courts and by interviewing legal practitioners and judges from various Member State courts of first instance to gain a better insight into the complex issues they face when confronted with consumer complaints, as well as the solutions they adopt. She wanted to see the doctrine in action. Dr. Beka concludes that the *ex officio* doctrine applies under two circumstances: when "mandatory law" is applicable to a specific context (e.g., a legislative presumption that one party to a transaction has a weaker negotiation position than the other); and when there is an imbalance in the consumer's legal relationship with the business. Dr. Beka reveals, for the first time, a clear formulation of the legal framework surrounding the *ex officio* doctrine. She also demonstrates that this legal framework not only forges a Europeanized model of an active consumer court, but also stands as a pillar of procedural consumer law, touching upon a fundamental aspect of civil procedure. She shows how the narrative of consumer procedural law has evolved, and will continue to evolve, to incorporate the specificities of consumer law into the procedures themselves and how it impacts different types of proceeding (payment, insolvency and mortgage). Dr. Beka, in light of her innovative empirical study of first instance court judges, also establishes that this doctrine has already transformed the judicial mind-set in different jurisdictions. Her collaboration with Spanish and English judges, as well as her first-hand observations at relevant court hearings, gives her work a unique, cutting-edge perspective. Finally, and perhaps most surprisingly, Dr. Beka's work reveals how seemingly technical, procedural rules can encompass a humanized perception of procedure. She is able to demonstrate that, behind the courts' procedural rulings, the *ex officio* doctrine allows citizens' true stories to unfold before the judges' eyes and allows courts, be they the CJEU or a first-instance national court, to take on the role of "guardian of EU fundamental rights". The need for such a guardian, and the courts' assumption of that role, is more crucial than ever because the on-going crisis transcends finance and now strikes at the very pillars of the Member States' and EU's polities; the courts' application of this doctrine in consumer law makes plain that, contrary to some frequently expressed opinions, EU law is not a disembodied set of rules interpreted by judges far removed from the citizens' daily reality.

However, Dr. Beka also acknowledges that judicial failure to act in accordance with the *ex officio* doctrine – that is, a judge's refusal to exercise the discretion he has to protect fundamental rights – can theoretically be sanctioned or corrected within the judicial system, but hardly will be in practice. Rather, Dr. Beka shrewdly suggests that, to solve that problem, extrajudicial measures must be taken. For example, she proposes judicial training in the exercise of *ex officio* power to accustom judges to such a legal mechanism. She also convincingly advocates raising judicial awareness of the human consequences of unfair contractual terms in consumer transactions and supporting judges in their attempt to identify and address such unfair or imbalanced provisions. Her conclusions and solutions are ground-breaking.

Those who will read Dr. Beka's book will not only learn about the active role of courts in consumer litigation. They will also be reminded that the law is not a mere conceptual process, but is made by and for human beings and that scholars should bear this in mind when they embark on a legal research. Anthi Beka never forgot it, even when she came across extremely complex legal issues. The understanding of this fact is evident in her book because she is not only an extremely talented lawyer, she is first and foremost, an extremely talented person.

Prof. Dr. Elise Poillot
Professeur en Droit civil
Director of the Consumer Law Clinic
University of Luxembourg

# INTRODUCTION BY JUDGE ETIENNE RIGAL

Le premier poste de juge que j'ai occupé a été celui de juge d'application des peines. Durant 8 années, j'ai été chargé d'accompagner et de surveiller des condamnés, parfois de les incarcérer, de ma propre initiative, d'office, au nom de leur apparente dangerosité, de la protection de la sécurité collective, de l'ordre public.

Puis je suis, presque par hasard, devenu juge d'instance, ce magistrat qui est tout à la fois appelé à être un civiliste généraliste de proximité et un spécialiste du droit de la consommation, notamment du droit du crédit.

Là, j'ai appris que je ne devais pas, d'office, m'intéresser à l'ordre public, au nom duquel j'avais pourtant tant puni. J'avais incarcéré tant d'hommes et de femmes, le plus souvent pleins de leurs faiblesses sociales et psychologiques. Je ne devais pas protéger, même ceux que la loi appréhendait comme les faibles au contrat.

On choisit d'être jugé dans l'idée de rendre justice et mon idée du juste est celle de l'unité sociale et de la cohérence. En cela je ne pouvais et je ne peux toujours pas penser le droit comme divisible; il n'y a pour moi qu'un ordre public, sans distinction entre sa part pénale et sa part civile. Protection et sanction ne se justifient l'une que par l'autre.

Penser l'unicité du droit et rester le juriste que j'avais choisi d'être, dans la cohérence de son office, voilà ce qui m'a guidé et me guide encore aujourd'hui.

Un autre refus m'habitait, celui de céder à la tentation de définir moi-même, seul, mon office, alors que je suis appelé à rendre la justice au nom du peuple français, comme le rappelle la loi, à servir. Exclure l'imperium du juge et pourtant résister à ce qui était la jurisprudence restrictive de notre Cour de cassation. Une seule voie était légitime, m'en remettre au dialogue des juges et au droit de l'Union.

Tout ce qui m'a conduit à interroger celle qui alors se nommait la CJCE est ici raconté.

Le code civil français en son article 1231-5 énonce que: « Le juge peut, même d'office, modérer ou augmenter la pénalité … convenue (au contrat) si elle est manifestement excessive ou dérisoire ».

J'appelle de mes voeux des juges en charge, au besoin d'office, d'être gardiens de l'excès et protecteurs de l'ordre public, cela dans l'exercice de toutes leurs fonctions civiles comme pénales.

Comment ne pas être heureux que ces questions, au-delà de se poser au juge, intéressent une doctrine enrichissant la pensée commune.

Pour toutes ces raisons, j'ai accepté sans aucune hésitation et avec gratitude de rédiger l'avant-propos de l'ouvrage de Madame Anthi Beka, *The Active Role of Courts in Consumer Litigation – Applying EU Law of the National Courts' Own Motion* qui retrace l'histoire, écrite avec d'autres, de juges nationaux qui s'en sont remis à la Cour de Justice de l'Union Européenne afin que la voie légitime du relevé d'office soit tracée. Mme Beka apporte à ces histoires un cadre scientifique, ce qui lui permet de prendre la hauteur de vue que nous n'avions pas et d'observer de façon posée et objective les conséquences légales qui en sont découlées. Qu'elle en soit ici remerciée.

Etienne Rigal
Vice-président du tribunal d'instance de Villefranche-sur-Saône
Vice-président de la commission des clauses abusives

[*Translated by the author*]:

The first judicial position I held was one of a sentencing judge. Over an eight year period, I was in charge of accompanying and monitoring condemned persons, sometimes having to incarcerate them, on my own initiative due to their apparent dangerousness, for the sake of protecting the general public and for public order. Then I became, almost by chance, a first instance judge, a judge that is in charge of civil law disputes and a specialist of consumer law, in particular consumer credit law, at the same time.

In this role, I learned that I should not raise pleas of public policy of my own motion in the name of which I had, nonetheless, sentenced in the past. I incarcerated many men and women, quite often, people who had many social and psychological weaknesses. My role was not to protect even those people that the law designated as the weaker party in the contract.

One decides to become a judge in order to deliver justice and my idea of justice is one of social unity and coherence. From this perspective, I could not, and I cannot still, envisage the law as divisible; for me there is only one public order, one without distinction between the penal element and the civil element. Protection and sanction are mutually justified.

To think of the unity of law and to remain the lawyer that I have chosen to be, heeding to the coherence of the legal function, is what has guided me and still guides me today.

I have also refused to concede to the temptation of defining my judicial role alone, as I am expected to provide justice in the name of the French people and to serve as the law requires. I have had to exclude the exercise of the power of the judge, while still having to resist what was, at the time, the restrictive case law of our court of cassation. The only legitimate way to reach a solution was to resort to the dialogue of judges and to Union law.

The reasons which led me to make a reference for preliminary ruling to the Court which, at that time, was called the European Court of Justice are discussed in this book.

Article 1231-5 of the French Civil Code provides: "The court may, even of its own motion, moderate or increase the penalty (…) decided (in the contract) if it is manifestly excessive or petty".

I invite full-heartedly judges to penalize excessive claims – if need be of their own motion – and to protect the public policy in the framework of the exercise of their civil or penal duties.

I can only be glad that such questions occupy not only the judiciary, but are also the focus of academic research, enriching reflection.

For these reasons, I accepted without any hesitation, and with gratitude, the offer to write an introduction for Anthi Beka's book, *The Active Role of Courts in Consumer Litigation – Applying EU Law of the National Courts' Own Motion*, which retraces the history of the national judges who addressed the Court of Justice of the European Union so as to establish the active role of the courts. Anthi Beka gives these stories a scientific framework, which allows her to take a high level view which we judges do not have and to observe, in a measured and objective way, the resulting legal consequences. For this, she should be thanked.

Etienne Rigal
Vice-President of the First Instance Court
of Villefranche sur Saône, France
Vice-President of the French Unfair Terms Law Commission

# ACKNOWLEDGMENTS

*As you set out for Ithaca hope the voyage is a long one, full of adventure, full of discovery.*

C.P. Cavafy, *1863–1933*

As the "voyage" on which this work has taken me comes to an end, I wish to take a pause and deeply thank those persons that made it fascinating.

I wish to start with the Dean of the Faculty of Law of the University of Maastricht, Professor Jan Smits, for supporting the publication of this book with Intersentia. It was after reading his dissertation more than ten years ago that I developed a particular research interest for the then emerging field of European private law. I seise this occasion to express my admiration for his work and for the leading research conducted by the M-EPLI Maastricht European Private Law Institute.

I also wish to thank Intersentia, in particular two of its excellent professionals, Ann-Christin Maak-Scherpe and Rebecca Moffat.

If this book comes to fruition, it will be thanks to the constant support of Judge Michail Vilaras, with whom I have the honor to work at the European Court of Justice. Working with him for the past two years provided me with a fresh insight into the subject of this work and motivated me to proceed with its publication. I thank my colleagues with the chambers and in particular the legal secretary, Flavien Mariatte, for all our discussions over the last two years. I also wish to thank the former legal secretaries, Kostas Popotas and Evelyne Tichadou.

I would next wish to express my gratitude toward Professor Elise Poillot, this excellent legal mind, whose innovative ideas "sail" the research in the field of European private law through new *terrains*. I had the chance to benefit from her wise guidance during the completion of my dissertation at the University of Luxembourg, upon which this book builds and expands. I would then wish to thank the members of the jury of my dissertation for providing the most useful comments which further nourished my reflection. I would first of all start with the late Professor Dr. Norbert Reich, the loss of whom has deeply saddened the academic community. He leaves behind a legacy that will guide the future generations of European private law scholars. I would like to thank the former President of the Court of Justice, Professor Vassilios Skouris, under the wise presidency of whom the consumer active court doctrine was established. Professor Skouris so kindly accepted to honor my work with his presence and to share his invaluable experience with me. I would like to thank Professor Christian Twigg-Flesner, Professor Eleftheria Neframi and the expert-member of the jury, Judge of the Court of Barcelona, José María Fernández Seijo.

Meeting Judge José María Fernández Seijo, this exceptional figure of the judiciary, was a turning point in my work. His "humanized" vision of law has deeply inspired me. I thank him so much for all the time and care he devoted to my work and for inviting me to participate in a conference of the Judicial Council (*Consejo General del Poder Judicial*) on the impact of the case law of the Court on the protection of mortgage debtors in the Spanish legal system.

My participation as a national rapporteur for Luxembourg to the empirical study of the Max Planck Institute (Luxembourg) on the strand pertaining to the procedural protection of consumers, carried out in 2016 on behalf of the European Commission, gave me the chance to hold interviews with national judges in Luxembourg. I would in particular like to thank Judge Françoise Hilger for explaining to me the particularities of the *ex officio* judicial role and for sharing with me her enthusiasm for a human vision of proceedings.

I also thank Judge Gérard Biardeaud, Vice-President of the *Tribunal de Grande Instance* of Limoges and Director of consumer law judicial training at the French National School of the Judiciary (École Nationale de la Magistrature), for inviting me to participate in a seminar on consumer credit and the case law of the Court of Justice which enhanced my understanding of the influence of this case law on the French legal order.

Back in 2013, I had the chance to meet with county court judges in England. It was a precious chance to gain an insight of English small claims and repossession proceedings in the County Court of Kingston upon Hull. I am thankful to Judge Besford, Judge Mclliwaine, Judge Knightinghale, Judge Neal and Judge Richardson, who took the time to answer my enquiries with much enthusiasm. The person who very kindly took care that I meet with the judges was clerk Stephen Jones.

I would like to thank the former Dean of the Faculty of Law of the University of Hull, Professor Christian Twigg-Flesner, for welcoming me on my visit to the faculty, which gave me the chance to hold fruitful discussions with Honorary Fellow Diana Wallis and Reader Dr. Lisa Whitehouse.

Finally, I met with judges in Greece at the height of the sovereign debt crisis and during a period where the first instance courts had to deal with a very high number of applications of over-indebted consumers, following the coming into force of the (then) new law on consumer insolvency. I visited the County Court of Thessaloniki and Volos. I wish to thank Judge Konsta, Judge Arvanitidis and Judge Kotsianis. I was very touched by the humanity with which they exercise their judicial role.

I would then like to thank the academic community of the FDEF of the University of Luxembourg, and more particularly Professor Séverine Menetrey.

Her theory of the procedure as a lever in recalibrating competing interests (*outil de réequilibrage des intérêts*) has followed me throughout my work. I had the important occasion to benefit from discussions with the Visiting Professor and former Judge in the General Court, Arjen Meij, who so kindly shares his wisdom with young scholars. The theoretical insight of Professor Johan van der Walt has been an incredible source of reflection. Particularly in the first stages of my research, I found a compass in my discussions with Professor Herwig Hofmann, Professor Gilles Cuniberti and Professor Jörg Gerkrath.

I will always remain intellectually indebted to the Professors of the Department of Civil Law, Civil Procedural and Labor Law at the Faculty of Law at Aristotle University of Thessaloniki (Greece). It is not easy to find the words to thank the person who I would wish to consider as my mentor in law, Professor Evangelia Podimata. Her writings are intellectual diamonds to which every young researcher can aspire. I also wish to thank Emeritus Professor Marianos Karasis, Professor Paris Arvanitakis, Professor Konstandinos Stamatis, Professor Nikoleta Paisidou, Professor Athanasios Pouliades, Professor Christina Deliyanni-Dimitrakou and Professor Eutuxia Kounougeri-Manoledaki.

It is a good occasion to say a heartfelt thank you to the people who welcomed me in the European Commission during my internship in 2007, Dr. Emil Ems, Dr. Francisco Caballero Sanz and Klaus Ossmann, who continue to follow my academic steps since then.

Coming to the end of these acknowledgments, I thank my family Nikolaos, Ifigeneia and Anna Beka, and my husband, Lorenzo Debay, for always being there and for embracing me with all their love. As the late Professor Norbert Reich used to tell me jokingly, your husband is the true "weaker party." On this occasion, I ask him to excuse me for all the time I deprived him of and to thank him for believing in me and for accompanying me in this effort.

Anthi Beka
Luxembourg, March 15, 2018

Disclaimer: All opinions expressed are strictly those of the author.

# CONTENTS

PART II. THE EMERGENCE AND DISTINCTIVE FEATURES OF THE ACTIVE CONSUMER COURT DOCTRINE

# LIST OF CASES*

## COURT OF JUSTICE OF THE EUROPEAN UNION



* Cases are in chronological order.

## EUROPEAN COURT OF HUMAN RIGHTS



## FRANCE



## THE NETHERLANDS

## SPAIN



## UNITED KINGDOM

# LIST OF ABBREVIATIONS

| | |
|---|---|
| ADR | Alternative Dispute Resolution |
| BGH | *Bundesgerichtshof* |
| Conv | Conveyancer and Property Lawyer |
| CMLR | Common Market Law Review |
| CPC | *Code de Procédure Civile* |
| CPR | Civil Procedure Rules |
| CJQ | Civil Justice Quarterly |
| ECHR | European Convention on Human Rights |
| ECJ | European Court of Justice |
| ECtHR | European Court of Human Rights |
| ELRev | European Law Review |
| ERCL | European Review of Contract Law |
| ERPL | European Review of Private Law |
| EuCML | Journal of European Consumer and Market Law |
| EUVR | *Zeitschrift für Europäisches Unternehmens- und Verbraucherrecht* |
| LEC | *Ley de Enjuiciamiento Civil* |
| MCD | Mortgage Credit Directive |
| RTDEur | *Revue Trimestrielle du droit européen* |
| ZEuP | *Zeitschrift für Europäisches Privatrecht* |
| ZPO | *Zivilprozessordnung* |

# INTRODUCTION

*[T]he system of protection laid down by the Directive [93/13] is based on the notion that the imbalance between the consumer and the seller or supplier may only be corrected by positive action unconnected with the actual parties to the contract.*

Joined Cases C-240/98–C-244/98, *Océano Grupo*, EU:C:2000:346, para. 27

*The court must consider whether the term is fair even if none of the parties to the proceedings has raised that issue or indicated that it intends to raise it*

Section 71 (2) Consumer Rights Act 2015

*Este capítulo recoge también la modificación del procedimiento ejecutivo a efectos de que, de oficio o a instancie de parte, el órgano judicial competente pueda apreciar la existencia de cláusulas abusivas en el título ejecutivo y, como consecuencia, decretar la improcedencia de la ejecución o, en su caso, su continuación sin aplicación de aquéllas consideradas abusivas*[1]

Preamble to the Spanish Law 1/2013 laying down measures for the strengthening of the protection of mortgagors, the restructuring of debt and social rent of 14 May 2013

*... Seule la reconnaissance du pouvoir dont dispose le juge de soulever d'office l'application d'une disposition protectrice du consommateur permettait de rétablir un équilibre dans le cadre d'un procès entre la partie faible et la partie dominante*[2]

*French Senate, Report no 111 (2007–2008), of December 5, 2007 by Senator M. Gérard Cornu*

If the sources of the passages above were omitted, one might have thought, but for the language, that it is the same court or the same legislator that recognizes the same issue: the consumer is in weak position not only in the contractual relationship but also as a party in the procedure, and this has to be compensated for by the courts. If Union law came to address this issue, that is thanks to the judiciary of the Union, which comprises the Court of Justice (hereinafter "the Court") and the national courts. When the Unfair Contract Terms Directive[3]

1 "This chapter establishes the reform of the enforcement procedure to the effect that the court, of its own motion or following a respective demand by the party, has the power to assess the existence of unfair terms in the enforcement title and, as a consequence, adopt an order to stop the enforcement, or, depending on the circumstances, its continuation without the application of the unfair terms" (translated by the author).

2 "Only the recognition of the power of the court to raise of its own motion the application of a protective rule in favor of the consumer would allow the balance to be re-established in the framework of a procedure inbetween the weaker party and the dominant party" (translated by the author).

3 Council Directive 93/13/EEC of 5 April 1993 on unfair terms in consumer contracts [1993] OJ L95/29.

was adopted 25 years ago, probably no one, not even the Member States, could have foreseen the impact it would exercise upon procedure. It is true that Article 7 of the said Directive already encapsulated a general clause of judicial protection, according to which Member States must provide for adequate and effective means to prevent the continued use of unfair terms, including the possibility of consumer associations to seek injunctive relief. The procedural dimensions of this *nucleus* were far-reaching, transforming the pattern of consumer judicial protection in a significant way. The extent of this transformation is on par with the developments in the procedural and societal context within which the Unfair Contract Terms Directive would have to be applied. The application of the Unfair Contract Terms Directive in the context of the global financial crisis and the Great Recession unearthed complex legal issues relating to judicial protection. The conceptual key to a novel and constructive procedural reading of the Unfair Contract Terms Directive was laid down in a series of cases before the Court pertaining to the powers of the courts to raise unfair terms of their own motion. This reading was progressively extended to other instruments of consumer legislation.

In the landmark ruling in *Océano Grupo*[4] dating back to 2000, the Court decided that national courts should have the power to raise the unfairness of standard terms of their own motion. Since then, the number and complexity of the references on this subject have increased in an exponential degree. The restoration of the contractual imbalance underlying the Unfair Contract Terms Directive, and more broadly the restoration of the market imbalance underlying consumer law legislation, was extended to the procedural level. This was translated, in particular, into an active role for the courts. The strict adherence to the principle of party presentation according to which the consumer would be obliged to put forward the legal submissions in favor of his position would have led to a *de facto* procedural crystallization of the power imbalance which the legislator intended to reverse. In acknowledging that the protective aim of the consumer law legislation could only be achieved by a positive action of the courts unconnected to the parties in the dispute, the Court advanced a *distinctive* European conception of the role of the courts and the parties in individual consumer litigation. The line of case law that supports this conception forms what is called in this work the "doctrine of the active consumer court" or the "consumer *ex officio* doctrine." The Latin term has been often used in European literature to denote the consideration by the courts of an issue of their own motion. To a lesser extent, use is made of the Latin term *sua sponte* employed in American legal English. The term "consumer court" does not denote the existence of a separate jurisdiction for consumer disputes. It is shorthand for the active role of the court in consumer litigation.

4 Joined Cases C-240/98–C-244/98, *Océano Grupo*, EU:C:2000:346.

This book attempts to uncover the theory underlying the *ex officio* doctrine. The main enquiry is whether and how this doctrine affects individual consumer litigation. It can be broken down into sub-lines of enquiry. First, there will be an analysis of the characteristics of the doctrine and the features that distinguish it from other lines of case law on the role of the courts with regard to the application of Union law. The role that the national courts have played in the construction of the doctrine and the implications that the latter had for specific jurisdictions will also be examined. The issue of the respective role of the courts and the parties touches upon the fundamentals of civil justice. The establishment a specific role for the courts with regard to a particular type of dispute governed by Union law points to a Europeanization of the pattern of civil justice in that regard. The concept of Europeanization has various meanings and interpretations.[5] For the purposes of this work, as it will be further analyzed in Chapter 1, the concept is understood, in a broad sense, as encompassing the influence of Union law upon domestic procedural law and judicial protection. Throughout this work it will be argued that the consumer *ex officio* doctrine does not "upset" civil procedural traditions. These traditions rather mold the theoretical underpinnings of the active court, resulting in a novel understanding of the concept at the European level.

This perception is underpinned by the idea of what the former President of the Court Vassilios Skouris has called "osmosis"[6] of Union law and national laws. The present study, as a work of European private law, has as its point of departure Union law. However, the next step is to explore the way in which the ruling of the Court was applied in the specific case by the referring court and, more broadly, to identify the extent to which the precedent set by the Court has affected the specific national jurisdiction from which the reference emanated as well as other jurisdictions. The Union relies upon an "interlocking system of jurisdiction[s],"[7] where Union law and national law concepts interact and interpenetrate. The multilevel structure of the Union and its legal system makes a "circular" method of enquiry on legal questions particularly relevant. In this book we seek to trace such a circular path, starting from the Union level of procedural law relevant for the consumer, moving to the domestic level and finally returning to the Union level.

The book is divided into two parts, each of which is subdivided in three chapters. The first chapter "sets the scene" of the consumer *ex officio*

---

5 C. Twigg-Flesner, *The Europeanisation of Contract Law: Current Controversies in Law* (Abingdon, Routledge, 2nd ed., 2013), 2.

6 V. Skouris, "The Principle of Procedural Autonomy and the Duty of Loyal Cooperation of National Judges under Article 10 EC" in M. Andenas and D. Fairgrieve (eds.), *Tom Bingham and the Transformation of the Law, A Liber Amicorum* (Oxford, Oxford University Press, 2009), 493–507, 493.

7 K. Lenaerts, "The Rule of Law and the Coherence of the Judicial System of the European Union" (2007) 44 *CMLR* 1625–1659, 1625.

doctrine placing it within the context of individual legal protection of consumers in Union law. This is achieved through a presentation of the legislative landscape and the broader constitutional context of the legal protection of Union law rights. It demonstrates the role of the principle of effectiveness as "a forceful impetus"[8] to individual consumer litigation by setting in stone the model of an active national court to ensure the full effect of mandatory consumer legislation. Chapter 2 gives an outlook on the "general" Union *ex officio* doctrine, shaped by the *Van Schijndel*[9] line of case law. Although the consumer *ex officio* doctrine has a common point of departure with the "general" doctrine, it has developed differently. It already seems to be established in the case law of the Court[10] and in literature[11] that the consumer *ex officio* doctrine is *specific* compared to the general position pronounced in *Van Schijndel*. The aim of Chapter 2 is to explain the general position so as to enable a better understanding of the considerations that justify the specific position of a Union consumer *ex officio* doctrine. Chapter 3 takes up the same problematic, but from a domestic perspective. The *Van Schijndel* judgment pays heed to the "conceptions prevailing"[12] in most Member States with regard to the principle of party presentation in civil adjudication. It also makes reference to the exceptional circumstances of public policy or public interest that can justify an intervention by the courts. Even if the reasoning of the Court may be inspired by domestic conceptual patterns, it gives them, finally, a "European legal significance."[13] Before embarking on a detailed analysis of the consumer *ex officio* doctrine, it is important to navigate by way of illustration on the role of the courts in selective jurisdictions with regard to points of law in general, and points of Union law

---

8 A. Hartkamp, *European Law and National Private Law* (Deventer, Kluwer, 2012), para. 109.

9 Joined Cases C-430/93 and C-431/93, *Van Schijndel and Van Veen*, EU:C:1995:441.

10 *See* Joined Cases C-222/05–C-225/05 *Van der Weerd*, EU:C:2007:318 and Case C-227/08 *Martín Martín*, EU:C:2009:792.

11 N. Reich, *Individueller und kollektiver Rechtschutz im EU-Verbraucherrecht, Von der "Nationalisierung" zur "Kostitutionalisierung" von Rechtsbehelfen* (Baden-Baden, Nomos, 2012), 36; V. Trstenjak and E. Beysen, "European Consumer Protection Law: *Curia Semper Dabit Remedium?*" (2011) 48 *CMLR* 95–124, 119; S. Whittaker, "Who Determines What Civil Courts Decide? Private Rights, Public Policy and EU Law" in D. Leczykiewicz and S. Weatherill (eds.), *The Involvement of EU Law in Private Law Relationships* (Oxford, Hart Publishing, 2013), 89–129, 123; K. Lenaerts, I. Maselis and K. Gutman, *EU Procedural Law* (Oxford, Oxford University Press, 2014), para. 4.41; A. Ó Caoimh, "Issues of EU Law Raised by National Courts of Their Own Motion" in P. Cardonnel, A. Rosas and N. Wahl (eds.), *Constitutionalising the EU Judicial System: Essays in Honour of Pernilla Lindh* (Oxford, Hart Publishing, 2012), 123–138, 134; M. Dougan, "The Vicissitudes of Life at the Coalface, Remedies and Procedures for Enforcing Union Law", in P. Craig and G. de Burca (eds.), *The Evolution of EU Law* (Oxford, Oxford University Press, 2nd ed., 2011), 412–424; M.J. Sørensen, "In the Name of Effective Consumer Protection and Public Policy" (2016) 5 *ERPL* 791–822.

12 Joined Cases C-430/93 and C-431/93 *Van Schijndel and Van Veen* (n. 9), para. 21.

13 S. Whittaker (n. 11), 92.

and consumer Union law in particular. This chapter also indicates the capacity of accommodation of the consumer *ex officio* doctrine and foreshadows some of the developments in Part Two with regard to the influence of the doctrine in the French and English legal orders.

Part II includes Chapters 4 to 6. Chapter 4 presents the underpinnings of the consumer *ex officio* doctrine as they have been laid down in the early judgments of the Court. The landmark rulings in that regard are *Océano Grupo, Cofidis*[14] and *Mostaza Claro*.[15] It also presents its refinement in subsequent case law that clarified its nature, its scope and its limitations. Chapter 5 concentrates mainly on two judgments, *Banco Español de Crédito*[16] and *Aziz*,[17] which are representative of the "transprocedural" character of the doctrine of the active court. The *ex officio* doctrine permeates various procedural constellations which were not adapted to power disparity and becomes their benchmark of effectiveness. Chapter 6 explores the influence of the consumer *ex officio* doctrine, concentrating in particular, on three jurisdictions: England, France and Spain. The book concludes with reflections on the effectiveness of the consumer *ex officio* doctrine and discusses its potential to become a reference model for litigation patterns bearing similar structural characteristics.

14 Case C-473/00 *Cofidis*, EU:C:2002:705.
15 Case C-168/05 *Mostaza Claro*, EU:C:2006:675.
16 Case C-618/10 *Banco Español de Crédito*, EU:C:2012:349.
17 Case C-415/11 *Aziz*, EU:C:2013:164.

# PART I

# THE DOCTRINE OF THE ACTIVE CONSUMER COURT IN CONTEXT

Part I introduces the thesis of the establishment of a doctrine of an active court in European consumer law proceedings, tracing its origins in Union constitutional law and, more particularly, in the effective judicial protection of Union law rights (Chapter 1), and in the application of Union law by national courts of their own motion (Chapter 2). Moreover, this part presents a selective perspective of three national jurisdictions on the respective role of the courts and the parties with regard to pleas in law in general and Union law in particular (Chapter 3). The argument towards which it points – an argument that will be taken up further particularly in Part II of this volume – is that the procedural protection of consumers in their *individual* capacity in *domestic* litigation has been *Europeanized* and considerably strengthened by a specific line of case law of the Court of Justice of the European Union (hereinafter "the Court"). The case law of the Court on the powers of the courts to raise certain mandatory rules of consumer law of their own motion was generated in the context of reference for preliminary ruling (Article 267 of the Treaty on the Functioning of the European Union (TFEU). The doctrine is therefore to be attributed to the Union courts, meaning the Court and the national courts in their *function* as Union courts. It is well established that the judicial dialogue is the prime feature of the judicial system of the Union[18] which, as the President of the Court Koen Lenaerts puts it, "hinges on [an] interlocking system of jurisdiction[s]."[19] In the same vein, the former President of the Court, Vassilios Skouris, points out that Union law, despite its autonomous character, is "*anchored* in national legal orders and draws, to a large extent, its inspiration from those orders".[20] In the particular field of consumer *ex officio* case law,

---

18 See Opinion 2/13 (*Accession of the European Union to the ECHR*) of 18 December 2014, EU:C:2014:2454, para 176 and the case law cited.

19 K. Lenaerts, "The Rule of Law and the Coherence of the Judicial System of the European Union" (2007) 44 *CMLR*, 1625–1659, 1625.

20 Translated by the author from the original citation: "Trozt seines autonomen, eigenen Charakters ist Europarecht tief in den nationalen Rechtsordnungen verankert und wird wesentlich von diesen inspiriert", V. Skouris, "Der Einfluss des nationalen Rechts und der Rechtsprechung der mitgliedstaatlichen Gerichte auf die Auslegung des Europarechts" (2014) 3 *Zeitschrift der Verwaltungsgerichtsbarkeit* ZVG, 203–208.

we may observe that national jurisdictions have been particularly active in prompting the Union law question (among which, most prominently, the Spanish and the French but also the Hungarian, the Dutch, the Slovakian and the Romanian jurisdictions). In the field of consumer contract law, national courts fully assume their competence as Union law judges.[21] The *ex officio* case law "sets in stone" the model of an *active court* in national proceedings to ensure the *full effect* of the Union mandatory consumer legislation guided by the weaker party normative paradigm.

21 *See*, in general, A. Barav, "La plénitude de compétence du juge national en sa qualité de juge communautaire", in *Mélanges en hommage à Jean Boulouis, L'Europe et le Droit* (Paris, Dalloz, 1991).

# CHAPTER 1

# SETTING THE SCENE

## Europeanization of Consumer Procedural Law and Judicial Protection of Union Rights

This chapter sets out the framework of individual legal protection of consumers within which the *ex officio* doctrine is placed. The extensive European Union consumer contract law affecting cross-border and domestic transactions alike lacks a comprehensive Union consumer procedural law. This is due to the allocation of competences between the European Union and the Member States. The procedural law governing the enforcement of substantive Union consumer law is, in principle, a matter for the Member States. However, the principles of effectiveness and effective judicial protection limit their procedural competence.

The *ex officio* doctrine was not provided for under any legislative instrument. Rather, it has been the result of a growing *indirect* Europeanization of consumer procedural law, which is understood as the impact of the principles of effectiveness and effective judicial protection upon national procedural law, applicable in litigation involving consumers. Even if the procedural rules governing the exercise of consumer rights before the courts are not harmonized, it needs to be noted, however, that the development of the *ex officio* doctrine occurred within a field of law (namely consumer law) marked by the extensive harmonization of rights and remedies. In essence, the *genesis* of the *ex officio* doctrine, pertaining to the respective role of the courts and the parties in litigation, relates to the effectiveness of the extensive rights and remedies provided for under secondary consumer legislation (for instance, the non-binding nature of unfair terms, the right to withdraw from a distance or off-premises contract, or the remedy of price reduction or rescission from a sales contract in case of lack of conformity of the consumer goods delivered).

As will be further analyzed in Part II, the establishment of the active court in consumer litigation signals a Europeanization of the role of the courts in consumer law proceedings predicated upon the protection of the *weaker* party. In a steady line of case law following the landmark ruling in *Océano Grupo*,[22] the Court has elevated the protection of the weaker party into the *normative*

---

[22] Joined Cases C-240/98–C-244/98 *Océano Grupo*, EU:C:2000:346.

*justification of an active bench*. From this perspective, the active consumer court could be considered as an important expression of the "principle of the weaker party" identified by Norbert Reich as a general principle of Union civil law.[23]

This chapter will be divided into two sections. Section 1 provides a brief account of the *direct* Europeanization of consumer procedural law. This covers the legislative instruments on procedural law either applicable to consumer litigation or of particular relevance for consumer litigation. These instruments have a specific and limited material and territorial scope of application. Section 2 deals with the *indirect* Europeanization of consumer procedural law which forms part of, to employ the terms of Bart Krans, the "invisible pillar" of the Europeanization of civil procedural law.[24] This is the result of the application of general principles of Union law in the enforcement of domestic disputes. The influence of Union law in this framework is diffuse or, as Michal Bobek puts it, "functional and transversal ... not limited to any field or area of law."[25] Through the application of these principles, national procedural laws can edge toward certain common procedural standards.

## 1. THE DIRECT EUROPEANIZATION OF CONSUMER PROCEDURAL LAW

The consumer law *acquis* comprises a wealth of harmonized substantive consumer rights and remedies forming the core of European contract law.[26] The Union law instruments that govern these rights take the form of directives,

23 N. Reich, *General Principles of EU Civil Law* (Cambridge, Intersentia, 2014), 37–38.

24 B. Krans, "EU Law and National Civil Procedure Law: An Invisible Pillar" (2015) 4 *ERPL* 567–588. P. Taelmann, "Some European Challenges for Belgian Civil Procedure" in A. Nylund and B. Krans (eds.), *The European Union and National Civil Procedure* (Antwerp, Intersentia, 2016), 5–17, who expands upon the idea of the "invisible pillar" in the field of the *ex officio* application of Union Consumer law. See more generally on the Europeanization of civil procedure E. Storskrubb, *Civil Procedure and EU Law: A Policy Area Uncovered* (Oxford, Oxford University Press, 2008).

25 M. Bobek, "The Effects of EU Law in the National Legal Systems" in C. Barnard and S. Peers (eds.), *European Union Law* (Oxford, Oxford University Press, 2012), 166.

26 On the conceptual distinction between rights, remedies and procedures, see the seminal study of W. Van Gerven, "Of Rights, Remedies and Procedures," (2000) 37 *CMLR* 501–536. On EU consumer law as the core of European contract law, see N. Reich, H.-W. Micklitz, P. Rott and K. Tonner, *European Consumer Law* (Cambridge, Intersentia, 2nd ed., 2014); E. Poillot, *Droit Européen de la consommation et uniformisation du droit des contrats* (Paris, LGDJ, 2006); C. Twigg-Flesner, *The Europeanisation of Contract Law: Current Controversies in Law* (Abingdon, Routledge, 2nd ed., 2013); S. Weatherill, *EU Consumer Law and Policy* (Cheltenham, Edward Elgar, 2nd ed., 2014); I. Ramsay, *Consumer Law and Policy* (Oxford, Oxford University Press, 3rd ed., 2012); H.-W. Micklitz, J. Stuyck and E. Terryn (eds.), *Cases, Materials and Text on Consumer Law* (Oxford, Hart Publishing, 2010); J. Devenney and M. Kenny, *European Consumer Protection, Theory and Practice* (Cambridge, Cambridge University Press, 2013).

requiring the intervention of the national legislator (Article 288 TFEU) for their proper implementation. The existing measures cover a wide array of aspects, such as unfair terms,[27] sales of consumer goods and guarantees,[28] distance selling and doorstep selling,[29] consumer credit[30] and, in the aftermath of the 2008 global financial crisis, residential mortgage credit.[31] The directives do not distinguish between cross-border and domestic transactions.[32] Thus, many consumer rights and remedies exercised at the domestic level stem from Union law.

The protection of the rights enshrined in the consumer law *acquis* depends upon their effective enforcement, which is, mainly, a matter for the Member States.[33] The enforcement powers are exercised at the national public-administrative level and at the national private-judicial level, with the

---

27 Council Directive 93/13/EEC of 5 April 1993 on unfair terms in consumer contracts [1993] OJ L95/29 (hereinafter the "Unfair Contract Terms Directive").

28 Directive 1999/44 of the European Parliament and of the Council of 25 May 1999 on certain aspects of the sale of consumer goods and associated guarantees [1999] OJ L171/12 (hereinafter the "Consumer Sales Directive").

29 The rights and remedies available in distance contracts and off-premises contracts are the main subject matters of Directive 2011/83/EU of the European Parliament and of the Council of 25 October 2011 on consumer rights, amending Council Directive 93/13/EEC and Directive 1999/44/EC of the European Parliament and of the Council and repealing Council Directive 85/577/EEC and Directive 97/7/EC of the European Parliament and of the Council [2011] OJ L304/64 (hereinafter the "Consumer Rights Directive").

30 Directive 2008/48/EC of the European Parliament and the Council of 23 April 2008 on credit agreements for consumers and repealing Council Directive 87/102/EEC [2008] OJ L133/66 (hereinafter the "Consumer Credit Directive").

31 Directive 2014/17/EU of the European Parliament and of the Council of 4 February 2014 on credit agreements for consumers relating to residential immovable property and amending Directives 2008/48/EC and 2013/36/EU and Regulation (EU) No 1093/2010 [2014] OJ L60/34 (hereinafter the "Mortgage Credit Directive").

32 The reasons for the wide scope of the consumer law directives covering both cross-border and domestic transactions are tested by C. Twigg-Flesner, "EU Law and Consumer Transactions without an Internal Market Dimension" in D. Leczykiewicz and S. Weatherill (eds.), *The Involvement of EU Law in Private Law Relationships* (Oxford, Hart Publishing, 2013), 317–331, who suggests a normative approach based on regulations governing only cross-border transactions, particularly online. See also C. Twigg-Flesner, "Time to Do the Job Properly: The Case for a New Approach to EU Consumer Legislation" (2010) 33 *Journal of Consumer Policy*, 355–375. It is important to note that according to the amendments proposed by the European Parliament (1st reading, as of February 26, 2014) to the Proposal for a Regulation of the European Parliament and of the Council on a Common European Sales Law, COM/2011/635 final, this one, if ever adopted, it would apply only to distance contracts, concluded particularly online, as an optional second national contract law regime for contracts falling within its scope.

33 See J. Stuyck, "Public and Private Enforcement in Consumer Protection: General Comparison EU-USA, Enforcement of Consumer Rights and Legal Redress for Consumers in the EU: An Institutional Model" in F. Cafaggi and H.-W. Micklitz (eds.), *New Frontiers of Consumer Protection: The Interplay between Private and Public Enforcement* (Cambridge, Intersentia, 2009); G. Howells et al. (eds.), *Handbook of Research on International Consumer Law* (Cheltenham, Edward Elgar, 2010); R. Brownsword, H.-W. Micklitz, L. Niglia and S. Weatherill (eds.), *The Foundations of European Private Law* (Oxford, Hart Publishing, 2011), particularly the contributions in Part Four: Enforcement and compliance;

regulatory authorities or consumer/professional organizations playing, respectively, a primary role.[34] The Member States need to provide for "adequate and effective means" to ensure compliance with the Union secondary legislation and for "effective, proportionate and dissuasive" penalties.[35] This is a "standard clause" embedding what Fabrizio Cafaggi and Paola Iamicelli call the "triad" of the principles of effectiveness, proportionality and dissuasiveness.[36]

The instruments that have, as their subject matter, judicial or out-of-court redress mechanisms applicable to consumer disputes or that can be of relevance for consumer redress (without being restricted to consumer disputes) could be considered to fall, in a broad sense, within Union "consumer procedural law". The vehicle for the *direct* Europeanization of consumer procedural law is secondary legislation (regulations or directives) or recommendations, governing specific procedural matters on the basis of the internal market harmonization clause (Article 114 TFEU). The backbone of consumer procedural law mainly consists of three mechanisms enhancing *access to justice*:[37,38] actions for injunction and collective redress,[39] Alternative Dispute Resolution (ADR)[40] and the European

---

H.-W. Micklitz, "The Transformation of Enforcement in European Private Law: Preliminary Considerations" (2015) 4 *ERPL*, 491–524.

34 F. Cafaggi and H.-W. Micklitz, "Introduction" in F. Cafaggi and H.-W. Micklitz (eds.) (n. 33), 1–44, who point out the "institutional complementarity" of courts and administrative authorities to ensure the effective protection of consumers.

35 See Article 7 (1( of the Unfair Terms Directive, which provides that "Member States shall ensure that, in the interests of consumers and of competitors, adequate and effective means exist to prevent the continued use of unfair terms in contracts concluded with consumers by sellers or suppliers." Article 23 (1) of the Consumer Rights Directive similarly provides that "Member States shall ensure that adequate and effective means exist to ensure compliance with this Directive". Art. 24 of the Consumer Rights Directive concentrates on the penalties for infringements, which shall be "effective proportionate and dissuasive."

36 F. Cafaggi and P. Iamiceli, "The Principles of Effectiveness, Proportionality and Dissuasiveness in the Enforcement of EU Consumer Law: The Impact of a Triad on the Choice of Civil Remedies and Administrative Sanctions" (2017) 25(3) *ERPL* 575–618.

37 On the access to justice movement, see the seminal work of M. Cappelletti (ed.), *Access to Justice and the Welfare State* (Florence, European University Institute, 1981).

38 Legal aid is not mentioned among the three limbs as it has an overarching application. It belongs to what Mauro Cappelletti and Bryant Garth call the "first wave" of the access to justice movement, along with the protection of collective interests and out-of-court settlement. See M. Cappelletti and B. Garth, "Introduction" in M. Cappelletti (ed.) (n. 37) 1–25. Legal aid is enshrined under Art. 47(3) of the Charter, while its modalities for cross-border disputes are governed by Council Directive 2002/8/EC of 27 January 2003 to improve access to justice in cross-border disputes by establishing minimum common rules relating to legal aid for such disputes [2003] OJ L26/41.

39 Directive 2009/22/EC of the European Parliament and of the Council of 23 April 2009 on injunctions for the protection of consumers' interests [2009] OJ L110/30; Commission Recommendation of 11 June 2013 on common principles for injunctive and compensatory collective redress mechanisms in the Member States concerning violations of rights granted under Union law [2013] OJ L201/60.

40 Directive 2013/11/EU of the European Parliament and of the Council of 21 May 2013 on alternative dispute resolution for consumer disputes and amending Regulation (EC)

small claims procedure.[41] The scope of application of these mechanisms is broader than consumer law. The European small claims procedure does not apply only to consumer disputes. The same is true for the common principles applicable to injunctive and compensatory collective redress, which cover collective claims for injunctions or damages in respect of violation of rights granted under Union law, including, but not restricted to, consumer law rights.[42]

The Union consumer procedural law would seem to support the observation made by Geraint Howells that "consumer protection is increasingly being integrated into [a] broader civil justice ... agenda."[43] As far as consumer law is concerned, this agenda pursues, in substance, "market-function"[44] goals. The underlying rationale is an economic one, in line with the market competence basis (Article 114 TFEU) and the prevalent "marketized" image of the consumer in Union law.[45] Pursuant to Article 169 TFEU, the consumer law policy, aims at the protection of the "economic interests" of consumers by means of the promotion of, inter alia, their "right to information". The "informed consumer" normative standard,[46] reflects, in turn, the dominant pattern of "market-rational welfarism" in European contract law, as demonstrated in the seminal paper of Thomas Wilhelmsson, with the rational consumer representing the "dominant consumer image".[47]

---

No 2006/2004 and Directive 2009/22/EC [2013] OJ L165/63(hereinafter "Directive on consumer ADR");Regulation (EU) 524/2014 of the European Parliament and of the Council of 21 May 2013 on online dispute resolution for consumer disputes and amending Regulation (EC) 2006/2004 and Directive 2009/22/EC [2013] OJ L165/1 (hereinafter "Directive on consumer ODR").

41 Regulation (EC) No 861/2007 of the European Parliament and the Council of 11 July 2007 establishing a European Small Claims Procedure [2007] OJ L199/1, amended by Regulation (EU) 2015/2421 of the European Parliament and of the Council of 16 December 2015 [2015] OJ L341/1 (hereinafter the "European Small Claims Regulation").

42 According to the Preamble (7) to the Commission Recommendation of 11 June 2013 on common principles for injunctive and compensatory collective redress mechanisms in the Member States concerning violations of rights granted under Union law, (n. 39). Amongst the areas where the supplementary private enforcement of rights granted under Union law in the form of collective redress is of particular importance, are consumer protection, competition, environment protection, protection of personal data, financial services legislation and investor protection. The principles set out in this Recommendation should be applied horizontally and equally in those areas, but also in any other areas where collective claims for injunctions or damages in respect of violations of the rights granted under Union law would be relevant.

43 G. Howells, "European Consumer Law," in C. Barnard and S. Peers (eds.) (n. 25), 702.

44 C. Hodges et al., *Consumer ADR in Europe* (Oxford, Hart Publishing, 2012), 191 *et seq.*

45 H.-W. Micklitz, "The Consumer: Marketised, Fragmented, Constitutionalised" in D. Leczykiewicz and S. Weatherill (eds.), *The Images of the Consumer in EU Law: Legislation, Free Movement and Competition Law* (Oxford, Hart Publishing, 2016), 21–41.

46 N. Reich, "Vulnerable Consumers in EU Law" in D. Leczykiewicz and S. Weatherill (eds.) (n. 45), 139–158, 146.

47 T. Wilhelmsson, "Varieties of Welfarism in European Contract Law" (2004) 10(6) *European Law Journal* 712–733. This model focuses on the creation of pre-contractual information

The efficiency of justice is viewed as a motor of growth of the EU economy. To illustrate this, the establishment of efficient ADR schemes offering "simple, affordable, expedient and accessible system of redress" is intended to "boost consumer confidence" serving an ultimate market goal.[48] If consumers know that such a framework is available, they will be more confident in engaging in cross-border shopping.[49] The European small claims procedure is a "genuine" access to justice instrument in the sense that it has been adopted on the basis of the Union competence for the creation of a civil justice area (Article 81 TFEU). Since the Treaty of Amsterdam, this provision vests the Union, with competence in the field of judicial cooperation in civil law matters which have *cross-border* implications (Article 81 TFEU).[50] Still, the market connection is strong. The amendment of the European Small Claims Regulation which governs this procedure made the market emphasis stronger. The ceiling of the value claims falling under its scope has been raised to €5,000 aiming, according to its Preamble (4) to "improve access to an effective and cost-efficient judicial remedy for cross-border disputes, in particular for SMEs."

The market orientation of the existing instruments presupposes empowered and active consumers who will take advantage of the schemes established in order to vindicate their rights. But they will be of little or no relevance for the individual consumer who is "taken" to court[51] by a sophisticated professional. As for the individual consumer redress, the ADR framework can only complement the conventional judicial redress avenue rather than compete with it or displace it.[52] Its establishment is certainly a very positive development for resolving

duties and cancellation rights as a means to enhance consumer confidence and the business access to consumer markets.

48 According to the Preamble (4) of the ADR Directive (n. 40): "Ensuring access to simple, efficient, fast and low-cost ways of resolving domestic and cross-border disputes which arise from sales or service contracts should benefit consumers and therefore boost their confidence in the market" and allow them (Preamble 7) "to exploit fully the potential of the internal market".

49 On the image of the "confident" consumer, see C. Twigg-Flesner, "The Importance of Law and Harmonisation for the EU's Confident Consumer" in D. Leczykiewicz and S. Weatherill (eds.) (n. 45), 183–201.

50 Important instruments have been adopted on this basis, in the field of international jurisdiction and choice of law, but also in the field of the advancement of effective access to justice, which is also relevant for consumer law proceedings. See E. Storskrubb (n. 24).

51 See J. Baldwin, *Small Claims in the County Courts in England and Wales: The Bargain Basement of Civil Justice* (Oxford, Clarendon Press, 1997), 15; C. Whelan, "Small Claims Courts: Heritage and Adjustment" in C. Whelan (ed.), *Small Claims Courts: A Comparative Study* (Oxford, Clarendon Press, 1990), 217.

52 See M. Stürner, "ADR and Adjudication by State Courts: Competitors or Complements?" in M. Stürner et al. (eds.), *The Role of Consumer ADR in the Administration of Justice* (Munich, Sellier, 2015). According to the Justice of the Supreme Court of Canada, Beverley McLachlin, "some cases should go to court … [because] they raise legal issues that should be considered by the courts for the good of the litigants and the development

consumer disputes that concern instant commercial transactions and/or transactions of limited financial scope. But the ADR fora are less appropriate for disputes concerning the performance of "*social lifetime contracts*",[53] covering goods and services that meet basic needs of the consumer as a *citizen*[54], such as contracts for the services of general economic interest, credit contracts, tenancy or residential mortgage contracts. Certain disputes that affect the performance of these contracts can only be subject to judicial adjudication (excluding out of court settlement). This is particularly the case for the setting aside of an unfair term, which has generated the biggest part of Union case law regarding procedures affecting consumers.

In sum, the direct harmonization of European consumer procedural law relies, largely, on the "confident consumer"[55] paradigm in litigation. The all-embracing "normative design"[56] for both consumer legislation and enforcement focus has long been the "empowered" consumer duly informed and educated.[57] This is an idealized vision which is not adapted for all consumers. Stephen Weatherill observes that:

> exalting the empowered consumer serves to humble consumers who are not so alert as "problem cases" needing remedial action – when an alternative vision treats the dauntingly intransparent and economically asymmetric market as the root cause at which corrective reform should be addressed.[58]

---

of the law.": HON. B. MCLACHLIN, P.C., "The Challenges We Face," Presented at the Empire Club of Canada, Toronto, March 8, 2007, available on the official portal of the Supreme Court of Canada under the section Speeches and quoted by S. MENETREY, *L'amicus curiae, vers un principe commun de droit procedural?* (Paris, Dalloz, 2010), 422.

53 L. NOGLER and U. REIFNER (eds.), *Life Time Contracts: Social Long-Term Contracts in Labour, Tenancy and Consumer Credit* (The Hague, Eleven Publishing, 2014); L. RATTI (ed.), *Embedding the Principles of Life Time Contracts: A Research Agenda for Contract Law* (The Hague, Eleven Publishing, 2018).

54 See H.-W. MICKLITZ, *Universal Services: Nucleus for a Social European Private Law* (EUI Working Paper 2009/12).

55 See indicatively T. WILHELMSSON, "The Abuse of the 'Confident Consumer' as a Justification for EC Consumer Law" (2004) 27 *Journal of Consumer Policy* 317–337; H.-W. MICKLITZ, "The Expulsion of the Concept of Protection from the Consumer Law and the Return of Social Elements in the Civil Law: A Bittersweet Polemic" (2012) 35 *Journal of Consumer Policy* 283–296.

56 H.-W. MICKLITZ, ibid.

57 See V. MAK, "The Myth of the 'Empowered Consumer': Lessons from Financial Literacy Studies" (2012) 4 *Journal of European Consumer and Market Law* 254–263; S. DE VRIES, "Consumer Protection and the EU Single Market Rules: The Search for the 'Paradigm Consumer'" (2012) 4 *Journal of European Consumer and Market Law* 228–242; V. MAK, "The 'Average Consumer' of EU Law in Domestic and European Litigation" in D. LECZYKIEWICZ and S. WEATHERILL (eds.) (n. 42), 333–356, who explains that in this framework "the protection through law is limited [and] mostly it takes the shape of rights which aim to equip and to encourage consumers to navigate the consumer (financial) market."

58 S. WEATHERILL, *EU Consumer Law and Policy* (Cheltenham, Edward Elgar, 2013), 312.

The gradual shift in paradigm, advanced along with the progressive prevalence of neoliberalism ideas, is explained by Hans Micklitz: "Consumer protection law became consumer law, while the protection of the weak became the protection of the ordinary informed and attentive consumer".[59]

The post-financial crisis consumer legislation might mark a turn in terms of the legislative perception of the consumer paradigm in the procedure and lean towards more, what Thomas Wilhelmsson has called, "need-rational welfarism"[60] regulatory patterns. In the Mortgage Credit Directive,[61] particular reference is made to the situation of arrears and foreclosure (Article 28). The stage of arrears represents what Hans Micklitz has called the "dark side of consumer credit".[62] The consumer-debtor in default represents the opposite of the "confident" consumer paradigm, namely the consumer who has lost confidence in the market and who is need of protection so as to live a decent life.[63] The aforementioned Article 28 of the Mortgage Credit Directive, provides for the obligation of the Member States to encourage creditors to exercise "reasonable forbearance" in residential mortgage repossession proceedings. Notably, in the Commission Accompanying Document to the said Directive, it is stressed that "where foreclosures do take place, which cannot be completely ruled out, common sense and humanity should always prevail at all levels (lender, authorities, courts, etc.) and throughout the whole procedure."[64]

---

59 H.-W. Micklitz (n. 55), 290. Indeed, one of the main indications of a normative shift is the change in the use of language. Alain Supiot recalls George Orwell's "Principles of Newspeak" and the necessity of restoring the meaning of the words in order to redefine our future: A. Supiot, *L'esprit de Philadelphie, la justice sociale face au marché total* (Paris, Seuil, 2010), 134, citing the following passage from George Orwell's "Principles of Newspeak" (Appendix to *Nineteen Eighty-Four*, 1949): "The purpose of Newspeak was not only to provide a medium of expression for the world-view and mental habits proper to the devotees of Ingsoc, but to make all other modes of thought impossible"

60 T. Wilhelmsson (n. 47), 725 and 730. This type of welfarism, generally absent from European contract law, refers to "regulation aimed at giving benefits to parties with special needs in comparison with other parties in similar situations". It concentrates upon the mitigation of the unbearable contractual consequences for the economically weaker in situations of social force majeure (as it is the case, for instance, with consumer bankruptcy schemes).

61 Directive 2014/17/EU of the European Parliament and of the Council of 4 February 2014 on credit agreements for consumers relating to residential immovable property and amending Directives 2008/48/EC and 2013/36/EU and Regulation (EU) No 1093/2010 [2014] OJ L60/34.

62 H.-W. Micklitz, "The Regulation of Over-indebtedness of Consumer in Europe" (2012) 35 *Journal of Consumer Policy* 417–419, 417.

63 A. Beka, "The Protection of the Primary Residence of Mortgage Debtors: Embedding the 'Basic Needs' Principle in Mortgage Repossession Proceedings" in L. Ratti (ed.) (n. 53), 247–276, 272.

64 Commission Staff Working Paper, National measures and practices to avoid foreclosure procedures for residential mortgage loans, Accompanying Document to the Proposal for a Directive of the European Parliament and of the Council on credit agreements relating to residential property, SEC (2011) 357 final, Brussels, 31 March 2011, 11.

We will come back to the residential mortgage repossession proceedings later.[65] The main point to be made here is that the direct Europeanization of consumer procedural law is less relevant for national procedural law governing individual judicial redress and is rather well adapted to a specific consumer model, the empowered and confident consumer. The broader horizontal impact of European law upon national proceedings concerning consumer disputes has rather been indirect and is associated with the "interplay"[66] between Union substantive consumer protection law and the effectiveness of national procedural law, to which we shall turn to now.

## 2. THE INDIRECT EUROPEANIZATION OF CONSUMER PROCEDURAL LAW

The indirect Europeanization of consumer procedural law refers to the impact of Union law on national procedural law resulting from the application of the principles of effectiveness and effective judicial protection. The case law on the individual judicial protection of consumers in domestic litigation has built *a procedural strand of protection* construed on the basis of the protective purposes of substantive consumer law. This strand of procedural protection is *complementary* to the existing harmonized procedural law of relevance for consumer disputes, discussed in the section above. In particular, the doctrine of the active court in consumer litigation was developed in case law, in the context of review of domestic procedural rules in light of the requirements of effective consumer judicial protection against the use of unfair terms. Its establishment was, from the beginning, associated with the attainment of the *full effectiveness* of the applicable rules of the substantive consumer law in order to ensure *effective consumer protection*. Before getting to a detailed analysis of the doctrine, it appears necessary, therefore, to place it within the broader constitutional framework of the judicial protection of Union law rights.

The Court has consistently held that, in the absence of harmonization of remedial and procedural rules of Union law rights, Member States remain competent to organize their judicial system and to provide for the remedial and procedural framework for the effective enforcement of Union law rights This competence is subject to the principles of equivalence and effectiveness and the principle of effective judicial protection. The standard formulation of the Court on the principle of national procedural autonomy, as it has evolved since the

65 Chapter 5, Section 3.

66 See H.-W. Micklitz, "The Constitutional Transformation of Private Law Pillars through the CJUE" in H. Collins (ed.), *European Contract Law and the Charter of Fundamental Rights* (Cambridge, Intersentia, 2017), 49–91, 89.

famous judgments in *Rewe*[67] and *Comet*[68] (customarily known as the "*Rewe/Comet* formula"), reads as follows:

> in the absence of [Union] rules in the field, it is for the domestic legal system of each Member State to designate the courts and tribunals having jurisdiction and to lay down the detailed procedural rules governing actions for safeguarding rights which individuals derive from [Union] law, provided, first that such rules are not less favourable than those governing similar domestic actions (principle of equivalence) and, second, that they do not render virtually impossible or excessively difficult the exercise of rights conferred by [Union] law (principle of effectiveness).[69]

The application of the principles of effectiveness and effective judicial protection results in a progressive and indirect Europeanization of procedural law, despite the lack of harmonization of domestic enforcement of Union rights.[70] The obligation of the Member States to ensure effective legal protection of Union rights is enshrined under the "constitutional tandem"[71] of Article 19 of the Treaty on European Union (TEU) and Article 47 of the Charter.[72] Both fundamental provisions encapsulate a decades-long judicial shaping of domestic procedures under the requirements of effectiveness and effective judicial protection. Michal Bobek explains the differences of the two distinct logics between procedural unification/harmonization on the one hand, and the influence exercised upon the domestic legal order governing the enforcement of Union law rights through the application of the imperatives of effective judicial protection on the other:

> the logic of EU legislation is one of area-specific, conferred competence. In contrast, the logic of the Court's engagement with national enforcement of EU law is functional and transversal. It is not limited to any field or area of law.[73]

---

67 Case 33/76 *Rewe-Zentralfinanz and Rewe-Zentral*, EU:C:1976:188, para. 5.

68 Case 45/76 *Comet*, EU:C:1976:191, para. 13.

69 See Joined Cases C-222/05–C-225/05 *Van der Weerd*, EU:C:2007:318, para. 28; Case C-268/06 *Impact*, EU:C:2008:223, paras. 42–47; Joined Cases C-317-320/08 *Alassini*, EU:C:2010:146, paras. 48 and 49.

70 On the consideration of *Europeanization* from the perspective of principles drawn from the case law, see W. Van Gerven, "The Case Law of the European Court of Justice and National Courts as a Contribution to the Europeanisation of Private Law" (1995) 3 *ERPL* 367–378. At the level of public law, J.H. Jans, R. de Lange, S. Prechal and R.J.G.M Widdershoven, *Europeanisation of Public Law* (Groningen, Europa Law Publishing, 2007) analyze the Europeanization of national procedural law in the context of the requirements of equivalence and effectiveness and effective judicial protection. See E. Storskrubb (n. 24), 12 *et seq.*, who analyzes the case law of the Court as a form of procedural harmonization leading to the Europeanization of civil procedural law.

71 N. Reich (n. 23), 91.

72 See Case C-243/15, *Lesoochranárske zoskupenie VLK*, EU:C:2016:838, para. 50.

73 M. Bobek, (n. 25), 166.

The basic pattern of the judicial enforcement of Union civil and consumer law rights is not different compared to the enforcement of other Union law rights. The objective of the following paragraphs is not to offer an exhaustive analysis of the landmark concept of national procedural autonomy or of the principles of effectiveness and effective judicial protection.[74] For our purposes, it suffices to adumbrate the constituents of the concepts, drawing as far as possible from civil law paradigms.

## 2.1. THE FUNCTION OF PROCEDURAL AUTONOMY: A MECHANISM UNDERPINNING THE SYSTEM OF DECENTRALIZED ENFORCEMENT OF UNION LAW

The EU legal system has a complex structure of mechanisms for its implementation and enforcement. The term "implementation" is broader than the term "enforcement" and encompasses both the executive power to adopt delegated norms as well as the administrative and judicial power to enforce legislation in individual circumstances.[75] The Treaties endorse the principle of indirect administration by providing that "Member States are responsible for adopting all measures of national law necessary to implement legally binding Union acts" (Article 291(1) TFEU). Article 197 TFEU reiterates this primary responsibility of Member States, but requires that implementation be "effective," as an element "essential for the proper functioning of the Union" which "shall be regarded as a matter of common interest." Such a rule is not a particularity of the Union, but is a common feature of the system of executive federalism (*Vollzugsföderalismus*), whereby the federal legislator adopts the law and the federal entities are entrusted with its application.[76]

---

[74] A wealth of literature exists on this issue by the most distinguished authors. See V. Skouris, "The Principle of Procedural Autonomy and the Duty of Loyal Cooperation of National Judges under Article 10 EC" in M. Andenas and D. Fairgrieve (eds.), *Tom Bingham and the Transformation of the Law: A Liber Amicorum* (Oxford, Oxford University Press, 2009), 493–507; K. Lenaerts, "Le traité de Lisbonne et la Protection Juridictionnelle des Particuliers en Droit de l'Union" (2009) *Cahiers de Droit Européen* 711–745; K. Lenaerts, "The Rule of Law and the Coherence of the Judicial System of the European Union" (2007) 44 *CMLR* 1625–1659; K. Lenaerts and P. Van Nuffel, *European Union Law* (London, Sweet & Maxwell, 2nd ed., 2011), paras. 21-001 *et seq.*; K. Lenaerts, I. Maselis and K. Gutman, *EU Procedural Law* (Oxford, Oxford University Press, 2014), paras. 4.01 *et seq.*; M. Safjan and D. Düsterhaus, "A Union of Effective Judicial Protection: Addressing a Multi-level Challenge through the Lens of Article 47 CFREU" (2014) 33 *Yearbook of European Law* 3–40; W. van Gerven (n. 26); C.N. Kakouris, "Do the Member States Possess Judicial Procedural Autonomy?" (1997) 6 *CMLR* 1389–1412; J.H. Jans et al. (n. 70), 35 *et seq.*

[75] The French version of the Treaties uses the term "mise en oeuvre" in Art. 291(1) TFEU with respect to the implementing powers of the Member States and the term "exécution" in Art. 291(2) TFEU with respect to the implementing powers of the Commission.

[76] B. Dubey, "Administration indirecte et fédéralisme d'exécution en Europe" (2003) *Cahiers Droit Européen* 87–133, K. Boskovits, *Le juge communautaire et l'articulation des*

The legal basis of the principle of indirect administration is the principle of conferral (Article 5 TEU) along with the principle of sincere cooperation (Article 4 TEU).[77] The principle of conferral in the administration level means that the Member States are entrusted with the implementation of Union law, unless the Treaties have provided otherwise. The prevailing decentralized model is complemented[78] by the centralized model, so that the European Union combines "both federal models in its own constitutional brand."[79] The principle of sincere cooperation requires that in the exercise of their implementation competences, Member States are bound to achieve the effectiveness of Union law.

The model of decentralized or indirect administration "straddles" the entire array of state powers, the legislative, the executive and the judiciary. Correspondingly, it takes three forms:[80] (i) the normative;[81]

---

*compétences normatives entre la Communauté européenne et ses Etats Membres* (Brussels, Bruylant, 2001) 347; K. Lenaerts and P. Van Nuffel (n. 74), 688; R. Schütze, "From Rome to Lisbon: 'Executive Federalism' in the (New) European Union" (2010) 47 *CMLR* 1385.

77 Opinion 2/13 (*Accession of the European Union to the ECHR*), EU:C:2014:2454, para. 173; K. Lenaerts and P. van Nuffel (n. 74), 687; G. Isaac and M. Blanquet, *Droit général de l'Union Européenne* (Paris, Dalloz, 10th ed., 2012), 442 *et seq.*; K. Boskovits (n. 76), 352 *et seq*; J. Jiller, "Exécution centralisée et exécution partagée" and L. Azoulai, "Pour un droit de l'exécution de l'Union Européenne" in J. Dutheil de la Rochère (ed.), *L'exécution du droit de l'Union, entre mécanismes communautaires et droits nationaux* (Brussels, Bruylant, 2009). On the thesis of effectiveness as a "lever" of allocation of competences, see F. Caulet: "Le principe d'effectivité comme pivot de répartition des compétences procédurales entre les États Membres et l'Union européenne" (2012) *RTDE* 594.

78 Executive federalism is not the sole constitutional pattern applicable for the enforcement of Union law. There are instances (although exceptional) of direct powers attributed to the Union to implement and enforce its own law, either through an explicit basis in the Treaties – the most representative example being competition law (Arts. 105, 106 and 108 TFEU) or through the general basis of Art. 291(2) TFEU. This provision is the legal basis for Union executive competence powers "where uniform conditions for implementing legally binding Union acts are needed." The existence of such a requirement is to be assessed in accordance with the general principles of subsidiarity (Art. 5(3) TFEU) and proportionality (Art. 5(4) TFEU). The constitutional reality is even more complex than that. Scholars in European administrative law study the phenomenon of European administrative governance in terms of novel executive forms of cooperation and shared administration, which go "beyond the dichotomy of direct and indirect administration": H.C.H. Hofmann, G.C. Rowe and A.H. Türk, *Administrative Law and Policy of the European Union* (Oxford, Oxford University Press, 2012), 259. On the model of "cooperative federalism": R. Schütze, *From Dual to Cooperative Federalism: The Changing Structure of European Union Law* (Oxford, Oxford University Press, 2009).

79 R. Schütze, *European Constitutional Law* (Cambridge, Cambridge University Press, 2012), 244.

80 G. Isaac and M. Blanquet (n. 77); M. Vaerini Jensen, *Exécution du droit communautaire par les Etats membres* (Helbing, Bruylant/L.G.D.J,. 2007), 15, who distinguishes between three categories of indirect administration: the normative, the administrative and the disciplinary. The disciplinary function can nevertheless be considered as a subcategory of the administrative and the judicial function.

81 The normative indirect administration requires legislative action by the Member States in order to complement Union legislation. The implementation of Union directives is the most representative example of normative indirect administration.

(ii) the administrative;[82] and (iii) the judicial. Article 291(1) TFEU encompasses the normative and the administrative indirect enforcement. The judicial indirect enforcement mainly finds its expression in Article 19(1) TEU. According to the second subparagraph of this provision: "Member States shall provide the remedies sufficient to ensure effective legal protection in the fields covered by Union law."

The aforementioned provision introduced in the Lisbon Treaty, represents the legislative "reaffirmation" of settled case law.[83] The Union defines at the central level the substantive rights, while the Member States, using their "powerful mechanisms" ("puissantes machineries" according to the eloquent expression of one of the founding fathers of the Union, Jean Monnet[84]) provide for the institutional framework, the administrative procedures, the judicial remedies and proceedings for the implementation and enforcement of Union law.[85] The "decentralized model of justice"[86] is constructed upon the premise that national courts are "the primary venue for the assertion of [Union] rights."[87] They therefore operate in a "jurisdictional" or "functional dualism."[88] The national

---

82 The administrative indirect administration requires the employment of the administrative mechanisms in a Member State so that Union law can effectively be applied. The sanctioning of the infringement of Union law is a subcategory of the administrative indirect administration.

83 Case C-583/11P *Inuit Tapiriit Kanatami and Others v. European Parliament and Council*, EU:C:2013:625, para. 101; Case C-274/12 P *Telefónica v. Commission*, EU:C:2013:852, para. 57, Opinion 1/09 (Agreement creating a Unified Patent Litigation System), EU:C:2011:123, para. 69; Case C-50/00 P *Unión de Pequeños Agricultores v. Council*, EU:C:2002:462, para. 41.

84 J. Monnet, *Mémoires* (Paris, Fayard, 1976), 436.

85 The role of the Member States as executive agents in the implementation of EU law and their "dédoublement fonctionnel" (relevant to all authorities applying Union law, including the courts) has been the subject of remarkable doctrinal elaboration. See indicatively J. Rideau, "Le rôle des États Membres dans l'application du droit communautaire" (1972) 18 *Annuaire Français de Droit International*, 864-903; A. Barav, "La plénitude de compétence du juge national en sa qualité de juge communautaire," in J. Boulouis (ed.), *L'Europe et le Droit, Mélanges en hommage à Jean Boulouis* (Paris, Dalloz, 1991), 1–20 ; G. Isaac and M. Blanquet (n. 77), 441; A. von Bogdandy and J. Bast, "The European Union's Vertical Order of Competences: The Current Law and Proposals for its Reform" (2002) 39 *CMLR* 227–268; D. Simon, *Le système juridique communautaire* (Paris, PUF, 3rd ed., 2001), 163; S. Kadelbach, "European Administrative Law and the Law of the Europeanised Administration" in C. Joerges and R. Dehousse (eds.), *Good Governance in Europe's Integrated Market* (Oxford, Oxford University Press, 2002), 167; A. Levade, "Les moyens des Etats" in L. Azoulai and L. Burgorgue-Larsen, *L'autorité de l'Union Européenne* (Brussels, Bruylant, 2006), 157; M. Vaerini Jensen (n. 80); J. Dutheil de la Rochère (n. 77).

86 T. Tridimas, *The General Principles of EU Law* (Oxford, Oxford University Press, 2nd ed., 2006), 418.

87 Ibid., 419.

88 C.N. Kakouris, "Do the Member States Possess Judicial Procedural Autonomy?" (1997) 6 *CMLR* 1389–1412, 1393; F. Grévisse and J.C. Bonichot, "Les incidences du droit communautaire sur l'organisation et l'exercise de la fonction jurisdictionelle dans les Etats Membres" and A. Barav, "La plénitude de compétence du juge national en sa qualité de juge communautaire" both in J. Boulouis, (n. 85) ; A. Rosas, "The National Judge as EU Judge: Opinion 1/09" in P. Cardonnel, A. Rosas and N. Wahl (eds.), *Constitutionalising*

courts, acting in their capacity as Union courts, enforce rules of a legal order in which, as Loïc Azoulai points out, the *jurisdictio* (law-making) function is disconnected from the *actio* (the execution of the law) function, being each assigned to different actors, the Union and the Member States respectively.[89] This separation of powers lies at the heart of the integration of Union law within the national legal orders. The founding fathers trusted this "ship so fragile in turbulent waters"[90] to the national courts, equipping them with the "compass" of the principle of loyal cooperation.[91]

The mechanism *par excellence* of the decentralized model of justice, the "keystone" in the words of the Court,[92] is the preliminary reference procedure (Article 267 TFEU). It is the symbol of the judicial dialogue[93] between the Court as the "Supreme Court of the Union"[94] and the national courts. The relationship is not hierarchical,[95] but rather one of judicial cooperation.[96] Opinion 1/09 summarizes the role of the national courts as follows:

> The system set up by Article 267 TFEU ... establishes between the Court of Justice and the national courts direct cooperation as part of which the latter are closely

---

*the EU Judicial System: Essays in Honour of Pernilla Lindh* (Oxford, Hart Publishing, 2012), 105–121; N. Fennelly, "The National Judge as Judge of the European Union" in *The Court of Justice and the Construction of Europe: Analyses and Perspectives on Sixty Years of Case-Law* (The Hague, T.M.C. Asser Press, 2013).

89 L. Azoulai, "Pour un droit de l'exécution de l'Union Européenne" in J. Dutheil de la Rochère (ed.) (n. 77).

90 The metaphor was coined by Lord Wilberforce in his inaugural speech in the 9th F.I.D.E. Congress in 1980 when he questioned to what extent the founding fathers of the Community would have realized the diversity among the national judicial systems "auraient eu la foi de confier un navire si fragile à une mer si agitée"; cited by A. Barav (n. 88), 17.

91 It has been settled case law since Case 14/83 *Von Colson and Kamann*, EU:C:1984:153 that the principle of loyal cooperation applies to all authorities applying Union law within a Member State, including the judiciary.

92 Opinion 2/13 (*Accession of the European Union to the ECHR*), EU:C:2014:2454, para. 176.

93 Ibid. The judicial dialogue and the role of preliminary reference as a mechanism of such dialogue are topics that have attracted elaborate academic reflection. See J. Rideau., (n. 85), 882; *Le dialogue des juges: actes du colloque organisé le 28 avril 2006 à l'Université Libre de Bruxelles* (Brussels, Bruylant, 2007); F. Lichère, L. Potvin-Solis and A. Raynouard (eds.), *Le dialogue entre les juges européens et nationaux: incantation ou réalité?, Actes de la journée d'études organisée le 10 février 2003 à la Faculté de droit, économie et administration de l'Université de Metz* (Brussels, Nemesis, Bruylant, 2004), A.M. Slaughter Burley, A.S. Sweet and J.H.H. Weiler, *The European Court and National Courts: Doctrine and Jurisprudence - Legal Change in its Social Context* (Oxford, Hart Publishing, 1998).

94 T. Tridimas, "The European Court of Justice and the Draft Constitution: a Supreme Court of the Union?" in T. Tridimas (ed.), *European Union law for the 21st Century, Vol. 1 Rethinking the New Legal Order* (Oxford, Hart Publishing, 2004), 113–141.

95 See J. Komarek, "In the Court(s) We Trust? On the Need for Hierarchy and Differentiation in the Preliminary Ruling Procedure," in F. Fontanelli, G. Martinico and P. Carrozza, *Shaping Rule of Law through Dialogue, International and Supranational Experience* (Groningen, Europa Law Publishing, 2010), 89–116.

96 See already from early case law Case 62/72 *Bollmann*, EU:C:1973:24; P. Pescatore, *Court of Justice of the European Communities: References for Preliminary Rulings under Article 177 of*

> involved in the correct application and uniform interpretation of European Union law and also in the protection of individual rights conferred by that legal order.[97]

In this process, Union law and national law become "communicating vessels." The former President of the Court, Vassilios Skouris, describes the influence of national law and case law upon the application of Union law in terms of building unity through law.[98] Despite its autonomous character,[99] Union law remains deeply "anchored" in the national legal orders so that they both build the *"corpus"* of Union law.[100] Provided that national and European courts engage in genuine dialogue, Hans Micklitz argues that the preliminary reference procedure makes "the principal democratic foundation of the European legal order."[101]

The decentralized model of justice is underpinned by the constitutional principles of the direct effect and primacy of Union law.[102] However, they are not sufficient in themselves for the judicial materialization of a Union right. Anthony Arnull[103] observes that the principles of primacy and direct effect, as well as the principle of state liability for violation of Union law, form a "skeleton" for which the "flesh" is filled by the principle of national procedural autonomy. In the Union legal order, as opposed to the legal orders of the Member States, the triptych of rights, remedies and procedures[104] is rarely complete. A Union right

---

*the EEC Treaty and Cooperation between the Court and National Courts* (Luxembourg, Office for Official Publications of the European Communities, 1986).

97 Opinion 1/09 (n. 83), para. 84.

98 V. Skouris, "Der Einfluss des nationalen Rechts und der Rechtsprechung der mitgliedstaatlichen Gerichte auf die Auslegung des Europarechts" *Zeitschrift der Verwaltungsgerichtsbarkeit* ZVG 2014/3, 203.

99 Opinion 2/13 (n. 92), paras. 179–200.

100 V. Skouris (n. 98).

101 H.-W. Micklitz, *The Politics of Judicial Cooperation – Sunday Trading, Equal Treatment and Good Faith* (Cambridge, Cambridge University Press, 2005), 425; P. Pescatore, "Van Gend en Loos, 3 February 1963 – A View from Within" in M. Poiares Maduro and L. Azoulai (eds.), *The Past and the Future of EU Law: The Classics of EU Law Revisited on the 50th Anniversary of the Treaty of Rome* (Oxford, Hart Publishing, 2010), 3, at 7, writes with regard to the potential of the preliminary reference procedure revealed in *Van Gend en Loos*: "The Court held that the vigilance of individuals concerned to protect their rights amounts to an effective supervision in addition to the supervision entrusted by Art. 169 and 170 in the diligence of the Commission and the Member States. This formulate is prophetic, since we would see later on that the preliminary reference procedure … will effectively become the infringement procedure for the European citizen."

102 On those fundamental principles of EU law, see indicatively A. Tizzano, J. Kokott and S. Prechal (organizing committee), *50th Anniversary of the Judgment in Van Gend en Loos (1963–2013), Conference Proceedings Luxembourg, 13 May 2013* (Curia), available online at https://curia.europa.eu/jcms/upload/docs/application/pdf/2013-12/qd30136442ac_002.pdf; R. Lecourt, "Quel eut été le droit des communautés sans les arrêts de 1963 et 1964 ?" in J. Boulouis (n. 85), 349–361.

103 A. Arnull, "The Principle of Effective Judicial Protection in EU Law: An Unruly Horse?" (2011) 36 *ELRev* 51–70, at 52.

104 On the conceptual contours of the notions, see the classic study of W. Van Gerven (n. 26).

will not necessarily be accompanied by a specific measure for its enforcement and even less by procedural rules for its vindication in courts. The principle of national procedural autonomy "fills in" this "gap," attenuating the risk to the effective application of Union law. When European law is silent, it falls back to national laws to ensure the effective transformation of a Union right into a specific remedy, accommodated within a procedural context. In the words of AG Jacobs in his Opinion in the *Van Schijndel* case:

> The assumption underlying the system established by the Treaties ... is that the need for effectiveness and proper judicial protection can normally be satisfied by national remedies enforced through the national courts in accordance with national procedural rules .... The underlying premise is that States based on the rule of law will organize their national legal systems in such a way as to ensure proper application of the law and adequate legal protection for their subjects. It is therefore only exceptionally that the Court will need to intervene to ensure that effect is given to Community law.[105]

This solution, this "initial pact, base line" as Clare Kilipatrick eloquently puts it,[106] stemming from the separation of powers in the Union legal order, ensures the application of Union law. To put it simply, Union law does not have its own rules of Union (civil or administrative) procedure before the national courts. It does not have either decentralized Union courts separate from the Member State courts functionally operating as Union courts for matters pertaining to Union law. Union law takes the Member States' courts "as it finds them", to employ the famous principle applying with reference to the US federal system of enforcement of federal law by state courts.[107] In turn, each Member State, as Koen Lenaerts explains, "contributes its own judicial system for the sake of ensuring the effective application and enforcement of EU law."[108]

Much has been written on the legal nature of Member States' procedural autonomy.[109] Sacha Prechal encapsulates neatly the relevant debate:

> Should it be considered to be an expression of national sovereignty? Or does it result directly from the decentralized nature of the enforcement and application of EU law,

---

105 Opinion of AG Jacobs in Joined Cases C-430/93 and C-431/93 *Van Schijndel v. Stichting Pensioenfonds voor Fysiotherapeuten*, EU:C:1995:185, paras. 29–30.

106 C. Kilipatrick, "The Future of Remedies in Europe" in C. Kilipatrick, T. Novitz and P. Skidmore, *The Future of Remedies in Europe* (Oxford, Hart Publishing, 2000), 1–31.

107 I refer to the principle as famously pronounced by H. Hart, "The Relations between State and Federal Law" (1954) 54 *Columbia Law Review*, 489, 508: "The general rule, bottomed deeply in belief in the importance of state control of state judicial procedure, is that federal law takes the state courts as it finds them." See J. Rideau., (n. 85), 884.

108 K. Lenaerts (n. 74).

109 For a detailed account, see D.U. Galetta, *Procedural Autonomy of EU Member States: Paradise Lost? A Study on the Functionalised Procedural Competence" of EU Member States* (Berlin, Springer, 2011).

in which Member States retain the power to determine the procedural rules governing the enforcement and application of Union law, only as long as Union legislation governing procedural rules have not been developed? [T]hose debates would seem, above all, to be prompted by a difference of approach rather than by fundamental theoretical insights.[110]

In his eminent contribution to the debate, Constantinos Kakouris rejects the understanding of procedural autonomy as a manifestation of Member States' sovereignty. In his view: "in point of fact, the Court has tended to regard national procedural law merely as an ancillary body of law the function of which is to ensure the effective application of substantive [Union] law".[111]

In his seminal study "On Rights, Remedies and Procedures," Walter Van Gerven suggests that it might be better:

to abandon the term procedural autonomy and to speak of procedural competence of Member States' in view of the fact that "competence in procedural matters remains the prime responsibility of the Member States so long as, as Prechal points out, no [Union] rules have been enacted and direct [Union] competence is absent."[112]

Indeed, in certain cases, the Court refers to a "competence" which falls within the Member States.[113] According to Vassilios Skouris "the institutional and procedural autonomy is somehow a specific expression of Article 5 [TEU] and the fundamental principle of subsidiarity pursuant to which each specific competence must be exercised at the most appropriate level".[114]

For the former President of the Court, the procedural autonomy is actually "one of the main consequences of ... division of labour" whereby the primary judicial enforcement of [Union] law falls upon the national judges.[115] However, he also notes that such a "privileged position" carries with it certain obligations deriving from the principle of loyal cooperation.[116]

The exercise of the procedural competence of Member States must be exercised, indeed, with due regard to the principle of loyal or sincere cooperation

110 S. Prechal and K. Cath, "The European Acquis of Civil Procedure: Constitutional Aspects" (2014) 19 *Uniform Law Review* 179–198, 180.

111 C.N. Kakouris (n. 74), 1390. See also M. Bobek, "Why There is No Principle of 'Procedural Autonomy' of the Member States" in H.-W. Micklitz and B. de Witte (eds.), *The European Court of Justice and the Autonomy of Member States* (Cambridge, Intersentia, 2014), 305–334.

112 W. Van Gerven (n. 26), at 502, with reference to S. Prechal, "Community Law in National Courts: The Lessons from *Van Schijndel*" (1998) 35 *CMLR* 681–706.

113 Case C-55/06 *Arcor*, EU:C:2008:244, para. 190(on the burden of proof). See also Case C-360/09 *Pfeiderer*, EU:C:2011:389, para. 24 and Case C-536/11 *Donau Chemie*, EU:C:2013:366, para. 27 (on the right to access to the file of cartel cases).

114 V. Skouris (n. 74), 493–507, 494.

115 Ibid.

116 Ibid.

(Article 4(3) TEU). The duty of loyal cooperation "is binding on all the authorities of the Member States" and in particular for the level of judicial enforcement, it is binding "on the courts."[117] Under this principle, since the judgment in *Rewe*,[118] it is settled case law that "it is for the courts of the Member States to ensure judicial protection of a person's rights under EU law".[119]

In the case law following the Lisbon Treaty, the Court complements this reference to the principle of loyal cooperation with the provision on effective remedies under Article 19(1) TEU: "In addition, Article 19(1) requires Member States to provide remedies sufficient to ensure effective legal protection in the fields covered by Union law".[120]

The obligation laid down in the effective remedies' rule of Article 19 TEU corresponds to the right to an effective judicial protection under Article 47 of the Charter. As stated in the judgment of the Court in *Berlioz Investment Fund*:

> According to Article 47 of the Charter, entitled "Right to an effective remedy and to a fair trial", everyone whose rights and freedoms guaranteed by the law of the Union are violated has the right to an effective remedy before a tribunal. The obligation imposed on the Member States in the second subparagraph of Article 19 (1) TEU, to provide remedies sufficient to ensure effective legal protection in the fields covered by Union law, corresponds to that right.[121]

The requirement of the Member States to provide for effective remedies under Article 19 TEU therefore appears to represent, as Eleftheria Neframi observes, the "procedural aspect" of the principle of loyal cooperation.[122] This in turn

117 Case 14/83 *Von Colson and Kamann* (n. 91), para. 26; Case 80/86 *Kolpinghuis Nijmegen*, EU:C:1987:431, para. 12.

118 Case 33/76 *Rewe* (n. 67), para. 5.

119 Case C-243/15 *Lesoochranárske zoskupenie VLK* (n. 72), para. 50; Case C-432/05 *Unibet*, EU:C:2007:163, para. 38.

120 Ibid., citing Case C-404/13 *ClientEarth*, EU:C:2014:2382, para. 52.

121 Case C-682/15 *Berlioz Investment Fund*, EU:C:2017:373, para. 44. See also Case C–243/15 *Lesoochranárske zoskupenie VLK* (n. 72), para. 50. The Court in its judgment in C–583/11 P *Inuit* (n. 83), para. 103, nevertheless confirmed the validity of the "no-new remedies" rules pronounced before the Lisbon Treaty in its judgment in Case C–432/05 *Unibet* (n. 119): "As regards the remedies which Member States must provide, while the FEU Treaty has made it possible in a number of instances for natural and legal persons to bring a direct action, where appropriate, before the Courts of the European Union, neither the FEU Treaty nor Article 19 TEU intended to create new remedies before the national courts to ensure the observance of European Union law other than those already laid down by national law." See J.H. Jans, "On *Inuit* and Judicial Protection in a Shared Legal Order" (2012) 21 *European Energy and Environmental Law Review* 188–191.

122 E. Neframi, "Quelques réflexions sur l'article 19, para. 1, alinéa 2, TEU et l'obligation de l'Etat Membre d'assurer la protection juridictionnelle effective dans les domaines couverts par le droit de l'Union" in *La Constitution, l'Europe et le droit, Mélanges en l'honneur de Jean-Claude Masclet* (Paris, Publications de la Sorbonne, 2013), 807. The author discusses the proposition whether Art. 19(1) TEU could be read as establishing an "autonomous

reflects the principle of "federal good faith" that applies in the exercise of a wide array of authorities' powers in a system of multi-level governance.[123]

As for the scope of procedural autonomy, it is a very broad one. It is an "umbrella" term that captures all "rules and principles that are of an organizational nature, governing actions at law intended to ensure the application and enforcement of Union law."[124] It covers first of all the institutional autonomy, the competence of Member States to "designate the courts and tribunals having jurisdiction" before which judicial redress may be sought.[125] Moreover, the concept of procedural autonomy embraces remedial autonomy, *stricto sensu* procedural autonomy and, more broadly, "enforcement autonomy."[126] Verica Trstenjak and Erwan Beysen have likewise observed that the Court "extends the concept of procedural autonomy to cases concerning national remedies for the enforcement of individuals' rights under Union law, thus mixing the concepts of remedial and procedural autonomy."[127]

---

obligation" of the Member States to achieve a particular result. The case law available after the coming into force of the Lisbon Treaty, in particular Opinion 1/09 [2011] ECR I-1137, which the author analyzes, would seem to imply that Art. 19(1) does not create an autonomous obligation and does not absorb the principle of loyal cooperation. The recent case law of the Court on the interrelationship of Art. 19(1) TEU and Art. 47 of the Charter seems to confirm the tentative proposition expressed by K. LENAERTS ET AL (n. 74), para. 4.12, according to which, against the background of the Charter, the case law of the Court might "transform the obligation to make best endeavours into an obligation to achieve a particular result." See also the Opinion of AG Jääskinsen in Case C-536/11 *Donau Chemie*, EU:C:2013:366, point 47: "Finally, due account needs to be taken of Article 19(1), and the extent to which it supplies a supplementary guarantee to the principle of effectiveness. Pursuant to Article 19(1), Member States are bound to provide remedies 'sufficient to ensure effective legal protection in the fields covered by Union law.' In other words, in the light of that Treaty provision, the standard of effective judicial protection for EU based rights seems to be more demanding than the classical formula referring to practical impossibility or excessive difficulty. In my opinion this means that national remedies must be accessible, prompt, and reasonably cost effective." On the relationship between Art. 19(1) TEU and Art. 47 of the Charter, see also M. SAFJAN and D. DÜSTERHAUS (n. 74).

123 K. LENAERTS and P. VAN NUFFEL (n. 74), para. 7-042. The Opinion of AG Warner in Case 33/76 *Rewe*, EU:C:1976:167, the landmark case that set the foundations for the development of the principle of national procedural autonomy, explains the thrust of the principle "*as a situation in which Community law and national law operate in combination, the latter taking over where the former leaves off, and working out its consequences.*" In the absence of uniform Union procedural rules, Union rights could risk become a dead letter and therefore, the Opinion continues, there is "*no alternative to the application of the remedies and procedures prescribed by national law*".

124 S. PRECHAL andK. CATH, (n. 110), 180.

125 This has been a settled formulation of the Court since Case 33/76 *Rewe* (n. 67); see for instance Case C-268/06, *Impact*, (n. 69), para. 44.

126 J. ENGSTROM, *The Europeanisation of Remedies and Procedures through Judge-Made Law: Can a Trojan Horse Achieve Effectiveness?* (Fiesole, EUI, 2009), 5–11, who merges remedies and procedures into "enforcement rules."

127 V. TRSTENJAK and E. BEYSEN, "European Consumer Protection Law: *Curia Semper Dabit Remedium*?" (2011) 48 *CMLR* 95–124, at footnote 34.

According to the classic definition proposed by Walter van Gerven,[128] the remedies are "classes of action, intended to make good infringements of the rights concerned." It is a fundamental obligation of the Member States to establish "a system of legal remedies and procedures which ensure respect for the fundamental right to effective judicial protection,"[129] an obligation reaffirmed under Article 19(1) TEU. The Member States also have to provide for the executive remedial rules, which according to Walter van Gerven can be defined as the "conditions and restrictions under which individuals are enabled to bring and maintain actions before courts of law in order to safeguard their rights." These cover for instance rules on standing and legal interest in bringing proceedings,[130] allocation of the burden of proof,[131] rules of evidence[132] and limitation periods.[133] Depending on the classification adopted by a given legal system, the same rules could be considered as *stricto sensu* procedural rules, understood as "practical rules according to which the remedy is to be pursued in a court of law."[134] Procedural autonomy may also be deemed to cover every rule that relates to the enforcement of Union law, such as rules governing the broader implementing framework of a certain right,[135] sanctions for the infringement of Union law[136] or the contractual consequences for non-compliance with the obligations laid down in the Directives.[137]

---

128 W. Van Gerven (n. 112), 524.

129 *Inuit* (n. 83) para. 100.

130 Joined Cases C-87/90–C-89/90 *Verholen and Others*, EU:C:1991:314, para. 24; Case C-12/08 *Mono Car Styling*, EU:C:2009:466, para. 49 (with further citations therein).

131 Case C-55/06 *Arcor*, (n. 113), paras. 179–192; Case C-449/13 *CA Consumer Finance*, EU:C:2014:2464.

132 Case C-276/01 *Steffensen*, EU:C:2003:228, para. 60; Case C-35/09 *Speranza*, EU:C:2010:393, para. 41.

133 Case 61/79 *Denkavit Italiana*, EU:C:1980:100, para. 23; Case C-326/96 *Levez v. Jennings, Ltd* EU:C:1998:577; Case C-63/08 *Pontin*, EU:C:2009:666; Case C-262/09 *Meilicke and Others*, EU:C:2011:438, para. 55; Joined Cases C-501/12 *Specht and Others*, EU:C:2014:2005, para. 112.

134 W. Van Gerven (n. 112), 524.

135 Case C-378/10 *VALE Építési*, EU:C:2012:440, para. 49. In this case the Court applied "the logic underlying" the case law on procedural autonomy with respect to the implementing framework for the exercise of a company's right to carry out a corporate conversion.

136 It is settled case law and standard formulation in the directives that the sanctions for infringement of Union law must be effective, proportionate and dissuasive: Case 14/83 *Von Colson and Kamann* (n. 91), para. 23; Case C-177/88 *Dekker*, EU:C:1990:383, paras. 23–26; Case C-271/91 *Marshall*, EU:C:1993:335, paras. 24–26; Joined Cases C-378/07–C-380/07 *Angelidaki and Others*, EU:C:2009:250, para. 186.

137 Case C-604/11 *Genil 48 and Comercial Hostelera de Grandes Vinos*, EU:C:2013:344, para. 57.

## 2.2. THE EFFECTIVE PROTECTION OF UNION RIGHTS RESHAPING PROCEDURAL AUTONOMY

The Member States remain competent to provide for the remedies and procedures that will allow for the judicial enforcement of Union law rights, provided that, first, these rules are not less favorable than those governing similar domestic claims (*principle of equivalence*) and, second, they do not render virtually impossible or excessively difficult the exercise of rights conferred by Union law (*principle of effectiveness*). The principles of equivalence and effectiveness "embody," according to settled case law, "the general obligation on the Member States to ensure judicial protection of an individual's rights under Union law."[138] In this way, Union law defines the outer limits of the Member States' procedural competence, but it may also, indirectly, reshape national procedural law if it falls short of guaranteeing an effective judicial protection. The reasoning followed by the Court within this framework, requires a careful and complex "balance between the duty of loyal cooperation and the principle of national procedural autonomy."[139]

As far as the principle of equivalence is concerned, it represents a specific application of the principle of non-discrimination. Member States must ensure that the same procedural conditions apply irrespective of the origin of the claim (Union law or national law). The difficulty with this test lies with the identification of the similarity of claims "as regards their purpose, cause of action and essential characteristics."[140] With regard to the principle of effectiveness, the original test requiring the assessment of the *impossibility* of judicial protection implied a minimum degree of scrutiny of procedural autonomy. This test was complemented by the *excessive difficulty* benchmark which has progressively evolved into a more positive test of adequate and effective judicial protection.[141] This jurisprudential development, has subsequently been reflected under Article 19 TEU and Article 47 of the Charter. The constitutionalization process at the level of remedies and procedures implies more than a simple limitation to the Member States' procedural autonomy. Under certain circumstances, it provides the impetus of reform of procedural law by strengthening the level of protection. This phenomenon of *osmosis* of national procedural standards and Union law

---

[138] Case C-268/06 *Impact* (n. 69), para. 47; Joined Cases C-317–320/08 *Alassini* (n. 69), para. 49; Case C-63/08 *Pontin* (n. 133) para. 44.

[139] V. Skouris (n. 74), 493.

[140] Case C-63/08 *Pontin* (n. 133), para. 45; Case C-591/10 *Littlewoods Retail and Others*, EU:C:2012:478, para. 31.

[141] W. van Gerven (n. 107) has eminently pleaded for a test of adequate judicial protection to replace the test of minimum effectiveness.

requirements to the effect of reinforcement of effective judicial protection, has been famously theorized by Norbert Reich in terms of the "hybridisation" of remedies and procedures[142] with emphasis at the level of consumer law remedies and procedures.[143]

The following sections will provide illustrations of the application of the principles of equivalence, effectiveness and effective judicial protection that have exercised an influence on private law remedies and civil procedures. It is mainly the principles of effectiveness and effective judicial protection that have functioned as the "driving force" of the Europeanization of private law remedies and procedures. The impact of the principle of equivalence has not been particularly decisive in this regard.

### 2.2.1. *The Principle of Equivalence: A Mild Impact Upon Member State Autonomy*

The principle of equivalence has had a milder impact upon remedial and procedural autonomy. It requires a comparison exercise between the rules governing the domestic claim in a certain field of law and the rules applicable for a comparable claim under Union law. It is relatively rare, in comparison to the principle of effectiveness, that the Court will concentrate its analysis on the principle of equivalence.[144] The Court has ruled that it is in principle for the national courts to ascertain whether a claim under Union law is subject to less favorable requirements compared to a similar form of action under domestic law.[145]

Discussing the principle of equivalence and the comparison exercise, Hans Micklitz observes that in reality the Court "compares substantive rules not procedural rules."[146] This observation appears particularly relevant in the field of

---

142 N. Reich, "Horizontal Liability in EC Law: Hybridisation of Remedies for Compensation in Case of Breaches of EC Rights" (2007) *CMLR* 705–742, at 708; N. Reich *General Principles of EU Civil Law* (Cambridge, Intersentia, 2014), 97–99.

143 N. Reich, *Individueller und kollektiver Rechtschutz im EU Verbraucherrecht, Von der "Nationalisierung" zur "Konstitutionalisierung" von Rechtsbehelfen* (Baden-Baden, Nomos, 2012).

144 *Cf.* a critical account of the principle of equivalence by M. Bobek, (n. 25), 166, who concludes that due to the difficulties in carrying out the test, it should instead be discarded.

145 See Case C-326/96 *Levez*, EU:C:1998:577; Case C-261/95 *Palmisani v. INPS*, EU:C:1997:351; Case C-63/08 *Pontin* (n.133); Case C-591/10 *Littlewoods Retail and Others* (n. 140). The Court elaborates further on the factors that have to be taken into account in order to proceed to the comparison of the procedural treatment between domestic and Union law claims. *See* also the Opinion of AG Mancini in Case 199/82 *San Giorgio*, EU:C:1983:247 and the Opinion of AG Lever in Case C–326/96 *Levez*, EU:C:1998:220.

146 H.-W. Micklitz, "The ECJ between the Individual Citizen and the Member States – A Plea for a Judge-Made European Law on Remedies" in H.-W. Micklitz and B. de Witte (eds.) *The European Court of Justice and the Autonomy of Member States* (Cambridge, Intersentia, 2012), 349–400, 399.

the *ex officio* application of Union law. In *Van Schijndel*,[147] the Court examined the compliance with the principle of equivalence by means of comparison between national mandatory law and Union mandatory law. It ruled that where domestic law confers on courts the discretion to apply of their own motion points of law based on binding domestic rules, there is an *obligation* with regard to rules of Union law that occupy a *similar* position. In this context, the principle of equivalence is transformed to a more substantive comparison test that could be termed the *public policy equivalence principle*, which will be extensively discussed in Chapter 2. For the purposes of this section, suffice it to say that its application may result in the broadening of the scope of the national concept of public policy/mandatory law in order to embrace pleas of Union law that have a comparable position in the Union legal order. The hybrid nature of the principle of equivalence in those circumstances, leads Tim Corthaut to speak of "effective equivalence."[148]

### *2.2.2. The Principle of Effectiveness in its Various Expressions and the Principle of Effective Judicial Protection*

The principle of effectiveness is the other limitation to the principle of national procedural autonomy and is the most decisive. The principle of effectiveness has a broader scope than being a "standard of review"[149] of national procedural autonomy. It is a general principle of Union law,[150] including Union civil law.[151] As Arthur Hartkamp puts it, the principle of effectiveness has provided "forceful impetus to the creation of the private law legal order within the European Union."[152] Koen Lenaerts et al.[153] demonstrate the "polymorphic" nature of the principle of effectiveness:

> Generally speaking, the principle of effectiveness can be said to be ventilated through three strands of the case-law concerning: first, the principle of effective judicial protection, which has been recognised by the Court of Justice as a general principle of Union law and underpins matters concerning effective access to court, effective judicial review, and the need for judicial supervision (or control); second, the full effectiveness of Union law in relation to upholding the principle of primacy of Union law vis-à-vis national (procedural) law; and third, the interface between national law on procedure

---

147 Joined Cases C-430/93 and C-431/93 *Van Schijndel v. Stichting Pensioenfonds voor Fysiotherapeuten* (n. 109).

148 T. Corthaut, *EU Ordre Public* (Alphen aan den Rijn, Wolters Kluwer, 2012), II-172.

149 A. Hartkamp, *European Law and National Private Law: Effect of EU Law and European Human Rights Law on Legal Relationships between Individuals* (Cambridge, Intersentia, 2nd ed., 2016), para. 109.

150 See T. Tridimas (n. 86), 421 *et seq.*

151 N. Reich, *General Principles of EU Civil Law* (n. 142), 89 *et seq.*

152 A. Hartkamp (n. 149).

153 K. Lenaerts et al. (n. 74), para. 4.05.

and sanctions and the Union framing principles of equivalence and effectiveness (i.e. the principle of effectiveness *sensu stricto*).

Norbert Reich distinguishes between three functions of the principle of effectiveness.[154] The first corresponds to the minimalist approach of the *Rewe/Comet* formula, which the author calls the "eliminatory" function. According to this function, the principle of effectiveness can "eliminate restrictions to protection, but do[es] not create remedies for protection." The second is the "hermeneutical" or interpretative function of effectiveness on the basis of which the Court "went beyond the merely 'eliminatory' approach ..." and developed the positive *effet utile* or "'full effectiveness' test" in order to identify the adequate remedy which protects the Union law right. Finally, the third one is the "remedial" function, which may lead to the "upgrading" of national remedies and procedures in order to meet the standard of the effective remedy required by Article 19(1) TEU and Article 47 of the Charter. The combination of Member State remedial or procedural autonomy with the need to enforce EU rights leads, according to the author, to an "hybridization" approach to remedies, whereby the remedy is rooted in national law but upgraded to meet, where need be, the higher effectiveness standard.[155] In the same vein, Arthur Hartkamp[156] distinguishes between the "gap-filling" function of the principle of effectiveness on the one hand and the "review" function on the other hand. The frontiers among the various functions of the principle of effectiveness are not rigid, as the functions are "intertwined"[157] and cannot be "sharply distinguished."[158]

---

154 N. Reich, *General Principles of EU Civil Law* (n. 142), 89 *et seq.* Another categorization of the principle of effectiveness is based on the *phases* of the case law of the Court on procedural autonomy. See T. Tridimas, "Enforcing Community Rights in National Courts: Some Recent Developments," in C. Kilipatrick, T. Novitz and P. Skidmore, *The Future of Remedies in Europe* (Oxford, Hart Publishing, 2000); M. Dougan, "The Vicissitudes of Life at the Coalface Remedies and Procedures for Enforcing Union Law," in P. Craig and G. de Burca (eds.), (n. 11), 412. According to this categorization, in the initial phase there seemed to be a tendency of deference to national laws, as demonstrated by the test of "practical impossibility" of exercise of the Community, at that time, rights as a minimum limitation to procedural autonomy. In the middle phase an approach of closer scrutiny and more positive can be identified with the recognition of the independent EU law remedies of state liability, injunction and restitution. The third phase is distinguished by a casuistic weighing of the effectiveness of EU law against the role and purposes of the national rules and thus, according to T. Tridimas (n. 86), 421, by a tendency for "selective deference to the national rules of procedure." The same author argues that these developments in case law "should not be taken as evidence of retreat on the part of the Court," but "[r]ather, they illustrate the directed use of judicial power as the legal system matures."

155 N. Reich, "Horizontal liability" in EC Law – "Hybridisation" of remedies for compensation in case of breaches of EC rights", (n. 142).

156 A. Hartkamp (n. 149), paras. 110–111.

157 K. Lenaerts et al. (n. 74).

158 A. Hartkamp (n.149), para. 112.

The application of the principle of primacy and the principle of effectiveness has led, furthermore, to the consideration of certain remedies as being "inherent" in the system of the Treaties.[159] Their establishment was "autonomized" from the national remedial and procedural framework. The most well-known remedies are the *Francovich*[160] remedy of reparation of damage resulting from Member State infringement of EU law, the *Factortame*[161] remedy to injunctive relief, the *San Giorgio*[162] remedy of restitution for unlawfully levied charges and the *Courage*[163] remedy of compensation for anticompetitive behavior. The premise for their establishment lies upon the *Simmenthal* reasoning of the "full force and effect" of Union law.[164] In *Francovich* the existence of a right of redress in the case of violation of rights derived from Union law derives from "the full effectiveness" of Union law.[165] Similarly, in *Factortame* the Court decided that "the full effectiveness of Community law would be just as much impaired"[166] if the national courts were not empowered to take measures of interim relief. In *Courage*[167] and *Manfredi*,[168] the Court established the principle of private liability for anti-competitive behavior[169] on the basis of the

159 Joined Cases C-6/90 and C-9/90 *Francovich and Bonifaci v. Italy*, EU:C:1991:428, para. 35.

160 Ibid. The landmark case is followed by Joined Cases C-46/93 and C-48/93 *Brasserie du Pêcheur SA v. Bundesrepublik Deutschland and The Queen v. Secretary of State for Transport ex parte Factortame Ltd and Others*, EU:C:1996:79; with respect to infringements attributable to the judiciary Case C-224/01 *Köbler*, EU:C:2003:513.

161 Case C-213/89 *Factortame*, EU:C:1990:257.

162 Case 199/82 *San Giorgio*, EU:C:1983:318, as developed in subsequent case law; see Case C-212/94 *FMC*, EU:C:1996:40, Case C-188/95 *Fantask*, EU:C:1997:580; Case C-192–218/95 *Comateb*, EU:C:1997:12; Case C-228/96 *Aprile*, EU:C:1998:544; Case C-343/96 *Dilexport*, EU:C:1999:59; Joined Cases C-397/98 and C-410/98 *Metallgesellschaft and Others*, EU:C:2001:134; Case C-591/10 *Littlewoods Retail and Others* (n. 140).

163 Case C-453/99 *Courage and Crehan*, EU:C:2001:465. The ground had already been prepared in the Opinion of AG Van Gerven in Case C-128/92 *Banks v. British Coal*, EU:C:1993:860, paras. 36 *et seq.*

164 Joined Cases C-6/90 and C-9/90 *Francovich* (n. 159), para. 32; Case C-213/89 *Factortame I* (n. 161), paras. 18 and 20; Case 199/82 *San Giorgio* (n. 162), para. 12; Case C-453/99 *Courage and Crehan* (n. 164), para. 25.

165 Joined Cases C-6/90 and C-9/90 *Francovich* (n. 159), para. 33. The definition of the precise substantive and procedural rules governing legal redress is a matter of national procedural autonomy, subject to the principles of equivalence and effectiveness: Joined Cases C-6/90 and C-9/90 *Francovich* (n. 159), para. 43; Joined Cases C-46/93 and C-48/93 *Brasserie du Pêcheur* (n. 160), para. 67.

166 Case C-213/89 *Factortame I* (n. 161), para. 21.

167 Case C-453/99 *Courage and Crehan*, (n. 164). The ground had already been prepared in the Opinion of AG Van Gerven in Case C-128/92 *Banks v. British Coal*, EU:C:1993:860, paras. 36 *et seq.*

168 Cases C-295/04–C-298/04 *Manfredi*, EU:C:2006:461.

169 There is abundant literature on the issue of private enforcement of competition law. See indicatively J. Basedow (ed.), *Private Enforcement of EC Competition Law* (Dordrecht, Kluwer Law International, 2007); A. Komninos, *EC Private Antitrust Enforcement* (Oxford, Hart Publishing, 2008).

"full effectiveness"[170] and the "practical effect" of the competition law provisions of the Treaties.

The *Francovich* and *Factortame* rulings appeared to erode the "no new remedies rule" that had been proclaimed in the early *Butter Buying Cruises*[171] case, according to which the Treaty is not intended to create new remedies in the national courts to ensure observance of Union law other than those already laid down by national law. In *Unibet*,[172] the Court explicitly provided for the exception, namely that the "no new remedies rules" will not apply "if it were apparent from the overall scheme of the national legal system in question that no legal remedy existed which made it possible to ensure, even indirectly, respect for an individual's rights under Community law".[173]

As Paul Craig has aptly observed, "membership of a Union naturally entails modification of substantive values and there is no reason why procedural values should be immune in this regard."[174] Herwig Hofmann writes that national courts are therefore required to offer "active protection"[175] of Union law rights.

The need to ensure the full effectiveness of Union law also covers secondary law. This might require the interpretation of national law in such a way as to safeguard its full effectiveness and, under certain circumstances, it might lead to the setting aside of a rule of national law or to the recognition of a remedy. In the early case of *Von Colson and Kamann*[176] the Court ruled that in order to ensure that the prohibition of gender-based discrimination is *fully effective*, the sanction chosen by the Member State – in the case in question, the sanction of compensation – had to be adequate in relation to the damage suffered. The existence of an appropriate remedy was considered both from the perspective

170 Case C-453/99 *Courage and Crehan* (n. 167), para. 26; Cases C-295/04–C-298/04 *Manfredi* (n. 168), para. 60. The right to claim damages for the violation of antitrust law has been codified under Directive 2014/104/EU of the European Parliament and of the Council of 26 November 2014 on certain rules governing actions for damages under national law for infringements of the competition law provisions of the Member States and of the European Union [2014] OJ L349/1. See N. Reich, "Horizontal Liability in EC Law: Hybridisation of Remedies for Compensation in Case of Breaches of EC Rights" (n. 142); N. Reich, "The Interrelation between Rights and Duties in EU Law: Reflections on the State of Liability Law in the Multilevel Governance System of the Union: Is There a Need for a More Coherent Approach in European Private Law?" (2010) 29 *Yearbook of European Law* 112–163.

171 Case 158/80 *Rewe v. Hauptzollamt Kiel (Butter Buying Cruises)*, EU:C:1981:163.

172 Case C-432/05 *Unibet* (n. 119), para 40. See also Case C-583/11 P *Inuit Tapiriit Kanatami and Others v. Parliament and Council* (n. 83), paras. 103–104.

173 According to A. Arnull (n. 103), 56, the judgment made clear that "the overriding consideration is the effective protection of Union law rights."

174 P. Craig, *EU Administrative Law* (Oxford, Oxford University Press, 2nd ed., 2012)., 726.

175 H.C.H. Hofmann, "Art 47 – Right to an Effective Remedy" Section III. Specific Provisions (Meaning)" in S. Peers et al. (eds.) *The EU Charter of Fundamental Rights: A Commentary* (Oxford, Hart Publishing, 2014), para. 47.56.

176 Case 14/83 *Von Colson and Kamann* (n. 91).

of effectiveness of the sanction and from the perspective of guaranteeing real and effective judicial protection for the aggrieved party.[177] According to Norbert Reich, the principle of effectiveness takes a "positive, remedial sense [which has] a constitutional dimension ... now well settled under Article 47 of the Charter."[178] To take an example from consumer contract law, in *Weber and Putz*,[179] the Court interpreted sales law remedies in a way that would guarantee that the consumer "as the weak party to the contract" would enjoy "complete and effective protection from faulty performance."[180]

The application of the principle of effectiveness is a complex exercise requiring a careful balancing of interests.[181] The most important "rule of thumb" informing the content of this exercise has been set out in the leading authority of *Van Schijndel*.[182] The Court sets out the balancing exercise that has to be performed: on the one hand, the application of Union law has to heed to the justifiable and due demands underlying the national judicial systems – a logic of the *Cassis de Dijon* rule of reason[183] or the "objective justification" model[184] – while, on the other hand, national law has to ensure that it can accommodate the enforcement of Union rights. This "procedural rule of reason," as coined by Sacha Prechal,[185] is reflected in the following standard formulation by the Court:

> Every case in which the question arises as to whether a national procedural provision makes the application of European Union law impossible or excessively difficult must be analysed by reference to the role of that provision in the procedure, its progress and its special features, viewed as a whole before the various national bodies. For those purposes, account must be taken, where appropriate, of the basic principles of the

177 Similarly, in Case C-271/91 *Marshall v. Southampton and South West Hampshire Area Health Authority*, (n. 136), the Court ruled that the award of full compensation for a breach of Council Directive 76/207/EEC of 9 February 1976 on the implementation of the principle of equal treatment for men and women as regards access to employment, vocational training and promotion, and working conditions [1976] OJ L39/40, required the recognition of interest as an essential component of compensation. Moreover, the same considerations plead against the setting of an upper limit.

178 N. Reich, *General Principles of EU Civil Law* (n. 142), 100.

179 Case C-65/09 *Gebr. Weber and Putz*, EU:C:2011:396.

180 Ibid., para.75. For an analysis of the case and its reception in German case law, see N. Reich, *General Principles of EU Civil Law* (n. 142), 106–108; N. Reich and H.-W. Micklitz, "Sale of Consumer Goods" in N. Reich et al. (eds.) (n. 26), 108 *et seq.*; Commentary note of A. Johnston and H. Unberath (2012) 49 *CMLR* 793–808.

181 See V. Skouris (n. 74), 506–507.

182 Joined Cases C-430/93 and C-431/93 *Van Schijndel and Van Veen*, EU:C:1995:441.

183 A. Biondi, "The Rule of Reason and National Procedural Limitations. Is it Really Reasonable?" in A. Schrauwen (ed.), *Rule of Reason: Rethinking Another Classic of European Legal Order* (Groningen, Europa Law Publishing, 2005).

184 M. Dougan, *National Remedies before the Court of Justice: Issues of Harmonization and Differentiation* (Oxford, Hart Publishing, 2004), 30.

185 S. Prechal (n. 112), 690.

domestic judicial system, such as protection of the rights of the defense, the principle of legal certainty and the proper conduct of procedure.[186]

The case law on the application of the test of effectiveness as a benchmark of review of national procedural autonomy has been developed in a wide array of issues affecting traditional areas of civil procedural (and remedial) law,[187] such as national limitation periods,[188] the principle of *res judicata*,[189] standing and legal interest in bringing proceedings[190] but also the contractual consequences of non-compliance with a directive[191] or access to documents in cartel proceedings.[192] To give an example from consumer law, in *CA Consumer Finance*[193] the considerations of effectiveness determined the question of the burden of proof for the demonstration of compliance with the pre-contractual information duties of the creditor and his obligations to proceed to creditworthiness assessment laid down in the Consumer Credit Directive.[194] The Court decided that the effectiveness of the consumer rights conferred by this directive preclude national rules which would place upon the consumer the burden of proving the actual performance by the creditor of his obligations.

The principle of effectiveness is not the sole benchmark of assessment of national procedural laws. The early case law has ranked the principle of effective

186 Joined Cases C-430/93 and C-431/93 *Van Schijndel*, (n. 182) para. 19. In consumer law cases, see Case C-40/08 *Asturcom Telecommunicaciones*, EU:C:2009:615, para. 39; Case C-618/10 *Banco Español de Crédito*, EU:C:2012:349, para. 49 and the case law cited therein.

187 See M. Dougan (n. 184), 412; S. Prechal and K. Cath (n. 110). For a critical discussion of the tension that the principle of effectiveness can cause to the principle of legal certainty, see P. Rott, "The Court of Justice's Principle of Effectiveness and its Unforeseeable Impact on Private Law Relationships" in D. Leczykiewicz and S. Weatherill (eds.) in D. Leczykiewicz and S. Weatherill (eds.), *The Involvement of EU Law in Private Law Relationships* (Oxford, Hart Publishing, 2013), 181–198.

188 See Case C-262/09 *Meilicke and Others*, EU:C:2011:438 (lack of transitional period allowing the shareholders to claim a tax credit); Joined Cases C-501/12–C-506/12, C-540/12 and C-541/12 *Specht and Others*, EU:C:2014:2005 (time limit for bringing an action to claim financial payments before the end of the financial year); Case C-362/12 *Test Claimants in the Franked Investment Income Group Litigation*, EU:C:2013:834 (curtailment of the limitation period for the applicable remedies without notice and retroactively); Case C-452/09 *Iaia and Others*, EU:C:2011:323 (five-year limitation period in respect of the right to payment of periodic remuneration).

189 Case C-234/04 *Kapferer*, EU:C:2006:178; Case C-69/14 *Târşia*, EU:C:2015:662, para. 38.

190 Case C-12/08 *Mono Car Styling* (n. 130), para. 49: "Thus, whilst it is, in principle, for national law to determine an individual's standing and legal interest in bringing proceedings, Community law nevertheless requires, in addition to observance of the principles of equivalence and effectiveness, that the national legislation does not undermine the right to effective judicial protection."

191 Case C-604/11 *Genil 48 SL*, EU:C:2013:344.

192 Case C-536/11 *Donau Chemie and Others* (n. 113 ).

193 Case C-449/13 *CA Consumer Finance*, EU:C:2014:2464.

194 Directive 2008/48/EC of the European Parliament and of the Council of 23 April 2008 on credit agreements for consumers and repealing Council Directive 87/102/EEC [2008] OJ L133/66.

judicial protection among the general principles of Union law stemming from the constitutional traditions common to the Member States, enshrined in Articles 6 and 13 of the European Convention on Human Rights (ECHR). This right is given expression in Article 47 of the Charter.[195] The application of Article 47 of the Charter presupposes that the respective national legislative provision comes within the scope of the Charter according to Article 51(1).[196] The fundamental right to effective judicial protection is "mirrored"[197] by the obligation of Member States to provide for effective remedies, an obligation well settled in case law and now "reaffirmed by the second subparagraph of Article 19(1) TEU."[198] The right to an effective judicial protection is not only applicable in disputes against the state/Union institutions, but also in private disputes.[199] However, in such horizontal relations, the effect of the constitutional right is only indirect as the claim to effective judicial protection is addressed against the state and the courts which have to ensure its observance.[200] In individual consumer litigation the issue of the application of Article 47 Charter arose mainly in relation to mortgage enforcement proceedings, to which we will come back later in detail in Chapter 5.[201]

---

195 Case 222/84 *Johnston v. Chief Constable of the Royal Ulster Constabulary* EU:C:1986:206, para. 18; Case 222/86 *Heylens* EU:C:1987:442, para. 14; Case C-50/00 P *Unión de Pequeños Agricultores v. Council* EU:C:2002:462, para. 39; Case C-263/02 P *Commission v. Jégo-Quéré*, EU:C:2004:210 para. 29; Case C-432/05 *Unibet* (n. 119), para. 38; Joined Cases C-402/05 P and C-415/05 P *Kadi and Al* Bakaraat, EU:C:2008:461, para. 335.

196 The application of the Charter to the Member States is subject to the condition that they are implementing Union law or that they are acting within the scope of Union law. As is apparent from the explanations to the Charter and the case law of the Court, the word "implementation" should be understood broadly to include Member State legislation falling within the scope of EU law: see Joined Cases C-411/10 and C-493/10 *N.S. and Others*, EU:C:2011:865; Case C-617/10 *Åkerberg Fransson*, EU:C:2013:105, Case C-682/15, *Berlioz Investment Fund*, EU:C:2017:373.

197 H.C.H. Hofmann (n. 175), para. 47.50.

198 Case C-583/11 *Inuit Tapiriit Kanatami and Others v. Parliament and Council* (n. 173), para. 101.

199 See *Von Colson and Kamann* (n. 91), para. 23 (financial sanctions for gender discrimination must guarantee real and effective judicial protection and have a deterrent effect on the employer); Case C-63/08 *Pontin* (n. 133), para. 75 (effective remedy for breach of the principle of equal treatment of pregnant workers); Joined Cases C-317/08–C-320/08 *Alassini* (n. 78) (mandatory out-of-court settlement before bringing proceedings); Case C-12/08 *Mono Car Styling* (n. 130), para. 47 (limitation of the right of individual workers to bring proceedings in order to ensure compliance with the right to information and consultation in collective redundancy proceedings); Judgment of 14 June 2017, *Menini and Rampanelli*, C-75/16, EU:C:2017:457 (system of mandatory mediation).

200 See H.C.H. Hofmann (n. 175) para. 47.72; C. Mak, "Rights and Remedies. Article 47 EUCFR and Effective Judicial Protection in European Private Law Matters" in H.-W. Micklitz, *Constitutionalisation of European Private Law* (Oxford, Oxford University Press, 2014), 236–258, 242–243, who notes that Art. 47 of the Charter "may be considered to impose a positive duty on courts, a duty to guarantee effective protection of those rights."

201 The requirement for effective judicial protection informs the analysis of Case C-415/11 *Aziz* EU:C:2013:164 and it is explicitly addressed in Case C-169/14 *Sánchez Morcillo and Abril García*, EU:C:2014:2099; and Case C-34/13 *Kušionová*, EU:C:2014:2189.

For the purposes of the present discussion, one case could be singled out: *Morcillo and García*.[202] This case raised an aspect of *inequality of arms or procedural inequality* which, in the words of the Court, "accentuates" the underlying horizontal relationship of contractual imbalance. The finding of a violation of the equality of arms is linked to "the balance of interests between the private parties involved":[203] the use of unfair terms by the party with the strongest bargaining position eliminates the contractual autonomy of the weaker party.

### *2.2.3. The Articulation between the Principle of Effectiveness and Effective Judicial Protection as Standards of Review*

It is clear from the preceding analysis that the establishment of rights derived from Union law has an impact upon the procedural competence of Member States. The binding effect of the Charter, which enshrined in Article 47 of the Charter the general principle of the right to an effective judicial protection, revived the old debate on the relevance and content of the principle of procedural autonomy. Is it still relevant in view of Article 47 of the Charter? Does it have to be reshaped?[204] Does it have to be abandoned? The choice is certainly not anodyne and it has serious implications for the intensity of interference with the competence of Member States to design their procedural rules. The terms under which the principle of effectiveness – as a limitation to procedural autonomy – is being couched in case law connotes a "minimum" test:[205] the exercise of Union law rights should not be rendered "impossible" or "excessively difficult." By contrast, the right to an effective judicial protection is a positive test and it implies an obligation of the Member States to achieve a specific result. On the other hand, as has already been explained in the preceding analysis, the application of the principle of effectiveness has evolved as a more positive test rather than a negative test. To grasp the interaction of the two principles, it is necessary to illustrate this through the various strands of case law.[206]

Already before the Charter, there have been cases where the Court applied a "double standard" of review, with the cumulative application of both principles.

202 Case C-169/14 *Sánchez Morcillo and Abril García* (n. 201).

203 See C. Mak (n. 200), 242, who discusses the implications of the famous suretyship case of the German Constitutional Court on the indirect horizontal effect of fundamental rights. On that basis the author observes that when courts analyze the right to effective judicial protection, they "cannot avoid looking into the balance of interests between the private parties (eg the restriction of a weaker party's autonomy caused by the almost unilateral determination of contracting terms by its stronger contracting partner."

204 *Cf.* Opinion of AG Jääskinsen in Case C-536/11 *Donau Chemie*, EU:C:2013:67, para. 5.

205 Eminently W. van Gerven (n. 26).

206 See M. Safjan and D. Düsterhaus (n. 74), who distinguish four configurations of the interaction of the principles in case law, namely "superposition, coexistence, infusion and exclusivity." See critically the penetrating views of A. Ostlund, *Effectiveness of European Union Law versus Procedural Protection, Tracing the Tension throughout the case-law of the Court of Justice on Ex-Officio Review by the National Judge* (2017, Dissertation, University of Luxembourg).

Probably the earliest example of a "two-stage" approach is *Steffensen.*[207] The compatibility with Union law of the national rules on the admission of evidence was assessed both in the light of the principles of equivalence and effectiveness and in the light of the right to an effective judicial protection. In subsequent judgments, namely in *Alassini,*[208] *Mono Car Styling*[209] and *Agrokonsulting-04,*[210] the Court elaborated further on the way in which the principles interact. We can single out *Alassini*, a case that is particularly interesting from a consumer law perspective. This case concerned the compatibility with Union law of a national mandatory out-of-court settlement procedure in electronic communications disputes. At the first level of assessment, the Court took into account certain factors which demonstrated the compatibility of this scheme with the principle of effectiveness: the settlement procedure did not prejudice the right of the parties to bring legal proceedings following its conclusion; no substantial delay or fees were involved; and, finally, for the duration of the settlement procedure, the period for the time-barring of the claims was suspended.[211] However, the compatibility with the principle of effectiveness was subject to the availability of other means than the electronic ones in order to access the settlement procedure and to the availability of interim measures. At the second stage of assessment, the Court found that the mandatory settlement procedure introduced an additional step for access to the courts which might prejudice implementation of the principle of effective judicial protection.[212] However, the Court pointed out that this right is not an "unfettered prerogative" and that it may be restricted, in accordance with the requirements set out in Article 52(1) of the Charter. In that regard, it found that the aim of the national provisions at issue, namely the "quicker and less expensive settlement of disputes" and "a lightening of the burden on the court system," pursued an objective of general interest. Finally, it proceeded with an assessment of the proportionality of the settlement procedure and concluded that "in the light of the detailed rules for the operation" of that procedure – the ones that were already taken into account in the framework of the effectiveness review – that measure did not appear disproportionate.

Although the "double-stage" review formally applies both standards, in essence the considerations which feed the analysis in each stage merge. This is particularly so at the level of assessment of the proportionality of a restriction to the exercise of the right to effective judicial protection resulting from a national procedural rule, as demonstrated in *Alassini.* Progressively, it would appear that the Court leans toward a more "assertive" approach in relation to the exclusive application of Article 47 of the Charter in circumstances where

207 Case C-276/01 *Steffensen* (n. 132).
208 Joined Cases C-317–320/08 *Alassini* (n. 69).
209 Case C-12/08 *Mono Car Styling* (n. 130).
210 Case C-93/12 *Agrokonsulting-04*, EU:C:2013:432.
211 Joined Cases C-317–320/08 *Alassini* (n. 69), paras. 48–49 and 52–57.
212 Ibid. paras. 62 *et seq.*

the Union legislator has set down more detailed rules on the content of judicial review. This would seem to particularly hold true in the field of public procurement, environmental protection and asylum law. Three judgments in each one of these fields, namely *Star Storage*,[213] *VLK*[214] and *Sacko*,[215] accordingly illustrate this tendency. In all of these cases, the details of judicial review are set in secondary legislation. The judgment of the Grand Chamber in *VLK* encapsulates the "upgraded" test of assessment of the principle of procedural autonomy:

> In the absence of EU rules governing the matter, it is for the domestic legal system of each Member State to lay down the detailed procedural rules governing actions for safeguarding rights which individuals derive from EU law, the Member States being responsible for ensuring compliance with the right to an effective remedy and to a fair hearing enshrined in Article 47 of the Charter.[216]

The sole application of Article 47 of the Charter would be the most appropriate standard of review in those situations in which the *core* elements of the right to an effective judicial protection are affected. These elements include, in particular "the rights of the defense, the principle of equality of arms, the right of access to a tribunal and the right to be advised, defended and represented".[217]

An example of this approach from earlier case law is the *DEB*[218] judgment on the right to legal aid and access to justice for legal persons. In this case, although the referring court had couched the question in terms of national procedural autonomy, the Court reformulated it in terms of effective judicial protection. An illustrating example in that regard in the field of consumer law is the judgment in *Menini and Rampanelli*.[219] The legal context of this case is similar to the one in the aforementioned *Alassini* case. This time the question related to the (then) newly enacted ADR Directive.[220] The referring court had enquired as to the compatibility with the ADR Directive of a scheme of mandatory recourse to mediation procedure for disputes on financial services. As was the case with

---

213 C-439/14 and C-488/14 *Star Storage and Others*, EU:C:2016:688, para. 45.

214 Case C -243/15 *Lesoochranárske zoskupenie VLK*, (n. 72), para. 65.

215 Case C-348/16 *Sacko*, EU:C:2017:591.

216 Case C-243/15 *Lesoochranárske zoskupenie VLK* (n. 72), para. 65.

217 Case C-199/11 *Otis and Others*, EU:C:2012:684, para. 48.

218 Case C-279/09 *DEB*, EU:C:2010:811. See P. Oliver, "Commentary in Case C-279/09, *DEB v. Germany*, Judgement of the European Court of Justice (Second Chamber) of 22 December 2010, nyr." (2011) 48 *CMLR* 2023–2040, 2038, suggests that the principles of effectiveness and effective judicial protection, even if they were once separate, "have both been subsumed under Article 47 [Charter] now."

219 Case C-75/16 *Menini and Rampanelli* (n. 199).

220 Directive 2013/11/EU of the European Parliament and of the Council of 21 May 2013 on alternative dispute resolution for consumer disputes and amending Regulation (EC) No 2006/2004 and Directive 2009/22/EC (Directive on consumer ADR) [2013] OJ L165/63.

*Alassini*, the condition of mandatory mediation introduced an "additional step" for access to courts. Therefore, the Court considered that the scheme would have to be assessed in light of the principle of effective judicial protection. Yet, contrary to *Alassini*, the Court made its analysis *exclusively* on the basis of the right to effective judicial protection. This appeared all the more appropriate as Article 1 of the ADR Directive explicitly provides for the possibility of Member States to make participation in ADR procedures mandatory "provided that such legislation does not prevent the parties from exercising their right of access to the judicial system."

There is, finally, a strand of consumer case law in which the review of national procedural rules is based on a *synthesis* of the requirements of effectiveness and effective judicial protection. This method of reasoning has, as its starting point, the requirement set out in Article 7(1) of the Unfair Contract Terms Directive, according to which the Member States must ensure "adequate and effective means" to prevent the continued use of unfair terms. By means of application of this method, demonstrated in *Morcillo and García*[221] the effectiveness *implies* a requirement effective judicial protection, with the analysis of the effectiveness being merged within the one of effective judicial protection:

> the obligation for the Member States to ensure the effectiveness of the rights that the parties derive from Directive 93/13 against the use of unfair clauses implies a requirement of judicial protection, also guaranteed by Article 47 of the Charter, that is binding on the national court.

In *Radlinger*[222] the Court found that the means that the Member State must provide according to Article 7(1) of the Unfair Contract Terms Directive in order to prevent the use of unfair terms "must include provisions enabling consumers to be guaranteed effective judicial protection."

The "effectiveness implies effective judicial protection" type of reasoning is a direct expression of the more covert "infusion" method. This connotes the application by the Court of the *Rewe* type of effectiveness test *imbued* by the positive considerations of the right to an effective judicial protection. Marek Safjan and Dominik Düsterhaus refer to it as the "*Rewe-47*"[223] test. An illustration from this method of reasoning from the consumer *ex officio* doctrine is the judgment in *Kušionová*.[224] This case concerned the question whether the right of a mortgage creditor to have recourse to simplified mortgage enforcement proceedings was liable to infringe the judicial protection of consumers.

221 Case C-169/14 *Sánchez Morcillo and Abril García* (n. 202), para. 35.
222 Case C-377/14 *Radlinger and Radlingerová*, EU:C:2016:283, para. 46.
223 M. Safjan and D. Düsterhaus (n. 74).
224 Case C-34/13 *Kušionová*, EU:C:2014:2189.

In order to assess the compatibility with the principle of effectiveness, the Court mainly took into account the parameters of access to court, namely the availability of interim relief. The question which then arises is whether the existence of the "infusion" type of reasoning means that the classic formulation of the principle of effectiveness will have to be abandoned.

In their study of the principle of effectiveness and the principle of effective judicial protection, Sacha Preschal and Rob Widdershoven[225] plead against the principle of effectiveness becoming "an overarching principle, absorbing the principles of equivalence and effectiveness."[226] The authors explain that despite the "partial overlap"[227] between the two principles, they are "driven by different rationales."[228] The main rationale behind the *stricto sensu* effectiveness test is the effective application of Union law within the context of the loyal cooperation of Member States in ensuring their obligations deriving from the Treaties. The rationale behind the principle of effective judicial protection is the protection of the fundamental right of the individual. Moreover, the balancing exercise operates on different terms. The assessment of the effectiveness as a limitation of procedural autonomy requires ponderation of the national values underlying a certain procedural provision (the "procedural rule of reason").[229] The limitation to the exercise of the right to an effective judicial protection follows the proportionality test laid down in Article 52(1) of the Charter. The extent to which the "procedural rule of reason" is embodied within this test of proportionality has yet to be explored.[230]

It should also be noted that the principle of effective judicial protection might in certain circumstances serve "contrasting purposes"[231] compared to the effective enforcement of a Union law right. This can be well demonstrated in *Banif Plus Bank*,[232] where it was held that when a national court exercises its duty of *ex officio* unfairness assessment of a contractual term, it also has an obligation to invite arguments from the parties. Thus, the full effectiveness of

225 S. Prechal and R. Widdershoven, "Effectiveness or Effective Judicial Protection: A Poorly Articulated Relationship," in T. Baumé et al. (eds.), *Today's Multi-layered Legal Order: Current Issues and Perspectives. Liber Amicorum in Honour of Arjen W.H. Meij* (Zutphen, Paris Legal Publishers, 2011), 283–297; S. Prechal and R. Widdershoven, "Redefining the Relationship between 'Rewe-Effectiveness' and Effective Judicial Protection" (2011) 4 *Review of European Administrative Law* 31–50.

226 S. Prechal and R. Widdershoven, "Redefining the Relationship between "Rewe-effectiveness" and Effective Judicial Protection" (n. 225), 46.

227 Ibid.

228 Ibid, 47.

229 S. Prechal (n. 112).

230 On this question, see Opinion of AG Kokott in Case C-73/16 *Puškár*, EU:C:2017:253, para. 50: "The principle of proportionality is also part of the principle of effectiveness. It is reflected in the limitation on excessive complication."

231 M. Safjan and D. Düsterhaus (n. 74), 15. See also A. Van Duin, "Metamorphosis? The Role of Article 47 of the EU Charter of Fundamental Rights in Cases Concerning National Remedies and Procedures Under Directive 93/13" (2017) 6 *EuCML*, 190–198.

232 Case C-472/11 *Banif Plus Bank*, EU:C:2013:88.

the right of the consumer to have the unfair clause set aside is circumscribed by the fair trial requirements applicable to both parties in the proceedings. The judgment in *Biuro podróży "Partner"*[233] is also telling in that regard. This case concerned, in essence, the *erga omnes* effect of a register of terms declared unfair by a judicial decision, even against professionals who were not party to the proceedings for as long as the term employed would be identical to the term declared unfair. The subsequent use of such term was deemed to be an unlawful act for which a fine could be imposed. It was beyond doubt that such a register enhances the effectiveness of the rights that consumers derive from the Unfair Terms Directive. Nonetheless, the Court had to verify whether such a scheme also respected the right to an effective judicial protection of the professionals.[234]Inversely, the effectiveness of Union law is in itself an objective of general interest that can justify, subject to the principle of proportionality, a limitation of the fundamental right to effective judicial protection.[235]

Therefore, it would appear that although the *Rewe* test was pronounced more than 40 years ago and even if its meaning has evolved ever since, it is still "good law." It is true that the overview of the various strands of case law might give the impression of an "amalgam." However, this plurality reflects the necessity to embrace diverse configurations and the different levels of harmonization of rights/remedies at the level of Union law. The degree of intensity of the judicial scrutiny on national procedural law should not be "straitjacketing," but should be capable of adapting. Following this logic, the Court rather seems to seek to achieve an appropriate articulation and a mode of "cohabitation" of the various standards of review.

---

233 Case C-119/15 *Biuro podróży "Partner"*, EU:C:2016:987.

234 Ibid. para. 26: "In the absence of a provision in Directives 93/13 and 2009/22 providing explicitly for a scheme of effective judicial protection for the seller or supplier, they must be interpreted in the light of Article 47 of the Charter."

235 The case law on access to documents in a civil action for cartel infringement and the weighing exercise that needs to be undertaken is a very good example: Case C-360/09 *Pfeiderer* (n. 113); Case C-536/11 *Donau Chemie* (n.113).

# CHAPTER 2

# THE GENERAL RULE ON THE APPLICATION OF UNION LAW BY NATIONAL COURTS OF THEIR OWN MOTION

This chapter situates the consumer *ex officio* doctrine within the broader theme of the *ex officio* application of Union law by national courts. The landmark ruling in that respect is *Van Schijndel.*[236] It has already become common ground in the case law of the Court[237] and in literature[238] that the consumer *ex officio* doctrine stands apart from the "general" position – the "droit commun" – on the application of Union law by the courts of their own motion pronounced in *Van Schijndel*. In order to substantiate this claim and to grasp the distinctiveness of the doctrine of active court in consumer litigation, the remaining developments of Part I are devoted to the *sua sponte*[239] consideration of Union law grounds before the national courts. In particular, this chapter presents the perspective of Union law, while the next (Chapter 3) will delve into certain Member States' procedural traditions in relation to the same question. This way of analysis reflects the "osmosis"[240] of Union law and national laws. While the Court draws on the prevailing traditions of Member States, it bestows them with a "European legal significance."[241]

---

236 Joined Cases C-430/93 and C-431/93 *Van Schijndel and Van Veen*, EU:C:1995:441.

237 See Joined Cases C-222/05–C-225/05 *Van der Weerd*, EU:C:2007:318 and Case C-227/08 *Martín*, EU:C:2009:792.

238 S. Whittaker, "Who Determines What Civil Courts Decide? Private Rights, Public Policy and EU Law" in D. Leczykiewicz, S. Weatherill (eds.), *The Involvement of EU Law in Private Law Relationships* (Oxford, Hart Publishing, 2013), 89–129, 92 and 123 *et seq.*; K. Lenaerts, I. Maselis and K. Gutman, *EU Procedural Law* (Oxford, Oxford University Press, 2014), para. 4.41; M. Dougan, "The Vicissitudes of Life at the Coalface. Remedies and procedures for enforcing Union Law" in P. Craig and G. de Burca (eds.), *The Evolution of EU Law* (Oxford, Oxford University Press, 2nd ed., 2011), 424.

239 In common law literature, the Latin term *sua sponte* implies the examination of a point that has not been suggested by the parties. In European literature the Latin term employed is "*ex officio*".

240 The term is borrowed from V. Skouris, "The Principle of Procedural Autonomy and the Duty of Loyal Cooperation of National Judges under Article 10 EC" in M. Andenas and D. Fairgrieve (eds.), *Tom Bingham and the Transformation of the Law, A Liber Amicorum* (Oxford, Oxford University Press, 2009), 493–507, 493.

241 S. Whittaker (n. 238), 92.

Both Chapters 2 and 3 trace the origins of the consumer *ex officio* doctrine from different perspectives and form the *passerelle* for Part II. The mandatory nature of consumer legislation and the considerations of inequality in legal representation underpin the doctrine of an active court in litigation involving the application of Union consumer law, which is distinct compared to the *ex officio* application of Union law. Its distinctiveness justifies a certain deviation from the principle of party autonomy and judicial passivity. The purpose of this chapter will be to demonstrate under which terms the *Van Schijndel* line "contrasts with"[242] the *Océano Grupo*[243] line of case law.

The position of principle is that Union law does not require a mutation in the role of the courts. National courts are neither required nor prohibited by Union law alone to "initiate the selection of arguments to be put in their balance"[244] from the field of Union law. Even if, as AG Jacobs observes in his Opinion in *Van Schijndel*,[245] a requirement imposed upon national courts to apply Union law of their own motion "might not be impossible to put into practice in any system, [it] would cause a degree of disruption which might vary in different systems but would probably be significant in all of them."

This case demonstrated that the observance of the rules of competition law laid down in the Treaties is mandatory, but the impact of this mandatory nature upon the role of the courts is left to the domestic procedural systems. The principle of equivalence might necessitate the application by the courts of a plea of Union law of their own motion, where the courts would be required to raise a similar type of plea based on national law. In this case, the *trigger* of the *ex officio* application is pulled by national law. When it comes to consumer law proceedings, the application of mandatory Union consumer law by the courts of their own motion is required *as a matter of Union law*, anchored upon a high "effectiveness threshold."[246] For as long as the trigger governing the *ex officio* application of Union consumer law is pulled by Union law considerations, one may discern the emergence of an autonomous Union consumer *ex officio* doctrine. Outside consumer litigation,[247] the precise role of the courts with regard to the *ex officio* application of EU law is defined on the basis of

242 K. Lenaerts, I. Maselis and K. Gutman (n. 238), para. 4.41.

243 Joined Cases C-240/98–C-244/98 *Océano Grupo*, EU:C:2000:346.

244 An expression borrowed from N.H. Andrews, "The Passive Court and Legal Argument" (1988) 7 *CJQ* 125–140, at 125.

245 Opinion of AG Jacobs in Joined Cases C-430/93 and C-431/93 *Van Schijndel and Van Veen*, EU:C:1995:185, point 37.

246 V. Trstenjak and E. Beysen, "European Consumer Protection Law: *Curia Semper Dabit Remedium*?" (2011) 48 *CMLR* 95–124, 121.

247 This is not meant to exclude the potential application of the reasoning upon which consumer litigation rests equally to other types of litigation bearing similar characteristics of disparity of contractual power, particularly in labor law. This possibility remains to be explored in case law. I discuss this in Chapter 6.

procedural autonomy, provided that a *genuine opportunity* for raising the EU law arguments exists. The Court does not endorse a general and abstract obligation of *ex officio* application of Union law as a consequence of the direct effect and primacy of Union law. Such a position would have given precedence to the uniform application of Union law, irrespective of the national legal environment in which Union law is applied.[248] This would result in a different role for the courts, depending on the domestic or Union origin of the plea and it would favor the application of the second over the first. By contrast, the application of the "balancing approach" to resolve the question of the *ex officio* application of Union law introduced in *Van Schjndel*, on the basis of which the restriction to the effectiveness of the application of Union law has to be balanced against the principles of the domestic judicial system, recognizes no "procedural superiority" for the Union law argument.

The situation is different in consumer law proceedings. There, the effective protection of the consumer requires by reason of Union law a *positive* action by the courts. It requires the establishment of a Union "positive action doctrine"[249] resting upon the premise that the consumer is deprived *ab initio* of the genuine opportunity of raising the consumer law defense. This lack of genuine opportunity does not, in principle, result from a procedural obstacle to access to the courts. It is the result of a "procedural handicap" stemming from the *imbalance in the underlying substantive relation*. To anticipate the argument that will become clearer through the course of this study, the capacity of one of the parties as the consumer/weaker party reflects upon the role of national courts, necessitating a uniform articulation of their role. The Union law perception of the role of the national courts in that regard is independent from the national procedural rules which determine the respective roles of the courts and the parties. Yet, there is no departure from national procedural traditions. According to the standard formulation by the Court, the doctrine of the active court rests upon the availability of all factual and legal circumstances and the strict adherence to the principle of due notice (*audi alteram partem*).

Section 1 of this chapter presents the main strands of reasoning underlying the position of principle with respect to the *ex officio* application of Union law under the *Van Schijndel* line. Section 2 delves into the conceptual elements of the *ex officio* application of Union law, pertaining to the notions of public policy and mandatory law.

---

248 *Cf.* AG Darmon in his Opinion in Joined Cases C–87/90–C–89,90 *Verholen* EU:C:1991:223. As to the reasons why this would not have been the correct approach, see S. PRECHAL, "Community Law in National Courts: The Lessons from Van Schijndel" (1998) 35 *CMLR* 681, 683, concluding that there is no antithesis between supremacy and procedural autonomy.

249 V. ZENO-ZENCOVICH and M.C. PAGLIETTI, "Le droit processuel des consommateurs" (2014) *Revue de droit international et de droit comparé* 321–355, 338.

# 1. THE GENERAL RULE ON THE *EX OFFICIO* APPLICATION OF UNION LAW: THE *VAN SCHIJNDEL* LINE OF CASE LAW

## 1.1. THE MAIN STRANDS OF REASONING

This section presents the main strands of reasoning on the position of principle with regard to the application of Union law by the courts of their own motion. The first one pertains to what could be termed as the "public policy equivalence principle."[250] The second one corresponds to the balancing approach, a type of "procedural rule of reason"[251] applicable in the context of the examination of the principle of effectiveness.

### *1.1.1. The Public Policy Equivalence Principle*

The public policy equivalence principle is the result of a simultaneous application of the "classic" principle of equivalence with the substantive concept of public policy. While the respect of the principle of equivalence requires "equal treatment of claims based on a breach of national law and of similar claims based on a breach of EU law".[252] Respect of the public policy equivalence principle requires the non-discrimination between domestic public policy grounds and the grounds that enjoy similar ranking at the level of Union law.

National laws usually bestow rules of public policy with specific procedural consequences, such as the power of the courts to apply those rules of their own motion, the right to raise for the first time the relevant plea in appeal/cassation or the establishment of a ground for review of an arbitration award. By virtue of the principle of loyal cooperation, the courts have an *obligation* to apply, of their own motion, the rules of Union law which occupy within the Union legal order a similar position to the national rules of public policy. This marks an extended understanding of the principle of equivalence, whereby "a national power implies a Union duty."[253] This shift, according to da Cruz Vilaça, brings the *effet utile* of Union law within the field of the effectiveness of Union law.[254]

---

250 See also T. Corthaut, *EU Ordre Public* (Alphen aan den Rijn, Kluwer Law International, 2012), II-172, who speaks of "effective equivalence."

251 S. Prechal (n. 248), 690.

252 Case C-69/14, *Târşia*, EU:C:2015:662, para. 34.

253 J.H. Jans et al., *Europeanisation of Public Law* (Groningen, Europa Law Publishing, 2007), 57.

254 J.L. da Cruz Vilaça, "Le Principe de l'effet utile du droit de union dans la jurisprudence de la Cour" in A. Rosas et al. (eds.), *The Court of Justice and the Construction of Europe: Analyses and Perspectives on Sixty Years of Case Law* (Springer, Asser Press, Curia, 2013), 279–306, 297 (in the original text in French "*pousse l'effet utile du droit de l'Union déjà sur le terrain de l'effectivité*").

Public policy is a very wide concept which can mean different things depending on the values each legal order holds dear.[255] Therefore, the application of the public policy equivalence can have far-reaching implications for national law if the Union law perception of public policy differs from the domestic perception.[256] Under specific circumstances, the Court has applied extensively the principle of equivalence in such a way as to broaden the contours of the domestic concept of public policy. In such cases, while it is national law which "sets the procedural stage," it is Union law which fills in the substance. As Martin Ebers puts it, Union law "defines the *tertium comparationis* itself."[257] According to the extended understanding of the principle of equivalence, if a rule of Union law is considered as binding or fundamental in the Union legal order, it shall qualify for the same procedural treatment as binding domestic rule or as a rule of national public policy, irrespective of the national qualification. This results, effectively, in a uniform understanding of public policy across the Union. The Court applied such a Heteronomous method of determination of the content of public policy in *Van Schijndel* and *Eco Swiss*.[258] In these cases, analyzed further below (section 1.2), even if the domestic rules of competition law did not qualify as rules of public policy which would have to be applied by the courts of their own motion, the Court considered that the rules of Union competition law should elevate to the same hierarchical rank and qualify for the same procedural treatment as the rules of domestic public policy. Nevertheless, the later judgment in *Bensada Benallal*,[259] discussed below (section 1.2), would seem to follow a more restrictive understanding of the public policy equivalence.

### *1.1.2. Minimum Effectiveness*

The second pattern of reasoning follows the application of the principle of effectiveness as a "minimum" benchmark, implying the least possible interference with national procedural law. Under this benchmark, it is examined whether the procedural restrictions in the advancement of the claim based on Union law, or upon the role of the courts, render the application of Union law "impossible or excessively difficult." To guide this examination, the Court in *Van Schijndel* developed the well-known balancing approach.[260] In the framework of this

---

255 See in more detail below Section 2.1.

256 See S. Prechal and N. Shelkoplyas, "National Procedures, Public Policy and EC Law. From Van Schjindel to Eco Swiss and Beyond" (2004) 12 *ERPL* 589–611, 594 *et seq.*, J.H. Jans et al., (n. 253), 312 *et seq.*

257 M. Ebers, "ECJ (First Chamber) 6 October 2009, Case C-40/08, *Asturcom Telecomunicaciones SL v. Cristina Rodríguez Nogueira*. From Océano to Asturcom: Mandatory Consumer Law Ex Officio Application of European Union Law and Res Judicata" (2010) *ERPL* 823–846, 839.

258 Case C-126/97 *Eco Swiss*, EU:C:1999:269.

259 Case C-161/15, *Bensada Benallal*, EU:C:2016:175.

260 See above Chapter 1, Section 2.2.2.

analysis – which, broadly, applies in the context of the assessment of the effectiveness of any domestic procedural provision – the purpose of the national procedural rules have to be taken into account, in particular the "basic principles of the domestic judicial system, such as protection of the rights of the defence, the principle of legal certainty and the proper conduct of procedure."[261] Initial critical reactions to the balancing approach saw in it the potential to create inroads into national procedural systems and found it in competition with the *Rewe's*[262] approach of setting a "more objective yardstick."[263] However, exactly the opposite would seem to hold true. As Jans et al. rightly argue, the balancing method is "a guarantee against unreasonable and far reaching infringements of Member States' procedural autonomy."[264]

In most of the cases that will be discussed below, the rationale underlying the domestic procedural provision prevailed over an unrestrictive advancement of the Union law claim, except where either the very specific circumstances of the case (*Peterbroeck*)[265] or the nature of proceedings (judicial review of an arbitration award in *Eco Swiss*) required a different approach.

It could be argued that the more leeway is left to national procedural law, the more the effective enforcement of Union law is undermined. This proposition is not correct for the simple reason advanced by AG Jacobs: "proper application of the law does not necessarily mean that there can be no limits on its application."[266]

In the same vein, Sacha Prechal has pointed out that in reality there is no paradox (what she famously calls the "*Rewe-Simmenthal* contradiction") between the application of the principle of effectiveness on the one hand and the principle of primacy on the other hand, but only a difference in perception.[267] A national court might consider that one of the parties should have traced a different line in their pleadings. But it is not Union law which empowers a court to restructure the litigation and to transform it from the parties' dispute into one which it "might have preferred to have before it."[268]

261 Joined Cases C-430/93 and C-431/93 *Van Schijndel and Van Veen* (n. 236), para. 19.

262 Case 33/76 *Rewe*, EU:C:1976:188.

263 M. Hoskins, "Tilting the Balance: Supremacy and National Procedural Rules" (1996) 21(5) *E.L. Rev.* 365–377. *Cf.* J. Delicostopoulos and E.M. Szyszczak, "Intrusions into National Procedural Autonomy: The French Paradigm" (1997) 22(5) *E.L. Rev.* 141–149.

264 J.H. Jans et al. (n. 253), 56, observing (at p. 59) that after all it is "*still [Union] law that forms part of national law and not vice versa*".

265 Case C-312/93 *Peterbroeck*, EU:C:1995:437.

266 F. Jacobs, "Enforcing Community Rights and Obligations in National Courts: Striking the Balance" in J. Lonbay and A. Biondi (eds.), *Remedies for Breach of EC Law* (Michigan, Wiley, 1997).

267 S. Prechal (n. 248), 683 *et seq.*

268 I borrow this expression from a differenct context used by J.A. Jolowicz, "*Da mihi factum dabo tibi jus:* A problem of demarcation in English and French law" in P. Feuerstein and C. Parry, *Multum non Multa, Festscrift für Kurt Lipstein* (Heidelberg, Müller Juristischer Verlag, 1980), 79–99, 91.

The only requirement that Union law imposes in that regard is the "*genuine opportunity* to raise a plea."[269]

The case law which is relevant in relation to the powers of the courts to raise a new plea of their own motion can be classified into two broad categories according to the type of proceedings involved: 1) the powers of the courts to raise a (new) point of Union law in ordinary civil proceedings, examined in *Van Schijndel*, the reasoning of which was then "exported"[270] in administrative proceedings[271] (*Peterbroeck*,[272] *Kraaijeveld*,[273] *Van der Weerd*,[274] *Heemskerk*[275] and, more recently, *Bensada Benallal*);[276] and 2) the powers of the courts in proceedings for review of an arbitration award to admit a point of Union law that has not been argued before the arbitrators (*Eco Swiss*).[277] The considerations which apply with regard to the powers of the courts to raise of their own motion a plea that has not been pleaded by the parties are equally relevant as to the possibility of the parties to invoke and the courts to accept a new plea in appeal/cassation that has not been argued before the trial courts.[278]

## 1.2. THE GENERAL RULE IN CIVIL AND ADMINISTRATIVE PROCEEDINGS

The earliest example of the *ex officio* application of Union law by national courts is *Verholen*.[279] As *Van Schijndel*[280] followed a few years later, *Verholen*

[269] Joined Cases C-222/05–C-225/05 *Van der Weerd* (n. 237), para. 41.

[270] J.H. Jans and A.T. Marseille, "Case Analysis in 'Joined Cases C–222/05, *Van der Weerd and others* v. *Minister van Landbouw, Natuur en Voedselkwaliteit*, Judgment of the Court (Fourth Chamber) of 7 June 2007, [2007] ECR I–4233'" (2008) 48 *CMLR* 853–862, 859.

[271] The preponderance of the references by Dutch administrative courts is not a matter of coincidence, but is due to the changes brought about to the Dutch administrative procedural rules in 1994. Under the system that was applicable before, as is explained by J.H. Jans et al. (n. 253), 313, the primary function of the courts was to review the administrative decision in light of all the relevant rules of law independent of the pleadings of the parties (*recours objectif*). Following the reform, the primary function of judicial review was no longer the *objective legality* of the decision, but the protection of rights *within the realm* sought by the individual.

[272] Case C-312/93 *Peterbroeck* (n. 265).

[273] Case C-72/95 *Kraaijeveld*, EU:C:1996:404.

[274] Joined Cases C-222/05–C-225/05 *Van der Weerd* (n. 237).

[275] Case C-455/06 *Heemskerk*, EU:C:2008:650.

[276] Case C-161/15, *Bensada Benallal*, EU:C:2016:175.

[277] Case C-126/97 *Eco Swiss China Time Ltd and Benetton International NV* (n. 258).

[278] It has to be noted that in Case C-312/93 *Peterbroeck* (n. 265), the ground of appeal on the basis of Union law had not been duly raised before the administrative authorities within the prescribed time limit set out for the specific tax dispute in question.

[279] Joined Cases C-87/90–C-89/90 *Verholen* (n. 248).

[280] Joined Cases C-430/93 and C-431/93 *Van Schijndel and Van Veen* (n. 236).

has been somewhat "overshadowed." The reason why the Court could not have been more conclusive on the issue of the *ex officio* application in *Verholen*, is probably due to the fact that the question referred was couched in negative terms. The referring court had asked whether Union law precludes a national court from assessing of its own motion the conformity of national rules with the unconditional and sufficiently precise rules of the Sex Equality Directive[281] after its implementation period has elapsed, when the parties have not relied upon it. Unsurprisingly, the Court ruled that Union law does not preclude such a judicial power. In order to reach such a conclusion, it did not have to consider the role of the courts and the parties in the procedure. For the purposes of the specific question, it was sufficient to take into account the obligation of the courts to refer a case for a preliminary ruling "as soon as the court perceives either of its own motion or at the request of the parties that the litigation depends on a point"[282] pertaining to Union law. It then found that:

> that power to raise of its own motion a question of [Union] law presupposes that the national court considers either that [Union] law must be applied and, if necessary, national law disapplied, or that national law must be interpreted in a way that conforms with [Union] law.[283]

It would not be until the reference made by the Dutch Supreme Court, the *Hoge Raad*, in *Van Schijndel* that the Court would be given the opportunity to decide on the impact of the effective application of Union law and the role of the courts in civil proceedings. The applicants in the case who had subscribed to a private pension scheme, challenged a decision adopted by the pension fund of the professional body to which they belonged. That decision refused to exempt them from the obligation to join the fund on the ground that they did not meet the exemption requirements. Before the lower courts, the applicants invoked the incorrect appreciation of the criteria for compulsory membership set out by the pension fund. On appeal, the appellants' claims were dismissed. In their application for cassation before the *Hoge Raad*, the applicants advanced, for the first time, arguments in relation to the alleged breach of the rules of Union competition law by the decree making membership to the pension fund compulsory. The facts in relation to the ground pertaining to competition law had not been established by the lower courts. The first limb of the question of the *Hoge Raad* was whether lower civil courts should have been obliged to raise a point of Union law of their own motion. If such an obligation exists, its breach constitutes a ground of cassation. The second limb of the question was whether

281 Council Directive 79/7/EEC of 19 December 1978 on the progressive implementation of the principle of equal treatment for men and women in matters of social security [1979] OJ L6/24.

282 Joined Cases C-87/90–C-89/90 *Verholen* (n. 248), para. 12.

283 Ibid., para. 13.

such an obligation exists even if the advancement of new points of Union law would require the courts to go beyond the ambit of the dispute defined by the parties and the examination of facts that have not been established by the lower courts.

According to Dutch law, as presented in the order for reference, lower courts are obliged to raise points of law of their own motion in the sense of requalification of the pleas of the parties.[284] The principle of judicial passivity entails that the courts are required to stay within the ambit of the dispute as defined by the parties and that they cannot rely on facts and circumstances other than those on which the claim is based.[285] At the level of cassation, the appeal is limited to pure points of law, being understood as points that do not require an examination of new facts. The essence of the question was whether the Union law origin of the new plead put forward required a change in the principle of party presentation which restricts the judicial assessment to the issues and materials as presented by the parties.

The reasoning of the Court is articulated on the basis of the concept of *binding rules* of Union law and the *principle of party presentation*. An *ex officio* obligation to raise pleas of Union law might be established depending on the national rules of procedural law and depending on the importance for the Union legal order of the provision allegedly breached. In the first place, the Court holds that the rules of competition law set out in primary law are "binding rules, directly applicable in the national legal order."[286] Moreover, on account of the principle of sincere cooperation, the national courts have an obligation to raise of their own motion points of law based on binding rules of Union law, where by virtue of domestic law they have an obligation or even a discretion to apply of their own motion binding rules of national law.[287] Nonetheless, so the reasoning of the Court goes, the courts are not obliged to proceed to an investigation of the Union law point if that would require a departure from the ambit of the dispute as defined by the parties, and if it would oblige them to examine facts that have not been put before them.[288] Indeed, the parties had not advanced at the trial stage the facts constitutive of anti-competitive behavior. The omission to invoke and establish the relevant facts at the trial level rendered the new plea raised "after the midnight bell" inadmissible at the level of cassation.

Later cases demonstrate that there are circumstances under which the courts would be obliged to raise a point of Union law of their own motion even if that would entail that they go beyond the ambit of the dispute as defined

---

284 As currently provided under Article 25 of the Netherlands Code of Civil Procedure (*Wetboek van Burgerlijke Rechtsvordering*): ("De rechter vult ambtshalve de rechtsgronden aan").

285 Joined Cases C-430/93 and C-431/93 *Van Schijndel and Van Veen* (n. 236), para. 11.

286 Ibid., para. 13.

287 Ibid., para. 14.

288 Ibid., para. 22.

by the parties' claims. That would be so if the dispute before them concerns "an agreement … manifestly illegal under Article [101 TFEU] of the Treaty."[289] In this sense, the Court held in *Manfredi*, in an *obiter dictum*, that: "Articles 101 TFEU and 102 TFEU are a matter of public policy which must be automatically applied by national courts."[290]

The obligation of an "automatic application" of the competition law rules was reaffirmed in *T-Mobile*.[291] In his Opinion in *Van Schijndel*, AG Jacobs had pointed out that such a situation pertaining to the performance of an illegal contract will fall under the principle of equivalence since "it can safely be assumed that no court would enforce a transaction which was manifestly illegal as a matter of national law, even if the illegality was not invoked by the parties."[292]

The judgment in *Van Schijndel* did not reason in this way because the matter raised did not concern the performance of a contract. The applicants in *Van Schijndel* changed the *basis* of their claim in the course of the proceedings. Before the trial courts they had pleaded that the criteria for the exemption from compulsory membership to the pension fund were not properly applied, whereas in cassation they pleaded that the legal act on the basis of which the pension fund took its decision ran counter to the competition law rules.[293]

Arthur Hartkamp observes that the Dutch courts seem to show "a tendency to consider article [101 TFEU] as a matter of public policy"[294] provided that

---

289 Opinion of AG Jacobs in *Van Schijndel* (n. 245), point 49.

290 Joined Cases C-295/04–C-298/04 *Manfredi*, EU:C:2006:461, para. 31; T. Corthaut (n. 250) II-178, argues that one could dismiss the reference to public policy in *Manfredi* as "a slip of the pen" since the issue "is not raised in respect of the merits, but *ex abundantia* to justify the admissibility of the questions referred to the ECJ by an apparently rather zealous national court." On the other hand, he points out that the Court has since then "not stopped from stressing the public policy status of the rules of competition law."

291 Case C-8/08 *T-Mobile Netherlands and Others*, EU:C:2009:343, where the Court ruled, in para. 49, that "article [101 TFEU], first, produces direct effects in relations between individuals, creating rights for the persons concerned which the national courts must safeguard and, second, is a matter of public policy, essential for the accomplishment of the tasks entrusted to the Community, which must be automatically applied by national courts."

292 Opinion of AG Jacobs in *Van Schijndel* (n. 245), point 49.

293 In detail, see A. Hartkamp, *European Law and National Private Law: Effect of EU Law and European Human Rights Law on Legal Relationships between Individuals* (Cambridge, Intersentia, 2016), paras. 125–128; A. Hartkamp, "Ex officio application in case of unenforceable contracts or contract clauses, EU Law and National Laws Confronted" in L. Gullifer and S. Vogenauer (eds.), *English and European Perspectives on Contract and Commercial Law, Essays in Honour of Hugh Beale* (Oxford, Hart Publishing, 2014), 467–484, 470; B. Fekete and A.M. Mancaleoni, "Application of Primary and Secondary EU Law on the National Courts' Own Motion" in A. Hartkamp, K. Sieburgh and W. Devroe (eds.), *Cases, Materials and Text on European Law and Private Law* (Oxford, Hart Publishing, 2017), 421–461, 426.

294 A. Hartkamp, *European Law and National Private Law* (Deventer, Kluwer, 2012), para. 125. The author cites in that regard, the judgment of the Dutch Supreme Court (*Hoge Raad*) in case *Vreugdenhil/ BVH* (HR 3 December 2004, NJ 2005, 118), pursuant to which the "courts deciding questions of fact (in the case under consideration the appeal court)

the relevant issue can be intimated on the basis of the allegations of the parties. Yet, this tendency does not seem to reflect an established practice. Balázs Fekete and Anna Maria Mancaleoni note that it is not the prevailing view in the Netherlands that the courts should declare a legal act null and void of their own motion if the rule violated is a mandatory rule which does not concern public policy, even if this rule entails absolute nullity.[295]

On the same day as *Van Schijndel*, another case was decided on the issue of the *ex officio* powers of the courts on a point of Union law. The judgment in *Peterbroeck*[296] is quite exceptional. The Court acknowledged that Union law precluded a legal provision which prevented the courts from raising a point of Union law of their own motion because, under the circumstances of the present case, the exercise of Union rights was made impossible.[297] The applicant was deprived of the opportunity to raise a plea of Union law not because of the principle that the courts decide on the basis of the issues put before them, but because of the specificities of the procedural system in place. A combination of factors – the court of appeal before which the applicant initiated proceedings was the first court that could make a reference for preliminary ruling, no other court would subsequently have the opportunity to consider the question, and the limitation period to lodge a complaint had already expired when the court was seised of the case – led to the conclusion that under these circumstances, the national court should have the power to consider a point of Union law of its own motion. The peculiarity of the procedural features of this case[298] makes it

must, insofar as necessary of [their] own motion, establish the invalidity of an agreement that is contrary to article [101 TFEU] if the allegations made by the parties do not imply the invocation of such invalidity with sufficient clarity." The author then refers to a subsequent judgment of the same court in case *Municipality of Heerlen v. Whizz* (HR 16 January 2009, NJ 2009, 54). This case did not involve the application of Union competition law, since there was no cross-border dimension. Yet, it is interesting to note that it was held that Article 6 of the Dutch Competitive Trading Act "did not comprise public policy law which the courts must automatically apply, even if it would thereby go beyond the ambit of the dispute defined by the parties."

295 B. Fekete and A.M. Mancaleoni, (n. 293), 455.

296 Case C-312/93 *Peterbroeck* (n. 265).

297 The case arose in the framework of administrative proceedings. A company contested before the responsible administrative authorities the tax rate applicable in its tax assessment. Following the rejection of its claims by the administration, it brought proceedings before the court of appeal (Cour d'Appel) on the basis of a new argument deriving from Union law that the rate applicable was an infringement of the freedom of establishment. The legal argument was considered as an inadmissible *new* plea within the meaning of the provisions of the income tax code, although the court of appeal was actually the first level of adjudication seised of the dispute. The tax code imposed a 60-day limitation from the lodging by the administration of a copy of the decision for the advancement of complaints. Not only was the applicant prevented from raising the new plea after the ending of the limitation period, but so too were the courts. As a result, the case could not be assessed from the perspective of Union law, nor was it possible that a reference for preliminary ruling be made.

298 Pointed out, to that effect, in Joined Cases C-222/05–C-225/05 *Van der Weerd* (n. 237), para. 40.

a rather "weaker" precedent, compared with *Van Schijndel*, on the matter of the *ex officio* powers of the courts.

The judgment in *Kraaijeveld*[299] builds upon *Van Schijndel*, although the context was different. The applicant had brought annulment proceedings against an administrative decision approving a zoning plan that would allegedly be ruinous for his business. The project would proceed without a prior environmental impact assessment being carried out. The national implementing legislation of the relevant applicable directive[300] provided for such minimum thresholds of the size of the works subject to prior environmental impact assessment, to the effect that such an assessment would be excluded for the project at issue. The referring court considered that the criteria set by the implementing legislation were an incorrect implementation of the requirements of the applicable directive. The administrative decision could therefore have been challenged on that basis. However, the applicant did not bring forward pleas as to the necessity of an environmental impact assessment and consequently as to the compatibility of national law with Union law. The case is important as the Court considered, in essence, that environmental protection law, in particular the obligation of the assessment of the effect of projects to the environment, forms part of Union binding law.[301] It was less conclusive as to the division of roles between the courts and the parties, as it concentrates on the judicial control of the exercise of their discretion by the national legislative or administrative authorities.[302]

In later case law, the Court in its judgment in *Heemskerk*[303] stressed the importance of observance of the principle enshrined in the national legal order from which the reference stemmed (Dutch law), that an individual bringing an action must not be placed in a less favorable position than if he had not brought that action (principle of the prohibition of *non reformatio in pejus*). This principle overrides an eventual obligation for the *ex officio* application of Union law.[304] The referring court had explained that the arguments based on Union

---

[299] Case C-72/95 *Kraaijeveld* (n. 273).

[300] Council Directive 85/337/EEC of 27 June 1985 on the assessment of the effects of certain public and private projects on the environment [1985] OJ L175/40.

[301] As it can be inferred from Case C-72/95 *Kraaijeveld* (n. 273), para. 60.

[302] Ibid., paras. 60–61.

[303] Case C-455/06 *Heemskerk* (n. 275).

[304] The dispute was raised in the context of administrative proceedings of two companies brought against the decision of an administrative authority ordering repayment of an export refund up to a certain amount. The referring court had identified certain pleas in law derived from the relevant Union legislation, which, however, have not been put forward by the parties. A possible consideration of those arguments would breach the principle of judicial passivity as expressed under Art. 8:69 of the General Administrative Law (*Algemene wet bestuursrecht*), according to which the courts decide the case within the ambit of the dispute as defined by the parties. The obligation, according to national law, for the courts to supplement pleas in law of their own motion is understood as an obligation to put the applicant's objections into the correct legal form and not to make an assessment of the court's own initiative.

law fell outside the ambit of the dispute as it had been defined by the parties.[305] Since the Court had already excluded the existence of an *ex officio* obligation on the basis of the principle of *non reformatio in pejus*, it did not have to elaborate further on the respective role of the courts and the parties.

The next important judgment within the *Van Schijndel* line of case law is *Van der Weerd*.[306] This judgment provided an excellent opportunity for the Court to *codify* the conditions under which the position of principle in *Van Schijndel* would apply, as well as distinguish the general rule from the solution that had already started to emerge in litigation involving the application of consumer law under the *Océano Grupo* line of case law.

The applicants in this case brought proceedings for annulment of a decision of the administration which was prejudicial to their business (the slaughtering of their cattle). They alleged that the decision was illegal due to misinterpretation of the applicable law. The referring court, although rejected the pleas put forward before it, observed that other pleas in law existed upon which the applicants could have relied. It pointed out that in similar pending cases before it, the validity of similar decisions had been challenged on the basis of different pleas in law, drawn from the directive on foot-and-mouth disease.[307] Such an alternative basis had not been put forward by the appellants in the main proceedings, although they could have eventually won their case if they had proceeded along this line of argumentation. The question raised was whether the *Van Schijndel* line of case law required that the courts essentially substitute the pleas of the parties for those deriving from Union law.

Dutch administrative law did not allow for such substitution. It provided that the court gives its ruling solely on the basis of the issues which are put before it. The courts are obliged to supplement the pleas in law of their own motion, but that duty is understood in the sense that the court shall put the objection made by the applicant in the correct legal form and not in the sense of an independent

---

305 If the ruling in *Van Schijndel* would be applied by analogy (since the proceedings in Case C-455/06 *Heemskerk* (n. 275) were administrative and not civil), an *ex officio* application would probably be excluded as it would violate the principle that the parties control the ambit of the matters in dispute. It is not, though, entirely clear, whether the legal arguments that the national courts envisaged would necessitate examination of novel facts or whether these arguments could already be derived on the basis of the facts brought forward by the parties. Dutch administrative law provides for a discretion of the courts to *supplement* the facts of their own motion on the basis though of the case made already by the parties in the dispute.

306 Joined Cases C-222/05–C-225/05 *Van der Weerd* (n. 237).

307 The national court in Joined Cases C-222/05–C-225/05 *Van der Weerd* (n. 251), para. 15, referred to Case C-28/05 *Dokter and Others* EU:C:2006:408, where similar decisions of the administration were successfully challenged. The argument that was put forward in that case was that the administrative authority was not entitled to proceed the way it did because the laboratory that had taken the tests was not authorized by the applicable directive to carry them out. The administration was also not entitled to base the measures solely on the content of the facsimile sent by the laboratory without prior verification of the file.

judicial assessment.[308] An analysis of the court's own initiative is required only on public policy grounds, which are construed as being issues concerning the powers of administrative authorities and those of the court itself, and provisions as to the admissibility of an objection or appeal.[309] Jan Jans and Bert Marseille explain that public policy has to be narrowly understood, that it covers only formal aspects while the "substantive defects will, in general, not qualify as public policy grounds."[310]

The Court distinguished *Van der Weerd* from *Van Schijndel* and set out the two main criteria which encapsulate or codify the general position on the *ex officio* application of Union law by national courts: the *importance* of the provision to the Union legal order, as well as the *genuine opportunity* to raise a plea based on Union law.

The reasoning follows the same pattern as in *Van Schijndel*, but the application of the "public policy equivalence" to the circumstances of the case led to a different result. First, the Court acknowledged that the provisions of the directive in relation to foot-and-mouth disease "do not occupy a similar position within the [Union] legal order" to the national rules of public policy which have to be raised by national courts of their own motion and that "they cannot therefore be considered as being equivalent to the national rules of public policy."[311] Furthermore, the Court pointed out that, were those provisions to form part of public health policy, the respective pleas would have been put forward "essentially in order to take account of the *private interests* of individuals" who were affected by the disputed measures.[312] From this statement, it may be gleaned that a provision of Union law shall be of *public interest* in order to occupy a position similar to that of a national rule of public policy. Moreover, the Court points out that to determine the existence of a duty of national courts to raise a plea based on Union law of their own motion, the "importance of that provision to the [Union] legal order" has to be taken into account.[313]

It is interesting to note that the *Hoge Raad* has fully endorsed the criterion of public interest served by a certain provision of Union law and its importance within the Union legal order in a case that concerned an issue similar to the one that had been raised in *Van der Weerd*. In its judgment in *Cagemax*, the *Hoge Raad* ruled that where a case involves "a [Union] interest of such fundamental

---

308 Article 8:69 of the General Law on Administrative Law. See Joined Cases C-222/05–C-225/05 *Van der Weerd* (n. 237), para. 16; J.H. Jans and A.T. Marseille (n. 285) who discuss the application of this provision by the highest national administrative courts.

309 Joined Cases C-222/05–C-225/05 *Van der Weerd* (n. 237), para. 29. See also Case C-455/06 *Heemskerk* (n. 275), para. 20.

310 J.H. Jans and A.T. Marseille (n. 270), 854.

311 Joined Cases C-222/05–C-225/05 *Van der Weerd* (n. 237), paras. 29–31.

312 Ibid., para. 32 (emphasis added).

313 Ibid., para. 41.

weight and in such a concrete degree ... the appeal court should of its own motion have applied [Union] law to safeguard that interest."[314]

Second, the Court clarified that the general rule on the *ex officio* application of a point of Union law rests upon the existence of a *genuine opportunity* of the parties to put forward the Union law argument.[315] The fact that the referring court was ruling in first and last instance was not decisive in that regard. The condition of the genuine opportunity already seems to underlie *Eco Swiss* and *Peterbroeck*. In his Opinion in *Van der Weerd*, AG Poiares Maduro explained that both of these cases raised the issue of the availability of a judicial remedy for the applicants, a situation which explained the different result reached by the Court in those cases compared to *Van Schijndel*.[316] According to the Opinion, the mere fact that the applicants in the main proceedings were not circumspect enough to rely on provisions of Union law in order to challenge the contested administrative decision "does not create an obligation for the national court to provide assistance and repair the omission on account of the principle of effectiveness."[317]

The requirement that each party is afforded a genuine opportunity to present his or her case is the expression of the principle of fair trail and equality of arms, which in turn form "an integral part of the fundamental right to effective judicial protection guaranteed by Article 47 of the Charter."[318] As *Van der Weerd* shows, the right to effective judicial protection does not, as such, require that the courts raise points of Union law of their own motion. By contrast, the Court itself acknowledged, in that same judgment, that the different approach in the framework of consumer disputes is justified by the need to ensure *effective consumer protection*.[319]

The last judgment in the line of case law informing the general position on the *ex officio* application of Union law, is *Bensada Benallal*.[320] This judgment took a rather restrained approach to the application of the principle of equivalence with regard to pleas based on public policy. The question referred to by the Belgian Council of State (*Conseil d'État*) was whether

---

314 *Cagemax v. State* (HR 11 September 2009, NJ 2010, 369), para. 3.32. The case is reported by A. Hartkamp, *European Law and National Private Law* (Kluwer, 2012), para. 128.

315 Joined Cases C-222/05–C-225/05 *Van der Weerd* (n. 237), para. 41.

316 Opinion of AG Poiares Maduro in Joined Cases C-222/05– C-225/05 *Van der Weerd*, EU:C:2007:124, points 27–29.

317 Ibid., point 30.

318 Opinion of AG Cruz Villallón in Case C-199/11 *Otis and Others*, EU:C:2012:388, point 57. In its judgment of 6 November 2012 in that case (EU:C:2012:684) the Court ruled that: "The principle of equality of arms, which is a corollary of the very concept of a fair hearing ... implies that each party must be afforded a reasonable opportunity to present his case, including his evidence, under conditions that do not place him at a substantial disadvantage vis-à-vis his opponent" (para. 71).

319 Joined Cases C-222/05–C-225/05 *Van der Weerd* (n. 237), para. 40.

320 Case C-161/15, *Bensada Benallal*, EU:C:2016:175.

the right of an individual to be heard under Union law carries with it in the legal system of the Union an *equivalent importance* to that held by the rules of public policy in the Belgian legal system, and whether the principle of equivalence would require that such a plea be raised for the first time before the *Conseil d'État*.

The facts can be summarized as follows.[321] The applicant was a Spanish national who had made use of his right to free movement, residing in Belgium as a salaried worker. The Belgian authorities subsequently withdrew the residence authorization and ordered him to leave the territory. The reason for this was that it appeared that Mr. Bensada Benallal provided misleading information to the administration and that the company in which he was supposed to be working was a sham. The applicant challenged the decision before the relevant authority for immigration, putting forward a single plea alleging, *inter alia*, infringement of the obligation to state reasons for the act and the breach of Article 35 of the Citizens' Directive,[322] which prescribes the conditions under which Union nationals may have their residence right withdrawn. Following rejection of his application, he brought an a appeal on a point of law before the referring court (the *Conseil d'État*), pleading for the first time, the infringement of the general principles of Belgian law of respect of the right to be heard, as well as the infringement of Article 41 of the Charter which enshrines the right to be heard. The referring court observed that a plea relying upon Article 41 of the Charter could not be raised for the first time before the court hearing an appeal on a point of law, unless that plea qualified as a matter of public policy.

According to the Opinion of AG Mengozzi,[323] the classification of the rules of Union law as public policy is a matter of Union law. Under this approach, in order to ensure a uniform application across the Union of the rules that would have to be considered as falling under the category of public policy, there has to be a prior Union definition of the nature of the respective rule, which does not depend upon the national classification.[324] Drawing in particular from case law on the *ex officio* application of Union law,[325] the Opinion suggests that it has to be determined whether "the rule at issue occupies, within the EU legal order, a 'position' which is at least equivalent to the position enjoyed by the rules which may or must be raised by the national courts of their own motion."[326]

---

321 Ibid., paras. 8–19.

322 Directive 2004/38/EC of the European Parliament and of the Council of 29 April 2004 on the right of citizens of the Union and their family members to move and reside freely within the territory of the Member States amending Regulation (EEC) No 1612/68 and repealing Directives 64/221/EEC, 68/360/EEC, 72/194/EEC, 73/148/EEC, 75/34/EEC, 75/35/EEC, 90/364/EEC, 90/365/EEC and 93/96/EEC, [2004] OJ L158/77.

323 Opinion of AG Mengozzi in Case-161/15 *Bensada Benallal*, EU:C:2016:3.

324 Ibid., point 58.

325 More particularly from Joined Cases C-222/05–C-225/05 *Van der Weerd* (n. 237), paras. 29–31 and Case C-40/08, *Asturcom Telecomunicaciones*, EU:C:2009:615, para. 49.

326 Opinion of Advocate General Mengozzi in Case-161/15 *Bensada Benallal*, (n. 323), point 49.

Following a thorough account of the case law on the right to be heard, the Opinion concludes that "respect for the right of a person to be heard by a national authority before any decision is taken by that authority that is likely to affect that person adversely does not have, in the EU legal order, a ranking or position equivalent to that held by the rules of public policy" in the respective national legal system.[327]

If the Court had applied the principle of equivalence in the same way as in *Van Schjndel* or in *Van der Weerd*, it would have, first of all, to enquire on the comparability between a plea based on the right to be heard, as guaranteed by Union law, and a plea based on national public policy *in abstract*. However, the Court seemed to construct its reasoning in more narrow terms. The level of equation is between a plea based on the right to be heard, as guaranteed in Union law and a plea based on failure to respect that same right *as guaranteed by national law*. Although the Court recalled its settled case law, according to which the right to be heard is a *fundamental principle* of EU law which must be guaranteed,[328] it did not require that this right enjoys the same procedural treatment as the domestic rules of public policy, irrespective of the classification of the right to be heard under Belgian law. It is only if, *under Belgian law*, the right to be heard would be a matter of public policy that the right to be heard under Union law would enjoy the same procedural treatment. In those circumstances, leaving it to the national court to decide on the applicability of the principle of equivalence, the Court found that: "it is for the national court to determine whether the right to be heard, as guaranteed by national law, satisfies the conditions required by national law for it to be classified as a matter of public policy."[329]

In line with this finding, the referring court decided that the principle of equivalence of Union law does not require it to admit a plea based on a violation of the right to be heard, raised for the first time in cassation proceedings, given that *such a right*, as safeguarded *within the Belgian legal order*, does not qualify for a plea of public policy.[330]

---

327 Ibid., point 101.

328 Case C-161/15, *Bensada Benallal* (n. 320), para. 33.

329 Ibid., para. 34.

330 *Conseil d'État*, Case no 236.440, *X contre l'État belge*, du 17 novembre 2016 (Council of State, Case no 236.440, X v Belgian state, 17 November 2016): "En conséquence, sans qu'il soit besoin de vérifier si la situation du requérant relève de la mise en œuvre du droit de l'Union européenne, il y a lieu de constater que le principe d'équivalence du droit de l'Union européenne ne requiert pas que le moyen tiré de la violation du droit d'être entendu, tel qu'il est garanti par le droit de l'Union, soulevé pour la première fois en cassation, soit declaré recevable étant donnée que ce droit, tel qu'il est garanti par le droit interne, ne remplit pas les conditions exigées pour être qualifiée de moyen d'ordre public." [Consequently, without it being necessary to verify whether the situation of the applicant falls under the application of Union law, it has to be stated that the principle of equivalence of Union law does not require that a plea derived from the violation of the right to be heard, as it is safeguarded by Union

Even if *Bensada Benallal* followed a more narrow understanding of the application of the principle of equivalence in matters of public policy for the purpose of determination of the role of the courts, it is probably not yet safe to draw the conclusion that the "public policy equivalence" approach established in *Van Schijndel* will be abandoned. The judgment does not proceed with distinguishing *Van Schijndel*; it is not even cited. Moreover, the plea based on infringement of the right to be heard in an administrative procedure is quite specific, even before the Union courts. The Opinion of AG Mengozzi in the case extensively discusses this aspect and concludes that the right to be heard does not fall within the category of pleas based on public policy that have to be raised by the courts of their own motion.[331] Further case law would be required to be more conclusive on whether the rather restrictive approach of *Bensada Benallal* will be confined in the context of application of the right to be heard or not.

## 1.3. THE GENERAL RULE IN PROCEEDINGS FOR REVIEW OF AN ARBITRATION AWARD

The decisive element in the judgment in *Eco Swiss*,[332] was the fact that the question of the *ex officio* application of Union law arose in relation to proceedings for review of an arbitration award, which was the first time when a question of Union law could be referred for a preliminary ruling.

More particularly, the question arose in the context of a dispute pertaining to the breach of contractual obligations due to the early termination of a licensing agreement between Benetton on the one hand and Eco Swiss and Bulova on the other hand. The parties referred their dispute to arbitration. An interim award acknowledged the contractual responsibility of Benetton toward Eco Swiss and Bulova, but the determination of the precise amount of the damages to be paid was left for the parties to decide. An appeal against the interim award could be entered within a period of three months from the date of lodging the award at the court registry. Benetton did not appeal, so the interim award acquired the force of *res judicata*. Due to the failure of the parties to agree on the amount of damages to be paid, the respective determination was made by the arbitrators in a final award. Benetton brought proceedings for annulment against both awards (the interim award and the final award) on the ground

law, raised for the first time in cassation, be declared admissible, for as long as this right, as it is safeguarded by national law, does not fulfill the conditions required in order to qualify as a plea of publicpolicy] (translated by the author).

331 Opinion of AG Mengozzi in Case-161/15 *Bensada Benallal* (n. 323), in particular points 88 and 99.

332 Case C-126/97 *Eco Swiss* (n. 258).

of breach of public policy. In the framework of these proceedings, Benetton invoked for the first time that the licensing agreements, the enforcement of which was being sought, violated EU competition law. Following the dismissal of its application for annulment, Benetton appealed before the *Gerechtshof*, which decided to stay the enforcement of the final arbitration award. According to that court, the respect of the competition law provisions of the Treaties is a matter of public policy which justifies the annulment of the arbitration award (under Article 1065(1)(e) of the Dutch Code of Civil Procedure). The final award had the purpose of enforcing a clause of an agreement that was in breach of the competition law rules. In the view of that same court, the failure by Benetton to challenge the interim award in time did not preclude the admission of the relevant ground of public policy. Eco Swiss brought proceedings in cassation before the referring court, the *Hoge Raad*, against the decision of the *Gerechtshof*.

The *Hoge Raad* observed that in Dutch law, an application for annulment of an arbitration award could be admitted only in exceptional circumstances, one of them being breach of public policy. However, the possible conflict of an arbitration award with competition law was not generally regarded, under Dutch law, as a ground of public policy justifying the application for annulment of the award. The *Hoge Raad* inferred from *Van Schijndel* that: "Article [101 TFEU] is not to be regarded as a mandatory rule which is so fundamental that no restrictions of a procedural nature should prevent it from being observed."[333]

Moreover, as the question of nullity of the licensing agreement had not been raised by the parties in the arbitration proceedings, the arbitrators could not have decided on that question of their own motion. If the arbitrators would have done otherwise, their ruling would be amenable to judicial review because they would have failed to comply with their terms of reference.[334] The referring court observed that the arbitrators could not be considered as a "court or tribunal" competent to make a reference for preliminary ruling.[335] Yet, the interim award had already acquired the force of *res judicata* and it could not be called into question in subsequent proceedings directed against the final award.

Against this factual and legal framework, the referring court enquired as to the impact of the mandatory nature of Union competition rules upon the powers of the arbitrators and those of the courts. First of all, the referring

333 Ibid., para. 25.

334 According to Article 1065(1)(c) of the Netherlands Code of Civil Procedure (Case C-126/97 *Eco Swiss* (n. 258), para. 26).

335 Case C-126/97 *Eco Swiss* (n. 258), para. 28, with reference to Case 102/81 *Nordsee*, EU:C:1982:107. In this case, the link between the arbitration procedure and the organization of legal remedies through the courts in the Member State in question was not sufficiently close for the arbitrator to be considered as "court or tribunal of a Member State" within the meaning of Article [267] TFEU.

court asked to what extent it would be possible to apply by analogy the ruling in *Van Schijndel* to arbitration proceedings, to the effect that the arbitrators would also be obliged to raise mandatory rules of Union law that have not been raised by the parties. As to the impact on the judicial proceedings, the question was whether a ground based on Union competition law should be admitted in the specific circumstances of the case, even if, first, that would be contrary to national procedural law, second, the issue fell outside the ambit of the dispute presented before the arbitrators and, third, the interim award acquired the force of *res judicata*.

The Court replied only to the questions in relation to the powers of the courts to examine a ground for annulment of an arbitration award based on Treaty competition law rules, by considering that its answer rendered unnecessary the response to the rest of the questions.[336] A difficult balance had to be struck among different values: procedural autonomy, the interest of ensuring efficient arbitration proceedings, the importance of the rules of competition law for the Union legal order and the particular position of arbitration tribunals as opposed to state courts, the first being excluded from the preliminary reference procedure.

The application of the "public policy equivalence" principle, led the Court to consider that where domestic rules of procedure require national courts to annul an arbitration award on the grounds of public policy, the same should apply where the application for annulment relies on the breach of the Union rules of competition law.

However, as previously mentioned, the domestic rules of competition law did not form part of the public policy grounds which could justify the annulment of an arbitration award. For this reason, the Opinion of AG Saggio observes that by:

> extend[ing] the ambit of the Netherlands rule on judicial review of arbitration awards to include matters of "public [Union] policy" ... the application of domestic law would still be ensured, with the minor sacrifice of the principle of procedural autonomy.[337]

The Court was ready to proceed with such a "minor sacrifice" to procedural autonomy, particularly for the reason that the arbitrators, unlike national courts

---

[336] The Opinion of AG Saggio in Case C-126/97 *Eco Swiss*, EU:C:1999:97, had also analyzed the first question, reaching the conclusion that Union law "does not require arbitrators, when they have been asked to rule on the performance of an agreement, to raise of their own motion questions about the compatibility of that agreement with [Union] competition law if consideration of those questions would oblige them to abandon the passive role assigned to them, going beyond the ambit of the dispute defined by the parties and relying on facts and circumstances other than those on which the party with an interest in application of those provisions relied in order to substantiate his claim," point 52(1).

[337] Ibid., point 38.

and tribunals, are not in a position to make a reference for preliminary ruling to the Court. Should the ground based on competition law not be admitted at the stage of proceedings for annulment of an arbitration award, there would be no possibility to examine the point based on Union law, and that would result in a divergence of interpretation of a provision of Union law.[338] As AG Maduro explained in his Opinion in *Van der Weerd*, the Court's main concern in *Eco Swiss*:

> appears to have been that a judicial remedy must be available in order to challenge an arbitration award that infringes article [101 TFEU] … The fact that the parties had an opportunity to rely on grounds based on [Union] law during the arbitration proceedings does not guarantee complete judicial protection, because those proceedings – like the administrative review procedure in *Peterbroeck* – do not constitute *judicial* proceedings in the strict sense.[339]

In the light of the above considerations, the present case was to be distinguished from *Van Schijndel* to the effect that:

> questions concerning the interpretation of the prohibition laid down in Article [101 TFEU] should be open to examination by national courts when asked to determine the validity of an arbitration award and … it should be possible for those questions to be referred, if necessary, to the Court of Justice for a preliminary ruling.[340]

That being said, the Court acknowledged that the principle of *res judicata*, a specific expression of the principle of legal certainty, places an *absolute limit* on the obligation of national courts, ruling on an application for annulment of an arbitration award, to admit a ground of review based on the infringement of Union competition law.[341] Thus, national courts are not required to refrain from applying domestic rules of procedure according to which an interim arbitration award has acquired the force of *res judicata*, even if this would be necessary in order to examine the compatibility of an agreement, which the interim award held valid, with Union competition law.[342] The importance of the principle of *res judicata* in the Union legal order has since then been stressed in the case law, to the effect that the principle should not be set aside,

---

338 Case C-126/97 *Eco Swiss*, (n. 258), para. 40: "However, it is manifestly in the interest of the [Union] legal order that, in order to forestall differences of interpretation, every [Union] provision should be given a uniform interpretation, irrespective of the circumstances in which it is to be applied."

339 Opinion of AG Maduro in Joined Cases C-222/05–C-225/05 *Van der Weerd* (n. 316), point 28.

340 Case C-126/97 *Eco Swiss*,(n. 258), para. 40.

341 Ibid., para. 46.

342 Ibid., paras. 47–48 and operative part point 2.

even if that would be liable to remedy a situation involving a violation of Union law.[343]

Following the decision in *Eco-Swiss*, the *Hoge Raad* decided that the public policy ("openbare orde") character of the Union rules of competition law requires their application by the courts in the framework of proceedings for annulment of an arbitration award.[344] However, the assessment of such a ground is no longer possible when this would oblige the courts to set aside an award that has become final. Consequently, the judgment of the *Gerechtshof*, which allowed the staying of the enforcement of the final arbitration award, was set aside.

## 2. THE CONCEPTUAL ELEMENTS OF THE *EX OFFICIO* APPLICATION OF UNION LAW

The general position on the *ex officio* application of Union law relies upon the qualification of a rule of Union law as binding which occupies a similar position to the domestic rules of public policy. As is the case with national legal orders, the concept of public policy at the Union level is "as much vague as it is fundamental."[345] The contours of the rules of Union law which could rank to the same hierarchical level of domestic rules of public policy – rules of a "Union public policy" – are not yet comprehensively drawn in case law. The theoretical analysis of this matter exceeds the scope of this work.[346] For our purposes, it suffices to have an understanding of the way in which the concept "ordre public" is being employed in the context of the *ex officio* application of pleas of Union law.

### 2.1. PUBLIC POLICY: AN ELUSIVE AND VARIABLE CONCEPT

The position that a rule of Union law occupies within the Union legal order is the decisive element that may trigger its *ex officio* application by national courts.

---

343 Case C-69/14 *Târşia*, (n. 266), para. 38; to that effect, see Case C-224/01 *Köbler*, EU:C:2003:513, para. 38 and Case C-453/00 *Kühne & Heitz*, EU:C:2004:17; Case C-234/04 *Kapferer*, EU:C:2006:178; Case C-2/06 *Willy Kempter*, EU:C:2008:78.

344 Hoge Raad R 96/057 (8850) of 25 February 2000.

345 Translation from French from the opinion of *Procureur Général Terlinden* in the case of the Belgian Supreme Court Cass. 12 mai 1922, *Pas.* 1922 I, p. 296 : "notion aussi vague que fondamentale … se sent bien plus qu' [il] ne se définit" [concept as much vague as it is fundamental … it can be felt much more more than it can be defined] (translated by the author), cited in P. Wéry, *Droit des Obligations, Vol. I Théorie générale du contrat* (Brussels, Larcier, 2010), para. 308.

346 For a thorough analysis, see T. Corthaut, (n. 250). See also the contributions concerning Union law in M.J. Redor (ed.), *L'ordre public: ordre public ou ordres publics? Ordre public et droits fondamentaux* (Brussels, Bruylant, 2001).

The question as to which rules of Union law should be regarded as so *fundamental* for the Union legal order as to have a similar rank to the national rules of public policy then becomes crucial. The terminology employed through the *Van Schijndel* line of case law does not appear uniform. This is due to the way in which the question has been articulated or due to the procedural context. The concept of public policy in Union law appears to be what Sacha Prechal and Natalya Shelkolplyas metaphorically call a "chameleon concept" that "changes its colours depending on the circumstances it is relied upon."[347] A similar observation was made by the Advocate General of the *Hoge Raad*, Tim Koopmans, in his (domestic) opinion to *Eco-Swiss*, pointing out that *ordre public* is a concept which varies according to the context to which it is used.[348]

To give some examples of the terminology employed, in *Van Schijndel* and in *Kraaijeveld* the term used for the rules of competition law enshrined in the Treaties is that of "binding [Union] rules" ("règles contraignantes").[349] Sacha Prechal observes that the term "mandatory" would be the appropriate translation of the original Dutch term "dwingende regels."[350] In the specific context of annulment of an arbitration award in *Eco-Swiss*, Article 85 EC [Article 101 TFEU] was qualified as "a fundamental provision which is essential for the accomplishment of the tasks entrusted to the [Union]," which "may be regarded as a matter of public policy within the meaning of the New York Convention [of 10 June 1958 on the Recognition and Enforcement of Foreign Arbitral Awards]."[351] Two other judgments, *Manfredi* and *T-Mobile*, refer to *Eco Swiss* to support the proposition that the rules of competition law are a matter of "public policy which must be automatically applied by national courts."[352]

The context is very different when the concept of public policy forms part of secondary Union law. That is the case in the field of recognition and enforcement of judgments, according to the Brussels I Regulation.[353] Article 45(1)(a) of said regulation provides that the recognition of a foreign judgment shall be refused "if such recognition is manifestly contrary to public policy (ordre public) in the Member State addressed." In accordance with the Court's settled case law,

347 S. Prechal and N. Shelkoplyas (n. 256), 600.

348 Reference made by S. Prechal (n. 248), 703.

349 Joined Cases C-430/93 and C-431/93 *Van Schijndel and Van Veen* (n. 236), para. 13 and Case C-72/95 *Kraaijeveld* (n. 273), para. 60.

350 S. Prechal (n. 248), 698.

351 Case C-126/97 *Eco Swiss* (n. 258), paras. 36 and 39 accordingly. See in detail N. Shelkoplyas, *The Application of EC Law in Arbitration Proceedings* (Groningen, Europa Law Publishing, 2003).

352 Joined Cases C-295/04–C-298/04 *Manfredi* (n. 290), para. 31; Case C-8/08 *T-Mobile Netherlands and Others*, (n. 291), para. 49.

353 Regulation (EU) No 1215/2012 of the European Parliament and of the Council of 12 December 2012 on jurisdiction and the recognition and enforcement of judgments in civil and commercial matters [2012] OJ L351/1.

first, this public policy clause "may be relied on only in exceptional cases,"[354] and second for the purposes of its application, "while Member States remain in principle free … to determine, according to their own national conceptions, what the requirements of their public policy are, the limits of that concept are a matter of interpretation of [Brussels I Regulation]."[355]

Within that specific context of the plea of public policy forming a ground for refusal of recognition of a judgment, the Court endorses a strict interpretation of the rules which may qualify as rules of public policy. It has accepted that the fact that the alleged manifest error which was made by the court of the state of origin concerned a rule of EU law, and not a rule of national law, does not alter the conditions for reliance upon the public policy clause.[356] The public policy clause would apply only if the recognition of the judgment in the Member State in which recognition is sought would result "in a manifest breach of an essential rule of law in the EU legal order and therefore in the legal order of that Member State."[357]

Despite the difference in context, it could be assumed that if a rule cannot be considered an "essential rule of law in the EU legal order" for the purposes of application of the harmonized public policy clause laid down in Brussels I Regulation, it could not be considered either to be a binding rule, having a position similar to national rules of public policy for the purposes of its *ex officio* application.

Finally, it has to be observed that the substance of the public policy concept varies not only among the different legal systems but also within a given legal system. The variables of the concept also relate to the "changing manners, morals and economic conditions"[358] in a society. The same observation is *a fortiori* valid at the Union law level, stemming from a "*sui generis* polity"[359] and begs for caution in the construction and application of a coherent European public policy doctrine.

## 2.2. UNION PUBLIC POLICY BEFORE UNION COURTS

In order to identify the boundaries of the concept of Union public policy as a ground that may trigger the *ex officio* application of Union law by national

---

354 Case C-420/07 *Apostolides*, EU:C:2009:271 para. 55 and the case-law cited; Case C-681/13 *Diageo Brands*, EU:C:2015:471, para. 41.

355 Ibid., *Apostolides*, para. 57; Ibid., *Diageo Brands*, para. 42; Case C-559/14, *Meroni*, EU:C:2016:349, paras. 39–40.

356 Case C-38/98 *Renault*, EU:C:2000:225, para. 32; Ibid., *Diageo Brands*, para. 48.

357 Ibid., *Diageo Brands*, para. 50.

358 E. Peel, *Treitel, The Law of Contract* (London, Sweet&Maxwell, 12th ed., 2007), paras. 11–104.

359 J.H.H. Weiler and U.R. Haltern, "The Autonomy of the Community Legal Order: Through the Looking Glass' (1996) 37 *Harvard International Law Journal* 411.

courts, one could suggest a comparison with the role of the Union courts on the *ex officio* application of grounds pertaining to public policy. Nevertheless, the difference in the level of the *ex officio* application (national level and Union level) probably does not allow for parallelisms.[360] To explain this statement, some general remarks on the *ex officio* application of Union law before the Union courts are necessary.

Union procedural law before the Union courts is governed by the principle of party presentation. In direct actions before the Union courts, the application by which the action is brought must state "the subject matter of the proceedings, the form of order sought, the pleas in law and arguments relied on and a summary of those pleas in law."[361] Exceptionally, the Union courts have jurisdiction to raise, of their own motion, pleas involving matters of public policy and by doing so, the Court has held that:

> the [Union] courts do not go beyond the scope of the dispute that has been brought before them, or in any way infringe the rules of procedure relating to the presentation in the application of the subject-matter of the dispute and the pleas in law.[362]

The pleas involving matters of public policy relate to the admissibility of the action[363] and to the lawfulness of the contested Union law measure, according to Article 263 TFEU. With regard to the lawfulness, the Union courts are, in particular, bound to raise, of their own motion, the pleas in relation to the lack of competence of the institution adopting the act and the infringement of an essential procedural requirement. Such pleas form public policy grounds vitiating the "external" or *procedural legality* ("*légalité externe*") of a measure. By contrast, pleas on the merits of a measure, pertaining to its "internal" or *substantive legality* ("*légalité interne*"), based on the ground of infringement of a Treaty provision or of any rule of law relating to the application of such provision need to be raised by the applicants. This classic distinction differentiating the scope of the *ex officio* judicial powers has long been established by case law.[364]

---

360 T. Corthaut, (n. 250), p. 483.

361 Article 21 of the Statute of the Court of Justice of the European Union; Article 120 of the Rules of Procedure of the Court of Justice; Article 76 of the Rules of Procedure of the General Court of 4 March 2015; Case C-89/08 P *Commission v. Ireland and Others*, EU:C:2009:742; Case C-165/08 *Commission v. Poland*, EU:C:2009:473; C-559/12P *France v. Commission*, EU:C:2014:217; Case C-209/13 *United Kingdom v. Council*, EU:C:2014:283 and Case C-122/16 P *British Airways v. Commission*, EU:C:2017:861.

362 Ibid., *British Airways v. Commission*, para. 90 and case law cited.

363 Such as the time limit for bringing an action and standing requirements. See the case law in K. Lenaerts, I. Maselis and K. Gutman (n. 238), para. 7.217.

364 The relevant rulings are Case C-166/95 P *Commission v. Daffix*, EU:C:1997:73, para. 24; Case C-367/95P *Commission v. Sytraval*, EU:C:1998:154, para. 67; See K. Lenaerts, I. Maselis and K. Gutman (n. 238), para. 7.146; B. Vesterdorf, "Le relevé d'office par le

In his Opinion in the landmark case on the *ex officio* application of Union law by the Union courts, *Salzgitter v. Commission*, AG Jacobs made the preliminary observation that the concept of public policy is inherently difficult to define due to the amount of variables on which it depends:

> which points a court may raise of its own motion ultimately depends on the fundamental values of the legal order concerned, on the respective roles of the parties and the court under the applicable rules of procedure, on the branch of the judiciary which is called upon to apply the concept, and on the level at which the proceedings take place.[365]

The Opinion, supported a broader understanding of the pleas based on public policy that could be raised by the Court of its own motion.[366] According to this approach, the Union courts should also be able to raise "a manifest and grave substantive illegality."[367] In order to determine which pleas are based on public policy, the criteria mainly identified, as summarized in the Opinion of AG Mengozzi in *British Airways*, are the following: whether the rule infringed serves a *fundamental objective* or a fundamental value of the EU legal order and whether the rule infringed has been laid down in the *public interest* and not merely in the interests of the persons directly concerned.[368] This broader understanding of the *ex officio* role has not been confirmed in case law though.[369]

The comparison between the *ex officio* application of Union law before the national courts, on the one hand, and before the Union courts, on the other hand, might give an impression of a certain mismatch. It would seem

---

juge communautaire," in N. Colneric et al. (eds.), *Festchrift für Carlos Rodríguez Iglesias, Une communauté de droit* (Berliner Wissenschafts-Verlag, 2003) and F. Castillo de la Torre, "Le relevé d'office par la juridiction communautaire" (2005) 3–4 *Cahiers de Droit Européen C.D.E* 395–463.

365 Opinion of AG Jacobs in Case C-210/98 P *Salzgitter v. Commission*, EU:C:2000:172, point 134.

366 Advocate General Mengozzi has also endorsed this view, see Opinion of AG Mengozzi in Case C-122/16 P *British Airways v. Commission*, EU:C:2017:406, point 103 and his Opinions cited therein.

367 Opinion of AG Jacobs in Case C-210/98 P *Salzgitter v. Commission* (n. 365), point 137.

368 Ibid., points 141–143; and Opinion of AG Mengozzi in Case C-122/16 P *British Airways* (n. 366), para. 103. AG Jacobs in his Opinion in Case C-210/98 P *Salzgitter v. Commission* (n. 365) also referred to a third criterion, according to which there should be a *manifest breach* of the fundamental provision laid down in the public interest.

369 In Case C-210/98 P *Salzgitter v. Commission*, EU:C:2000:397, para. 56, the Court, without making reference to the public policy concept or to the criteria suggested in the Opinion of AG Jacobs (n. 365), decided that the contested Commission decision was vitiated by lack of competence, which necessitated that the relevant ground be raised by the Court of its own motion. The General Court has applied of its own motion a ground in relation to the *scope of application* of the law in Joined Cases T-576/93–T-582/93 *Browet v. Commission*, EU:T:1994:93, para. 35.

that while national courts are obliged to raise of their own motion binding rules of Union law – rules which rank equally to the domestic rules of public policy – in proceedings for judicial review of an administrative act or in civil law proceedings, Union courts do not have to raise pleas in relation to the substantive legality of a Union act. Nevertheless, as hinted above, there is no common "denominator" for the comparison.[370] The level of comparison is different because the role of the judiciary involved in the comparison is not the same. The Union courts "ensure that in the interpretation and application of the Treaties the law is observed" (Article 19 TEU), while Member State courts ensure effective legal protection in the system of *decentralized enforcement* of Union law.

The procedural realization at the national level of a binding rule of Union law passes through the channel of national procedural law. The *ex officio* application of material Union law by national courts remains exceptional. The exceptional situations that can arise at the level of the national judicature requiring that a point of Union law be taken by the courts of their own motion, cannot be the same as at the level of the Union judicature. To give an example, a civil law case concerning the performance of a contract between two private parties vitiated by illegality due to a manifest breach of a provision of mandatory Union law, can only arise at the level of national jurisdictions. Tim Corthaut observes that the *effet utile* of the mandatory provisions of Union law is particularly compromised in cases of risk of persistent under-enforcement or "systemic failure,"[371] or in cases of "inequality between the parties,"[372] the latter being a main feature in individual consumer litigation. Such situations of "under-enforcement" of Union law or of inequality of the parties cannot, as a matter of fact, be present at the level of the Union judicature. Whether or not the Court should admit the *ex officio* review of the substantive legality of a Union measure and endorse the criteria suggested in that regard by its advocates-general, this is an issue which will depend upon considerations proper to the Union judicature and not comparable to those applicable at the level of judicial enforcement of Union law rights before national courts. That being said, even if the position of principle of the *ex officio* application is not the same between the two levels of Union jurisdiction and the national jurisdictions, the aforementioned criteria on the basis of which the Union public policy may be identified – the fundamental rule of law and the public interest – remain relevant for both levels.

---

370 *Contra*, S. Prechal and N. Shelkoplyas (n. 256), 611, according to whom "there should be a kind of alignment ... national courts should, in principle, not be asked to apply certain – substantive – [Union] law provisions ex officio and as a matter of public policy, if the Luxembourg courts do not do so either."

371 With reference to the rules on free movement or state aid whereby: "Member States may have an interest to bend the rules and create such systemic failures, as demonstrated by the state-aid case in *Lucchini*" (Case C-119/05 *Lucchini*, EU:C:2007:434).

372 T. Corthaut (n. 250), 438.

## 2.3. UNION PUBLIC POLICY AND MANDATORY LAW BEFORE NATIONAL COURTS

In the *Van Schijndel* line of case law, the rules of Union law which may qualify for *ex officio* application before national courts are not qualified as such rules of "Union public policy." The term employed is either, as has already been mentioned, that these rules should be "binding" ("contraignantes") or that they should occupy, within the Union legal order, a *similar position* to the domestic public policy rules. In the *Océano Grupo* line of case law, the rules of consumer law which have to be raised by the courts of their own motion have been qualified as "mandatory provisions" ("dispositions imperatives").[373] In addition, certain rules of consumer protection, notably Article 6(1) of the Unfair Contract Terms Directive, which lays down the rule that the unfair terms are not binding on the consumer, have been qualified as provisions of *public interest* in light of which they must be regarded as of *equal standing* to that of national rules that have, within the domestic legal system, the character of rules of *public policy*.[374]

The concept of "mandatory" law or "loi impératif" has its roots in civil legal theory. It is understood as encompassing the binding rules from which the parties may not derogate, without the public interest necessarily being at stake, as it is the case with rules of public policy. Mandatory law is devoid of the moral connotations of ordre public. In the French and Belgium legal traditions, there is a basic distinction between public policy rules designed to order society, adopted in the general interest and which the courts may raise of their own motion ("ordre public de direction"), and public policy rules designed to protect a specific category of persons, adopted in their proper interest and which may be relied upon only by them ("ordre public de protection").[375] The idea which used to prevail is that the courts have to raise of their own motion the first category of rules because they concern the public interest, but not the second category of rules. Modern legal doctrine distances itself from the traditional division of mandatory rules according to the public/private

---

373 See for instance Case C-168/05 *Mostaza Claro*, EU:C:2006:675, para. 36; Case C-243/08 *Pannon GSM*, EU:C:2009:350, para. 25; Case C-137/08 *Pénzügyi Lízing*, EU:C:2010:659, para. 47; Case C-488/11 *Asbeek Brusse*, EU:C:2013: 341, para. 38.

374 Case C-154/15, C-307/15 and C-308/15, *Gutiérrez Naranjo and Others*, EU:C:2016:980, para. 54, citing to that effect Case C-488/11 *Asbeek Brusse* (n. 373), para. 44. With regard to the "public interest" underlying Article 5(3) of Directive 1999/44/EC of the European Parliament and of the Council of 25 May 1999 on certain aspects of the sale of consumer goods and associated guarantees [1999] OJ L171/12 see Case C-497/13 *Faber*, EU:C:2015:357, para. 56.

375 See indicatively for France P. Malaurie et al., *Les Obligations* (LGDJ, 6th ed., 2013) with further references to the literature; and for Belgium P. Wéry, (n. 345), paras. 307 *et seq.*

interest divide.[376] The former Counselor of the Belgian *Cour de Cassation* Albert Meeùs, relying upon the early writings of De Page,[377] has argued that all mandatory laws partake of the nature of a rule of public policy but to a different degree.[378] He explains that where the legislator decides to establish rules to protect one party, this is in order to serve a general interest purpose for reasons of equity, equality between the parties, of social piece and of economic stability. He incisively concludes that the protection of the private interest might be the immediate objective, but this does not exclude reasons pertaining to the public interest.[379] The practical effect of the identification of a certain rule as a mandatory law of protection is the *relative* nullity of the contract, which restricts the *class* of persons who may invoke nullity only to the party whom that rule intends to protect. Moreover, the person whom the rule intends to protect may decide to *renounce* protection after being informed of the nullity of the contract. By contrast, the courts should always have the power to raise mandatory rules of protection of their own motion.[380]

This view on the role of the courts with respect to mandatory laws of protection was not necessarily reflected in case law, however. In general, the procedural status of mandatory rules, as opposed to rules of public policy, is subject to debate. In France for instance, as will be explained in more detail in Chapter 3,[381] the prevailing view was that mandatory rules of consumer law cannot be raised by the courts of their own motion. In the Netherlands, the prevailing view is that the courts do not have the power to raise, of their own motion, mandatory rules that do not reflect public policy, even if their violation results to absolute nullity of the contract.[382] This position evolved with regard to consumer law following a judgment of the Netherlands

---

376 A. Meeùs, "La notion de loi impérative et son incidence sur la procédure en cassation et sur l'office du juge", *Note sous Cour de Cassation, 3e chambre, 17 mars 1986* (1988) *Revue critique de jurisprudence belge* 495–527; J. Ghestin, "L'annulation d'office d'un contrat" in *Mélanges offerts à Pierre Drai, Le juge entre deux millénaires* (Dalloz, 2000), 593–607.

377 De Page, *Droit civil belge*, vol. IV, (E. Bruylant 1st ed., 1938).

378 A. Meeùs (n. 376). In the same sense P. Malaurie et al., *Droit des Obligations* (LGDJ, 8th ed., 2016), para. 650.

379 Ibid., A. Meeùs (n. 376), 511: "Si le législateur organise une telle protection, c'est parce que l'intérêt général la commande pour des raisons d'équité, d'égalité entre les contractants, de paix sociale, de stabilité économique. Il serait plus exact de dire que la protection des intérêts privés est le but immédiat et principal du législateur, mais n'exclut pas les motifs d'intérêt général." [If the legislator puts in place such a protection, that it is because general interest so requires for reasons of equity, of equality between the contractual parties, of social peace, of economic stability. It would be more precise to say that the protection of private interests is the immediate and main objective of the legislator, but this does not exclude reasons pertaining to the public interest] (translated by the author).

380 See J. Ghestin (n. 376).

381 Chapter 3, Section 2.2.4.

382 B. Fekete and A.M. Mancaleoni (n. 295), 455.

Supreme Court, in which national law was interpreted in such a way as to imply an obligation of the courts to raise the nullity of unfair terms of their own motion.[383]

The case law of the Court follows a progressive and pragmatic vision of mandatory law and the procedural consequences attached. Union law also has its "economic public policy" or mandatory law of the market and its "social protection public policy" or mandatory law of protection.[384] However, such classification does not imply any sharp dividing line.

The rules falling under the pillar of the mandatory law of the market are of a fundamental nature for the attainment of the objectives of the Treaties and serve the public interest for the internal market organization. In *Eco-Swiss*, the Court referred to Article 101 TFEU (then Article 85, on the prohibition of anti-competitive agreements) as "a fundamental provision which is essential for the accomplishment of the tasks entrusted to the [Union] and, in particular, for the functioning of the internal market."[385] The "importance of such a provision" is underlined by the sanction provided for its breach in that same provision, which is absolute nullity.[386]

The rules falling under the pillar of the mandatory law of protection are also of a fundamental nature and they serve the public interest, but they are equally intended to protect a certain category of persons, considered as weaker compared to the other party in the contract, such as the consumer and the worker. The mandatory rules of consumer law partake of both the "economic" sphere[387] and of the sphere of "protection." Pursuant to the classic formulation of *Océano Grupo* and now the standard motto in all cases relevant for the active consumer court doctrine:

> the system of protection introduced by the [Unfair Terms] Directive is based on the idea that the consumer is in [a] weak position vis-à-vis the seller or supplier, as regards both his bargaining power and his level of knowledge.[388]

---

383 Hoge Raad der Nederlanden, 13 September 2013, *Heesakkers v Voets*, NJ 2014, 274, NL :HR2013 :691. The judgment with its most important excerpts is reported in English by B. Fekete and A.M. Mancaleoni (n. 295), 436.

384 According to the classic French model of *ordre public de direction* and *ordre public de protection*, see J. Carbonnier, *Droit Civil*, vol. IV, *Les Obligations* (P.U.F., Collection Thémis privé, 22nd ed., 2000); P. Malaurie et al., (n. 378) with further references to the literature.

385 Case C-126/97 *Eco Swiss* (n. 258), para. 36. In his Opinion in *Eco-Swiss* AG Saggio (n. 336), explains that the distortion of the competition rules leads "to the detriment of the public interest, individual undertakings and consumers" (point 36) citing Joined Cases 46/87 and 227/88 *Hoechst*, EU:C:1989:337, para. 25.

386 Case C-126/97 *Eco Swiss* (n. 258), para. 36.

387 See Opinion of AG Saggio in Joined Cases C-240/98–C-244/98 *Océano Grupo Editorial and Salvat Editores*, EU:C:1999:620, point 25.

388 Joined Cases C-240/98–C-244/98 *Océano Grupo* (n. 257), para. 25.

The rules falling under the Union mandatory law of protection have some important differences compared to the rules belonging to mandatory law of the market in terms of the consequences of their breach. The breach in a contract of a Union mandatory rule of protection results in *relative nullity* – not absolute nullity – in favor of the consumer. However, this is without prejudice to the obligation of the courts to raise the breach of such a rule of their own motion.[389] The *ex officio* powers of the courts to raise the cause of relative nullity should not be confused with the question which one of the parties is entitled to raise the exception of nullity, namely the consumer as opposed to the professional.[390] Moreover, as the Court has established, the consumer has the right to renounce protection *a posteriori*, after having been informed by the courts of the existence of an unfair term.[391] As Arthur Hartkamp rightly puts it, the case law of the Court on the active consumer court:

> has not replaced the concept of relative nullity by absolute nullity, which would run counter to the need of consumer protection, but has added to the concept of "relative" nullity an additional protection by extending the power of the courts.[392]

The consequence of the relative nullity of the contract is that the consumer may renounce his or her rights based on *informed consent*. This means that his or her *procedural omission* alone to raise the protective provision, or his or her *absentia*, is not sufficient. The case law of the Court places emphasis on the "real risk" that the consumer will not make his case "particularly because of ignorance of the law," not as a result of deliberate choice. Due account is thus taken of the procedural imbalance of the parties. The professional is, usually, to employ the classic categorization by Marc Galanter, a "repeat player" of the law, while the consumer is a "one shotter."[393] In view of this situation, the courts are required to intervene to restore the imbalance. The objective of protection, in conjunction with the procedural imbalance, forms the basis of reasoning of the doctrine of the active consumer court.

Moreover, the provisions of consumer law belonging to the mandatory rules of protection serve the general interest. This interest corresponds to the good functioning of the internal market and undistorted competition.

---

389 See P. Wéry, "Les clauses abusives relatives à l'inexécution des obligations contractuelles dans les lois de protection des consommateurs du 14 juillet 1991 et du 2 aout 2002" (2003) *Journal des Tribunaux* 797–809, 808.

390 J. Ghestin (n. 336), 603.

391 Case C-243/08 *Pannon GSM* (n. 373), para. 33.

392 A. Hartkamp, "*Ex Officio* Application in Case of Unenforceable Contracts or Contract Clauses, EU Law and National Laws Confronted," in L. Gullilfer and S. Vogenauer (n. 293), 467–484, 480.

393 M. Galanter, "Why the "Haves" Come Out Ahead: Speculations on the Limits of Legal Change" (1974–1975) *Law and Society Review* 95–160.

However, this is not the only interest. The "high level of consumer protection" is a self-standing value figuring in Article 38 of the Charter of the Union. The Court has stressed out that the Union has not only an economic but also a *social purpose*.[394] The creation of the internal market is, thus, only the means to achieve the ultimate aim proclaimed in Article 3 TEU, the "well-being" of the peoples of the Union. In the words of Alain Supiot: "La libre circulation des marchandises et des capitaux n'est pas un objectif en soi. Elle n'a de valeur que dans la mesure où elle sert réellement l'amélioration du sort des hommes." [The free movement of goods and capital is not an objective on its own. It is of value only to the extent that it effectively serves to improve peoples' lives] (translated by the author).[395]

394 Case C-201/15 *AGET Iraklis*, EU:C:2016:972, para. 77.

395 A. Supiot, *L'Esprit de Philadelphie, La justice sociale face au marché total* (Paris, Editions du Seuil, 2010), 110.

# CHAPTER 3

# NATIONAL PERSPECTIVES ON THE APPLICATION OF UNION LAW BY NATIONAL COURTS OF THEIR OWN MOTION

The *Van Schijndel* line of case law has demonstrated that the national procedural rules which reflect "conceptions prevailing in most of the Member States as to the relations between the State and the individual"[396] do not "bend" before the enforcement of Union law. The question of the power of the courts to address certain issues of Union law of their own initiative touches upon the fundamentals of civil justice by "cutting across," as Simon Whittaker puts it, "the existing national pattern of the relative roles of the parties and courts in determining the subject matter of the case, whether in fact or in law".[397]

The leading procedural principles which determine the respective roles of the courts and the parties in civil adjudication[398] are the principle of party presentation, according to which the delimitation of the ambit of the dispute belongs to the parties (*principe dispositif* – *Dispositionsgrundsatz*) and the principle of adversarial proceedings according to which the court decides on the basis of the materials which have been put forward and debated by the parties (*principe de la contradiction* – *Beibringungsgrundsatz*).

This chapter discusses the *ex officio* application of Union law from a domestic law perspective. It would be beyond the scope of the present work to elaborate upon all the details of the legal systems of Member States with respect to the division of roles between the parties and the courts[399] However, as the

---

396 Joined Cases C-430/93 and C-431/93 *Van Schijndel and van Veen* EU:C:1995:441, para. 21.

397 S. Whittaker, "Who Determines What Civil Courts Decide? Private Rights, Public Policy and EU Law," in D. Leczykiewicz and S. Weatherill (eds.), *The Involvement of EU Law in Private Law Relationships* (Oxford, Hart Publishing, 2013), 89–129, 91.

398 In this chapter the term "civil process" is taken to refer to the adjudication of private law disputes without distinction of the venue of adjudication. This clarification is important in view of the broad understanding of disputes conferred in civil courts in the English legal context, which also includes judicial review or administrative action: S. Whittaker, (n. 397), 89–129, at fn. 1 and 3; N. Andrews, *English Civil Procedure, Fundamentals of the New Civil Justice System* (Oxford, Oxford University Press, 2003) para. 1.53.

399 See in that regard the comparative study of N. Trocker and V. Varano (eds.), *The Reforms of Civil Procedure in Comparative Perspective, An International Conference dedicated to Mauro Cappelletti* (Torino, Giappichelli, 2005).

*Van Schijndel* line of case law touches upon this issue, it is essential to adumbrate the theoretical assumptions underlying the principle of party presentation. Illustrations will then be drawn from the relative roles of the parties and courts in three jurisdictions – the English, the French and the German, with some references also to the Belgian and Luxembourg jurisdictions – in civil law adjudication with regard to points of mandatory Union law. The application of the consumer *ex officio* doctrine in national legal orders will then be examined in detail in Chapter 6.

## 1. THE "PREVAILING CONCEPTIONS" WITH REGARD TO THE ROLE OF THE COURTS AND THE PARTIES: ON THE PRINCIPLE OF PARTY PRESENTATION

The Court in *Van Schijndel* seems to imply that there exists a common procedural core as to the role of the courts and the parties in the Member States, moving beyond the traditional dividing lines between common law and civil law. The Opinion of AG Jacobs[400] follows an analysis transcending divisions. The acknowledgment in *Van Schijndel* of the "prevailing conceptions" as to the relative role of the courts and the parties in judicial proceedings could be considered as proof of a spirit of "osmosis"[401] between the Union legal order and the national legal orders. Antonio Tizzano, delving into the relationship between the two normative levels of Union law and national law, explains that Union law influences national law, but that the national legal systems are also a source of inspiration of values, principles and concepts. These values, principles and concepts materialize "the frame of reference or the environment of the common law of the Union".[402] By making the principle of party presentation the reference point of the prevailing procedural conceptions of Member States, the Court sees in it what Rolf Stürner calls the foundation of all legal families of procedural law ("le fondement incontesté des toutes les familles de droit processuel").[403]

---

400 Opinion of AG Jacobs in Joined Cases C-430/93 and C-431/93 *Van Schindel and van Veen*, EU:C:1995:185.

401 A. Tizzano, "Quelques Considérations sur le Rôle de la Cour de Justice" (2010) 4 *Revue de la Faculté de Droit de l'Université de Liège* 493–504, 499.

402 Ibid. (translated by the author from the original: "*constituent à leur tour la source d'inspiration des valeurs, des principes et des concepts qui matérialisent le cadre de référence, 'l'environnement' du droit commun*").

403 R. Stürner, "Procédure Civile et Culture Juridique" (2004) 4 *Revue Internationale de Droit Comparé R.I.D.C.* 797–824. The *ALI/Unidroit Principles and Rules on Transnational Civil Procedure* is perhaps the largest-scale project that has been undertaken thus far in the field of establishing a common procedural framework. For an analysis, see P. Fouchard (ed.), *Vers un Procès Civil Universel? Les Règles Transnationales de Procèdure Civile de l'American*

The "prevailing" conceptions with regard to the principle of party presentation to which the *Van Schijndel* judgment refers relate to the "relations between the State and the individual," being a principle which "safeguards the rights of the defense" and which "ensures proper conduct of proceedings."[404] The principle is grounded, indeed, upon deep political, constitutional and philosophical considerations as to the role of the judiciary in a liberal democracy. It is the reflection of a legal culture which respects private autonomy, participation and "human individuality,"[405] but also judicial impartiality.[406] The role of the judge is, to employ the metaphor of Herve Croze, to read the balance of justice and not to make it weigh towards one side or the other.[407]

In the same way that the principle of party autonomy is a fundamental pillar of private law, in civil procedural law it is the parties who remain "masters of the litigation" (*dominus litis*).[408] The parties "hold the reins" of the initiation and termination of the procedure, but also of the delineation of the subject matter of the dispute, defined by the legally significant material facts advanced in their pleadings and supported by the evidence they adduce.

If one party is at liberty to decide whether to enforce a substantive right or not, it ensues that that party should be at liberty to decide the terms of his case. That being said, the considerations of substantive law do not necessarily coincide with the considerations proper to procedural law.[409] If a legal rule qualifies as

*Law Institut* (Editions Panthéon-Assas, 2001); R. Stürner, "The Principles of Transnational Civil Procedure" (2005) *Rabels Zeitschrift* 201–254; N. Andrews, (n. 398), Chapter 43. At the European level, the first comprehensive research effort for an "*Approximation of Judiciary Law in the European Union*" was carried out under the direction of Marcel Storme; see M. Storme (ed.), *Rapprochement du Droit Judiciaire de l'Union Européenne* (Kluwer, 1993). Currently there is an ongoing project carried out by UNIDROIT and ELI in order to set out European Rules of Civil Procedure. More information and updates on the project can be found at the site http://www.europeanlawinstitute.eu/projects-publications/current-projects-feasibility-studies-and-other-activities/current-projects/civil-procedure (last access January 4, 2018).

404 Joined Cases C-430/93 and C-431/93 *Van Schijndel and van Veen* (n. 396), para. 21.

405 See R. Stürner (n. 403), 800, who refers to the existence of a link between the principle of party disposition and an individualist legal culture that places the subjective right of the individual in the centre of all economic and judicial actions. On the liberal underpinnings of the adversarial principle, see M.R. Damaska, *The Faces of Justice and State Authority: A Comparative Approach to the Legal Process* (New Haven & London, Yale University Press, 1986).

406 H. Croze, "Le juge doit-il dire le droit?" in *Mélanges en l'Honneur de Serge Guinchard, Justices et droit du procès, du légalisme procédural à l'humanisme processuel* (Dalloz, 2010), 225–232, 229, who observes that it is difficult for an "overpowerful court" to remain neutral (translated by the author of the original "*il est difficile à un juge tout puissant de rester neutre*").

407 Ibid.

408 Opinion of AG Jacobs in Joined Cases C-430/93 and C-431/93 *Van Schindel and van Veen* (n. 400), point 34.

409 On the relationship between substantive and procedural law, John Anthony Jolowicz explains in a type of word game that "subjection to substantive law is, subjection to civil procedural

mandatory law, this does not mean that the courts should investigate the facts to ensure its application.[410]

On the other hand, the fact that the parties seek to resolve their individual dispute before the courts is without prejudice to the public interest underlying court adjudication. To quote the Hon. James J. Spigelman: "A court is not simply a publicly funded dispute resolution centre."[411] The public interest dimension of the civil process does not imply, still, the requirement of a judicial intervention *in abstracto* for the determination of the elements of the dispute.[412] In the eloquent terms of Eduardo Couture, the process is at the crossroads of public law and private law, being for the parties an instrument of private law, but for the state, it is a means of realization of the law.[413]

It has not been uncommon in the past, particularly in the English legal literature, to oppose sharply the continental legal system and the English legal system as to the role of the courts,[414] with at one end of the spectrum,

---

law is not, involuntarily" and that "substantive law is, procedural law is not, 'self-executing'": J.A. Jolowicz, "On the nature and purposes of civil procedural law" in I.R. Scott (ed.), *International Perspectives on Civil Justice: Essays in Honor of Sir Jack I. H. Jacob, QC* (London, Sweet & Maxwell, 1990), 27–45, 32.

410 See also S. Amrani Mekki, "Les catégories de Common Law et de Civil Law à l'épreuve de l'office du juge et des parties" in *Mélanges en l'Honneur de Serge Guinchard, Justices et droit du procès, du légalisme procédural à l'humanisme processuel* (Dalloz, 2010), 157–173, 168, who explains that despite the parties being the masters of the "judicial space" ("espace judiciaire,") they have to respect court management rules.

411 J.J. Spigelman, "Judicial Accountability and Performance Indicators" (2002) 21 *C.J.Q.* 18, 26 (quoted by J.A. Jolowicz, "Substantive and Procedural Justice in Civil Litigation: A Measure of the Role of Civil Litigation" in *De Tous Horizons, Mélanges Xavier Blanc-Jouvan* (LGDJ, 2005, 549–566, 564), who opposes the proposition that the courts provide a "service" to the litigants: "Litigants are, and should be, treated in the courts as citizens not consumers. The courts do not deliver a 'service'. The courts administer justice in accordance with the law. They no more deliver a 'service' in the form of judgments and decisions, than a parliament delivers a 'service' in the form of debates and statutes. Courts serve the people but they do not provide services to the litigants."

412 See J. Heron and T. Le Bars, *Droit Judiciaire Privé* (Lextenso, 5th ed., 2012), para. 261.

413 E. Couture, "Le procès comme institution" (1950) *Revue Internationale de Droit Comparé*, 276–281: *"Le procès est situé au carrefour des chemins du droit public et du droit privé. Pour les parties, le procès est un instrument de satisfaction du droit privé; mais, pour l'Etat, c'est une forme de réalisation du droit … d'un point de vue absolument privé du procès, le juge est un spectateur presque impassible du drame judiciaire, mais dans une conception publique du procès le juge est un protagoniste, il prend sa place au milieu de la scène."* [The process is situated at the crossroads of public and private law. For the parties, the process is an instrument of materialization of a private right, but for the state, it is a form of realization of the law … from an absolutely private point of view of the process, the court is an almost passive observer of the judicial drama, but from a public conception of the process, the court is a protagonist; it takes its place in the middle of the scene] (translated by the author). J.A. Jolowicz (n. 409), 45, observes that: "The process of civil litigation serves purposes other than that of doing justice to those who appear before the courts, and those purposes must be reflected in our procedural law."

414 See J.I. Jacob, *The Fabric of English Civil Justice* (Stevens, 1987), 7 *et seq.*

England with a purely adversary system of civil procedure,[415] and at the other end, the civil law countries with, supposedly, an inquisitorial system.[416] Nonetheless, studies from authors like John Anthony Jolowicz have paved the way for a more conciliatory vision.[417] To take the example of France, civil justice is not inquisitorial but adversarial (*accusatoire*), whereby the parties play an essential role in the procedure, moderated only by certain "inquisitorial" elements, especially with respect to the management of the evidence. But even within the confines of a single judicial system, the study of the role of the courts and the parties in terms of categorization of that sort has been heavily criticized. Jacques Héron, one of the leading authors of French procedural theory, has rejected the analysis of the civil process in terms of an accusatorial/inquisitorial divide as a simplification to the extent of being somewhat "Manichean."[418] This is why he suggests that the civil process is hybrid (mixed accusatory and inquisitorial: "mi-accusatoire, mi-inquisitoire").[419]

---

415 See J.I. Jacob (n. 414); M. Cappelletti and J.A. Jolowicz, *Public Interest Parties and the Active Role of the Judge* (Milan, 1975); J.A. Jolowicz, "The Woolf Report and the Adversary System" (1996) 15 *Civil Justice Quarterly* 183; N. Andrews, *Andrews on Civil Processes, Court Proceedings*, vol I (Cambridge, Intersentia, 2013), Chapter 1, Section 2.7.

416 This distinction can be epitomized in the following quotation by Sir J.I. Jacob: "whereas under the civil law inquisitorial system, the court plays an active, authoritative, interventionist role; and correspondingly, under the adversary system, the parties play a major, dominating, independent role to persuade the court to adjudicate or otherwise resolve the dispute in their favor whereas under the inquisitorial system, they play a minor, tentative, supportive role to enable the court to perform its function to inquire into and determine the dispute"; J.I. Jacob (n. 414), 7.

417 J.A. Jolowicz, "*Da Mihi Factum Dabo Tibi Jus*: A Problem of Demarcation in English and French Law" in *On Civil Procedure* (Cambridge, Cambridge University Press, 2000); J.A. Jolowicz, "Adversarial and Inquisitorial Models of Civil Procedure" (2003) 52 *International & Comparative Law Quarterly*, 281–295; J.A. Jolowicz, "Substantive and Procedural Justice in Civil Litigation: A Measure of the Role of Civil Litigation" in *De Tous Horizons, Mélanges Xavier Blanc-Jouvan* (LGDJ, 2005), 549–566. If there would be such a sharp distinction between the English legal process and the continental civil process, maybe the *ALI/Unidroit* Principles would have never become reality. According to M. Taruffo, "La Genèse et la Finalité des Règles Proposées par l'American Law Institut," in P. Fouchard (ed.) (n. 403), 20: "nous ne cherchons pas un compromis ou une médiation entre les deux modèles essentiels, puisque nous ne croyons pas que ces deux modèles existent et qu'ils s'opposent de façon antithétique." [We do not seek for a compromise or a mediation between the two essential models, as we do not believe that such two models exist or that they oppose each other] (translated by the author).

418 J. Heron and T. Le Bars (n. 412), paras. 259–263,: "on peut même penser qu'elle est parfois nuisible: par son simplisme quelque peu manichéen, l'opposition de l'accusatoire et l'inquisitoire risque de détourner des données véritables du procès civil, qui sont seules à même inspirer le législateur" [we may even think that at times it is even harmful: due to its somewhat Manichean simplicity, the divide between the accusatory and the inquisitorial system risks distracting from the true elements of the civil process, which they are the only ones to interest the legislator] (translated by the author).

419 Ibid. Also, E. Jeuland, "Remarks on the power of French judge in a European perspective" in *Festschrift für Rolf Stürner zum 70. Geburstag* (Mohr Siebeck, 2013), 1545–1553, who describes the French civil procedure as hybrid.

The above gives also the background to the position of AG Jacobs in his Opinion in *Van Schijndel*, in which he contests the thesis of sharp contrasts between the different legal systems. He has considered the contradiction as "exaggerated" and one which "can hardly be sustained."[420] The principle *jura novit curia* in the continental civil systems is accompanied by the principle *da mihi factum, dabo tibi jus.* As AG Jacobs explains, where civil courts may raise a new point of law, this should not involve new issues of fact, while if there are circumstances under which courts have the power to raise a new point, the parties are invited to submit their observations.[421] The English courts, on the other hand, are "in no way precluded from raising a point of law which the parties have not relied upon."[422] On the contrary, it is a matter of course that "like any other court [the English court] will take of its own motion a point which is a matter of public policy," as is notably the case with the refusal of enforcement of illegal contracts. Based on the comparative study of John Anthony Jolowicz, AG Jacobs in his Opinion in *Van Schijndel* concludes that the differences in the approach on that matter of the English and French courts "are not great".[423]

In that vein, the procedural systems are considered by John Anthony Jolowicz as placed in a scale "at the one end of which there is the theoretically pure adversary system and at the other the theoretically pure inquisitorial".[424]

Each procedural system needs then to be situated somewhere across the scale according to the prevailing element. Besides, the extent to which a given system of civil process is considered to bear characteristics of the one or the other sort also depends on the reader of the scale.[425]

Within the framework of such nuanced understanding, the civil justice systems would then appear to oscillate between the two models in an attempt to achieve the *right balance* in the role distribution between the courts and the parties, and, ultimately, a model of civil justice which promotes the dialogue between the courts and the parties. The dialogue represents, according to Serge Guinchard, one of the principles of the civil process of the future.[426]

---

420 Opinion of AG Jacobs in Joined Cases C-430/93 and C-431/93 *Van Schindel and van Veen* (n. 400), point 34.

421 Ibid.

422 Ibid.

423 Ibid. J.A. Jolowicz, "Da mihi factum dabo tibi jus: a problem of demarcation in English and French law" (n. 417), 196:, who concludes that "both English and French law express their continued allegiance to the general principle that it is the parties' dispute with which the court must deal, not the dispute which the court might have preferred to have before it: the law maybe for the judge, but he is bound by the parties' choice of material facts."

424 J.A. Jolowicz, "Adversarial and Inquisitorial Models of Civil Procedure" (n. 417), 281.

425 "La procédure y est plus accusatoire ou inquisitoire que la sienne" [the procedure is more accusatory or inquisitorial compared to our own] (translated by the author): S. Amrani Mekki (n. 410), 161.

426 S. Guinchard, "Quels Principes Directeurs pour les Procès de Demain?" in *Mélanges Jacques van Compernolle* (Brussels, Bruylant, 2004), 201–248, 222.

The absolute limit is the observance of the right to fair trial, the universal model (*modèle universel*), which brings about, in the beautiful words of the same author, "la modélisation des procès par la mondialisation des procédures" [the standardization of process through the globalization of the procedures] (translated by the author).[427]

# 2. ILLUSTRATIONS FROM THE NATIONAL COURTS' PERSPECTIVE ON THE APPLICATION OF UNION LAW OF THEIR OWN MOTION

This section takes the inquiry on the application of Union law by the courts of their own motion to the national level and intends to add flesh to the "conceptions prevailing in most of the Member States as to the relations between the State and the individual" referred to in the *Van Schijndel* judgment. Illustrations will mainly be drawn from the perspective of three jurisdictions (English, French and German). Given that the delimitation of the role of the courts and the parties in the civil law dispute touches upon the fundamentals of each civil procedural system, it would go beyond the scope of this work to embark upon an extensive comparative analysis of such fundamentals. The objective here is only to demonstrate the methodological path to be followed in the study of the implications of the general position on the *ex officio* application of Union law in a given national legal order.

## 2.1. THE ENGLISH COURT PERSPECTIVE

### *2.1.1. General Observations on the Relative Role of the Courts and the Parties*

The backbone of English civil justice is the adversarial system.[428] The case management introduced by the Civil Procedure Rules (CPR) tempered the conception of a "highly concentrated form of the adversarial principle,"[429]

427 S. Guinchard, "Les Métamorphoses de la Procédure à l'Aube du Troisième Millénaire" in *Clés pour le Siècle* (Dalloz, Université Panthéon-Assas, 2000), 1134–1211, 1138; S. Guinchard et al., *Droit Processuel, Droits Fondamentaux du Procès* (Dalloz, 7th ed., 2013), paras. 216 *et seq.*

428 On the philosophical underpinnings of the adversarial principle, see M.R. Damaska, *The Faces of Justice and State Authority: A Comparative Approach to the Legal Process* (New Haven & London, Yale University Press, 1986). Critically, see D. Luban, *Lawyers and Justice: An Ethical Study* (Princeton, Princeton University Press, 1988).

429 N. Andrews, "A New Civil Procedural Code for England: Party-Control 'Going, Going, Gone'" (2000) 19 *Civil Justice Quarterly*, 19–38, 22.

synonymous with the party-control of all aspects of the litigation, in order to enable the courts to deal with cases "justly and at proportionate cost."[430] But the move from the parties to the courts under the CPR has only shifted "the procedural centre of gravity."[431] The determination of the scope of the dispute, including legal issues, rests upon the pleadings of the parties, as has always been the case.[432]

In English law there is no principle comparable to the *ius novit curia* principle, which places the ultimate responsibility for the application of the law with the courts.[433] As Neil Andrews explains, the English courts "adhere to the tradition that it is the parties' lawyers who set the parameters of legal analysis" and they will, therefore, "not examine legal points or doctrine which are not covered by these submissions."[434] That being so, as is stressed in the Opinion of AG Jacobs in *Van Schijndel*, the courts are not precluded from raising a new point of law, provided that the principle of due notice is adhered to.[435] In order

---

430 CPR 1.1 (1) See R. Turner, "Actively: The Word that Changed the Civil Courts" in D. Dwyer (ed.), *The Civil Procedure Rules Ten Years On* (Oxford, Oxford University Press, 2009), 77–88, 82, who speaks of a culture of "proactive interventionism" in the litigation process. Lord Woolf, Final Report on Access to Justice (1997), para. 3 (Lord Woolf is the architect of the CPR reforms) explains that the managerial justice does not encroach upon the core elements of the adversarial English civil justice: "The responsibility of the parties and the legal profession for handling cases will remain. The legal profession will, however, be performing its traditional adversarial role in a managed environment governed by the courts and by the rules which will focus effort on the key issues rather than allowing every issue to be pursued regardless of expense and time, as at present."

431 N. Andrews (n. 429), 24.

432 See *Lombard North Central plc v. Automobile World (UK) Ltd* [2010] EWCA Civ 20, per *Rimer* LJ: "There can, in my judgment … be no duty on a judge to inquire as to whether such a litigant wishes to apply to amend his pleadings to raise any particular issue that he has not pleaded. It is for the litigant to decide what case he wishes to make and how to make it. It is not for the judge to step into the arena and inquire of him whether he wishes to make some additional case" (para. 78).

433 The emphatic quotation from F.A. Mann, "Fusion of the Legal Professions?" (1977) *Law Quarterly Review* 367, 369, that "perhaps the most spectacular feature of English procedure is that the *curia novit legem* rule has never been and is not part of English law" is well known.

434 N. Andrews (n. 415), para. 25.52; N. Andrews, "The Passive Court and Legal Argument" (1988) *CJQ* 125–140, arguing for a more active role of the courts, for as long as the principle of due notice is observed. In *Darlington BC v. Wiltshier Northern Ltd* [1995] 1 WLR 68 (CA), *Steyn LJ* (as he then was) said that "courts of law in our [English] system are the hostages of the arguments deployed by counsel". Lord Denning M.R. has famously militated in favor of more active courts in taking the path of independent legal reasoning in *Goldsmith v. Sperrings Ltd* [1977] WLR 478. In his famous citation from the case (at 486): "an erroneous proposition should not be accepted as good law simply because counsel has passed it by in silence. By that means it gains currency and is never remedied. Better to correct it now while the opportunity offers rather than let it continue to disturb the course of justice."

435 Opinion of AG Jacobs in Joined Cases C-430/93 and C-431/93, *Van Schijndel and van Veen* (n. 400), point 34. In the same vein, see J.A. Jolowicz, "*Da mihi factum dabo tibi jus*" (n. 417), 190, arguing that for as long as the fundamental requirement of due notice is observed, there is nothing in English law requiring that the court should give judgment contrary to his belief of what the law is, "merely because counsel for one party failed through incompetence

for the courts to raise a new legal issue, all the necessary materials have to be introduced by the parties.[436]

Exceptionally, the courts have an obligation to take an issue of their own motion irrespective of the pleadings of the parties. The parties' dominance over the ambit of the dispute does not reach so far as to impose judicial passivity over the enforcement of an illegal contract. English law does not accept that the courts become facilitators for enforcement of illegality, a centuries-old rule which AG Jacobs also pointed out in his Opinion in *Van Schijndel*, quoting *Bank of India v. Trans Continental Commodity Merchants Ltd*, *per* Bingham J:[437]

> where a transaction is on its face manifestly illegal the Court will refuse to enforce it whether the point is pleaded or not and whether either party raises the point or not, and even if the point arises for the first time on appeal. The reasons for this rule is that the Queen's Courts may not be used to enforce unlawful contracts, whatever the wishes of the parties.

However, this exceptional role of the courts is activated only if illegality can be clearly deduced from the facts put before the court.[438] As per Donaldson J,

---

or inadvertence to rely in argument on the applicable rule of law." Even F. A. MANN (n. 433), 369, who spoke of a "principle of judicial unpreparedness" in England, as opposed to the *curia novit legem* principle, accepts that courts should have a power but not a duty to intervene, provided they respect the rights of defense of the parties: "The court may raise questions, suggest new lines of argument or amendments of the pleadings, draw attention to authorities overlooked by counsel. But it is not its duty to do so. In any event points or authorities that occur to the judge ought (and are expected) to be put to counsel to prevent surprise."

436 S. WHITTAKER, "Who Determines What Civil Courts Decide? Private Rights, Public Policy and EU Law" in D. LECZYKIEWICZ and S. WEATHERILL (eds.), (n. 397), 89–129, 97, explains that: "A court being able to raise an issue is not the same as a court being entitled to determine an issue".

437 [1982] 1 Lloyd's Reports 427, 429. J.A. JOLOWICZ, "Da mihi factum dabo tibi jus" (n. 417), citing further *Holman v. Johnson* (1775) 1 Cowper 341, 343, per Lord Mansfield "[i]f, from the plaintiff's own stating or otherwise; the cause of action appears to arise ex turpi causa, or the transgression of a positive law of this country, there the Court says he has no right to be assisted"; *North-western Salt Co. Ltd v. Electrolytic Alkali Co Ltd.* [1914] A.C. 461; *Edler v. Auerbach* [1950] 1 K.B. 359; *Snell v. Unity Finance Ltd.* [1964] 2 Q.B. 203. A very interesting case is *Moase v. Secretary of State for the Environment* [2001] Env.L.R. 13, which the Court of Appeal distinguished from the ECJ ruling in Case C-72/95 *Kraaijeveld*, EU:C:1996:404: "We would enter one caveat that of course there may be circumstances in which an illegality even as a matter of domestic law is so plain that the reviewing court will have an obligation to take the point of its own motion. That might well be established by fresh evidence. Since the court should take the point, it will take it if it is raised by a party although it was not raised before the Inspector. But that is not the case."

438 See H. BEALE ET AL. (ed.), *Chitty on Contracts*, Vol. I (Sweet & Maxwell, 30th ed., 2010), para. 16-205, explaining that as long as the court will be "satisfied that all the relevant facts are before it and it can clearly see from them that the contract had an illegal object, it may not enforce the contract, whether the facts were pleaded or not." S. WHITTAKER (n. 436), 96, clarifies that "where a contract is not illegal on its face, then evidence of extraneous

"illegality, once brought to the attention of the court, overrides all questions of pleading."[439] The court's intervention of its own motion to ensure that the illegal contract will not be enforced intends to ensure that "its process is not being abused by inviting it to enforce *sub silentio* a contract whose enforcement is contrary to public policy".[440]

### 2.1.2. *Mandatory Rules of Union Law and the Role of the Courts*

The relative roles of the courts and the parties in the procedure do not change when the dispute raises an issue of mandatory Union law. It falls upon the parties to plead points of Union law and not upon the courts to raise them.[441] John Temple Lang explains the impact of *Van Schijndel* on the English legal order as follows:

> national courts must raise points of [Union] law on their own initiative where the public interest requires this, just as they would with comparable points of national law, but need not alter their normal role or go outside the facts alleged by the parties and the dispute as defined by the pleadings.[442]

The following passage from a judgment on environmental law, referring to the judgment of the Court in *Kraaijeveld*,[443] offers an insight into the perception of the role of the courts in public law proceedings with regard to arguments pertaining to Union law:

> where a court is entitled to take points of its own motion, as it undoubtedly is in public law proceedings, then it should take a point considering breach of a directive even if the parties to the case have not taken that point. If, for example, the challenges in the present case were brought on domestic grounds and the court saw a point concerning breach of the environmental assessment Directive, the court could, and should, raise that point of its own motion.[444]

With regard, more particularly, to proceedings pertaining to the performance of a contact in breach of a mandatory rule of Union law, the theory of

---

circumstances tending to show that it has an illegal object should not be admitted unless the circumstances relied on are pleaded."

439 *Belvoir Finance Co Ltd v. Harold G Cole & Co* (1969) 2 All ER 904, 908.

440 *Birkett v. Acorn Business Machines Ltd* [1999] 2 All ER (Comm) 429, *per* Mr. Justice Colman.

441 See for instance cases where breach of the Treaty free movement of services provision had to be alleged and proved by the plaintiffs: *Wilander and Novacek v. Tobin and Jude* (1997) 1 Lloyd's Rep 195; *Paul Edwards v. The British Athletic Federation and the International Amateur Athletic Federation* [1998] 2 CMLR 363.

442 J. Temple Lang, "The duties of national courts under Community constitutional law" (1997) 22 (1) *E.L.Rev.*, 3-18, 14.

443 Case C-72/95, *Kraaijeveld* (n. 437).

444 *R. v. London Borough of Hammersmith & Fulham* [2000] Env. L. R. 532.

*prima facie* manifest illegality, mentioned above, is fully applicable. The contracts in breach of the domestic rules of competition law are void[445] and illegal.[446] Therefore, as is the case with an agreement restrictive of trade that is affected by illegality,[447] the court may refuse to enforce a contract breaching the Union competition rules if it is manifestly illegal or if there is before the court persuasive and comprehensive evidence of illegality, even if illegality has not been pleaded.[448] In any other case, per Parker J in *Panayiotou (George Michael) v. Sony Music Entertainment*: "it is not for the court to raise and to adjudicate upon an issue of [Union] law which [the plaintiff] has not himself raised, and which [counsel] submits (albeit wrongly, in my judgment) is irrelevant."[449]

With regard to consumer contracts and in particular the control of unfair terms, in the immediate aftermath of the *Océano Grupo* judgment,[450] Simon Whittaker had connected the obligation of the courts to raise the unfairness of contract clauses with the English doctrine of illegality. In his view, that case law:

> could be seen as establishing a new category of illegality of contract term, according to which national courts should refuse to apply the term either if it is unfair (and therefore "illegal") on the face of the record or capable of being held unfair on the facts before them.[451]

---

445 Competition Act 1998, s. 2(4).

446 *Gibbs Mew Ppc v. Graham Gemmell* [1999] E.C.C. 97, 112, para. 40: *per* Gibson LJ "I do not accept [counsel's] argument that an agreement in breach of Article [101 TFEU] is not 'illegal in the strict sense'. Article [101 TFEU] not only makes the agreement automatically void but contains a prohibition and is a penal provision. For an agreement to be illegal it not be in breach of the criminal law." Gibson LJ then refers further to the Opinion of AG Jacobs in *Van Schijndel* (n. 400) (point 49, in particular) as unambiguously assimilating a breach of the Union competition law provisions with the English concept of illegality.

447 On the issue of illegality in restraint of trade, see H. Beale et al. (ed.), (n. 438), para. 16-075 *et seq.*; E. Peel, *Treitel, The Law of Contract* (London, Sweet & Maxwell, 12th ed., 2007), para. 11-086 *et seq.*

448 See the case law cited by E. Peel (n. 447), fn. 621 on the consideration of grounds of illegality by the courts on their own motion: *Birkett v. Acorn Business Machines Ltd* [1999] 2 All ER (Comm) 429, para. 433; *Snell v. Unity Finance Co Ltd* [1964] QB 203; *Charlton v. Fisher* [2001] EWCA Civ 112 [2002] QB 518, para. 80.

449 [1994] ECC 395, 419 para. 74.

450 Joined Cases C-240/98–C-244/98 *Océano Grupo Editorial and Salvat Editores*, EU:C:2000:346.

451 S. Whittaker, "Judicial Interventionism and Consumer Contracts" (2001) 117 *Law Quarterly Review* 215–220, 218. See also S. Whittaker, in H. Beale et al (ed.), (n. 438), para. 15–119, and idem., "The Relative Roles of the Court of Justice of the EU, National Courts and the Parties" in H. Beale et al (ed.), *Chitty on Contracts* (Vol. II, 32nd ed., 2015, Sweet&Maxwell), paras. 38-302–38-310, at para. 38-309, according to whom the active role of the national courts to assess unfair terms of their own initiative can be understood in terms of "neutral judicial assessment" and not proper for the imposition of a burden of proof of the unfairness on either party. The author draws an analogy with unfair dismissal disputes, where the tribunal will assess the question whether the employer "acted reasonably or unreasonably" as a "neutral" issue, although the parties may adduce facts or arguments in support of their positions (citing *Boys and Girls Welfare Society v. McDonald* [1996] IRLR 129, at 132).

The doctrine of the active consumer court is now embedded in the Consumer Rights Act 2015, but only as far as the control of unfair terms is concerned. According to section 71 of the Act, in proceedings before a court which relate to a term of a consumer contract: "The court must consider whether the term is fair even if none of the parties to the proceedings has raised that issue or indicates that it intends to raise it," but only for as long as "the court considers that it has before it sufficient legal and factual material to enable it to consider the fairness of the term."

This is an important development for the reception of the *ex officio* doctrine in national jurisdictions and will be examined further in Chapter 6.

## 2.2. THE FRENCH COURT PERSPECTIVE

### *2.2.1. General Observations on the Relative Role of the Courts and the Parties*

The French Civil Procedure Code (*Code de Procédure Civile* (CPC)) lays down explicitly in Article 12 the maxim *ius novit curia*, according to which the courts decide the case on the basis of the applicable rules of law and apply the proper legal qualification to the facts, except where the parties have bound the court on the points of law on which they wish to restrict their case, by means of an express agreement pertaining to rights which they can freely dispose of.[452] The *ius novit curia* principle has to be read within the context of the other leading procedural principles, particularly the principle of party presentation and the adversarial principle.[453]

---

452 Article 12 CPC: "Le juge tranche le litige conformément aux règles de droit qui lui sont applicables. Il doit donner ou restituer leur exacte qualification aux faits et actes litigieux sans s'arrêter à la dénomination que les parties en auraient proposée. Toutefois, il ne peut changer la dénomination ou le fondement juridique lorsque les parties, en vertu d'un accord exprès et pour les droits dont elles ont la libre disposition, l'ont lié par les qualifications et points de droit auxquels elles entendent limiter le débat." Translation: "The court settles the dispute in accordance with the rules of law applicable thereto. He must give or restore their proper legal definitions to the disputes facts and deeds notwithstanding the denominations given by the parties. However, he may not change the denomination or legal ground where the parties, pursuant to an express agreement and in the exercise of such rights that they may freely alienate, have bound him by legal definitions and legal arguments to which they intend to restrict the debate. Where a dispute has arisen, the parties may, under the same matters and conditions, confer upon the judge a mandate to determine a case as an amicable compounder subject to an appeal where the parties have not expressly abandoned their right of appeal.".

453 On the civil procedural principles in France: J. Héron and T. le Bars, *Droit Judiciaire Privé* (Lextenso, 5th ed.); E. Jeuland, *Droit Procéssuel Général* (Lextenso, 2nd ed.); L. Cadiet and E. Jeuland, *Droit Judiciaire Privé* (LexisNexis, 8th ed., 2013); L. Cadiet, J. Normand and S.A. Mekki, *Théorie Générale du Procés* (PUF, 2013, 2nd ed.); S. Guinchard, F. Ferrand and C. Chainais, *Procédure Civile* (Dalloz, 2012, 3rd ed.); G. Couchez and X. Lagarde, *Procédure Civile* (Sirey, 2014, 13th ed.); J. Normand, "Principes Directeurs du Procès"

According to the principle of party presentation (*principe dispositif*), the subject matter of the dispute is defined by the submissions of the parties.[454] The principle is complemented by the rule that the court cannot adjudicate *infra petita* or *ultra petita*.[455] The principle of party disposition also applies to the factual allegations of the parties and the means of evidence that support their legal submissions.[456] The court may base its judgment only upon the facts that have been adduced by the parties, even if those facts have not been specifically relied upon.[457] The parties not only bring forward the facts but also propose their legal arguments.[458] The court has active powers in the management of evidence with the power to order measures to investigate facts.[459] In all circumstances, the court shall observe and ensure the observance of the adversarial principle (*principe de la contradiction*), the quintessential expression

in L. Cadiet (ed.), *Dictionnaire de la justice* (PUF, 2004); J. Normand, *Le juge et le litige* (LGDJ, 1965); L. Cadiet, "Et les Principes Directeurs des Autres Procès? Jalons pour une Théorie des Principes Directeurs du Procès" in *Mélanges J. Normand* (Paris, Litec, 2003), 71; G. Cornu, "Les Principes Directeurs du Procès Civil par eux-mêmes (Fragment d'un état des questions)" in *Etudes offertes à P. Bellet.* (Paris, Litec, 1991), 83–100.

454 Article 4 CPC: "L'objet du litige est déterminé par les prétentions respectives des parties. Ces prétentions sont fixées par l'acte introductif d'instance et par les conclusions en défense. Toutefois l'objet du litige peut être modifié par des demandes incidentes lorsque celles-ci se rattachent aux prétentions originaires par un lien suffisant."Translation: "The subject matter of the disputes is determined by the respective claims of the parties. The originating process and the defense submissions define such claims. However, the subject matter of the dispute may be modified by the interlocutory claims where they relate to the initial claims by a sufficient link."

455 Article 5 CPC: "Le juge doit se prononcer sur tout ce qui est demandé et seulement sur ce qui est demandé." Translation: "The judge must rule upon all what is claimed and only upon what is claimed."

456 Article 6 CPC: "A l'appui de leurs prétentions, les parties ont la charge d'alléguer les faits propres à les fonder." Translation: "In support of their claims, the parties put forward the relevant facts supporting their claims." Article 9 CPC: "Il incombe à chaque partie de prouver conformément à la loi les faits nécessaires au succès de sa prétention." Translation: "Each party must prove, according to the law, the facts necessary for the success of his claim."

457 Article 7 CPC: "Le juge ne peut fonder sa décision sur des faits qui ne sont pas dans le débat. Parmi les éléments du débat, le juge peut prendre en considération même les faits que les parties n'auraient pas spécialement invoqués au soutien de leurs prétentions." Translation: "The judge may not base his decision on facts not in the debate. Among the facts mentioned in the debate, the judge may even take into consideration such facts that the parties have not expressly relied upon to support their claims."

458 A formal expression of this is provided under Article 56 CPC, according to which the claim form (*assignation*) must contain the object of the action with a statement of the arguments. Before the *Tribunal de Grand Instance* and in the *Cour d'Appel*, the pleadings of the parties (*conclusions*) need to contain the factual and legal grounds supporting their claims (Articles 753 CPC and 954 CPC respectively).

459 Article 10 CPP: "Le juge a le pouvoir d'ordonner d'office toutes les mesures d'instruction légalement admissibles." Translation: "The judge has the authority to order *sua sponte* any legally appropriate investigation measures."

of the right to fair trial.[460] This particularly applies when the court intends to base its decision on legal arguments which it has raised of its own motion.

The issue of the application by the courts of legal pleas of their own motion is inextricably linked to the facts which determine the subject matter of the dispute. What are the facts of the dispute? They are certainly those which have been *specifically relied upon* by the parties in support of their submissions.[461] They are also those which were urged by the court and which have in this way been *integrated* into the dispute.[462] This can result from the power of the court to invite the parties to provide factual explanations that it deems necessary for the resolution of the dispute (Article 8 CPC) and from its power to order investigative measures (Article 10 CPC).[463] But the courts also have the power to take into consideration the facts which are in the debate but that have not been expressly relied upon by the parties in support of their claims (Article 7 CPC). A well-known metaphor is the court's "basket, (*panier du juge*) of facts,

460 Article 16 CPC: "Le juge doit, en toutes circonstances, faire observer et observer lui-même le principe de la contradiction. Il ne peut retenir, dans sa décision, les moyens, les explications et les documents invoqués ou produits par les parties que si celles – ci ont été à même d'en débattre contradictoirement. Il ne peut fonder sa décision sur les moyens de droit qu'il a relevés d'office sans avoir au préalable invité les parties à présenter leurs observations." Translation: "In all circumstances, the judge must supervise the respect of, and he must himself respect, the adversarial principle. In his decision, may take into consideration grounds, explanations and documents relied upon or produced by the parties only if the parties had an opportunity to discuss them in an adversarial manner. He shall not base his decision on legal arguments that he has raised *sua sponte* without having first invited the parties to comment thereon".

461 J. Heron and T. Le Bars (n. 453), para. 274, explain that when a party specifically invokes a fact, it presents it in such way as to heed the attention from the other party and the court. In this way is articulated a proper plea in law, namely reasoning which seeks the acknowledgment of the well-founded of the claim ("consiste à le présenter de telle sorte qu'il est censé attirer l'attention de l'adversaire et du juge … l'articuler dans un 'moyen', c'est-à-dire un raisonnement tendant à faire reconnaitre le bien-fondé de la prétention de son auteur"). As to the facts that have not been specifically invoked, according to the same authors, they form part of the dispute and the court may resort to them in order to found its decision ("ont été mis dans le débat (fut-ce en vrac) et le juge peut les utiliser pour fonder sa décision"): J. Normand, (1974) *Révue Trimestrielle de Droit civil (RTD civ.)* 450-1, explains that the facts which form part of the debate include not only the facts upon which the parties have concentrated, by invoking a given rule of law or by suggesting a legal qualification to the facts, but also those facts which, exceeding the border of this more or less delimitated "circle", are directly or indirectly available from the file, those which are directly adduced or those ones which may only be deduced ("non seulement les faits sur lesquels les parties ont, en invoquant une règle ou proposé une qualification, concentré leur attention, mais également tous ceux qui, débordant de ce cercle plus ou moins étroit, ressortent directement ou indirectement du dossier, ceux qui se trouvent expressément relates, ceux qui n'apparaissent que par analyse ou par déduction").

462 L. Cadiet, J. Normand and S.A. Mekki. (n. 453), para. 222.

463 In this way the court exercises an "influence over the facts of the dispute"; M. Storm "Le juge et son panier" in *Mélanges J. Héron* (LGDJ, 2009), 474. See G. Bolard, "Les faits tirés du dossier" in *Justice et Droits Fondamentaux Mélanges offertes à J. Normand* (Litec, 2003), 43–50, 46.

from the "bottom" of which it can "pick up" the facts to base its decision.[464] Those are the facts, famously termed by Henri Motulsky as "faits adventices."[465] The classification of the facts as *faits adventices*, or facts that have not been specifically relied upon by the parties in support of a submission, plays an important role in the determination of the question whether the courts have discretion or an obligation to raise a point of law.

### *2.2.2. The Obligation and Faculty to Raise a Point of Law: Pure Points of Law and Points of Mixed Fact and Law*

The *ex officio* powers of the courts with regard to pleas of law (*relevé d'office d'un moyen de droit*) have attracted an exceptional theoretical elaboration in French procedural theory. One of the leading legal procedural theorists, Henri Motulsky, had long pleaded for the recognition of an obligation of the courts to raise *ex officio* pure points of law. The court is the "master of the law" ("maître du droit")[466] and should therefore have the power to proceed with independent legal inquiry – in the eloquent words of Henri Motulksi "faire le tour complet" of the legal question[467] – provided that the court remains within the factual ambit of the dispute and the *audi alteram partem* principle is observed.

As mentioned in the introduction above, French civil procedural law provides that the courts shall decide the dispute in accordance with the applicable law and give the proper legal qualification to the facts invoked by the parties without being restricted to their submissions (Article 12 CPC). There is no doubt that this provision covers the situation where no legal grounds are invoked by the parties. This scenario is unlikely when the parties are represented by counsel.[468]

---

464 J. Heron/T. le Bars (n. 453), para. 274, according to whom the court may seek the facts in the bottom of the "basket" placed before it ("Le juge peut aller chercher les faits au fond du panier que l'on a posé devant lui"), quoting C. Parodi, *L'ésprit général et les innovations du nouveau Code de procédure civile* (Paris, 1976); M. Storm (n. 463), 475.

465 H. Motulsky, "La cause de la demande dans la délimitation de l'office du juge" in *Ecrits, Etudes et notes de procédure civile* (Dalloz, 2010), 101–129, 110.

466 Ibid., 107, according to whom, the invoked legal rule and the legal qualification do not form part of the cause of action, and provided that the court does not interfere with the facts presented before it to support the claim, the court remains the "master of law". Da mihi factum, dabot tibi jus: this maxim seems (to the author) to find perfectly its place in the framework of the cause of action. ("La vérité nous semble être, par suite, que, ni la règle de droit invoquée, ni la qualification utilisée ne font partie de la cause de la demande. À la seule condition de ne point toucher à l'édifice de fait présenté comme soutien de la demande, le juge demeure donc maître du droit. Da mihi factum, dabo tibi jus : la maxime nous parait, pour notre part, avoir parfaitement sa place dans le domaine de la cause de la demande.")

467 Ibid.

468 Counsel has actually a legal and deontological duty to argue in law. According to Article 56(2) CPC: "In addition to the particulars prescribed for processes served

More problematic as to the possibility of application of the *ius novit curia* principle is the situation where the parties identify an erroneous legal basis which the court considers that it should be substituted by another one or where the court considers that an alternative legal foundation not explored by the parties should have been followed.

In its previous version, Article 12 CPC was more precise as to the application of the *ius novit curia* principle. According to its former wording, the court may raise of its own motion the pleas of "pure law" ("moyens de pur droit"), irrespective of the legal basis upon which the parties' submissions are founded ("[le juge] peut relever d'office les moyens de pur droit quel que soit le fondement juridique invoqué par les parties").

For the purposes of the powers of the trial courts, the pleas of pure law (*moyens de pur droit*) are understood as the pleas based on the facts *specifically relied upon* by the parties. This is a broader understanding compared to the scope of the matters of pure law admitted at the level of cassation.[469] At the level of cassation, the pleas of "pure law" are understood as these ones which are based on the facts which have been established at the lower instance level and which therefore do not require the examination of new facts. By contrast, the points based on facts which have not been specifically relied upon by the parties, but which form part of the file (*faits adventices*), "simplément allégués et non pas invoqués", are qualified as grounds of "mixed fact and law" ("moyens mélangés de fait et de droit"). The part of the wording of Article 12 CPC in relation to the "relevé d'office" of a pure point of law was annulled as a result of a judgment by the French Council of State (*Conseil d'Etat*) in 1979.[470] This judgment had annulled the then first sentence of Article 16 CPC, considering that it breached the adversarial principle.[471] The then third sentence of Article 12 CPC (on the *relevé d'office* of a pure point of law) was annulled as being indivisible from the annulled provision of Article 16 CPC.

The old provision of Article 12 CPC on the powers of the courts to raise of their own motion a pure point of law has maintained, since that time, a type

through bailiffs, the writ of summons, under penalty of nullity, must contain: the object of the action with a statgement of the arguments."

469 See O. Deshayes, "L'office du juge à la recherche de sens. A propos de l'arret d'assémblée plénière du 21 décembre 2007" (2008) *Recueil Dalloz* 1102, explaining that the source of the facts necessary for the application of the law is different between the level of the trial court (*juge de fond*) and the cassation level. The source of the facts for the trial court is the ambit of the dispute, while for the *Cour de Cassation* it is the lower instance judgment.

470 *Conseil d'Etat*, 12 October 1979, *Rassemblement des nouveaux avocats de France et autres*, JCP 1980, II, 19288; note A. Benabent, *Gazette de Palais* 1980, 6.

471 The then wording of Article 16 CPC was challenged on the ground that it gave the impression of exempting the court from observing the adversarial principle when raising a point of law of its own motion ("le juge doit, en toutes circonstances, faire observer le principe de la contradiction").

of unofficial judicial authority as a "customary acquis" ("autorité officieuse"),[472] "une évidence et un acquis coutumier" in the words of Gérard Cornu,[473] provided that the right of the parties to be heard on the point of law raised *ex officio* is observed. Moreover, the old formulation of Article 12 CPC, according to which the court *may* raise of its own motion pleas of "pure law" ("peut relever d'office les moyens de pur droit"), could be taken to mean that the judicial power to raise a pure point of law is a *faculty* and not an obligation. Gérard Cornu considered this approach to be balanced; a step that should not be crossed between a principle on the one hand and an *absolute* principle on the other hand ("un pas (à ne pas franchir) entre principe et principe absolu").[474] If that power would be translated into an obligation, this would bear the risk, according to the father of the CPC, of unmeritorious applications for cassation in circumstances in which there would be no real complaint against the judgment apart from criticizing the court for failing to explore all the possible legal paths. In his penetrating view, the criterion should be flexible, so that a court does not breach its duties if it does not raise an issue which it could not reasonably have noticed.[475]

Yet, the procedural legal literature has mainly followed the thesis of Henri Motulsky. According to the "Motulskian" philosophy, the courts have an obligation to raise pure points of law of their own motion as opposed to a mere faculty. Motulsky's remarkable writings explain how such an obligation is intrinsically linked to the jurisdiction of the court.[476] With respect to the points of law based on facts upon which the parties did not specifically rely, the points of mixed fact and law, it has further been maintained in legal literature that the courts are *empowered* to raise them, but they are not obliged to do so.[477] Such a power does not modify the cause of action.[478] The French *Cour de Cassation* has quashed judgments in which the court raised of its own motion points of mixed fact and law not because of a supposedly modification of the cause of action, but for the reason that such points had not been subject to contradictory

---

472 L. Cadiet and E. Jeuland (n. 453), para. 548.

473 G. Cornu (n. 453), 89.

474 Ibid., 90. "Le juge ne méconnait son devoir que s'il ne relève pas ce qu'il ne devait raisonnablement voir, critère souple".

475 Ibid.

476 H. Motulsky (n. 465).

477 J. Normand "Principes Directeurs du Procès," in L. Cadiet (ed.) (n. 453), 932; S. Guinchard et al. (n. 453), para. 743; L. Cadiet and E. Jeuland (n. 453), para. 548. Critically, see R. Martin, "Le relevé d'office par le juge d'un moyen de droit. Une question mal posée"*Recueil Dalloz* 2005, 1444, on the transposition of the concept of *moyen de pur droit* from the level of cassation level to the trial level. He rejects the power of the trial courts to "invent" new submissions by "manipulating the facts".

478 Henri Motulsky defines the cause of action as comprising the factual circumstances invoked in order to establish the subjective right which forms the submission put forward to the court ("les circonstances de fait invoquées en vue d'établir le droit subjectif par lequel se traduit juridiquement la prétention soumise au juge").

debate by the parties.[479] If the courts would be obliged to also raise of their own motion points of law based on facts which have not been specifically relied upon by the parties, this would lead to a "factual" activism which does not form part of the role of the courts.[480] It is the role of the parties to bring to the attention of the courts the facts which are capable of founding their cause of action and in this way to formulate a proper legal argument.[481] In practical terms, it would probably be an insurmountable challenge for the courts[482] if they were obliged

479 Cass. Civ. 1re, 13 Nov. 2008, finding that, by founding its decision upon such a plea which none of the parties had invoked, without inviting them beforehand to submit their observations in that regard, the court of appeal had disregarded the requirements of article 16 CPC. ("Qu'en fondant sa décision sur un tel moyen qu'aucune des parties n'avait invoqué, sans inviter au préalable celles-ci à présenter leurs observations à cet égard, la cour d'appel a méconnu les exigences du texte [de l'article 16 CPC].")

480 J. Heron and T. Le Bars, (n. 453), para. 283, explain the responsibilities that the parties bear for properly formulating properly their pleas in law as follows: "… when the parties allege the facts, it is their responsibility to allege them properly, that is to say to rely upon those one which they consider relevant. In sum, it is their responsibility to develop proper pleas in law, that is to say a reasoning which supports their claim. The facts articulated in pleas in law are the foundation of those pleas. They are 'specifically invoked'. The court should not be obliged to raise of its own motion the law on the basis of facts 'simply alleged', even if its decision would reveal the existence of such facts." ("En quelque sorte, quand les parties allèguent des faits, il leur appartient de bien les alléguer, c'est-à-dire de faire ressortir ceux qu'elles estiment être véritablement concluants. Bref, il leur appartient de développer de vrais moyens, c'est-à-dire des raisonnements tendant à la reconnaissance du bien-fondé de leur prétention. Les faits articulés dans ces moyens apparaissent comme le fondement de ceux-ci. Ils sont "spécialement invoqués". En présence de faits qui ne seraient que "simplement allégués", le juge ne doit donc pas être tenu de relever d'office la règle applicable, quand bien même il relèverait l'existence de ces faits dans sa décision.")

481 R. Martin (n. 477), 1444, explains that the court is obliged to raise of its own motion the appropriate legal provision for as long as the party enabled it to do so, that is to say if the party has alleged the appropriate facts in order to support a new qualifcation. By contrast, the court is not obliged, but has merely the discretion, to deduce from the file facts that have ("… relever d'office la règle de droit adéquate si la partie l'a mis en état de le faire, c' est à dire si elle a allégué les faits propres à soutenir une nouvelle qualification … Le juge, par contre, n'a pas l'obligation d'extraire du dossier des faits adventices pour les lire à travers une grille juridique nouvelle. Il n'en a que la possibilité.")

482 A "charge colossale", as pointed out by S. Menetrey and V. Bolard, "Le plein office du juge et le rôle des parties", *Juris News* Vol. 2 No 3-4/2013, 21-28, 25, because without this jurisprudential limitation, the obligation to requalify would shift upon the court the colossal duty to seek for all possible pleas in law and for any legal basis potentially applicable to a considerable amount of not well delimitated facts. The authors point out that the court shall only draw the legal consequences of those facts that lie at the heart of the debate, which it is possible to circumscribe and which need attract its attention. By contrast, as the authors underline, the court does not have the necessary means to appreciate the heteroclite mass of facts that have not been invoked ("A l'inverse, sans cette limite jurisprudentielle, l'obligation de reaqualifier ferait peser sur le juge le charge colossale de rechercher tous les moyens et les fondements juridiques applicables à une masse de faits considérable et mal délimitée. Le juge peut et doit tirer les conséquences juridiques des faits au coeur du débat, que l'on peut circonscrire et qui, par hypothèse, doivent retenir son attention. Sauf à promouvoir le mythe d'un 'juge providence', il n'a nullement les moyens d'appréhender la masse hétéroclite des faits adventices ").

to examine unpleaded facts which do not form part of the core of the dispute (presented *en vrac*)[483] against all possible legal avenues.

### 2.2.3. *National Case Law on the Powers of the Courts to Raise a Point of Law of Their Own Motion: Perspectives from the French, Belgian and Luxembourgian Case Law*

An important authority in French case law on the issue of the application of points of law by the courts of their own motion, is the judgment of the *Cour de Cassation* of 2007.[484] The reasoning does not go along the lines of the distinction, discussed above, between pleas of "pure law" ("moyens de pur droit") and pleas of "mixed fact and law" ("moyens mélangés de fait et de droit"). It establishes the obligation for the courts to act of their own motion only as far as the legal qualification of the material facts is concerned, without however covering the substitution of legal grounds by the courts of their own motion. The relevant ground of cassation in the specific case concerned an alleged breach by the Court of Appeal of the requirements of the fundamental principle under Article 12 CPC. The applicant, a purchaser of a default second-hand car, claimed the cost of repair, the reduction of the purchase price and compensation on the basis of the existence of a latent defect (*vice cache*). The price reduction claim was rejected because, according to the Court of Appeal, the existence of the latent defect had not been proved. However, the applicant claimed that the court should have examined *ex officio* an alternative foundation for his claim, namely that of the obligation of the seller to guarantee the good functioning condition of the vehicle in conformity with the contract.[485]

In its judgment, the *Cour de Cassation* ruled that the *ius novit curia* principle does not, in principle, imply an obligation of the courts to change the legal foundation of the submissions of the parties.[486]

The stance of the *Cour de Cassation* has been critically received in the French doctrine for breaking the logical path from the appropriate legal classification of the material facts to the attribution of the appropriate legal consequences and for creating an "artificial" distinction between the requalification of the facts and the change of the legal foundation of the claim.[487] The wider or

---

483 J. Heron and T. Le Bars (n. 453).

484 Cass. ass. plén., 21 déc. 2007, *Bull. civ.* 2007, ass. plén., no 10.

485 According to Article 1603 of the Civil Code.

486 " Parmi les principes directeurs du procès, l'article 12 du nouveau code de procédure civile oblige le juge à donner ou restituer leur exacte qualification aux faits et actes litigieux invoqués par les parties au soutien de leurs prétentions, il ne lui fait pas obligation, sauf règles particuliers, de changer la dénomination ou le fondement juridique de leurs demandes."

487 J. Heron and T. Le Bars (n. 453), para. 284; L. Cadiet et al. (n. 453), para. 226; Couchez and Lagarde (n. 453) para. 237-1; S. Guinchard, "L'autorité de la chose qui n'a pas été jugée à l'épreuve des nouveaux principes directeurs du procès civil et de la simple faculté pour le

narrower understanding of the *ex officio* powers is intrinsically linked to the scope of *res judicata*. The year before the plenary judgment on the *office du juge*, the judgment of the *Cour de Cassation* in *Césario*[488] established the rule of concentration of legal submissions. This means that all alternative legal foundations which have not been invoked for the same factual setting are covered by the principle of *res judicata*.[489]

The tenet of the French *Cour de Cassation* can be tested against the position of the Belgian *Cour de Cassation* and also of the Luxembourgian *Cour de Cassation*.

The judgment of the Belgian *Cour de Cassation* of 2005[490] is among the most important judgments in Belgium on the question of the *ex officio* powers of the courts. It accedes to the thesis of the factual qualification of the cause of action, in the sense that only the facts pleaded by the parties form part of the cause of action and not the rules of law applicable in the dispute.[491] The courts are obliged to take a point of law on their own motion for as long as the principle *audi alteram partem* has been observed. In that case, the appeal court had rejected the counterclaim of the appellants for damages for the reason that the ground invoked in support of their claim – quasi-tortious liability – had not been proved, while the contractual liability of the respondents could not be engaged as this legal basis had not been invoked by the applicants.

juge de changer le fondement juridique des demandes" in *De code en Code, Mélanges en l'honneur du Doyen Georges Wiederkehr* (Dalloz, 2009), 379–395, 391; H. Croze, "Le juge doit-il dire le droit?" in *Mélanges en l'Honneur de Serge Guinchard, Justices et droit du procès, Du légalisme procedural à l'humanisme processuel* (Dalloz, 2010), 225–232, 230; V. Bolard, "La Cour de Cassation consacre l'obligation de requalifier. A propos de l'arrêt de la Cour de Cassation du 10 mars 2011" (2012) 19 *Journal des Tribunaux Luxembourg* 01/2012, 8.

488 Cass. ass. plén., 7 juill. 2006, *Césareo*, *Bull. civ.* 2006, citations to commentaries L. Cadiet and E. Jeuland, *Droit Judiciaire Privé* (n.453), para. 740, fn. 181. According to the ruling, the claimant has to put forward from the beginning of the litigation the entire arsenal of legal submissions ("de presenter dès l'instance relative à la première demande l'ensemble des moyens qu'il estime de nature à fonder celle-ci"). The situation is different only if there are new elements which arise after the dispute (Cass. 3e civ., 25 avr. 2007, *Bull. civ.* 2007, citations to commentaries L. Cadiet and E. Jeuland (n. 453), para. 740, fn. 182). Similarly the defendant has to put forward all his legal means of defense (Cass. com, 20 févr. 2007, *Bull. civ.* 2007). See, rather critical of this case law, E. Jeuland, "Remarks on the power of the French judge in a European perspective" in *Festschrift für Rolf Stürner zum 70. Geburstag* (Mohr Siebeck, 2013), 1546–1553, at 1549.

489 S. Guinchard, "L'autorité de la chose qui n'a pas été jugée à l'épreuve des nouveaux principes directeurs du procès civil et de la simple faculté pour le juge de *changer le fondement juridique des demandes*", in *Mélanges en l'honneur de Georges Wiederkhr, De code en code*, 393. L. Cadiet et al. (n. 453), para. 271 consider this judgment as the expression of "procedural politics" ("politique processuelle") aiming at the dilatory practices and negligence of the parties ("une ferme volonté de lutter contre les manœuvres dilatoires et la négligence des parties"), provided that the parties will still have the opportunity to bring a fresh action on a new foundation if no negligence can be attributed to them.

490 Cass., 14 avr. 2005, JT 2005, 659 *et seq*.

491 J. van Compernolle, "La cause de la demande: une clarification décisive" (2005) *Journal des Tribunaux* 661–663, with reference to the influential doctoral thesis of J.-F. van Drooghenbroeck, *Cassation et juridiction* – Jura dicit curia, (Brussels – Paris, 2004).

The *Cour de Cassation* rejected this interpretation and decided that a proper reading of Article 774 of the *Code Judiciaire Belge* implies that the court is obliged to decide the case in accordance with the applicable law and that it has the obligation, in observance of the rights of the defense, to raise of its own motion those pleas in law that the application follows from the facts specifically invoked by the parties in support of their submissions.[492]

Jacques van Compernolle explains that the courts should be empowered to apply the law without making a distinction in that regard between the requalification of facts, the substitution of the legal basis and the application of the rule of law that has not been invoked by the parties.[493] Moreover, Belgium case law has recognized the powers of the courts to annul of their own motion an agreement which is contrary to rules of competition law, stemming either from national law of Union law.[494]

In the same vein as the Belgian case law, the Luxembourg judgment of the *Cour de Cassation* of 10 March 2011 is being considered as a procedural judgment of great importance.[495] The provision of Article 61 of the Luxembourg Civil Procedural Code (*Nouveau Code de Procédure Civile* (NCPC)) interpreted in this judgment is directly inspired from Article 12 of the French CPC.[496] However, the Luxembourgian *Cour de Cassation* did not follow the path of the French *Cour de Cassation* as to the interpretation of the said provision. The case concerned a public procurement dispute where the bidder, considering his offer

492 According to the original text of the decision: "Le juge est tenu de trancher le litige conformément à la règle de droit qui lui est applicable; qu'il a l'obligation, en respectant les droits de la défense, de relever d'office les moyens de droit dont l'application est commandée par les faits spécialement invoqués par les parties au soutien de leurs prétention."

493 J. van Compernolle, "Le rôle actif du juge dans l'application de la règle de droit: la consécration par la jurisprudence belge de la conception factuelle de la cause de la demande" in *Mélanges Dédiés à la Mémoire du Doyen Jacques Héron* (LGDJ, 2009), 477–483, 482, arguing that it has to be possible for the court to apply every legal rule relevant for the case as it is the mission of the court to give to the dispute the solution that the law calls for ("Toute norme juridique dès lors qu'elle s'applique au règlement du litige, doit pouvoir être appliquée, fut-ce d'office, par le juge qui a pour mission de donner à ce litige la solution que le droit commande").

494 Hof van Berop Brussel (Court of Appeal Brussels), 10 October 2008, TBH 2009, 5, Bima NV v Sodrepe NV. The judgment with its most important excerpts is reported in English by B. Fekete and A.M. Mancaleoni, "Application of Primary and Secondary EU Law on the National Courts' Own Motion" in A. Hartkamp, C. Sieburgh and W. Devroe (eds.), *Cases, Materials and Text on European Law and Private Law* (Oxford, Hart Publishing, 2017), 421–461, 446.

495 C. Cass., 10 mars 2011, No 18/11, analyzed in the study of V. Bolard, "La Cour de Cassation consacre l'obligation de requalifier. A propos de l'arrêt de la Cour de Cassation du 10 mars 2011" (2012) 19 *Journal des Tribunaux Luxembourg* 01/2012, 8.

496 According to Art. 61 NCPC, the court decides the case in accordance with the applicable rules of law and it gives the exact qualification to the facts and relevant acts without being restrained to the qualification proposed by the parties ("Le juge tranche le litige conformément aux règles de droit qui lui sont applicables. Il doit donner ou restituer leur exacte qualification aux faits et actes litigieux sans s'arreter à la dénomination que les parties en auraient proposée").

to be unfairly rejected, introduced a claim for damages. The plaintiff did not specify in the statements of case (*assignation*) the legal basis of his claim. The appeal court (*Cour d'Appel*) inferred that the claim was brought on the basis of contractual liability. Considering that this was actually a case of tortious liability, but that such legal submission had not made, it rejected the claim for damages. This judgment was quashed at the cassation level on the ground that the appeal court should have enquired of its own motion whether tortious liability could have been engaged on the basis of the facts brought forward by the applicant, provided that the rights of the defense would be respected.[497]

### *2.2.4. Ordre Public, Mandatory Law and Role of the Courts*

As French law currently stands, the courts have a *faculty* to raise pure legal grounds, unless there is an explicit provision to the effect of a duty[498] and generally in the presence of a rule of public policy. It should be noted that in the view of Henri Motulsky and contemporary authors, the courts should have a broad obligation to raise points of law, irrespective of whether they qualify as public policy or not.[499]

---

497 The relevant finding of the judgment reads as follows in the original: "Qu'en statuant ainsi, sans rechercher, en respectant les droits de la défense, si sur la base des faits spécialement invoqués par la société X à l'appui de ses prétentions, la responsabilité délictuelle de l'association [...] n'était pas engagée, les juges d'appel ont violé l'article 61 du Nouveau Code de procédure civile." Two more cases followed in that vein in 2013. The first one repeated the obligation of the courts to raise *ex officio* pure points of law (C. Cass., 24 October 2013, no 63/13, no 3231). In this case the plaintiff claimed a certain sum of rent as damages from the conclusion of an invalid contract (concluded by an incapable without the assistance of the curator) on the basis of contractual liability and at subsidiary level on the basis of non-contractual liability. The nullity of the contract had been declared, whereas the claim for damages had been rejected as the court considered that there was no fault. The *Cour de Cassation* quashed the judgment, deciding that the appeal court should have enquired, with due respect to the rights of the defense, whether the claim could be found on the basis of a restitution claim based on the general principle of the retroactive effects of the nullity of the annuled contract ("Les juges de la Cour d'appel auraient du rechercher, en respectant les droits de la défense, si la demande de [...] n'était pas fondée au titre d'une demande en restitution sur base du principe général du droit de 'rétroactivité de la nullité' de la convention annulée.") The second case highlighted that the observance of the rights of defense is a necessary corollary to the obligation of the court to raise of its own motion points of law (Luxembourg Cour de Cassation 24 october 2013, no 62/13). In this case the *Cour de Cassation* quashed the judgment of the *Cour d'Appel* because it gave the parties the possibility to take a position on a point of law it had raised of its own motion only at the stage of the oral hearing and not at the stage of the written submissions. For both cases, see the analysis of S. Menetrey and V. Bolard (n. 482).

498 This is, for instance, the case where a fixed-term employment contract has been concluded in violation of the conditions set out by the law, for which case the contract is considered to be concluded for an indeterminate duration (Article L-1245-1 and L-1245-2 *Code du Travail*).

499 "Le juge est tenu d'appliquer la loi parce qu'elle est la loi, et non parce qu'elle est d'ordre public" : H. Motulsky, (n. 465), no 25; L. Cadiet et al. (n. 453) para. 225 at 776; L. Cadiet and E. Jeuland (n. 453), para. 548.

### 2.2.4.1. Public Policy and *Ex Officio* Obligation

The obvious difficulty with the establishment of an obligation to raise a plea in law only in the presence of a rule of public policy lies with the identification of the grounds deemed to fall within the scope of public policy. The meaning of *ordre public* in French law is maybe one of the most conceptually challenging issues in civil legal theory.[500] Article 6 of the French Civil Code (*Code Civil*) provides that it is not possible to derogate from the laws of public policy and public morals by means of private contractual arrangements.[501] The laws which cannot be derogated from by the parties are mandatory laws.[502] While mandatory laws and the meaning of the respective concept are easier to identify than public policy, it is complex to trace the normative purview of the concept of mandatory law with respect to public policy. There is a line of thought according to which only the mandatory rules of public interest are expressions of public policy and another one according to which the two concepts actually have the same content.[503] For the purposes of the analysis of the powers of the courts, of great importance is the theory which relies upon the nature of the interest which the legislator intends to pursue with a given provision.

More specifically, the civil law theory distinguishes between the classic concept of public policy and modern public policy. The classic concept has a rather negative meaning, placing outer limits to the contractual autonomy of the parties, in order to preserve the fundamental principles in society.[504] The second concept of modern public policy comprises elements of the economic and social organization of society and imposes more positive obligations than prohibitions. The degree or intensity of the public interest element within a given provision forms a scale on the basis of which a distinction is drawn between two categories: on the one hand, the public policy rules of general interest designed to order society (*ordre public de direction*); and, on the other hand, the public policy rules of private interest designed to protect certain category of individuals who are deemed to be in weak position (*ordre public de protection*

---

500 See the following classic studies on the concept: P. Malaurie, *Les contrats contraires à l'ordre public* (Thèse Paris, Ed. Madot-Braine, 1953); J. Ghestin, "L'ordre public, notion à contenu variable, en droit privé français" in C. Pelerman and R. Vander Elst (eds.), *Les notions à contenu variable en droit* (Bruylant, 1984); P. Catala, "A propos de l'ordre public" in *Mélanges P. Drai, Le juge entre deux millénaires* (Dalloz, 2000).

501 According to the original text of Article 6 CC: "On ne peut déroger, par des conventions particulières, aux lois qui intéressent l'ordre public et les bonnes mœurs."

502 See C. Pérès-Dourdou, *La règle supplétive* (LGDJ, 2004).

503 See M. Mekki, *L'intérêt général et le contrat. Contribution à une étude de la hiérarchie des intérêts en droit privé, thése* (LGDJ, 2004), para. 353 with references to the literature on the relevant discussion.

504 P. Malaurie, L. Aynes and P. Stoffel-Munck, *Les Obligations* (LGDJ, 2013, 6th ed.), paras. 648 *et seq.*

or *ordre public de protection sociale*).[505] However, even if the private interest is dominant in the provisions of the public policy of protection, this does not mean that considerations of public interest are excluded.

Despite the vague lines upon which lies the distinction between *ordre public de direction* and *ordre public de protection*, this distinction acquired great practical importance for the role of the courts once considered in association with the regime of contractual nullities.[506] The theory of contractual nullities relies upon the distinction between public interest and private interest.[507] The violation of a rule of public policy of general interest is sanctioned by absolute nullity, which the courts are obliged to raise of their own motion, even in the absence of a respective submission by the parties.[508] This obligation is subject to the observance of a contradictory debate and to the availability of the facts required for the establishment of nullity.[509] The parties may not renounce absolute nullity. By contrast, the violation of a rule of public policy of protection is sanctioned by relative nullity which can be invoked only by the affected party.[510] The affected party may renounce protection (*confirmation du contrat*).[511]

Originally, the *Cour de Cassation* regarded the power of the courts to raise the relative nullity as a matter of pure law.[512] A change in case law was marked in 2000 when the civil chamber of the *Cour de Cassation* (in the so-called *Grine* case) quashed the decision of the lower court for having raised the relative nullity arising out of a breach of the mandatory consumer credit rules.[513] It took a long

---

505 J. Carbonnier, *Droit Civil*, vol. IV, *Les Obligations* (P.U.F., Collection Thémis privé, 2000, 22nd ed.). See also M. Mekki (n. 503), para. 345 *et seq.* for a wealth of references to the literature.

506 Since the leading work of R. Japiot, *Des nullités en matière d'actes juridiques. Essai d'une théorie nouvelle*, th. Dijon (Thèse Dijon, 1909) (reprinted by the publisher La Mémoire du Droit, 2017).

507 See the extensive discussion in N. Sauphanor-Brouillaud et al., *Les contrats de Consommation Règles Communes* (LGDJ, 2013), para. 970; M. Mekki (n. 503), para. 322.

508 It is admitted that *a fortiori* the courts can substitute a ground of absolute nullity that has been put forward by another ground: Cass. Ch. mixte, 10 July 1981, *Dalloz* 1981, p. 637.

509 See J. Ghestin, "L'annulation d'office d'un contrat" in *Mélanges offerts à Pierre Drai, Le juge entre deux millénaires* (Dalloz, 2000), 593–607, 594 *et seq.*

510 On the theory of nullities see the classic work of J. Ghestin, G. loiseau and Y.M. Serinet, *La Formation du Contrat, L'objet et la cause, Les nullités, Traité de Droit Civil, Vol. II* (LGDJ, 4th ed., 2013); P. Malaurie et al. (n. 504) para. 701; A. Bénabent, *Droit des Obligations* (LGDJ, 5th ed., 2016), paras. 203 *et seq.*

511 Following the reform of contract law in France of 10 February 2016, the distinction of the regime of nullities on the basis of the public/private interest divide is encapsulated under Articles 1179, 1180 and 1181 of the *Code Civil*.

512 Cass. civ. 1re, 22 May 1985, *Bull. civ. I*, no 159, p. 145; Cass. civ. 3e, 28 January 1987, *Bull. civ.*, III, no 13, p. 8.

513 Cass. civ. 1re, 15 February 2000, *Bull. civ.* I, no 49, which found that the violation of the rules of the consumer code applicable in the case could only be examined upon the objection of the person whom those provisions are intended to protect ("la méconnaissance des textes susvisés (C. consom., art. L. 311-2, L-311-8 et L. 311-10), même d'ordre public, ne peut être opposée qu'à la demande de la personne que ces dispositions ont pour objet de protéger").

time to reverse the *Grine* case law, which has attracted heavy criticism from the lower courts and the literature.[514]

The French doctrine has long pleaded against an approach that would draw important practical consequences out of the distinction between *ordre public de direction* and *ordre public de protection.* Jacques Ghestin pointed out that the relative nullities should be subject to a proper regime, but not at the level of the remit of the powers of the courts.[515] The protective purpose of the legislator in establishing relative nullity would require that the nullity should not "backfire" against the person to be protected, notably by means of excluding the other party from invoking the nullity. By contrast, the role of the courts is different. There should be no confusion, Jacques Ghestin explains, between the power of the court to raise a relative nullity of its own motion and the determination of the party to the contract which is entitled to invoke nullity.[516] The protective purpose of the relative nullity is also demonstrated by the right of the party to *renounce* the protection that the law confers as the result of an informed decision.[517]

It is important to note that in Belgium, the same concerns had been voiced against refusing the powers of the courts to raise mandatory laws of their own motion in the case of a relative nullity.[518] In an eminent study on the concept of mandatory law and its effect upon the role of the courts, the Emeritus counselor of the Belgian *Cour de Cassation*, A. Meeùs, explains that mandatory law requires judicial intervention, subject to the caveat that there is no objection by

514 See G. Poissonier, "Mode d'emploi du relevé d'office en droit de la consommation" *Contrats Concurrence Consommation* no 5, Mai 2009, étude 5, fn. 5; G. Biardeaud and P. Flores, *Le Contentieux du droit de la consommation Vol. I, Le crédit aux consommateurs* (École Nationale de la Magistrature, 2005), 88 *et seq.*

515 J. Ghestin et al. (n. 510), para. 2332; J. Ghestin (n. 509), 603.

516 J. Ghestin (n. 509), 603. This is demonstrated by the difference in the term used between the court raising the nullity and the party putting forward the nullity ("*relever*" and "*demander*"respectively. As the author rightly points out, the court never becomes a party to the contract, or even a third party who would have the right to object to the contract; the court decides a case in relation to a contract, which is absolutely not the same thing. Nonetheless, the same author explains, the court's intervention in order to ensure the protection of the party that the law intends to protect cannot run against this party ("Le juge n'est pas une partie au contrat, ni même à proprement parler un tiers, qui invoquerait un droit de critique. Il tranche un litige relatif au contrat, ce qui n'est pas du tout la même chose. Ensuite, l'intervention d'office du juge afin d'assurer la protection de la partie que la loi entendait protéger ne peut normalement se retourner contre cette dernière.")

517 According to Article 1181 of the Civil Code, the relative nullity can be renounced by the party for whom it has been established ("peut être couverte par la confirmation"). On the issue, see P. Malaurie et al. (n. 504), para. 704; M. Fabre-Magnan, *Droit des obligations, 1- Contrat et engagement unilatéral* (PUF, 3rd ed., 2013), 479, with further references to the literature.

518 See particularly A. Meeùs, "Note: La notion de loi impérative et son incidence sur la procédure en cassation et sur l'office du juge" (1988) 4 *Revue Critique de Jurisprudence Belge* 495–527. His theory is followed by one of the leading Belgian authors of civil law: P. Wéry, *Droit des Obligations, Vol. I, Théorie générale du contrat* (Larcier, 2010), paras. 326 *et seq.*

the protected party to that effect.[519] A renunciation of the right to invoke nullity should not be deduced from the absentia of the protected party or from his failure to invoke mandatory law, attributed to his inadvertence or ignorance.[520] The doctrine of the active consumer court relies upon the same premise (of ignorance of the law) when it comes to the procedural consequences of the omission of the consumer to plead the mandatory rules for his protection.

The introduction of an explicit procedural provision in the French consumer code (currently Article R-632-1 *Code de la Consommation*) and the influence of the case law of the Court on the doctrine of the active consumer court brought about an important change in the perception of the role of the courts in France as to relative nullities, in particular those which result from the breach of the provisions of consumer law. The rules of consumer protection are explicitly qualified by the legislator as *ordre public*. Indeed, the rules of consumer protection serve a double purpose, protecting the consumer while regulating the market.[521] Elise Poillot speaks of an "ordre public univoque" which does not sit comfortably with the bipolar *ordre public de direction/ordre public de protection*.[522] Pursuant to the *Cornu* Report of the French Senate on the reform of the *Code de la Consommation*, only a positive action makes it possible to address the imbalance in the framework of a procedure between parties of unequal economic strength. From this perspective, a passive court in consumer proceedings would even amount to a negation of the right to a fair trial according to Article 6 ECHR.[523] The doctrine of the active consumer court in France will be taken up in more detail in Chapter 6.

#### 2.2.4.2. Mandatory Union Law and Role of the Courts

It has been argued in French literature that the role of the French courts has been modified as a result of the *Van Schijndel* judgment because the courts would have an obligation to raise matters of pure law and also matters of mixed fact and law.[524] However, the obligation established in *Van Schijndel* does not concern any kind of plea of Union law but only pleas of mandatory rules of Union law. Moreover the courts are not obliged to go outside the ambit of the dispute. Under these conditions, the courts would not be obliged to raise of their own

---

519 A. Meeùs (n. 518) 527.

520 Ibid., 525.

521 See G. Poissonier, "Office du juge en droit de la consommation : une clarification bienvenue" (2008) *Recueil Dalloz* 1285, with further references.

522 E. Poillot (n. 507).

523 French Senate in *Rapport no 111 au nom de la commission des Affaires économiques sur le projet de loi, pour le développement de la concurrence au service des consommateurs par M. Gérard Cornu*, Sénat de la session ordinaire de 2007–2008, 99-103.

524 J. Delicostopoulos and E. M. Szyszczak, "Intrusions into national procedural autonomy: the French paradigm" (1997) 22(2) *E.L. Rev.* 141–149.

motion a point, for instance, of competition law which has not been pleaded by the parties and for which no facts have been adduced. Such examination would normally require complex factual assessments and it will therefore be a matter of mixed fact law which the courts are not obliged to raise, if it does not fall outside the ambit of the dispute overall.[525]

Therefore, it would not seem correct to infer from *Van Schijndel* that the decisions of the lower courts would be quashed for not having applied any possible rule of Union law to facts that have not been brought forward by the parties, or to which the parties have not drawn their attention through their submissions. A case before the *Cour de Cassation* of 1993 demonstrates that the facts which support a point of Union law have to be properly pleaded before the trial courts, so that this point can be brought forward at the level of cassation. In this case, a new plea on the basis of Union law was brought forward at the level of cassation in order to challenge the tax imposition at issue. The new plea was rejected, as the relevant facts had not been advanced (and consequently they had not been established) at the level of the trial court.[526] In another judgment of the *Cour de Cassation* of 1994,[527] the applicants challenged the judgment of the lower court for not having examined whether the provisions of the French legislation allowing the exclusive distribution of optical products from opticians infringed the Treaty provisions on competition law. The *Cour de Cassation* rejected the ground which was advanced in the absence of specific complaints before the trial courts demonstrating the existence of discriminatory practices or abuse of dominant position.

French law seems to similarly well accommodate the *Eco-Swiss*[528] obligation of the courts to admit a point of mandatory Union law in the annulment proceedings of an arbitration award, even if this point has not been pleaded before the arbitration tribunal. The breach of international public policy, including Union law, is a ground for the annulment of an arbitration award.[529] However, the breach needs to be manifest. A judgment of the Paris Court

---

525 See G. Canivet and J.G. Huglo, "L'obligation pour le juge judiciaire national d'appliquer d'office le droit communautaire au regard des arrêts *Jeroen van Schijndel* et *Peterbroeck*"(1996) *Europe* April 1–4, 3.

526 Cass., 23 November 1993, *Bull. civ.* no 424, p. 308, finding that the alleged incompatibility with Union law of the disputed tax, had not been invoked by the company before the trial court; that the complaint implies a prior assessment of the tax basis, its rate and the modalities of its recovery, namely factual circumstances which were not put before the Court of Appeal and which are therefore inadmissible at the level of cassation. ("L'incompatibilité de la taxe litigieuse avec les dispositions du droit communautaire n'a pas été invoquée par la société devant les juges du fond; que ce grief qui implique l'examen de l'assiette, du taux et des modalités de recouvrement de l'impôt, donc de circonstances de fait que la cour d'appel n'a pas connues, est irrecevable devant la Cour de Cassation.")

527 Cass., 1re civ., 4 January 1994 *Bull civ.* 1994 IV No 2, p.1.

528 Case C-126/97 *Eco Swiss*, EU:C:1999:269.

529 Article 1520-5 CPC.

of Appeal illustrates the readiness of French courts to consider points of Union law in such proceedings, yet taking into account the principles of legal certainty and the exceptional character of review of the substance of an arbitration award.[530] In that case, the applicants sought the annulment of an arbitration award on the ground that its enforcement would lead to the performance of an illegal contract in breach of the Treaty rules on competition law. The court accepted, on the one hand, that the question of Union law that had not been raised before the arbitral tribunal had not been covered by *res judicata* and that in principle it should be open for examination, since this is the first jurisdiction that can make a reference for preliminary ruling. On the other hand, it found that the breach would have to be manifest. This condition intends in particular to avoid tactics by the defense where one of the parties would deliberately choose not to advance certain points before the arbitration tribunal and, if necessary, to bring them forward only at the stage of annulment proceedings.

From this brief overview of the French perception of the role of the courts and the parties, it appears that the adage *da mihi factum, dabo tibu jus* (give me the facts, I will give you the law) cannot properly be understood within a static vision of the civil process, but it is important to consider the *dialectics* of civil procedure. The fundamental principles of the civil procedure form "a charter of the division of the roles between the courts and the parties,"[531] express a "monument of equilibrium"[532] and establish a "principle of cooperation" between the parties and the courts.[533] More broadly, the civil process should be governed by a "principle of dialogue," eminently envisaged by Serge Guinchard as one of the future leading procedural principles.[534]

---

530 Cour d'Appel de Paris, 1re chambre, 18 November 2004, finding that the violation of the international public policy, pursuant to Article 1520-5 Civil Procedure Code, has to be flagrant, real and specific and that the court before which proceedings for annulment of an arbitration award are brought may certainly proceed to an appreciation in law and in fact of the elements of the arbitral award deferred to its control, but the court cannot rule on the substance of a complex case, on the issue of an eventual illegality of certain contractual provisions, which has never yet been pleaded or decided before the arbitration court. ("Considérant que la violation de l'ordre public international au sens de l'article 1520-5 du NCPC doit être flagrante, effective et concrète, que le juge de l'annulation peut certes, dans le cadre de ses pouvoirs de nature disciplinaire, porter une appréciation en droit et en fait sur les éléments qui sont dans la sentence déférée à son contrôle, mais pas statuer au fond sur un litige complexe qui n'a jamais encore été ni plaidé, ni jugé devant un arbitre concernant la simple éventualité de l'illicéité de certaines stipulations contractuelles.")

531 L. Cadiet (n. 453), para. 18.

532 Ibid.

533 H. Motulsky, "La réforme du Code de Procédure Civile par le décret du 13 Octobre 1965 et les principes directeurs du procés", in *Ecrits* (n. 465), para. 4; J. Normand "Principes Directeurs du Procès," in L. Cadiet (ed.) (n. 453), 1040–1041.

534 S. Guinchard, "Quels principes directeurs pour les procès de demain ?", in *Mélanges J. van Compernolle* (Brussels, Bruylant, 2004), 201.

## 2.3. THE GERMAN COURT PERSPECTIVE

### 2.3.1. *General Observations on the Relative Role of the Courts and the Parties*

As an introduction to the perspective of German civil proceedings on the respective role of the courts and the parties, Peter Murray and Rolf Stürner point out that:

> German civil proceedings involve a sophisticated balance and coordination of activity and responsibility between parties, their counsel and the court designed to promote fair and just outcomes of civil disputes efficiently and at reasonable cost.[535]

The two fundamental legal principles which govern the relative role of the parties and the courts in German civil proceedings are the principle of party presentation (*Dispositionsgrundsatz*) and the adversarial principle (*Verhandlungsgrundsatz* or *Beibringungsgrundsatz*).[536] Both principles are prime features of the fundamentals of the civil process (*Verfahrensgrundsätze*) and even if they express different aspects of the powers of the parties, they are tightly linked.[537] Under the first fundamental guiding principle, the *Dispositionsgrundsatz*, the parties have the control over the subject matter of the dispute (*Verfügungsfreiheit über den Streitgegenstand*) as defined by their claims (*Anträge*). It refers in particular to their power of disposition over the initiation, the subject matter, the course and the termination of the proceedings.[538] The second principle, the *Verhandlungsgrundsatz*, refers to the power of the parties to bring forward the factual elements (*tatsächlicher Prozessstoff*) and to produce the means of evidence (*Beweismittel*) that will

---

535 P. Murray and R. Sturner, *German Civil Justice* (Carolina Academic Press, 2004), 155.

536 Those principles are discussed in every commentary of the German Civil Procedure Code – *Kommentar Zivilprozessordnung-ZPO* (ZPO) and every monograph on the fundamentals of German civil justice. In these commentaries the paragraphs correspond to the German "Rn." See indicatively T. Rauscher, "Einleitung" in W. Kruger and T. Rauscher (eds.), *Münchener Kommentar zur ZPO (MünchKomm-ZPO)* (ZPO) (Munich, Beck, 4th ed., 2013), paras. 290–305; L. Rosenberg, L.H. Schwab and P. Gottwald (eds.), *Zivilprozessrecht* (Munich, Beck, 17th ed., 2010), paras. 77–79; D. Leipold, "Vorbermerkungen vor §128 ZPO" in F. Stein and M. Jonas (eds.), *Kommentar zur ZPO* (Tübingen, Mohr Siebeck, 22nd ed., 2005); H. Prütting and M. Gehrlein, "Einleitung" in H. Prütting and M. Gehrlein (eds.), *Kommentar zur ZPO* (Luchterhand Verlag, 5th ed., 2013); H.J. Musielak, "Einleitung" in H.J. Musielak (ed.), *ZPO*, paras. 35–44 (Munich, Beck, 11th ed., 2014).

537 D. Leipold in F. Stein and M. Jonas (eds.) (n. 536), para. 138.

538 The main provisions of the *Dispositionsgrundsatz* are §308 ZPO on the determination of the subject matter of the dispute by the parties' claims, §269 ZPO on withdrawal of the action and §§306–307 ZPO on renunciation (*Verzicht*) and acknowledgment (*Anerkenntnis*), respectively, of the claim. On further illustrations of the principles, see Prütting and Gehrlein (n. 536), paras. 26–28.

form the basis of the judgment (*iudex secundum allegata et probate iudicare debet*).[539] Both principles reflect the discursive and liberal character of the German civil procedure and are the procedural expression of private autonomy (*Parteifreiheit und Parteiverantwortung*) governing the private relationships of the parties.[540]

The legal characterization of the parties' claims lies with the court, provided that the relevant factual elements are available. By contrast, the courts do not have the power to raise legal grounds that lead to legal consequences different from those envisaged by the parties in view of their submissions[541] or that require an examination of facts which lie outside the ambit of the dispute.

An important feature of the German judicial proceedings lies with the "managerial" obligations (§139 ZPO – *Materielle Prozessleitung*)[542] that the courts bear, going beyond formal judicial management. Whenever that is

---

539 The *Verhandlungsgrundsatz* is mainly inferred from §282 ZPO on the timely advancement of all submissions and objections (*Angriffs- und Verteidigungsmittel, insbesondere Behauptungen, Bestreiten, Einwendungen, Einreden, Beweismittel und Beweiseinreden*) but also *a contrario* from provisions establishing the inquisitorial system (*Amtsermittlungsgrundsatz*) (for instance §616 I ZPO for family issues). H. Prütting and M. Gehrlein (n. 536), para. 28.

540 T. Rauscher (n. 536), paras. 290 and 307; L. Rosenberg, L.H. Schwab and P. Gottwald (n. 536), section 76, para 1.

541 On the concept of the submission, see the classic works: J. Goldschmidt, *Der Prozess als Rechtlage* (Berlin/Heidelberg, Springer-Verlag, 1925); G. Baumgärtel, *Wesen und Begriff der Prozesshandlung einer Partei im Zivilprozess* (Köln/Berlin/Bonn/München, Carl Heymanns, 2nd ed., 1972). In Greek literature the classic work of G. Mitsopoulos, *Διαδικαστικαί πράξεις, Μελέται Γενικής Θεωρίας Δικαίου και Αστικού Δικονομικού Δικαίου* (Athens, Komotini, 1983) (in Greek).

542 It is worth reproducing the provision of §139 ZPO (based on the English translation of the provision of the German ministry of Justice) upon which broad powers of the courts may find their foundation:

*Direction in substance of the course of the proceedings*

1) The court has to discuss with parties the facts and legal issues of the dispute, to the extent required and ask questions. It has to ensure that the parties present all the material facts in a timely and complete manner, by particularly complementing insufficient references, that they designate the means of proof and that they bring forward the relevant claims on the basis of the facts advanced.
2) The court may base its decision on a point [of law or fact], other than a subsidiary claim, which a party has apparently overlooked or had considered insignificant, provided that it has called the parties' attention to the point and has given to them the opportunity to comment on it. The same provision applies if the court's understanding of a point differs from the understanding of both parties.
3) The court has to draw attention to the parties upon its reservations with respect to points that have to be considered by the court on its own motion.
4) The advice according to this provision need to be communicated to the parties as soon as possible and documented in the records. Their communication can only be proved through the record. Against the content of the record only proof of forgery is admitted.
5) If a party is not in the position to respond immediately to a judicial request for clarification then the court upon motion of that party sets a time limit so that the clarification can be brought by means of written pleadings.

necessary, the courts have the power to make such suggestions and questions to the parties so as to ensure that the submissions of the parties are properly advanced and clarified (*Hinweis- und Aufklärungspflicht*). If one party seems to have overlooked a material point (*Gesichtspunkt*), the court is obliged to bring it to the attention of both parties and invite their argument. The parties should not therefore be taken by surprise (*Verbot von Überraschungsentscheidung*). The same applies if the court adopts a view on the case that is different from the view of one of the parties. However, it needs to be underlined that those powers are not considered to be in contradiction with the procedural principles guiding the role of the courts and the parties, nor do they transform the nature of the proceedings into inquisitorial. The objective of the court's duty to structure the proceedings is to achieve the aim of the civil procedure, namely the effective materialization of the rights of the parties.[543] It should be viewed as expressing an "intelligent dialogue between the court and counsel [that] leads to a better quality of the judicial product overall."[544]

The courts exercise their duty to give hints and feedback within the subject matter of the dispute in due observance of the principle of judicial impartiality. In that delicate operation they have "to steer a careful course between too little and too much judicial engagement."[545] The parties remain first of all free to follow or not the indications of the court, assuming of course the procedural risk that any omission attributable to them may entail.[546] The suggestions of the courts should not be understood as an invitation to the parties to bring forward entirely new submissions, claims or objections, but should be based on the pleadings already advanced by them.[547] Indications in the pleadings of the parties (*Anhaltspunkte*) must already exist for a point to be raised by the court.[548] On the basis of such concrete indications (*konkretem Anlass*), the court will suggest a more comprehensive articulation so that certain submissions can be clarified and completed. Otherwise, the decision can be quashed for lack of impartiality (*Besorgnis der Befangenheit*). The respect of the principle of judicial neutrality marks the borderline between, on the one hand, lawful guidance and, on the other hand, unlawful support for one of the parties.[549]

---

543 D. Leipold, "§139 ZPO," in Stein and Jonas (eds.) (n. 536), para. 1.

544 P. Murray and R. Sturner (n. 535), 170.

545 Ibid., 176.

546 T. Rauscher, "Einleitung", (n. 536), para. 303.

547 G. Wagner, "§139 ZPO", in *MünchKomm-ZPO* (n. 536), paras. 9–10; H. Prütting, "§139 ZPO" in H. Prütting and M. Gehrlein (n. 536) para. 2; A. Herb, *Europäisches Gemeinschaftsrecht und nationaler Zivilprozess* (Mohr Siebeck, 2007), 60 with further references.

548 D. Leipold, "§139 ZPO," in Stein and Jonas (eds.) (n. 536), para. 52; G. Wagner, "§139 ZPO" (n. 547), paras. 11–21.

549 Ibid., D. Leipold, para. 52.

It is accepted in literature that the managerial powers of the courts under §139 ZPO is not a means to make "social policy," but a means to protect and enforce the rights of the parties afforded by law.[550] Dieter Leipold argues that the proposition that §139 ZPO could be considered as an ideological foundation of a social vision of civil procedure (*soziale Zivilprozess*) for the protection of the socially weaker party does not find strong support in the text of the law.[551] However, the same author does not exclude other considerations coming into play where the substantive legal relationship underlying the dispute is guided by considerations of power inequality, economic behavior and lack of experience.[552] This observation would appear particularly relevant for the doctrine of the active consumer court. Already it is acknowledged that the *Hinweis- und Aufklärungspflicht* is stronger where the parties are not represented by counsel.[553] Achieving substantive justice might thus require the adaptation of the role of the courts in certain types of proceedings and this is exactly the case with respect to consumer proceedings, which should be governed by considerations of the protection of the weaker party.[554]

The obligation of German courts to provide guidance (called, as aforementioned, *Hinweispflicht*) empowers the courts to raise a material point (*Gesichtspunkt*)[555] that has been overlooked by the parties, provided that it is brought to their attention and that they are heard. The power embraces important aspects. The courts are obliged to examine the plaintiff's claim on an alternative legal basis, provided that the parties are given the opportunity to debate. To that effect, they are bound by the facts brought forward by the parties, but not they are not restricted to the facts which the parties adduce to

550 Ibid., para. 149.

551 Ibid., para. 1.

552 Ibid., para. 149, pointing out that the civil court is responsible not for doing social policy, but for protecting the rights of individuals and for enforcing the law. It is a different issue that in the framework of each legal relationship, there are factors which play a role, such as power equality, economic behaviour and lack of experience. ("Der Zivilrichter hat nicht die Aufgabe, Sozialpolitik zu betreiben, sondern seine Sache is es, das Recht des einzelnen zu schützen und durchsetzen. Dass im Rahmen des jeweiligen materiellen Rechtsverhältnisses in erheblichen Masse Faktoren wie Machtunggleichkeit, wirtschaftliche Verhältnisse, Unerfahrenheit eine Rolle spielen, steht auf einem anderen Blatt".) P. Murray and R. Sturner (n. 535), 177.

553 D. Leipold (n. 536), para. 150.

554 This is the case with respect to consumer proceedings, which should be governed by considerations of the protection of the weaker party, an assertion which will be substantiated in Part II.

555 It should be noted that before the reform brought about in 2001, the *Hinweispflicht* was limited on legal points (*rechtliche Gesichtspunkte*). D. Leipold, (n. 536), paras. 64–65, explains that the elimination of this limitation rendered, in essence, obsolete the need for delimitation of the concept of legal points. The *Hinweispflicht* encompasses then, legal as well as factual aspects, including the appreciation of evidence.

support a specific claim or defense. A claim for damages, for instance, rejected on the basis of tortious liability might have to be examined under the basis of contractual liability or under the basis of unjustified enrichment.[556] The issue of the contractual validity or the validity of general contractual terms is considered as such a material point (*Gesichtspunkt*) that can be raised by the court in the framework of its *Hinweispflicht*.[557] However, the relevant factual background needs to be brought forward by the parties. The duty to raise a legal foundation does not, therefore, arise if it would imply the need to explore a new set of facts (*Tatsachenkomplex*).[558]

In the third paragraph of §139 ZPO, the German legislator provides for the obligation of the court to communicate to the parties its reservations with respect to points that it has to take into account on its own motion. These are points related to an absolute bar to proceedings (*unverzichtbare Prozessvoraussetzungen*) or to the requirements for the exercise of a remedy (*Rechtsbehelfsvoraussetzungen*).[559] The court will examine of its own motion the relevant issue and will communicate its findings to the parties. The burden then lies upon the parties to bring forward the necessary submissions and evidence. There is therefore no swift to an inquisitorial mode of proceedings.[560] In practice, the *Amtsprüfung* obligation is established when there are concrete indications that point to the absence of a certain procedural requirement.[561] Factual circumstances that point to the nullity of a contractual relationship (such as the absence of the necessary form or illegality) do not fall within the *ex officio* control of §139 III ZPO, but within the remit of the advice obligation of §139 I-II ZPO. It is then only within the scope of the parties' submissions

---

556 G. Wagner (n. 547), para. 33, explains that the court has to examine whether the claim is justified on the basis of all relevant legal rules, and if need be, to support its judgment on another legal basis than the one suggested by the applicant; D. Leipold, (n. 536), para. 67.

557 Ibid. D. Leipold, (n. 536), para. 67; *OLG Düsseldorf* MDR 1982, 855; *BGH* NJW RR 1987, 112.

558 Ibid., *OLG Düsseldorf*, para. 34, explaining that the court will not examine whether a claim for damages based on tortious liability should rather be found upon the "equitable liability" (*Billigkeitshaftung*: §829 BGB), or whether a claimant lacking legitimacy should cede his claim to the person that would normally be entitled to exercise the claim.

559 D. Leipold, (n. 536), para. 91. According to Article 56 ZPO, the courts have to review *ex officio* the capacity of the party to be party in the proceedings (*Parteifähigkeit*), the capacity to sue and be sued (*Prozessfähigkeit*), the legitimization of a legal representative and the authorization to purse legal proceedings. Courts would also have to draw the attention to the parties to questions of legal interest (*Rechtschutzinteresse*) or to the conditions for the proper lodging of an appeal (*Einlegung eines Rechtsmittels*).

560 G. Wagner (n. 547), para. 51.

561 Ibid., bringing the example of the posting date that indicates the belated lodging of a means of appeal, or the documents disposed by the court that indicate the legal incapacity of the claimant.

that a point of substantive law can be examined,[562] although the position can be further nuanced in the case of mandatory rules of public policy.[563]

The *Hinweispflicht* embraces an obligation which is important for the articulation of the defense. As the courts have an obligation to provide guidance for the proper articulation of the legal submission, in the same way they are obliged to guide the defendant, provided that a relevant objection can be derived from the submissions advanced. When the party advances the facts that can found – for instance, an objection of set-off (*Aufrechnung*) or withdrawal (*Rücktritt*) – the court is obliged to consider the application of the relevant objection even if it has not been submitted as such by the party.[564] This is particularly important for the objections which can only be brought forward by their beneficiary and rely upon his will to do so ("genuine objections" – *echte Einreden*).[565] The court may raise of its own motion such an objection only if its effects follow unequivocally from the facts advanced by the beneficiary. With respect, for instance, to the objection of limitation, the relevant constitutive elements have to be unequivocally *inferred* from the submissions of the defendant. The same applies for *the intended consequence* of the relevant facts presented in the defense.[566] Under those circumstances, Gerhard Wagner points out,[567] the courts do not actually raise a new objection, but elucidate the proper way of proceeding.

The lack of jurisdiction is examined by the courts of their own motion. This power is particularly important where the defendant does not appear in the proceedings.[568] This obligation does not arise where submission by appearance is possible and the defendant has not raised the relevant objection (*rügelose Verhandlung*, §39 I ZPO). However, at the level of local courts (*Amtsgerichte*),[569] submission to the jurisdiction by appearance is subject to prior judicial advice (§39 II ZPO).[570] The prorogation of jurisdiction is prohibited in

562 G. Wagner (n. 547), para. 51; D. Leipold, (n. 536), para. 92.

563 See below Section 2.3.2.1.

564 G. Wagner (n. 547), para. 36; D. Leipold, (n. 536), para. 53, pointing out that whether the submissions of the party contain an indication of the relevant exception (*Anhaltspunkte*) is a matter that has to be clarified in every particular circumstance.

565 D. Leipold, (n. 536), para. 158.

566 That would be the case, for instance, when the defendant points out that after the passing of x years (corresponding to the limitation period), he could no longer prove the payment with the receipt or that he is unwilling still to have to deal with this issue which he considered settled: G. Wagner, "§139 ZPO" (n. 547), para. 38.

567 Ibid. G. Wagner, (n. 547), para. 36.

568 L. Rosenberg, L.H. Schwab and P. Gottwald (n. 536); R. Bork, in F. Stein and M. Jonas (eds.) (n. 536), para. 70.

569 The ordinary courts are competent for lower monetary value disputes up to €5,000 and certain other disputes for which exclusive jurisdiction exists (§23 GVG). For an overview in English of the organization of the courts in Germany, see P. Murray and R. Stürner (n. 535), 47 *et seq.*

570 The relevant provision for the *Amtgerichte* provides that in the event of a lack of territorial jurisdiction or competence *rationae materiae*, the court shall make a relevant indication

consumer litigation.[571] Such prohibition raised by the courts of their own motion is perfectly in line with the Union consumer judicial protection requirement for an obligation of national courts to raise of their own motion the unfairness of contractual terms conferring jurisdiction to the seat of the trader, unless the consumer intends to submit to jurisdiction.[572] The consequence in German law would be to dismiss the claim and refer it to the competent court.[573]

An important feature of the German ordinary (*ordentliche*) jurisdiction is the existence of a simplified procedure before the local courts (*Amtgerichte*) for claims falling beyond a certain threshold (currently €5,000).[574] In those courts, representation by lawyer is not obligatory and the written preparation of the case is limited. The *Amtsgerichte* jurisdiction allows for a simplified procedure while maintaining the quality of justice. Already in the early literature, Klaus Rohl was pointing out certain features of this procedure that also appear to be of particular relevance for the doctrine of the active consumer court:

> this court is able to integrate into the regular procedure important simplifications. Beyond that, a fairly long tradition of practicing the judicial task of assisting the parties has largely protected the judge against a conflict of roles when seeking to reach a settlement and enables him to a certain extent to compensate for the parties' unequal strengths.[575]

---

to the defendant prior to holding the hearing on the merits of the case and shall draw the defendant's attention to the consequences of entering an appearance on the merits of the case without filing the relevant objection (§504 ZPO). R. Bork, in F. Stein and M. Jonas (eds.) (n. 536), para. 3; D. Leipold, (n. 536), para. 94 points out that under exceptional circumstances, the obligation to give advice could arise even in proceedings before the regional courts (*landgerichtlichen Verfahren*).

571 The personal scope of application of the provision of §38 ZPO concerns only merchants, legal persons of public law or special assets under public law. Article 38 provides for very exceptional circumstances under which a proroationg agreement could still be admissible. See L. Rosenberg, L.-H. Schwab and P. Gottwald (n. 536), Section 37 ZPO, para. 20.

572 Joined Cases C-240/98–C-244/98 *Océano Grupo and Salvat Editores* (n. 446); Case C-243/08 *Pannon GSM*, EU:C:2009:350; Case C-137/08 *VB Penzugyi Lízing*, EU:C:2010:659. See F. Möslein, "Richtlinienkonforme Auslegung im Zivilverfahrensrecht? – Uberlegungen zur Auswirking der EuGH – Urteile Océano Grupo und Cofidis, aufgezeigt am Beispiel des §281 Abs. 2 S. 4 ZPO" (2004) *Zeitschrift für Gemeinschaftsprivatrecht-GPR* 59–66, 61; G. Borges, "AGB-Kontrolle durch den EuGH" (2001) *NJW* 2061, noting that given the *ex officio* obligation of the German courts with respect to consumer jurisdictional agreements, there is no need for the "implementation" of that case law.

573 L. Rosenberg, L.-H. Schwab and P. Gottwald, "39 ZPO", (n. 536), paras. 17–18. F. Möslein (n. 562) discusses further the implications of the Court's case law for the application of the binding effect of the judgment referring jurisdiction to another competent court (§281 Abs. 2 S. 4 ZPO); see J. Heinig, "Die AGB-Kontrolle von Gerichtsstandsklauseln-zum Urteil Pannon des EuGH" (2009) *Europäische Zeitschrift für Wirtschaftrecht* 885, discussing further the implications for German legal order of accepting that this case law also implies a power to raise the unfair term *in limine litis*.

574 Section 23 of the *Gerichtsverfahrungsgesetz-GVG*.

575 K. Rohl, "Small Claims in West Germany" in C. Whelan (ed.), *Small Claims Courts: A Comparative Study* (Oxford, Clarendon Press, 1990), 167–181, 180; see also H. Koch, *Verbraucherprozessrecht* (Heidelberg, Müller, 1990), 81 *et seq.*

### 2.3.2. *Mandatory Law and Powers of the Courts*

Following the brief sketch of the conceptual tools that define the division of the roles between the parties and the courts, we shall attempt to examine how *Van Schijndel* has been received in the German legal order. To do this, we need to find out the impact of a mandatory provision of national law upon the principle of party presentation, and then find out the impact of a mandatory provision of Union law. The question is linked to the problem of the limitations of disposition of the parties over the dispute when mandatory rules of substantive law are concerned.[576] Andreas Cahn observes that an unlimited procedural freedom of disposition over mandatory rules of substantive law would ensure that the same legal relationship be governed differently depending on whether the same rights are exercised procedurally or not.[577] Following this logic, the considerations of mandatory substantive law should be reflected upon procedural law by means of *ex officio* consideration. On the other hand, it could be argued that substantive law and procedural law are governed by distinct considerations and that the mandatory nature of the former cannot automatically imply an *ex officio* control or the lack of procedural restrictions in the way in which the relevant submissions are brought forward.

#### 2.3.2.1. National Mandatory Law

An important demonstration of the extent of the power of the parties over mandatory law in civil proceedings comes with the power of the parties to acknowledge a claim (*Anerkenntnis* §306 ZPO) and to forgo a claim (*Verzicht* §307 ZPO). The power of disposition of the parties in the civil procedure cannot be entirely disconnected from the limitations that are set by substantive law.[578] On the other hand, it could be argued that mandatory law only forbids *ex ante* the creation of claims and not their disposition *ex post*.[579] In accordance with the prevailing opinion in literature, the acknowledgment of the claim is ineffective if it would lead to a contractual performance that would be forbidden by law (§134 BGB) or *contra bonos mores* (§138 BGB) or against public policy (§6 EGBGB), the latter comprising the essential foundations of the European and German legal order.[580]

---

576 See the study of A. Cahn, "Prozessuale Dispositionsfreiheit und zwindgendes materielles Recht" (1998) 198 *Archiv für die civilistische Praxis* 35–71, with further references; G. Wagner, *Prozessverträge* (Mohr Siebeck, 1998) 97.

577 Ibid., A. Cahn, 37.

578 On the relevant debate *see* A. Herb (n. 547) 43–44 and T. Heiss, *Anerkenntnis und Anerkenntnis Urteil im Zivilprozess* (Mohr Siebeck, 2012) 77 *et seq.*

579 G. Wagner (n. 576) 106 *et seq.*; ibid., A. Herb, 44.

580 L. Rosenberg, L.H. Schwab and P. Gottwald "§132 (3)" (n. 536); H.-J. Musielak, "§307 ZPO" (n. 536), para. 17.

The power of the parties to bring forward the factual elements that will form the basis of the judgment and to advance their submissions is not replaced by an inquisitorial principle (*Untersuchungsmaxime*) in the field of mandatory law. In order for the application of a rule of mandatory law to be established, the parties have to bring forward the necessary facts through their submissions, unless the contrary is provided for within the framework of certain procedures.[581] The power of the parties over the facts is qualified by the obligation of procedural honesty (§138 ZPO). However, there are instances of mandatory law which can be considered by the courts of their own motion independently from the parties' submissions.

The ZPO provides for certain circumstances in which the *Verhandlungsgrundsatz* is limited when mandatory rules are involved in the dispute. The *ex officio* control (*Amtsprüfung* or *Amtsberücksichtigung*) implies a judicial assessment which is independent of the submissions and overall procedural behavior of the parties.[582] There is no need, for instance, for the defendant to bring forward a relevant objection so that the court can assess the lack of the requirements to sue and be sued. However, the concept does not imply an independent judicial investigation of the facts (*Amtsermittlung*).[583] There is no shift in the burden of proof and the courts do not bear an obligation to order measures of investigation.[584] The principle of *Amtsprüfung* therefore stands at the crossroads between the *Verhandlungsgrundsatz* and the *Untersuchungsgrundsatz*.[585]

In the general observations made above regarding the role of the courts in Germany, it has been explained that they have the power to indicate to the parties the application of rules of law when the relevant submissions are made by the parties. *A fortiori*, it should then follow that when the submissions of the parties imply the application of a mandatory rule of law, the courts are obliged to bring it to the attention of the parties. This is in accordance with the *Verhandlungsmaxime*, requiring that the court bases its decision on facts

---

581 Ibid., L. Rosenberg, L.H. Schwab and P. Gottwald, §77 II; T. Rauscher,"Einleitung," in W. Kruger and T. Rauscher (eds.) (n. 536), paras. 306–313. It is interesting to note that in Greek law, where the *ex officio* control is established by law, this is a lawful exception from the principle of party presentation; see for instance Areios Pagos 8/1993 (in plenary) *Elliniki Dikaiosini* 1994, 1241; Areios Pagos 22/2005 (in plenary) *Elliniki Dikaiosini* 2005, 715. For the relevant discussion in Greek law, see K. Kalavros, *Claims and Submissions in Civil Suits* (Sakkoulas, 2013), 92 *et seq.*, S. Kousoulis, *Submissions in Civil Suits* (Sakkoulas, 2003).

582 D. Leipold, (n. 536), para. 163; B. Rimmelspacher, *Zur Prüfung von Amts wegen im Zivilprozess* (Verlag Otto Schwarz, 1966), 33 *et seq.*

583 T. Rauscher, "Einleitung," in W. Kruger and T. Rauscher (eds.) (n. 536), paras. 328–333; L. Rosenberg, L.H. Schwab and P. Gottwald (n. 536), §77 paras. 45–78.

584 T. Rauscher, (n. 536), para. 331; D. Leipold, (n. 536), para. 171.

585 Ibid., D. Leipold, para. 163; ibid., T. Rauscher, para. 329.

advanced by the parties.[586] But what is the case when the material facts have not been advanced by the parties (*nicht vorgebrachte Tatsachen*) but form part of the case file and involve the application of a mandatory rule of law? There are at least four approaches on this issue:

1. The restrictive view on the *ex officio* control (*Amtsprüfung*): Wolfgang Brehm takes the view that the court is bound by the submissions of the parties even when mandatory law is concerned.[587] The sanction of nullity does not prevent the parties from renouncing their right to invoke nullity.[588] It is only exceptionally that the *Verhandlungsgrundsatz* should be restricted, where the recognition of a certain legal relationship by the judgment would result in a contractual performance which is illegal or *contra bonos mores*.[589] Dieter Leipold explains that the right of the parties to determine the factual scope of the dispute is based upon a different premise from the one prohibiting the parties to exclude the application of mandatory rules of substantive law.[590]
2. The *ex officio* examination (*Amtsprüfung*) in the presence of specific indications resulting from the case file (*Anhaltspunkte*): Andreas Cahn argues that the public interest considerations in the field of substantive mandatory law, in circumstances where the parties do not have freedom of disposition, should result in the application of those substantive provisions by the courts of their own motion, in the same way that public interest considerations lead to the *ex officio* application of the standing requirements.[591] If it were otherwise, the author argues, the parties could essentially circumvent the prohibitions set out in substantive law by omitting to advance the relevant rules of mandatory law.[592] The existence of a mandatory provision limiting the freedom of the parties for an autonomous construction of their legal relationship demonstrates, according to Cahn, that the legislator cannot rely exclusively upon the plaintiff/defendant in order to safeguard a reasonable balancing of the interests involved.[593] An obligation to raise mandatory provisions should, however, be attached to specific indications (*Anhaltspunkte*) arising from the file.[594] Thus, an *ex officio* application of a rule of mandatory law should not be understood

---

586 Ibid., D. Leipold, para. 153.

587 W. Brehm, in F. Stein and M. Jonas (eds.) (n. 536), paras. 95–96.

588 Ibid.

589 Ibid.

590 D. Leipold, (n. 536), para. 167.

591 A. Cahn (n. 576), 70, fn. 148.

592 A. Cahn, "Gemeinschaftsrecht und nationales Verfahrensrecht" 6 (1998) *Zeitschrift für europäisches Privatrecht – ZeuP* 969–980, 979.

593 Ibid.

594 A. Cahn (n. 576), 70.

in the sense of independent investigation of the facts that could potentially and *in abstracto* found a point of mandatory law not brought forward by the parties. It should rather be understood in the sense of a neutral judicial clarification and classification of the factual elements of the dispute.

3. *Ex officio* control (*Amtsprüfung*) on the basis of the *purpose* of the provision: this approach starts from the premise that not all rules of mandatory law need automatically to be reflected in an *ex officio* role for the courts. There are substantive rights which, although they form part of *ius cogens*, can be disposed of *ex post*. Taking the example of a contract which is void because of lack of the legal form (§125 BGB), does *ipso iure* nullity imply that the party entitled to object to the contract cannot confirm its validity in the procedure or that the court has to consider the nullity of its own motion? The literature gives a response to this question on the basis of the *purpose* of the mandatory provision: whether the purpose of the prohibition by the mandatory law is exhausted at the stage of establishment of the right (*Rechtsgestaltung*) or whether it also applies at the stage of its enforcement (*Rechtsdurchsetzung*).[595] Taking, for instance, the mandatory provision on the formality of real property transactions (§311b BGB), the law prescribes the notarial form, but it is possible that a lack of form will be remedied in the future. If the parties choose to litigate on a different basis from the question of form of the contract, that is not the same as if they would decide to enforce the contract.[596] But if we take the example of an illegal transaction (§134 BGB – *Gesetzliches Verbot*) or a transaction *contra bonos mores* (§138 BGB – *Sittenwidriges Rechtsgeschäft*), there is an important difference which also needs to be reflected at the procedural level. The prohibition set by the legislator is not set only to the benefit of the aggrieved party but also to the *public interest* and to the *legal order* in its entirety. The state cannot provide through its courts the facility of enforcement of illegality.[597] Therefore, the nullity established is *absolute*, in the sense that the courts can consider it of their own motion.[598] The courts should therefore be empowered to apply of their own motion all those provisions for which the confirmation or acknowledgment of illegality (*Anerkenntnis*) is not possible as their protective scope extends beyond the parties in the dispute.
4. The objection based on breach of good faith: the breach of good faith in the contractual relationship, including the plea of *abuse of right*, is taken into

---

595 T. Heiss (n. 578), 82–83, with references mainly to M. Würthwein, *Umfang und Grenzen des Parteienflusses auf die Urteilgrundlagen im Zivilprozess* (Duncker & Humblot, 1977), 115.

596 T. Heiss (n. 578), 82, 85.

597 Ibid.

598 On the distinction between absolute and relative nullity (*absolute* and *relative Nichtigkeit*), see indicatively C. Armbrüster, "§134 BGB" in F.J. Säcker (ed.), *Münchener Kommentar zum Bürgerlichen Gesetzbuch: BGB (MünchKomm-BGB)* (Beck, 7th ed., 2015).

consideration by the courts of their own motion.[599] In general, the courts will review of their own motion *unreasonable* clauses in general conditions as a result of the *Schlüssigkeitsprinzip*, according to which the courts have to investigate whether the facts brought forward by a party justify the award of the claim or defense.[600] For as long as the necessary factual elements derive from the court file, the courts need to deduce the legal consequences of abuse of right of their own motion. Once the material facts form part of the file, it is not relevant which of the parties adduced them in litigation and it is not necessary that the aggrieved party advances the breach of good faith *ope exceptionis* for the court to consider it of its own motion. In that regard, it therefore suffices that the courts have available all the material facts which nullify the right upon its constitution (the objection that is based upon such facts is called *rechtsvernichtende Einwendung*). The provision of §242 BGB on the requirement of contractual performance in observance of the principle of good faith operates, according to Roth and Schubert as an inherent limitation of the right to perform a contract which violates such a requirement.[601]

#### 2.3.2.2. Mandatory Union Law

The role of German courts does not change depending on the domestic or Union origin of the mandatory rule. The mandatory rules that have to be considered *ex officio* are those that serve the *public interest*. This corresponds to the case law of the Court, which provides for an *ex officio obligation* only for such rules that *have an importance for the Union legal order* which exceeds the individual interest of the parties.[602] Let us concentrate on the question posed by *Van Schijndel*: do German courts have to apply *ex officio* the provisions of competition law?

As far as the breach of competition law provisions affects the validity of a contract, it is admitted in the literature that courts should consider the ensuing nullity of their own motion, even if the relevant objection has not been brought forward, as long as the facts founding nullity derive from the court file.[603]

599 H. Roth and C. Schubert, "§242 BGB," in F.J. Säcker (ed.), *MünchKomm-BGB* (n. 598), paras. 82–85.

600 See the explanations on the application of the *Schlüssigkeitsprinzip* in A. Hartkamp, "*Ex Officio* Application in Case of Unenforceable Contracts or Contract Clauses, EU Law and National Laws Confronted" in L. Gullilfer and S. Vogenauer (eds.), *English and European Perspectives on Contract and Commercial Law: Essays in Honour of Hugh Beale* (Oxford, Hart Publishing, 2014), 467–484, 473.

601 H. Roth and C. Schubert, (n. 598), para. 82.

602 See Joined Cases C-222/05–C-225/05 *Van der Weerd*, EU:C:2007:318.

603 A. Herb (n. 547), 66–67; P. Stockenhuber, "Art. 101 AEUV" in E. Grabitz, M. Hilf and M. Nettesheim *Das Recht der Europäischen Union* (EUV/AEUV) (Beck, 53rd ed., 2014),

The *ex officio* role for the court corresponds to the purpose of the prohibition. The interests served by the provisions of competition law and the legal consequence of nullity lie beyond the disposition of the parties and relate to the good functioning of the internal market.[604] That is so, Schmidt explains, because the power of the parties exists over the subject matter of the dispute and the facts, but does not cover the judicial assessment of those elements.[605] However, the dominance of the parties in litigation (*Parteiherrschaft*) is maintained upon the facts on which the judgment will be founded.

It seems settled in German case law that those litigants who wish to rely upon the competition law provisions of Union law have to bring forward and prove the required conditions.[606] The Federal Civil Court (BGH) has rejected the view that the courts should examine the question of a breach of competition law provisions irrespective of the parties' submissions or where an examination of new facts would be required.[607] Thus, courts will not apply competition law provisions where the breach has not been adequately advanced by the parties. Besides, the civil courts are not the only ones responsible for the application of the competition provisions; there exist special administrative procedures of investigation in that respect.[608] It would not be correct to deduce that this stance does not meet the Union requirements. If the parties bring forward all the factual elements constitutive of a breach of competition law, then German courts would indeed be able to raise the ensuing nullity *ex officio*. However, in the absence of specific submissions to that effect and considering the high level of complexity in competition law litigation, it is hard to imagine that the courts would dispose of the necessary factual and legal elements in order to proceed to an *ex officio* control.

As far as consumer litigation is concerned, it would appear from the above that the German judicial system is equipped with the conceptual tools to accommodate the doctrine of the active court. There are certain features of the German judicial system regarding the independent judicial assessment of mandatory rules of substantive law which are particularly relevant in the field of consumer law. It has been already said that the breach of good faith does not have to be brought *ope exceptionis*. Thus, in a consumer contractual dispute, once the court infers from the facts before it that there is a potential breach of

---

paras. 231–232; K. Schmidt, "Art. 101 Abs. 2 AEUV" in U. Immenga and E. J. Mestmäcker (eds.), *EU-Wettberwerbsrecht* (Beck, 5th ed., 2012), para. 14.

604 See A. Cahn (n. 584), 978.

605 K. Schmidt, "Art. 101 Abs. 2 AEUV," in U. Immenga and E. J. Mestmäcker (eds.) (n. 603), para. 14.

606 BGH, NJW 1998, 156, 159; BGH, NJW 1992, 2145, 2145.

607 BGH, NJW 1998, 156, 159.

608 A. Herb (n. 547), 68, with further references to case law: *OLG Karlsruhe*, EuZW 1991, 31, 32.

the requirement of good faith by means of the use of an unfair term,[609] it has the power to assess such a term of its motion, despite the silence or even the absence of the consumer. The *ex officio* power is accompanied by the obligation of the court to hear the parties in relation to the respective plea. If the consumer is present, the court will resort to its advice duty (*Hinweispflicht*) in order to inform the consumer of the existence of an unfair term or another mandatory rule of consumer law. Probably thanks to those features, Arthur Hartkamp assumes that the case law of the Court on the *ex officio* application of the unfair terms legislation "has met much less resistance in Germany (and related legal systems) than initially in the Netherlands."[610]

## 2.4. FINAL REMARKS ON *VAN SCHIJNDEL* AND THE NATIONAL LEGAL PERSPECTIVES

The presentation of the national legal perspectives on the respective roles of the courts and the parties in civil proceedings brings us to the end of Part I. It has been demonstrated that the *Van Schijndel* line did not require any change in the relative role of the courts and the parties in the proceedings. This line relies principally upon the principle of equivalence and the principle of loyal cooperation, by virtue of which the Union binding rules or mandatory rules are subject to the same procedural rules as similar domestic mandatory rules or public policy rules. The national procedural preferences are admitted, provided that the parties have a genuine opportunity to put forward the Union law claim. In brief, Union law does not require that Member States abandon their fundamental "prevailing conceptions" of procedural law, predicated upon the principle of party presentation and the adversarial character of the proceedings.

Of course, when it comes to the exact application of those principles, in particular with regard to the powers of the courts to raise a point of law of their own motion, the responses in each system differ. National courts might be obliged to examine rules of mandatory law, but this will depend upon the availability of the facts of the dispute and the parties' submissions. Differences exist on the exact determination of the judicial role with regard to facts advanced but not canvassed (or improperly canvassed) in legal submission or with regard to facts of the case file which have not been pleaded. From the overview of the three legal systems that have been examined here, there would seem to be at

609 Article 307 (1) al. 1 BGB which provides for the ineffectiveness of standard contract terms if they unreasonably disadvantage the other party to the contract with the user.

610 A. Hartkamp, "*Ex Officio* Application in Case of Unenforceable Contracts or Contract Clauses, EU Law and National Laws Confronted," in L. Gullilfer and S. Vogenauer (eds.) (n. 600), 474.

least some common themes, despite the various nuances. Courts are not obliged to raise a point of mandatory law which could not have been brought to their attention. If the pleadings of the parties do not contain at least an indication of the application of a mandatory rule, the breach of that rule should be manifest so that the court would raise it of its own motion. A judgment cannot be quashed for not having applied a mandatory law that it was not in position to apply in view of the facts available. At the level of cassation, the new points of law that depend upon novel facts which have not established at a lower level are not admitted. Depending on the legal system, courts can still have the discretion to raise a point of mandatory law which arises from the case file even if it is not clearly advanced by the parties. The main requirement which, however, is common to all of them is the respect of contradictory debate.

The question whether the courts have the power to raise a point of law of their own motion and upon which conditions therefore has to be considered within the framework of the fundamental principles governing the civil dispute in each legal order. A court raising an issue independently of the parties' submissions is of course the exception to the normal course of disputes. Courts can be more or less active in legal enquiry depending on the legal system, but this "activism" is carefully circumscribed so that courts keep their jurisdictional role without losing their impartiality. The existence of mandatory Union law obeys the same rules without requiring a different procedural framework.

*Van Schijndel* is certainly a landmark case bringing about welcome clarifications on the relative role of the courts and the parties in the proceedings and on the parameters of the balancing exercised with regard to the assessment of the effectiveness of national procedural law. Since it does not require a change in the role of the courts, subject to the respect of the principle of equivalence and effectiveness, it could be assumed that if it had not existed, there would not have been any change in the course of the application of Union law. That statement is not the same with regard to the *Océano Grupo* line of case law. This is one of the cases for which we could ask ourselves "what the Union consumer law would have been without *Océano Grupo*?"[611]

Since 2000 and particularly in the aftermath of the financial crisis, the Court has literally been flooded by questions concerning the role of the courts in individual consumer litigation originating from various jurisdictions. The effectiveness of consumer legislation required that the Court takes its jurisprudence one step further compared to *Van Schijndel*. This step would

[611] I paraphrase here the famous observation made by Robert Lecourt with regard to the impact of Case 26/62 *van Gend & Loos*, EU:C:1963:1 and Case 6/64 *Costa v. ENEL*, EU:C:1964:66, R. Lecourt, « Quel eut été le droit des Communautés sans les arrêts de 1963 et 1964?" in *L'Europe et le droit ; mélanges en hommage à Jean Boulouis* (Paris, Dalloz, 1991), pp. 349–361.

not require a fundamental deviation from the basic tenets of civil procedure, but it would require the recognition of a Union court model in consumer law proceedings that would temper the principle of party disposition. This is already huge progress in terms of the conception of the *office* of the courts where established practices and mindsets would not easily allow change. Part II, will delve into the details of this fascinating that would leave its imprint on civil procedural law for consumers and for weaker parties. *Océano Grupo* rewrote the history of individual consumer litigation.

# PART II

# THE EMERGENCE AND DISTINCTIVE FEATURES OF THE ACTIVE CONSUMER COURT DOCTRINE

The purpose of this part is to examine the role of the case law of the Court in the strengthening of individual consumer procedural protection. The development of a specific line of case law on consumer procedural protection did not have its basis in a procedural legislative instrument. The existing legislation on consumer law does not cover the course of domestic litigation before national courts. The "springboard" for the creation of the doctrine has been Article 7(1) of the Unfair Contract Terms Directive,[612] which requires that Member States ensure that "adequate and effective means exist to prevent the continued use of unfair terms." This provision, as Peter Rott puts it, "codifies" effectiveness.[613] The protective purpose of the rules of substantive consumer law led to the inference of their procedural implications. In practice, the reading of the Union consumer protection legislation in light of the principle of effectiveness resulted in a *conceptual reappraisal* of the standards of judicial protection applicable in consumer litigation.

This conceptual reappraisal is based upon two premises. The first one is the qualification of the mandatory rules of consumer protection as an expression of *European public interest* with the result that those procedural rules should be elevated to the same procedural ranking as domestic rules of public policy. This premise alone would not be sufficient to establish the distinctiveness of the role of the courts in the consumer procedural litigation framework. It is shared by other internal market rules that have been characterized as expressions of European public policy, namely the rules of competition law. The second premise, which is distinctive in consumer litigation, is the presumption set at the Union level of the existence of a situation of *procedural imbalance*, a procedural

612 Council Directive 93/13/EEC of 5 April 1993 on unfair terms in consumer contracts [1993] OJ L95/29 (the "Unfair Contract Terms Directive").

613 P. Rott, "The Court of Justice's Principle of Effectiveness and its Unforeseeable Impact on Private Law Relationships" in D. Leczykiewicz and S. Weatherill (eds.), *The Involvement of EU Law in Private Law Relationships* (Oxford, Hart Publishing, 2013), 181–198, 182.

expression of the underlying structural weakness of one of the parties compared to its sophisticated counterparty.

While the general rule on the application of Union law by the courts of their own motion does not require any change in the respective role of the courts and the parties, provided that the parties have a genuine opportunity to raise the Union law argument, the position is inverted at the level of Union consumer law. A presumption is set at the European level that the absence of an *ex officio* role for the courts involving consumers *ab initio* deprives the consumer of the genuine opportunity to raise the argument based on Union consumer law. In theory, the consumer has the opportunity to state his case like any other litigant. But, such an opportunity will normally be illusory not due to a procedural obstacle per se, but due to the underlying imbalance. The combination of the two premises, the expression of European public interest and of the weaker party, lead to the recognition of a distinct role of an active court intended to restore procedural equality.

The second part of this study is divided into three chapters. Chapter 4 presents the fundamental judgments for the active consumer court doctrine. In essence, the theoretical underpinnings of the doctrine, particularly with regard to the element of the procedural imbalance, are set in those first judgments. Moreover, Chapter 4 covers the case law which refined the doctrine as to its scope, prerequisites and consequences of application.

Chapter 5 delves into some representative examples in case law of what could be called the "meta-*ex officio*" era. This term connotes a phase in case law where the already well-established doctrine became the standard of assessment of the effectiveness of various procedural contexts involving consumers. In this sense, it acquires a transversal and trans-procedural character. This perspective is reflected in the following part of the reasoning of the Court, according to which:

> the specific characteristics of court proceedings, which take place under national law between sellers or suppliers and consumers, cannot constitute a factor which is liable to affect the legal protection from which consumers must benefit under the provisions of that directive.[614]

The interventionist role of the Court, taking a "positive action unconnected with the actual parties to the contract"[615] in order to remedy procedural imbalances, therefore becomes a permanent feature of any type of procedural setting where the consumer is involved.

---

614 Case C-618/10 *Banco Español de Crédito*, EU:C:2012:349, para. 55; Case C-415/11 *Aziz*, EU:C:2013:164, para. 62.

615 Joined Cases C-240/98–C-244/98 *Océano Grupo Editorial and Salvat Editores*, EU:C:2000:346, consistently cited in subsequent case law.

Chapter 6 illustrates the influence of the active consumer court doctrine in three different jurisdictions: Spain, France and England. It also advances reflections on the effectiveness of the active consumer court doctrine as such as well as on its potential for transposition to other fields of Union law.

Before embarking on the detailed analysis of the cases which form the active consumer court doctrine, some further preliminary observations are necessary on the two "phases" of the doctrine (covered in Chapters 4 and 5 accordingly). The first "phase" represents the establishment of the doctrine and its "autonomization" compared to the general position of the *Van Schijndel* line. The Court, as AG Sharpston observed in *Faber* "has developed that case law separately from cases involving similar questions in the context of other parts of EU law."[616] In the second "phase" the doctrine evolves into a benchmark of effectiveness.

## 1. THE AUTONOMOUS DETERMINATION OF THE ROLE OF THE COURTS IN CONSUMER LAW PROCEEDINGS AS A MATTER OF EFFECTIVENESS

Compared to the *Van Schijndel* line of case law, Koen Lenaerts et al. point out that the Court in the *Océano Grupo* line "frames [the reasoning] primarily in the context of the full effectiveness of Union law ... with the principle of national procedural autonomy playing a less prominent role."[617]

If the courts would be prevented from raising the consumer law provisions of their own motion solely because the consumer omitted to raise a respective claim "the regime of special protection" established by consumer law "would be definitely undermined."[618] The Court encapsulated the full effectiveness argument in the following terms:

> effective consumer protection could be achieved only if the national court were required, of its own motion, to examine compliance with the requirements which flow from EU law on consumer law.[619]

Following the *Océano Grupo* line of case law, courts bear an obligation to raise of their own motion the unfair nature of contractual terms "irrespective of the degree of passivity national courts must usually adhere to as a matter of national

---

616 Opinion of AG Sharpston in Case C-497/13 *Faber*, EU:C:2014:2403, point 62. Similarly, J.H. Jans et al., *Europeanisation of Public Law* (Groningen, Europa Law Publishing, 2007), 312, explains that the *ex officio* application of Union law is "not always approached exclusively along the lines of Van Schijndel and Peterbroeck".

617 K. Lenaerts et al., *EU Procedural Law* (Oxford, Oxford University Press, 2014), para. 4.41.

618 Case C-168/05 *Mostaza Claro*, EU:C:2006:675, para. 31.

619 Case C-377/14 *Radlinger and Radlingerová*, EU:C:2016:283.

law."[620] The active consumer court doctrine, although inspired by domestic doctrines on *ordre public*, mandatory law of protection and illegality does not rely upon domestic procedural configurations or classifications in order to define the role of the courts in consumer law proceedings. The result, in the view of Verica Trstenjak and Erwin Beysen, is "a less stringent application of the concept of procedural autonomy."[621] The provisions of consumer law are considered to express the general interest which exceptionally requires an active court raising the respective argument, even if that would mean under domestic procedural law that the court would go beyond the ambit of the dispute.[622] This justifies the necessity for the Court to rise "over and above the application of [domestic] concepts and rules of national procedural law" and, in essence, afford an autonomous procedural status to consumer law claims.[623] In order to enable the national courts to assume their active role, the Court held in *Pénzügyi Lízing*[624] that, as a matter of effectiveness, they must "in all cases and whatever the rules of its domestic law, determine whether or not the contested term was individually negotiated between a seller or supplier and a consumer," taking, if necessary, measures of investigation. The clarification of the nature of the judicial power as an obligation which might even entail measures of investigation has clear normative implications: Union law sets an autonomous standard of procedural protection for consumers.

Following the principle that "the fair process is a differentiated process,"[625] individual consumer litigation also deserves differentiated application of the principle of effectiveness compared to the general line of reasoning drawn in *Van Schijndel*. The creed of the reasoning in the establishment of an active role for the courts lies in considerations of both *substance* and *procedure*, of the *protection of the weaker party* and the *redress of the power imbalance*. In the absence of such a role, the courts would be impotent observers of the transformation of the power imbalance of the contractual parties into *procedural imbalance*. To that effect, a connection is required between procedural law and substantive law, which Vincenzo Zeno Zencovich and Maria Cecilia Paglietti eloquently call a "redimensionnement de la séparation traditionnelle entre le droit substantiel et le droit processuel" [bringing a new dimension to the traditional separation between substantive law and procedural law] (translated by the author).[626]

620 T. Corthaut, *EU Ordre Public* (Dordrecht, Wolters Kluwer, 2012), II-175.

621 V. Trstenjak and E. Beysen, (n. 11), 119.

622 See Case C-227/08 *Martín Martín*, EU:C:2009:792, paras. 20–21.

623 Opinion of AG Mengozzi in Case C-429/05 *Rampion and Godard*, EU:C:2007:575, point 82.

624 Case C-137/08 *VB Pénzügyi Lízing*, EU:C:2010:659, para. 51.

625 See M. Cappelletti, *The Judicial Process in Comparative Perspective* (Oxford, Clarendon Press, 1989), 268.

626 V. Zeno-Zencovich and M. C. Paglietti, "Le droit processuel des consommateurs" (2014) *Revue de droit internationale et de droit comparé* 321–355, 325. More generally,

The premise of the protection of the weaker party renders the field of consumer law proceedings perfectly amenable to what Michael Dougan has identified as "a distinct sectoral conception of the principle of effectiveness."[627] This feature, together with the mandatory nature of consumer law, results in the evolution of the "public policy equivalence" principle – the main thread of reasoning in the *Van Schijndel* line – to the setting of an autonomous mode of judicial protection. As a result of the importance of the *public interest* recognized with regard to consumer protection rules, these could be considered to express a "public policy of protection"[628] within Union law.

Although the establishment of the active consumer court doctrine has been the concretization of the principle of effectiveness in consumer law proceedings, it could be argued that the considerations of power imbalance draw the doctrine closer to the principle of effective judicial protection. The need for the establishment of an active consumer court would appear to presume *a priori* the lack of a "genuine opportunity"[629] for the consumer as the weaker party to make his case. Therefore, if the courts are not empowered to restore the imbalance whenever the factual and legal elements are available for them to do so, this could potentially raise concerns of denial of justice.[630]

## 2. THE EVOLUTION OF THE ACTIVE CONSUMER COURT DOCTRINE AS A TRANS-PROCEDURAL BENCHMARK OF EFFECTIVENESS

While the first phase of case law on the active consumer court relates to the establishment of the doctrine in individual consumer law proceedings *as a matter of Union law*, there is a second, more complex phase in which the question arises as to the *operation* of the doctrine within the framework of specific proceedings and overall the way in which it is accommodated in proceedings involving consumers. From this perspective, procedural rules which appear unconnected to the *ex officio* question, such as payment order proceedings,

see E. Jeuland, "Autour de la Forme et du Fond, Problèmes de Procédure" in *De Code en Code, Mélanges en l'honneur du Doyen Georges Wiederkehr* (Paris, Dalloz, 2009).

627 M. Dougan, "The Vicissitudes of Life at the Coalface Remedies and Procedures for Enforcing Union Law" in P. Craig and G. de Burca (eds.), *The Evolution of EU Law* (Oxford, Oxford University Press, 2nd ed., 2011), 412, 424.

628 P. Malaurie et al., *Les Obligations* (LGDJ, 6th ed., 2013), para. 650, discussed in the context of French law.

629 Case C-222/05 *Van der Weerd and Others* EU:C:2007:318, para. 41.

630 See H. CH. Hofmann, "Art. 47 Right to an Effective Remedy," in S. Peers et al. (eds.), *The EU Charter of Fundamental Rights: A Commentary* (Oxford, Hart Publishing, 2014), paras. 47.77 *et seq*, who associates the *ex officio* application of Union law with the potential of denial of justice.

mortgage enforcement proceedings or debt restructuring proceedings, are drawn within the ambit of the *ex officio* doctrine. The starting point to assess the interaction of the active court doctrine with specific procedural rules is the principle of national procedural autonomy as limited by the principles of equivalence and effectiveness. In particular, when it comes to the assessment of the principle of effectiveness, this, as Verica Trstenjak and Edward Beysen have noted, is "pinched upon" a "high threshold."[631] More precisely, the obligation for the Member States to ensure the effectiveness of the rights that consumers derive from Union law "implies"[632] or is anchored on a requirement of effective judicial protection. The application of the principle of effectiveness would then appear to be "infused" by the considerations of Article 47 of the Charter.[633]

The judgment in *Aziz*,[634] for example, recognized that in an action for mortgage repossession, the court hearing the declaratory proceedings on the issue of contractual unfairness should be empowered to grant interim relief. Although implicit, the principle of effective judicial protection was the underlying consideration, as demonstrated by the respective citation made to the judgment in *Unibet*.[635] In *Kušionová*,[636] the Court reformulated the reference for preliminary ruling. Although the question referred only to Article 38 of the Charter, the Court took into account Article 47 of the Charter which enshrines the right to an effective judicial protection. Moreover, the above cases brought within the scope of analysis a second constitutional imperative, the right to respect of one's family life and home according to Article 7 of the Charter. The need to safeguard effective judicial protection is underscored by the quality of the property at stake, in consideration of ECtHR jurisprudence that "the loss of a home is one of the most serious breaches of the right to respect of the home."[637]

The approach in the first and the second phase of the active consumer court doctrine is to be explained in terms of evolution rather than in terms of opposing methods of reasoning. As the national courts became more confident in its application, the doctrine entered a new phase and assumed a *trans-procedural* character. In the first phase, the *ex officio* doctrine was built. In the second phase, it became the yardstick for the effectiveness of national procedural rules. In this phase, the reasoning had to take into account the specificities of different

---

631 V. Trstenjak and E. Beysen (n. 11), 121.

632 Case C-169/14 *Sánchez Morcillo and Abril García*, EU:C:2014:2099, para. 35.

633 See M. Safjan and D. Düsterhaus, "A Union of Effective Judicial Protection: Addressing a Multi-level Challenge through the Lens of Article 47 CFREU" (2014) 33 *Yearbook of European Law* 3–40, 12, who explain that "procedural rules which globally comply with the requirements of Article 47 Charter may ... fail to do so where they would jeopardise the protection of consumers against unfair terms".

634 Case C-415/11 *Aziz*, EU:C:2013:164.

635 Case C-432/05 *Unibet*, EU:C:2007:163, para.38.

636 Case C-34/13 *Kušionová*, EU:C:2014:2189.

637 Ibid., para. 64 with the citations to the ECtHR case law.

procedural contexts within which the *ex officio* application of consumer law was to be confronted and the "fine margins"[638] of balancing involved in such types of adjudication.

In many references for preliminary ruling, the national courts suggested that the review of national procedural law be carried out in light of Article 38 of the Charter[639] or in conjunction with Article 47 of the Charter.[640] Article 38 of the Charter provides that the Union policies must ensure a high level of consumer protection. The origins of this principle can be traced back to the Treaties, particularly Articles 12 and 169 TFEU. While its integration into the Charter "carries an immediate appearance of a statement of significant constitutional weight,"[641] its nature of "principle" places limits on its justiciability (Article 52(5) of the Charter). From the way in which Article 38 of the Charter has been woven into the reasoning of the Court, two conclusions could be drawn. The first is that the high level of consumer protection guaranteed by the Charter and the Treaties is a normative benchmark which supports the "high threshold" of effectiveness in cases involving individual consumer protection.[642] The second observation relates to the limits of interpretation due to the limited judicial cognizance of a principle couched in vague terms. *Pohotovost*[643]is a good example in that regard. The question was whether the effectiveness of consumer protection against unfair terms required the existence of an autonomous right of consumer associations to intervene in proceedings for enforcement of a judicial decision or a final arbitration award. The Court asserted the character of Article 38 of the Charter as a principle which does not confer individual rights "by itself."[644] In light of the above, the conclusion of Stephen Weatherill seems justified, in that Article 38 "is becoming common currency in consumer law cases" but, without "seem[ing] apt to add anything of substance to the directions already found in Articles 12, 114(3) and 169 TFEU."[645]

The case law of the Court on the active consumer court is presented following a "circular" method. It is only after the national context of each case is properly grasped that we can go back to the answer of the Court and, whenever this has been possible to trace, we shall examine its application by the national court and

638 S. Weatherill, "Art. 38 – Consumer Protection" in S. Peers et al. (eds.), *The EU Charter of Fundamental Rights: A Commentary* (Oxford, Hart Publishing, 2014), para. 38.57.

639 Case C-227/08 *Martín Martín*, EU:C:2009:792.

640 See Case C-34/13 *Kušionová* (n. 636) where the question was reformulated by the Court to include Article 47 of the Charter.

641 S. Weatherill (n. 638), para. 38.13.

642 Ibid., para. 38.64, suggests that it can "strengthen an interpretative preference to adopt a pro-consumer approach".

643 Case C-470/12 *Pohotovosť v. Miroslav Vašuta*, EU:C:2014:101.

644 Ibid., para. 52.

645 S. Weatherill (n. 638), para. 38.64.

the overall impact upon the respective national legal order. Such an approach follows the inherent balance between the general effect that a judgment of the Court has for Union law and its concrete application by the national court which made the reference. On the one hand, the case law of the Court creates a precedent for all jurisdictions, while, on the other hand, it has to respond to a specific legal issue that arose within the specific context of a given legal order. In any event, the case law needs to be read bearing in mind the well-known tenet that the Court does not decide its own docket. This is quite obvious in the context of the consumer *ex officio* doctrine. It is the national courts (not their counsellors, since the consumers were not represented or present) which brought to the fore the serious impediments in consumer procedural protection and viewed the Court as their partner in strengthening the procedural protection for the Union consumer and citizen.

# CHAPTER 4

# THE ESTABLISHMENT, REFINEMENT AND CONSEQUENCES OF APPLICATION OF THE ACTIVE CONSUMER COURT DOCTRINE

This chapter analyzes the case law of the Court that sets in stone the doctrine of the active consumer court. The first three sections are devoted to the "trio" of fundamental judgments where the Court sets the theoretical underpinnings of the doctrine. The landmark judgment in that regard is *Océano Grupo*,[646] together with *Cofidis*[647] and *Mostaza Claro*.[648] Section 4 analyzes the case law that sets the basis for the extension of the scope of application of the active consumer court in other fields of consumer protection law. It also covers the case law that "refines" the doctrine of the active court. This case law provided for crucial clarifications on the nature of the judicial power the doctrine entails (an obligation) as well as the precision of the boundaries of that power linked to the availability of all the factual and legal elements and the observance of the *audi alteram partem* principle. Section 5 delves into the consequences of the exercise of the *ex officio* powers of the courts. The final Section 6 takes up the problematic of application of the doctrine of active consumer court to collective proceedings, concluding that the doctrine is applicable, for the moment, only in individual consumer proceedings. Although there are certainly matters that have to be clarified in relation to the doctrine, the wealth of the case law developed over the last 15 years at least and analyzed in this chapter demonstrates the existence of a doctrine at a relatively important state of "maturity."

646 Joined Cases C-240/98–C-244/98 *Océano Grupo*, EU:C:2000:346.
647 Case C-473/00 *Cofidis*, EU:C:2002:705.
648 Case C-168/05 *Mostaza Claro*, EU:C:2006:675.

## 1. *OCÉANO GRUPO*: LAYING THE FOUNDATIONS OF AN ACTIVE CONSUMER COURT

The question in *Océano Grupo*[649] was referred by the industrious *Juzgado de Primera Instancia de Barcelona*. This was the same court which more than a decade later would make the reference in the other groundbreaking judgment within this line of case law, *Aziz*.[650] Those two cases can be considered the most important for the establishment of the active consumer court doctrine. As Fernanda Nicola and Evelyne Tichadou have discerned, it is the second one which revealed the "social relevance" of the first, allowing *Océano Grupo* to live today "a life of its own."[651] So it is only with the benefit of hindsight that this judgment stayed in the history of the landmark judgments of Union private law due to its laying down of the foundations of an active court in consumer litigation. However, at the time it was decided, the most challenging question was the potential horizontal effect of the Unfair Contract Terms Directive[652] which had not yet been transposed in Spain, although the period of transposition had elapsed.[653]

The issue arose within the framework of the "juicio de cognición" procedure, a summary procedure available only for actions involving limited amounts of money.[654] The actions were initiated by a professional against consumers who purchased encyclopedias by installments and defaulted on the sums due. The contracts of purchase included an exclusive jurisdiction clause in favor of the seat of the trader (*cláusula de sumisión*) in Barcelona, a city where none of the defendants was domiciled. The referring court considered such a clause to be unfair, in which case it would have to declare the action inadmissible.

649 *Océano Grupo* (n. 646).

650 Case C-415/11 *Aziz*, EU:C:2013:164. When asked, Judge Dr. José María Fernández Seijo, who referred the questions in both cases (*Aziz* and *Océano Grupo*), which judgment he considered more fundamental for the doctrine of the active consumer court, he said that he considered it to be *Océano Grupo*, despite the fact that the second case, *Aziz*, attracted more publicity due to the mortgage crisis in Spain.

651 F. Nicola and E. Tichadou, "Océano Grupo: A Transatlantic Victory for the Consumer and a Missed Opportunity for European Law" *in* F. Nicola and B. Davies (eds.) *EU Law Stories, Contextual and Critical Histories of European Jurisprudence* (Cambridge University Press, 2017), 369–390, 372 and 388.

652 Council Directive 93/13/EEC of 5 April 1993 on unfair terms in consumer contracts [1993] OJ L95/29 (hereinafter the Unfair Contract Terms Directive).

653 F. Nicola and E. Tichadou (n. 651) delve extensively on this aspect of the judgment. The fact that the Court maintained its position with regard to the absence of horizontal effect of directives and followed the conventional approach of harmonious interpretation, is considered by the authors as a "missed opportunity" for the constitutionalisation of European private law.

654 Between approximately €480 and €4,800.

The preliminary issue was whether the court was actually empowered to make the finding of unfairness of its own motion.

To begin with, the Court concurred with the view of the national court (itself following the case law of the *Tribunal Supremo*)[655] that the disputed contractual term was unfair. A term that confers exclusive territorial jurisdiction on the place where the seller or supplier has its principal place of business "satisfies all the criteria enabling it to be classed as unfair."[656] Due to the fact that the consumer is obliged "to submit to the exclusive jurisdiction of a court which may be a long way from his domicile," the costs related to appearing before the court especially in low-value cases, might lead him to "forgo any legal remedy or defense."[657] Such a term falls within the category of terms under the Annex of the Unfair Contract Terms Directive (paragraph 1(q)), which "have the object or effect of excluding or hindering the consumer's right to take legal action"[658] and it "must be regarded as unfair."[659]

The point which the national court intended to clarify was whether it should be possible for the national court considering a term to be unfair to raise the issue of its own motion. In the absence of procedural rules applicable specifically in the field of unfair terms, such intervention seemed be precluded pursuant to the civil procedural provisions applicable at that time.[660] A reference to the

655 The national court has made reference to the relevant jurisprudence of the *Tribunal Supremo* (Spanish Supreme Court) (*Océano Grupo* (n. 646), para. 18). On the unfairness of the "cláusula de sumisión", see Sentencia Tribunal Supremo, STS 4793/1997; Sentencia Tribunal Supremo, STS 1137/1998.

656 *Océano Grupo* (n. 646), para. 21.

657 Ibid., para 22.

658 A contractual term "conferring exclusive territorial jurisdiction on the seat of the trader" was explicitly included within the list of terms which may be regarded as unfair, according to the Spanish legislation transposing the Unfair Contract Terms Directive, Ley 7/1998 sobre condiciones generales de la contratación (Law 7/1998 on General Contractual Conditions) of 13 April 1998 (BOE No 89 of 14 April 1998), Chapter VI (see the Opinion of AG Saggio in *Océano Grupo*, (n. 646), point 19). However, the respective legislation was not in force at the material time (see *Océano Grupo* (n. 646), paras. 30–32).

659 In Case C-237/02 *Freiburger Kommunalbauten*, EU:C:2004:209, para. 23, the Court explains its rather conclusive stance on the unfairness of the term of exclusive jurisdiction in the *Océano Grupo* case. The disputed term in the latter case "was solely to the benefit of the seller and contained no benefit in return for the consumer … it thereby undermined the effectiveness of the legal protection of the rights which the [Unfair Terms] Directive affords to the consumer". Later case law would flesh out the abstract concepts of "good faith" and "significant imbalance" employed in the Unfair Contract Terms Directive, prompting H.-W. Micklitz and N. Reich, "The Court and Sleeping Beauty: The Revival of the Unfair Contract Terms Directive" (2014) 51 *CMLR* 771–808, to consider that we are edging towards a common EU understanding of unfairness.

660 The Spanish Civil Procedure Code of 3 February, 1881 (Ley de Enjuiciamiento Civil (LEC)) (BOE No 36 of 5 February 1881), Art. 74 provided that: "*En ningun caso se promoveran de offício las cuestiones de competencia en los asuntas civiles*" [In no case will questions of competence be raised by the courts of their own motion] (translated by the author). This law

Court of Justice on this specific point was needed as the decisions of national courts on the matter were inconsistent.[661] In addition, the Spanish state Counsel's Office (*Public Ministero*), when asked by the national court, had given a negative response as to the possibility of raising the issue of absence of jurisdiction of its own motion.[662]

The Court could have reasoned in terms of procedural autonomy to the effect that it falls upon each jurisdiction to govern the role of the courts and the parties in relation to pleas pertaining to unfair terms or reproduce the *Van Shijndel* reasoning. This was not the case. A purposive interpretation of the Unfair Contract Terms Directive would change the course of the application of Union law by the courts of their own motion.

*Océano Grupo* establishes a novel procedural rule intended to ensure effective consumer protection against the imposition of unfair terms. It is an innovative judgment in that it considers judicial empowerment as a matter inherent in the substantive content of the Unfair Contract Terms Directive and a corollary for its enforcement. The active stance of the national court in restoring the imbalance between the contractual parties/litigants is not a matter of procedural technicality. It encapsulates the materialization of the protection of the weaker party. To perceive the matter in this way presupposes a teleological[663] understanding of the Unfair Contract Terms Directive in light, today, of the constitutional references on a high level of consumer protection (Article 12 TFEU and Article 38 of the Charter). This approach is essential in order to enable the enforcement of the substantive rights conferred upon the consumer and to connect the positions of the weaker party in the contract and the weaker party in litigation. It is true that the Unfair Contract Terms Directive makes no direct reference to the procedural consequences of the finding of unfairness.[664] It is only by discerning the purpose of the related instrument that

was repealed by the new Spanish Civil Procedure Code (Ley de Enjuiciamiento Civil (LEC)) (Law 1/2000 of 7 January 2000 (BOE No 7 of 8 January 2000).

661 *Océano Grupo* (n. 646), para. 18.

662 Opinion of AG Saggio in *Océano Grupo* (n. 658), point 13.

663 On the teleological method in the Court's reasoning, see for example N. Fennelly, "Legal Interpretation at the European Court of Justice" (1996) 20 *Fordham International Law Journal* 656–679; M. Καράσης, "Σκέψεις για μία Ευρωπαική Μεθοδολογία του Δικαίου" (2011) *ΧρΙΔ* 401–407 (translated as: M. Karasis, "Reflections on European Legal Methodology" (2011) *Chronicles of Private Law* 401–407). On the teleological reasoning in the *Océano Grupo* line of case law, E. Ποδημάτα, "Η δικονομική μεταχείριση του ισχυρισμού από το άρθρ. ΑΚ 281. Αποτίμηση ορισμένων νομολογιακών θέσεων ιδίως σε αναφορά με τον έλεγχο καταχρηστικότητας ΓΟΣ κατ'άρθρ. 2 παρ. 6 ν. 2251/1994" (2008) Η *Χρονικά Ιδιωτικού Δικαίου* 673–679 (translated as: E. Podimata, "The procedural qualification of the objection deriving from Article 281 of the Civil Code: Assessment of the jurisprudential position in particular with respect to the control of unfairness under Article 2 para. 6 Law 2251/1994" (2008) H *Xronika Idiotikou Dikaiou* 673–679).

664 See the criticism voiced by G. Borges, "AGB-Kontrolle durch den EuGH" (2001) *Neue Juristische Wocherschrift* 2061–2062, at 2062, who considers that by contrast with the view

the consequences on the level of judicial empowerment could be established by means of extending the legal consequences of unfairness into the procedural field. This is corroborated by the qualification of the rules on unfair terms as a matter of public interest exceeding the judicial sphere of the individual consumer.

## 1.1. THE PURPOSIVE INTERPRETATION OF THE UNFAIR CONTRACT TERMS DIRECTIVE ALONG THE LINES OF THE FULL EFFECTIVENESS OF UNION LAW

The purposive interpretation of the Unfair Contract Terms Directive demonstrates that an active judge is the corollary to achieve the *effet utile* of the system of protection introduced by the Unfair Contract Terms Directive. An active court constitutes:

> a proper means both of achieving the result sought by Article 6 of the [Unfair Terms] Directive, namely, preventing an individual consumer from being bound by an unfair term, and of contributing to achieving the aim of Article 7, since if the court undertakes such an examination, that may act as a deterrent and contribute to preventing unfair terms in contracts concluded between consumers and sellers or suppliers.[665]

In view of this finding, the power of the courts to raise points of consumer law of their own motion is therefore considered to be the appropriate and necessary means to achieve both the aim of consumer protection in the specific case brought before them and the general aim of eliminating distortions in the market because of the persistence of unfair contractual practices which undermine consumer confidence.[666]

According to the reasoning of the Court, the entire scheme of the Unfair Contract Terms Directive is construed upon "the idea that the consumer is in a weak position vis-à-vis the seller or supplier, as regards both his bargaining power and his level of knowledge."[667]

---

of the Court, the Unfair Contract Terms Directive cannot be relied upon to determine the consequences of an ineffective jurisdiction clause for civil proceedings.

665 *Océano Grupo* (n. 646), para. 28.

666 As a result of the acknowledgment of the general aim of deterrence, the active role for the courts may also appear, to a certain extent, to be a means of policing the market. In Case C-472/10 *Invitel*, EU:C:2012:242, the Court established a connection between the remedy of seeking the invalidity of an unfair contractual term and the effectiveness of injunctive proceedings through extension of the force of *res judicata* to the consumers that were not party to the proceedings, but were bound by the same unfair term with the same professional. This connection prompts F. Cafazzi and S. Law, "Unfair Contract Terms – Effect of collective proceedings, Comment *Invitel*" in E. Terryn, G. Straetmans and V. Colaert (eds.), *Landmark Cases of EU Consumer Law in Honour of Jules Stuyck* (Cambridge, Intersentia, 2014), 653–676, 671, to speak of "a stronger regulatory function of national courts in policing contractual terms".

667 *Océano Grupo* (n. 646), para. 25.

There are two elements of procedural inequality that are identified. The first is that the consumer might not appear before the court because he is deterred by the costs of legal representation. The second is that where self-representation is allowed, there is the risk that the unsophisticated party ignores the law and the procedural means to defend his case. In view of those elements, the purpose of the Unfair Contract Terms Directive is to protect the weaker party in the contract, and the courts must be vested with the procedural means to ensure that this purpose is fulfilled. No decisive significance needs to be attached to the procedural behavior of the consumer in the same way that the substantive law does not accord legal significance to the fact that the consumer has signed the contract that contains the unfair terms.[668] Empowering the courts to evaluate the terms of the contract of their own motion therefore becomes a necessary procedural vehicle to achieve effective consumer protection. The need for a "positive action unconnected with the actual parties to the contract" as a means to correct the imbalance is corroborated by reference to Article 7 of the Unfair Contract Terms Directive, according to which Member States are required to implement adequate and effective means to prevent the continued use of unfair terms (Article 7, paragraph 1) and that those means are to include actions by consumer associations (Article 7, paragraph 2).[669]

It follows that the *Océano Grupo* authority was not construed upon the principle of national procedural autonomy and its limitations, but relied upon a purposive interpretation of the substantive provisions.

The *effet utile* of the Unfair Contract Terms Directive and the *effective protection* for the consumer required the acknowledgment of procedural consequences which flow from the weaker party protection *rationale*. According to the Opinion of AG Saggio, it did not appear to be possible to interpret national law in such a way as to recognize an active role for the court in such circumstances.[670] There were some indications to that effect, such as the negative opinion of the Public Minister Council's office and the legal assessment on behalf of the Spanish government.[671] Noting this incompatibility, AG Saggio argued along the lines of *Simmenthal*[672] and the principle of primacy of Union law. In his view, national procedural law should be set aside, given that: "in accordance with the general principle of primacy of Community law, national procedural provisions cannot be applied by a court unless they afford effective protection of the rights conferred by Community law."

---

668 Opinion of AG Saggio in *Océano Grupo* (n. 658), point 23.
669 *Océano Grupo* (n. 646), para. 27.
670 Opinion of AG Saggio in *Océano Grupo* (n. 658), points 27–30.
671 Reference to the observations of the Spanish government in Opinion of AG Saggio in *Océano Grupo* (n. 658), point 21.
672 Case 106/77 *Simmenthal*, EU:C:1978:49, paras. 17–24.

The principle of national procedural autonomy is only referred to in a footnote to the Opinion.[673] But overall, the Opinion makes a rather ingenious twist in the reasoning to the direction of "European procedural primacy."[674]

The reasoning of the Court is less explicit in relation to the primacy argument. However, by choosing to frame the case in terms of the full effectiveness of Union law, it would appear to belong to what Koen Lenaerts et al. have called the "second strand" of case law on the principle of effectiveness "in relation to upholding the principle of the primacy of Union law vis-à-vis national (procedural) law."[675]

The recognition of the powers of the courts as a matter of Union law could, however, encounter, in the specific case, a serious obstacle: the lack of horizontal effect of the directives. As has already been mentioned, when the case in the main proceedings arose, the Unfair Contract Terms Directive had not yet been transposed into national law.[676] Given that, according to the Opinion of AG Saggio, the conforming interpretation was not possible, he argued in favor of the application of the so-called "exclusionary" effect of directives,[677] according to which the rule of community law operates as a "parameter of legality."[678] Following this approach, the national court would not actually apply a provision of the non-transposed directive between private individuals, but "between two possible interpretations of the national provisions," it would simply be "called upon to give preference to the one that enables the result envisaged by the directive to be achieved."[679]

The Court contented itself with the *Marleasing*[680] doctrine of harmonious interpretation. Therefore, it left it to the national court to follow an interpretation of the national legislation on unfair terms applicable at the material time and pre-dating the Unfair Contract Terms Directive,[681] in a way that would allow it to "decline of its own motion the jurisdiction conferred on it by virtue of an unfair term."[682] It should be noted that the absence of the timely implementation

---

673 Opinion of AG Saggio in *Océano Grupo* (n. 658), note 14.

674 On which, J. Delicostopoulos, "Towards European Procedural Primacy in National Legal Systems" (2003) 9:5 *European Law Journal* 599–613.

675 K. Lenaerts et al., *EU Procedural Law* (Oxford, Oxford University Press, 2014), para. 4.05. see Chapter 1, Section 2.2.2.

676 The applicants brought their actions before the entry into force of the law transposing the Unfair Contract Terms Directive into Spanish law, namely Law 7/1998 (n. 658).

677 For which see, inter alia, P. Craig and G. De Búrca, *EU Law Texts and Materials* (Oxford, Oxford University Press, 5th ed., 2011), 207. *et seq.*

678 See the discussion on the related case law in the Opinion of AG Saggio in *Océano Grupo* (n. 658), points 30 *et seq.*

679 Ibid., point 31. See M. Carballo fidalgo and G. Paisant, "Première interprétation par la CJUE de la directive du 5 avril 1993 relative aux clauses abusives" *La Semaine Juridique Edition Générale*, no 15, 11 Avril 2001, II 10513, para. 14.

680 Case C-106/89 *Marleasing*, EU:C:1990:395.

681 The legislation pre-existing transposition was Ley General 26/1984 para la Defensa de los Consumidores y Usuarios (General Law 26/1984 for the Protection of Consumers and Users) of 19 July 1984 (BOE No 176 of 24 July 1984).

682 *Océano Grupo* (n. 646), paras. 30–32.

of the Unfair Contract Terms Directive into Spanish law did not impede the *Tribunal Supremo* from affirming its applicability along with the at that time existing legislation on unfair terms for the purpose of declaring the exclusive jurisdiction terms (*cláusula de sumisión*) unfair.[683]

## 1.2. THE PROTECTION OF THE CONSUMER AS MANDATORY LAW

Later case law would entrench the doctrine of the active consumer court within the quality of the provisions of the unfair terms legislation and of other rules of consumer protection law as "mandatory"[684] and as of "equal standing, to that of national rules that have, within the domestic legal system, the character of rules of public policy,"[685] pertaining to the "public interest."[686] In a broad sense, the protection of consumers from unfair terms has become a matter of *European public policy of protection.*[687]

### *1.2.1. The Original Consideration of the Unfair Terms Legislation as a Reflection of the Mandatory Rules of Economic Public Policy*

The Opinion of AG Saggio in *Océano Grupo*[688] foreshadows later developments with regard to the consumer protection legislation being viewed as mandatory law. Pursuant to Article 6(1) of the Unfair Contract Terms Directive, the unfair terms are "not [to] be binding on the consumer." Although the choice of the

683 See Tribunal Supremo STS 4793/1997: "Tal Directiva debía ser transpuesta al Derecho español, a más tardar el 31 de diciembre de 1994 … Lo cual no ha sucedido … En conclusión, aplicando tanto la Ley general para la defensa de los Consumidores y usuarios como la Directiva comunitaria, se estima abusiva la cláusula de sumisión del contrato de autos, lo que implica la nulidad de la misma (art. 10.4. de aquella ley) y su ineficacia (art. 6 de la Directiva)." [This Directive had to be tranposed into Spanish law, by 31 December 1994 at the latest … This did not occur … To conclude, applying both the [Law 26/1984 for the Protection of Consumers and Users], as well the Community Directive, the disputed exclusive jurisdiction clause should be regarded as unfair, which implies its nullity (Art. 10.4 of that law) and its inapplicability (Art. 6 of the Unfair Contract Terms Directive)." (translated by the author).

684 Case C-168/05 *Mostaza Claro* (n. 648), paras. 36–38; Case C-137/08 *VB Pénzügyi Lízing*, EU:C:2010:659; Case C-243/08 *Pannon GSM*, EU:C:2009:350, paras. 25–31.

685 Joined Cases C-154/15, C-307/15 and C-308/15, *Gutiérrez Naranjo*, EU:C:2016:980, para. 54.

686 Ibid., para. 56; Case C-227/08 *Martín Martín*, EU:C:2009:792, para. 28.

687 See N. Reich, "More clarity after '*Claro*'?" (2007) 1 *European Review Contract Law* 41–61, 60, arguing that the concept of "'ordre public' [(public policy)] … has now become a Community concept". By contrast J. Stuyck, "Case note under *Pannon GSM* and *Asturcom Telecommunicaciones*" (2010) 47 *CMLR* 879–898, 892, does not support the view that case law has established such a link but that the "consumer protection would rather seem to be a 'mere' 'public interest', not belonging, at the EU level, to 'public policy' or 'ordre public'.

688 Opinion of AG Saggio in *Océano Grupo* (n. 658).

specific civil law sanction is left to the Member States,[689] it is clear, according to the Opinion of AG Saggio, that:

> the choice effected by that wording entails conferring upon the provisions of the [Unfair Contract Terms Directive] the character of "mandatory" rules of "economic public policy" and that such mandatory character "cannot fail to be reflected in the powers conferred upon the national court."[690]

It follows that whatever sanction the Member States choose to impose for the use of an unfair term under national law, the plea of unfairness should not be construed as an objection to be raised by the consumer. Such a construction would be incompatible with the protective system of the Unfair Contract Terms Directive.

The interests defended therein, being "part of economic public policy, extend beyond the specific interests of the parties concerned."[691] The unfairness in consumer contracts "disperses" its detrimental effects beyond the legal sphere of the specific consumer that has signed the contract, undermining the legal order, and it cannot therefore be tolerated.[692] It should not be legally relevant for the judicial review of unfairness whether the consumer perceives himself the term as unfair and whether he makes a submission to that effect.[693] It is a different issue whether the consumer may opt to renounce protection, if after being informed of the unfairness, he does not wish to assert the non-binding status of the contested term.[694] Moreover, the independent judicial assessment on unfairness must be subject to contradictory debate.[695]

---

689 G. Paisant, "La lutte contre les clauses abusives des contrats dans l'Union européenne", in *Vers un code européen de la consommation, sous la direction de F. Osman* (Bruylant, Brussels 1998), 165–177, 174 ; H.-W. Micklitz, J. Stuyck and E. Terryn, *Cases, Materials and Text on Consumer Law, Ius Commune Casebooks for the common law of Europe* (Hart Publishing, 2010), 299. In particular, the German provision on unfair terms deprives them of any effect ("*unwirksam*", BGB §307 s1). In France the unfair terms are considered non-existent ("*non écrites*": L 241-1 Code de la Consommation). In Luxembourg they are deemed void and non-existent ("*nulle et non écrite*" : L. 211-2(1) Code de la Consommation). All provisions have the effect of absolute nullity. In the much later judgment of 21 December 2016 in Joined Cases C-307/15 and C-308/15 *Gutiérrez Naranjo and Others* (n. 685), para. 65, the Court clarified with regard to the provision of Art. 6 (1) of the Unfair Contract Terms Directive that the regulation by the national legislator of the protection guaranteed to consumers may not alter the "substance of that protection and thus affect the strengthening of the effectiveness of that protection".

690 Opinion of AG Saggio in *Océano Grupo* (n. 658), point 25.

691 Ibid, point 26.

692 For a cogent analysis of this point E. Podimata, "Standard Contract Terms and Rules of Procedure" in *Essays in Honour of Konstantinos D. Kerameus* (Sakkoulas/Bruylant, 2009), 1079–1105.

693 Later confirmed in Case C-397/11 *Jőrös*, EU:C:2013:340, para. 42.

694 As clarified in later case law in Case C-243/08 *Pannon GSM* (n. 684).

695 As clarified in later case law in Case C-472/11 *Banif Plus Bank*, EU:C:2013:88; Case C-488/11 *Asbeek Brusse*, EU:C:2013:341.

In order to establish the connection between the "economic public policy" expressed in the rules on the Unfair Contract Terms Directive, on the one hand, and the judicial powers, on the other hand, the Opinion of AG Saggio drew conclusions from comparative law. Maybe the most important influence was drawn from Italy, where AG Saggio had formerly served as a judge in the *Corte di Cassazione*. He observed that under the (then) new Article 1469(d) of the Italian Civil Code, unfair terms "are ineffective only in respect of the consumer and that ineffectiveness may be raised of its own motion by the court."[696] This provision is today to be found in Article 36(3) of the Italian Consumer Code (*Codice del Consumo*).[697]

The Opinion also referred to the provision of the French Consumer Code (*Code de la Consommation*) according to which the provisions on the unfair terms are an expression of "ordre public."[698] In his view, this classification should imply an *ex officio* role for the courts. Nevertheless, at the time of the Opinion, the *Cour de Cassation* refused to establish such a connection. Later cases, namely *Cofidis*[699] and *Rampion and Godard*,[700] would bring to light the "polemic" surrounding this restrictive approach of the *Cour de Cassation*.

Finally, the AG Opinion makes reference to Belgium, relying in particular on a study of Eric Balate,[701] who was arguing in favor of an *ex officio* role as a result of the *economic* public policy nature of the respective provisions on unfair terms. However, as a commentary by Jules Stuyck written at that time reveals,[702] the issue had not yet been settled in Belgium.[703] With the benefit of hindsight, it could be said that the position of Eric Balate was certainly progressive and

696 Opinion of AG Saggio in *Océano Grupo* (n. 658), note 12.

697 "La nullita 'opera soltanto a vantaggio del consumatore e puo' essere rilevata d'ufficio dal giudice". This is a "nullity of protection" (*nullità di protezione*). See M. Ebers, "Unfair Contract Terms Directive", in H. Schulte-Nölke, C. Twigg-Flesner, M. Ebers (eds.), *European Consumer Law Compendium* (Munich, Sellier, 2008), 243.

698 Then Art. L-132-1 *in fine*: "Les dispositions du présent article sont d'ordre public" (currently Art. L-212-3 which reads as follows: "Les dispositions du présent chapitre sont d'ordre public" (translation: "the provisions of this chapter [on unfair terms] are of public policy").

699 Case C-473/00 *Cofidis* (n. 647).

700 Case C-429/05 *Rampion and Godard*, EU:C:2007:575.

701 E. Balate, "Le contrôle des clauses abusives : premier bilan" (1997) *Droit de la consommation* DCCR 321–361; see also idem, "Le contrôle des clauses abusives : juge gardien du Code civil ressuscité ou juge entraineur" (1996) *Revue de Droit Commercial* R.D.C. - T.B.H 947–955.

702 J. Stuyck, "Case note *Océano Grupo*" (2001) 38 *CMLR* 719–737, 731 citing *Stijns* who in a publication of 2000 (Stuyck et al. (eds.), "Onrechtmatige bedingen" in *Recente wetswijzigingen inzake handlelspraktijken* (Kluwer, 2000), 230–235, concluded that the provisions of unfair terms served only private interests and that, therefore, they are not of public policy nature and cannot be invoked by the courts of their own motion.

703 See also with reference to case-law M. Ebers (n. 697) referring to a judgment of CA Mons, judgment of 29 Mars 1999, *Journal des Tribunaux* 1999, 604 which "pointed out that given the relative nullity it did not have the competence to assess the unfair character of terms of its own motion".

ahead of its time. It was a position that was also in line with that of Counsel Albert Meeùs, according to whom when a court raises of its own motion the provision of mandatory legislation intended for the protection of one of the parties, the jurisdiction of the court is actually "seised by the law."[704] Relying on this doctrinal approach, the Opinion of AG Saggio perhaps made a selective reading of the theories to be taken on board for the establishment of the Union active consumer court.

### 1.2.2. *At the Crossroads of Concepts*

It would appear from the above that at the time of the Opinion of AG Saggio (in 1999), there was no truly shared understanding on the role of the courts with regard to the rules pertaining to the protection from unfair terms. The Court draws inspiration from certain national legal theories on "mandatory law," "public interest" and "relative nullity." But then the Court molds the concepts into an autonomous Union understanding of the role of the courts in the context of Union consumer law litigation. It would still take a few years for the *ex officio* doctrine to mature and signal an evolution in the perception of the judicial role. The case law of the Court would be particularly influential to that effect.

Taking into account the fact that Member States remain competent to translate in their own legal orders the legal consequences of the finding of unfairness, the reasoning of the Court does not employ concepts which may have different nuances in the various national legal orders. The point of departure is the weaker position of the consumer and the attainment of the aim of not having him bound by unfair terms which would not be achieved if the latter were obliged to plead the unfairness. Whatever civil law consequences the Member States adopt, the sanctioning of the unconscious professional behavior needs to be performed by the courts of their own motion and not only *ope exceptionis*. The Court adopts a nuanced approach, somewhere at the *crossroads* of relative nullity and the consequences of absolute nullity. It is an approach that invites us to stop thinking across strict dichotomies and to privilege, as Patrick Wéry so intelligibly puts it, a "third path, between relative nullity with an ex officio power to the courts" ("troisième voie: celle de la nullité relative avec un pouvoir d'office reconnu au juge").[705] In the same vein, Elise Poillot suggests that the field of consumer law

---

704 A. Meeùs, "La notion de loi impérative et son incidence sur la procédure en cassation et sur l'office du juge", note sous Cass., 17 mars 1986 (1988) *Revue Critique de Jurisprudence Belge* 527.

705 P. Wéry, "Les clauses abusives relatives à l'inexécution des obligations contractuelles dans les lois de protection des consommateurs du 14 juillet 1991 et du 2 aout 2002" (2003) *Journal des Tribunaux*, 797–810, 808. See also C. Delforge, "Clauses abusives, office du juge et renonciation" (2008) 3 *Jurisprudence de Liege, Mons et Bruxelles* J.L.M.B., 93–100, naming this "voie hybride".

establishes a *sui generis* public policy, an "ordre public univoque," the intensity of which varies according to the type of interest protected.[706]

The Advocate General of the Belgian *Cour de Cassation*, Michel Palumbo, also held that the distinction between the provisions of mandatory law and the provisions of public policy is no longer absolute in substantive law, particularly in the field of consumer protection.[707] He found a reflection of this approach in the Preamble of the new sales law adopted in 2004, according to which:

> "Contrairement à la règle généralement admise selon laquelle une nullité relative ne peut jamais être soulevée d'office par le juge, il y a lieu de tenir compte, en cette matière, de la jurisprudence résultant de l'arrêt dit *Océano* ..."[708] [Contrary to the generally admitted rule that a relative nullity can never by raised by the court of its own motion, it is necessary to take into account, as far as this field of law [consumer law] is concerned the case law resulting from the *Océano* judgment] (translated by the author).

### *1.2.3. The Active Court and Impartiality*

If the various national approaches as to the contractual nullities and to the consequences attached with regard to the role of the courts cannot be a proper obstacle to the positive role of the courts, there is however an objection that is serious and has to be carefully considered. The objection is on the level of judicial independence. Do the courts breach their duty of impartiality by raising a plea in law of mandatory consumer law? The answer is in the negative. Being required to act positively in order to ensure the application of mandatory law, the court is not neutral (since it has to raise a plea that would otherwise not be pleaded), but it is impartial. Raising a rule of a mandatory nature to the benefit of the weaker party which the legislator intended to protect, the court does not take sides with the party by "whispering"[709] a plea in law. It exercises its function to adjudicate according to the law, provided that the facts are available and provided that the right of the parties to be heard on the plea raised by the court of its own motion is respected.[710] It acts, in the view of Magistrate Ghislain

---

706 E. Poillot, "Moyen d'ordre public"in N. Sauphanor-Brouillaud et al. (eds.), *Les Contrats de Consommation Règles Communes* (Paris, LGDJ 2013), para. 970.

707 Cour de Cassation, 3e Chambre, 28 Octobre 2013, *Pasicrisie Belge* No 556, 2066.

708 Preamble to the law of 1 September 2004, extract cited also in P. Wéry, *Droit des Obligations Vol. I* (Paris, Larcier, 2010), 320, note 52.

709 The expression is a translation in English from the following passage of J. Ghestin, G. Loiseau and Y. M. Serinet, *La formation du contrat, Vol. II : L'objet et la cause – Les nullités* (LGDJ, 4e ed., 2013), para. 2323 : "Le juge n'entend pas manquer à l'impartialité en 'soufflant' un moyen de nullité à l'une des parties".

710 This point is underlined by all authors supporting the judicial activism in consumer law proceedings. See Magistrat G. Poissonier, "Mode d'emploi du relevé d'office en droit de la consommation", *Contrats Concurrence Consommation* no 5, Mai 2009, étude 5; G. Poissonier, "Office du juge en droit de la consommation : une clarification bienvenue" (2008) *Recueil*

Poissonier, as a counterweight (*contre-pouvoir*) to the benefit of ensuring application of mandatory law.[711] By contrast, if the courts were required to stay neutral and passive in the name of judicial impartiality and let the weaker party forgo protection, without probably ever being aware of his rights, that would in essence amount to a breach of the right to a fair trial for the weaker party.[712] This is a distorted vision of impartiality. Judges Philippe Flores and Gérard Biardeaud[713] explain this as a phenomenon of "judicial Darwinism":

> Il est douteux de considérer que le juge qui ... reste inerte et, dans une espèce de darwinisme judiciaire, laisse la solution du litige dépendre uniquement de l'habileté respective des parties, respecterait son obligation d'impartialité ... Le rôle du juge n'est pas d'entériner le rapport des forces établi par les parties dans le cadre de la procédure, mais d'assurer le respect de l'équilibre voulu par le législateur ... En procédant au relevé d'office, le juge ne vole pas au secours d'une partie mais, au contraire, agit simplement en serviteur de la loi.[714]

## 1.3. THE TERMS COVERED BY THE DOCTRINE

*Océano Grupo* also sets the basis for the delineation of the ambit of the judicial control of unfairness, although the matter would be further clarified in subsequent judgments. Despite the fact that the question concerned specifically unfair jurisdiction terms, the reasoning would already seem to allow for a broader vision of the type of unfair terms covered, whether procedural or substantive.[715] Indeed, the underlying need to correct the imbalance between

---

*Dalloz* 1285; P. Flores/G. Biardeaud, "L'office du juge et le crédit à la consommation" (2009) *Recueil Dalloz* 2227.

711 G. Poissonier, "La CJCE franchit une nouvelle étape vers une réelle protection du consommateur" (2009) *Recueil Dalloz* 2312.

712 See on this point the observations of the French Sénat in *Rapport no 111 au nom de la commission des affaires économiques sur le projet de loi, pour le développement de la concurrence au service des consommateurs par M. Gérard Cornu*, Sénat de la session ordinaire de 2007–2008, 99–103.

713 P. Flores and G. Biardeaud, "L'office du juge et le crédit à la consommation" (2009) *Recueil Dalloz* 2227.

714 [One could doubt whether the passive court, which, in a kind of judicial Darwinism, lets the solution to the case depend solely upon the resourcefulness of the parties, respects its obligation of impartiality. The role of the courts is not to endorse the state of [the] power-relationship of the parties in the framework of the procedure. By taking positive action, the court does not assist one of the parties but, on the contrary, acts simply as [a] servant of the law](translated by the author).

715 In the paragraphs that form the core of the Court's reasoning (paras. 26–28) references is made to "*a term*" or "*une clause de contrat*" as opposed to "*the jurisdictional term*", thus leaving open a wider application of the *ex officio* powers to *any* term. *Cf.* an opposite understanding at the time J. Stuyck, "Note in *Océano Grupo*" (2001) 38 *CMLR* 719–737, 732 that "... the ruling of the Court is limited in two respects: only the unfair character of jurisdiction clauses

the trader and the consumer through positive action unconnected to the parties cannot be restricted only to terms conferring jurisdiction. An all-embracing approach for the unfairness control, nevertheless, entails evidential difficulties. Examining whether a term conferring jurisdiction is unfair for the consumer will probably require no more evidence than the contract (adduced by the party who relies on it) and elementary knowledge of geography (in order to ascertain the distance of the seized court on the basis of the unfair clause from the residence of the consumer). But the determination of unfairness of terms pertaining to the substance of the contractual relationship will not normally be an easy task. The Court will therefore correctly, in later case law constructing the details of application of the *ex officio* doctrine,[716] point out that the exercise of the judicial intervention is subject to the availability of *all the legal and factual elements* to the court, irrespective of which party advances them.[717]Yet, national courts are obliged to order investigation measures in order to ascertain the scope of application of the Unfair Contract Terms Directive.[718] The importance of the observance of fundamental procedural right of the parties to be heard before the court pronounces its judgment on a point it has raised of its own motion will also be stressed in future judgments.[719]

Even if future case law would still clarify the parameters of application of the doctrine, *Océano Grupo* is a very important judgment from a double perspective. It is the first preliminary reference on the application of the Unfair Contract Terms Directive and it is the first judgment on the *ex officio* role of the courts decided on the basis of the effectiveness and purpose of the law. It sets the main elements for a Union standard of procedural consumer protection at the level of the role of the courts.

---

is confirmed and only with respect to the admissibility of the claim must the national court be able to invoke that the clause is unfair".

716 See Case C-243/08 *Pannon GSM* (n. 684), para. 32; Case C-618/10 *Banco Español de Crédito*, EU:C:2012:349, para. 53.

717 Commenting on the importance of the role of the parties in advancing the facts, S. Whittaker, "Judicial interventionism and Consumer Contracts", (2001) 117 *The Law Quarterly Review* 215–220, at 217.

718 Case C-137/08 *VB Pénzügyi Lízing* (n. 684). With regard to the other consumer law directives, the Court would later adopt a more nuanced approach, ruling in its judgment in Case C-497/13 *Faber*, EU:C:2015:357, para. 46, that the principle of effectiveness requires the national court to determine whether the purchaser may be classified as a consumer, as soon as it has at its disposal the matters of facts and law necessary for that purpose or "*may have them at its disposal simply by making a request for clarification*".

719 Case C-472/11 *Banif Plus Bank* (n. 695); Case C-488/11 *Asbeek Brusse* (n. 695). On the application of the adversarial principle in case of *ex officio* assessment of the contractual unfairness in consumer contracts, see M. Carballo fidalgo and G. Paisant, "Première interprétation par la CJUE de la directive du 5 avril 1993 relative aux clauses abusives", *La Semaine Juridique Edition Générale no 15*, 11 Avril 2001, II 10513.

### 1.4. THE NATIONAL JUDGMENT

On the basis of the Court's ruling, the *Juzgado de Primera Instancia no 35 de Barcelona* rejected the application of the professionals concerned (the editorial companies) as inadmissible and ruled that the competent jurisdiction was that of the place in which the defendant was domiciled.[720] It is interesting to see in more detail the reasoning of the judgment which was based on a combined application of domestic case law and the ruling of the Court. The Unfair Contract Terms Directive was held to have direct effect, in accordance with the case law of the *Tribunal Supremo.*[721] In the assessment of the question as to whether the unfairness has to be considered *de oficio*, the judgment takes into account certain elements. The first element is drawn from the final consideration of the preamble of the Unfair Contract Terms Directive, which provides that "the courts ... of the Member States must have at their disposal adequate and effective means of preventing the continued application of unfair terms in consumer contracts," as well as from Article 7(1) of the Unfair Contract Terms Directive. The judgment further takes into account the case law of the *Tribunal Supremo* on the unfairness of exclusive jurisdiction clauses inserted into standard terms. Such clauses "operate in general to the detriment of the weaker party and distort the competence of the courts on the basis of the sole and unacceptable criterion of the convenience of one of the parties."[722] Reference is also made to case law from another first instance provincial court (the *Audiencia Provincial de Barcelona*) deciding in favor of a control *de oficio* of such unfair terms. The second part of the judgment cites the findings of the Court in *Océano Grupo.* On the basis of the above, the referring court reaches the conclusion that it has the power to raise the unfairness of the term concerned, that it lacks competence and that the nullity of such term means that only the courts of the consumer's domicile are competent.

## 2. *COFIDIS*: TURNING THE TIDE, FROM BARCELONA TO VIENNA VIA LUXEMBOURG

*Cofidis*[723] was a groundbreaking judgment, particularly for the French legal order with regard to the role of the courts in individual consumer proceedings. Its legacy would later be enshrined in the French law. Besides contributing to

---

720 Auto 200 of 28 June 2000.

721 According to the case law of the Tribunal Supremo referred to in the discussed national case (n. 720), even if the transposition of the Unfair Contract Terms Directive has not taken place, the Spanish courts have to act as Union courts.

722 Judgment of the Tribunal Supremo of 29 october 1993.

723 Case C-473/00 *Cofidis* (n. 647).

the building of the consumer *ex officio* doctrine, it demonstrates well the virtues of the judicial dialogue in the Union. The national court in the *Cofidis* case made its reference after finding in *Océano Grupo* the means to challenge the course of domestic case law. If the Barcelona court had recourse to Union law to derive the necessary powers to set aside of its own motion an unfair jurisdiction clause, could the court of Vienna do the same and raise of its own motion the unfairness of contractual clauses pertaining to substance, despite the elapse of a foreclosure period? The judge who made the reference in *Cofidis*, Etienne Rigal, would indeed find in *Océano Grupo* the means to challenge the powerful but much-contested case law of the *Cour de Cassation* with regard to the role of the courts in consumer law proceedings. He discovered, as novelist Emmanuel Carrère so eloquently describes it, "the crucial move that [would] change the tide of battle."[724]

*Cofidis*, decided two years after the *Océano* judgment, contributed to the theoretical construction of the active consumer court doctrine as an autonomous Union procedural standard. Such a procedural standard would prevail over national procedural rules that undermine the effectiveness of the protective consumer legislation. The restriction of the application of the doctrine only to matters of jurisdiction is implicitly rejected. The setting of limitation periods or foreclosure periods for the raising of unfairness, either as a claim or more often as an objection of the consumer-defendant, is excluded.

## 2.1. THE "POLEMIC" SURROUNDING THE QUESTION IN *COFIDIS*

The question referred from the French court (*Tribunal d'instance de Vienne*) concerned the compatibility of a legal provision (former Article L-311-37 of the French Consumer Code), with effective consumer protection. This provision stated that the actions brought before the first instance court (*tribunal d'instance*) "must be raised within two years of the events which give rise to them and are otherwise time-barred."[725] The biannual foreclosure period has been interpreted

724 In E. Carrère, *Other lives but mine* (tr. Linda Coverdale) (London, Serpent's Tail, 2012), 179, we are immersed in the emotions of the moment when Judge Etienne Rigal reads the ruling in *Océano Grupo*: "One October day in 2000, Étienne is in his office leafing through some law reviews. He comes across a commentated decision by the European Court of Justice, which he begins to read casually, then with increasing attention ... Étienne and Juliette have been fighting a battle the outcome of which will affect the lives of tens of thousands of individuals. For months they've been suffering one rout after another; they were about to admit defeat, and now Étienne has discovered the crucial move that will change the tide of the battle."

725 "Le Tribunal d'instance connait des litiges nés de l'application du présent chapitre. Les actions engagées devant lui doivent être formés dans les deux ans de l'évènement qui leur a donné naissance à peine de forclusion."

in such a way as to cover not only actions brought by the creditor but also actions by the borrower who could no longer contest, either in the form of a claim or defense, the credit contract on the basis of the breach of the legal formalities set out by the law for the conclusion of the consumer credit contract.[726] The starting date for the calculation of the biannual period was moreover determined as from the date of the conclusion of the contract. The wording and the systematic reading of the provision left doubts as to whether the plea of unfairness should also be deemed to be covered by the foreclosure period.[727] With the benefit of hindsight, in view of the subsequent legislative amendment that clarified the true meaning of the provision,[728] now it can be stated with certainty that the purpose of that provision was not to impose a time limit upon the raising of the plea of unfairness. According to the current wording of the provision: "The first instance court is competent for the disputes which arise out of the application of the present chapter [on consumer credit]. The actions for payment that are brought before it by reason of default by the borrower shall be time-barred two years after the event giving rise to them occurred [...]."[729]

The law had been respectively modified when the Court had to decide the case, but it was applicable in the material time. If the meaning of the provision is now clear, this was not the case back in 2001. Certain observations appear necessary in order to put the question into its national context. If the facts of *Cofidis* are read in isolation from the national legal context, there might be a first impression that the French law had established a blunt unfairness to the detriment of the consumer. But such an impression could be rebutted, considering that it would appear at least absurd that the legislator[730] would establish forthright procedural unfairness within an instrument that intends to protect consumers. Once we delve deeper into the national context, the reasons behind the doubts as to the meaning of the law entertained by the national court clearly appear. The reference is a conscious move (if not a move of resistance) from a lower court to change the course of the much-criticized case law of the *Cour de*

---

726 See G. Biardeaud and P. Flores, *Le contentieux du droit de la consommation, Vol. I Le crédit aux consommateurs* (Bordeaux, Ecole Nationale de la Magistrature, 2005); G. Biardeaud and P. Flores, *Crédit à la consommation, Protection du consommateur* (Delmas Express, 2012).

727 The Opinion of AG Tizzano in Case C-473/00 *Cofidis*, EU:C:2002:239, makes it much clearer that the Court had to decide on the basis of a certain *assumption* of the legal meaning of the disputed provision that it could also cover the defence of unfairness.

728 Loi 2001-1168 du 11 décembre 2001 portant mesures urgentes de réformes à caractère économique et financier (Law 2001-1168 of 11 December 2001 on urgent measures of reform of an economic and financial nature, the so called "Loi MURCEF").

729 Article R 312-35 Code de la Consommation "*[...] Les actions en paiement engagées devant lui à l'occasion de la défaillance de l'emprunteur doivent être formées dans les deux ans de l'événement qui leur a donné naissance à peine de forclusion [...]*" (translated by the author).

730 The original law was Law 78-23 of 10 January 1978, known also as *Loi Scrivener*, from the name of the responsible secretary of state for consumer law matters (*Sécretaire d'Etat à la Consommation*) Ms. Christiane Scrivener (known as "Madame consommation").

*Cassation* and to ensure that it would not be applicable to the plea of unfairness. Even the personal story behind the scenes of *Cofidis* reveals the commitment of the referring judge, Etienne Rigal, toward the defense of the protective spirit of consumer law. Like many of his colleagues, he firmly believed that:

> "la loi est là pour tout le monde ... elle protège les esprits faibles contre ceux qui veulent en profiter" [The law is made for everyone ... it protects the weak against those who wish to take advantage of their weakness] (translated by the author).[731]

Setting a foreclosure period in putting forward a plea of unfairness, would appear to be a "Trojan horse" to strip consumer law of its protective scope. Only a purposive interpretation could reveal that the true purpose should have been to prevent the accrual of interest and consumer overindebtedness by inciting the creditor to act promptly and with due diligence.[732] Nevertheless, the interpretation of the provision in question by the *Cour de Cassation* has resulted in the obscuring of its true meaning.[733] According to its case law (developed under the original version of the provision), the borrower could no longer contest, in the claim or defense, the credit contract on the basis of breach of the legal formalities once the biannual foreclosure period had elapsed. The starting date for the calculation of the biannual foreclosure period was considered to be the conclusion of the contract.[734] The principle of legal certainty was the reason behind the adoption of this stance by the *Cour de Cassation*.[735] The particular chapter of the French Consumer Code, within which the foreclosure period is integrated, sets specific formality requirements that need to be respected by the creditor in the conclusion of the contract. The borrower has two years to peruse the contract and to raise any formal irregularities. The breach of certain of those formalities results in depriving the creditor of the right to

731 Interview by Claire Chartier of M. Etienne Rigal: C. Chartier, "Etienne Rigal, juge des plus faibles" *L'Express* 19.03.2009, <http://www.lexpress.fr/actualite/economie/etienne-rigal-juge-des-plus-faibles_748039.html> accessed 02.10.2017. Judge Etienne Rigal has inspired the novelist E. Carrère to write the book *Other lives but mine*, (n. 724), upon which the film "Toutes nos envies" is based (directed by P. Lioret, the role of the judge is brilliantly played by Vincent Lindon).

732 P. Flores and G. Biardeaud, "La protection de l'emprunteur : une notion menacée" (2000) *Recueil Dalloz* 191; G. Biardeaud and P. Flores (n. 726), para. 2001.

733 Cass. avis, 9 octobre 1992, *Bull. avis* no 4 ; Cass. civ. 1re, 15 décembre 1998, Bull. civ. I, no 365; Cass. civ. 1re, 15 juillet 1999, Bull. civ. I, no 246; Cass. civ. 1re, 15 février 2000, Bull. civ. I, no 49.

734 Cass. avis 9 octobre 1992, Bull. avis no 4 ; Cass. civ. 1re, 15 décembre, Bull. civ. I, no 365 ; Cass. civ. 1re. 15 juillet 1999, Bull. civ. I, no 246 (application to guarantee contracts), Cass. civ. 1re, 15 février 2000, Bull. civ. I, no 49;

735 Cass. civ. 1re., 15 décembre 1998, *Dalloz Affaires* 1999, 330; X. Lagarde, "Forclusion biennale et Crédit à la Consommation. Réforme de l'article L.311-37 du Code de la Consommation" (2002) *La Semaine Juridique, Edition Générale* no 4, I 106.

contractual interest.[736] The position favoring the application of the biannual foreclosure period considered that under the principle of legal certainty, the severity of the sanction imposed required that a certain period be set within which those irregularities could be raised.[737] Xavier Lagarde considered that the foreclosure is a way to constrain an act of bad faith (*mauvaise foi*) on the part of the consumer, in the case of which he might initiate an action of breach of the formal requirements for the formation of the contract years after the conclusion of the contract with the purpose of obtaining a free credit.[738]

The objective of combatting bad faith being legitimate as such, the restrictive interpretation of the application of the foreclosure period actually led to unfair results. The starting point of the foreclosure period was interpreted in such a way as to create different treatment between the creditor and the consumer. The creditor had two years to make his claim from the moment of default on the part of the consumer,[739] but the consumer could only raise the eventual breach of the provisions of the law (set for his protection) within two years from the conclusion of the contract.[740] Given that the foreclosure period was interpreted to cover all disputes in relation to the consumer credit contract either initiated by the creditor or the consumer, it then also covered all procedural means of action and defense on the part of the consumer.[741] The resulting effect was the creation of a procedural imbalance between creditors and consumers, which was rigorously criticized not only in academia but also by first instance judges.[742] The creditor could legally initiate action for payment after the elapse of the two-year foreclosure period, while at that stage it would be no longer possible for

736 Currently Art. L341-2 Code de la Consommation.

737 See also V.N. Monachon-duchene, "La forclusion en matière de crédit à la consommation" *Jurisclasseur Périodique Edition Générale* 1995, I, 3655; A. Gourio, "Le délai de forclusion en matière du crédit à la consommation" (2000) *RD bancaire et financier* 201 et seq.

738 X. Lagarde (n. 735).

739 Cass. civ. 1re, 7 février 1995, Bull. civ. I, no 77; Cass. civ. 1re., 4 juin 1996, Bull. civ. I, no 238; Cass. civ. 1re., 10 avril 1996: Bull. civ. I, no 178.

740 Cass., opinion, 9 Octobre 1992: Bull. civ. Avis no 04: "Le point de départ du délai de forclusion opposable à l'emprunteur qui conteste la régularité de l'offre préalable, par voie d'action ou d'exception, est la date à laquelle le contrat de crédit est définitivement formé". [The start date of the foreclosure period that can be objected to the borrower who contests the regularity of the preliminary offer, by means of action or defense, is the date on which the credit contract is definitely concluded] (translated by the author).

741 Cass., opinion, 9 October 1992, Bull. civ. Avis no 04, finding that when a foreclosure period is set, the rule according to which *l'exception survit à l'action* (the objection "survives" the action) is not applicable.

742 G. Biardeaud and F. Flores, "La protection de l'emprunteur, une notion menacée" (2000) *Recueil Dalloz* Chron. No 12, 191. Indirectly, the position of the *Cour de Cassation* was criticized by the opposing decisions of the first instance courts that were quashed at the supreme judicial level (see the judgment of the *Cour d Appel* de Bourges, 8 December 1993, quashed by the *Cour de Cassation* in Cass. civ. 1re,3 janvier 1996, Bull. civ. I, no 11; also CA Bordeaux, 30 avr. 1998, Contrats, conc., consom. 1998, no 138; CA Versailles, 1re ch. B, 19 mars 1999, (1999 *Dalloz Affaires* 895).

the consumer to contest payment on the basis of the breach of the legal provisions. This is a vicious effect[743] of deviation from the *quae temporalia sunt ad agendum, perpetua sund ad excipiendium* rule, which allows submissions that can no longer be adduced as claims to be invoked as a defense. In commercial relations, legal certainty might have to prevail over the foundation of "morality"[744] underlying the principle *queae temporalia.* But a deviation is not justified with regard to non-sophisticated parties protected by consumer legislation. In principle, the consumer will seek professional advice and discover irregularities to the contract once the default occurs and he will be taken to court. The default can easily occur after the elapse of two years (the foreclosure period) since the conclusion of the contract. As Judges Philippe Flores and Gérard Biardeaud note, by contrast with professionals, who have no difficulty in adapting to the requirements of the provision in question, the consumer-borrower will not seise the courts, fearing a lengthy and costly litigation process.[745] In addition, according to the prevailing, at the time interpretation, not only the consumer was stripped of his means of defense but also the courts did not have the power to raise of their own motion the irregularities of the contract.[746] For those reasons, the aforementioned authors took a highly critical view on the way in which the contested provision was interpreted at the time, speaking of a "procedural paralysis" and of a "movement of evaporation of consumer law."[747]

As to the extension of the application of the biannual foreclosure period to the plea of unfairness of a contractual term, this was still in doubt when the national court made the reference. The French government had acknowledged the existing uncertainty since the *Cour de Cassation* had not yet had the occasion

---

743 See obs. L. Leveneur, in Cass. civ. 1re civ., 19 déc. 1995, D. 1996, Somm. 327.

744 See M. Storck, "L'exception de nullité en droit prive" (1987) *Recueil Dalloz* Chron. No 10, 67–72; See G. Biardeaud and P. Flores, "La protection de l'emprunteur, une notion menacée" (n. 742), II A.

745 Ibid., G. Biardeaud and P. Flores, II B: "Or, si les professionnels n'ont guère eu de difficulté à s'adapter aux exigences de l'art. L-311-37 c. consom. pour mettre en place des systèmes de recouvrements rapides et efficaces, il n'en va pas de même pour les emprunteurs. Nos concitoyens répugnent en effet à se présenter devant une justice dont ils ignorent et craignent le fonctionnement et le coût." [If professionals have had no difficulty in adapting to the requirements of Art. L-311-37 of the Consumer Code in order to put in place rapid and efficient systems of debt recovery, the same is not true for the borrowers. Our fellow citizens are reluctant to appear before a justice they do not know, and they fear the operation and cost] (translated by the author).

746 Cass. civ. 1re, 15 février 2000, Bull. civ. I, no 49 : "Vu les articles L. 311-2, L-311-8 et L.311-10 du Code de la Consommation; Attendu que la méconnaissance des exigences des textes susvisés, même d'ordre public, ne peut être opposée qu'à la demande de la personne que ces dispositions ont pour objet de protéger." [Considering articles L.311-2, L-311-8 and L.311-10 of the Consumer Code, and considering that the breach of the requirements set out in those articles, even of public policy nature, cannot only be invoked by the person which those provisions have as an objective to protect] (translated by the author).

747 See G. Biardeaud and P. Flores (n. 742).

to rule on the point.[748] The referring court therefore intended to ensure that the objection of unfairness would not be subject to the same procedural regime of foreclosure as the plea based on the breach of the provisions on the formalities on the conclusion of the consumer credit contract.[749] If that would be the case, the national law would jeopardize the effectiveness of Union law on unfair terms. Hence, the Court's ruling was given on the basis of the assumption that the foreclosure period also referred to the raising of the plea of unfairness.[750]

## 2.2. THE CONTRIBUTION OF *COFIDIS* ON THE BUILDING OF THE ACTIVE CONSUMER COURT DOCTRINE

In substance, the reasoning of the Court was made along the lines of *Océano Grupo*.[751] In order to ensure effective protection of the consumer, the courts should have the power to determine of their own motion the unfairness of contractual terms. This is so in view of the real risk that the consumer is unaware of his rights or that he encounters difficulties in enforcing them.[752] Such power

748 Case C-473/00 *Cofidis* (n. 647), para. 19.

749 The French Judge G. Poissonier, "Panorama des clauses abusives en droit français du crédit à la consommation" (2006) 3 *Revue européenne de droit de la consommation* 171–198, 174, explains that a contractual clause that would contravene the legal requirements of "model contracts" set out in the *Code de la Consommation* (following legislative reform by the Law of July 1 2010, the various model contracts were substituted by a unique form of precontractual information and a unique model contract), would be deemed *illegal* with respect to the public policy legislation but also *unfair* since it infringes the rights that this law guarantees for the consumers. (Original text: "Une disposition 'contractuelle' contraire aux dispositions du modèle type ou aux mentions légales obligatoires est nécessairement abusive en ce sens qu'elle octroie au professional un avantage et impose au consommateur un renoncement à un droit garanti par la loi. Ce faisaint, le juge constate que la clause 'contractuelle' crée 'un désequilibre significatif au détriment du consommateur entre les droits et les obligations du contrat' ... alors même que la loi a précisément crée les modèles types pour établir un équilibre contractuel entre les parties inégales").

750 Case C-473/00 *Cofidis* (n. 647), para. 24: "As to the question whether or not the limitation period under Article L.311-37 of the Code de la consommation applies to unfair terms, that is a question of national law which as such is not within the jurisdiction of the Court."

751 It has to be noted that *Cofidis* had argued that the question was inadmissible. More specifically, it had argued that the disputed terms in the contract merely reflected mandatory provisions (reproducing a model contract set up by the law) and were therefore excluded from the scope of the Unfair Contract Terms Directive. It was also contesting the premise upon which the national court was based, in the sense that that provision would applicable to the unfair terms. The Court ruled that it was not obvious that the terms employed in the contract fell outside the scope of the Unfair Contract Terms Directive as the referring court criticized their legibility. The national court found that *Cofidis* did not respect the rules of model contracts set by the law law or from the Commission on Unfair terms in relation to the presentation of interest clauses. The disputed contractual clause was illegible and the reference in the first side of the leaflet to an ostensible gratuity of the credit could deceive the consumer.

752 Case C-473/00 *Cofidis* (n. 647), para. 33.

does not exist merely in relation to the examination by the national court of its own jurisdiction. The French government attempted to distinguish the present case from the *Océano Grupo* case on the basis of the difference between a legislative provision setting a time-limit as opposed to a term conferring exclusive jurisdiction. This argument did not prosper. The active role of the court had started to take shape as a doctrine of European origin that would have to infiltrate national procedural rules. The Court rejected the argument of the French government by explaining that a time limit, such as that in the main proceedings in *Cofidis*, which would also cover the powers of the courts to raise an unfair terms of their own motion, would be "liable to affect the effectiveness of the protection" intended by the Unfair Contract Terms Directive. If it were otherwise, the risk of moral hazard would arise as: "sellers or suppliers would merely have to wait until the expiry of the time-limit fixed by the national legislature before seeking enforcement of the unfair terms they would continue to use in contracts."[753]

The moral hazard argument has deeper origins in the equity rationale expressed in the adage *quae temporalia sunt ad agendum, perpetua sunt ad excipendium.*[754]

Reference is also being made in the judgment to the criterion of *excessive difficulty* of enforcement of the rights derived from the Unfair Contract Terms Directive.[755] Given that the procedural rule in question prevented the national court from exercising its powers to ensure the unenforceability of an unfair term, it rendered the realization of the protection that the Unfair Contract Terms Directive intended to confer on the consumers excessively difficult. For this reason it was incompatible with Union law.

An important aspect of the *Cofidis* judgment is that it confirms the all-embracing remit of the *ex officio* powers as to the scope of the contractual terms covered. The Court indirectly rejected the submission that the power of the courts pronounced in *Océano Grupo* concerned merely a power to decline jurisdiction. The acknowledgment of the scope of the *ex officio* powers with respect to substantive terms is a very important finding. The control of jurisdictional terms by the courts of their own motion can be considered a specific expression of the principle that the courts examine *ex officio* the compliance with the general procedural requirements for initiating proceedings.[756] There is no

---

753 Ibid., para. 35.

754 See M. Storck, "L'exception de nullité en droit privé" (1987) *Recueil Dalloz* Chron. No 10, 67–72, 67.

755 Case C-473/00 *Cofidis* (n. 647), para. 36.

756 When it comes specifically to territorial jurisdiction national laws may provide that it is upon the defendant to put forward the defense of incompetent jurisdiction. This was besides the case under the general rules (not with regard to the consumers) of Spanish civil procedural law (as explained in *Océano Grupo* case above Section 1) as well as French law (Art. 93 of the French civil procedural law (Nouvelle Code NCPC) provides that: "En matière gracieuse,

doubt that such a limited remit of the *ex officio* powers would have been more evident for national legal systems to accommodate and more straightforward to implement compared to the control of substantive terms. In such a case, it would probably have even gone unnoticed and it would not bring about the significant enhancement of the procedural protection of consumers resulting from the active consumer court doctrine.

## 2.3. THE NATIONAL JUDGMENT AND THE EVOLUTION IN LEGISLATION AND CASE LAW

Following the ruling in *Cofidis*, the *Tribunal d'Instance de Vienne* proceeded with an unfairness assessment and ruled against those particulars of the creditor's claim that corresponded to the unfair clauses.[757] In particular, the national court considered that the clauses on the contractual interest and on the default interest rate were not transparent, lacked legibility and could therefore induce the consumer to err in the conclusion of the contract.[758] On the basis of those

---

le juge peut relever d' office son incompétence territoriale. Il ne le peut, en matière contentieuse, que dans les litiges relatifs à l'état des personnes, dans les cas où la loi attribue compétence exclusive à une autre juridiction ou si le défendeur ne comparait pas". (Translation: "In non-contentious matters, the judge may raise *sua sponte* his lack of territorial jurisdiction. He may do so, in contentious matters, only in litigations relating to the status of persons, in cases where the law has conferred exclusive jurisdiction to another court or where the defendant does not appear"). Restrictive conditions can nevertheless be placed for recourse to exclusive jurisdiction agreements when the contracting parties are not legal persons. This is the case in Germany, see §38-40 ZPO and in France (Art. 48 NCPC: "Toute clause qui, directement ou indirectement, déroge aux règles de compétence territoriale est réputée non écrite à moins qu'elle n'ait été convenue entre des personnes ayant toutes contracté en qualité de commerçant et qu'elle n'ait été spécifiée de façon très apparente dans l'engagement de la partie à qui elle est opposée." (Translation: "Any clause that departs, directly or indirectly, from the rules of territorial jurisdiction will be deemed non-existent unless it has been agreed between parties to a contract entered into as merchants and the same has been provided for in an explicit manner in the undertakings of the party against whom it will be enforced").

757 Tribunal d'Instance de Vienne, Judgment of 16 May 2003, No 11-00-001014, *Cofidis c/Fredout* (Base de données Dalloz): "La Cour a retenu que la fixation d'une limite temporelle au pouvoir du juge d'écarter de telles clauses était de nature à porter atteinte à l'effectivité de la protection du consommateur voulue par la directive". [The Court decided that the setting of a temporal limitation upon the power of the court to set aside such clauses would breach the effectiveness of the consumer protection intended by the Directive] (translated by the author).

758 Ibid.: "Mais, surtout, comme l'a relevé la Cour de justice des Communautés Européennes, les dites clauses ne se limitaient pas à cette reproduction [du modèle type], l'ambigüité étant, avant tout, la conséquence de l'emploi d'un intitulé ("demande gratuite de réserve d'argent"), qui ne figure bien évidemment pas au modèle réglementaire". : [But, above all, as the Court ruled, those clauses did not limit themselves to the reproduction [of the model type of consumer credit contract], their ambiguity resulting, above all, from the use of a title ('cost-free request of credit facility'), which it is evident does not appear in the regulatory model.] (translated by the author).

findings, the French court declared "non écrites" the stipulations on contractual and default interest, which in essence sanctioned the creditor by divesting him of the remuneration of the credit.[759] The consumer, Mr Fredout, was ordered to pay only the capital due.

By the time the judgment was rendered, the disputed provision had been amended, putting an end to the ambiguity which led to situations of procedural inequality. The amendment would bring about clarity as to the personal ambit of the contested provision, to the effect that only the payment action brought by the creditor would be subject to the biannual foreclosure period.[760] With the new wording, the purpose of the law was reinstated. It became clear that the foreclosure period aims to avoid situations of overindebtedness due to the accumulation of default interest. The foreclosure period did not impede the consumer, acting either as a plaintiff or most commonly as a defendant, from raising the irregularities of the contract or, *a fortiori*, the unfairness of the contract. However, its temporal effect was restricted only to contracts concluded *after* its promulgation.[761] As far as contracts concluded prior to the promulgation of the new law, the *Cofidis* case should serve as a bastion against any interpretation that

759 Ibid.: "La société COFIDIS indique que l'annulation de ces clauses d'intérêts et de pénalité constituerait une sanction excessive, aboutirait à modifier l'équilibre contractuel, en transformant indument un crédit à intérêts en crédit gratuit. Elle ajoute que déclarer nulles les dites clauses opérait 'un dévoiement de la notion de clauses abusives'. Une telle annulation manquerait de 'base légale'. Cependant, il n'appartient pas au juge d'apprécier le bien-fondé de la sanction prévue par le législateur, en l'article L 132.1 alinéa 6 du code de la consommation, lequel dispose que les clauses abusives sont 'réputées non écrites'. Il doit être ajouté que la dite sanction est applicable y compris s'agissant des clauses relatives au prix. Le tribunal annulera la stipulation d'intérêts conventionnels et la clause pénale du contrat objet du litige." [The company Cofidis notes that the annulment of the interest rate clauses and the penalty clause would be an excessive sanction and would result in modifying the contractual balance by unduly transforming a credit with interest to a free credit. It adds that if the relevant clauses would be declared invalid this would lead to 'a misuse of the concept of unfair terms'. Such annulment would lack a 'legal basis'. However, it is not for the court to assess the legitimacy of a sanction provided for by the legislator, in Art. L. 132-1(6) of the Consumer Code, which provides that the unfair terms are 'deemed unwritten'. It should be added that this sanction is applicable also with regard to terms related to the price. The court annuls the term on contractual interest and the penalty clause of the contract in question.] (translated by the author).

760 Loi MURCEF (n. 728). The actions or objections on the basis of breach of the formal requirements set out by the law would then have to be subject to the common regime of limitations according to X. LAGARDE, "Forclusion biennale et Crédit à la Consommation. Réforme de l'article L.311-37 du Code de la Consommation" (2002) *La Semaine Juridique, Edition Générale* no 4, I 106; the author criticizes the new law, pointing out that it could also lead to the unintended effect of inciting the consumer to take advantage to the formalities set out in the Consumer Code in order to obtain the civil sanction of the divestiture of interest. Instead, the author proposes that the entire regime of the formalities set should be replaced by a rigorous judicial unfairness control and pre-formulated contractual terms agreed at collective level.

761 Art. 16 (II-3) Loi MURCEF (n. 728).

would impose a limitation period for the raising of pleas of contractual unfairness. The same should apply with regard to contracts vitiated by formal irregularities. Although this had not originally been the approach of the *Cour de Cassation*,[762] in subsequent case law, that court employed the biannual foreclosure in a way that Philippe Flores and Gérard Biardeaud acknowledge as "inventive", with the objective of penalizing "certain practices of granting excessive credit."[763] This is in line with the central finding of *Cofidis*. The powers of the courts cannot be subject to the same limitations as the actions of the parties because these powers are recognized in order to uphold the law.[764] Moreover, in the French context, the European or domestic origin of the formality requirements does not appear to be decisive for the exercise of the *ex officio* powers. The French legislator includes among the rules qualified as *ordre public* the provisions pertaining to the formalities that have to be respected in the conclusion of consumer credit contracts (L314-26 *Code de la Consommation*). It also extends the *ex officio* powers of the courts to all the provisions of the Consumer Code. (R632-1 *Code de la Consommation*). From the moment that the *ex officio* doctrine applies to all the protective provisions of the code, the modalities of its application (including the exclusion of a time-limit within which the *ex officio* powers should be exercised) should be uniform.[765]

In his Opinion in *Cofidis*, AG Tizzano[766] notes the importance of the precedent setting by this judgment for the national legal orders on the issue of unfairness

762 Cour Cass. civ. 1re, 2 octobre 2002, Bull. civ. I no 229. The reasoning of the *Cour de Cassation* reiterates its case law prior to the Loi MURCEF, given its lack of temporal applicability.

763 P. Flores and G. Biardeaud, "L'office du juge et le crédit à la consommation" (2009) *Recueil Dalloz* 2227. The authors (both judges in France) give case law examples in which the court had applied the peremptory time-limit to contracts under which the grant of credit had been tacitly (not explicitly) renewed and had exceeded the initial amount borrowed, and the court thereby declared as inadmissible the creditors' actions. The creditors had not, as was required by law, made a prior offer to the debtors (Cass. civ. 1re, 7 décembre 2004, Bull. civ. I, no 304 and 305; Cass. civ. 1re, 30 mars 2005, Bull. civ. I, no 159).

764 Rightly therefore, Ghislain Poissonier criticizes a jurisprudential line of the Paris Court of Appeal (CA Paris of 6 July 2017 RG 16/14519 and of 11 January 2018, RG 16/12948) according to which the courts are barred from raising of their own motion formal irregularities in the consumer credit contract and from applying the penalty of forfeiture of interest if five years have elapsed after the conclusion of the contract, in application of the respective limitation period set out in Article L-110.4 of the Commercial Code: G. Poissonier, "Credit à la consommation : prescription quinquennale et relevé des moyens d'office" (2018) *Recueil Dalloz*, 238.

765 To that effect, Joined Cases C-297/88 and C-197/89 *Dzodzi*, EU:C:1990:360 ; Case C-482/10 *Cicala*, EU:C:2011:868. Following the *Dzodzi* line of case law, the Court is competent to give a reference for preliminary ruling when Union law has been made applicable by national provisions "directly and unconditionally" (*Cicala*, para. 19 and case law cited). This is in order to ensure that "every [Union] provision should be given a uniform interpretation irrespective of the circumstances in which it is to be applied" (*Dzodzi*, para. 37). Even if the *ex officio* doctrine is not established by a Union law provision, it forms a case law built mandatory feature of consumer protective legislation in order to ensure its effectiveness.

766 Opinion of AG Tizzano in *Cofidis* (n. 727), note 43.

and limitation: "I think it distinctly significant that in the other Member States no limitation period is imposed in regard to pleading the unfairness of terms included in standard contracts".

Importantly, the *Cofidis* case demonstrated the high level of awareness and sensitivity of national courts as to the issues of consumer protection (particularly trial courts which are better placed with regard to practical aspects of the litigation arising out of these issues) and their determination, if necessary, to change the course of an established line of case law that may prove detrimental to the effective judicial protection of consumers.

## 3. *MOSTAZA CLARO* AND *ASTURCOM TELECOMUNICACIONES*: THE MANDATORY NATURE AND PUBLIC INTEREST QUALITY OF CONSUMER PROTECTION LAW

*Mostaza Claro*[767] is the first judgment which explicitly recognizes the mandatory nature of Union rules on consumer protection from unfair terms and their qualification as rules of public interest. The public interest is not merely associated with the functioning of the internal market. Although consumer protection furthers this aim as well, the public interest of the respective rules is equally associated with the aim of "raising the standard of living and the quality of life" in the Union. The judgment suggests that national courts have an obligation to raise of their own motion the unfairness of a contractual term as the procedural consequence of "the nature and importance of the public interest" underlying the consumer protection rules of the Unfair Contract Terms Directive. The rule that the unfair terms do not bind consumers is considered as being of *the same type* as domestic rules of public policy, rephrased in *Asturcom Telecomunicaciones*[768] as a provision "of equal standing to national rules which rank, within the domestic legal system, as rules of public policy."

The Court has been cautious not to qualify directly the consumer law provisions as rules of (Union) public policy. Interestingly, in *Mostaza Claro*, the Commission expressed the view that the rules on unfair terms could be regarded as rules of public policy.[769] It is only in a broad sense that the rules on consumer protection could be considered to express a Union public policy of protection. This category could be understood as comprising mandatory rules which protect

767 Case C-168/05 *Mostaza Claro* (n. 648).

768 Case C-40/08 *Asturcom Telecommunicaciones*, EU:C:2009:615.

769 In its observations the Commission had considered that in view of the importance attached to consumer protection, the provisions of the Unfair Contract Terms Directive can be regarded as rules of public policy (Opinion of AG Tizzano in Case C-168/05 *Mostaza Claro*, EU:C:2006:265, point 55).

private interests, but also have a public interest objective and which the courts are required to raise of their own motion, without prejudice to the right of the protected party to renounce protection.

*Mostaza Claro* refers to the public policy equivalence principle on which the earlier judgment in *Eco Swiss*[770] (on the judicial review of arbitration awards) was based. There the Court found that competition law rules have equal status to domestic rules of public policy for the purposes of admitting a claim for annulment of an arbitration award on the grounds of public policy. It was recognized that the questions in relation to the breach of competition law should be open to examination by the courts, even if this would result in the extension of the ambit of the dispute as set by the parties in the arbitration proceedings. However, the reason for accepting such a result was due to the specific context of review of an arbitration award where, unlike in *Van Schijndel*, the courts are the first venue which can make a reference for a preliminary ruling. By contrast, the recognition of the mandatory nature of the Unfair Contract Terms Directive provisions in *Mostaza Claro* and the consequences for the active role of courts was not only relevant in the arbitration context but also had a broad reach over a wide range of consumer law disputes pertaining to Union consumer law.[771] In *Mostaza Claro* it is the capacity of the consumer as the weaker party and the need to compensate for the imbalance which is decisive for the positive action by the courts. This premise permeates every type of procedural context.

## 3.1. *MOSTAZA CLARO*: THE CONTRIBUTION TO THE THEORETICAL CONSTRUCTION OF THE DOCTRINE

The question in *Mostaza Claro* arose in the context of annulment proceedings of an arbitration award. It intended to clarify whether the national court had the power to raise of its own motion the unfairness of an arbitration agreement, despite the fact that the applicant had not contested its validity in the course of arbitration proceedings, but only during the annulment proceedings. The facts were as follows. A consumer, Ms Mostaza Claro, had contracted a telephone subscription contract with a professional of the sector. The contract contained an arbitration clause under which any dispute in relation to the contract would be referred for arbitration to an arbitration tribunal. Actually this tribunal was

770 Case C-126/97 *Eco Swiss*, EU:C:1999:269. The case is discussed in Chapter 2, Section 1.3.

771 See Case C-377/14 *Radlinger and Radlingerová*, EU:C:2016:283; Case C-243/08 *Pannon GSM* (n. 684), paras. 31–32; Case C-137/08 *VB Pénzügyi Lízing* (n. 684), para. 47; Case C-227/08 *Martín Martín* (n. 686), para. 28; Case C-453/10 *Pereničová and Perenič*, EU:C:2012:144, para. 28; Case C-618/10 *Banco Español de Crédito* (n. 715), para. 40; Case C-472/11 *Banif Plus Bank* (n. 695), para. 20; Case C-397/11 *Jőrös* (n. 693), paras. 25–30; Case C-488/11 *Asbeek Brusse*, EU:C:2013:341(n. 695), paras. 42–46.

the one drafting the terms employed in the contract.[772] The professional initiated the arbitration proceedings against the consumer, as she did not comply with the minimum subscription period. In a letter addressed to her, she was given 10 days in which to refuse arbitration. The consumer presented herself before the arbitration tribunal and put forward arguments on the merits, but she did not contest the validity of the arbitration agreement. Unsurprisingly, the arbitrators found against her. This award was contested by the consumer before the referring court, submitting that the arbitration agreement was null and void because of the unfair nature of the arbitration clause. The referring court had not doubt that the arbitration clause was unfair. However, the procedural law would not allow the relevant ground to be made at that stage.

The applicable law on arbitration at that time[773] provided that an objection to arbitration on the basis *inter alia* of nullity of the arbitration agreement had to be raised at the same time as the parties made their initial submissions. As to the applicable (at the time) law on consumer protection,[774] it did not yet[775] provide for effective safeguards against unfair recourse to arbitration clauses by professionals. Arbitration agreements were deemed valid, provided that, in addition to the legal requirements for their validity, they were clear and explicit.[776]

### 3.1.1. *The Issue of Unfairness of the Arbitration Clause*

As opposed to *Océano Grupo*, where the Court examined in more detail the elements which contribute to the finding of unfairness of an exclusive jurisdiction clause to the benefit of the professional, in the present case the reasoning was limited to the procedural question of the powers of the court upon the finding that a term was unfair. The judicial assessment of the unfairness of the disputed term, the arbitration clause, was left for the national court to decide.[777] The same

772 This aspect was revealed in the framework of Case C-40/08 *Asturcom Telecomunicaciones* (n. 768).

773 Ley 36/1988 de Arbitraje (Law 36/1988 on Arbitration) of 5 December 1988 (BOE No 293 of 7 December 1988), Art. 23(1).

774 Law 7/1998 (n. 658).

775 The respective provision, as it will be explained below in Section 3.1.1, was amended in 2006.

776 Art. 10 (4) Law 7/1998 (n. 658): "Los convenios arbitrales establecidos en la contratación a que se refiere este artículo serán eficaces si, además de reunir les requisites que para su validez exigen las leyes, resultan claros y explícitos. La negativa del consumidor o usuario a someterse a un sistema arbitral distinto del previsto en el artículo 31 de esta Ley no podrá impedir por sí misma la celebración del contrato principal." [The arbitration agreements to which this article refers are effective if, in addition to complying with the legal requirements, they are clear and explicit. Refusal by the consumer or user to submit himself/herself to a system of arbitration distinct from the one provided under Art. 31 of the present law [note: arbitral system set by the government] does not impede conclusion of the contract] (translated by the author).

777 Case C-168/05 *Mostaza Claro* (n. 648), paras. 21–23 with reference to the deferential approach in Case C-237/02 *Freiburger Kommunalbauten*, EU:C:2004:209.

approach was followed in *Sebestyén*,[778] which concerned specifically the question of the unfairness of a clause in a mortgage contract providing for the exclusive competence of an arbitration tribunal. Certain criteria have been provided in this judgment which could assist the referring court in pinning down the contours of the concept of unfairness in the specific situation of arbitration clauses. The most important indication is the Annex of the Unfair Contract Terms Directive, which contains the 'gray list' of terms. Pursuant to this Annex, a term *may* be regarded as unfair if it has the object or effect of "excluding or hindering the consumer's right to take legal action or exercise any other legal remedy, particularly by requiring the consumer to take disputes exclusively to arbitration not covered by legal provisions."[779]

In its assessment, the national court would also have to consider the fact that general information provided to the consumer, in plain and intelligible language, as to the disadvantages of arbitration compared to ordinary proceedings is not sufficient by itself to rule out the unfairness of the relevant clause.[780]

As the national court had already established that the arbitration clause was unfair, the Court did not, in any event, have to pronounce on the issue of its fairness in *Mostaza Claro*. A deferential approach on the matter of consumer arbitration also seemed at that time prudent in view of the variance of Member States' approaches. Provisions governing the matter can be found either in specific arbitration legislation or under the unfair terms legislation with differing degrees of control.[781] In France, for instance, the Civil Code (*Code Civil*) provides that an arbitration clause (*clause compromissoire*) cannot be used against non-professionals.[782] Particularly with regard to consumer arbitration, the French Consumer Code includes the arbitration agreement under the terms that are *presumed* to be unfair (with the possibility of the professional producing proof to the contrary), for as long as the consumer would be obliged to seise an arbitration tribunal not covered by legislative provisions or to resort exclusively to alternative dispute resolution (ADR) in relation to the

---

778 Case C-342/13 *Sebestyén*, EU:C:2014:1857.

779 Point 1(q) of the Annex to the Unfair Contract Terms Directive.

780 *Sebestyén* (n. 778), paras. 33–34.

781 For a comprehensive analysis of the various approaches in consumer arbitration see N. Reich, "More clarity after 'Claro'? Arbitration clauses in consumer contracts as an ADR (alternative dispute resolution) mechanism for effective and speedy conflict resolution, or a 'deni de justice'?" (2007) 1 *ERCL* 41–61, proceeding to a comparative overview of Member States' and US approaches to arbitration and discussing also the distinction between cross-border and internal arbitration clauses; M. Piers, "Consumer Arbitration and European Private Law: A Seminal Consumer Arbitration Model Law for Europe" (2013) 21: 1 *ERPL* 247–288; M. Piers, "Consumer Arbitration in the EU. A Forced Marriage with Incompatible Expectations" (2011) 2 *Oxford Journal for International Dispute Settlement* 2–5; M. Piers, "Spillovers of European Consumer Law: Validity of Arbitration Agreements ... and beyond" (2011) 22 *American Review of International Arbitration* 635–659.

782 Article 2061 Code Civil.

settlement of disputes.[783] A rather arbitration-friendly approach is followed in the Netherlands and Germany, provided that certain standards are met.[784] The Union legislator, as has just been mentioned in the previous paragraph, classifies mandatory arbitration among the list of 'gray' terms, leaving it to the courts to assess whether a mandatory consumer arbitration clause could jeopardize the rights to effective judicial protection.[785]

The model of consumer dispute resolution that the Union legislator advances in ADR legislation is based on the observance of strict quality standards.[786] Expertise, independence, impartiality, transparency, effectiveness, fairness, liberty and legality are the governing principles with which every national ADR scheme has to comply.[787] The meaning of the principle of liberty is that an agreement to submit complaints to an ADR entity should not be binding if it has the effect of depriving the consumer of his right to bring an action before the courts.[788] In that respect, Union legislation has a clearly advanced consumer protection approach compared to the much-criticized consumer arbitration system in the US.[789]

783 R. 212-2 (10) Code de la Consommation. See G. Brunaux in N. Sauphanor-Brouillaud, *Les contrats de consommation, Règles communes* (LGDJ, 2012), 618–621; G. Poissonier, "Note sous *Asturcom Telecomunicaciones*" *Gazette du Palais* 2010 no 49, 12.

784 Discussing the Dutch approach, M. Piers, "Consumer Arbitration and European Private Law: A Seminal Consumer Arbitration Model Law for Europe" (n. 781), note 81, explains that the legal history of Book 6 of the new Dutch Civil Code that did not include consumer arbitration among the clauses that could be considered as "*unreasonably burdensome*" was explained by the "improved procedural guarantees that warrant the quality and impartiality in arbitration". As far as Germany is concerned, the German Civil Code allows arbitration clauses but under strict formality requirements (Art. 1031(5) German Procedural Code (ZPO) *Form der Schiedsvereinbarung*).

785 It is interesting to note, that under the Proposal for a Common European Sales Law, COM (2011) 0635, the arbitration clause that would require the consumer "to take disputes exclusively to an arbitration system not foreseen generally in legal provisions that apply to contracts between a trader and a consumer" is under the list of "black" terms which always have to be considered unfair (Art. 84(d)).

786 Directive 2013/11/EU of the European Parliament and of the Council of 21 May 2013 on alternative dispute resolution for consumer disputes and amending Regulation (EC) No 2006/2004 and Directive 2009/22/EC (Directive on consumer ADR) [2013] OJ L165/63; Regulation (EU) No 524/2013 of the European Parliament and of the Council of 21 May 2013 on online dispute resolution for consumer disputes and amending Regulation (EC) No 2006/2004 and Directive 2009/22/EC (Regulation on consumer ODR) [2013] OJ L165/1.

787 On the issue of access to justice and ADR schemes see Chapter 1, Section 1.

788 See Case C-75/16 *Menini and Rampanelli*, EU:C:2017:457.

789 The validity of arbitration agreements "in commerce" is provided under the Federal Arbitration Act. Its scope of application had been extended by the Supreme Court to consumer disputes without making a distinction as to the imbalance of sophistication power of the parties involved: see *Green Tree Fin Corp-Ala v Randolph* (2000) 531 US 79 (The consumer had contended that the arbitration agreement was unenforceable due to the high costs it would incur. The Supreme Court disagreed: "... to invalidate the agreement would undermine the liberal federal policy favoring arbitration agreements [...] and would conflict with this Court's holdings that the party resisting arbitration bears the burden of proving

### 3.1.2. *The Powers of the Courts in Proceedings for Annulment of a Consumer Arbitration Award:* Eco Swiss *Tuned to* Océano Grupo *Purposiveness*

The reasoning of the Court on the question whether the courts should have the power to annul an arbitration award in proceedings for annulment despite the fact that the consumer did not plead invalidity in arbitration proceedings is articulated through the application of the principle of procedural autonomy and the weaker party protection.

#### 3.1.2.1. The Principle of National Procedural Autonomy

The premise of the reasoning of the Court is the principle of national procedural autonomy. It will be recalled that in *Océano* and *Cofidis*, the powers of the courts to apply of their own motion the protection of consumers from unfair terms was inferred by means of a purposive reading of the Unfair Contract Terms Directive. In *Mostaza Claro*, the pattern of reasoning resembles that of the judgment in *Eco Swiss*; however it is imbued with all the purposive elements

---

that Congress intended to preclude arbitration of the statutory claims at issue [...] Thus a party seeking to invalidate an arbitration agreement on the ground that arbitration would be prohibitively expensive bears the burden of showing the likelihood of incurring such costs [...]"); and *Buckleye Check Cashing Corp v John Cardegna*, (2006) 546 US 440 (the applicants had contested the validity of the credit agreement as a whole and they had sued in court instead of submitting to arbitration. The Supreme Court upheld the application of the rule of severability of the arbitration agreement from the remainder of the contract to the consumer contracts: "... unless the challenge is to the arbitration clause itself, the issue of the contract's validity is considered by the arbitrator in the first instance"). The rulings are analyzed in N. Reich (n. 781), 49–52; For a comparative transatlantic approach see C. R. Drahozal and R. J. Friel, "Consumer Arbitration in the European Union and the United States" (2002) 28 *North Carolina Journal of International Law & Commercial Arbitration* 357–394.

In the much disputed case *AT&T Mobility, 131* S.Ct. 1740 (2011) the US Supreme Court confirmed the validity of the collective-arbitration waivers in consumer contracts. It held that the Federal Arbitration Act preempted California's judicial rule regarding the unconscionability of class arbitration waivers in consumer contracts and overturned *Discover Bank* 36 Cal. 4th 148 (2005). For a detailed analysis of *AT&T Mobility*, F. Blechschmidt, "Comment, All Alone in Arbitration: AT & T Mobility v. Conception and the Substantive Impact of Class Action Waiver" (2012) 160 *University of Pennsylvania Law Review* 541.

A Bill on an "Arbitration Fairness Act" has been introduced several times before Congress but has not become law. Such a law would have marked a breakthrough on the matter of consumer arbitration as it intends to restore the scope of application of the Federal Arbitration Act (FAA) as applicable only "*to disputes between commercial entities of generally similar sophistication and bargaining power*". The Bill proposes an amendment to title 9 of the United States Code with respect to arbitration in order to declare invalid any pre-dispute arbitration agreement on consumer disputes, but also employment, antitrust or civil rights disputes. The applicability of the proposed provisions to an agreement to arbitrate and the validity and enforceability of an arbitration agreement would have to be determined by a court, rather than an arbitrator "*irrespective of whether the party resisting arbitration challenges the arbitration agreement specifically or in conjunction with other terms of the contract containing such agreement.*"

of *Océano Grupo* and it contributes to building the doctrine of the active court even further. As the case law on the active doctrine evolved, the reasoning on the basis of national procedural autonomy would become the standard one, in circumstances under which the powers of the courts would have to be applied in specific proceedings.[790]

Within the context of review proceedings of an arbitration award involving the consumer, the Court found that national courts are required to determine the validity of an arbitration clause even if the consumer did not plead that ground in the course of the arbitration proceedings.[791] To that effect, the balancing of competing interests was necessary: efficiency and certainty of arbitral proceedings reflected in the restricted scope of grounds of annulment on the one hand against effective consumer protection on the other hand. Indeed, the professional and the German government pointed out the interest of effectiveness of arbitration awards that needs to be safeguarded against the unrestricted revision of the merits of the award. Nevertheless, such a submission omits reference to the safety net of public policy. Thus, in its decision, the Court did not intend an overhaul of the principle of limited control of arbitration, recognizing the value of efficient arbitration proceedings.[792] However, it ensured that consumer protection from unfair terms would figure among the *public policy exceptions.*

As has already been expressed in *Océano Grupo*, the prevalent consumer model in individual litigation is that of the *weaker* party.[793] The average consumer model that the Court has advanced in other contexts[794] has been, as Maud Piers observes, "effectively eliminated from the context of consumer arbitration."[795]

790 This phase of case-law will be discussed in Chapter 5.

791 Case C-168/05 *Mostaza Claro* (n. 648), para. 30.

792 Ibid., para. 34.

793 However, recognizing the weakness of the consumer does not imply an *absolute* protection either, as it has been demonstrated later in Case C-40/08 *Asturcom Telecommunicaciones* (n. 768)(below Section 3.2).

794 The model of a "reasonably well informed and reasonably observant and circumspect"' consumer has been advanced mainly in the context of assessing the compatibility of national rules with the internal market (see for instance Case C-220/98 *Estée Lauder*, EU:C:2000:8, para. 27; Case C-30/99 *Commission v Ireland*, EU:C:2001:346, para. 32; Case C-44/01 *Pippig Augenoptik*, EU:C:2003:205, para. 55; Case C-356/04 *Lidl Belgium*, EU:C:2006:585, para. 78) and in trade mark cases (see for instance Case C-53/01 *Linde and Others*, EU:C:2003:206, para. 41; Case C-363/99 *Koninklijke KPN Nederland*, EU:C:2004:86, para. 34; Case C-265/09 P *OHIM* v *BORCO-Marken-Import Matthiesen*, EU:C:2010:508, paras. 32 and 35; Case C-217/13 *Oberbank*, EU:C: 2014: 12, para. 39). It has also been employed as a criterion for the national courts to assess the extent to which a consumer can effectively assess the implications of the use of a contractual term (see Case C-26/13 *Kásler and Káslerné Rábai*, EU:C:2014:282, para. 74).

795 M. Piers (n. 781), 266, observing that "even the most nonchalant consumer should be protected against an unfair arbitration clause", citing in the same vein V. Mak, "Standards of Protection: in Search of the "Average Consumer" of EU law in the Proposal for a Consumer Rights Directive" (2011) 1 *European Review of Private Law* 30.

In *Mostaza Claro*, the professional and the German government seemed in their observations to defend a model of a more normatively optimized consumer as a party to the proceedings. They had maintained that the arbitration clause respected consumer rights since the consumer remained at liberty to refuse arbitration and argue that the clause in question was void in the initial statement of defense submitted to the arbitrator. The Court was not convinced by this approach and remained within the lines drawn in *Océano Grupo* and *Cofidis* of a consumer that is in a weaker position and runs the risk of not raising the unfair term either because he is unaware of his rights or because he is deterred by the costs entailed. In his Opinion, AG Tizzano explained that this *rationale* is similarly (or even *a fortiori*) applicable in the arbitration proceedings initiated by the seller, as the consumer might not exercise the power to refuse arbitration "out of ignorance or fear of the costs of an action before the ordinary judicial authorities."[796] The extremely short limitation period (10 days) within which the consumer had to decide on whether to submit to arbitration would even amount, according to the Opinion, to a breach of the right to a fair hearing.[797]

### 3.1.2.2. The Mandatory Law and Public Interest Nature of the Protection Against Unfair Terms

The qualification of the rules on unfair term protection as mandatory law expressing the *public interest* has a played a decisive role in the argumentation of the Court for the determination of the powers of national courts.

The Spanish legislation on arbitration, like most of the national and international instruments on the subject of arbitration,[798] includes public policy among the restrictive reasons that can justify an action for the annulment of an arbitration award.[799] If domestic procedural rules allow for the annulment of an arbitration award on the grounds of domestic rules of public policy, the principle of equivalence requires that the same should be applicable to Union rules "of this type."[800] This requirement of integration of the Union mandatory laws within public policy grounds that can justify the annulment of an arbitration award already derived from *Eco Swiss*.[801] There the Court held that the public policy nature of the rules of Union competition law justifies that courts should review an arbitration award on that basis, despite the fact that the applicants presented the issue for the first time in court proceedings. The Union rules of competition

796 Opinion of AG Tizzano in Case C-168/05 *Mostaza Claro* (n. 769), point 47.
797 Ibid., point 48.
798 Ibid., point 52, note 20.
799 According to Art. 45(5) of the Law of Arbitration (n. 773) applicable at the time of the dispute: "El laudo sólo podrá anularse en los siguientes casos ... (5) Cuando el laudo fuese contrario al orden público" (Translation: "The arbitration award may be annulled only in the following cases ... (5) Where the award is contrary to public policy").
800 Case C-168/05 *Mostaza Claro* (n. 648), para. 35.
801 Case C-126/97 *Eco Swiss* (n. 770).

law therefore had to be placed on the same footing as national rules of public policy, although competition rules were not perceived as such in domestic level. Similarly, in *Mostaza Claro*, there was no indication that Spanish national law included within the core of public policy exceptions the review of unfair contractual terms, whether of domestic or European origin. The principle of public policy equivalence was therefore applied in such a way as to bring the unfair terms protection within the core of domestic public policy exceptions.

The discrepancy between the domestic perception of grounds based on consumer law and the Union law perception blurs the demarcation between the application of the principle of equivalence and the creation of a new category of rules of public policy. This is an example of what has been elsewhere described as "heteronomous" method of determination of the public policy content.[802] Moving "beyond a basic understanding of equivalence"[803] would appear to situate the ruling in a rather "gray zone" between the principle of equivalence and the principle effectiveness.

In his Opinion, AG Tizzano had suggested a different path of reasoning as he was worried about opening the "floodgates of public policy" by giving an: "excessively wide scope to a concept, namely that of public policy, which traditionally refers only to rules that are regarded as being of primary and absolute importance in a legal order."[804]

Even without resort to the public policy concept, the Opinion concluded in favor of judicial review of the arbitration award.[805] Its reasoning goes along the lines of a breach of the *fundamental right to a fair hearing*, which as "a fundamental principle of [Union] law" and as "one of the fundamental rights deriving from the constitutional traditions common to the Member States"[806] forms part of the Union concept of public policy. Indeed, the disputed arbitration clause had been drafted in such a way as to offer the appearance of respecting the liberty of the consumer to choose to submit the case in arbitration, whereas its practical effect (providing for the short period of 10 days in which the consumer could refuse arbitration and if he did not refuse, to file submissions and present evidence in his defense)[807] severely limited the fundamental right of the consumer to a fair hearing.[808]

---

802 Chapter 2, Section 1.1.1.

803 M. Ebers, "ECJ (First Chamber) 6 October 2009, Case C-40/08, *Asturcom Telecomunicaciones SL v. Cristina Rodríguez Nogueira* From Océano to Asturcom: Mandatory Consumer Law Ex Officio Application of European Union Law and Res Judicata" (2010) *ERPL* 823–846, 839.

804 Opinion of AG Tizzano in Case C-168/05 *Mostaza Claro* (n. 796).

805 However, the Opinion (ibid.) did not exclude the approach suggested by the Commission to consider the rules of the Unfair Contract Terms Directive as rules of public policy.

806 Ibid., points 59–60.

807 Ibid., point 48.

808 The breach of the right to the fair hearing is corroborated by the fact that the arbitration panel lacked independence. As previously mentioned, it was drafting itself the contracts which were subsequently used by the telecommunications undertakings.

The Court followed a path of reasoning which was not restricted to the consumer arbitration, but it would have broader implications. In order to justify the reason why national courts should apply to the rules on the protection of the consumers from unfair terms the same procedural rules as applicable to the domestic public policy rules grounds with regard to the annulment of an arbitration award, it qualified Article 6(1) of the Unfair Contract Terms Directive as a "mandatory provision." Moreover, the aim promoted by the Unfair Contract Terms Directive, the strengthening of consumer protection:

> constitutes, according to [then] Article 3(1)(t) EC, a measure which is essential to the accomplishment of the tasks entrusted to the Community and, in particular, to raising the standard of living and the quality of life in its territory.[809]

This is a fundamental statement. Consumer protection is not merely viewed as a functional instrument for the internal market, in the same way as competition law rules.[810] Those rules are an important contribution to the Union's aim to promote the "well-being" of its peoples (Article 3 (1) TEU).

The "nature and importance of the public interest" underlying the consumer protection rules consequently justified, according to the Court, that the national courts be "required" to assess of their own motion the unfairness of a contractual term and thus compensate for the imbalance in the relationship between the parties.[811] With the use of the term "required,"[812] the Court for the first time alludes to the nature of the power of the courts as an obligation, as opposed to a mere discretion.[813]

### *3.1.3. National Legislative Developments and the Judgment of the National Court*

Since the ruling in *Mostaza Claro*, there have been important legal developments in Spanish law to the effect of enhancing consumer protection with regard to unfair consumer arbitration. Following subsequent amendments to the law of consumer protection,[814] the current position is to consider as unfair

809 Case C-168/05 *Mostaza Claro* (n. 648), paras. 36–37.

810 *Cf.* Case C-126/97 *Eco Swiss* (n. 770), para. 36.

811 Case C-168/05 *Mostaza Claro* (n. 648), para. 38.

812 In Spanish "deba apreciar de officio", in French "soit tenu d' apprécier d'office".

813 One possible explanation for the use of the term "required" could be that it reflects the wording of the question referred by the national court. In later case law, it would become clear that the role attributed to national courts "is not limited to a mere power to rule on the possible unfairness of a contractual term but also consists of the obligation to examine the issue of its own motion": Case C-243/08 *Pannon GSM* (n. 684), para. 32.

814 Initially, Art. 10.4 of Law 26/1984 (n. 681) (as amended by Law 7/1998 (n. 658)) allowed consumer arbitration agreements provided they were clear and express. ("Los convenios arbitrales establecidos en la contratación a que se refiere este artículo serán eficaces si, además de reunir los requisitos que para su validez exigen les leyes, resultan claros y explícitos.

any arbitration agreement outside the framework of the system of consumer arbitration governed by the state (*Sistema Arbitral del Consumo*) and unless it is covered by legal provisions with respect to a specific sector or case.[815] However, arbitration agreements (falling within the *Sistema Arbitral del Consumo*) shall not be binding on the consumer if they were concluded before the dispute has arisen.[816] The law of arbitration has also been modified. The new law on

---

La negativa del consumidor o usuario a someterse a un sistema arbitral distinto del previsto en el artículo 31 de esta Ley no podrá impedir pro sí misma la celebración del contrato principal." [The arbitration agreements to which this article refers are valid if, in addition to the requirements the law provides, they are clear and express. The objection of the consumer or user to subject himself to an arbitral system distinct from the one provided for in Article 31 of this law, may not impede the conclusion of the principal contract.] (translated by the author). However, if those agreements formed part of the general terms and conditions, they had to be regarded as unfair: "A los efectos previstos en el artículo 10bis, tendrán el carácter de abusivas al menos las cláusulas o estipulaciones siguentes: 'La sumisión a arbitrajes distintos del de consumo, salvo que se trate de órganos de arbitraje institucionales creados por normas legales para un sector o un supuesto espcífico.'" (Translation: "To the effects provided for under Art. 10bis, the clauses or following provisions are unfair: 'Submission to arbitration other than consumer arbitration, except for institutional arbitration bodies established by law for a specific sector'").

Subsequently, Ley 44/2006, de mejora de la protección de los consumidores y usuarios (Law 44/2006 on improved consumer protection ) of 26 December 2006 (BOE No 312 of 30 December 2006), considering that the law was not effective enough in preventing the use of unfair arbitration agreements on consumers, modified the aforementioned Art. 31(4) and provided for the nullity of mandatory pre-dispute arbitration agreements: "Los convenios arbitrales con los consumidores distintos del arbitraje de consumo previsto en este artículo, sólo podrán pactarse una vez surgido el conflicto material o controversia entre las partes del contrato, salvo que se trate de la sumisión a órganos de arbitraje institucionales creados por normas legales o reglamentarias para un sector o un supuesto específico. Los convenios arbitrales pactados contraviniendo lo dispuesto en el párrafo precedente serán nulos." [Arbitration agreements with consumers other than consumer arbitration provided for in this article, may only be concluded after the material conflict or the dispute between the parties to the contract has arisen, where this does not concern the submission of the dispute to institutional arbitration bodies established by legal norms or regulated for a specific sector or case. The arbitration agreements concluded in violation of the provision of this paragraph will be considered null.] (translated by the author).

815 Arts. 57, 58 and 90 of Real Decreto Legislativo 1/2007, por el que se aprueba el texto refundido de la Ley General para la Defensa de los Consumidores y Usuarios y otras leyes complementarias (Royal Decree Law 1/2007 approving the revised text of the general law for the protection of consumers and users and other complementary laws) of 16 November 2007 (BOE No 287 of 30 November 2007).

Under Art. 90(1) of this law: "Son, asimismo, abusivas las cláusulas que establezcan: La sumisión a arbitrajes distintos del arbitraje de consumo, salvo que se trate de órganos de arbitraje institucionales creados par normas legales para un sector o un supuesto específico." [Terms that require submission to arbitration other than consumer arbitration, except in the case of submission to institutional arbitration bodies created by legal rules for a specific sector or case, are equally unfair] (translated by the author).

816 According to Royal Decree Law 1/2007 (n. 815), Art. 57(4): "No serán vinculantes para los consumidores les convenios arbitrales suscritos con un empresario antes de surgir el conflicto. La suscripción de dicho convenio, tendrá para el empresario la consideración de aceptación del arbitraje para la solución de las controversias derivadas de la relación

arbitration,[817] to which the Court also made reference, no longer required that the submissions on invalidity grounds of the arbitration agreement be made at the same time as the parties make their original claims in the arbitration process.[818]

In its decision delivered following the ruling of the Court on the preliminary reference, the *Audiencia Provincial* in Madrid annulled the contested arbitration award.[819] On the basis of the national law on consumer protection,[820] the Spanish court decided first that the arbitration clause was unfair and void. This solution was supported by the amendments that had already been made to the Consumer Protection Law, providing for the clear sanction of nullity of arbitration clauses.[821] On the basis of the nullity of the arbitration clause, the national court then proceeded to annul the arbitration award. It did so in accordance with the first of the restrictively prescribed grounds of annulment of arbitration awards, according to which an award can be nullified when the agreement is *void*.[822] The national court did not follow the path of *Mostaza Claro* reasoning with respect to the equivalence of consumer protection rules to domestic rules of public policy. Such reasoning would have led the national court to nullify the award rather on the basis of the public policy ground. But it did cite *verbatim* the ruling

---

jurídica a la que se refiera, siempre que el acuerdo de sometimiento reúna los requisitos exigidos por las normas aplicables." [Arbitration agreements concluded between a consumer and a professional before a dispute has arisen will not be binding on the consumer. For the professional, provided that the arbitration agreement meets the requirements of the law, it will be implied that the professional accepts the arbitration agreement and is bound to follow its terms in the event of a dispute] (translated by the author).

817 Ley 60/2003 de Arbitraje (Law 60/2003 on Arbitration) of 23 December 2003 (BOE No 309 of 26 December 2003).

818 According to Art. 22(2) of Law 60/2003 (n. 817): "Las exceptiones a las que se refiere el apartado anterior deberán oponerse a más tardar en el momento de presentar la contestación [...]." [The objections to which the previous paragraph refers have to be put forward at the latest at the moment of entering the opposition] (translation by the author).

819 Audiencia Provincial de Madrid (Sección 21ª) Sentencia num. 9/2007 of 16 January 2007 (JUR/2007/159346).

820 Law 7/1998 (n. 658) which added an additional provision to Law 26/1984 (n. 681). Under point 26 of that additional provision, it shall be deemed to be unfair the submission to arbitration other than consumer arbitration, apart from arbitration by bodies created by law for a specific sector.

821 Law 44/2006 (n. 814).

822 Law 36/1988 on Arbitration (n. 773), Art. 45: "El laudo sólo podrá anularse en los siguientes casos: 1) Cuando el convenio arbitral fuese nulo." [The arbitration award may be annulled only in the following cases: 1. Where the arbitration agreement is null and void] (translated by the author). At the time of the main proceedings, the law already in force, namely Law 60/2003 (n. 817), Art. 41(a) was worded as follows: "El laudo sólo podrá ser anulado cuando la parte que solicita la anulación alegue y pruebe: a) Que el convenio arbitral no existe o no es válido." [The arbitration award may be annulled when the party which claims the annulment alleges and proves that: a) The arbitration agreement does not exist or is invalid] (translation by the author). The national judge applied Law 36/1988 on the basis of the transitional provisions of Law 60/2003 (n. 817).

of the Court in order to confirm its power to declare the nullity of an arbitration award on the basis of the nullity of the arbitration agreement, despite the fact that the consumer had invoked the nullity for the first time in the course of the annulment proceedings.[823]

## 3.2. *ASTURCOM TELECOMUNICACIONES*: PROTECTION FROM UNFAIR TERMS OF EQUAL STANDING TO RULES OF DOMESTIC PUBLIC POLICY

The *Mostaza Claro* judgment was the reference point for the subsequent judgment in *Asturcom Telecomunicaciones*,[824] a case related to the proceedings for enforcement of a final arbitration award and the powers of the courts. The judgment in *Asturcom Telecomunicaciones* was, in turn, the reference point in the Order of the Court in *Pohotovosť v Korčkovká (Pohotovosť I)*.[825] In both cases, the Court was invited to explore the powers of the courts in the context of proceedings for enforcement of an arbitration award which has become final after the elapse of the time-limit for its contestation before the courts. The unfairness of the contract enforced by the award can more particularly concern either the arbitration clause itself (*Asturcom Telecomunicaciones*) or a clause of substance (*Pohotovosť I*).

### *3.2.1.* Asturcom Telecomunicaciones: *Proceedings for Enforcement of a Final Arbitration Award and the Powers of the Courts*

The factual background in *Asturcom Telecomunicaciones* has similarities to that in *Mostaza Claro*. The consumer concluded a subscription contract for a mobile

---

823 In the words of the national judgment: "Por tanto la recurrente podía alegar como motive de anulación del laudo que el convenio arbitral era nulo por contener una cláusula abusiva, conforme al artículo 45.1 de la Ley de Arbitraje de 1988 [...]., aun cuando en el procedimiento arbitral no hubiera utilizado esta argumentación, y, en consecuencia, procede estimar el recurso de anulación del laudo arbitral [...]."[The applicant may invoke as ground for the annulment of the arbitral award that the arbitration agreement is null because it includes an unfair term, in accordance with Art. 45.1 of the Law on Arbitration of 1988 [...] even when during the arbitration proceedings she did not make this argument, and as a consequence, we need to examine the application for annulment of the arbitration award] (translation by the author).

824 Case C-40/08 *Asturcom Telecommunicaciones* (n. 768).

825 Order of 16 November 2010 in Case C-76/10 *Pohotovosť v Korčkovká*, EU:C:2010:685 *(Pohotovosť I)*. The judgment of 27 February 2014 in Case C-470/12 *Pohotovosť*, EU:C:2014:101 (*Pohotovosť II)*, involves the same Slovak credit institution (Pohotovosť) and the same procedural context of enforcement of a final arbitration award against the consumer. The problem raised in that latter case was, however, distinct compared to the one raised in the earlier case. It raised a question of the standing of consumer associations and their right to intervene in proceedings for enforcement of a final arbitration award. That case will be

telephone which contained an arbitration clause, a dispute arose and it was brought before an arbitration panel (the same as in *Mostaza Claro*). From this point onwards, the procedural evolution of the two cases diverges and it is this difference which accounts for the different solutions between the two judgments. The consumer neither participated in the arbitration proceedings nor initiated annulment proceedings, as had been the case in *Mostaza Claro*. Thus, the award became final and the company brought an action for its enforcement which has not been contested by the consumer.

As was also the case in *Mostaza Claro*, the referring court had already established that the arbitration clause in the subscription agreement was unfair. Two main reasons were given to that effect. The first one related to the violation of the right to *access to justice* and the second to the violation of the right to a *fair trial* due to the breach of the principles of fairness and independence of the proceedings. The costs that the consumer would have incurred in order to travel to the seat of the arbitration tribunal would have exceeded the amount in dispute (€669.60), since that seat – which in passing was not even indicated in the contract – was located a considerable distance from the consumer's place of residence. As to the fair trial concerns, the referring court observed that the body constituting the arbitration tribunal was the same that drafted the contracts used by the telecommunication undertakings (the same contracts the terms of which the arbitration tribunal was supposed to control). The referring court found that the arbitration proceedings failed to ensure effective consumer protection, since the arbitrators were not required nor allowed under the applicable national law on arbitration[826] to examine of their own motion the unfairness of the arbitration agreement (or of any other contractual clause). The Spanish civil procedural rules applicable to the enforcement of an arbitration award[827]

discussed below in section 6, devoted to the distinct line of reasoning when it comes to the question of application of the *ex officio* doctrine in collective proceedings.

826 Law 60/2003 on Arbitration (n. 817).

827 Spanish Civil Procedure Code (n. 660), Art. 548 *et seq.* The enforcement procedure for final arbitration awards is the same as the one for judgments. The competent court issues an enforcement order after having verified all requirements set out by law (*orden general de ejecución*). This is a different procedure from the *exequatur* procedure, followed, for instance, in Germany (§1060 ZPO: "Die Zwangvollstreckung findet statt, wenn der Schiedsspruch für vollstreckbar erklärt ist." (Translation: "The enforcement takes place when the arbitration award has been declared enforceable"). In the course of this process, the German courts have the power to refuse enforcement if the subject-matter of the dispute cannot be a matter of litigation under German law or if it leads to a result which is contrary to public policy (§1060 ZPO(2) in conjunction with §1059(2)(b) ZPO). It is accepted in German literature that the core of consumer protection provisions, on unfair terms in particular, is covered by the *ordre public* ground of refusal of enforcement. See K. Hilbig, "Absoluter Verbraucherschutz bei unzulässigen ABG-Schiesvereinbarungen?", SchiesVZ 2010, 74, 81, with further references. However, the author explains that the qualification of the rules on unfair terms as part of *ordre public* in the sense of §1059(2)(b) ZPO does not bode well with the case-law of the BGH. The judgment cited to that effect (BGH, Schieds VZ 2009, 66; NJW 2009, 1215) concerned

did not provide for an independent judicial assessment of the potential nullity of an arbitration award on the ground of unfairness of the arbitration clause entailed in the contract enforced by the award. The question of the referring court was whether the effectiveness of consumer protection would require that the arbitration award be set aside, even if the latter has already become final and was covered by the force of *res judicata* (*cosa juzgada*).

### 3.2.1.1. Prevalence of the *Res Judicata* Principle

The reasoning of the Court was structured along the lines of procedural autonomy. However, the order of examination of the limitations to procedural autonomy was reversed, with the principle of effectiveness being examined before the principle of equivalence. The solution results from a combined application of *Mostaza Claro* with *Eco Swiss.* To recall the finding of *Eco Swiss*, Union law does not require national courts to refrain from applying the rules on the force of *res judicata* and examine an arbitration award that has become final, even if that would be necessary in order to examine the validity of an agreement with the rules of competition law. As will be argued later on, the transposition of *Eco Swiss* within the framework of proceedings for annulment of an arbitration award enforced against a consumer is perhaps not the best outcome.

The Court examined first whether the principle of effectiveness required that the courts refrain from applying the *res judicata* principle so that they set aside the arbitration award of their own motion on the ground of enforcement of an unfair arbitration clause. The Court framed the issue in terms of whether the positive action required on behalf of the courts in order to re-establish equality between the parties would imply that the consumer be afforded "absolute protection," in derogation from the *res judicata* principle.[828] Reference was made not only to *Eco Swiss*, but also to the judgments in *Kapferer*[829] and *Falimento Olimpiclub,*[830] which highlighted the "importance, both for the [Union] legal

provisions on the law on the quality of grains. There, the BGH distinguished between rules that form the core of ordre public and other mandatory provisions that do not form part of this core: "Wenn der Schiedspruch eine Norm verletz, did die Grundlagen des staatlichen oder wirtschaftlichen Lebens regelt, oder wenn er zu deutschen Gerectigkeitsvorstellungen in einem untragbaren Widerspruch steht; der Schiedspruch muss mithin die elementaren Grundlagen der Rechtsordnung verletzen." [When the arbitration award violates a legal norm which governs the foundations of the state or economic life, or when it runs against the German conceptions of justice in an untolerable way; the arbitration award must, therefore, violate the elementary foundations of the legal system] (translation by the author). "Nicht jeder Widerspruch der Entscheidung des Schiedsgerichts zu zwingenden Vorschriften des deutschen Rechts stellt danach eien Verstoss gegen den ordre public dar." [Not every opposition of the decision of the arbitration court against the mandatory provisions of the German law represents an obstacle against the public policy] (translation by the author).

828 Case C-40/08 *Asturcom Telecomunicaciones* (n. 768), para. 34.

829 Case C-234/04 *Kapferer*, EU:C:2006:178.

830 Case C-2/08 *Falimento Olimpiclub*, EU:C:2009:506.

order and for the national legal systems, of the principle of *res judicata*."[831] In those latter judgments, it was decided that Union law:

> does not require a national court to disapply domestic rules of procedure conferring finality on a decision, even if to do so would make it possible to remedy an infringement of a provision of [Union] law regardless of its nature on the part of the decision at issue.[832]

In *Asturcom Telecomunicaciones*, the Court observed that the arbitration award became final because the consumer did not have the procedural diligence to bring an action for annulment within the two-month time limit. Such a peremptory time limit is considered to be "reasonable" for the due exercise of the right of defense. The fact that the dispute in the main proceedings concerned the application of consumer law did not require derogation from the observance of the force of the *res judicata* of the final arbitration award. At this point, in a rather strong tone, the Court puts forward the "total inertia" argument, according to which the *ex officio* doctrine is not intended to compensate for the consequences of the omissions of the totally passive consumer:

> In any event, the need to comply with the principle of effectiveness cannot be stretched so far as to mean that, in circumstances as those in the main proceedings, a national court is required not only to compensate for a procedural omission on the part of the consumer who is unaware of his rights, as in the case of the judgment in Mostaza Claro, but also to make up fully for the total inertia on the part of the consumer concerned who, like the defendant in the main proceedings, neither participated in the arbitration proceedings nor brought an action for annulment of an arbitration award, which therefore became final.[833]

#### 3.2.1.2. Rules Protecting Against the Use of Unfair Terms of Equal Standing to Domestic Laws of Public Policy

After finding that the principle of effectiveness did not require the courts to compensate for the *total inertia* of the consumer, the Court indicated, however, that the solution could be different on the basis of application of the principle of equivalence. It stated that Article 6(1) of the Unfair Contract Terms Directive: "must be regarded as a provision of equal standing to national rules which rank, within the domestic legal system, as rules of public policy."[834]

---

[831] Case C-40/08 *Asturcom Telecomunicaciones* (n. 768), para. 35. On the importance of the *res judicata* principle outside the consumer law context *see* Case C-69/14, *Târşia*, EU:C:2015:662, paras. 28-29 and case law cited.

[832] Ibid., para. 37.

[833] Ibid., para. 47.

[834] Ibid., para. 52.

This extensive application of the principle of equivalence, the 'public policy equivalence', requires the *conceptual extension* of domestic public policy in order to accommodate the imperatives at the Union law level and in particular the rules on protection from unfair terms. In taking this stance, the Court might have also been influenced by the developments in Spanish case law toward the direction of admitting the powers of the courts to refuse the enforcement of an arbitration award based on unfair terms. The Spanish government had submitted that the courts responsible for the enforcement of an arbitration award do have jurisdiction to assess of their own motion whether or not an arbitration clause is null and void, on the ground that such a clause is contrary to public policy.[835] Some Spanish courts had already ruled that an arbitration award that violates public policy cannot be enforced, in particular where the fundamental right to a fair hearing has been breached.[836]

The Order of the *Audiencia Provincial de Madrid* of 28 July 2005 is particularly instructive in that regard.[837] A combined and purposive reading of the provisions on arbitration law and civil procedural law led that court to the conclusion that Spanish law can be interpreted in such a way as to refuse the enforcement of an arbitral award against the consumer that contravenes public policy.[838] This was so as the arbitration tribunal was not impartial. According to the order:

> We believe that in this case the minimum guarantees of the principle of impartiality have been breached. We are in fact aware that the contracts have been drafted, following a similar model by AEADE … The consequence of this affirmation is clear; the impartiality necessary for the good functioning of the arbitral procedure does not exist. The association prepares the contracts for the business of the sector, renders the accession to the arbitration clause binding without any prior negotiation with the consumer … the award is therefore void being contrary to the public policy (translated by the author).[839]

835 References are made in Audiencia Provincial de Madrid, orders 189/2005 of 28 July 2005 (No de Recurso 302/2005), 29 July 2005 (No de Recurso 155/2005), 186/2008 of 10 June 2008 (No de Recurso 694/2007), all cited in the Opinion of AG Trstenjak in Case C-40/08 *Asturcom Telecomunicaciones*, EU:C:2009:305, notes 37–40.

836 Ibid.

837 Auto 189/2005 (n. 835).

838 The Order reads as follows: "… deberá denegarse la ejecución cuando el contenido sea contrario al orden público, entendido, desde la perspectiva constitucional, como el conjunto de principios jurídico públicos, privados, políticos, morales y económicos que son absolutamente obligatorios para la conservación de un modelo de sociedad en un pueblo y época determinados (SSTC 11/87 de 11 de febrero, 116/1988 de 20 de junio y 54/1989 de 23 de febrero)." [… the enforcement has to be refused when its content would be contrary to public policy, understood from the constitutional perspective, as the set of the public, private, political, moral and economic legal principles that are absolutely necessary for maintaining a model of society for a specific people and point in time] (translated by the author).

839 The original text reads as follows: "Pues bien, creemos que en este caso se han violentado las garantías mínimas del principio de imparcialidad objetiva. En efecto conocemos que los

### 3.2.1.3. The Total Inertia Argument and the Alternative Approach on the Basis of the Right to Effective Judicial Protection

*Asturcom Telecomunicaciones* introduces into the doctrine of the active consumer court the caveat of the total passivity of the consumer. This notion is quite puzzling. The powers of the courts on the mandatory rules of protection cannot depend upon the procedural behavior of the weaker party, whatever that may be. Either a rule is mandatory law and the courts have to raise it of their own motion or it is not mandatory law and they are not obliged to raise it. Therefore, if a rule is classified as mandatory, the courts should be able to raise the plea of their own motion, irrespective of whether the consumer participated in the proceedings or not. What the impact of the passivity of the consumer will be on the decision of the court is a different question. If the consumer participates in the proceedings, it is more likely that he will bring to the court's attention points of fact that will enable it to discharge its *ex officio* role. To put it simply, the consumer's participation can be beneficial for his case. But his passivity should not be penalized. Moreover, it is not easy to find a safe criterion in order to distinguish among 'procedural omission', 'passivity' and 'total passivity.' It is also a different question whether the fact that the consumer has to enter an objection is in itself liable to undermine the effectiveness of consumer protection. Later case law of the Court would clarify that the effective legal protection guaranteed by the Unfair Terms Directive "is based on the premise that one of the parties to the contract will bring an action before the national courts."[840] But from the moment that proceedings have been brought, as Advocate General Sharpston observes in her Opinion in *Karel de Grote*, the courts "must, of their own motion, in all cases and whatever the rules of their domestic law, examine whether a contract falls within the scope of Directive 93/13."[841]

It can also be argued that the passivity line of reasoning was maybe not really necessary for the purposes of the solution in *Asturcom Telecomunicaciones*. The case raised first and foremost the problem of a breach of the right to a fair trial. In her Opinion, AG Trstenjak[842] followed a path of reasoning inspired by the right to effective judicial protection and shares, in essence, the considerations

contratos están redactados, siguiendo un mismo modelo, por AEADE, que incluso llegó a incluir su anagrama en los mismos y tras visitar la página Web de la citada asociación … La consecuencia de esa afirmación es clara; no existe la imparcialidad objetiva necesaria para la buena llevanza del proceso arbitral. La asociación prepara los contratos para las empresas del sector a instancias de esas mismas empresas, lo hace bajo la fórmula de contratos de adhesión con efecto obligatorio para todos los contratantes, sin posibilidad alguna de discusión; … el laudo también es nulo por ser contrario al orden público."

840 Case C-527/10, *ERSTE Bank Hungary*, EU:C:2012:417, para. 63.

841 Opinion of AG Sharpston in *Karel de Grote – Hogeschool Katholieke Hogeschool Antwerpen*, C-147/16, EU:C:2017:928, point 33.

842 Opinion of AG Trstenjak in Case C-40/08 *Asturcom Telecomunicaciones*, EU:C:2009:305.

that certain Spanish courts had already adopted.[843] The Opinion considered that in the circumstances of the case, the *res judicata* principle had *exceptionally* to be disregarded in light of the principle of effective judicial protection as enshrined in Article 47 of the Charter. In his comment on the case, Judge José María Fernández Seijo observed that although the reasons that led the Court to follow the path of legal certainty were understandable, the Opinion of AG Trstenjak corresponded better to the reality of the existing imbalance in consumer disputes.[844]

To be sure, the Court did not question the procedural failures of the arbitration procedure. Besides, the referring court had already decided that the arbitration clause was unfair. The real question was whether this breach could have an impact upon the procedural question of the power of the court to refuse to enforce the award of its own motion. It is true that the Spanish procedural law provided the consumer with the possibility to challenge the arbitration clause in the course of the arbitration proceedings or to introduce proceedings for annulment of the arbitration award (as the consumer did in *Mostaza Claro*). Since the consumer did not exercise her rights, so the argument goes, there is no violation of the right to effective judicial protection. However, there is a preliminary question that has to be asked: did the consumer have a genuine procedure opportunity to exercise her rights in the circumstances of the case?

To answer this question, it would have to be taken into account that the consumer faced important obstacles in defending herself before the arbitration panel as well as before the courts. The arbitration proceedings were held in a location situated far from the residence of the consumer and the costs of travelling there would have been greater than the disputed debt. The seat of the arbitration was not even specified in the arbitration agreement and there was no

---

843 (n. 835). These judgments reached the conclusion that an arbitration award violating the minimum procedural guarantees of impartiality contravenes public policy and therefore the courts should have the power to declare such an award void *ex officio* and refuse enforcement.

844 J. M. Fernández Seijo, *La defensa de los consumidores en las ejecuciones hipotecarias* (Dordrecht, Wolters Kluwer, Bosch, 2013), 191, observing in particular that: "… lo cierto es que comprendiendo las razones que han llevado al TJUE a una interpretación tan restrictiva en aras a garantizar la seguridad jurídica, sin embargo creo que las conclusiones de la Abogado General al asunto *Asturcom Telecomunicaciones* se adecúan mucho más a la realidad puesto que la situación de desequilibrio frente a los consumidores es tan acentuada en muchas ocasiones que el consumidor no llega a alcanzar las posibilidades de intervención efectiva en los procedimientos judiciales, arbitrales o de mediación, y el coste económico e incluso personal de esa intervención frustra su presencia en el procedimiento". [… I certainly understand the reasons that led the Court to such a restrictive interpretation for the sake of legal certainty, nonetheless, I believe that the Opinion of the Advocate General in the Case *Asturcom Telecomunicaciones* corresponds much more to reality since the situation of imbalance towards consumers is so pronounced on many occasions that the consumer does not seize the opportunity for an effective intervention in judicial, arbitration or mediation proceedings, and the economic as well as the personal cost of such intervention thwarts his presence in the procedure] (translated by the author).

choice between possible locations. The consumer had practically no chance to challenge the arbitration clause except for the moment when proceedings would be brought against her. Given that the objections with regard to the jurisdiction of the arbitrator had to be raised no later than the statement of defense,[845] and that the arbitrators are not required nor permitted to examine the potential unfairness of the arbitration clauses of their own motion, the consumer would have been obliged "to take part in the arbitration proceedings, the very lawfulness of which is questioned by the referring court."[846]

Therefore, the failure to participate in the arbitration proceedings should not be a relevant factor in the appreciation of the role of the court in the enforcement proceedings of the arbitration award. The Court pointed to consumer apathy also with regard to the proceedings for annulment of the arbitration award. The problem with that (apart from the general reservations with regard to the 'total inertia' argument discussed above) is that the territorially competent court for issuing the enforcement order was that of the place where the arbitral award was issued.[847] If the consumer had decided to oppose the enforcement proceedings, she would have faced the same obstacles of access to justice (court far from domicile) as she faced in entering defense before the arbitration tribunal. Moreover, the action for annulment has to be brought within two months of the date of notification of the arbitration award.[848] Although such a peremptory time limit is, according to the Court, "reasonable," there is an open question as to the awareness of this right by the consumer. It is not clear from the case whether the notification of the arbitration award contained information on the rights available to the consumer for the purpose of challenging the award.

The national court had already expressed doubts as to the impartiality of the arbitration tribunal.[849] There was a close link between the arbitrators and one of the parties, as they were drafting the contracts used by the telecommunication undertakings.[850] This indicated a strong conflict of interest in the dispute, as it

845 Art. 23(1) Law 36/1988 on Arbitration (n. 822).

846 Opinion of AG Trstenjak in Case C-40/08 *Asturcom Telecomunicaciones* (n. 842), point 64.

847 Art. 8 (5) Law 36/1988 on Arbitration (n. 822).

848 Ibid., Art. 41(4).

849 It should be remembered that the principle of independence and impartiality is of central importance in consumer alternative dispute resolution proceedings according to Art. 6 of the Directive 2013/11/EU of the European Parliament and of the Council of 21 May 2013 on alternative dispute resolution for consumer disputes and amending Regulation (EC) No 2006/2004 and Directive 2009/22/EC (Directive on consumer ADR) [2013] OJ L165/63.

850 The Spanish judgment of the Audiencia Provincial de Madrid of 28 July 2005 (n. 835) distinguished between a situation where the panel would recommend the arbitration process be employed and would determine the arbitration clause, and the current situation in which the arbitration body drafts the contract which imposes the arbitration: "una cosa es recomendar el arbitraje y determinada cláusula arbitral, y otra bien distinta es preparer los contratos, inserter obligatoriamente la cláusula arbitral, y después administrarlo, de forma que el arbitraje resulta prácticamente obligatorio cuando se quiere obtener un determinado

could not be expected that the arbitrators would ever consider the terms that they had themselves drafted to be unfair. If it would have been recognized that the courts should have the power to review a final arbitration award in the exceptional circumstances of the case, there would have been no departure from the basic position of the recognition of the *res judicata* principle. If the arbitration proceedings involving consumers violate the right to a fair trial, there is no reason to uphold the award of such 'scam' proceedings. The rule of law cannot tolerate the fact that a blatant breach of procedural justice produces the force of *res judicata*.

It is important at this point to make a clarification. The situation in the main proceedings, i.e. enforcement of an arbitral award adopted on the basis of an unfair arbitration clause and a partial body, where the consumer was effectively deprived of her rights of defense, has to be distinguished from that of the enforcement of a final judgment. If the grounds of defense pertaining to consumer law are covered by the *res judicata* principle, they can no longer be raised in the course of the enforcement of a judgment.[851] But this should not amount to the breach of the right to effective judicial protection.[852] In judicial proceedings the consumer is "given a genuine opportunity to raise a plea"[853] while the application of the *ex officio* doctrine ensures the effective protection of his mandatory rights. The *res judicata* principle and the value of the proper administration of justice it represents are meaningful only within the broader context of procedural fairness. The fact that the consumer may claim damages because of the omission of a court to raise a plea of its own motion is a different question.[854] In her Opinion, AG Trstenjak concluded that:

> the assessment of whether an unfair arbitration clause is void may not be given over to the arbitrator alone ... this task must be the responsibility of the court, which fully guarantees the judicial impartiality required in a State governed by the rule of law.[855]

In view of the position of quite a few courts in Spain (but not of the *Tribunal Supremo*) to the effect of refusing to enforce arbitration awards, the Court might

tipo de teléfono móvil, y por ultimo ejecutarlo". [It is one thing to recommend the arbitration and to determine the arbitration clause, and another, very different, thing to prepare the contract, insert the arbitration clause, and then decide on this basis, in such a way that the arbitration becomes in practice obligatory when one wishes to obtain a specific type of mobile phone, then ultimately enforce that arbitration clause] (translated by the author).

851 See the Spanish Civil Procedure Code, Art. 564 and J. M. Fernandez Seijo, *La defensa de los consumidores en las ejecuciones hipotecarias* (n. 844), 183 *et seq*.

852 See *De Haan v. the Netherlands* (App. 22839/93), 26 August 1997, §52–55, 1997-IV according to which no violation of the right to fair trial could be established if the decision of the Appeals Tribunal was subject to subsequent control by a judicial body that had full jurisdiction and did provide the guarantees of Article 6 of the ECHR.

853 Cases C-222/05–C-225/05 *Van der Weerd*, EU:C:2007:318.

854 Case C-168/15 *Tomášová*, EU:C:2016:602.

855 Opinion of AG Trstenjak in Case C-40/08 *Asturcom Telecomunicaciones* (n. 842), point 66.

have been satisfied that a reasoning based on the principle of public policy equivalence would in any event be sufficient to ensure a fair solution for the consumer. But at the material time the whole issue in Spain was still subject to controversy.[856] After the judgment was given, the referring court, in its own judgment, took the view that it did not have the power to refuse enforcement of its own motion.[857] The order issued obliged the consumer to pay the principal amount owed, but only up to a certain amount of the costs and interests that had originally been claimed for.[858]

### 3.2.2. Pohotovost': *Unfair Terms in the Consumer Credit Contract Enforced by Means of a Final Arbitration Award*

*Asturcom Telecomunicaciones* was the main authority for the Order of the Court in *Pohotovost' I*.[859] That ruling confirms that the reasoning of *Asturcom Telecomunicaciones* with regard to the powers of the courts to refuse to enforce an arbitration award where they have such powers under their domestic law is applicable in situations where not only is the arbitration clause unfair but also the substantive content of a final arbitration award contravenes the mandatory rules of the Unfair Contract Terms Directive. There is one more interesting aspect of the Order with regard to the powers of the courts to raise of their own motion a civil sanction. We shall come back to this aspect within the framework of the analysis of the judgment in *Radlinger and Radlingerová*.[860]

The facts in *Pohotovost' I* reveal strongly aggressive practices on behalf of the credit company which enforced the proceedings for an enforcement order of a final arbitration award. The district court decided to discontinue the enforcement proceedings on the ground that they contravened basic morality as regards the costs of legal representation, but also the default interest penalty. Under the Slovakian rules on arbitration proceedings, courts are required "to discontinue the enforcement of a payment laid down by an arbitration award where that payment is prohibited by law or where it contravenes basic morality."[861] This provision allowed for the application of the public policy equivalence principle as applied in *Asturcom Telecomunicaciones*, this time with respect to the *substance* of the arbitration award. The Court held that:

> where the court seised with a view to the enforcement of an arbitration award may, of its own motion, discontinue the application of that arbitration award where that award

856 Ibid., point 69.
857 Order of 26 October 2009 (JUR\2011\403897).
858 The reason was that the amount claimed exceeded the legal threshold set out by law.
859 Case C-76/10 *Pohotovost' I* (n. 825).
860 Case C-377/14 *Radlinger and Radlingerová*, EU:C:2016:283, discussed in Section 5.5.
861 *Pohotovost' I* (n. 825), para. 52.

> imposes on the party concerned an objectively impossible payment, prohibited by law or contrary to basic morality, that court must, where it has available to it the legal and factual elements necessary for that task, examine, of its own motion, within the context of the enforcement proceedings, whether the penalty laid down by the credit contract concluded between a creditor and a consumer is unfair.[862]

The national court was also seeking further guidance on the assessment of the unfairness of the contract. This was the occasion for the Court to clarify the incidence of the breach of a mandatory provision of consumer law upon the assessment of unfairness. More particularly, the consumer credit contract made a misleading reference to the Annual Percentage Rate of Charge (APR), which is an essential information under Article 10 of the Consumer Credit Directive. Although not explicitly mentioned, it is evident that the national court had considered that it had the power to raise of its own motion the breach of the relevant provision. The Court held that such a breach of mandatory consumer law "may be a decisive factor" for the assessment of the requirement of *transparency* of the clauses regarding the cost of credit.[863] Employing other legislative instruments on consumer protection as a yardstick of unfairness was also a technique in *Pereničova*,[864] this time with regard to the Unfair Commercial Practices Directive. The method of intertwining the protective logic of consumer directives is considered to be a very positive development by Hans Micklitz and Norbert Reich.[865] The technique of cross-referencing and intertwining instruments of consumer protection is, according to their view, an important indication among others of the emergence of "an autonomous and substantive interpretation of the good faith clause."

The impact of the finding of an unfair term in the credit agreement enforced by means of a final arbitral award upon the enforcement proceedings was left to the national court to decide on the basis of its national law and the guidance that the Court had already provided. The question of the national court was whether upon the finding that the credit would be interest-free, as a result of the application of a civil sanction, it should discontinue enforcement or limit the enforcement only to the principal amount. It appears that four years later, as *Pohotovst II*[866] reveals, this remained a disputed question in the Slovakian legal

862 Ibid., para. 53.

863 Ibid., para. 71.

864 Case C-453/10 *Pereničová and Perenič*, EU:C:2012:144, para. 43. The Court ruled that "a finding that a commercial practice is unfair is one element among others on which the competent court may base its assessment of the unfairness of the contractual terms under Article 4(1) of Directive 93/13".

865 H.-W. Micklitz and N. Reich, "The Court and Sleeping Beauty: The Revival of the Unfair Contract Terms Directive" (2014) 51 *CMLR* 771–808, 788 citing their study in N. Reich and H.-W. Micklitz, "AGB-Recht and UWG – (Endlich) eine Ende des Kastchendenkens?" (2012) *Europäisches Wirtschafts-und Steuerrecht* (EWS), 257, 259.

866 Case C-470/12, *Pohotovosť II* (n. 825).

order. In that later case, the national court had *partially* rejected the application for enforcement of the arbitration award as far as default interest and costs were concerned, upholding it for the remaining debt. The consumer association seeking leave to intervene had claimed that the enforcement proceedings should be suspended in their *entirety*. However, in *Pohotovost' II* the question concerned only the right of the consumer association to intervene. It is then national law that would need to spell out the consequences of the finding of a term unfair upon the proceedings.[867] A plausible choice would seem to be that the court refuses enforcement if the arbitration award is invalid due to the invalidity of the arbitration clause and in all other cases it orders enforcement without application of the unfair term. In any event, the Court in *Pohotovost' I* considered that the reply to such a question involved an actual application to the facts of the case at issue of the interpretation it had already given and that this is the task of the national court.

## 4. BROADENING AND REFINING THE DOCTRINE OF THE ACTIVE CONSUMER COURT

In the years following the "trio" of judgments which laid down the theoretical underpinnings of the doctrine of the active consumer court, national courts started to discharge their role, as a consequence of which new references from preliminary ruling reached the Court. With their questions, the national jurisdictions gave to the Court the possibility, first, to clarify the scope of application of the doctrine, extending its application to all Union consumer law legislation (section 4.1), and, second, to "refine" the doctrine, in the sense of clarifying aspects for its application (section 4.2). This refinement concerned in particular its nature as a faculty or an obligation and the procedural requirements that have to be observed for its exercise. The following subsections will analyze the relevant case law around these two broader thematics.

### 4.1. BROADENING THE SCOPE OF APPLICATION OF THE DOCTRINE

The first important question which was clarified in subsequent case law was the scope of the consumer protection legislation covered by the doctrine. Was it

867 In the framework of enforcement proceedings, the Spanish legislation leaves it up to the judge to decide whether, in the finding of a term as unfair in an action for enforcement of non-judicial titles, either to terminate the enforcement or to allow its continuation without

only applicable with regard to the legislation on the protection from the use of unfair terms which has an impact upon the legality of the respective terms or would it also be applicable to other rules of Union consumer protection law irrespective of their impact upon the validity of the contract? That was not an easy question as the *Van Schijndel* doctrine does not require the courts to raise of their own motion an issue which would oblige them to go beyond the ambit of the dispute as defined by the parties. From early on, the Court extended the reach of the doctrine beyond the unfair terms legislation to other rules of consumer law conferring protection, which similarly had the quality of *mandatory rules* serving the *public interest*. The public interest of those rules justified the *exceptional* character of the intervention of the courts. Initially, the courts were merely empowered to raise those latter rules, but were not obliged to do so. Subsequently the Court moved towards an all-embracing approach to establish an obligation for the courts to raise all the requirements which flow from the Union consumer legislation, provided that all legal and factual elements are available and that the adversarial principle is observed.

### *4.1.1.* Océano Grupo *Extended: The Rules of Consumer Protection Legislation Coming Under the Public Interest*

In two cases of the early period of the *ex officio* doctrine, *Rampion and Godard*[868] and *Martín Martín*,[869] the Court extended the reasoning of *Océano Grupo* to other provisions of mandatory consumer law, unrelated to the issue of contractual validity.

#### 4.1.1.1. *Rampion and Godard*: Moving Beyond National Classifications Which Impede the Powers of the Courts

In *Rampion and Godard*, the referring court faced comparable procedural constraints to the referring court in *Cofidis* with regard to its powers in the proceedings. This time, the issue was not about a time limitation on the powers of the courts to raise unfair terms, nor was it even connected to contractual unfairness. The consumers had purchased goods financed by a credit facility. The credit was concluded on the same day as the purchase of goods, the credit limit was equal to the sale price and the credit offer identified the seller. The twist

application of the unfair term (Spanish Civil Procedure Code, Art. 561). With respect to the consequences of the application of the civil sanction of forfeiture of interest, the French law provides for the repayment by the debtor of the remaining capital due, pursuant to the schedule of repayments provided for. The interest already paid is restituted to the debtor or is allocated to the capital due (Art. L311-48 Code de la Consommation).

868 Case C-429/05 *Rampion and Godard*, EU:C:2007:575.

869 Case C-227/08 *Martín Martín*, EU:C:2009:792.

in the tale was that the credit did not specify the goods being financed. When the consumers realized that the goods purchased were defective, they brought proceedings against both the trader and the creditor seeking a termination of both the credit and the sale contract. However, in order to support their claim, they did not invoke the remedies provided for under the Consumer Credit Directive[870] for linked credit contracts (notably, its Article 11(2)).[871] They merely claimed that the contract of sale did not indicate the date of delivery of the goods. The objection raised by the credit professional was that the two contracts were not linked because the goods financed were not indicated in the offer of credit and the credit facility was not tied to the financing of the sale. Should the consumers be expected to respond to this legal question and construe their counter-defense or could the national court intervene and raise pleas in law in relation to the conditions of the interconnection of linked credit contracts or other mandatory provisions governing consumer credit? By asking this question, the French national court intended in essence to know whether the *Océano Grupo* case law could extend to national provisions implementing a directive on mandatory consumer protection other than the Unfair Contract Terms Directive.

The national court considered itself impeded from raising the matter of its own motion because of the case law of the *Cour de Cassation* on the issue of the *ex officio* powers of the courts (*relevé d'office*) and more particularly on the distinction between rules of public policy intended to order society (*ordre public de direction*) and rules of public policy intended to protect private interests (*ordre public de protection*). The courts were empowered to raise of their own motion only those rules which belonged to the *ordre public de direction*, but not those which belonged to the *ordre public de protection*.[872] The rules on consumer credit belonged to those latter rules that impeded the courts from raising them of their own motion. As was discussed in Chapter 3,[873] the denial of the powers of the courts on the basis of this dichotomy has been a fiercely debated matter in France. The French judge Ghislain Poissonier, echoing many of his colleagues

---

870 Council Directive 87/102/EEC of 22 December 1986 for the approximation of the laws, regulations and administrative provisions of the Member States concerning consumer credit [1987] OJ L42/48, repealed by Directive 2008/48/EC of the European Parliament and of the Council of 23 April 2008 on credit agreements for consumers and repealing Council Directive 87/102/EEC [2008] OJ L133/66.

871 Now Art. 15(1) of the Consumer Credit Directive. On linked credit agreements see P. Rott, "Consumer Credit" in N. Reich et al., *European Consumer Law* (Cambridge, Intersentia, 2nd ed., 2014), 226 *et seq.*

872 The referring court cites Cass. civ. 1re, 23 novembre 2004, Bull. civ. I, no 287, 241. On further citations of French case law see G. Poissonier, "La C.J.C.E. donne au juge national le pouvoir d'appliquer d'office le droit communautaire de la consommation" (2007–2008) 1 *Revue Européenne de Droit de la Consommation* 131–142, at 138–140.

873 Chapter 3, Section 2.2.4.

in the first instance judiciary considered that the distinction derived from a classical doctrinal conception "disconnected from the procedural reality of consumer litigation."[874]

The Court did not enter into this debate and it did not take up the proposition of the national court to "reclassify" the rules of consumer credit legislation as *ordre public de direction*, so that the courts could raise them of their own motion. Such a move would have most probably led the Court into the turbulent waters of direct engagement with the national legal concepts and classifications. Instead, it took up the invitation of AG Mengozzi to construct the active role of the courts "over and above the application of the ... domestic concepts and rules of national procedural law."[875] The Court recalled first the double finality of the Consumer Credit Directive: to ensure both the creation of a common consumer credit market and the protection of the consumers who take the credit.[876] It continued with a consideration of the difficulties the consumers were facing in ensuring their rights against the professionals (as they had been set out in the trio of the judgments in *Océano Grupo, Cofidis* and *Mostaza Claro*) and which render the powers of the courts to raise of their own motion the unfair terms of a contract "necessary for ensuring that the consumer enjoys effective protection."[877] These considerations were deemed to be valid not only with regard to the Unfair Contract Terms Directive, but equally with regard to other provisions governing consumer protection, such as the rules in relation to linked credit contracts set out in the Consumer Credit Directive. These rules aim to confer on the consumer rights against the grantor of credit over and above the consumer's normal contractual rights. Therefore, the Court found that:

> That aim could not be effectively achieved if the consumer were himself obliged to invoke the right to pursue remedies which he enjoys against the grantor of credit in accordance with the provisions of national law transposing Article 11(2) of [the Consumer Credit Directive], in particular because of the real risk that the consumer may be unaware of his rights or may encounter difficulties in exercising them.[878]

The Court also pointed out that the premise of structural inequality underlying this finding does not depend on whether the consumer enjoys legal representation or not "as the issue must be settled independently of the specific circumstances of the case."[879]

---

874 Translation from the following passage of G. Poissonier (n. 872), note 27: "Cette jurisprudence était issue d'une conception doctrinale classique, coupée de la réalité procédurale du litige de la consommation."

875 Opinion of AG Mengozzi in Case C-429/05 *Rampion and Godard*, EU:C:2007:199, point 82.

876 Case C-429/05 *Rampion and Godard*, (n. 868), para. 59 with references to earlier case law.

877 Ibid., para. 62.

878 Ibid., para. 65.

879 Ibid.

It should be noted that *Rampion and Godard* raised another very interesting question, although on which the Court did not have to decide as it exceeded the ambit of the order of reference. The professional contended that the true purpose of the question of the referring court was to authorize it to impose, of its own motion, the penalty of forfeiture of interest for failure to include certain mandatory under French law information in the prior offer relating to tied credit. The Court would have the occasion to complete the "missing piece" of *Rampion and Godard* and address the issue of the *ex officio* application of civil sanctions in the order in *Pohotovosť*[880] as well as in *Radlinger*,[881] an issue which will be discussed later.[882]

#### 4.1.1.2. *Martín Martín*: The Public Interest of Consumer Protection Legislation Which Exceptionally Justifies a Positive Intervention by the Courts

The main issue raised in *Martín Martín*[883] was whether the courts should have the power to pronounce of their own motion the nullity of a contract concluded in breach of a mandatory provision of the Doorstep Selling Directive,[884] namely Article 4 on the notification to the consumer of the right of cancellation of the contract. The consumer, Ms. Martín Martín, signed an off-premises contract for the purchase of certain goods. The goods were delivered to her, but the company did not receive payment. The professional applied for an order for payment procedure and obtained a judgment against the consumer, who subsequently brought an appeal before the Spanish referring court. This court considered that the contract signed by the consumer should be declared void inasmuch as she was not informed of her right to withdraw from the contract within a period of seven days from the delivery of the goods, or of the conditions and the consequences of exercise of that right. As it follows from Spanish legislation, the infringement of the provisions for the conclusion of an off-premises contract affords to the consumer the right to cancel the contract.[885] However, Ms Martín Martín did

880 Case C-76/10 *Pohotovosť I* (n. 825).

881 Case C-377/14 *Radlinger and Radlingerová*, EU:C:2016:283.

882 Section 5.5.

883 Case C-227/08 *Martín Martín* (n. 869).

884 Council Directive 85/577/EEC of 20 December 1985 to protect the consumer in respect of contracts negotiated away from business premises [1985] OJ L372/31, repealed by Directive 2011/83/EU of the European Parliament and of the Council of 25 October 2011 on consumer rights, amending Council Directive 93/13/EEC and Directive 1999/44/EC of the European Parliament and of the Council and repealing Council Directive 85/577/EEC and Directive 97/7/EC of the European Parliament and of the Council [2011] OJ L304/64.

885 Ley 26/1991 sobre contratos celebrados fuera de los establecimientos mercantiles (Law 26/1991 on Contracts Negotiated Away from Business Premises) of 21 November 1991 (BOE No 283 of 26 November 1991) Art. 4 (in force until 1 December 2007), provided that a contract that was concluded or proposed in violation of the requirements set out in the law, could be annulled upon request of the consumer. This law had been amended by Royal

not submit a plea of nullity before the court of first instance or during the appeal proceedings. The referring court considered that it was uncertain whether it could declare the contract void, given, on the one hand, that national law leaves it up to the consumer to request the cancellation and, on the other hand, that Spanish civil proceedings are governed by the *principio de justicia rogada*, a principle on the basis of which the court cannot assess, of its own motion, facts, evidence and claims which the parties have not raised.[886]

In order to address the question of the power of a court to raise of its own motion the *nullity* of a contract resulting from the breach of a mandatory provision of consumer protection law, the Court had to examine two separate issues. The first issue was whether Article 4 of the Doorstep Selling Directive was a provision that could be raised by the courts of their own motion. The second issue concerned whether the national court seised can raise of its own motion the consequences from the breach of that provision, as set out in national law.

The first issue was, in essence, a matter of the extension of the scope of application of *Océano Grupo*. However, the Court did not refer to that case. Rather, it established the *ex officio* powers within the framework of the consumer legislation at issue as an *exception* to the approach of the principle pronounced in *Van Schijndel*, justified on the basis of the *public interest* served by that legislation and the *effectiveness* of legislation on consumer protection. Taking this path of reasoning, it recalled first that:

> [Union] law does not, in principle, require national courts to raise of their own motion an issue concerning the breach of provisions of Community law, where examination of that issue would oblige them to go beyond the ambit of the dispute defined by the parties themselves and rely on facts and circumstances other than those on which the party with an interest in application of those provisions has based his claim.[887]

However, the court should be able to act of its own motion "*only in exceptional cases where the public interest requires its intervention.*"[888] To that effect, the Court cites *van Schijndel* and *van der Weerd*. It had therefore to be ascertained whether the provision at issue (Article 4 of the Doorstep Selling Directive) could be considered to be founded upon such a public interest. The Court finds that the system of protection established by that directive "assumes not only that the consumer, as the weaker party, has the right to cancel the contract, but also that he is made aware of his rights by being specifically informed of them in writing."[889] It follows, from that, that the obligation to give notice of the right

Legislative Degree 1/2007 (n. 815), Art. 112 of which had similar wording to the legislative provision in force until that time.

886 Case C-227/08 *Martín Martín* (n. 869), para. 16.

887 Ibid., para. 19.

888 Ibid., para. 20.

889 Ibid., para. 26.

of cancellation "plays a central role in the overall scheme of that directive as an essential guarantee [...] for the effective exercise of that right and, therefore, for the effectiveness of consumer protection sought by the Community legislature."[890] It follows that such a provision comes under the *public interest* justification, within the meaning of the exceptional circumstances justifying the derogation from the principle of *Van Schijndel* and the establishment of:

> a positive intervention by the national court in order to compensate for the imbalance between the consumer and the trader in the context of contracts concluded away from business premises.[891]

In those circumstances, the Court finds that the national court seised "may" raise of its own motion the infringement of the requirement of notification of the right of cancellation laid down in the Doorstep Selling Directive. By employing the verb "may," the Court did not frame yet the respective power of the courts as an obligation. By contrast, with regard to unfair terms, it had already established that the courts have an "obligation" to raise the matter. This discrepancy had puzzled the commentators.[892] The position of the Court would eventually evolve and it is on this evolution we shall now turn.

The second issue, pertaining to the possibility for the court to pronounce the nullity of the contract of its own motion, is a matter associated with the consequences of the finding of the violation of consumer legislation and it will be discussed later under the respective section.[893]

### *4.1.2. The Obligation of the Courts to Examine of Their Own Motion Infringements of EU Consumer Protection Legislation*

The first two judgments deciding in favor of the extension of application of the active court doctrine to other provisions of consumer law, *Rampion and Godard*

---

890 Ibid., para. 27.

891 Ibid., para. 28.

892 See E. Poillot, "L'Encadrement Procédural de l'Action des Consommateurs" in N. Sauphanor-Brouillaud et al., *Les Contrats de Consommation Règles Communes* (Paris, LGDJ 2013), 971, 986, who, inspired by the theory of the classic authors Planiol and Ripert (M. Planiol and G. Ripert, *Traité de droit civil français* (Paris, LGDJ, 2nd ed., t. VI, no 295), searches for an explanation of the discrepancy between the importance of the protected interest and the mandatory character of a provision or its connection with ordre public: "C'est donc bien le critère de l'importance de l'intérêt protégé et non pas celui du caractère impératif d'une norme ou son rattachement à l'ordre public qui élève le relevé d'office au rang d'obligation, ce qui finalement nous ramène à la théorie de Planiol et Ripert". [It is then the criterion of the importance of the protected interest and not the one pertaining to the mandatory character of a rule or its connection with public policy which elevates the obligation of the courts to raise a plea in law of their own motion into the rank of an obligation, which finally takes us back to the theory of Planiol and Ripert] (translated by the author).

893 Section 5.1.

and *Martín Martín*, raised some questions as to the remit of this extension. Would it apply only to those provisions of consumer legislation which come under the ambit of *public interest*? If so, which provisions should be considered to fall under this category and do the courts have a faculty or an obligation to raise them? These questions now seem to be settled following the judgment in *Radlinger.*[894] But before getting there, there are two other cases on the powers of the courts to raise of their own motion provisions of the Consumer Sales Directive,[895] which have prepared the ground for *Radlinger.*

#### 4.1.2.1. *Duarte Hueros*: The Powers of the Courts to Recognize of Their Own Motion the Right of the Consumer to Obtain a Remedy in the Sales Contract

The question referred to in *Duarte Hueros*[896] concerned the impact of the *res judicata* principle (*cosa juzgada* in the Spanish legal order from which the question originated) and the principle of 'concentration' of claims upon the exercise of the consumer sales remedies and the power of the courts to grant those remedies of their own motion. In essence, taking into account the procedural circumstances of the case, the judgment introduces a limited derogation to the *ne ultra petita* principle, allowing the courts to grant an alternative remedy to the consumer in circumstances where her initial claim was rejected and she was not entitled to refine her initial application or to bring a fresh action to that end.

The consumer, Ms. Duarte Hueros, purchased a vehicle with a sliding roof which turned out to be defective. After attempting in vain to have it repaired, the consumer asked the car to be replaced. As the professional refused to do so, the consumer brought an action before the referring court and sought rescission of the contract of sale and an order that the seller and the manufacturer be ordered to repay the purchase price of the vehicle. The national court decided that the default was minor and therefore had to reject the claim for rescission. This left the consumer with the alternative remedy of reduction of the price on the basis of Article 3(5) of the Consumer Sales Directive.[897] However, she had failed to put forward such subsidiary claim in the proceedings. The alternative remedy could not be raised by the court of its own motion in view of the principle that judicial decisions must be commensurate with the requests made by the parties (*ne ultra petita*).[898] Moreover, it was not possible for the consumer to bring new proceedings and claim the reduction of the price. This was the case

894 Case C-377/14 *Radlinger and Radlingerová* (n. 881).
895 Directive 1999/44/EC of the European Parliament and of the Council of 25 May 1999 on certain aspects of the sale of consumer goods and associated guarantees [1999] OJ L171/12.
896 Case C-32/12 *Duarte Hueros*, EU:C:2013:637.
897 Directive 1999/44/EC of the European Parliament and of the Council of 25 May 1999 on certain aspects of the sale of consumer goods and associated guarantees [1999] OJ L171/12.
898 Art. 218.1 Spanish Civil Procedure Code.

due to the combined application of the 'principle of concentration' and the *res judicata* principle: if the claimant did not bring forward all the facts and legal grounds which he could have advanced at earlier proceedings, these grounds were covered by the force of *res judicata* and could no longer be examined in subsequent proceedings.[899]

According to the Opinion of AG Kokott,[900] there would be no need to recognize an obligation for the courts with regard to the exercise of remedies in a consumer sales contract because the consumer in that case should not be considered to be "in a comparably weak position with regard to the implementation of the contract,"[901] unlike the case of enforcement of a contract which contains unfair terms. The Opinion therefore concluded that: "action by a national court of its own motion would not strengthen consumer protection, but would rather provide the consumer with an additional means of attack."[902]

The Court did not endorse this line of reasoning. Its reasoning is based upon the principle of national procedural autonomy within the framework of which the Court assessed whether the procedural rules at issue were liable to undermine the effectiveness of consumer protection. This way of reasoning might come as a surprise in the beginning. The older cases, *Rampion and Godard* and *Martín Martín* concentrated upon the public interest of the provisions that had to be raised by the courts of their own motion in order to achieve the effectiveness of consumer protection. Moreover, an explicit reference is made to the effect that Article 3 of the Consumer Sales Directive does not contain any provision pursuant to which the national courts would be obliged to grant of their own motion the remedy of price reduction. However, this way of reasoning could be explained by the fact that the case at hand was the result of a particular interpretation of the rules on the presentation of the claims in the course of the proceedings. This is why it might have seemed more prudent to examine the case through the lens of the particular circumstances of the procedural system in question.

The Court found that the combined application of the Spanish civil procedural principles with regard to pleas in law that can be put forward in the proceedings, within the context of a consumer sales dispute, may lead to the result that the consumer is "definitely deprived of the possibility of benefitting from the right to seek an appropriate reduction in the price" of the defected goods.[903] In order to avoid this situation, the consumer could certainly include in her application an alternative claim seeking the price reduction. But the Court recognizes that:

> such an eventuality must be regarded as very improbable because there is a significant risk that the consumer in question will not put forward an alternative claim which

---

899 Article 400 Spanish Civil Procedure Code.
900 Opinion of AG Kokott in Case C-32/12 *Duarte Hueros*, EU:C:2013:128.
901 Ibid., point 48.
902 Ibid.
903 Case C-32/12 *Duarte Hueros* (n. 896), para. 37.

> would seek, moreover, relief inferior to that sought in the principal claim, either on account of the particularly rigid requirement that the alternative claim be presented at the same time as the principal claim or because the consumer is unaware of, or does not appreciate, the extent of his rights.[904]

This part of the reasoning demonstrates the high threshold of effectiveness which the Court adopts in consumer disputes. The procedural provisions which would normally apply in any other type of litigation, without raising concerns as to their effectiveness, have to be adapted within the framework of consumer litigation in order to take into account the lack of sophistication of the party which the law intends to protect. However, the Spanish system did not match this high threshold as it seemed to require the same procedural diligence from the consumer as from any other party by:

> essentially oblig[ing] the consumer to anticipate the outcome of the competent court's analysis of the legal characterization regarding the lack of conformity in the goods, which is final, making the protection provided for the consumer under Article 3(5) of [the Consumer Sales Directive] completely uncertain in nature, and thereby rendering that protection inadequate.[905]

Under such circumstances, the Court held that the Spanish procedural rules were "liable to undermine the effectiveness of the consumer protection intended by the European Union legislature" and that the national court should therefore be allowed to recognize of its own motion the right of the consumer to obtain an appropriate reduction in the price of the goods.[906] That being so, it is left to the national court "taking the whole body of domestic law into consideration and applying the interpretative methods recognized by domestic law" to ensure that the right conferred by the consumer legislation is "fully effective."[907] In that regard, it is interesting to note that the Opinion of AG Kokott argued that the whole issue could be resolved as a matter of proper interpretation of domestic procedural law rather than in terms of setting an obligation of the court to raise the plea of its own motion.[908]

#### 4.1.2.2. *Faber*: Public Interest of the Rule Relating to the Burden of Proof and Equal Standing to Domestic Public Policy

*Faber*[909] gave to the Court the possibility to examine the powers of the courts with regard, this time, to another mandatory provision of the Consumer Sales

904 Ibid., para. 38.
905 Ibid., para. 40.
906 Ibid., para. 39.
907 Ibid., para. 42.
908 Opinion of AG Kokott in Case C-32/12 *Duarte Hueros* (n. 900), point 50.
909 Case C-497/13 *Faber*, EU:C:2015:357.

Directive. The case also raised the preliminary question of whether the courts are required to examine of their own motion the capacity of the purchaser as a consumer within the meaning of that Directive, even though the party has not relied on that status. This aspect of the case will be discussed in the next section.[910]

The plaintiff in the case, Ms. Faber, had purchased a second-hand vehicle on May 27, 2008 at a garage. The contract of sale bore the heading "contract of sale to a private individual." On September 26, 2008 (i.e. less than six months after the delivery of the vehicle) it caught fire during a journey and was completely destroyed. The car was towed to the garage and later scrapped. Ms. Faber maintained that already on the occasion of the accident, the parties spoke about the possible liability of the garage. At the beginning of 2009, there was a new contact between Ms. Faber and the garage in view of the imminent police report on the cause of the accident. It was only by a letter of May 11, 2009, that she informed the professional that she was holding them liable for the damage resulting in the destruction of the vehicle. On October 26, 2010, she brought proceedings against them. In support of her action, she submitted the lack of conformity of the vehicle with the contract, but she did not claim to have made her purchase in her capacity as a consumer. The defendant disputed the lack of conformity and submitted that the rights of Ms. Faber were in any event foreclosed, as she did not give them notice of the contested lack of conformity in a timely manner after its discovery. The first instance court rejected the claim of Ms. Faber on the basis that the contact between the two parties took place more than three months after the vehicle caught fire. It also held that there was no need to examine whether the purchaser was a consumer.

The referring Dutch court essentially asked two questions in relation to the powers of the courts.[911] The first question, which as mentioned will be dealt with in the next section,[912] was whether the courts should be obliged to investigate the status of the purchaser as a consumer within the framework of appeal proceedings. In case the national court determined that the contract in question came within the material scope of the Consumer Sales Directive, the next issue was whether Article 5(3) of that Directive should be considered as a rule of equal standing to the domestic rules of public policy. This article establishes the rule of apportionment of the burden of proof on the lack of conformity of the goods with the contract according to which, unless proved otherwise, any lack

---

910 Section 4.2.2.

911 There were also two more questions as to the application of the rule on the notification by the consumer to the seller of the alleged lack of conformity, and the rule on the apportionment of the burden of proof, in particular, which matters it is for the consumer to establish. See P. Rott, "Improving consumers' enforcement of their rights under EU consumer sales law: *Froukje Faber*" (2016) *CMLR*, 509–526.

912 Section 4.2.2.

of conformity which becomes apparent within six months of the delivery of the goods is, in principle, to be presumed to have existed at the time of delivery.

The Court found that such apportionment of the burden of proof in favor of the consumer was, in accordance with Article 7 of the Consumer Sales Directive:

> binding in nature both for the parties, who may not derogate from it by means of an agreement, and for the Member States, which must ensure that it is complied with. It follows that that rule relating to the burden of proof must be applied even though it has not been expressly relied on by the consumer who may benefit from it.[913]

By using the term "must be applied," the Court made it clear, for the first time outside the field of unfair terms, that the courts are actually obliged to raise the respective mandatory rule of consumer protection.

The next question was whether this obligation would also apply at the level of appeal proceedings. According to Dutch procedural law, at that level of proceedings the court "may rule only on the complaints which were put forward by the parties in the first claims lodged on appeal."[914] However, the provisions of public policy have to be applied by the courts of their own motion, even if they have not been invoked by the parties. On this basis, the Court constructed its reasoning on the 'public policy equivalence' principle resorting to the *public interest* underlying the protection conferred by the provision of consumer law in question. In view of this *public interest* quality, the rule on the apportionment of the burden of proof "must be regarded as a provision of equal standing to a national rule which ranks, within the domestic legal system, as a rule of public policy."[915]

Moreover, according to the method of application of the public policy equivalence, according to which the discretion is raised into an obligation (on the basis of the principle of loyal cooperation), the Court concluded that:

> where, under its domestic legal system, it has a discretion as to whether to apply such a rule of its own motion, the national court must of its own motion apply any provision of its domestic law which transposes Article 5(3) of [the Consumer Sales Directive].[916]

#### 4.1.2.3. *Radlinger* and the All-Embracing Approach

*Duarte Hueros* and *Faber* paved the way for the all-embracing approach of the Court in *Radlinger and Radlingerová* as to the scope of the active consumer

913 Case C-497/13 *Faber* (n. 909), para. 55.
914 Ibid., para. 15.
915 Ibid., para. 56.
916 Ibid.

court doctrine.[917] One of the questions in this case was whether the courts are required to examine of their own motion the breach by the creditor to provide the mandatory information to be included in the credit agreement, pursuant to Article 10(2) of the Consumer Credit Directive.

The Court first recalled the existing case law with regard to an *obligation* of the courts to examine of their own motion infringements of Union consumer protection legislation. *To that effect*,[918] the judgment cites *Pannon*[919] with regard to the Unfair Contract Terms Directive, *Martín Martín*[920] with regard to the Doorstep Selling Directive and *Duarte Hueros*[921] with regard to the Consumer Sales Directive. The reasoning continues with the well-established arguments on the *weak position* of the consumer vis-à-vis the seller, on the *fundamental importance* of the provision on the information of the consumer at the moment of conclusion of the credit contract, and the *real risk* that the consumer, particularly because of a lack of awareness, will not rely on the legal rule that is intended to protect him. From these elements it follows that "effective consumer protection could be achieved only if the national court were required, of its own motion, to examine compliance with the requirements which flow from EU law on consumer law."[922]

This proposition is supported, *by analogy*, by the findings of the very first judgment where the Court ruled in favor of the extension of the application of the active consumer doctrine to other instruments of consumer legislation, which is none other than *Rampion and Godard*.[923] With reference to the latter judgment, the Court makes a *leap forward* and furthers its case law by recognizing a wide scope of application of the doctrine of the active court.

## 4.2. REFINING THE DOCTRINE

The judgment that set in stone the exact nature of the powers of the courts to raise unfair terms as an obligation depending on the elements of the case file is *Pannon*.[924] Subsequent references for preliminary ruling allowed the Court

---

917 Case C-377/14 *Radlinger and Radlingerová*, EU:C:2016:283.

918 Citing case law "*to that effect*" allows the Court to develop its case law while supporting its path of reasoning on precedent. This is evident here, as in one of the cases cited, Case C-227/08 *Martín Martín* (n. 869), para. 29, the Court established only a discretion and not an obligation of the courts to raise the rules of consumer law in question, while the other judgments cited covered a specific field of consumer legislation without making broader statements as to the scope of the rules covered by the active consumer court doctrine.

919 Case C-243/08 *Pannon GSM*, EU:C:2009:350, discussed in the following Section 4.2.1.

920 Case C-227/08 *Martín Martín* (n. 869).

921 Case C-32/12 *Duarte Hueros* (n. 896).

922 Case C-377/14 *Radlinger and Radlingerová* (n. 917), para. 66.

923 Case C-429/05 *Rampion and Godard* (n. 868).

924 Case C-243/08 *Pannon GSM* (n. 919).

to refine further the contours of the active consumer court in proceedings pertaining to the protection from unfair terms particularly on the following issues: the eventual obligation of the courts to order measures of investigation; the observance of an adversarial process; the role of the consumer in the proceedings; and the eventual application of the doctrine at the level of appeal proceedings.

The refinement of the doctrine addresses two major concerns that could be raised against the active role of the courts in consumer litigation: that it might undermine the judicial duty of impartiality and that it places an insurmountable burden upon the courts them. The elements that will follow give a more precise idea not only of how the active court is supposed to discharge its role but also of what it means to be an active consumer court in negative terms. An active court is *not an inquisitorial court*. It bears an obligation to raise the unfairness of a contractual clause as long as it has all the legal and factual elements available. It has to classify the matters of law and of fact which the parties have submitted to it, if necessary by requesting the parties to provide any useful details. An active court is *not a partial court*. It applies the law and in this way ensures the protection which the legislator itself intended to afford to the weaker party. An active court is *not an authoritative court*, in the sense of a court which ignores fundamental procedural guarantees. As soon as it raises a point of law of its own motion, it is required to urge argument from the parties and observe the right to a fair trial. Finally, an active court is *not a "paternalistic" court*. The consumer is free to renounce *a posteriori* the protection of the law once he has been respectively informed by the judge. The "deviation" which an active consumer court requires from national procedural laws is to abandon a dogmatic perception of absolute judicial passivity when that would be necessary to *terminate the procedural crystallization of market imbalance*. The positive action by the courts in consumer disputes is the procedural "reflection" of the intention of the legislator to remedy the *asymmetries at the contractual level*. Within such a perception of their role, the courts do not "take sides." On the contrary, they remain neutral by redressing the failures which prevent the full effect of the protection the law intends to confer.

### *4.2.1. The Obligation of the Courts Attached to the Availability of All Factual and Legal Elements*

As mentioned earlier, *Pannon* is the first case in which the Court:

> clearly stated that the role assigned by EU law to national courts is not limited to a mere power to rule on the possible unfairness of a contractual term … but also consists of an obligation to examine that issue of its own motion, where it has available to it the legal and factual elements necessary for that task.[925]

[925] Case C-168/15 *Tomášová* (n. 854), para. 30.

Even if the Court in *Mostaza Claro*[926] hinted at the existence of an obligation of the courts to raise unfair terms, in that judgment (as the Court explained in a later judgment) "it did not attach any significance to that fact"[927] since it was ruling on a different question. The legal issue raised in *Pannon* was similar to the one raised in *Océano Grupo*. The consumer had concluded with the trader a mobile telephone subscription contract which contained an exclusive jurisdiction clause. The trader applied for an order for payment for failure of compliance with the contractual obligations. The consumer filed a statement of opposition against the order, without however challenging the exclusive jurisdiction term. The Hungarian court noted that the disputed clause conferred jurisdiction on a court which was far away from the place of residence of the consumer, and to which there was only limited access by public means of transport. The Hungarian Civil Procedure Code provides that the courts must raise of their own motion the issue of territorial jurisdiction. However, as the jurisdiction is not exclusive, the prorogation was deemed to be confirmed after the first filing of the defense as to the substance of the dispute. Thus, the law deprived the courts from raising of their own motion the issue of absence of their jurisdiction, even if it originated from an unfair term.

In order to establish an obligation of the courts to raise the unfair term under those circumstances, the Court referred to *Mostaza Claro* and the established "nature and importance of the public interest underlying the protection" which justify that the national court be "required" to assess of its own motion whether a contractual term is unfair. The obligatory character of the active consumer court doctrine insinuated in *Mostaza Claro* now becomes perfectly clear:

> Consequently, the role thus attributed to the national court by [Union] law in this area is not limited to a mere power to rule on the possible unfairness of a contractual term but also consists of the obligation to examine that issue of its motion, where it has available to it the legal and factual elements necessary for that task, including when it is assessing whether it has territorial jurisdiction.[928]

Moreover, the Court continued on the possibility for the consumer to renounce protection:

> In carrying out that obligation, the national court is not, however, required under the [Unfair Contract Terms Directive] to exclude the possibility that the term in question

---

926 Case C-168/05 *Mostaza Claro* (n. 648), para. 38.

927 Case C-168/15 *Tomášová* (n. 854), para. 29. Indeed, the judgment in *Mostaza Claro* (ibid) concentrated on the question whether a consumer may invoke the invalidity of an arbitration agreement for the first time before the national court hearing an action for annulment of an arbitration award, although he has not invoked the nullity ground in the arbitration proceedings.

928 Case C-243/08 *Pannon GSM* (n. 919), para. 32.

may be applicable, if the consumer after having been informed of it by that court, does not intend to assert its unfair on non-binding status.[929]

Let us delve into the first important clarification brought by this judgment, the existence of a duty to consider the fairness of the term subject to the availability of all legal and factual material necessary for that task. This proviso has constantly been repeated ever since.[930] The *availability* of all the necessary factual and legal elements points to the requirement that these elements should actually *enable* the court to consider the issue of fairness. For a court to be enabled to consider an issue, the matter must somehow be *brought to its attention*. The usual way for this to occur is that the professional *relies* upon a term or a list of terms in order to request the performance of the contract. It would then appear justified to conclude that the court is not obliged to consider the fairness of all terms of the contract, even those unrelated to the dispute at issue. The situation would be different if the other contractual terms influence the assessment of the unfair nature of the term upon which the action is based. As the Court clarified in *Banif Plus Bank*, "the national court must, in order to determine whether the contractual term on which the claim before it is based may be unfair, take account of all of the other terms of the contract."[931]

The *ex officio* obligation still operates within the framework of an adversarial system. Even if the principle of party presentation is *tempered* in order to accommodate the underlying power imbalance of the parties, the consumer proceedings do not become inquisitorial. The requirement to observe the factual ambit of the dispute is the "borderline"[932] which the courts cannot cross. This limitation counters, according to Judge Ghislain Poissonier,[933] any criticism that could be made that the *ex officio* doctrine supposedly gives a "blank check" to the courts. Moreover, the same judge observes, it dispels any concerns that the judiciary could have that the *ex officio* doctrine could open up the floodgates of unjustified professional or civil liability.[934] That is so since, in view of the limitation pertaining to the availability of all the necessary elements for the own motion assessment, the parties cannot challenge a decision of a lower court for that court not having proceeded upon an enquiry which *it was not in*

929 Ibid., para. 33. This aspect will be further discussed below under Section 4.2.4.

930 Case C-618/10 *Banco Español de Crédito* (n. 715), para. 44; Case C-472/11, *Banif Plus Bank* (n. 695), para 23.

931 Case C-472/11 *Banif Plus Bank* (n. 695), para. 41 and operative part number 2.

932 G. Biardeaud and P. Florés, *Credit à la Consommation, Protection du Consommateur* (Paris, Delmas Express, 2012), para. 2902: "En fait, la nécessité de respecter l'objet du litige constitue une frontière infranchissable pour le juge, que le moyen soit de droit interne ou de droit communautaire." [Actually, the necessity to observe the ambit of the dispute is the borderline which the courts may not cross, irrespective whether the plea in law concerned is of national or Union law origin] (translated by the author).

933 G. Poissonier (n. 937).

934 See Case C-168/15 *Tomášová* (n. 925), analyzed in Chapter 6, Section 4.2.

*a position* to undertake in view of the elements of the case file.[935] The former Advocate General of the Court, Verica Trstejnak, writing on the procedural aspects of European consumer protection law, has stressed the importance of the clarifications brought about by *Pannon* in the following terms:

> [the] knowledge [of the courts] about the legal and factual elements as well as the attitude and the intentions of the consumers are taken into consideration for determining the scope and the consequences of the duty of the national courts to intervene in consumer protection proceedings.[936]

So the courts are not obliged to check each consumer contract for potential unfair terms *in the abstract*, if those terms are not crucial for the dispute which is put before them. That being said, they should retain the *faculty* to raise any other term of the contract from the moment that they have available all the legal and factual material, without being constrained by the principle of party presentation.

The establishment of an obligation might at first sight appear intrusive for the national procedural systems. However, from the moment that a provision is qualified as mandatory law, that law serves the public interest and all the necessary elements to conduct an own motion assessment are available to the court, there is no valid justification in framing the power in terms of discretion. This would mean that the same rule qualified as mandatory Union law of protection, laid down in the public interest, would be raised by some national courts and not by others. The establishment of an obligation ensures and reinforces, on the one hand, the equality of the parties before the law.[937] On the other hand, it confirms that the unfair terms legislation defends the core of the Union consumer protection values which has to uphold in a uniform way across national jurisdictions. The Unfair Contract Terms Directive, by providing that the consumer is not bound by unfair terms "is intended to accord a right to the citizen, in his role as a consumer."[938]

---

935 G. Poissonier (n. 937): "Quant à ceux qui craignent que la responsabilité professionnelle ou civile du juge puisse être engagée en cas de manquement à son 'devoir', ils seront surement rassurés par la règle selon laquelle les parties ne peuvent pas reprocher au juge ne pas avoir procédé à une recherche qu'elles ne lui ont pas permis de réaliser, règle rappelée régulièrement par la Cour de Cassation justement à propos de la forclusion biennale." [As for those who fear that the professional or civil responsibility of the judge may be engaged due to failing to observe his "duty" [to raise of its own motion the mandatory provision of consumer law], they will certainly be reassured by the rule according to which the parties may not criticize the court for not having proceeded with a research that they did not allow it to make, rule noted regularly by the Cassation Court exactly with regard to the biannual foreclosure period] (translated by the author).

936 V. Trstenjak, "Procedural aspects of European Consumer Protection Law and the Case Law of the CJEU" (2013) 2 *ERPL* 451–477, 468.

937 G. Poissonier, "La CJCE franchit une nouvelle étape vers une réelle protection du consommateur" (2009) *Recueil Dalloz* 2312.

938 Case C-243/08 *Pannon GSM* (n. 919), para. 21.

In view of the importance of consumer protection, this obligation does not depend upon the role that each jurisdiction confers upon its courts with respect to points of law. It is a positive standard of effective consumer protection required by the Unfair Contract Terms Directive. It is true that under Article 6(1) of the Unfair Contract Terms Directive, Member States have to ensure that consumers are not bound by unfair terms "as provided for under their national law." However, such deference to national laws cannot be understood as enabling Member States to subject the non-binding status of an unfair term to the condition that the term can only be declared unfair if the consumer has successfully challenged it.[939] The same logic could apply as to the power of the courts. The deference to national laws cannot be understood as allowing some courts to apply the doctrine of the active court and others not.

On the other hand, it has to be noted that even when the Court framed the doctrine simply in terms of a *power* for the courts, such power was not to be understood as leaving room for judicial arbitrariness. *Judicial* discretion is always circumscribed by law. The clarification of the obligatory nature of the *ex officio* doctrine at the Union level is more associated with ensuring the uniformity of its application.

It is interesting to consider the understanding that a national highest court (the *Hoge Raad* – the Supreme Court of the Netherlands), has of the link between a court's obligation to raise an unfair term and the availability of all factual and legal elements of a case. In the landmark judgment of *Heesakkers v. Voets*[940] regarding the effective application of consumer law by Dutch courts, the *Hoge Raad* stated that the lower courts are obliged to raise an unfair term of their own motion when the facts in the complaint give the courts "*cause for the presumption*" that the relevant term falls within the scope of the Unfair Contract Terms Directive and that it is unfair. Therefore, a complaint in appeal proceedings which pertains to the omission by a lower court to raise an unfair term of its own motion will be successful: "if it is *incomprehensible* that the facts that emerged in the proceedings did not give the court cause for the suspicion referred to above."

As analyzed in the previous section,[941] the obligation of the courts to raise a plea of consumer law applies not only with regard to the violation of the rules on protection from unfair terms but also with regard to all infringements of EU consumer protection legislation As the Court clarified in *Radlinger*, "effective consumer protection could be achieved only if the national court were required,

---

939 See Case C-472/11 *Banif Plus Bank* (n. 695), para. 28.

940 Hoge Raad der Nederlanden, 13 September 2013, *Heesakkers v. Voets*, NJ 2014, 274, NL:HR2013: 691. The judgment with its most important excerpts is reported in English by B. Fekete and A.M. Mancaleoni, "Application of Primary and Secondary EU Law on the National Courts' Own Motion" in A. Hartkamp, C. Sieburgh and W. Devroe (eds.), *Cases, Materials and Text on European Law and Private Law* (Oxford, Hart Publishing, 2017), 421–461, 436.

941 Section 4.1.3.

of its own motion, to examine compliance with the requirements which flow from EU law on consumer law."[942] Yet, to carry through this examination the courts must have available all the factual and legal elements necessary for that task.[943]

Coming back to the judgment in *Pannon*, following its pronouncement, the referring Hungarian court declined jurisdiction and referred the case to the territorially competent court. It is also important to note that the ruling in *Pannon* accelerated a long-awaited legislative amendment in the French Consumer Code, to the effect of the precision that the courts have an obligation to set aside an unfair term where the unfairness may be derived from the elements of the dispute before it.[944]

### *4.2.2. The Limited Obligation to Order Investigation Measures*

As a follow-up to *Pannon*, a second reference from a Hungarian court in *Pénzügyi Lízing*[945] was the occasion for the Court to clarify, in the Grand Chamber, a very important aspect that was still left unanswered. If the court does not dispose of all the factual elements necessary, is it nevertheless required to establish them of its own motion in order to proceed to an assessment of unfairness? What motivated the Hungarian court to ask this question is that under the Hungarian Civil Procedure Code, it is up to the parties to file a motion for evidence discovery and courts may not do so of their own motion. The judgment proceeds upon the distinction of two stages of examination. In the first stage, the national court must ascertain, "in all cases and whatever the rules of its domestic law,"[946] whether a contractual term falls *within the scope* of the Unfair Contract Terms Directive, investigating, if necessary, the question of its own motion. If the court decides that the term does fall within the scope of the Unfair Contract Terms Directive, it proceeds, at a second stage, upon the legal assessment of the term. The second level of obligatory assessment remains, however, dependent upon the availability of all factual and legal elements necessary. Thus, according to the Opinion of AG Trstenjak, effective legal protection does not require that "the principle of the active role of the parties in civil proceedings ... be abandoned in favor of the principle of court-directed and court-investigated proceedings," but it "requires only that the Member States take appropriate measures to protect the individual from loss of the rights conferred on him by Community law through ignorance of what steps to take and how to take them in legal proceedings."[947]

---

942 Case C-377/14 *Radlinger* (n. 917), para. 66.
943 Ibid., para. 70.
944 Article R632-1 Code de la Consommation. See below Chapter 6, Section 2.
945 Case C-137/08 *VB Pénzügyi Lízing*, EU:C:2010:659.
946 Ibid., para. 51.
947 Opinion of AG Trstenjak in Case C-137/08 *VB Pénzügyi Lízing*, EU:C:2010:401, point 115.

Indeed, *Pénzügyi Lízing*, although it adds investigative elements to consumer law proceedings in relation to the examination of the scope of application of the unfair terms legislation, is not a departure from the pronouncement in *Pannon*. It is true that the first level assessment is genuinely investigative. The courts are not merely empowered to order any investigative measure they deem appropriate in order to examine a fact which forms part of the dispute. Such a power is not unknown in civil procedural systems.[948] By virtue of *Pénzügyi Lízing* it would appear that they are actually obliged to introduce into the debate facts by ordering the necessary investigative measures.[949] Nevertheless, this "factual activism" is *limited* to only one aspect: whether a particular term falls within the *scope* of the Unfair Contract Terms Directive. By contrast, the assessment of unfairness in relation to all the circumstances attending the conclusion of the contract remains dependent upon the availability of facts. The measures of investigation will concentrate only upon the facts that determine the scope of application *rationae materiae* and *rationae personae*.

In this connection it is useful to recall that the Unfair Contract Terms Directive covers standard terms that have not been the object of individual negotiation (*objective scope of application*) and is applicable in contracts between a consumer and a professional (*subjective scope of application*).[950] As far as the subjective scope of application is concerned, the term must be included in a contract between a *consumer* – any natural person who acts for purposes which are outside his trade, business or profession – and a *seller or supplier* – any natural or legal person who is acting for purposes relating to his trade, business or profession.[951] A contract term falls under the Unfair Contract Terms Directive if it is a standard or pre-formulated term that has not been individually negotiated.[952] The disputed term is not subject to review if it reflects mandatory or regulatory provisions[953] or if it relates to the definition of the main subject matter of the contract or to the adequacy of the price and remuneration insofar as it is drafted in plain and intelligible language.[954]

---

948 See for instance Art. 10 of the French Civil Procedure Code: "Le juge a le pouvoir d'ordonner d'office toutes les mesures d'instruction légalement admissibles". (Translation: "The judge has the authority to order *sua sponte* any legally appropriate investigation measures.) This provision should be read in conjunction with Arts. 143–154 of the French Civil Procedure Code circumscribing the role of the court in the administration of evidence.

949 See E. Poillot (n. 892), para. 975.

950 See further, H.-W. Micklitz, "Unfair Terms in Consumer Contracts" in N. Reich et al., *European Consumer Law* (Cambridge, Intersentia, 2nd ed., 2014).

951 On the question of consumer capacity Case C-537/13 *Šiba*, EU:C:2015:14, pertaining to a lawyer-client relationship; Case C-488/11 *Asbeek Brusse* (n. 695) where the Court rules that a residential tenancy agreement falls within the scope of the Unfair Contract Terms Directive, with further references to case law.

952 Art. 3(1) Unfair Contract Terms Directive.

953 Ibid., Art. 1(2).

954 Ibid., Art. 4(2). As the Unfair Contract Terms Directive envisages only partial harmonization (Art. 8), Member States remain free to afford a higher level of consumer protection by

Among the above conditions for the application of the Unfair Contract Terms Directive, those which are liable to involve rather pure factual questions and for which measures of investigation might have to be envisaged according to *Pénzügyi Lízing* is the capacity of the purchaser as a consumer and the question of whether individual negotiation has taken place or not.[955] Already with regard to the issue of negotiation, the law sets a *presumption* against individual negotiation.[956] With respect to the consumer capacity, the contract on the basis of which either party exercises his claim will in principle be sufficient evidence for the court to determine the application of the respective condition. If that is not sufficient, the most appropriate and simple measure of investigation would seem to be the appearance of the parties in person so that they can provide additional information. In *Pénzügyi Lízing*, it can be assumed that the existence of the contract on the basis of which the professional pursued the claim and knowledge of basic geography would have been enough to allow the court to include the contested term of exclusive jurisdiction within the scope of the Unfair Contract Terms Directive.[957]

It needs to be noted that even if *Pénzügyi Lízing* introduces a *limited* obligation to investigate facts in order to ensure the effective application of consumer law, national legal orders are free to go beyond this limitation and to establish a more *extensive* obligation. This would seem to be what is happening in the Netherlands following the judgment of the *Hoge Raad* in *Heesakkers v. Voets*.[958] The *Hoge Raad* has found that:

> If not all the relevant facts have been established, the court will have to take the necessary measures of inquiry to ensure the full effect of [the Unfair Contract Terms

extending the scope of examination even to such terms. On the possibility of extension of the judicial assessment to the core terms of the contract see Case C-484/08 *Caja de Ahorros*, EU:C:2010:309. In France, Belgium, Luxembourg, the Czech Republic, Latvia, Malta and Slovenia the scope of application of national legislation on unfair terms extends to individually negotiated terms (P. Rott and E. Terryn, "Right of Withdrawal and Standard Terms" in H.-W. Micklitz, J. Stuyck and E. Terryn (eds.), *Cases Materials and Text on Consumer Law, Ius Commune Casebooks for the common law of Europe* (Oxford, Hart Publishing, 2010), 288).

955 As S. Whittaker, "Judicial Interventionism and Consumer Contracts" (2001) 117 *Law Quarterly Review* 215–220, 219 observes, the question of whether a specific term reflects the subject matter or the adequacy of the price and whether they are drafted in plain intelligible language is rather a matter of mixed fact and law.

956 Art. 3(2) Unfair Contract Terms Directive.

957 At the national level, the case was dismissed as the claimant ceased its business. This information was given by the referring judge in the case, Dr. Andras Osztovits, in his speech during the Conference on the Issue of the Preliminary Reference in European Private Law (organized by the University of Luxembourg, Faculty of Law Economics and Finance, under the scientific direction of Professor Elise Poillot - November 25, 2011).

958 *Heesakkers v. Voets* (n. 940), translated by B. Fekete and A.M. Mancaleoni (n. 940), 438. This excerpt of the judgment backs the statement made by these authors (in p. 439) that

> Directive], both as regards the applicability of the directive, as the possible unfairness of the clause.

That being so, a later case, *Faber*, provided the Court with the possibility of demonstrating that there might be national procedural rules which enable the courts to clarify the factual ambit of the dispute as to the scope of application of EU consumer protection legislation, without actually involving measures of investigation. One of the questions raised in that case was whether a national court is required to examine of its own motion whether the purchaser is to be regarded as a consumer within the meaning of the Consumer Sales Directive, even though that party has not relied on that status. The case had been referred by a Dutch Court of Appeal, after having observed that the first instance court had not raised the potential capacity of the applicant-purchaser as a consumer and that this applicant had not brought forward a respective challenge in her appeal.

The Court made a very important clarification. It pointed out that in the first place, the qualification of the purchaser as a consumer may simply derive from the "legal classification" of the facts of the dispute, which is not tantamount to an *ex officio* application. The adjudicating court would in essence apply the *ius novit curia* principle by "establishing and ascertaining whether there is a statutory condition which determines the applicable legal rule."[959] In accordance with the principle of equivalence, the national court should therefore assign the appropriate legal classification to the facts:

> In the same way that, within the context of the detailed procedural rules of its domestic legal order, the national court is called upon, for the purpose of identifying the applicable rule of national law, to classify the matters of law and of fact which the parties have submitted to it, if necessary by requesting the parties to provide any useful details, it is required, in accordance with the principle of equivalence, to carry out the same process for the purpose of determining whether a rule of EU law is applicable.[960]

The possibility within a given legal system for the courts to ask the parties for clarifications of their claims or to provide certain documents relating to the case (consider the obligation of the German courts to provide advice – the *Hinweispflicht*)[961] can therefore be a mechanism which allows the courts to clarify the scope of application of a given legal provision without having to

"in this case the Dutch Supreme Court accorded a wide scope to the obligation to examine [unfair term clauses], even beyond what the [Court] itself required in *VB Pénzügyi Lízing*".

959 Case C-497/13 *Faber* (n. 909), para. 38.

960 Ibid., para. 39.

961 Chapter 3, Section 2.3.1. see P. Rott, "Improving consumers' enforcement of their rights under EU consumer sales law: Froukje Faber" (2016) 53 *CMLR* 509–526, 517.

resort to an *ex officio* investigation. In the main proceedings in *Faber*, it would appear that an "indication" existed with regard to the capacity of the purchaser as a consumer. Ms. Faber had herself produced the purchase contract which was entitled "contract of sale to a private individual."[962] For this reason, the Court explained that it is only if the rules of the domestic legal order did not provide the national courts with "any means" which would make it possible to give to the facts and acts at issue the appropriate legal classification that the question of compatibility with the principle of effectiveness would arise.[963] In this case, if the procedural rules would prevent the courts from proceeding with the legal classification that:

> would be tantamount to making the consumer subject to the obligation to carry out a full legal classification of his situation himself, failing which he would lose the rights which the EU legislature intended to confer on him.

The Court stays at the level of the requirement for the courts to be able to make the appropriate legal classification, as soon as they have at their disposal the matters of law and fact that are necessary for that purpose or they may easily obtain them by making a request for clarification. This way of proceeding satisfied the principle of effectiveness of the exercise of consumer rights. It would therefore not be necessary to actually order measures of investigation, since apparently the procedural means existed, but they would have to be applied so as to allow the national court to discharge its role and to examine whether the situation before it falls within the scope of the legislation on consumer sales.

### *4.2.3. An Obligation Subject to the Observance of Adversarial Proceedings*

When the court raises a plea of law of its own motion, the principle of a fair trial, enshrined in Article 47 of the Charter, requires that it brings this point to the attention of the parties so as to allow for a contradictory debate. The Court had the occasion in *Banif Plus Bank*,[964] as well as in *Asbeek Brusse*,[965] to make clear that in implementing Union law, the national court must also respect the requirements of effective judicial protection:

> Among those requirements is the principle of *audi alteram partem*, as part of the rights of defense which is binding on that court, in particular when it decides a dispute on a ground that it has identified of its own motion.[966]

---

962 Case C-497/13 *Faber* (n. 909), para. 40.
963 Ibid., para. 41.
964 Case C-472/11 *Banif Plus Bank*, EU:C:2013:88.
965 Case C-488/11 *Asbeek Brusse*, EU:C:2013:341.
966 Case C-472/11 *Banif Plus Bank* (n. 964), para. 29.

The importance of observance of the principle of adversarial proceedings which forms part of the rights of defense and fair trial has already been highlighted outside the context of consumer litigation.[967] Therefore, in *Banif Plus Bank*, the Court referred to its case law on the observance of the adversarial principle with regard to points of law that can be raised of its own motion by the Union judicature:

> the principle of *audi alteram partem* does not merely confer on each party to proceedings the right to be apprised of the documents produced and observations made to the court by the other party and to discuss them, but it also implies a right for the parties to be apprised of pleas in law raised by the court of its own motion, on which it intends to base its decision, and to discuss them.[968]

Therefore, when a court establishes that a term comes within the scope of the Unfair Contract Terms Directive and has assessed that the term is unfair, it is then:

> required to inform the parties to the dispute of that fact and to invite each of them to set out their views on that matter, with the opportunity to challenge the views of the other party.[969]

The court might have to reopen the proceedings or simply require from the parties to submit additional statements as to the issue of unfairness that has been raised by the court of its own motion.

### *4.2.4. An Obligation to Raise the Unfair Term Independent of the Consumer Submission in that Regard, but not Against his Will*

The mirror side of the obligation of the courts to raise a plea of consumer legislation of their own motion is the absence of a requirement on the part of the consumer to advance the respective submission. In particular with regard to a contract containing unfair terms, although the Unfair Contract Terms Directive provides for a neutral term to designate that unfair terms are "not binding,"[970] such finding cannot be subject by procedural law neither to existence of a declaratory judgment nor to a submission on behalf of the consumer.[971]

---

[967] Case C-300/11 *ZZ*, EU:C:2013:363, para. 55; Case C-450/06 *Varec*, EU:C:2008:91, para. 45.

[968] Case C-472/11 *Banif Plus Bank* (n. 964), para. 30, making reference to Case C-89/08 P *Commission v Ireland and Others*, EU:C:2009:742, paras. 55–56.

[969] Case C-472/11 *Banif Plus Bank* (n. 964), para. 31.

[970] Acknowledging, in this way, the diversities in the various legal systems, see Opinion of AG Trstenjak in Case C-472/10 *Invitel*, EU:C:2011:806, point 48.

[971] From the perspective of the law of contracts, the *ex officio* doctrine excludes the consequence of "voidability", in the sense of a requirement of declaration of the non-binding status of the

The effect of the unfair term not being binding upon the consumer is *ipso iure*[972] so that the consumer cannot be required to have first successfully contested the validity of the term.[973] Therefore, as is stated in *Pannon*, the reference to the national laws in Article 6(1) of the Unfair Contract Terms Directive, according to which the unfair terms shall not be binding, "cannot be understood as enabling Member States to subject the non-binding status of an unfair term"[974] to the condition that the consumer has first to successfully challenge the term.

Consequently, as has been further elaborated in *Banif Plus Bank*,[975] with *Asbeek Brusse*[976] and *Jőrös*[977] following suit, when the Court finds that the contract is affected by a ground of invalidity because of the existence of unfair term(s), the "full effectiveness of the protection" provided for by the [Unfair Contract Terms Directive] requires that the national court which has found of its own motion that a term is unfair be able to establish all the necessary consequences of this finding and in particular to pronounce the nullity of the term:

> without waiting for the consumer, who has been fully informed of his rights, to submit a statement requesting that term be declared invalid.[978]

If the consumer submission is not decisive for the exercise of the powers of the courts, his presence or absence in the proceedings should not play a role either. The active consumer court doctrine is founded upon the mandatory nature and the public interest character of consumer legislation. The courts proceed upon an independent determination of the application of the mandatory provision in question so that the own motion assessment many not rely upon the procedural behavior of the weaker party. That being said, as it has already been pointed out

contract by a judicial decision after the consumer invokes the ground of unfairness. This is however, what the term *vernietigbaar*, employed by the Dutch Civil Code (Art. 6:233 NBW), would seem to imply. M. Ebers, "Unfair Contract Terms Directive" in H. Schulte-Nölke, C. Twigg-Flesner and M. Ebers (eds.), *European Consumer Law Compendium* (Munich, Sellier, 2008) 197, 242–243, notes that the requirement that the consumer invoke the unfairness of the contractual clause, as was the case (at the time that the comparative study was written) in the Czech Republic, Latvia and the Netherlands, is contrary to the *ex officio* powers of the courts. See also R. Steennot, "Public and Private Enforcement in the field of Unfair Contract Terms" (2015) 4 *CMLR* 589–620, 600, who explains that the requirement of Belgian law to seek the remedy of the relative nullity only by court decision is not compatible with the Unfair Contract Terms Directive. By contrast, German law employs the term *unwirskam* and French law *non écrites*. See H.-W. Micklitz, J. Stuyck and E. Terryn, *Cases, Materials and Text on Consumer Law* (Oxford, Hart Publishing, 2010), 299.

972 See the Opinion of A G Trstenjak in Case C-137/08 *Pénzügyi Lízing* (n. 947), point 105.

973 Explicitly to that effect, Case C-472/11 *Banif Plus Bank* (n. 964), paras. 28 – 36; Case C-488/11 *Asbeek Brusse* (n. 965), para. 50; Case C-397/11 *Jőrös* (n. 659), para. 42.

974 Case C-243/08 *Pannon GSM* (n. 919), para. 27.

975 Case C-472/11 *Banif Plus Bank* (n. 964), para. 28.

976 Case C-488/11 *Asbeek Brusse* (n. 965), para. 50.

977 Case C-397/11 *Jőrös*, EU:C:2013:340.

978 Case C-472/11 *Banif Plus Bank* (n. 964), para. 28.

above,[979] the presence of the consumer in the proceedings and the explanations he may provide in the questions of the court (in the usual case of self-representation) may assist the court to derive from the case file the necessary facts which will allow an own motion assessment. From this perspective, the presence of the consumer in the proceedings enhances his case.

It is also clear from the early judgment in *Rampion and Godard*[980] (reiterated in *Faber*[981]) that the legal representation of the consumer does not alter the obligation of the courts to carry out an independent judicial assessment of the capacity of the party as a consumer, of the potential unfairness of a contractual term or of the application of mandatory provisions of consumer law. This flows again from the mandatory nature of the consumer protection legislation but also from the fact that "the interpretation of EU law and also the scope of the principles of effectiveness and equivalence are independent of the specific circumstances of each case."[982] From this point of view, the Court, Peter Rott observes, "not only protects the consumer against his or her own ignorance, but also against bad legal advice."[983]

Yet, the effectiveness of consumer protection does not stretch that far as to imply that the nullity of the unfair term – and *a fortiori* the eventual nullity of the contract, if it is not capable of continuing in existence without the unfair term – be pronounced *against the will* of the protected party. The fact that the consumer is not obliged to invoke the unfairness of the term or to submit a statement requesting the declaration of invalidity of that term does not mean that he loses his role as a *party* in the litigation or that he can no longer dispose of the rights conferred on him. The Court held in *Pannon* that the term that the national court considers unfair:

> may be applicable, if the consumer, after having been informed of it by that court, does not intend to assert its unfair or non-binding status.[984]

The main idea underlying that finding is that the unfair terms legislation serves a public interest, but it is primarily intended to protect the individual. From this perspective, there is no contradiction between the general interest, which justifies a positive judicial action, and the ultimate aim, which is to protect the individual consumer as the weaker party and which justifies his capacity to forgo *ex post* protection.[985] The model promoted by the *ex officio* doctrine is that of an

979 Section 3.2.1.3, with reference to the Opinion of Advocate General Sharpston in *Karel de Grote – Hogeschool Katholieke Hogeschool Antwerpen*, C-147/16, EU:C:2017:928, point 33.

980 Case C-429/05 *Rampion and Godard* (n. 868), para. 65.

981 Case C-497/13 *Faber* (n. 909), para. 47.

982 Ibid.

983 P. Rott (n. 961), 518.

984 Case C-243/08 *Pannon GSM* (n. 919), para. 33.

985 *Contra* A. Osztovits and Z. Nemessányi, "Missbräuchliche Zuständigkeitsklauseln in der Ungarischen Rechtssprechung im Licht der Urteile des EuGH" (2010) 01 *Zeitschrift*

*informed consent* – it is not about imposing protection and being "paternalistic." If the declaration of unfairness has an impact upon the continuation of the contract as a whole,[986] the consumer might wish to assert the validity of the contested term so as to maintain the contractual relationship.[987] The French or Belgian lawyer will certainly find an echo of the right of the consumer to renounce *ex post* the protection in the context of the theory of "renunciation of nullity" by the protected person ("confirmation de nullité").[988] We may here recall Patrick Wéry, who explains that the type of nullity which results from the active consumer court doctrine is situated in a middle ground (a "third path"): it is a relative nullity with an *ex officio* power for the courts.[989] In a similar vein, Arthur Hartkamp rightly observes that the case law of the Court on the active court:

> has not replaced the concept of relative nullity by absolute nullity, which would run counter to the need of consumer protection, but has added to the concept of "relative" nullity an additional protection by extending the power of the courts.[990]

### 4.2.5. *An Obligation of the Lower Courts and Eventually of the Courts of Appeal*

The majority of the rulings concerning the obligation of the courts to raise unfair terms arose before first instance courts. However, there are some instances

---

*für Internationales Privat- und Zivilverfarhrensrecht* 22–26, at 25, mentioning (at fn.27) that with the possibility given to renounce protection, the role of the judge is degraded to that of a mediator. *Cf.* G. Paisant, "L'obligation de relever d'office du juge national" *La Semaine Juridique Edition Générale* 2009 42, 336, observing that it is difficult to envisage that a consumer duly informed of his/her rights will renounce protection.

986 Art. 6 of the Unfair Contract Terms Directive. In Case C-453/10 *Pereničová and Perenič* (n. 864), paras. 33–35, the Court ruled that the question of whether a contract may continue to exist without the unfair terms should be based upon an objective examination of the contractual relationship and not solely on a possible advantage for the consumer. But Member States should not be precluded from providing a different solution where that would ensure better protection for the consumer.

987 See Case C-227/08 *Martín Martín* (n. 869), para. 35, where the Court ruled that "the national court seised may also have to take account, in certain circumstances the consumer's wish not to have the contract at issue cancelled".

988 On which see J. Ghestin, G. Loiseau and Y. M. Serinet, *La formation du contrat, Vol. II : L'objet et la cause – Les nullités*, paras. 2421 *et seq.*; F. Terré, P. Simler and Y. Lequette, *Précis Droit Civil Les obligations* (Paris, Dalloz, 11th ed., 2013), para. 389 *et seq.*; M. Fabre-magnan, *Droit des Obligations* (Thémis PUF, 3rd ed., 2012), 479. In Belgian law, P. Wéry, *Droit des Obligations Vol. I* (Paris, Larcier, 2010), para. 327. See Chapter 3, section 2.2.4.

989 P. Wéry, "Les clauses abusives relatives à l'inexécution des obligations contractuelles dans les lois de protection des consommateurs du 14 juillet 1991 et du 2 aout 2002", (2003) *Journal des Tribunaux* 797–810, 808. See also C. Delforge, "Clauses abusives, office du juge et renonciation" (2008) 3 *Jurisprudence de Liège, Mons et Bruxelles* J.L.M.B. 93–100, naming this approach hybrid ("*voie hybride*").

990 A. Hartkamp, "Ex officio application in case of unenforceable contracts or contract clauses, EU Law and National Laws Confronted" in L Gullifer and S. Vogenauer (eds.), *English*

where the question of the *ex officio* application arose before the courts of appeal. The first such case is *Martín Martín*,[991] which concerned the powers of the courts to raise of their own motion the infringement of the requirement of prior notification of the right of cancellation applicable in the off-premises contracts. In this case, the referring court did not insist on the fact that the proceedings before it were at the stage of appeal. As such, the Court did not have to delve into this particular aspect.

In one case from Hungary, *Jőrös*,[992] and two cases from the Netherlands, *Asbeek Brusse* and *Faber*, there was an explicit question as to the powers of the courts at the level of appeal. In *Jőrös*, the referring court stated that the relevant ground of invalidity of the contract was not raised in the proceedings at first instance and that under national law, new facts and evidence cannot generally be taken into consideration in appeal proceedings. Similarly, in *Asbeek Brusse* and *Faber*, the referring court explained that in Dutch law, the court hearing an appeal is required in general to keep to the complaints submitted by the parties and to base its decision on those complaints, unless a provision of public policy is at issue, in which case the court would be allowed to apply it of its own motion.

In all these latter cases, the analysis of the Court is based on the application of the *public policy equivalence principle*. The existence of an unfair term affecting the validity of the contract is accorded the *same procedural treatment* as one reserved, within the domestic legal system, to rules of public policy. Therefore:

> where the national court has the power, under internal procedural rules, to examine of its own motion the validity of a legal measure in the light of national rules of public policy ... it must also exercise that power for the purposes of assessing of its own motion, in the light of the criteria laid down in the [Unfair Contract Terms Directive], whether a contractual term coming within the scope of that directive may be unfair.[993]

Under both the Hungarian and Dutch jurisdictions from which the references for preliminary ruling originated, it appeared that the courts of appeal had a power to raise the issue of nullity of their own motion, provided that the respective grounds could be established from the case file.[994] In *Faber*, the principle of

*and European Perspectives on Contract and Commercial Law, Essays in Honour of Hugh Beale* (Oxford and Portland, Oregon, Hart Publishing, 2014), 467–484, 480.

991 Case C-227/08 *Martín Martín* (n. 869).

992 Case C-397/11 *Jőrös* (n. 977).

993 Case C-488/11 *Asbeek Brusse* (n. 965), para. 45 and Case C-397/11 *Jőrös* (n. 977), para. 30.

994 Ibid., *Asbeek Brusse*, para. 45 and ibid., *Jőrös*, paras. 33–34, with reference to the Opinion of the Mixed Civil Chamber of the Hungarian Supreme Court that "the appeal court must make a finding of invalidity of its own motion if grounds of invalidity can be established clearly from the circumstances of the proceedings at first instance. That Opinion also stipulates ... that if the facts set out by the applicant give the application a different legal basis to that relied upon by that party, the court seised can redefine appropriately, in law, the basis of the request submitted to it".

public policy equivalence was applied, this time, not with regard to a ground of contractual nullity, but with regard to the application of a mandatory provision of the Consumer Sales Directive (the rule on the burden of proof due to lack of conformity). In those circumstances, the Court concluded that this rule:

> must be regarded as a provision of equal standing to a national rule which ranks, within the domestic legal system, as a rule of public policy and that the national court must of its own motion apply any provision which transposes it into domestic law.[995]

On the basis of the judgment of the Court in *Asbeek Brusse*, the *Hoge Raad* (Netherlands Supreme Court) confirmed in *Heesakkers*,[996] that both first instance courts and the courts of appeal are obliged to raise of their own motion an unfair term "[even] if this means that the Court of Appeal has to go beyond the limits set by the grounds of appeal." To that effect, the *Hoge Raad* acknowledged the equivalence of the Unfair Contract Terms Directive to national public policy rules:

> under Dutch law on appeal procedure the national court must in principle apply public policy rules [even] beyond the limits set by the grounds of appeal, with the [proviso] that the national court must respect the ambit of the parties' legal dispute. The national court is therefore not required to make this assessment when the parties did not appeal the award or the rejection of the relevant claim.

Moreover, in the same judgment, the *Hoge Raad* confirmed the obligation of the Dutch courts to assess the unfair nature of general contractual terms in default proceedings, on the basis of Article 139 of the Dutch Civil Procedure Code (*Wetboek van Burgerlijke Rechtsovordering*). This article provides that in the absence of a defendant who has been summoned, the court grants the claim unless it appears *unlawful or unfounded*. Since "the directive involves law that is equivalent to public policy rules," the Dutch courts have to raise the relevant rules even in the absence of the defendant.

## 5. CONSEQUENCES OF THE EXERCISE OF THE POWERS OF THE COURTS TO RAISE OF THEIR OWN MOTION PLEAS OF CONSUMER LAW

The case law that built the doctrine of the active consumer court covers important aspects with regard to the consequences for the courts of raising

995 Case C-497/13 *Faber* (n. 909), para. 57.
996 (n. 940).

a plea of consumer law of their own motion and, in particular, the consequences of the *ex officio* finding of a ground affecting the validity of the contract. The general rule is that when the court finds that a contract term is unfair or that a provision of consumer law has been infringed, it must establish all the consequences thereby arising from national law.

In particular, with regard to Article 6(1) of the Unfair Contract Terms Directive, the Court has ruled that national courts which find that a contract term is unfair are required:

> first, to draw all the consequences that follow under national law, so that the consumer is not bound by those terms ... and, secondly, to assess whether the contract in question can continue to exist without application of those unfair terms.[997]

The case law sheds light as to what those consequences might be and as to the requirements flowing from Union law, be that secondary law or the Charter.

## 5.1. THE ASSESSMENT OF THE VALIDITY OF THE CONTRACT

It is clear from the case law that the court which finds a term unfair should be able to establish all the consequences of that finding without waiting for the consumer to submit a statement requesting that the term be declared invalid. The question is whether the powers of the courts in that regard also imply a power to pronounce the nullity of the contract. The first case which raised the question of the consequences from the finding by a court of its own motion of the existence of a ground affecting the validity of the contract was *Martín Martín*.[998] The first finding of that judgment was that national courts have the power to raise of their own motion the breach of the requirement of notification to the consumer of his right of cancellation of a contract concluded away from businesses premises (Article 4 of Directive 85/577 on off-premises contracts).[999] As to the consequences of that breach, Spanish law provided that the contract "may be cancelled at the request of the consumer." The national court asked whether it should have the power to declare the nullity of the contract of its own motion. In that regard, the Court recalls that the directive from which the obligation of notification flows affords to the national authorities a discretion in determining the consequences which should follow a failure to give notice, provided that the aim of protection of that directive is safeguarded. As the directive is of minimum

---

997 Case C-453/10 *Pereničová and Perenič* (n. 864), para. 30, with reference to Case C-40/08 *Asturcom Telecomunicaciones* (n. 768), paras 58–59 and Case C-76/10 *Pohotovost' I* (n. 825), paras. 61–62.

998 Case C-227/08 *Martín Martín* (n. 869).

999 N. 884.

harmonization (Article 8), Member States may provide for the sanction of *nullity* of a contract concluded in breach of the requirement of notification of the right of withdrawal. However, other solutions can be envisaged in other legal systems, which may also ensure an adequate level of protection:

> such as, for example, the resetting of the relevant time-limits relating to the cancellation of the contract, thus placing the consumer in a position to exercise the right which is granted to him by article 5 (1) of the Directive.[1000]

If the sanction provided for by the relevant national legal system is nullity, the court should then have the power to declare the contract void of its own motion. This would actually amount to the court acting "ultra petita", since the consumer has not asked for the nullity. However, this is justified in light of the application of the legal consequences of a finding of the breach of the mandatory requirements set out in consumer law. That being so, it is clarified, by analogy to *Pannon*, that the court could should also take account of the consumer's wish *not to have* the contract cancelled.[1001] This approach demonstrates that the doctrine of the active court strengthens protection, but does not *impose* protection.

After receiving the judgment in *Martín Martín*, the *Audiencia Provincial de Salamanca* decided to declare of its own motion the off-premises contract void on the ground that the consumer had not been informed of her right of cancellation.[1002]

With regard to the finding of unfairness of a contractual term, it has been mentioned in the introduction to this section that the courts are obliged "to assess whether the contract in question can continue to exist without application of those unfair terms." In that regard, the Court has insisted upon an objective assessment of the validity of the contract. Upon the *ex officio* finding of unfairness, the national court has to assess whether the contract may continue to bind the parties. The Unfair Contract Terms Directive rests upon the premise that the validity of the contract has to be preserved where that is possible following the setting aside of the unfair terms. *Pereničová*[1003] concerned the effects of the finding of unfairness on the validity of the contract and offers guidance on how this assessment should be carried out. Following the Opinion of AG Trstenjak in that regard, the Court found that the criterion underpinning the logic of the Unfair Contract Terms Directive on this question is an *objective* one and is

---

1000 Case C-227/08 *Martín Martín* (n. 869), para. 35.

1001 Ibid.

1002 Sentencia num. 79/2010 de 22 febrero, JUR\2010\145869.

1003 Case C-453/10, *Pereničová and Perenič* (n. 864). On the other aspect of the judgment regarding the impact upon the assessment of unfairness of a finding that the term constitutes unfair commercial practice, see the comment B. Keirsbilck, "The interaction between consumer protection rules on unfair contract terms and unfair commercial practices: *Pereničová and Perenič*" (2013) 50 *CMLR* 247–264.

based on the possibility of continuation of the contract. Thus, the court cannot base its decision to annul the contract "solely on a possible advantage for the consumer of the annulment of the contract as a whole."[1004] However, since this is a minimum harmonization directive, the Member States are not precluded from providing a higher level of protection and from laying down that:

> a contract concluded between a trader and a consumer which contains one or more unfair terms may be declared void as a whole where that will ensure better protection of the consumer.[1005]

## 5.2. THE PROHIBITION OF REVISION OF AN UNFAIR TERM AND THE QUESTION OF SUBSTITUTION BY A STATUTORY PROVISION

A term which the court finds to be unfair is not binding and is not applicable against the consumer. The court which establishes the unfairness of certain term must ensure its straightforward *non-application* by setting that term *aside* without revising its content. This important pronouncement was the second limb of the reference in *Banco Español de Crédito*.[1006] In the aftermath of *Banco Español de Crédito*, new references arose from Spain (*Unicaja Banco*)[1007] and the Netherlands (in *Asbeek Brusse*)[1008] on aspects of application of this rule. The reference from Hungary (in *Kásler*)[1009] concerned the possibility of substitution of an unfair clause by a supplementary provision of national law in cases where its non-application would result in the consumer being worst off. The following paragraphs will begin with the presentation of the position of principle in *Banco Español de Crédito* and will then move on to the application and refinement of that principle in subsequent judgments.

### *5.2.1. Prohibition of Revision of the Content of an Unfair Term in Order to Bring it to Compliance Levels*

The dispute in *Banco Español de Crédito* arose in the context of a consumer credit contract concluded between the bank and a consumer for the purchase of a vehicle for the sum of €30,000. The nominal interest rate was 7.950%, the Annual Percentage Rate of Charge (APR) was 8.890% and the rate of interest

---

1004 Case C-453/10 *Pereničová and Perenič* (n. 864), para. 33.
1005 Ibid., para. 35.
1006 Case C-618/10, *Banco Español de Crédito*, EU:C:2012:349.
1007 Joined Cases C-482/13, C-484/13, C-485/13 and C-487/13 *Unicaja Banco and Caixabank*, EU:C:2015:21.
1008 Case C-488/11 *Asbeek Brusse* (n. 965).
1009 Case C-26/13 *Kásler and Káslerné Rábai*, EU:C:2014:282.

on late payments was 29%(!). Following the default by the consumer on paying seven monthly installments, the bank applied for an order for payment for the amount of €29,381.95, corresponding to the amount of the unpaid monthly installments plus contractual interest and costs. The court before which the application was brought declared of its own motion that the 29% rate of interest for late payment was unfair. First, with regard to the form, this rate was fixed in a typed term which could not be distinguished from the rest of the text as regards the font, the size of the letters used or any specific acceptance by the consumer and, second, in relation to the content, it was more than 20 points greater than the nominal interest rate and it largely exceeded the Euribor and the ECB rates of interest. Taking into account those elements, it found that the clause on the interest for late payment was automatically void.

The applicable Spanish law at the time of the reference for preliminary ruling provided for the power of the courts to modify the content of the unfair term in accordance with the principle of good faith (*proceso de integración*).[1010] Therefore, the Spanish court, after finding the disputed term to be unfair, fixed the rate at 19% by reference to the statutory interest rate and to the interest rates for late payment included in the national budget laws from 1998 to 2008, and ordered the applicant to recalculate the amount of interest for the period at issue in the dispute before it. The applicant appealed against the order before the referring court (the *Audiencia Provincial de Barcelona*), submitting that the court could not, at that stage of the procedure, hold of its own motion that the term relating to interest of late payment was unfair or modify that term. One of the questions of reference for the preliminary ruling concerned the power for judicial revision modification.[1011]

The Court, following the Opinion of AG Trstenjak, ruled that such revision powers are incompatible with Article 6(1) of the Unfair Contract Terms Directive.[1012] The prohibition of revision of unfair terms is placed within

---

1010 Royal Decree Law 1/2007 (n. 815), Art. 83.

1011 The other aspect of the question on the powers of the courts in an order for payment procedure will be addressed in the next Chapter 5, Section 1.

1012 The Opinion of AG Trstenjak in Case C-618/10 *Banco Español de Crédito*, EU:C:2012:74, fn. 105, cites German literature according to which the "partial retention of the validity" (*geltungserhaltende Reduktion*) of an unfair term, i.e. maintaining the term with the lawful content following the setting aside of the illegal element, is incompatible with the Unfair Contract Terms Directive. See also E. Hondius, "Unfair contract terms – revising the content of a term" in E. Terryn, G. Straetmans and V. Colaert (eds.), *Landmark Cases of EU Consumer Law* (Intersentia, 2014), 625–631, 630; P. Rott, "Case note on Banco Español de Credito v Joaquín Calderón Camino" (2012) 8:4 *ERCL* 470–480, 477, favorable to the positition taken by the Court. The practice of the Federal Court (BGH) to modify unfair terms using the method of supplementary interpretation of the contract (*ergänzende Vertragsauslegung*) has also been criticized in that it amounts to "partial retention of the validity" of the unfair term which is incompatible with Union law. See H.-W. Micklitz and N. Reich, "The Court and Sleeping Beauty: The Revival of the Unfair Contract Terms Directive" (2014) 51 *CMLR* 771–808, 793, criticizing BGH, judgment of 14 March 2012, NJW (2012), 1865 para. 25; BGH

"the broader regulatory function of unfair contract terms law."[1013] The main reason lies in its deterrent effect. If the courts were empowered to revise the content of the unfair term to render it valid in order to restore the hypothetical will of the parties, the professionals could be tempted to continue using unfair terms, relying on the prospect that even if declared invalid, they would still be modified and would still gain an advantage. If that were the case, it would certainly:

> contribute to eliminate the dissuasive effect on sellers or suppliers of the straightforward non-application with regard to the consumer of those unfair terms.[1014]

In her Opinion, AG Trstenjak also drew arguments from an earlier Opinion of AG Tizzano in the *Yvos* case.[1015] AG Tizzano had found a rule of national law, by virtue of which the impact of the finding of a term unfair upon the contract was dependent on the question whether the parties would have concluded the contract without that term, to be incompatible with the Unfair Contract Terms Directive. Obviously, the unfair term was to the trader's advantage and possibly he would no longer wish to be bound by the contract if he could no longer skim off the profit he counted on. According to the Opinion:

> the aim of the Directive is to rebalance the contractual position of the consumer by preventing him "from being bound by an unfair term" rather than to safeguard the contractual freedom of the parties, and particularly that of the seller or supplier, who might indeed have every interest in escaping the obligations of a contract which, when the balance has been adjusted, would be less advantageous to him.[1016]

The judgment of the national court, rendered following the judgment of the Court, ruled on the second part of its decision that the term was unfair and for

---

23 January 2013, NJW 2013, 991. See also K. Uffmann, "Vertragsrechtligkeit als Leitbild der Inhaltskontrolle. Der BGH und die ergänzende Vertragsauslegung" (2012) *NJW*, 2225.

1013 P. Rott (n. 1012), 476.

1014 Case C-618/10, *Banco Español de Crédito* (n. 1011), para. 69.

1015 Opinion of AG Tizzano in Case C-302/04 *Yvos*, EU:C:2005:576. The Court in its judgment of 10 January 2006 in Case C-302/04 *Ynos*, EU:C:2006:9 held that it lacked jurisdiction to rule on the question.

1016 Opinion of AG Tizzano in Case C-302/04 *Yvos* (ibid), point 80. The disputed provision of Hungarian law has been amended and now Art. 239(2) of the Hungarian Civil Code reads as follows: "In the event of partial ineffectiveness of a contract concluded with a consumer, the contract shall fail in its entirety only if it is impossible to perform it without the ineffective part". A similar line of thinking on the dissuasive effect of the pronouncement of unfairness can be found in an English judgment quoted by P. Rott (n. 1012), fn. 28, that is *Stewart Gill Ltd v Horatio Myer & Co Ltd* [1992] 2 All ER (CA) 257, at 263 (per Stuart-Smith LJ): "Nor does it appear to me to be consistent with the policy and purpose of the Act to permit a contractor to impose a contractual term, which taken as a whole is completely unreasonable, to put a blue pencil through the most offensive parts and say that what is left is reasonable and sufficient to exclude or restrict his liability in a manner relied upon".

that reason was ineffective.[1017] In accordance with the ruling in *Banco Español de Crédito* on the incompatibility of the judicial revision of unfair terms with the Unfair Contract Terms Directive, the decision of the national court confirmed that the *integración* of the unfair term (its interpretation in light of the principle of good faith) was not possible. The unfair term on default interest was set aside and the rest of the contract was held to be valid. But the creditor did not lose its right to demand interest for late payment. The legal provisions on late payment interest remained applicable, but the onus was on the creditor to claim *in different proceedings* the damage resulting from the delay. The final amount that the consumer was ordered to pay was only calculated upon the unpaid installments and the capital outstanding, which made an amount approximately €3,500 less than what had originally been claimed by the creditor.

Following the decision of the Court in *Banco Español de Crédito*, the Spanish legislator amended the disputed provision. Law 3/2014, which brought about this change, in its recital makes an express reference to the need to conform to the said judgment of the Court.[1018] Article 83 has been modified to the effect that the court, after having heard the parties, declares the nullity of the unfair terms, while the contract remains binding between the parties if it is capable of continuing in existence without those terms.[1019,1020]

The Court confirmed the approach taken in *Banco Español de Crédito* in a subsequent judgment referred from the Netherlands, *Asbeek Brusse*.[1021]

1017 Audiencia Provincial de Barcelona, order 222/2012 of 29 October 2012 (No de Recurso 586/2010).

1018 Ley 3/2014 por la que se modifica el texto refundido de la Ley General para la Defensa de los Consumidores y Usuarios y otras leyes complementarias, aprobado por el Real Decreto Legislativo 1/2007, de 16 de noviembre (Law 3/2014 amending the revised text of the General Law for the Protection of Consumers and Users and other supplementary lawsapproved by the Legislative Decree 1/2007, of 16 November) of 27 March 2014 (BOE No 76 of 28 March 2014), Preamble point III.

1019 Artículo 83. "Nulidad de las cláusulas abusivas y subsistencia del contrato. Las cláusulas abusivas serán nulas de pleno derecho y se tendrán por no puestas. A estos efectos, el Juez, previa audiencia de las partes, declarará la nulidad de las cláusulas abusivas incluidas en el contrato, el cual, no obstante, seguirá siendo obligatorio para las partes en los mismos términos, siempre que pueda subsistir sin dichas cláusulas." [Article 83. Nullity of the unfair terms and continuation in existence of the contract. The unfair terms will be held null and invalid. To this effect, the court, after having heard the parties, will declare the nullity of the unfair terms included in the contract, which, nonetheless, will continue to engage the parties in the same terms, as long as it can subsist without the unfair terms] (translated by the author).

1020 It has to be noted that the first question of a pending reference for preliminary ruling from the Spanish Supreme Court (Tribunal Supremo) in Case C-70/17 *Abanca Corporación Bancaria* [2017] OJ C121/17, intends to clarify the question whether Article 6 (1) of the Unfair Terms Directive must be interpreted to the effect that a national court, in its assessment of the unfairness of an accelerated repayment clause in a mortgage credit contract, may find as unfair only that part of the clause which concerns the acceleration on account of default of one sole instalment and maintain the validity of the rest of the clause concerning the accelaration on account of default of multiple instalments.

1021 Case C-488/11 *Asbeek Brusse* (n. 965).

One of the questions in this case concerned the powers of the courts to "moderate" penalty clauses in residential tenancy agreements. Under Dutch contract law,[1022] courts have, at the debtor's request, the power to mitigate a penalty if this would be equitable. On the basis of that provision, the consumer had requested a reduction of the penalty stipulated in his tenancy agreement, due to the discrepancy between the sums requested and the detriment suffered by the landlord. He had submitted this claim for the first time at the level of appeal. If the court were to consider of its own motion that the stipulated term were unfair, should the penalty clause be set aside or reduced? Pursuant to the dissuasive effect against the use of unfair terms line of reasoning, the Court found that the clause should be set aside. The result of this would be that Dutch contract law would have to admit an exception to the judicial powers of moderation when a penalty clause falls within the scope of the Unfair Contract Terms Directive. The court would not have to wait until the consumer-debtor made a submission with respect to the unfairness of a penalty clause, and the courts' powers would not be reduced to mitigation of the effects of the unfair clause. This example of prohibition of the moderation of an unfair penalty clause demonstrates the "spillover effects" of the Unfair Contract Terms Directive on general contract law.[1023]

### *5.2.2. Substitution of an Unfair Term by a Supplementary Provision of National Law*

*Banco Español de Crédito* made it clear that the courts may not revise the content of an unfair term in order to restore it to the hypothetical will of the parties as if the term would be legal. The question is whether this means that the courts may never apply a supplementary provision of national law. Later case law demonstrated that the rule of *Banco Español de Crédito* could apply only to the benefit of the consumer and not in order to disadvantage his position. Simon Whittaker observes that in certain circumstances, if the underlying law to the contractual relationship that is otherwise applicable benefits the consumer, then it can still apply "as in the case of a non-binding exemption clause which leaves intact the trader's liability."[1024] The *Kásler*[1025] case falls within that framework.

---

1022 Art. 6:94 (1) Burgerlijk Wetboek.

1023 On the "*spillover*" effects between EU law and national private law see A. Johnston, "Spillovers" from EU Law into National Law: (Un) intended Consequences for Private Law Relationships" in D. Leczykiewicz and S. Weatherill (eds.), *The Involvement of EU Law in Private Law Relationships* (Hart Publishing, 2013), 357–394. From the perspective of principle of legal certainty P. Rott, "The Court of Justice's Principle of Effectiveness and its Unforeseeable Impact on Private Law Relationships" in D. Leczykiewicz and S. Weatherill, ibid, 181–198.

1024 S. Whittaker, "Distinctive Features of the new consumer contract law" (2017) 133 *Law Quarterly Review* 47–72, 55.

1025 Case C-26/13 *Kásler and Káslerné Rábai*, EU:C:2014:282.

The case was referred by the Supreme Court in Hungary (*Kúria*) and touched upon the "forex loan issue," an issue that has been a major concern for Hungarian mortgage borrowers (but also for many others in Poland, Croatia, Romania and Greece) of loans denominated in foreign currency (Swiss francs). These loans had been concluded before the global financial crisis to benefit from lower interest rates. The loan was advanced and disbursed in the domestic currency, the forint, but the monthly repayment installments were linked to the current rate for Swiss francs. The reference for that rate was not the *buying rate* applicable when the loan had been advanced, but the *selling rate.* A plunging forint following the credit crunch[1026] led to a surge of defaults by consumers who had borrowed under this mechanism.[1027] The Court held that such a mechanism of a foreign exchange margin was covered by the scope of judicial consideration of unfairness and that the requirement of transparency should be understood in a broad sense "so that the consumer can foresee, on the basis of clear, intelligible criteria, the economic consequences for him which derive from it."[1028]

With regard to the consequences of the finding of unfairness of a clause, the referring court had asked whether *Banco Español de Crédito* should be understood as precluding courts from restoring the invalidity of the unfair term by substituting a supplementary provision of national law. In the instant case the court of appeal decided that the conversion should be performed on the basis of the buying rate, excluding the unfair margin between the two reference points (i.e. between the selling rate and the buying rate).[1029] The problem was that if the invalid term would not be substituted, the contract could no longer operate and the consumer would be obliged to repay the entire debt. The Court held that a substitution with the national provision was consistent with the Unfair Contract Terms Directive.[1030] Following the Opinion of AG Wahl,[1031] the judgment held in particular that:

> if, in a situation such as that at issue in the main proceedings, it was not permissible to replace an unfair term with a supplementary provision, requiring the court to annul

1026 The domestic currency had lost as much as 60% of its value against the franc, see the article in *Financial Times* of 4 July 2014 "Hungary Acts on Foreign-Exchange Loans."

1027 To appreciate the extent of the problem in financial terms, by March 2013 Hungary had over Ft 3.55tn ($15.8bn) of foreign currency mortgages outstanding, equivalent to 12% of GDP, as reported in *Financial Times* of July 25, 2013 "Hungary struggles with foreign currency loan burden".

1028 Case C-26/13 *Kásler and Káslerne Rábai* (n. 1025), para. 73. See also Case C-143/13 *Matei*, EU:C:2015:127, para. 74; Case C-96/14, *Van Hove*, EU:C:2015:262.

1029 In accordance with the position applicable by default under Art. 231 of the Hungarian Civil Code.

1030 See also 306(2) BGB "Soweit die Bestimmungen nicht Vertragsbestandteil geworden oder unwirksam sind, richtet sich der Inhalt des Vertrags nach den gesetzlichen Vorschriften" (Translation: "To the extent that the terms have not become part of the contract or are ineffective, the contents of the contract are determined by the statutory provisions").

1031 Opinion of AG Wahl in Case C-26/13 *Kásler and Káslerné Rábai*, EU:C:2014:85.

> the contract in its entirety, the consumer might be exposed to particularly unfavorable consequences, so that the dissuasive effect resulting from the annulment of the contract could well be jeopardized.[1032]

Worse than that, a perverse effect would be produced, penalizing the consumer:

> In general, the consequence of an annulment is that the outstanding balance of the loan becomes due forthwith, which is likely to be in excess of the consumer's financial capacities and, as a result, tends to penalize the consumer rather than the lender who, as a consequence, might not be dissuaded from inserting such terms in its contracts.[1033]

The ruling in *Kásler and Káslerne Rábai* was a judgment ahead of its time. Future developments demonstrate the extent of the problem and the necessity to address it at the national and European levels. The European legislator first of all took account of the excessive risks implied in the offer of foreign currency loans and inserted a provision on this matter into the Mortgage Credit Directive.[1034] The consumers who contract such loans must be made aware of the risk and must have the possibility to *convert the currency* of the loan, or other regulatory means should be made available to limit exposure.[1035] The Hungarian legislator passed a law in 2014 by virtue of which there was established a presumption of unfairness of clauses providing for a unilateral increase in the interest rate and there was imposed a conversion on the foreign currency loans to national currency at the historical exchange rate.[1036]

Another question in relation to the question of substitution of an unfair term arose in *Unicaja Banco*[1037] in the context of Spanish mortgage enforcement proceedings. It concerned the compatibility with Union law of a legislative provision[1038] that required the moderation by the national court hearing

---

1032 Case C-26/13 *Kásler and Káslerne Rábai* (n. 1025), para. 83.

1033 Ibid., para. 84.

1034 Directive 2014/17/EU of the European Parliament and of the Council of 4 February 2014 on credit agreements for consumers relating to residential immovable property and amending Directives 2008/48/EC and 2013/36/EU and Regulation (EU) No 1093/2010 [2014] OJ L60/34 (hereinafter the "Mortgage Credit Directive").

1035 Article 23 of the Mortgage Credit Directive.

1036 See in detail J. Fazekas, "The Consumer Credit Crisis and Unfair Contract Terms Regulation" (2017) 6 *EuCML* 120–124. In November 2014, Hungary's government agreed with banks to convert up to €9bn of foreign currency loans into forints at the historic market rate. See reports in the press in *Financial Times* of 9 November 2014 "Hungary agrees official foreign exchange mortgage conversion rate" and 28 January 2015 "Beware Hungary's cure for the Swiss Franc mortgages hangover". For Poland, see *Financial Times* article of 10 February 2017 on the Polish plan for reconversion "Polish bank shares jump on Kaczynski forex loan comments".

1037 Joined Cases C-482/13, C-484/13, C-485/13 and C-487/13 *Unicaja Banco and Caixabank* EU:C:2015:21.

1038 The second transitional provision of Ley 1/2013 de medidas para reforzar la protección a los deudores hipotecarios, reestructuración de deuda y alquiler social (Law 1/2013 laying down

mortgage enforcement proceedings of a default interest rate stipulated in the mortgage contract when this rate would exceed the threshold of three times the statutory rate. The referring court expressed doubts as to whether this "automatic" adjustment was compatible with the obligation of the courts to set aside the unfair terms without revising their content. The Court, concurring with the Opinion of AG Wahl,[1039] ruled in favor of the compatibility of the Spanish legislation with Union law. Two elements were decisive in that regard. The first was that the legislation in question applied to all mortgage loan contracts, without being specific to contracts containing unfair terms. The second was that this legislation did not prejudice the powers of the national courts to assess the fairness of a default interest rate, even where this would be set below the threshold set out by the law. Moreover, it did not prejudice the powers of the courts to draw all the necessary consequences from the finding of potential unfairness of a default interest rate clause, without being limited to its moderation to the cap set out by the legislation.

In the aftermath of the judgment in *Unicaja Banco* (but also in the judgment in *Aziz*,[1040] in which the Court sets out guidance for the assessment of unfairness of default interest rate clauses), the Spanish Supreme Court (*Tribunal Supremo*) established in a series of judgments a presumption of unfairness of clauses included in consumer credit contracts which set the default interest rates (*intereses de demora*) at a rate exceeding two percentage points the ordinary interest rate.[1041] The result of this line of case law is that the lower jurisdictions

measures for the strengthening of the protection of mortgagors, the restructuring of debt and social rent) of 14 May 2013 (BOE No 116 of 15 May 2013).

1039 Opinion of AG Wahl in Joined Cases C-482/13, C-484/13, C-485/13 and C-487/13 *Unicaja Banco and Caixabank*, EU:C:2014:2299.

1040 Case C-415/11 *Aziz*, EU:C:2013:164, para. 74.

1041 With regard to personal (unsecured) consumer credit contracts, TS Judgment No 265/2015 of 22 April 2015, STS 1723/2015, ES:TS:2015:1723 (plenary); Judgment No 470/2015 of 7 September 2015, STS 3828/2015, ES:TS:2015:3828 and Judgment No 469/2015 of 8 September 2015, STS 3829/2015, ES:TS:2015:3829. With regard to mortgage consumer credit contracts, Judgment No 705/2015 of 23 December 2015, STS 5618/2015, ES:TS:2015:5618 (plenary); Judgment No 79/2016 of 18 February 2016, STS 626/2016 ES:TS:2016:626; Judgment No 364/2016 of 3 June 2016, STS 2401/2016, ES:TS:2016:2401 (plenary).
In the second reference for preliminary ruling in the pending (at the time of writing) Joined Cases C-96/16 and C-94/17 *Banco Santander and Escobedo Cortés* [2016] OJ C 145/24, the Tribunal Supremo brought before the Court the question of compatibility of its own line of case law on default interest rates with Union law on consumer protection. In the pending (at the time of writing) Case C-70/17 *Abanca Corporación Bancaria* [2017] OJ C 121/17, the Tribunal Supremo, with its second question, brought before the Court the issue of compatibility of its own case law regarding the appraisal of a term of acceleration of a mortgage loan due to default of one single instalment, set out in the aforementioned Judgment No 705/2015 of 23 December 2015 and confirmed by Judgment No 79/2016 of 18 February 2016. In these judgments, the Tribunal Supremo ruled that once a term on acceleration in a mortgage contract due to failure to pay one single instalment is declared unfair, the court may still allow the continuation of the mortgage enforcement proceedings and apply the supplementary provision of national law according to which the right of the creditor to call in the totality of the loan is subject to

will first, automatically consider as unfair every term which meets the criteria pronounced by the Tribunal Supremo without further appraisal of "all the circumstances attending the conclusion of the contract" (Article 4 (1) Unfair Terms Directive) and second, set aside the respective term.

## 5.3. DECLARATION OF UNFAIRNESS IN COLLECTIVE PROCEEDINGS AND CONSEQUENCES FOR THE INDIVIDUAL ACTION

The *ex officio* doctrine requires national courts to establish all the consequences provided under national law of the finding of a term to be unfair, not only when this finding results from their own assessment but also when it has been made in an action for injunction. Since the judgment of the Court in *Invitel,*[1042] the first to explore the interrelationship between collective and individual action, there have been few judgments which have dealt with this complex issue. The following paragraphs concentrate on the elements which are of particular relevance for the *ex officio* doctrine.

### 5.3.1. *Erga Omnes Effect of the Finding of a Term Unfair in Collective Proceedings:* Invitel *and Beyond*

The issue in *Invitel* arose in the context of a collective action brought by a Hungarian consumer association against a telecommunications company with regards to a term providing that the company could unilaterally amend the price of its services. For the purposes of the present discussion, it is necessary to examine the question of the referring court on whether Article 6(1) of the Unfair Contract Terms Directive read in conjunction with its Article 7(1) and (2) should be interpreted as not precluding national law that provides for an *erga omnes* effect of a declaration of invalidity in an action for injunction. The judgment in *Invitel* offers, according to Fabrizio Cafaggi and Stephanie Law, "new perspectives on the blurring of lines between individual and collective enforcement"[1043] by linking the effectiveness of the respective remedies provided

default of at least three monthly instalments and to an express agreement of the parties in that regard (Art. 693(2) of the Spanish Civil Procedure Code). The continuation of the mortgage enforcement proceedings is in particular allowed when the court, taking into account the criteria of appraisal of the unfairness of an acceleration clause as enounced in Case C-415/11 *Aziz* (n. 1040), para. 73, considers that the consumer would be better off than if the mortgage enforcement proceedings would be stayed and the creditor would instead initiate ordinary civil law proceedings to terminate the contract.

1042 Case C-472/10 *Invitel*, EU:C:2012:242.

1043 F. Cafaggi and S. Law, "Unfair Contract Terms – Effect of Collective Proceedings" in E. Terryn, G. Straetmans and V. Colaert (eds.), *Landmark Cases of EU Consumer Law – In Honour of Jules Stuyck* (Cambridge, Intersentia, 2014).

within each context. Concurring with the Opinion of AG Trstenjak,[1044] the Court held that the effective implementation of the objectives of the actions for injunction:

> requires … that terms of the GBC [general business conditions] of consumer contracts which are declared to be unfair in an action for injunction brought against the seller or supplier concerned … are not binding on either the consumers who are parties to the actions for an injunction or on those who have concluded with that seller or supplier a contract to which the same GBC applies.[1045]

A decision in a collective action to the effect of finding a term unfair then has to be accorded "fairly wide applicability"[1046] extending the scope of *res judicata* beyond the parties to the dispute to all those consumers who concluded a contract with the *same* seller or supplier.[1047] This translates into an *erga omnes* effect *limited* to the consumers that were not party to the injunction proceedings but who have concluded a contract with the same seller or supplier.[1048]

The recognition of a limited *erga omnes* effect in a collective action for injunction has an impact upon future individual proceedings. In such individual proceedings, the national courts are more particularly required:

> of their own motion, and also as regards the future, to draw all the consequences provided for by national law in order to ensure that consumers who have concluded a contract to which those GBC apply will not be bound by that term.[1049]

This means that in individual proceedings between *any* consumer bound by a term that has been declared unfair in a previous collective action against the *same* seller, the courts are required, according to the Opinion of AG Trstenjak, to eliminate the disputed term "at a stroke from all contracts in which it was used, without [the] individual consumer having to contest it before the courts."[1050] At the time that the judgment was pronounced, the question raised by Fabrizio

1044 Opinion of AG Trstenjak in Case C-472/10 *Invitel*, EU:C:2011:806.

1045 Case C-472/10 *Invitel* (n. 1042), para 38.

1046 Opinion of AG Trstenjak in Case C-472/10 *Invitel* (n. 1044), point 51.

1047 Such type of extension of *res judicata (Rechtskrafterstreckung)* is provided for in German law under §11 S. 1 Gesetz über Unterlassungsklagen bei Verbraucherrechts- und anderen Verstößen (UKlaG), see M. Ebers, "EuGH: Missbräuchlichkeit einer Preisanpassungsklausel und Wirkung von Unterlassungsurteilen" (2012) *LMK Kommentierte BGH-Rechtsprechung*, 333520.

1048 See H.-W. Micklitz, "Unfair Terms in Consumer Contracts" in N. Reich et al., *European Consumer Law* (Cambridge, Intersentia, 2014), 125–64, 154.

1049 Case C-472/10 *Invitel* (n. 1042) para. 43.

1050 Opinion of AG Trstenjak in C-472/10 *Invitel* (n. 1044), point 57. Commenting on this finding in German legal order, M. Ebers (n. 1047), observes that it could be problematic to reconcile with the requirement under §11 S. 1 UKlaG that the contracting party has itself to rely upon the of the judgment on the injunction.

Cafaggi and Stephanie Law was whether the Court was actually "attempting to reconfigure the relationship between the effects of invalidity and those of injunctions."[1051] Hans-W. Micklitz had suggested that further clarifications might still be required before concluding that Member States are now obliged to afford an *erga omnes* effect to the judgments finding a contractual term unfair in injunctive proceedings.[1052] Micklitz has long pleaded for a legislative interconnection of the subjective right to have an unfair term declared void and the collective right to have such terms removed.[1053]

In a later judgment that arose in the field of private international law, the Court was given the opportunity to provide for further clarifications of paragraph 43 of the judgment in *Invitel* with regard to the relationship between individual actions and collective actions. More particularly, in *Verein für Konsumenteninformation,*[1054] the Court explained that *Invitel* establishes "the consistency of assessment" between collective actions and individual actions. Without prejudice to the particularities of each national legal system, it would now appear that a system that would impede such consistency of assessment by depriving national jurisdictions of the power to raise of their own motion in individual proceedings a term that has been declared unfair in injunctive proceedings against the same seller would not be consistent with the principle of effectiveness. Ensuring the "consistency of assessment" between the two different kinds of proceedings is the main argument underpinning the distinction which the Court operated in *Verein für Konsumenteninformation* with regard to the applicable law in an action for injunction.

On the one hand, the law applicable in an action for injunction brought by a consumer association against a professional established in another Member State, for the purpose of preventing a trader from using terms considered to be unfair in consumer contracts, is determined on the basis of the Rome II Regulation applicable to non-contractual obligations. This is the result of the consistent application of the rules determining the applicable law with the rules determining the jurisdiction and enforcement of judgments under the

1051 F. Cafaggi and S. Law (n. 1043), 667.

1052 H.-W. Micklitz, "Unfair Terms in Consumer Contracts" (n. 1048).

1053 H.-W. Micklitz, "Reforming European Unfair Terms Legislation in Consumer Contracts" (2010) 4 *ERCL* 347–383. The author argues that if the two procedures are kept separate it seems as if there are two separate purposes serving each of them – market cleansing and individual protection of consumers – and that they do not fit together, a result which is not satisfactory both politically and legally. He proposes the following formulation of a legislative provision (at 359): "Member States shall provide for appropriate and adequate measures which enable consumers in individual litigation, where the outcome of the litigation depends on the validity of a certain contract term, to benefit from national final regulatory actions and/or final judgments of national courts which have declared the identical or a similar contract term void in injunction proceedings".

1054 Case C-191/15 *Verein für Konsumenteninformation*, EU:C:2016:612, para. 56.

Brussels I Regulation.[1055] Indeed, in *Henkel*,[1056] the Court held that a preventive action brought by a consumer association is a matter relating to tort, delict or quasi-delict within the meaning of Article 5(3) of the Brussels Convention (this interpretation also being valid under the Brussels I Regulation and the Brussels I Regulation Recast). In this way, consumer associations were recognized as having the right to bring preventive actions not only before the courts where the trader is domiciled but also before the courts of the Member State of their own domicile where the infringement of consumer legislation produces its effects. The damage consists of the "undermining of legal stability by the use of unfair terms."[1057] The same logic applies to the law which is applicable in an action for an injunction within the meaning of Directive 2009/22. Such action relates to a non-contractual obligation within the meaning of the Rome II Regulation.[1058] The applicable law in relation, for instance, to the prescription of the action or the legitimation of a consumer association will therefore be deemed to be a non-contractual matter governed by the Rome II Regulation. The provision of the Rome II Regulation which governs the applicable law in such an action is Article 6(1). This provision applies in the field of unfair competition the *lex loci domni* principle, designating as applicable the law of the country "where competitive relations or the collective interests of consumers are, or are likely to be, affected." As explained in the judgment, unfair competition within the meaning of Article 6(1) of the Rome II Regulation also covers the use of unfair terms "as this is likely to affect the collective interests of consumers as a group and hence to influence the conditions of competition on the market."[1059] The country where the collective interests are affected is "the country of residence of the consumers to whom the undertaking directs its activities and whose interests are defended by the relevant consumer protection association by means of that action."[1060]

On the other hand, the law applicable to the assessment of the validity of the terms challenged by the action of injunction is determined in accordance with the contractual nature of those terms under the Rome I Regulation. As mentioned earlier, this "disjunction" of the applicable law, determined under the Rome II Regulation as to the action for injunction and under the Rome I Regulation as to the assessment of the contractual terms, serves the purpose of the consistency of assessment between collective actions and individual actions. To ensure such consistency, in both types of actions, the applicable law for the assessment of the terms will have to be the same, so that in individual proceedings, the courts may raise of their own motion the unfairness of a term that has already been declared unfair in collective proceedings with regard to the

1055 Ibid., para. 39.
1056 Case C-167/00 *Henkel*, EU:C:2002:555.
1057 Ibid., para. 42.
1058 Case C-191/15 *Verein für Konsumenteninformation* (n. 1054), para. 39.
1059 Ibid., para. 42.
1060 Ibid., para. 43.

same professional. This solution carries with it the risk, as AG Øe rightly pointed out in his Opinion,[1061] that the professional is the one to decide on the applicable law that will determine the validity of the terms employed, not only at the level of individual contracts but also at the level of the abstract control of terms carried through in collective proceedings. To this risk could be added the potential of "centralization" of the control of unfairness of terms used by multinational companies in one sole jurisdiction, to the detriment of the national preferences of each of the 28 Member States. However, against this risk, the Court set out the appropriate safeguard: the application of Article 6(2) of the Rome I Regulation. From this provision, it follows that:

> the choice of the applicable law is without prejudice to the application of the mandatory provisions laid down by the law of the country of residence of the consumers whose interests are being defended by means of [the collective] action.[1062]

Such provisions include, among others, the national provisions which transpose the Unfair Contract Terms Directive, provided that they ensure a higher level of consumer protection, in accordance with Article 8 of the Unfair Contract Terms Directive.[1063] In the circumstances of the *Verein für Konsumenteninformation* case, this would result in the assessment of the unfair terms being carried out in accordance with Luxembourg law as the law applicable in the contract, without prejudice, however, to the application of the mandatory provisions of Austrian law on the unfair terms protection (the law of residence of the consumers the interests of whom are being defended by the consumer association).[1064]

Another issue in relation to the *erga omnes* effect of the declaration of invalidity pertains to the remit of such declaration as against other sellers or suppliers that have not been party to the proceedings. Commenting on *Invitel*, Hans-W. Micklitz had already observed that the open formulation in paragraph 40 of that judgment:

> leaves more leeway … and would make it theoretically possible to extend the *effet utile* to the term, regardless of the original user, for example if a Member State wants to

[1061] Opinion of AG Saugmandsgaard Øe in Case C-191/15 *Verein für Konsumenteninformation*, EU:C:2016:388, point 60.

[1062] Case C-191/15 *Verein für Konsumenteninformation* (n. 1054), para. 59. The Court then examines the question of the potential unfairness of the choice-of-law clause of the place of the establishment of the trader (paras. 61 *et seq*). See critically G. Rühl, "The Unfairness of Choice-of-Law Clauses, or: The (Unclear) Relationship Between Article 6 Rome I Regulation and the Unfair Terms in Consumer Contracts Directive: *VKI v. Amazon*" (2018) 55 *CMLR* 201–224.

[1063] Ibid.

[1064] Following the publication of the judgment in Case C-191/15 *Verein für Konsumenteninformation* (n. 1054), the referring court, the Austrian Supreme Court (Oberster Gerichtshof) issued its judgment on 14 December 2017 (OGH 2 Ob 155/16g) in which it decided that the choice of Luxembourgian law was invalid and examined the contested unfair terms in light of Austrian law.

> use some sort of system of *ex parte* court order by which each and every trader has to abstain from using the banned terms, with the penalty being fines or other sanctions, that seems to be up to that Member State.[1065]

The Court had the possibility of clarifying the issue of the compatibility of a national scheme bearing such features in its judgment in *Biuro podróży 'Partner'* (hereinafter *Biuro Partner*).[1066] The question was referred by a Polish jurisdiction and arose in proceedings between, on the one hand, a professional in the tourism sector and, on the other hand, the responsible authority for competition and consumer protection in Poland. It concerned the use by that professional of unlawful terms in its standard conditions of business, equivalent to those that had already been declared unfair by a national court and entered in a public register. The core of the problem in *Biuro Partner* was to draw the right balance between the effective protection of consumers, by means of establishing a "blacklist" of unfair terms, and the effective judicial protection of professionals, with regard to the entering of a term they employ in such a list and their defense against the imposition of a penalty.

To understand the case, it is necessary to have an overview of the Polish system of consumer protection with regard to the different types of review of unfair terms. Three types of review may be distinguished, as they result from the presentation of the legal framework of the case and as explained in detail in the Opinion of AG Øe.[1067] The first is individual review carried out by the ordinary courts between consumers and sellers, and relates to the unfairness of terms in specific contracts. This is the "standard" control of unfairness whereby all the circumstances attending the conclusion of the contract have to be taken into account, pursuant to Article 4(1) of the Unfair Contract Terms Directive. The second type of judicial review concerns an *in abstracto* control, carried out by a specialist court (the SOKiK), and relates only to terms contained in standard conditions of business, without taking into account the way in which that term is used in particular contracts. As opposed to individual review, an application for *in abstracto* review may be brought by any consumer, whether or not bound by the contract, by consumer associations or by the responsible authority for the protection of consumers. The final judgment which declares a term unfair in this type of proceedings is communicated to the aforementioned responsible authority, which, in turn, enters the respective term into the public register. From this point onward, the judgment produces *erga omnes* effect against all traders, irrespective of whether they participated in the original

---

1065 H.-W. Micklitz, "Unfair Terms in Consumer Contracts" in N. Reich et al., *European Consumer Law* (Intersentia, 2014), 125–164, 154.

1066 Case C-119/15 *Biuro podróży 'Partner'*, EU:C:2016:987.

1067 Opinion of AG Saugmandsgaard Øe in Case C-119/15 *Biuro podróży Partner*, EU:C:2016:387, points 24–30. See also in detail J. Luzak, "You Too Will be Judged: *Erga Omnes* Effect of Registered Unfair Contract Terms in Poland" (2017) 6 *EuCML*, 120–124.

application for the declaration of unfairness or not. The third stage of control, linked essentially to the second one, is carried out by the administration in order to determine whether a certain term is identical or equivalent to a term entered in the aforementioned register. This administrative verification is made with regard to the content of the contested term and its effect on consumers. If it leads to a positive finding of use of a term already entered in the register, it results in a decision ordering the cessation of such use and, where appropriate, the imposition of a (heavy) fine. The professional may challenge this decision only as to the equivalence of the term actually employed with that in the register, but not as to its unfairness in the particular circumstances at issue.

It results from the above that the Polish scheme of "blacklisting" of unfair terms proceeds upon a double stage of judicial and administrative review. The Court ruled in favor of the compatibility of such a scheme with Union law, a finding which was, essentially, supported by two elements. The first one is the provision of the Union law itself regarding the possibility of Member States to maintain a "blacklist" of unfair terms. According to Article 8a of the Unfair Contract Terms Directive, Member States commit to inform the Commission of provisions they adopt which go beyond the minimum harmonization level, in particular where those provisions "contain lists of contractual terms which shall be considered as unfair." As opposed to the Opinion of AG Øe, the Court does not seem to distinguish as to the origin of the list, be it legislative or judicial, at least for as long as the responsibility of drawing up and publishing such list relies upon the administration.[1068] However, the possibility of Member States to provide for a scheme of a "blacklist" of unfair terms has to comply with Union law. Achieving the objective of enhancing the effectiveness of the prohibition of use of unfair contract terms should not come at the cost of legal uncertainty for professionals or deprive them of effective judicial protection. On this basis, the second element in favor of the compatibility of the national scheme with Union law relied upon its particular features offering satisfactory standards also for professionals. In particular, a register, such as that at issue in the case at hand, has to meet the requirements of transparency, be structured in a clear manner and be kept up to date.[1069] Moreover, the principle of effective judicial protection must be observed.[1070] As the Court clearly stated, the Unfair Contract Terms Directive as well as the Directive on injunctive actions[1071] must both be interpreted in the light of the right to effective judicial protection, according to

---

1068 Case C-119/15 *Biuro podróży 'Partner'* (n. 1066), para. 36: "It follows from those provisions that those lists or registers drawn up by national departments are, as a rule, done so in the interest of consumer protection under Directive 93/13". The original French text makes reference to "instances nationales".

1069 Case C-119/15 *Biuro podróży 'Partner'* (n. 1066), paras. 38–39.

1070 Ibid., para. 39 *et seq.*

1071 Directive 2009/22/EC of the European Parliament and of the Council of 23 April 2009 on injunctions for the protection of consumers' interests, [2009] OJ L110/30.

Article 47 of the Charter. This interpretation concerns not only consumers, but also professionals. In the context of the establishment of a "blacklist" of unfair terms, this concretely translates into a right for the professional to challenge both the assessment of the conduct considered to be unlawful and the amount of the fine fixed by the competent national body. In the Polish system, the professional is entitled to challenge the equivalence of the terms it uses with those entered in the register, while the courts must examine whether those terms are "materially identical" with the previous ones "in the light of *inter alia* the effects they produce."[1072] By contrast, it would seem to result from the judgment that the absence of a right to challenge anew the assessment of the unfairness of the term used did not breach as such the right to a fair hearing of the professional.

No specific reference is made in *Biuro Partner* with regard to the *ex officio* role of the courts as there was no specific enquiry in that regard. However, it can reasonably be inferred from *Invitel* that if a national court is obliged to raise of its own motion the unfairness of a contractual term which has been declared unfair in collective proceedings, with *erga omnes* effect, this holds *a fortiori* true with regard to a term that is entered into a national register ("blacklist"). Such a system has multiple virtues. It facilitates the task of the courts, which do not have to embark into an *ex officio* assessment *ab nihilo*, but can rely on the register. Moreover, as the Court noted in *Biuro Partner*, it affords legal certainty, contributes to the transparency of a consumer protection scheme and rationalizes the use of judicial resources, thus contributing to the proper functioning of the national judicial system.[1073]

### 5.3.2. *Impact of Ongoing Collective Proceedings Upon Pending Individual Proceedings*

Both individual action and collective action for the prevention of use of unfair terms have the same main objective: to ensure effective judicial consumer protection. Article 7(1) of the Unfair Contract Terms Directive provides consumers with the possibility to challenge effectively unfair terms in their contract by requiring Member States to ensure that, in the interests of consumers and competitors, adequate and effective means exist to prevent the continued use of unfair terms. Under Article 7(2) of the Unfair Contract Terms Directive, those means shall include the possibility for the competent consumer associations to take action in order to obtain a judicial decision as to whether contractual terms drawn up for general use are unfair.[1074] Individual action concerns the individual review of a term employed in one specific contract between the consumer and the professional. The terms of the assessment of the contractual

1072 Case C-119/15 *Biuro podróży 'Partner'* (n. 1066), para. 42.
1073 Ibid., para. 35.
1074 See Case C-472/10 *Invitel* (n. 1042), para. 36.

term are provided for in Article 4(1) of the Unfair Contract Terms Directive requiring the consideration of all the circumstances attending the conclusion of the specific contract in which the contested term is employed. By contrast, collective action envisages an abstract judicial review of a term drawn up for general use. As the Court explained in *Invitel*:

> the deterrent nature and dissuasive purpose of actions for an injunction, together with their independence of any particular dispute, mean that such actions may be brought even though the terms which it is sought to have prohibited have not been used in specific contracts.[1075]

That same case, as has already been analyzed above, laid out the consistency of assessment between the two actions, by virtue of which national courts should be allowed to draw, of their own motion, including for the future, all the conclusions provided for in national law that follow from the finding, in an action for injunction, that a term included in the general terms and conditions of consumer contracts is unfair. For the rest, Member States remain competent to provide for the detailed procedural rules governing the relationship between individual and collective actions.

Indeed, the relationship between the two types of action is not harmonized at the Union level. However, when exercising their competence in that regard, Member States are meant to enhance consumer protection and not the contrary. This absolute limit on the national design of that particular procedural relationship has been clearly set out in the judgment of the Court in *Sales Sinués*.[1076] This case arose in the broader context of the "floor clauses"' litigation (*clausulas suelo*), which culminated in the judgment of the Grand Chamber of the Court in *Gutiérrez Naranjo*.[1077] The applicants, like thousands of Spanish consumers, had concluded their mortgage contract which contained a "floor clause," by virtue of which the variable interest rate was capped at a certain threshold. They brought an individual action before the Barcelona court requesting that the clause be declared unfair due to its lack of transparency. Meanwhile, a collective action was pending before another court in Madrid, brought by a consumer association (the ADICAE) against 72 banks, including the banks against which the applicants had initiated proceedings (Caixabank and Catalunya Caixa). The defendant bank relied upon national procedural law and requested that the individual actions against them be stayed until the final decision concluding the collective proceedings would be rendered.

The Spanish procedural law establishes mechanisms for avoiding the risk of conflicting judgments. Apart from the classical procedural mechanism of the force of *res judicata* and *lis pendens*, Article 43 of the Spanish Civil Procedure

1075 Ibid., para. 37.
1076 Joined Cases C-381/14 and C-385/14 *Sales Sinués and Drame Ba*, EU:C:2016:252.
1077 Joined Cases C-154/15, C-307/15 and C-308/15 *Gutiérrez Naranjo and Others*, EU:C:2016:980.

Code provides for the possibility of suspending proceedings while a decisive preliminary issue is pending.[1078] By virtue of this Article, in order to give a ruling on the subject matter of a dispute that is pending before a civil court, "it is necessary to decide an issue which itself constitutes the main subject-matter of other proceedings pending before the same or a different civil court" and where it is not possible for the two actions to be joined, the court seised may stay the proceedings "until such time as the proceedings concerning the preliminary issue are concluded." From the case file submitted before the Court, it appeared that this provision had given rise to divergent interpretations before the various national instances with regard to its application in the relationship between individual and collective proceedings.[1079] Certain courts would take the view that this provision establishes an incidence of "civil procedural precedence" and would stay individual proceedings pending the delivery of the judgment in collective proceedings. A minority of Spanish trial courts would consider this to be a situation of *lis pendens* of the individual actions vis-à-vis the collective actions because, in their view, the cause of action and the parties are the same. On this ground, they would therefore remove from the register the individual actions. Finally, some courts would take the view that there is neither an issue of civil procedural precedence, nor a situation of *lis pendens*, as neither the parties nor the causes of action are the same; these courts would therefore conclude that individual consumers retain *locus standi* in order to defend their interests. In view of this divergence and the considerable number of consumers involved, the referring court of Barcelona brought to the attention of the Court this important question in order to obtain an interpretation of Union law that would allow, in turn, a consistent interpretation and equality of treatment for all consumers.

The reasoning of the Court is guided by the specific characteristics of the two types of actions, the competence of Member States in matters governing the relationship between collective and individual actions, and the need to ensure the effectiveness of consumer protection intended by the Unfair Contract Terms Directive. The Court took note, first of all, of the "different purposes and legal effects" of the two types of actions.[1080] Next to the considerations mentioned a few paragraphs above, pertaining to the distinct nature of the control associated with each action (individual review as opposed to abstract review), there is particular reference to the possibility, already recognized by the case law, for the consumer to assert the application of the term to the contract despite the declaration of unfairness.[1081] The differences between the two types of action

1078 See the Opinion of AG Szpunar in Joined Cases C-381/14 and C-385/14 *Sales Sinués and Drame Ba* (n. 1076), para. 27. For a detailed analysis of the Spanish system of collective action and the relationship with the individual actions, see J. M. Fernández Seijo, *La Tutela de los Consumidores en los procedimientos judiciales* (Bosch, Wolters Kluwer, 2017), 133 *et seq.*

1079 Joined Cases C-381/14 and C-385/14 *Sales Sinués and Drame Ba* (n. 1076), paras 30–33.

1080 Ibid., para. 30.

1081 Ibid., para. 25.

justify the fact that their procedural relationship corresponds to procedural requirements relating to the sound administration of justice and to the need to avoid incompatible judicial decisions. However, as the Opinion of AG Szpunar points out, the interaction of the actions should be "favourable to the consumer, not one which poses an obstacle to individual actions or replaces individual actions by collective actions for an injunction."[1082]

Therefore, the design of the procedural interaction at issue should not lead to a weakening of consumer protection. That would be the case if the consumer could not disassociate himself from the ongoing collective action and if he could not maintain independent *locus standi* before the courts. The possibility of introducing independent proceedings appears to have various advantages. The Court pointed out that such possibility allows the consumer to put forward particular circumstances attending the conclusion of his own contract and it allows the court before which the case is brought to conduct its own analysis.[1083] Moreover, the suspension of individual actions while the collective proceedings are ongoing makes the consumer dependent on the time period within which the latter will be concluded.[1084] This consideration is of particular importance when the consumer intends to draw a (considerable) financial advantage from the finding of unfairness. Finally, the consumer faces an additional difficulty if he cannot disassociate himself from the collective proceedings. If he wishes to take part in the collective action, he is subject to constraints relating to the determination of the competent court and the pleas that he may put forward.

In light of the above, the Court concluded that the national rule at issue – or at least its interpretation in such a way as to oblige national courts to suspend individual proceedings while the collective action is pending – does not comply with the requirements of Article 7(1) of the Unfair Contract Terms Directive. This solution is compatible with the need to respect consistency between judicial decisions and the sound administration of justice. As the Court explained, the difference in nature of the judicial control exercised in each type of proceedings should prevent the risk of incompatible judicial decisions.[1085] The argument in favor of the suspension pertaining to the economy of judicial resources (the need to "avoid overburdening the courts") did not convince the Court either. The effective exercise of consumer rights may not be called into question by considerations connected to the organization of a Member State's judicial system. Although the Court did not engage with an analysis of hierarchical relationship between collective action and individual action, it results from the judgment that the two are complementary means of attaining effective consumer protection.

---

[1082] Opinion of AG Szpunar in Joined Cases C-381/14 and C-385/14 *Sales Sinués and Drame Ba*, point 59.

[1083] Joined Cases C-381/14 and C-385/14 *Sales Sinués and Drame Ba* (n. 1076), para. 37.

[1084] Ibid., para. 38.

[1085] Ibid., para. 41.

## 5.4. SCOPE OF THE FORCE OF *RES JUDICATA* OF A JUDGMENT DECLARING A TERM UNFAIR

One of the most important limits to the extent of the effectiveness of procedural consumer protection is the force of *res judicata*, which ensures stability of the law and legal relations, as well as the sound administration of justice. It is settled case law that the importance of the principle of *res judicata* justifies that a national court is *not* required:

> to disapply domestic rules of procedure conferring finality on a decision, even if to do so would make it possible to remedy an infringement of a provision, regardless of its nature contained in the Unfair Contract Terms Directive.[1086]

In *Banco Primus*, the Court had to answer whether this case law is applicable in the specific situation that national courts were not afforded the power to examine, at the request of the parties or of their own motion, the unfairness of a clause contained in a mortgage contract, in circumstances where another term of the same contract had been declared unfair at a previous stage of the proceedings.

The case was referred by a Spanish jurisdiction, in the usual context of mortgage repossession proceedings, in the aftermath of the amendment of the Spanish legislation following the judgment in *Aziz*.[1087] The enforcement proceedings against the mortgage debtor were initiated in 2010. In 2011 the property was auctioned and awarded to the bank for half of its value, due to a lack of bidders. The possession of the property by the bank was deferred following consecutive suspension applications, one of which led to an order which considered one clause of the contract relating to default interest unfair. A decision adopted in 2014 terminated the suspension of the eviction. After this decision, the consumer mortgage debtor lodged an extraordinary application on the basis of the new provision of the Civil Procedure Code (Article 695 *Ley de Enjuiciamiento Civil* – LEC), which afforded the debtor with the right to enter an objection on the ground of the unfairness of a term of the mortgage contract constituting the basis for the enforcement. The ground for his objection relied upon the unfairness of the clause of his loan agreement relating to default interest, i.e. that same clause that had already been declared unfair by the order adopted the year before. Yet, the referring court expressed doubts as to the unfairness of other terms of the loan agreement, namely the clause relating to the method

---

1086 Case C-421/14 *Banco Primus*, EU:C:2017:60, para. 47 with reference, to that effect, to Case C-40/08 *Asturcom Telecomunicaciones* (n. 768), para. 37 and Joined Cases C-154/15, C-307/15 and C-308/15 *Gutiérrez Naranjo and Others* (n. 1077), para. 68.

1087 Case C-415/11 *Aziz*, EU:C:2013:164. See Chapter 5, section 3.3.1 and Chapter 6, Section 1.2.1.

of calculation of the ordinary interest and the clause relating to the accelerated payment. However, it considered that the *res judicata* principle, as provided for in Spanish civil procedural law (Article 207 LEC), impeded the consideration of the unfairness of these other clauses.

Essentially, the Court had to delve into the remit of the force of *res judicata* with regard to the question of law that has been decided. The reasoning followed a basic distinction between a decision that rules upon the lawfulness of the entirety of the clauses contained in a contract and a decision that rules upon the unfairness of a specific clause.[1088] In the first case, the judicial assessment of the unfairness may not be called into question in subsequent proceedings. To the extent that national procedural law would provide such a scope for the *res judicata*, it would be compatible with Union consumer law. In the second case, where the judgment concentrates on a specific term or terms of the contract, the courts should not be impeded from examining the unfairness of other terms in subsequent proceedings. Indeed, the remit of the force of *res judicata* may not be drawn so as to cover a legal matter that has not been examined and in this way impede the courts from assessing, at the request of the parties or of its own motion, the potential unfairness of other terms of the contract. Although it is for national laws to set the conditions upon which consumers may not be bound by unfair terms, such conditions:

> may not adversely affect the substance of the right that consumers acquire under that provision not to be bound by a term deemed to be unfair.[1089]

In the proceedings in the case at hand the Court did not dispose precise information as to the exact scope of the clauses that have been examined in previous proceedings. It left it, therefore, for the national court to assess whether the decision which has become *res judicata* covered the lawfulness of all the terms of the contract or just one clause.[1090]

The limitation of the force of *res judicata* principle only to these terms which the national court raised of its own motion, which leaves intact the obligation of the court to examine in subsequent proceedings the potential unfairness of other clauses of the contract, can also be justified by the fact that the own motion assessment does not cover an abstract assessment of the validity of the consumer contract as a whole but only the assessment of unfairness of specific clauses. Moreover, the limited remit of the force of *res judicata* would appear to support the proposition that the own assessment *obligation* does not extend to all the terms of the contract but only to these terms upon which one of the parties relies

1088 Case C-421/14 *Banco Primus* (n. 1086), paras. 49, 50.

1089 Ibid., para. 51, citing Joined Cases C-154/15, C-307/15 and C-308/15 *Gutiérrez Naranjo and Others* (n.1077), para. 71.

1090 Ibid., para. 53.

in order to base his or her claim and for the assessment of which the court is in possession of the legal and factual elements.[1091]

## 5.5. APPLICATION BY THE COURTS OF THEIR OWN MOTION OF A PENALTY PROVIDED FOR THE INFRINGEMENT OF THE CONSUMER LEGISLATION

The power of the national courts to apply of their own motion a penalty (*sanction civile*) provided for in their national law for the violation of the consumer legislation derives from their general obligation to "draw all the consequences arising under national law" as soon as they establish a violation of such legislation. To this end, it suffices that the penalty sanctions the infringement of a national provision adopted in the context of transposition of EU consumer law.[1092] The application of a penalty as part of the *ex officio* application of national law transposing EU consumer law could already be inferred from the Order of the Court in *Pohotovosť I*.[1093] In its Order, applying *Rampion and Godard* by analogy, the Court found that, without it being necessary to examine the unfair nature of a term which failed to mention the APR in a consumer credit contract, the Consumer Credit Directive should be interpreted as allowing national courts to apply of their own motion the provisions transposing into national law the obligation to include a statement of the APR.[1094] In the case at issue, the Slovak law provided that the failure to mention the APR renders the credit interest-free and free of charge. The application by the courts of their own motion of the penalties provided for the violations of the consumer legislation was clearly couched in *Radlinger and Radlingerová*[1095] in terms of an obligation. With regard to the obligation of the creditor to provide information (pursuant to Article 10(2) of the Consumer Credit Directive), the national court is not only obliged to examine the issue of a potential violation of the respective provision of its own motion, where it has available to it the legal and factual elements necessary for that task.[1096] It will also have to draw of its own motion all the consequences arising under national law from that infringement, including the application of a national sanction without having "to wait for the consumer to

---

1091 See, to that effect Case C-472/11 *Banif Plus Bank*, EU:C:2013:88, paras. 37-41, if interpreted in the sense that the obligation of the court, in determining whether the term upon which the claim brought before it is based is unfair, consists into taking into account all of the other terms to the contract in order to examine the unfairness of this term, but does not imply an obligation to examine the potential unfairness of those other terms.

1092 See Case C-565/12, *LCL Le Crédit Lyonnais*, EU:C:2014:190, para. 35.

1093 Case C-76/10 *Pohotovosť I* (n. 825).

1094 Ibid, para. 76. This obligation was laid down in Art. 4(2)(a) of Directive 87/102 and in Art. 5(1)(g) of the Directive 2008/48 currently in force (n. 870).

1095 Case C-377/14 *Radlinger and Radlingerová* (n. 917).

1096 Ibid., para. 70.

make an application to that effect, provided always that the principle of *audi alteram partem* has been complied with."[1097]

The application of the sanction of forfeiture of interest to the violation of the rules of consumer legislation may not be made subject to a limitation period. This follows from *Cofidis*,[1098] according to which the *ex officio* power of the courts may not be made subject to a foreclosure period. The above case law leads to the conclusion that the *ex officio* power of the courts may not be subject to a limitation period not only with regard to violations of mandatory consumer law, but also with regard to the consequences arising under national law from its infringement. The penalty of forfeiture of interest is not to be treated as a counterclaim.[1099] It is a sanction imposed by law and it should be applicable automatically. Yet, the situation would differ in claims against a creditor for restitution of sums based on unjust enrichment. Such a claim would arguably have to be raised by the consumer in separate proceedings and may be subject to a limitation period.[1100] This is not the same as the application of a penalty by the courts of their own motion.

The penalty to be applied by the court of its own motion will have to be "effective, proportionate and dissuasive," as laid down under Article 23 of the Consumer Credit Directive and in accordance with the interpretation which the Court gave in *LCL Le Crédit Lyonnais.*[1101]

The case of *LCL Le Crédit Lyonnais* did not concern, as such, the *ex officio* application of sanctions, but instead the issue of their effectiveness.[1102] The French Consumer Code vests the national courts with the power to raise of their own motion *all the provisions* of the respective code,[1103] including those on sanctions. The sanction which was applicable in that case was the forfeiture of the entitlement of the lender to interest, on the ground of the failure of the latter to examine the creditworthiness of the borrower, by means of consultation of the national (French) register of individual credit repayment defaults.[1104]

---

1097 Ibid., para. 71.

1098 C-473/00 *Cofidis* (n. 647).

1099 Contra Cour d'Appel Paris, 6 July 2017, RG 16-14519, according to which the claim of the debtor for the forfeiture of interest is not a defense which aims at the partial rejection of the claim of the bank, but it is a counterclaim which should be subject to the 5 year-limitation of Art. L 110-4 of the Commercial Code (*Code de Commerce*).

1100 Cf. Joined Cases C-154/15, C-307/15 and C-308/15 *Gutiérrez Naranjo* (n. 1077), para. 69: "Likewise, the Court has previously held that in the interests of legal certainty it is compatible with EU law to lay down reasonable time-limits for bringing proceedings", citing Case C-40/08 *Asturcom Telecomunicaciones* (n. 755), para. 41.

1101 Case C-565/12 *LCL Le Crédit Lyonnais*, EU:C:2014:190.

1102 Making it a "petit grand arrêt", in the eloquent terms of E. Poillot, in F. Picod (dir.), *Grands Arrêts, Jurisprudence de la CJUE 2014, Décisions et Commentaires* (Bruylant, 2015), 743–752.

1103 The respective power was provided, at that time, under Art. L. 141-4 of the Code de la Consommation, currently laid down under Art. R 632-1 of the same code.

1104 The sanction of forfeiture of the interest was provided, at that time, under Art. L. 311-48 of the Code de la Consommation, and currently it is provided under Art. L. 341-2 of the same code.

The referring court raised of its own motion a plea concerning the possible forfeiture of the lender's entitlement to interest, and the lender (*LCL Le Crédit Lyonnais*) acknowledged the violation of its obligation, resulting in the application of the respective sanction. However, the issue which arose was the remit of the sanction: whether it covered only the contractual interest or whether it could be considered to also refer to the statutory interest.

At the origins of the doubts of the referring court was a specific line of case law of the *Cour de Cassation*, according to which the penalty of forfeiture of entitlement to interest should be considered to apply only to the contractual interest, while the statutory interest, as provided under the French Civil Code for the delay in performance of any type of debt (Article 1153 of the *Code Civil*), remains payable. Moreover, the referring court pointed out that by virtue of a provision of the Monetary and Financial Code (Article L. 313-3), the statutory rate is to be increased by five percentage points if the borrower has not repaid his debt in full within a period of two months after the decision of the court has become enforceable. Both the interest at the statutory rate and the increase of five percentage points apply by operation of law, even if it has not been claimed or if the decision does not provide for the granting of such interest.

The result of the above legislative framework, as interpreted by the highest national court, was to deprive the penalty of its practical effect. In the circumstances of the specific case, the contractual rate of interest was 5.60%, whereas after the declaration of forfeiture of entitlement to that interest, the creditor could still claim interest at the statutory rate, which increased by five percentage points two months after the judicial decision became enforceable – this would amount to 5.71% for 2012, securing, in reality, an advantage for the creditor.[1105] The penalty of forfeiture of interest might prove to be effective only where the consumer pays in full the outstanding amounts of the credit within two months of the judicial decision becoming enforceable (as the statutory rate is lower than the contractual rate). However, such a possibility is considered illusory by the referring court, taking into account that the proceedings on behalf of the creditor are instituted due to the inability of the consumer to meet his contractual obligations. Similarly hypothetical is the possibility that the consumer will seise the court, pursuant to the aforementioned provision of the Monetary and Financial Code, to request an exemption from the increase of the interest at the statutory rate or a reduction of the amount thereof. This is because the consumer is usually not aware of such a possibility and even if he does apply for the benefit, the decision for an eventual exemption/reduction depends upon the financial situation of the debtor and not upon an eventual violation of the obligations on behalf of the creditor.[1106]

1105 Case C-565/12 *LCL Le Crédit Lyonnais* (n. 1101), para. 21.
1106 Ibid., para. 24.

The examination by the Court of the "genuinely dissuasive" character of the penalty of forfeiture of contractual interest relies upon a "comparison test" which will have to be applied by the national jurisdiction. More particularly, the national jurisdiction is invited to compare two amounts: on the one hand, the amount which the creditor would have received by way of repayment of the loan if he had complied with his obligations to assess the creditworthiness of the debtor before the conclusion of the loan and, on the other hand, the amount which he would receive if the penalty for breach of that pre-contractual obligation were applied. If the result of this comparison is that the application of the penalty of forfeiture of contractual interest would lead to an advantage for the creditor because the right to statutory interest would be maintained and because this interest would be eventually increased by five percentage points, then that means the national system of penalties is not genuinely dissuasive. In any event, a penalty of forfeiture of interest will not qualify as being genuinely dissuasive if the amount which the creditor is likely to receive following the application of that penalty are not "significantly less" than the amount that he would have received had he complied with that obligation.[1107]

An argument in favor of the application of the statutory interest, notwithstanding the forfeiture of the contractual interest, is that the two types of interest are due to a different cause and do not serve the same purpose. Indeed, the contractual interest is the remuneration of the creditor for providing the credit service, while the statutory interest is to compensate for the damage resulting from delay in performance. However, the difference between the function of the two types of interest should not be of relevance when it comes down to the assessment of the genuinely dissuasive character of a penalty. As the referring court notes, the creditor's breach of its obligation to assess the consumer's creditworthiness may have contributed to the latter's overindebtedness.[1108] The creditor therefore should not be entitled to claim statutory interest as damages for a situation for which it could be held liable. If the creditor had complied with its obligation, perhaps it would not have granted the loan, or it may have granted a lower amount and the consumer would not have ended up in a situation of overindebtedness. Therefore, the Court rightly did not go along the path of an argument based on the different *raison d'être* of types of interest.

The *ex officio* application of sanctions is a corollary to the *ex officio* application of the provision of the law the violation of which results in the sanction. By contrast, any claim which may arise from the finding of unfairness, in particular the payment of unduly paid monies and/or damages, will have to be made by the consumer. In that regard, the Court clarified in *Gutiérrez Naranjo*[1109] that Member States are required, pursuant to Article 7(2) of the Unfair Contract Terms

1107 Ibid, paras. 50–52.

1108 Ibid., para. 23.

1109 Joined Cases C-154/15, C-307/15 and C-308/15 *Gutiérrez Naranjo* (n. 1077).

Directive, to provide for a right to restitution of advantages wrongly obtained, to the consumer's detriment, by the professional on the basis of the application of the unfair term. Even if Member States remain competent to provide for the particular means in order to ensure that the consumer will not be bound by unfair terms, national law "may not alter the scope and, therefore, the substance" of the protection which the consumer enjoys and "thus affect the strengthening of the effectiveness of that protection."[1110] Furthermore, the right to restitution which the consumer draws from Union law may not be subject to a temporal limitation of its effects by national jurisdictions, as that would jeopardize the "substance of the right that consumers acquire under that provision."[1111]

## 6. THE "WEAKER POSITION" RATIONALE TESTED AGAINST CONSUMER ASSOCIATIONS

The case law analyzed up to this point concerned the legal position of the consumer in individual litigation. The weaker position of the individual consumer against the supplier was pivotal in the empowerment of the courts to raise unfair terms of their own motion. Two rulings of the Court raise the question of the effectiveness of national procedural rules that affect the procedural position of consumer associations acting independently of an individual dispute (control *in abstracto* of unfair terms) or when acting in connection with an individual dispute. In the first case, *Asociación de Consumidores Independientes de Castilla y León,*[1112] the issue raised was whether the imbalance *rationale* with respect to the procedural position of consumers should also be applicable to consumer associations. This time, it was not in order to determine the existence of own motion assessment powers, but in order to guide the assessment of the effectiveness of certain procedural rules applicable to them when they initiate an action for injunction. The second case, *Pohotovst' v Miroslav Vašuta,*[1113] concentrated on the standing of a consumer association to intervene in an individual dispute as a means to strengthen the position of the consumer involved. A common theme in both cases is the application of the principle of effectiveness in the nexus between procedural rights of consumer associations and the advancement of consumer protection.[1114]

---

1110 Ibid., para. 65.

1111 Ibid., para. 70.

1112 Case C-413/12 *Asociación de Consumidores Independientes de Castilla y León*, EU:C:2013:800.

1113 Case C-470/12 *Pohotovosť II* (n. 812).

1114 See T. Dolny, "Procedural treatment of consumer organisations in the judicial proceedings concerning the use of unfair terms" (2014) 1 *Revue Européenne de Droit de la Consommation* 31–51.

## 6.1. INJUNCTIVE RELIEF, RULES ON JURISDICTION AND THE STRUCTURE OF LEGAL REMEDIES

The judgment in *Asociación de Consumidores Independientes de Castilla y León* sheds light on one aspect of the unfair terms protection in relation to injunction proceedings brought in the interests of consumers. It concentrates in particular on the question of how the principle of effectiveness can impact upon procedural rules on jurisdiction applicable to such proceedings. Pursuant to Spanish civil procedural law, injunction proceedings initiated to defend the collective interests of consumers have to be brought before the court where the defendant is established.[1115] Moreover, no appeal lies against orders ruling on questions of territorial jurisdiction while the court to which proceedings are referred is bound by that decision.[1116] In the instant case, a small sized consumer association, the *Asociación de Consumidores Independientes de Castilla y León*, had initiated proceedings in its own territorial jurisdiction in Salamanca against a professional established in Barcelona. The national court, after hearing the parties, declined jurisdiction and held the court in Barcelona to be competent. The consumer association appealed against the order, alleging that due to its limited financial means, it could not pursue the action in another court. National rules according to its view were contrary to the objectives pursued by the Unfair Contract Terms Directive. Rejecting the arguments of the Spanish government, the Court found the case admissible in that it:

> concerns the effectiveness of a procedural rule intended to safeguard a right which individuals enjoy under European Union law.[1117]

The Court, concurring with the Opinion of AG Mengozzi,[1118] did not transpose the logic of procedural imbalance applying in individual consumer actions to a collective action context:

> as regards the procedural remedies available to consumer protection associations in order to prevent the continued use of unfair terms, they are not in an inferior position vis-à-vis the seller or supplier.[1119]

---

1115 Art. 52(1)(16) Spanish Civil Procedure Code.

1116 Arts. 60(1) and 67 Spanish Civil Procedure Code.

1117 Case C-413/12 *Asociación de Consumidores Independientes de Castilla y León* (n. 1112), para. 25.

1118 Opinion of AG Mengozzi in Case C-413/12 *Asociación de Consumidores Independientes de Castilla y León*, EU:C:2013:532.

1119 Case C-413/12 *Asociación de Consumidores Independientes de Castilla y León* (n. 1112), para. 49.

After stressing the importance of the role that the Union legislator assigns to consumer associations for achieving a high level of consumer protection, the Court further held that:

> it must nevertheless be recognized that an action for an injunction pitting such an association against a seller or supplier is not characterized by the same imbalance that is present in an individual action brought by a consumer against a seller or supplier.[1120]

The criterion of procedural imbalance is a powerful yardstick in the light of which national procedural rules are to be assessed.[1121] Besides, the Court noted that it was not the procedural rules themselves that impeded the association to bring its action, but its financial situation.[1122] However, the general interest for the sound administration of justice and foreseeability cannot depend upon the subjective situation of each litigant.[1123] The Court was satisfied that several guarantees existed that safeguarded the right to access to justice for the association. It observed first of all that access to court is guaranteed since the jurisdiction designed as territorially competent is bound to decide on the merits. Second, there was no indication that if the association would bring the proceedings, it would have to be present at all stages. Third, legal aid could be available to offset the financial constraints. Moreover, the issue on jurisdiction was not final since it could be reopened if an appeal would be brought against the decision ruling on the merits. Fourth, the rule on one-tier jurisdiction aims at preventing contradictory decisions contributing to legal certainty.[1124] The argument that a privileged forum for consumer associations could be derived from the judgment in Case *Henkel*[1125] was rejected as that case concerned

1120 Ibid., para. 50.

1121 Ibid., para. 51, the Court notes that such a differentiated approach can also be supported by Art. 4(1) of Directive 2009/22/EC of 23 April 2009 on injunctions for the protection of consumers' interests [2009] OJ L 110/30 "under which it is the courts of the Member State where the defendant is established or has its address which have jurisdiction to hear actions for an injunction brought by consumer protection associations from other Member States in the event of an intra-EU infringement of European Union consumer protection legislation". This passage should not be understood as implying that this provision lays down a general rule of territorial jurisdiction (something which the Court stresses in the beginning of the judgment at para. 29). The provision covers only cross-border cases. This provision is rarely used, as it is explained in the Commission Report concerning the application of Directive 2009/22/EC of the European Parliament and of the Council on injunctions for the protection of consumers' interests, 06.11.2012, COM (2012) 635 final. The more common situation with a cross-border dimension is that the association will sue in its own jurisdiction, towards which the trader against whom the action is addressed, directs his activities (p. 6 of the Report).

1122 Case C-413/12 *Asociación de Consumidores Independientes de Castilla y León* (n. 1112), para. 37.

1123 Ibid., para. 38.

1124 Ibid., paras. 40–45.

1125 C-167/00 *Henkel*, EU:C:2002:555.

cross-border proceedings and could not be transposed to the present circumstances.[1126] The legal issue in *Henkel* was different and concerned the definition of a broad scope for the concept of a "harmful" event in the Brussels Convention so that the *lex loci damni* covers "not only situations where an individual has personally sustained damage but also, in particular, the undermining of legal stability by the use of unfair terms which it is the task of [consumer] associations ... to prevent."[1127] Besides, the Court in *Henkel* had rejected the application by analogy to consumer associations of the special rules of jurisdiction concerning the individual consumer.[1128]

## 6.2. INTERVENTION OF CONSUMER ASSOCIATIONS IN INDIVIDUAL CONSUMER LAW PROCEEDINGS

The judgment in *Pohotovosť v Miroslav Vašuta (Pohotovosť II)*,[1129] has to be distinguished from the 2010 Order of the Court bearing the same name.[1130] Both cases arose in the context of enforcement of an arbitration award, but the procedural issue which arose is different. In the *Pohotovosť II* case, the referring court from Slovakia was seeking to clarify whether the important role assigned to consumer associations by the Unfair Contract Terms Directive for the protection of consumers should be understood, in conjunction with Articles 38 and 47 of the Charter, as precluding national procedural law which does not give standing to consumer associations to intervene in individual disputes involving consumers for the enforcement of a final arbitration award. The Court upheld the compatibility of Slovak procedural law.[1131] The reasoning is particularly interesting with respect to the interpretation in light of the Charter.

According to Article 38 of the Charter "Union policies shall ensure a high level of consumer protection." The Court did not endorse an interpretation by virtue

1126 Case C-413/12 *Asociación de Consumidores Independientes de Castilla y León* (n. 1112), paras. 46–47.
1127 C-167/00 *Henkel* (n. 1125), para. 42.
1128 Ibid., para. 33.
1129 Case C-470/12 *Pohotovosť II* (n. 1113). There was one more case referred by a Slovak jurisdiction on the same issue. The question was dismissed as the Court found that it lacked manifestly jurisdiction to answer the questions referred by the national court, as the disputed contract was concluded before 1 May 2004, the date of accession of the Slovak Republic to the EU: Case C-153/13 *Pohotovosť*, EU:C:2014:1854.
1130 Case C-76/10 *Pohotovosť I* (n. 825).
1131 See the case note A. BEKA, *ECJ upholds national law precluding intervention of consumer associations in enforcement proceedings of an arbitration award*, 23 March 2014, available at <http://conflictoflaws.net/2014/ecj-upholds-national-law-precluding-intervention-of-consumer-associations-in-enforcement-proceedings-of-an-arbitration-award/> accessed 02.10.2017.

of which this provision can "by itself" be interpreted in a way that encompasses a right of intervention. As long as the Unfair Contract Terms Directive does not establish a right of intervention, such a right cannot find a constitutional foundation in Article 38 of the Charter alone.[1132] This reasoning is aligned with the rights' reasoning of the Court in the Grand Chamber case *Association de médiation sociale*.[1133] This was a case raising the issue of the horizontal application of the principle of the Charter laid down in Article 27 on the right of workers to information and consultation when given specific expression in Directive 2002/14.[1134] The Court, distancing itself from the Opinion of AG Cruz Villalón,[1135] held that:

> since that article by itself does not suffice to confer on individuals a right which they may invoke as such, it could not be otherwise if it is considered in conjunction with [Directive 2002/14].[1136]

Should the same line of reasoning be followed in *Pohotovosť II* with respect to Article 38 of the Charter, it would follow, as the Opinion of AG Wahl explains, that this article:

> which has nothing to say about a directly defined individual legal position, establishes a principle and not a right and is therefore judicially cognisable under Article 52 (5) of the Charter, only in the interpretation of Union acts and in the ruling on their legality, in this instance Directive 93/13.[1137]

Yet, Directive 93/13, AG Wahl continues:

> does not establish a right for such associations to intervene in individual disputes involving such consumers [i.e. protected by the Unfair Contract Terms Directive] and, in this regard, Article 38 of the Charter cannot require an interpretation of the directive in favour of recognition of such right.[1138]

---

1132 Case C-470/12 *Pohotovosť II* (n. 1113), para. 52.

1133 Case C-176/12 *Association de médiation sociale*, EU:C:2014:2.

1134 Directive 2002/14 of the European Parliament and of the Council of 11 March 2002 on a general framework for informing and consulting employees in the European Community [2002] OJ L80/29.

1135 Opinion of AG Cruz Villalón in Case C-176/12 *Association de médiation sociale*, EU:C:2013:491.

1136 Case C-176/12 *Association de médiation sociale* (n. 1133), para. 49.

1137 Opinion of AG Wahl in Case C-470/12 *Pohotovosť II*, EU:C:2013:844, point 66. See also the analysis on the horizontal application of fundamental rights and on the conditions of invocability of Charter principles in the Opinion of AG Cruz Villalón in Case C-176/12 *Association de médiation sociale* (n. 1135).

1138 Opinion of AG Wahl in Case C-470/12 *Pohotovosť II* (n. 1137), point 67.

The above sheds light on the limits of Article 38 of the Charter as a principle that cannot be the source of individual rights independent of the rights conferred in the directives.[1139]

With respect to Article 47 of the Charter, the Court decided that, as far as the consumer is concerned, the lack of an intervention right of consumer associations does not breach the right to an effective remedy of the individual consumer, "to the extent that Directive 93/13 requires that the national court hearing disputes between consumers and sellers or suppliers take positive action unconnected with the actual parties to the contract".[1140]

This passage elevates the *ex officio* doctrine in individual consumer litigation to a *necessary* component of the effective judicial protection of consumers. If the *ex officio* obligation did not exist, then the response of the Court with regard to the right of a consumer association to intervene would perhaps have been different. In the *ex officio* case law, it is well established that a positive action "unconnected to the parties" is required in order to strengthen the individual position of the consumer. Consumer associations play an important role for consumer protection too, but this is done, AG Wahl points out, "at a very different level and from a very different perspective to that required of the court."[1141] Moreover, the intervention of consumer associations is "not comparable to the legal aid which under Article 47 of the Charter must be made available, in certain cases, to those who lack sufficient resources."[1142]

As far as the consumer association is concerned, the refusal to grant it leave to intervene "does not affect its right to an effective judicial remedy to protect its rights as an association of that kind, including its rights to collective action."[1143] Besides, consumer associations can acquire a procedural role in individual proceedings since under the national law of the referring jurisdiction, they "may directly represent consumers in any proceedings, including enforcement proceedings, if mandated to do so by the latter."[1144]

1139 However, it should not be inferred from this that Art. 38 of the Charter has a mere declaratory value. Its effect is deployed on a different level as it can be demonstrated in Case C-12/11 *McDonagh*, EU:C:2013:43. In that case of rights' balancing, the principle of the Charter was employed as a counterweight to the freedom to conduct a business and the right to property. Interpreted in that way, the respective regulation was considered to comply with the requirement of striking a fair balance between the competing rights.

1140 Case C-470/12 *Pohotovosť II* (n. 1113), para. 53.

1141 Opinion of AG Wahl in Case C-470/12 *Pohotovosť II* (n. 1137), point 60.

1142 Case C-470/12 *Pohotovosť II* (n. 1113), para. 53.

1143 Ibid., para. 54.

1144 Ibid., para. 55.

# CHAPTER 5

# THE IMPACT OF THE ACTIVE CONSUMER COURT DOCTRINE IN SPECIFIC PROCEEDINGS

The Opinion of AG Wahl in *Unicaja Banco* starts with the observation that: "at the time of its inception, it is likely that most Member States would not have foreseen the impact that Directive 93/13/EEC was to have on their legal orders some 20 years later."[1145] Indeed, when the Court decided the *Océano Grupo* case, the *ex officio* doctrine was in its infancy. But even then, the weaker party protection and the procedural imbalance line reasoning bore with it an enormous potential of reconceptualization of individual consumer litigation. As the references for preliminary ruling on the own motion assessment became more frequent, they would explore a new facet of the *ex officio* doctrine as a standard against which to measure the adequacy of national standards of effective procedural protection. Progressively the doctrine acquired a *transprocedural* character where the powers of the courts would have to be tested within specific procedural settings. This phase or evolution of the doctrine of the active consumer court can metaphorically be named the "meta-*Océano Grupo*" or the "meta-*ex officio*" era. This evolution is a specific procedural expression of a broader perspective of what Judge José María Fernández Seijo calls the "transversal character" of consumer protection, which percolates a common standard of protection across the entire field of that legal discipline.[1146] In a broad sense, this idea may be reflected in Article 12 TFEU, according to which consumer protection has a transversal character expressed in the definition and implementation of other Union policies and activities.

Within the framework of the case law exploring the tranprocedural character of the active consumer court doctrine, the assessment of the compatibility of national procedural law with the principle of effectiveness of the exercise of consumer rights is carried out on the basis of the *Van Schijndel* balancing

1145 Opinion of AG Wahl in Joined Cases C-482/13, C 484/13, C-485/13 and C-487/13 *Unicaja Banco and Caixabank*, EU:C:2014:2299, point 1.

1146 J. M. Fernández Seijo, "La audacia del Derecho" (2013) 2 *Revista Aranzadi Doctrinal* 195–203.

approach. Such an approach considers the role, progress and special features of the national procedural system, taking due account of its basic legal principles. In this assessment, the basic tenets of the active court doctrine as set out in the *Océano Grupo* judgment and its "progeny" themselves become a benchmark of effectiveness and infuse national procedure.

This chapter presents the operation of the *ex officio* doctrine against the background of three procedural settings: the order for payment procedure (section 1), consumer insolvency proceedings (section 2) and proceedings for mortgage repossession (section 3). It is mainly the Spanish courts, followed by the Slovakian, which have taken the lead in making references for preliminary ruling, particularly in the field of mortgage repossessions. The case law developed in that regard is representative of the capacity of the *ex officio* doctrine to infuse its requirements into different procedural settings. Two landmark judgments in that regard, *Banco Español de Crédito* (followed by *Finanmadrid*) and *Aziz*, were at the origin of important reforms of the Spanish Civil Procedure Code (*Ley de Enjuiciamiento Civil* – LEC) that would set in stone the control of unfairness in order for payment proceedings and mortgage repossession proceedings. More broadly, these reforms marked the beginning of a legislative *redesign* of such proceedings tuned to enhanced protection for residential mortgage debtors. At the Union level, the Mortgage Credit Directive[1147] also moves toward this direction of strengthening protection.

## 1. POWERS OF THE COURTS IN ORDER FOR PAYMENT PROCEEDINGS

The judgment in *Banco Español de Crédito*[1148] is characteristic of the reach of the impact of the protective scope of the Unfair Contract Terms Directive upon the procedural rules of Member States.[1149] It makes clear that the type of the proceedings and their particular features cannot be an impediment to the exercise of the duty of courts to assess the fairness of contractual terms. The legitimate aim of quick enforcement of a liquidated debt in summary proceedings such as the order for payment procedure does not outweigh the imperative of effective consumer judicial protection, achieved by means of application of the *ex officio* doctrine by the court responsible for issuing the order. The judgment

[1147] Directive 2014/17/EU of the European Parliament and of the Council of 4 February 2014 on credit agreements for consumers relating to residential immovable property and amending Directives 2008/48/EC and 2013/36/EU and Regulation (EU) No 1093/2010 [2014] OJ L60/34 (hereinafter the "Mortgage Credit Directive").

[1148] Case C-618/10 *Banco Español de Crédito*, EU:C:2012:349.

[1149] Analysis in A. Beka, "Commentary note on Case C-618/10 Banco Español de Crédito SA v Joaquín Calderón Camino, judgment of 14 June 2012" (2012) 6 *Zeitschrift für Gemeinschaftsprivatrecht*, 326–328.

in *Finanmadrid*,[1150] dealt with the question of the compatibility with the effective protection of consumers from the use of unfair terms of a specific feature of the Spanish order for payment procedure related to the implication of the legal secretary in the process and the impact upon the powers of the courts.

### 1.1. APPLICATION OF THE *EX OFFICIO* DOCTRINE IN THE ORDER FOR PAYMENT PROCEEDINGS: *BANCO ESPAÑOL DE CRÉDITO*

In *Banco Español de Crédito*, a credit institution, Banesto, appealed before the referring court (the *Audiencia Provincial de Barcelona*) against an order made within the framework of an order for payment procedure (*procedimiento monitorio*). It was issued against a borrower of Banesto who was in default in terms of his credit installments. The lower court held of its own motion and *in limine litis*, before a statement of objection being lodged by the defendant, that the term of 29% interest on late payment set in the loan contract was unfair. The judicial order declared the term void and fixed the rate at 19%. The bank challenged before the court of appeal the exercise of the power of the first instance court to hold at that stage of the procedure and of its own motion that the disputed contractual term was void or to modify that term. The referring court entertained doubts as to the appropriate interpretation of Spanish legislation with regard to the Unfair Contract Terms Directive on a double prong. The first issue related to the fact that the Spanish civil procedural law[1151] did not empower the courts to raise of their own motion the unfairness of a term *in limine litis* within the framework of the *processo monitorio.* The consumer could challenge the unfair term only by means of introducing an objection against the order. The second issue was that the Spanish law on consumers provided (at that time) that courts shall proceed to the *modification* of a term that has been held to be unfair (*facultad de integrar el contrato*). This last aspect has already been discussed in the previous chapter.[1152]

The Court recognized that in the absence of harmonized rules on national mechanisms for the recovery of uncontested claims, the matter is left to Member States in accordance with the principle of national procedural autonomy, subject to the principles of equivalence and effectiveness. The Court found no breach of the principle of equivalence; national law did not provide for a duty to consider

---

1150 Case C-49/14 *Finanmadrid EFC*, EU:C:2016:98.

1151 The procedure of *procedimiento monitorio* is governed by the Spanish Civil Procedure Code Art. 812 *et seq*. The procedure can become *inter partes* if the consumer lodges an objection. On the procedure see J. L. Gómez Colomer, "Kreditschutz und Mahnverfahren in Spanien. Ein wirskames Instrument in Krisenzeiten?" in *Festschrift für Rolf Stürner zum 70. Geburstag, 2. Teilband* (Tubingen, Mohr Siebeck, 2013), 1507–1524.

1152 Chapter 4, Section 5.2.1.

fairness of contractual terms in an order for payment procedure based either on EU law or on national rules of *public policy*. Although the principle of equivalence is not decisive in this case, it is important that the Court underlines the parity level of the provisions on unfair terms with domestic public policy. With respect to the principle of effectiveness, the Court proceeded upon a balancing exercise in the context of national procedural law. It found that the national legislation was liable to seriously undermine the effectiveness of the protection intended by the Unfair Contract Terms Directive. Such a finding was justified by:

> the significant risk that the consumers concerned will not lodge the objection required either because of the particularly short period provided for that purpose, or because they might be dissuaded from defending themselves in view of the costs which legal proceedings would entail in relation to the amount of the disputed debt, or because they are unaware of or do not appreciate the extent of their rights, or indeed because of the limited content of the application for the order for payment submitted by the sellers or suppliers, and thus the incomplete nature of the information available to them.[1153]

This position reflects, according to Peter Rott, "a practical and realistic approach to the protection of consumers as the weaker party," who faces obstacles in seeking judicial protection.[1154] The existence of such obstacles might incite professionals to resort to an order for payment procedure instead of ordinary civil proceedings as a means to avoid the normal judicial control and to avoid, in this way, the application of the protective consumer legislation. Moreover, the specific characteristics of court proceedings which take place under national law, in the instant case the specific characteristics of *proceso monitorio*: "cannot constitute a factor which is liable to affect the legal protection from which consumers must benefit under the provisions of the [Unfair Contract Terms Directive]."[1155] The *ex officio* doctrine transcends, therefore, the specific characteristics of the proceedings.

The Court did not follow the reasoning of the Opinion of AG Trstenjak,[1156] according to whom the *ex officio* case law is applicable to jurisdictional terms

1153 Case C-618/10 *Banco Español de Crédito* (n. 1148), para. 54.

1154 P. Rott, "Case note on *Banco Español de Credito v Joaquín Calderón Camino*" (2012) 8:4 *ERCL* 470–480. On the difficulties facing the consumers in lodging objections he notes: "Experience from debt-counselling shows that overindebted consumers tend to be passive towards bills and their enforcement. First, they are aware that, in principle, their creditors are right to bring claims since they have not been paid in accordance with the contract; whilst consumers may fail to fully understand the details of all the side-claims made, such as claims related to interest or to the costs of legal representation. Second, overindebted as they are, consumers do not have the means available to seek legal advice or even to contest the first stage decision of the court. This type of consumer has nothing to do with the active information seeker that AG Trstenjak appears to have in mind".

1155 Case C-618/10 *Banco Español de Crédito* (n. 1148), para. 55.

1156 Opinion of AG Trstenjak in Case C-618/10 *Banco Español de Crédito*, EU:C:2012:74.

and not to substantive terms on the ground that the establishment of the unfairness of the latter terms requires a complex assessment.[1157] There is no distinction to be drawn with respect to the application of the *ex officio* doctrine depending on the type of term. Yet, the eventual complexity in the assessment of a substantive term is liable to reflect upon the extent of availability by the court of "all the legal and factual elements necessary"[1158] to proceed to the assessment of unfairness. The Opinion of AG Trstenjak also stressed the difference between the *ex parte* proceedings as opposed to proceedings for a declaratory judgment. The recognition of *ex officio* powers at the *ex parte* stage would, according the Opinion, compromise the fundamental right to hearing.[1159] The consequence in her view would be "a fundamental modification of the operation of the order for payment procedure," which would unduly restrict the procedural autonomy of Member States.[1160]

It should be noted that the judicial control *in limine litis* of a payment order containing an illegal default interest rate is not unknown to national legal traditions, which often provide for safeguards against attempts to obtain a payment order for clearly unjustified claims such as excessive costs and interest.[1161] Under German law, for instance, summary proceedings for a payment order (*Mahnverfahren*) cannot be initiated if the interest rate exceeds the legal threshold.[1162] The judgment takes into account that in Member States' legal traditions, the initiating stage of such proceedings is *ex parte* with no in-depth assessment of the merits.[1163] The ruling of the Court does not imply a comprehensive obligation of the courts to investigate and to assess the possible unfairness of complex terms of their own motion outside the framework of adversarial proceedings which would not be compatible with the procedural model of a payment order.[1164] Besides, considerable complications could emerge

1157 *Cf.* J. Stuyck, "Unfair Terms" in G. Howells and R. Schulze (eds.), *Modernising and Harmonising Consumer Contract Law* (Berlin, Sellier, 2009), 115, who, commenting on the case law on the *ex officio* doctrine issued up to 2008, took the position that the unfairness assessment should be limited to clauses limiting access to justice.

1158 Case C-618/10 *Banco Español de Crédito* (n. 1148), para. 53. Indeed, in the absence of party submissions, the court is less likely to have available all the legal and factual elements to carry through an own motion assessment of a complex term.

1159 Opinion of AG Trstenjak in Case C-618/10 *Banco Español de Crédito* (n. 1156), point 52. The national court addressed this point explicitly because the breach of the fundamental right to a fair hearing was one of the grounds of complaint of the appellant credit institution.

1160 Ibid., para. 77; see V. Trstenjak and E. Beysen, "European Consumer Protection Law: *Curia Semper Dabit Remedium*?" (2011) 48 *CMLR* 95124.

1161 See Green Paper on a European Order for Payment Procedure and on measures to simplify and speed up small claims litigation, COM (2002) 746 final, 31.

1162 §688, II 2 ZPO. For the Austrian approach when there is suspicion of abuse *see* §245 ZPO.

1163 See W. Rechberger and G. Kodek, "Das Mahnverfahren in den Mitgliedsstaaten der EU – Generalbericht" in W. Rechberger and G. Kodek, (eds.), *Orders for Payment in the European Union* (The Hague, Kluwer, 2001).

1164 This is also how the national court understood the judgment, discussed in the paragraph below.

when national law provides for an automated processing of the applications.[1165] The obligation of own motion assessment applies *only* insofar as the court *is in a position* to perform the control on the basis of the elements of the case file before it, as was the case with regard to a claim accrued by a default interest rate of 29%. It is a different question if an alternative model for payment recovery needs to be envisaged when the defendant is a consumer; a model designed to meet the structural inequality of the parties, but with due respect to the right to fair trial. In any event, a court which entertains doubts as to the fairness of the contractual terms upon which the claim is based, should be invested with the power to refuse to issue a payment order and invite the claimant to initiate ordinary proceedings. The Court is guided by a "real life"[1166] approach to the principle of effectiveness anchored upon the image of consumers as litigants who lack the same degree of sophistication in comparison to their more powerful counterparty.

The main ground of appeal of the creditor in the national proceedings was that the *ex officio* declaration of unfairness was in breach of its right to an effective judicial protection according to the Spanish Constitution (Article 24). In its judgment following the decision in *Banco Español de Crédito*, the national court[1167] held that there should be an *ex officio* power to declare the unfairness of a contractual term even *inaudita parte* without that being a breach of the right to fair hearing. The reason for this is that this decision is taken within the framework of a provisional procedure and it is not a judgment on the merits which would have the effect of *res judicata*. The analysis of the possible unfairness of a term relating to a default interest rate, carried out *ex officio* and *in limine litis*, is done in a summary way, in light of the elements available in the case file. Thus, nullity can only be declared *in limine litis* in cases of blatant or manifest unfairness ("en casos flagrantes, evidentes"), otherwise the question should be left to the court of the declaratory proceedings deciding *inter partes*. There must therefore be a close connection with the evidence presented in the case file, taking into account the risk that the procedure would lose its efficiency if the court had to take measures of investigation. Such an approach reserves the judicial intervention, according to the national court, only for extraordinary cases and preserves party autonomy. In the words of the national judgment:

> the appreciation on unfairness and *in limine litis* of a clause on default interest can only be justified because the clause was void in a manifest and incontestable way, without raising any doubt on its abusive character, without seeking to replace the general principle of party autonomy with a voluntary judicial interventionism.[1168]

---

1165 This can be the case in Germany (§689 ZPO) and Austria (§250 ZPO).

1166 P. Rott (n. 1154), 479.

1167 Audiencia Provincial de Barcelona, order 222/2012 of 29 October 2012 (No de Recurso 586/2010).

1168 "El juicio de abusividad de oficio y ab limine de una cláusula de intereses moratorios sólo puede venir justificado porque la cláusula sea nula de forma patente y incontestable,

The issue of the *ex officio* powers of the courts within the framework of *proceso monitorio* did not settle with the aforementioned judgment of the referring court. A year later, the *Audiencia Provincial de Madrid* in plenary session was called to provide clarifications on the scope of the *ex officio* doctrine within the Spanish civil procedural system of *proceso monitorio.*[1169] The need for clarification arose following the appeal introduced by a financial institution against the order of a lower court, which rejected the claim as inadmissible on the ground that the Spanish procedural framework *as such* was incompatible with the protection required for the consumers following *Banco Español de Crédito.* This approach was rejected on appeal. After citing the lessons from the *ex officio* doctrine and in particular the requirement of interpretation in conformity with Union law in *Océano Grupo*, it was decided that the *proceso monitorio* could be interpreted in that sense:

> we interpret the national legislation on payment order procedure in the light of the wording and purpose of the Union norm, as it had been decided in *Océano Grupo*; in this way we save the Spanish procedure on order for payment procedure; were it be otherwise the certainty of the procedure would be seriously affected, in addition to the implications that a contrary position would have in the ambit of the European order for payment procedure.[1170]

The order of the lower court was therefore revoked as it should have first proceeded with an *ex officio* examination of the question of unfairness. This did not mark the end of the tale either. A new reference questioned the compatibility with the Unfair Contract Terms Directive and the powers it confers to national courts of a specific feature of the Spanish procedural law in relation to the implication in the payment ordered procedure of the judicial secretary.

## 1.2. ENTRENCHING THE POWERS OF THE COURTS IN THE ORDER FOR PAYMENT PROCEEDINGS: *FINANMADRID*

At the time when the reference in *Banco Español de Crédito* was made, it was the court that had the power to adopt a decision to make an order for payment, but, as has been mentioned, it did not have the power to decide of its own motion

---

sin duda sobre la abusividad, sin que estemos sustituyendo la general prevención y respeto del principio de autonomía de la voluntad por un voluntarismo judicial intervencionista" (translated by the author).

1169 Audiencia Provincial de Madrid, Recurso de apelación 811/2012, 4 March 2013.

1170 "Interpretamos la normativa nacional del procedimiento monitorio a la luz del tenor literal y de la finalidad de la Directiva comunitaria, como nos pedía la sentencia [Océano Grupo]; y salvamos el proceso monitorio español, que de otra forma recibiría una carga de profundidad que afectaría seriamente a su estabilidad, amén de las implicaciones que una postura contraria tendría en el ámbito del proceso monitorio europeo …".

on the potential unfairness of a contractual term. The case in *Finanmadrid*,[1171] arose in the context of the introduction of specific powers afforded to the judicial secretary (*Secretario judicial*) in the order for payment procedure, which were not in force at the material time of the reference in *Banco Español de Crédito* was made.[1172] In particular, the judicial secretary was afforded specific powers within the order for payment procedure and his decisions were vested with effects analogous to a judicial decision. This posed particular concerns for the effective defense of consumers throughout the process. It is important to note that at the time the reference was made, Spanish law had not yet introduced the reform of the Spanish Civil Procedure Code (Ley de Enjuiciamiento Civil – LEC) prompted by *Banco Español de Crédito*. Spanish Law 42/2015 introduced, more particularly, a specific regime applicable into the powers of the courts in order for payment proceedings where the debt claimed arises from a consumer contract.[1173]

The reasoning of the judgment is a logical continuation of *Banco Español de Crédito*, confirming that the recognition of *ex officio* powers of the courts in the framework of the order for payment procedure cannot be called into question by the specific features and the configuration of the national procedural system. The potential role that non-judicial bodies may have in specific proceedings should be without prejudice to the duty of court to assess the unfairness of terms. Two elements are of particular interest in this case. The first element is the finding of incompatibility with Union law of a national rule implementing the *res judicata* principle in the specific circumstances of the case at hand. The second element refers to the question of the interrelation between the principle of effectiveness, as a limitation to the principle of procedural autonomy, and the right to an effective judicial protection under Article 47 of the Charter in consumer law cases. This last element had not been addressed by the Court as it considered that the referring court had not stated the reasons which would make it possible to consider a potential incompatibility of the national legislation with the Charter. The Opinion of AG Szpunar[1174] addressed the question and concluded that the national legislation did not comply with the principle of effectiveness, but that it did not breach the principle of effective judicial protection.

More particularly, in order to understand the particularities of the application of the *res judicata* principle in this case, it is necessary to outline

---

1171 Case C-49/14 *Finanmadrid*, EU:C:2016:98.

1172 The reform was made by Ley 13/2009 de reforma de la legislación procesal para la implantación de la nueva Oficina judicial (Law 13/2009 on reform of the procedural legislation through the establishment of the new judicial office of 3 November 2009 (BOE No 266 of 4 November 2009).

1173 Law 42/2015 of 5 October 2015, reforming Law 1/2000, of 7 January, on Civil Procedure (BOE No 239 of 6 October 2015). That law modified, among others, Art. 815 of the Spanish Civil Procedure Code.

1174 Opinion of AG Szpunar in Case C-49/14 *Finanmadrid*, EU:C:2015:746.

the national procedural framework. The judicial secretary has the power to decide upon an application for a payment order and to issue such an order where the documents attached to the application for payment constitute *prima facie* evidence of the applicant's right. At this stage, the debtor has the possibility to appear within a period of 20 days before the judicial secretary and to file a statement of objection (Article 815 LEC). If the debtor lodges an objection in due time, the procedure is transformed into normal declaratory proceedings (*proceso declarativo*) and a definitive decision is made on the issue, vested with the force of *res judicata* (Article 818(1) LEC). If the debtor fails to comply with the order for payment or fails to appear, the judicial secretary issues a "direction" (*decreto*) bringing the order for payment procedure to a close and calls upon the creditor to seek an enforcement order for the claim on the basis of his application alone (Article 816(1) LEC). From that stage onward, the procedure applicable to the enforcement of judgments is followed, although the objections that can be raised therein cannot relate to the amount claimed in the order for payment procedure (Article 816(2), LEC). This means that the merits of the claim enforced may no longer be challenged and that the order of the *Secretario judicial* is vested, effectively, with the force of *res judicata*.

This procedural framework applicable to the order for payment procedure did not distinguish, at the time of the reference in *Finanmadrid*, between consumer law claims and other civil claims. As a result, the consumer against whom the claim was addressed, in the absence of lodging an objection, could be deprived of the procedural guarantee of the *ex officio* judicial control of unfair terms contained in an enforcement instrument. That is so as, first, the power to proceed with such a control lies outside the competences of the judicial secretary and, second, it was no longer possible to take place at the stage of the enforcement of the order. The decision of the judicial secretary to close the proceedings acquired the force of *res judicata*. The only possibility for an *ex officio* judicial review of the contractual terms would be for the consumer to lodge an objection. However, the Court points to the "significant risk" that the consumer would not lodge the objection:

> be it because of the particularly short period provided for that purpose, or because they might be dissuaded from defending themselves in view of the costs which legal proceedings would entail in relation to the amount of the disputed debt, or because they are unware or do not appreciate the extent of their rights, or indeed because of the limited content of the application for the order for payment submitted by the sellers or suppliers, and thus the incomplete nature of the information available to them.[1175]

The Court referred, to that effect, to the judgment in *Banco Español de Crédito*. It followed the same logic with regard to the difficulties faced by the consumer

1175 Case C-49/14 *Finanmadrid* (n. 1171), para. 52.

in defending his rights. The application made of the principle of effectiveness in this case is such as to allow the court to redress the procedural handicap of the weaker party without penalizing his procedural omission. Taking into account those particular circumstances, the Court decided that the implementation of the *res judicata* in that particular case breached the principle of effectiveness.

The judgment concluded as to the incompatibility of the national Spanish legislation only with reference to the principle of effectiveness. It did not rule as to the existence of a potential violation of the right to an effective judicial protection, in view of the absence, as it stated, of the necessary elements allowing it to do so. By contrast, the Opinion of AG Szpunar went on to examine the national legislation through the prism of Article 47 of the Charter. The Opinion found that the aforementioned right was not violated because the right to access to a court does not include an *ex officio* review. The Opinion states clearly that such a review amounts to "a special feature of proceedings characterized by an imbalance between the parties"[1176] and that such a requirement can only flow from the need to ensure consumer protection and not from Article 47 of the Charter. According to the Opinion, the protection of this right would also not prevent a non-judicial body taking certain decisions falling within the exercise of judicial functions, provided, however, that such decisions could be subject to judicial review.[1177]

The Opinion rightly observes that the level of judicial protection of consumer rights under the Unfair Contract Terms Directive is higher than the one provided by Article 47 of the Charter for the parties in every other civil action involving EU law.[1178] This observation can be well demonstrated in the case in *Sánchez Morcillo and Abril García*,[1179] where the Court took into account a number of factors in relation to the particularities of consumer litigation in order to conclude that the consumer debtor, in the specific circumstances of that case, should have to right to enter an appeal, even if Article 47 of the Charter does not afford, *in general*, the right to access to a second level of jurisdiction. Disputes involving contractual imbalance are not the same as any other civil law dispute. Where one of the parties embarks on the procedure with a "procedural handicap," in the light of his weaker position, the absence of recognition of special powers for the courts would perpetuate the imbalance. Specific rules would therefore be required which would derogate from those applicable to every other civil disputes, so as to compensate for the procedural imbalance. It is the fact that the structurally weaker party lacks the capacity to take advantage of the generally applicable rules to every party in litigation irrespective of its

1176 Opinion of AG Szpunar in Case C-49/14 *Finanmadrid* (n. 1174), point 92.
1177 Ibid., point 91.
1178 Ibid., point 90.
1179 Case C-169/14 *Sánchez Morcillo and Abril García*, EU:C:2014:2099, discussed below, Sections 3.2.1 and 3.3.1.1.

capacity which hinders the access to court. This is the reason why specific procedural rules are required and are designed for the structurally weaker party.

The Spanish legislator acknowledged the incompatibility of the regime applicable in the order for payment proceedings with the judicial protection of consumers and introduced a reform of the relevant Spanish procedural provisions.[1180] Law 42/2015 added a new paragraph (4) to Article 815 LEC governing the order for payment proceedings.[1181] We will come back to the details of this reform in Chapter 6.[1182]

## 2. THE DUTY OF COURT TO CONSIDER CONSUMER PROTECTION LAW IN CONSUMER INSOLVENCY PROCEEDINGS: *RADLINGER*

Consumer insolvency is not a matter regulated at the Union level.[1183] For the time being, this sensitive field of policy is governed by national law, even if the risk of overindebtedness associates with fields of law that are regulated by Union law. The impact that Union consumer law exercises is indirect and concerns rather the prevention of overindebtedness, an objective that the Consumer Credit Directive[1184] is intended to serve. The Mortgage Credit Directive[1185] refers in a more direct way to overindebtedness, requiring that Member States ensure that following the sale of a mortgaged asset, measures are put in place to facilitate the repayment of outstanding debt. But the legislation on unfair terms and the strengthening of consumer protection as a result of the case law of the Court on the *ex officio* control by the courts still remains the most important pillar of protection for overindebted consumers. That being said, the qualification criteria and the detailed conditions for debt restructuring and for an eventual debt discharge are matters regulated by national law.[1186]

1180 See M. Rodríguez-Piñero Bravo-Ferrer, "Cláusulas contractuales abusivas y proceso monitorio" *Diario La Ley* (XXXVII) 174, 21 al 27 de marzo de 2016.

1181 Art. 76 of Law 42/2015, reforming Law 1/2000, of 7 January, on Civil Procedure (BOE No 239 of 6 October 2015).

1182 Chapter 6, Section 1.1.

1183 See F. Ferretti, "The over-indebted European consumers: quo vadis personal insolvency law?' (2016) *ELRev* 843–864.

1184 Directive 2008/48/EC of the European Parliament and of the Council of 23 April 2008 on credit agreements for consumers and repealing Council Directive 87/102/EEC [2008] OJ L133/66.

1185 Directive 2014/17/EU of the European Parliament and of the Council of 4 February 2014 on credit agreements for consumers relating to residential immovable property and amending Directives 2008/48/EC and 2013/36/EU and Regulation (EU) No 1093/2010 [2014] OJ L60/34.

1186 In detail, I. Ramsay, "Two Cheers for Europe: Austerity, Mortgage Foreclosures and Personal Insolvency Policy in the EU" in H-W. Micklitz and I. Domurath (eds.), *Consumer Debt and Social Exclusion in Europe* (Farnham, Ashgate, 2015), 189–227.

Union consumer law may interfere with such proceedings as long as their application has an impact over the *ex officio* powers of the courts. The judgment of the Court in *Radlinger*[1187] concerned this specific aspect of interrelation.

The referring Czech court was the responsible insolvency court before which the Radlinger couple filed for bankruptcy. The debt which the consumers had not been capable of honoring and led them to bankruptcy was a loan contracted with a credit institution, Smart Hypo, which later transferred that debt to the defendant in the current proceedings, Finway. The characteristics of the loan provide the perfect example of unconscionability. The couple borrowed, on 29 August 2011, the sum of €43,300. Less than a month later, the lender initiated proceedings against them and accelerated the repayment of the entire debt on the ground that they had misrepresented the fact that a seizure had been ordered of their property for the amount of approximately €160. At that stage, they would already owe more than double of the money the borrowed (€106,300). This was the result of an (effectively stipulated but in reality undervalued) APR of 28.9% and the combination of a number of contractual penalties in case of default (a contractual penalty of 0.2% of the principal sum for every day of default, a single contractual fine of approximately €4,320 in the event of a default exceeding one month and a lump sum of approximately €1,846 toward the lender's costs in recovering the amounts owed). On top of that, the consumers never actually received the monies of the loan (!). The credit was used to settle earlier debts owed to a bailiff, notarial fees, the costs of the lender and even the first installment and part of the following installments. By the following year, the Radlingers owed the amount of €140,500 for a debt which was never disbursed to them. In the context of the insolvency proceedings initiated by the consumers, who were unable to meet their debt, the lender registered two claims: the highest one was secured by mortgage and the second one, representing the contractual penalty, was unsecured. The consumers contested the amounts of the debt registered on the ground that the credit agreement contravened "accepted principles of morality" and made an incidental application as to the unlawfulness of the claims registered.

However, the examination by the court of the unlawfulness of the credit agreement underlying the debt registered in the insolvency proceedings was impeded at two stages of the proceedings. These stages were the application of the debtor for a discharge and the incidental application for the contestation of the registered claims. To start with, the examination of the credit agreement was not possible at the moment of application to the insolvency court by the debtor. At that stage, the court could only examine the fulfillment of the conditions to which the authorization of the debt discharge was subject, namely the absence of bad faith on behalf of the debtor and the reasonable presumption that the registered unsecured creditors will recover, in the discharge, at least 30% of

[1187] Case C-377/14 *Radlinger and Radlingerová*, EU:C:2016:283.

the established debts. By contrast, issues in relation to the validity, amount or the ranking of claims fell outside the ambit of judicial control, including the question whether the claim contained unfair terms or whether the underlying credit was concluded in violation of the relevant regulatory requirements. It is not until the insolvency court had approved the resolution of the bankruptcy by way of discharge that the debtor could lodge an incidental application to contest the registered debt. But even at this stage, there were serious restrictions as to the remit of the consumer opposition against the registered debt. His application was limited to the enforceable unsecured claims and could cover only a restrictive number of grounds, either that the claim has been satisfied or that it is time-barred. This means that the judicial control would not cover the validity of claims secured by mortgage or any issue in relation to the potential unfairness of unsecured claims. The referring court asked, in essence, two important questions in relation to the *ex officio* role of the courts: first, whether the insolvency court should have the power to examine of its own motion the potential unfairness of the consumer credit contractual clauses to which the consumer debt originates, without awaiting an incidental application to that effect by the consumer debtor and what is the remit of this power; and, second, whether the obligation to provide information, set out in Article 10(2) of the Consumer Credit Directive, is a provision that the court is obliged to raise of its own motion. Furthermore, the referring court asked for clarifications as to the meaning of the concepts of "total amount of credit" and "amount of drawdown," pursuant to the Consumer Credit Directive, as well as for guidance in assessing whether the amount of compensation required of a consumer who does not fulfill his obligations is disproportionately high.

In response to the questions of the referring court, the Court in *Radlinger* was given the opportunity to make a double step forward in building the *ex officio* doctrine. It extended the *ex officio* doctrine in consumer insolvency proceedings and opened up the remit of consumer law which the courts are *obliged* to raise of their own motion.

With regard to the recognition of the *ex officio* powers of the insolvency court, the response followed the case law on effective judicial protection in consumer proceedings. The Court confirmed Member States' procedural autonomy in the organization of insolvency proceedings. However, in the terms of the settled case law, the "specific characteristics" of court proceedings cannot constitute a factor which is liable to affect the legal protection from which consumers must benefit under the provisions of the Unfair Contract Terms Directive. The considerations of the necessity to redress contractual imbalance in the procedural plane by means of a positive action underlying the *ex officio* doctrine apply equally to insolvency proceedings.[1188]

[1188] Case C-377/14 *Radlinger and Radlingerová* (n. 1187), paras. 52–54.

Moreover, ensuring the right of the consumer to an *effective judicial remedy* is not compatible with the existence of restrictions as to the type of claims that may be contested in declaratory proceedings or as to the grounds which may found the contestation.[1189]

To be sure, the application of the *ex officio* doctrine in insolvency proceedings is without prejudice to the choice of the organizational aspects of each national legal system and in particular to the arrangement of the stage at which the merits of the claims registered may be examined. The Czech system provided for a distinct procedural avenue to challenge the merits of the claims by means of an incidental application before the insolvency court. The problem was that such a court was completely deprived of the ability to exercise its *ex officio* powers and that the merits of the registered claims could be examined only once the bankruptcy has been declared. It could be argued that the recognition of *ex officio* powers in the insolvency proceedings might, in practice, be of limited effect. As long as the debt discharge takes place, so the argument goes, the result will be the same, if not more beneficial, for the consumer compared to the hypothesis where some terms of the credit agreement would be declared unfair. This argument cannot, however, prosper. There is a fundamental distinction between a debt that is owed, but which the consumer is unable to pay, and a debt which is actually not owed because it is premised upon an illegal term or because it results from a contract where the consumer legislation has not been observed. Moreover, the *ex officio* control either of the contractual terms or of the observance of other mandatory consumer law provisions is attached with all the consequences that the court is obliged to draw, according to its national law. A consequence such as forfeiture of the creditor's right to interest might result, in itself, to important debt relief. Finally, the fact that the "right" to a debt relief is strictly circumscribed needs to be taken into consideration. If a debtor makes recourse to such a possibility unduly for an illegal debt, this may impede him from asking in the future, within a specified time-span, for new debt relief for a debt that would be legally due.

With regard to the scope of provisions covered by the *ex officio* doctrine, the Court found that the obligation to provide information in a consumer credit contract is a provision that the courts are *obliged* to raise of their own motion. This finding relies and expands upon the existing case law on the question of whether the courts should have the power to apply in the case before them the rules of consumer protection, even if those rules do not relate to the validity of the contract. The Court recalled the fields in which it has already ruled in favor of the *ex officio* application of the consumer legislation, which covers not only the legislation on unfair terms but also the legislation on contracts negotiated away from business premises, on the sale of consumer goods and

[1189] Ibid., paras. 55–58.

on consumer credit.[1190] This power had been qualified as an obligation only with regard to the legislation on unfair terms. It is true that in *Faber*[1191] the Court has ruled that Article 5(3) of the Consumer Sales Directive[1192] (regarding the presumption of lack of conformity if this one becomes apparent within six months of the delivery of the goods) must be considered as a provision of equal standing to a national rule which ranks, within the domestic legal system, as a rule of public policy and that the national court must of its own motion apply any provision which transposes it into domestic law. Within that framework, the *ex officio* obligation was pronounced as a consequence of the application of the principle of equivalence. In *Radlinger*, the *ex officio* application of the consumer protection legislation was elevated to an obligation, irrespective of the provisions of national law.[1193]

Establishing an "ex officio" obligation across the spectrum of consumer legislation is a welcoming clarification of the case law on this point and brings about coherence on the role of the courts. Until that time, the reference in case law to a discretion of the courts with regard to legislation outside the unfair terms legislation probably demonstrated a rather more cautious note. As has been already analyzed above,[1194] the Court made the breakthrough in *Rampion and Godard*[1195] with the finding that the public interest considerations which require the application of the *ex officio* doctrine in the field of the unfair terms legislation are equally valid in other fields of consumer protective legislation. What mattered there was to establish an exception to the principle of party presentation by reference to the weaker party and public interest considerations. In that sense, the national legislative framework should not impede the exercise of the *ex officio* powers. The obligation of Member States to ensure that unfair terms shall "not be binding on the consumer," pursuant to Article 6(1) of the Unfair Contract Terms Directive, is a firm anchor for the establishment of an *ex officio* obligation. Such an anchor is missing from the legislative instruments on consumer legislation. *Radlinger* makes a connection between the obligation of Member States to provide for dissuasive penalties for the infringements of national provisions adopted under the Consumer Credit Directive (Article 23) on the one hand and the *ex officio* obligation on the other hand.[1196] However, the objection could be made that the active role of the courts in consumer litigation is not a sanction but a procedural rule. The purpose of the *ex officio* doctrine is not to sanction the professional, but to restore equality between the parties

1190 See in detail above, Chapter 4, Section 4.1.
1191 Case C-497/13, *Faber*, EU:C:2015:357.
1192 Directive 1999/44/EC of the European Parliament and of the Council of 25 May 1999 on certain aspects of the sale of consumer goods and associated guarantees [1999] OJ L171/12.
1193 Case C-377/14 *Radlinger and Radlingerová* (n. 1187), para. 62.
1194 Above, Chapter 4, Section 4.1.1.1.
1195 Case C-429/05 *Rampion and Godard*, EU:C:2007:575.
1196 Case C-377/14 *Radlinger and Radlingerová* (n. 1187), para. 69.

and ensure that the law is applied for the person whom the legislator intended to protect. The procedural inequality and the public interest considerations underlying consumer mandatory legislation, as well as the necessity to ensure its uniform application across national jurisdictions already constitute a sufficient basis for the own motion assessment obligation.

The *ex officio* obligation of the courts to raise of their own motion the infringement of the duty to provide information according to the Consumer Credit Directive is followed by an obligation of the courts to draw all the necessary consequences from this finding. In its case law, the Court had already held that the courts need to draw all the necessary consequences from the finding of the unfairness of a contractual term, without waiting for the consumer to submit a statement to that effect.[1197] In *Radlinger*, the same finding is applied *by analogy* with regard to the violation of consumer legislation other than unfair terms.[1198] The courts are therefore obliged to raise of their own motion the penalties provided for under national law, even if the consumer has not raised an objection to that effect, provided that the *audi alteram partem* principle has been complied with.[1199] This is without prejudice to the assessment by the court of the dissuasive, proportionate and effective character of the penalties, as has been interpreted in the case law of the Court.[1200]

## 3. THE LEGACY OF *AZIZ* FOR THE DEVELOPMENT OF A CONSTITUTIONAL APPROACH

More than a decade after the decision in *Océano Grupo* that set the foundations of the active consumer court doctrine in Union consumer law, the judgment in *Aziz*[1201] opened up a whole new perspective with regard to the potential of the doctrine for mortgage reform. The judge in both references for preliminary ruling was Dr. José María Fernández Seijo.[1202] An article appeared in the press portraits about him as a judge who, while remaining impartial in his judicial role, "has a special inclination to protect the weaker parties and to defend the

1197 Case C-472/11 *Banif Plus Bank*, EU:C:2013:88, para. 36 and Case C-32/14 *ERSTE Bank Hungary*, EU:C:2015:637, para. 42.

1198 Case C-377/14 *Radlinger and Radlingerová* (n. 1187), para. 71.

1199 Ibid., paras. 71–74.

1200 Case C-565/12 *LCL Le Crédit Lyonnais*, EU:C:2014:190.

1201 Case C-415/11 *Aziz*, EU:C:2013:164.

1202 The judge published two books on the subject of consumer procedural protection with special emphasis on mortgage enforcement proceedings: J. M. Fernández Seijo, *La defensa des los Consumidores en las ejecuciones hipotecarias* (Dordrecht, Wolters Kluwer, 2013) and J. M. Fernández Seijo, *La tutela de los consumidores en los procedimientos judiciales, Especial referencia a las ejecuciones hipotecarias* (Dordrecht, Wolters Kluwer, 2017).

public interest."[1203] On the occasion of this groundbreaking case, the case law on consumer litigation for the first time entered the sphere of the mortgage crisis, which was particularly pressing in Spain, but also in other countries of the European Union, especially those hit by the sovereign debt crisis and the measures of austerity. Therefore, Hans Micklitz observes that this "is not just a case," it is "a test case, one where the [Court] is faced with the social and the societal dimension of the current economic crisis"[1204] and by virtue of which it is "involved in post-crisis management."[1205] It is one of the cases which reflect the social sensitivity of the judiciary and where the Court raises a high benchmark of protection for the citizen in the Union. Under the weight of the extraordinary economic turmoil and social emergency due to the global financial crisis, the imbalances in the repossession procedure were inexorably exposed. The failures of irresponsible and predatory consumer finance exacerbated the consequences of an imbalanced procedural system of mortgage repossession. The imbalance arises from a *mismatch* of the procedure with the underlying substantive relationship, i.e. when the design of the procedure does not take into account the underlying contractual relationship. The procedure might be designed in such a way that lends disproportionate weight to the economic interests of the mortgagee.[1206] There is a wealth of literature on the roots and consequences

1203 Interview of the judge in El Périodico, Barcelona, 6 April 2013, "José María Fernández Seijo: 'Los desahucios son la imagen de la crisis': "Es imparcial, pero tiene una especial inclinación a proteger a los más débiles y defender el interés público". In another interview given in *El Pais*, on 30 November 2012 "Entrevista al Juez Antidesahucios – El Gobierno se ha asustado a la hora de cambiar la legislación hipotecaria. Entrevista con el juez que ha logrado meter una china en el sistema de desahucios", José María Fernández Seijo recalls the first time he was faced with mortgage repossession proceedings in the beginning of his career as a judge. He had to accompany the bailiff for the eviction of a young couple with a small child. The young mother threatened to jump from the balcony. The judge tried to stop her. The young woman could not believe that this kind person who tried to understand her was actually the judge. Since then, Judge Fernández Seijo affords care to the personal situation of the people facing eviction: "Después de aquello he intendado siempre hacer un seguimiento personalizado de las ejecuciones. En el sistema español, el juez, si no quiere, ni siquiera llega a conocer al afectado". (Translation: "Since then, he has always tried to consider the personal dimension in the enforcement proceedings. In the spanish legal system, if the judge does not want, he does not even need to have any personal contact with the mortgage debtor").

1204 H.-W. Micklitz, "Unfair Contract Terms – Public Interest Litigation before European Courts" in E. Terryn, G. Straetmans and V. Colaert (eds.), *Landmark Cases of EU Consumer Law – In Honour of Jules Stuyck* (Cambridge, Intersentia, 2013) 633, 650. M. Józon, "Unfair Contract Terms Law in Europe in Times of Crisis: Substantive Justice Lost in the Paradise of Proceduralisation of Contract Fairness" (2017) 6 *EuCML* 157–166, develops the idea of the use of the preliminary reference procedure as a "tool of domestic judicial policy" to tackle the consequences of the financial crisis.

1205 H.-W. Micklitz, "The Constitutional Transformation of Private Law Pillars Through the CJEU" in H. Collins (ed.), *European Contract Law and the Charter of Fundamental Rights* (Cambridge, Intersentia, 2017), 49–91, 83.

1206 See L. Whitehouse, "Mapping the Boundaries of the Law of Mortgage: The Repossession Process in Practice" in C. Twigg-Flenser and G. Villata Puig (eds.) *Boundaries of*

of the mortgage credit crunch,[1207] a major expression of the "failure of capitalism."[1208] If the legislator does not employ the regulatory powers in order to cope swiftly with the consequences of defaulting borrowers and relies upon the "invisible hand"[1209] of the mortgage market (the same market that has produced the property "bubble"), the consequences can be devastating. The European Union did not provide for any regulatory responses to revamp the mortgage market until the adoption in 2014 of the Mortgage Credit Directive.[1210] Coming too late and not applicable to contracts existing before 21 March 2016, its adoption could not have been of much help to those mortgage debtors who had been entangled in debt since the outbreak of the crisis. At the level of Union law, it was mainly the case law of the Court which contributed to the strengthening of the judicial protection of this category of citizens.

This section will be structured into four subsections. The first subsection presents the Spanish constitutional "antecedents" of *Aziz* (section 3.1). Section 3.2 analyzes the issue of effective judicial protection of mortgage debtors dealt with in *Aziz* in the light of subsequent jurisprudential developments. Section 3.3 presents the legacy of *Aziz* for setting in stone the strengthening of due process in mortgage repossession proceedings. Finally, section 3.4 delves into the substantive guidance on the concept of unfairness which the *Aziz* case offers and concludes with the national judgment.

## 3.1. THE ANTECEDENTS OF *AZIZ*: THE CONSTITUTIONAL CHALLENGE OF MORTGAGE ENFORCEMENT LAW

As the mortgage credit crisis evolved in Spain, the lower courts proved "the maturity of the judiciary in facing up to the realities of the times."[1211] They were

*commercial and trade law* (Munich, Sellier, 2011), 51; S. Nield, "Mortgage finance: who's responsible?" in J. Devenney and M. Kenny, *Consumer Credit, Debt and Investment in Europe* (Cambridge, Cambridge University Press, 2012), 160.

1207 To name only few J. Stiglitz, *Free Fall: Free Markets and the Sinking of the Global Economy* (Penguin, 2010); J. Stiglitz, *The Price of Inequality* (Penguin, 2013); R. Posner, *The Crisis of Capitalist Democracy* (Cambridge – MA, Harvard University Press, 2010); N. Rubini and S. Mihm, *Crisis Economics, A Crash Course in the Future of Finance* (Penguin, 2010); T. Judt, *Ill fares the Land, A treatise on our present discontents* (Allen Lane, 2010); A. Supiot, *L'Esprit de Philadelphie, La crise sociale face au marché totale* (Seuil, 2010); A. Tourain, *Après la crise* (Seuil, 2010).

1208 R. Posner, *A Failure of Capitalism, The Crisis of '08 and the Descent into Depression* (Cambridge – MA, Harvard University Press, 2011).

1209 A. Smith, *The Wealth of Nations* (1776).

1210 Directive 2014/17/EU of the European Parliament and of the Council of 4 February 2014 on credit agreements for consumers relating to residential immovable property and amending Directives 2008/48/EC and 2013/36/EU and Regulation (EU) No 1093/2010 [2014] OJ L 60/34.

1211 L. Whitehouse, "Mapping the Boundaries of the Law of Mortgage: The Repossession Process in Practice" (n. 1206), 51.

called to decide upon issues surrounding foreclosures amid a mortgage crisis of a scale that had not been envisaged when the legal framework of repossessions had been originally designed. Before the first timid legislative efforts in 2011 to mitigate the effects of the evictions for the most vulnerable,[1212] there have been judgments of lower courts questioning the legitimacy of pursuit of a deficiency judgment. This was done on the basis of prohibition of "abusive" or "anti-social" exercise of the right (Article 7(2) of the *Código Civil*), but also on the basis of an interpretation of the law "according to the social reality" at the time of its application (Article 3(1) of the *Código Civil*).[1213] In order to perform their tasks, the courts could not remain alienated from social reality.[1214]

It is worth reiterating an extract from a 2011 judgment of the Court of First Instance of Lleida which attempts to draw arguments from general principles in order to address the situation of creditors pursuing the remaining debt against the mortgage debtors whose property has been repossessed following the plunge in property prices:[1215]

> the 2011 economic outlook has nothing to do with the economic outlook of 2006, 2007 and 2008 when the crisis was still emerging. Nowadays, the Spanish economy, as well as the world economy, suffers a deep economic crisis and for this reason, surely, the property adjudicated to the bank ... now has a market value below the price agreed in the mortgage loan, but is it fair that the debtor suffers all the consequences of this fall? Would it not be fairer that the financial institutions also bear part of this decline? Economists are unanimous in considering that the real estate value losses have been caused by the financial institutions themselves with their mismanagement of the financial system. Hence, if the laws should be interpreted according to the reality at the time when they are applied (Article 3 of the Spanish Civil Code) ... [it] is not acceptable that the stronger party in the mortgage loan contract obtains an unjustified benefit with the further execution at the expense of the debtor as a consequence of applying the legal rules which aim to obtain reimbursement, not enrichment, of the creditor.

But this approach of certain lower courts had not been shared by the Spanish Supreme Court (*Tribunal Supremo*).

---

1212 See Chapter 6, Section 1.2.

1213 See J. M. Molina, "Spanish Law in 2010–2012: The influence of European Union Law and the Impact of the Economic Crisis" 6 (2013) *Journal of Civil Law Studies* 419, 426 *et seq.*

1214 The judge, J.M. Fernández Seijo, "La audacia del derecho" (2013) 2 *Revista Aranzadi Doctrinal* 195–203, stresses the importance of Art. 9(2) of the Spanish Constitution. According to this provision, public authorities have to ensure that citizens can exercise their rights *effectively*. The text of the constitutional provision (in translation) reads as follows: "It is the responsibility of the public authorities to promote conditions ensuring that freedom and equality of individuals and of the groups to which they belong are real and effective, to remove the obstacles preventing or hindering their full enjoyment, and to facilitate the participation of all citizens in political, economic, cultural and social life."

1215 Juzgado de Primera Instancia de Lleida, December 29, 2011, ejecución hipotecaria 1895/2009, as cited and translated in J. M. Molina, (n. 1213), 429.

### 3.1.1. *The Decision of the Spanish Supreme Court on Anti-Deficiency Challenge*

In a pre-crisis ruling of 2006, the Supreme Court had rejected the argument that the personal action for debt outstanding after a foreclosure sale has generated negative equity could be held to be an abuse of a right that results in unfair enrichment for the creditor.[1216] For as long as the legal procedure has been followed, any challenge based on elements alien to the mortgage and the evaluation of the property as such would be unfounded, according to this judgment, because the right is not exercised beyond the limits of its socio-economic function.[1217]

### 3.1.2. *The Decision of the Spanish Constitutional Court on the Limitation of Grounds of Defense*

The issue of the limitation of grounds of defense within the framework of enforcement proceedings did not arise for the first time in *Aziz*. It had already been constitutionalized in 2011 when a question of constitutionality review had been made before the *Tribunal Constitucional*.[1218] The challenged provisions of the Spanish Civil Procedure (LEC) were the same as in *Aziz*, namely Articles 695 and 698, as well as Article 579 on the pursuance of the deficiency debt after auction. The challenge was in relation to the right to effective judicial protection (Article 24 of the Spanish Constitution), the principle of equality before the law (Article 14 of the Spanish Constitution), the right to decent and adequate housing (Article 47 of the Spanish Constitution) and the principle of prohibition of arbitrary action of the public authorities (Article 9(3) of the Spanish Constitution). The constitutional review was restricted only in relation to the limitation of the means of defense laid down under Article 695 LEC.[1219]

---

1216 Tribunal Supremo 128/2006, No de Recurso 2557/1999, of 16 February 2006.

1217 See the fifth point of the judgment, ibid.: "... el provecho que pueda haber obtenido ... resulta de lo dispuesto en el ordenamiento jurídico con el fin de facilitar la realización de las garantías hipotecarias, ante la falta de uso por el deudor de sus facultades para elevar el precio del remate, y, por consiguiente, no puede estimarse que el acreedor sobrepase los límites normales del ejercicio del derecho, desde el punto de vista de su función económico-social, por el hecho de que no renuncie a resarcirse del total de su crédito y, al propio tiempo, trate de obtener del bien adjudicado ventajas económicas admisibles en el tráfico negocial". (Translation: "... the profit that was obtained ... resulted from the relevant procedural provisions which aim at the enforcement of the procedural guarantees, in the absence of use by the creditor of his remedies provided in order to raise the price of the property; as a result it is not possible to consider that the creditor overstepped the normal limits of the exercise of the right, from the point of view of its socio-economic function, just because he did not waive his right to the entirety of his claim, and at the same time he purported to obtain from the property that has been auctioned economic advantages that are admissible in commerce").

1218 Tribunal Constitucional Pleno order 113/2011 of 19 July 2011 (BOE No 197 of 17 August 2011).

1219 With regard to Arts. 579 and 698 the question had been declared inadmissible for being irrelevant: see the third consideration of STC 113/2011.

The *Tribunal Constitucional* rejected the question as "manifestly unfounded" ("notoriamente infundado"), referring to its settled case law on the subject since 1981, which had already established that there is no violation of the right to effective judicial protection due to the extremely limited grounds of objection against repossession.[1220] However, the court which had referred the matter to the *Tribunal Constitucional* was envisaging a *novel* reading of the relevant provisions in light of the time that had elapsed since those rulings, the changing circumstances that no longer resemble those of 30 years ago and the fact that the foreclosure procedure concerned the family home of the mortgagor. The dissenting opinion to the judgment advanced the thesis of the sensitivity of the law to social reality.[1221] According to this opinion, the issue should have been considered in light of the new economic and social context, the features of which are radically distinct from those prevalent in the 1980s and have had a direct incidence upon mortgage contracts. But, the judgment of the Spanish Constitutional Court concluded that a constitutional challenge of the actual design of the legal regime on mortgage enforcement *in abstracto* with reference to an alternative hypothetical mortgage model would raise concerns of "competence creep" at the expense of the legislator. This passage touches upon the broader problematic of legal theory on the limits of judicial review and democratic legitimacy.[1222]

When the *Aziz* judgment was rendered, an important reform of the LEC was already in the pipeline. Some timid steps toward reform had been taken in 2011 and 2012.[1223] However, they were not rigorous enough to address the mounting pressure for reform. The new law (Law 1/2013) embraced a wide

1220 Reference had been made in particular to STC 41/1981 of 18 December 1981 and STC 217/1993 of 30 June 1993. There, it had been established that the possibilities of contradictory debate are not limited, since the court of the declaratory proceedings can decide on the issue. According to the judgment, what is being limited is solely the *suspensory effect* that the objection against repossession can have upon the ongoing enforcement proceedings.

1221 Voto concurrente que formula el Magistrado don Eugeni Gay Montalvo respecto del Auto dictado en la cuestión de inconsitucionalidad 7223–2010.

1222 On this fundamental question see R. Dworkin, *Taking Rights Seriously* (London, Bloomsbury, 1997), 163 *et seq.*; R. Dworkin, *Justice for Hedgehogs* (Cambridge – MA, Harvard University Press, 2011), 395 *et seq.*; R. Hirschl, *Towards Juristocracy: The Origins and Consequences of the New Constitutionalism* (Cambridge – MA, Harvard University Press, 2007); J. van der Walt, *The Horizontal Effect Revolution and the question of sovereignty* (Berlin, De Gruyter, 2014), 361 *et seq.*; P. Pescatore, "La legitimité du juge en régime démocratique" (2000) 90 *Commentaire*, 339–351; T. Koopmans, "Judicialisation" in N. Colneric, D. Edward, J.P. Puissochet and D. Ruiz-Jarabo Colomer (eds.) *Une communauté de droit, Festschrift für Gil Carlos Rodríguez Iglesias* (Berlin, BWV, 2003), 51–57.

1223 Real Decreto-ley 8/2011 de medidas de apoyo a los deudores hipotecarios [...] (Royal Decree Law 8/2011 on means to support the mortgage debtors) of 1 July 2011 (BOE No 161 of 7 July 2011) and Real Decreto-ley 6/2012 de medidas urgentes de protección de deudores hipotecarios sin recursos (Royal Decree Law 6/2012 on urgent measures to protect mortgage debtors without resources) of 9 March 2012 (BOE No 60 of 10 March 2012). See below Chapter 6, Section 1.2.

array of provisions in relation to mortgage enforcement and included the lessons from *Aziz*. The changes in the law will be discussed below in Chapter 6. Here the analysis is devoted to this remarkable case in light of the subsequent case law.

## 3.2. EFFECTIVE JUDICIAL PROTECTION OF THE CONSUMER IN THE MORTGAGE ENFORCEMENT PROCEEDINGS

To understand the ruling in *Aziz*, it is necessary to place it within the Spanish procedural framework of mortgage enforcement (*ejecución hipotecaria*). We shall then concentrate on the constitutional elements of the case, which were further highlighted in the subsequent case law.

### *3.2.1. The Procedural Question: Limitation of the Grounds of Defense and Lack of Interim Relief*

The provisions on mortgage enforcement proceedings are set out in the LEC as well as in the Law on Mortgages (*Ley Hipotecaria*).[1224] A separate chapter of the LEC is devoted to the particularity of mortgage enforcement, linked to the rapid materialization of the security right of the mortgagee. However, the particularity in relation to the procedural position of the weaker party, to the effective protection from unfair terms and to the nature of the property as the family residence of the mortgagor do not appear to have played a particular role. Enforcement proceedings can be initiated directly against the property,[1225] with the mortgage contract serving mainly as a basis for the enforcement title. The enforcement proceedings commence with the issuance of an injunction for payment (*requerimiento de pago*), whereby the role of the court is restricted to a formal control of the right to seek enforcement. The control pertains to the examination of the accompanying documentation to verify issues such as that the mortgage is established by notarial deed.[1226] The enforcement action can also be initiated by means of extrajudicial sale before the notary, a procedure which is governed by the *Ley Hipotecaria*.[1227] Under the law applicable in *Aziz*, the mortgagor could invoke very limited grounds to enter a defense against a repossession order, among which was not included any objection on the

1224 Decree of 8 February 1946 (BOE No 58 of 27 February 1946).

1225 Art. 681 Spanish Civil Procedure Code (LEC) and Art. 129 Law on Mortgages (Ley Hipotecaria).

1226 This point is explained by the referring court in the second case in the Order of the Court in Joined Cases C-537/12 and C-116/13 *Banco Popular Español and Banco de Valencia*, EU:C:2013:759, para. 31; J. M. Fernández Seijo, *La defensa des los Consumidores en las ejecuciones hipotecarias* (Dordrecht, Wolters Kluwer, 2013), 226.

1227 Art. 129 Ley Hipotecaria.

basis of the invalidity of the title giving rise to the debt due to the existence of unfair terms.[1228] An application in that regard could only be brought in separate declaratory proceedings, without however having the effect of staying the enforcement proceedings.[1229] The only possibility that a claim based on the validity of the mortgage title could suspend proceedings depended upon the unlikely event of the consumer contesting the unfair term by making a preliminary registration of annulment of the mortgage before registration of the marginal note regarding the issue of the security certificate.[1230] The judicial effect of annulment of the title could only then have *ex post* effect, after the auction of the property, giving rise to a claim of distribution of the proceeds of the enforcement or to a claim for damages. This procedural constellation raised concerns as to its compatibility with the effective judicial protection of consumers.

As has been previously explained, the limitation of the grounds of objection (and in particular of the ground based on the existence of unfair terms) had already been the objective of an unsuccessful constitutional challenge before the *Tribunal Constitucional*.[1231] As the *Aziz* case was brought before the court of the ordinary proceedings (and not the court of enforcement), the bank and the Spanish government had contested the relevance of the question with regard to the limitation of the grounds of objection. However, this argument did not convince the Court, which easily perceived the *connection* in between the two types of proceedings. Following in that regard the suggestion of the Commission and the Opinion of AG Kokott,[1232] the question had to be construed more broadly and reformulated as seeking to ascertain the compatibility with the Unfair Contract Terms Directive of the lack of *interim relief* against repossession in the declaratory proceedings *in light* of the restricted grounds for objection in mortgage enforcement proceedings. The procedural circumstances in *Aziz* did not yet require a clarification on the issue of whether at the stage of mortgage enforcement proceedings, the *ex officio* doctrine would require an assessment of the unfairness of the mortgage instrument by the court of its own motion and/or a new ground of objection.[1233] This was the subject at issue in *Banco Popular Español*.[1234]

The starting point in the reasoning of the Court was the principle of national procedural autonomy, given that the field of grounds of objections and powers of the courts in the course of mortgage enforcement proceedings is not an

1228 Art. 695 LEC (as applicable at that time).
1229 Art. 698 LEC (as applicable at that time).
1230 Art. 131 Ley Hipotecaria.
1231 See above Section 3.1.2.
1232 Opinion of AG Kokott in Case C-415/11 *Aziz*, EU:C:2012:700, point 36.
1233 Ibid., point 56.
1234 Order of the Court in Joined Cases C-537/12 and C-116/13 *Banco Popular Español*, EU:C:2013:759.

issue governed by Union law. The second stage was the assessment of national law through the prism of the principles of equivalence and effectiveness. In order to assess the principle of equivalence, the Court made a comparison between the powers of the courts with respect to a clause breaching domestic public policy and a clause which is unfair according to Article 6 of the Unfair Contract Terms Directive. With respect to the principle of effectiveness, the Court proceeded with a balancing exercise in the context of Spanish civil procedural law.

A wealth of elements substantiate the position of the Court that it would be contrary to the principle of effectiveness if the court of the declaratory proceedings (but also of the enforcement proceedings, as would later be confirmed in *Banco Popular Español*) would not have the power to grant interim relief while examining the substance of the challenge based on the existence of unfair terms. The full effectiveness of the protection sought by the Unfair Contract Terms Directive would be impaired since the potential finding of the term as unfair would have no effect upon the vesting of the property as such in a third party. In the words of the Court:

> the final vesting of mortgaged property in a third party is always irreversible, even if the unfairness of the term challenged by the consumer before the court hearing the declaratory proceedings results in the annulment of the mortgage enforcement proceedings.[1235]

The possibility that the consumer will obtain the staying of the enforcement proceedings by means of the preliminary registration mechanism of the *Ley Hipotecaria* is hypothetical:

> because there is a significant risk that the consumer in question will not make that preliminary registration within the period prescribed for that purpose, either because of the rapidity of the enforcement proceedings in question or because he is unaware of or does not appreciate the extent of his rights.[1236]

With reference to *Unibet*,[1237] the Court held that the procedural rules in question impair the effectiveness of the protection sought by the Unfair Contract Terms Directive insofar as the court of the declaratory proceedings has no power to grant *interim relief* which would be necessary to ensure the *full effectiveness* of its final decision.[1238]

1235 Case C-415/11 *Aziz* (n. 1201), para. 57.
1236 Ibid., para. 58.
1237 Case C-432/05 *Unibet*, EU:C:2007:163, para. 77.
1238 Case C-415/11 *Aziz* (n. 1201) para. 59.

The Court then drew attention to the inadequate protection that the procedural system concerned entailed for the consumer. It allowed only for:

> subsequent protection of a purely compensatory nature, which would be incomplete and insufficient and would not constitute either an adequate or effective means of preventing the continued use of that term, contrary to Article 7(1) of Directive 93/13.[1239]

What corroborates the inadequacy of the existing remedy in guaranteeing effective protection for the consumer is the fact that the mortgaged property is "the family home of the consumer" so that the subsequent payment of damages and interest "does not make it possible to prevent the definitive and irreversible loss of that dwelling."[1240] In light of all those elements, the Court concluded that the lack of interim relief in the Spanish declaratory proceedings, in view of the limited grounds of objection in the enforcement proceedings, was not compatible with the system of protection sought by the Unfair Contract Terms Directive.

At this juncture, it already seems appropriate to introduce the clarification that came with the Order of the Court in *Banco Popular Español.*[1241] *Aziz* did not address the specific question of application of the *ex officio* doctrine directly in the enforcement proceedings (*procedimiento de ejecución*), since the instant case arose within the framework of the subsequent declaratory proceedings. However, the powers of the court in the declaratory proceedings (*procedimiento declarativo*) have been confirmed *in light of the lack of powers* of the court in the enforcement to raise an objection of its own motion (*procedimiento de ejecución*). Authors discussing the question inferred from *Aziz* that such a power should also be available in

1239 Ibid., para. 60.

1240 Ibid.

1241 Order of the Court in Joined Cases C-537/12 and C-116/13 *Banco Popular Español* (n. 1234). It is interesting to note that in the first of the joined cases, in C-537/12 *Banco Popular Español*, the ground of objection raised to the mortgage proceedings was in relation to the "floor" clause ("clausula suelo") stipulated in the contract. That is a clause governing the variable interest rate, according to which that rate cannot go below a specified minimum rate. The question of unfairness of the *clausulas suelo* has been the subject of an important judgment of the Tribunal Supremo of 9 May 2013 (STS 1916/2013, No de Recurso 485/2012). The judgment declared the relevant terms used by three banks null on the ground of lack of transparency. Another judgment of the Tribunal Supremo of 8 September 2014 (STS 3903/2014, No de Recurso 1217/2013, No de Resolución 464/2014) annulled eight such clauses employed by one bank for lack of transparency and failure to render the term comprehensible to the consumer. The question referred in *Banco Popular Español* concerned only the procedural aspects, so the Court did not have to rule on the possible unfairness of the disputed clause. The highly controversial issue of the *clausula suelo* finally came before the Court in Joined Cases C-154/15, C-307/15 and C-308/15, *Gutiérrez Naranjo*, EU:C:2016:980, where the Court decided that the limitation of the temporal effects of the judgment of the *Tribunal Supremo* ruling upon the unfairness of a contractual clause is not compatible with Art. 6(1) of the Unfair Contract Terms Directive.

*procedimiento de ejecución*.[1242] However, the Opinion of AG Kokott in *Aziz* sounded a cautionary note on the application of *Banco Español de Crédito* in this procedural context because "in a case like the present one an enforcement order already exists in the form of the notarial instrument and it must be recognized that the creditor has an interest in seeking enforcement quickly."[1243]

According to the same Opinion, the need for the consumer to initiate separate declaratory proceedings in order to establish the unfairness would not necessarily mean that this should be regarded "*a priori* as an excessive impediment to the legal protection of the consumer."[1244] A direct inference of the duty of the court to examine the unfairness of contractual terms in mortgage enforcement proceedings would not then be evident on the basis of *Banco Español de Crédito* alone. The Court finally applied in *Banco Popular Español* the reasoning of *Aziz* by analogy in order to establish the same powers for the court in enforcement proceedings (*juez de ejecución*):

> in so far as they completely prevent the court responsible for enforcement either to assess of its own motion or at the consumer's request, the unfairness of a term contained in the contract which give rise to the debt claimed and which constitutes, in the present case, the basis of the right to enforcement, or to grant interim relief capable of staying or terminating the mortgage enforcement proceedings, where such relief is necessary to ensure the full effectiveness of the final decision of the court hearing the declaratory proceedings liable before which the consumer argues that the term is unfair, are liable to undermine the effectiveness of the protection which Directive 93/13 seeks to achieve.[1245]

This admittedly long phrase is necessary to encapsulate all the elements that *completely* deprived the court responsible for the enforcement of any powers and the consumer of any meaningful defense. It stresses the particularity of the procedural system where the *impermeability* in the course of two separate proceedings (mortgage and declaratory) led to a breach of the principle of effectiveness. After the coming into force of the legislative changes in Spain with Law 1/2013, the question arose as to whether *Aziz* should still be considered relevant.[1246] In view of the fact that the court of the enforcement proceedings was empowered to consider of its own motion the fairness of terms of the enforcement instrument, it remained open whether the court hearing

---

1242 E. Cordero Lobato, "Control Judicial sobre cláusulas abusivas y ejecuciones hipotecarias" (2013) 2 *Revista Aranzadi Doctrinal*, 205–212, 207; S. I. Sánchez, "Unfair terms in mortgage loans and protection of housing in times of economic crisis: *Aziz v. Catalunyacaixa*", (2014) 51 *CMLR* 955–974, 969, 963.

1243 Opinion of AG Kokott in Case C-415/11 *Aziz* (n. 1232), point 55.

1244 Ibid.

1245 Joined Cases C-537/12 and C-116/13 *Banco Popular Español* (n. 1234), para. 55.

1246 S. Sanchez (n. 1242), 964. The point will be revisited later during the discussion of the changes of Spanish civil procedural law.

the declaratory proceedings should still maintain a distinct power to grant interim relief or to assess of its own motion the unfairness of the mortgage instrument.[1247] *Morcillo and García*,[1248] a ruling that had been delivered following the coming into force of the Spanish legislative reforms, seems to confirm the tenure of application of *Aziz* in declaratory proceedings even after reform. The fact that "the enforcing court may have, at most, delivered a rapid assessment of the validity of the contractual clauses"[1249] could not "offset"[1250] the risk to which the consumer is exposed of losing his dwelling if in the course of the declaratory proceedings there is no power of the court to order interim relief. I will come back to this ruling in the section pertaining to the legacy of *Aziz*.

### *3.2.2. Constitutional Dimension of the Protection of the Mortgage Debtor*

Hans Micklitz has spoken of the "hidden" constitutionalization[1251] in the *Aziz* judgment. This "hidden" constitutionalization would be more clearly revealed in two subsequent rulings, *Morcillo and García*[1252] and *Kušionova*.[1253] The following developments are devoted to the elements informing the constitutional path traced in *Aziz* and followed in the aforementioned subsequent judgments on the subject of mortgage enforcement proceedings. They relate to the observance of the right to an effective judicial protection of the mortgage debtor and his family life and home. The constitutional elements involved in mortgage repossession proceedings necessitate an enhanced level of procedural protection of the mortgage debtor in order to take into account the importance of the mortgaged property as the family home of the consumer. From this perspective, the *Aziz* case demonstrates the necessity to redesign procedures which involve an asset representing an essential need of the consumer as a citizen. The redesign of procedure is accompanied by a more fundamental reconceptualization of the consumer in Union law: from the "marketised" consumer, as Hans W. Micklitz[1254] has brilliantly put it, to the consumer as citizen and as a weaker party who requires protection against the forces of the market.

---

1247 The problem is discussed by J. M. Fernández Seijo in *La tutela de los consumidores en los procedimientos judiciales, Especial referencia a las ejecuciones hipotecarias* (n. 1202), 115 *et seq*, taking the position that the consumer should have both defense strategies available.

1248 Case C-169/14 *Morcillo and García*, EU:C:2014:2099.

1249 Ibid., para. 43.

1250 Ibid.

1251 H.-W. Micklitz, "Unfair Contract Terms – Public interest litigation before European Courts" (n. 1204), 648; H.-W. Micklitz and N. Reich, "The Court and Sleeping Beauty: The Revival of the Unfair Contract Terms Directive" (2014) 51 *CMLR* 771–808, 800.

1252 Case C-169/14 *Morcillo and García* (n. 1248).

1253 Case C-34/13 *Kušionová*, EU:C:2014:2189.

1254 H.-W. Micklitz, "The Consumer: Marketised, Fragmentised, Constitutionalised" in D. Leczykiwicz and S. Weatherill (eds.), *The Images of the Consumer in EU Law, Legislation, Free Movement and Competition Law* (Oxford, Hart Publishing, 2016), 21–41.

### 3.2.2.1. Effective Judicial Protection

The constitutional implications of the limited grounds of objection upon the right to effective judicial protection were already the subject of litigation before the Spanish Constitutional Court (*Tribunal Constitucional*). The ruling of this court of 2011 had confirmed the compatibility of the (then applicable) system of mortgage enforcement with the fundamental right to an effective judicial protection, as it is enshrined in the Spanish Constitution (Article 24.1).[1255] The main line of argumentation of this judgment, was to consider that the mortgagor was not deprived of the right to an effective judicial protection and that the right to challenge the enforcement procedure initiated against him was not compromised. The only limitation upon his right, so the reasoning went, was the absence of *suspensive effect* upon the enforcement procedure "and nothing else" *(y nada más)*. This absence, however, of *suspending effect* was the reason that led the Court to consider specific features of the Spanish mortgage enforcement system incompatible with Union consumer law.

Let us pause to clarify that the Court did not engage into a direct "constitutional dialogue"[1256] with the *Tribunal Constitutional.* As a matter of fact, there is no reference to the Charter. However, all the elements that point to Article 47 of the Charter as well as to Article 19(1) TEU are present. Interim relief must be available to the mortgagor in order to ensure the full effectiveness of the final decision which assesses the unfairness of terms contained in the enforcement instrument. If there is no suspending effect upon the proceedings, while the court of the declaratory proceedings decides upon the validity of the claim, the protection that the consumer derives from the Unfair Contract Terms Directive is rendered nugatory. A subsequent protection "of a purely compensatory nature" is "incomplete and insufficient" and cannot therefore meet the standard of effective judicial protection required under Article 47 of the Charter. The link between interim relief and the right to an effective judicial protection was clearly established in *Factortame*[1257] and then in *Unibet*,[1258] to which the Court made reference:

> the principle of effective judicial protection of an individual's rights under [Union] law must be interpreted as requiring it to be possible under the legal order of a Member

---

1255 Above Section 3.1.2.

1256 H. Micklitz and N. Reich, "The Court and Sleeping Beauty: The Revival of the Unfair Contract Terms Directive" (n. 1251), 801, making the point that a reason for the "covert" constitutional approach in *Aziz* might have been to avoid engaging in such a constitutional dialogue with the *Tribunal Constitucional.* On constitutional conversations and relevant literature see M. Dawson, "The political face of judicial activism: Europe's law-politics imbalance" in M. Dawson, B. de Witte and E. Muir, *Judicial Activism at the European Court of Justice* (Cheltenham, Edward Elgar, 2013), 11–31, 18.

1257 Case C-213/89 *Factortame*, EU:C:1990:257, para. 21.

1258 Case C-432/05 *Unibet* (n. 1237), para. 77.

> State for interim relief to be granted until the competent court has given a ruling on whether national provisions are compatible with [Union] law, where the grant of such relief is necessary to ensure the full effectiveness of the judgment to be given on the existence of such rights.

Under this perspective, Hans Micklitz names the *Aziz* interim relief remedy as a "variation on *Factortame*."[1259]

If it were otherwise, the mortgagee could escape control of unfair terms by initiating repossession proceedings, depriving the consumer of the legal protection conferred by the Unfair Contract Terms Directive,[1260] as well as of his rights of defense against the ongoing repossession. The ruling in *Banco Popular Español* extended the *Aziz* logic with regard to the court hearing the enforcement proceedings. By the time that *Banco Popular Español* was decided, the Spanish legislator had already adopted Law 1/2013, by virtue of which the existence of unfair terms was established as an additional ground of objection within the framework of enforcement proceedings which could also be raised by the court of its own motion.

Although the Court had already ruled on the application of Article 47 of the Charter in relation to national procedural rules in order to guarantee the full effect of a substantive right conferred by Union law on individuals,[1261] this had not yet been the case within the framework of individual consumer litigation. The first direct reference to Article 47 of the Charter within the context of ensuring the *full effect* of the exercise of consumer rights under the Unfair Contract Terms Directive is the judgment in *Morcillo and García.*[1262] This Spanish case arose in the context of the new legislative regime following reform.[1263] For the purposes of the present discussion, it is important to point out the leveling of the requirement of the effectiveness of consumer protection law standard to a requirement of effective judicial protection. Just after having recalled the principle of effectiveness and the judgments within the line of the *ex officio* doctrine in consumer proceedings, the Court held that:

> the obligation for the Member States to ensure the effectiveness of the rights that the parties derive from Directive 93/13 against the use of unfair clauses implies a requirement of judicial protection, also guaranteed by Article 47 of the Charter that is binding on the national court.[1264]

---

[1259] H.-W. Micklitz, "The Transformation of Enforcement in European Private Law: Preliminary Considerations" (2015) 4 *European Review of Private Law* 491–524, 513.

[1260] Case C-415/11 *Aziz* (n. 1201), para. 62.

[1261] Case C-279/09 *DEB*, EU:C:2010:811; Joined Cases C-317/08–C-320/08 *Alassini*, EU:C:2010:146: see Chapter 1, Section 2.2.3.

[1262] C-169/14 *Morcillo and García* (n. 1248).

[1263] See below Chapter 6, Section 1.2.

[1264] Case C-169/14 *Morcillo and García* (n. 1248), para. 35.

The judgment that is cited in support of the inference, from the principle of effectiveness, of a requirement for judicial protection is *Banif Plus Bank*.[1265] There, the reasoning had also been predicated upon Article 47 of the Charter, although the context was different. It concerned the principle that the parties must be heard on a ground that the court has raised of its own motion. In *Banif Plus Bank*, the principle of effective judicial protection was actually a justification for a limitation on the effectiveness of consumer law. A national court raising the unfair term of its own motion had to seek argument from the parties and in particular from the professional against whom the finding of potential unfairness would operate, without this requirement undermining the effectiveness of consumer law. In *Morcillo and García* the principle of effectiveness and effective judicial protection interrelate in a different way, to the effect that the former principle is *infused* with considerations of the latter. The issue raised in *Morcillo and García* related to an aspect of the right to a fair hearing, namely the inequality of arms due to the imbalance that occurred in the exercise of the rights of appeal between the consumer mortgage debtor and the mortgage creditor. In a contribution to the discussion of procedural and remedial autonomy and the *ex officio* doctrine, former Advocate General Trstenjak and Edward Beysen have pointed out that "by emphasizing the weak position of the consumer, the ECJ implicitly raised the effectiveness threshold which national procedural rules for the enforcement of rights under the consumer protection directives must meet."[1266]

As *Morcillo and García* raised the question of access to the court for the mortgage debtor, this high effectiveness threshold embodies[1267] the requirement of effective judicial protection. The right to effective judicial protection is corroborated by the link with a second constitutional element, the right to respect of one's family life and one's home, to which we shall now turn.

#### 3.2.2.2. The Right to Respect for One's Family Life and One's Home

An additional constitutional layer to the argumentation in *Aziz* arose from the capacity of the defendant not only as a consumer but also as a *residential* mortgage debtor. The violation of the right to effective judicial protection

1265 Case C-472/11 *Banif Plus Bank*, EU:C:2013:88.

1266 V. Trstenjak and E. Beysen, "European Consumer Protection Law: Curia Semper Dabit Remedium?" (2011) 48 *CMLR* 95–124, 121.

1267 Term used in Joined Cases C-317/08–C-320/08 *Alassini*, EU:C:2010:146, para. 49 and case law cited; Opinion AG Bot in Case C-93/12 *Agrokonsulting-04*, EU:C:2013:172, point 30. See K. Lenaerts, "Exploring the Limits of the EU Charter of Fundamental Rights" (2012) 8 *European Constitutional Law Review* 375–403, 382.

from the absence of suspensive effect upon foreclosure is corroborated by the fact that:

> the mortgaged property is the family home of the consumer whose rights have been infringed, since that means of consumer protection is limited to payment of damages and interest and does not make it possible to prevent the definitive and irreversible loss of that dwelling.[1268]

Subsequent judgments clearly echo the European Court of Human Rights (ECtHR) jurisprudence in that respect. The qualification of the mortgage property as a family home accentuates the *vulnerability* of the consumer.[1269] The loss of such an asset in repossession proceedings without proper judicial control of the enforcement instrument is liable to seriously undermine not only the consumer right not to be bound by unfair terms, but also to place "the family of the consumer concerned in a particularly vulnerable position."[1270]

In *Kušionová* (echoing the observations of AG Wahl in *Macinský*),[1271] the Court engaged in a "constructive dialogue"[1272] with the ECtHR. National proceedings must provide for adequate procedural safeguards for the mortgage debtor:[1273]

> in that regard, the European Court of Human Rights has held, first, that the loss of a home is one of the most serious breaches of the right to respect for the home and, secondly, that any person who risks being the victim of such a breach should be able to have the proportionality of such a measure reviewed.[1274]

The ECtHR judgments cited to that effect were *McCann v. United Kingdom*[1275] and *Rousk v. Sweden.*[1276]

---

1268 Case C-415/11 *Aziz* (n. 1201), para. 61.

1269 See I. Domurath, "The case for vulnerability as the normative standard in European consumer credit and mortgage law: An inquiry into the paradigms of consumer law" (2013) 2 *Zeitschrift für europäisches Unternehmens- und Verbraucherrecht* 124–137, arguing for *vulnerability* as a competing normative paradigm in consumer mortgage credit against the information paradigm.

1270 Order of the President of the Court in Case C-169/14 *Morcillo and Garcia*, EU:C:2014:1388, also referred to in Case C-34/13 *Kušionová* (n. 1253).

1271 Opinion of AG Wahl in Case C-482/12 *Macinský and Macinská*, EU:C:2013:765.

1272 Borrowed from the expression used by the House of Lords in *R* v *Horncastle* [2010] 2 AC 373, cited by D. Cowan, *Housing Law and Policy* (Cambridge, Cambridge University Press, 2011), 387.

1273 See Opinion AG Wahl in Case C-482/12 *Macinský* (n. 1271). This case was removed from the Court register by Order of the Court on 7 February 2014.

1274 Case C-34/13 *Kušionová*, EU:C:2014:2189, para. 64; ECtHR *Rousk v. Sweden*, App. No 27183/04, para. 137.

1275 ECtHR *McCann* v *United Kingdom* (2008) 47 EHRR 40, para. 50. See also *Connors v. United Kingdom* (2004) 40 EHRR 189.

1276 ECtHR *Rousk v. Sweden* (n. 1274), para. 137.

In that same judgment in *Kušionová*, the Court connects the requirement of the existence of interim measures in residential mortgage repossession proceedings and the judicial control of the enforcement instrument with Article 7 of the Charter, which provides for the fundamental right for the respect of one's *home*:

> Under EU law, the right to accommodation is a fundamental right guaranteed under Article 7 of the Charter that the referring court must take into consideration when implementing Directive 93/13.[1277]

It should be pointed out that Article 7 of the Charter refers to "respect of one's home" and not to "the right to accommodation" (or "le droit au logement" in the original French text of the judgment). The right to *accommodation* connotes the right to housing or the *right to a home*, which is a *social right* distinct from the negative right for respect of one's home. If the right to a home is not enshrined in the Charter, under the solidarity principles, reference is made to a right to "social and housing assistance" (Article 34(3) of the Charter). It might be that the Court intended to confer a more social dimension on Article 7 of the Charter.

Even if such a bold proposition would require further argumentation and case law development, the case law of the Court on residential mortgage repossession proceedings sets in stone the interpretation of the Unfair Contract Terms Directive in light of the right to respect of one's home, which has resulted in enhanced procedural protection for residential mortgage debtors.[1278] If the mortgage debtor is to enjoy adequate procedural safeguards under Union consumer law in such proceedings, he should be able, on the one hand, to challenge the enforcement instrument and allege the existence of unfair terms and, on the other hand, to seek interim relief and suspend the ongoing proceedings.

Making a harmonious integration of ECtHR jurisprudence, the Court accepted unreservedly that mortgage repossession proceedings can *interfere* with the respect of one's home under Article 7 of the Charter.[1279] The rights understanding of the concept of *home* is broader than the strict proprietary

---

1277 Case C-34/13 *Kušionová* (n. 1274), para. 65.

1278 *See* A. Beka, "The Protection of the Primary Residence of Mortgage Debtors: Embedding the 'Basic Needs' Principle in Residential Mortgage Repossession Proceedings" in L. Ratti (ed.), *Embedding the Principles of Life Time Contracts, A Research Agenda for Contract Law* (The Hague, Eleven Publishing, 2018), 247–276.

1279 To appreciate the importance of this proposition, one could compare the hesitation of Lord Scott in *Qazi* v *Harrow LBC* [2003] UKHL 43, as mentioned by S. Nield, "Clash of the Titans: Article 8, Occupiers and their Home" in S. Bright (ed.), *Modern Studies in Property Law* (Oxford, Hart Publishing, 2011) 106. For Lord Scott, due respect to the home should be limited to the protection of privacy and freedom from State interference, a view which had not been shared by the majority. For an account of the UK litigation on social housing mandatory possession proceedings culminating in *Manchester CC v. Pinnock* [2010] 3 WLR 1441, see R. Cowan (n. 1272), 378 *et seq.*

law perspective. It is settled ECtHR case law that "whether a property is to be classified as a 'home' is a question of fact and does not depend on the lawfulness of the occupation under domestic law."[1280] From the perspective of the law of mortgage, a mortgage creditor has a contractual and statutory right to repossess and the debtor in arrears loses his weaker proprietary interest due to his default in meeting the repayment obligations. However, from a fundamental rights perspective, when the property is the residence of the debtor, it remains his dwelling even if he loses the right to occupation according to the contract. Therefore, Article 7 of the Charter, in the same way as Article 8 ECHR, provides, as Sarah Nield observes, a "new form of proprietary entitlement" by opening up the respect due to the home enshrined in those provisions "to possibilities beyond the traditional boundaries of property law."[1281]

The rights reasoning in *Kušionová* echoes a previous case, *Macinský*,[1282] in which AG Wahl delivered his Opinion before the case was removed from the register of the Court.[1283] The issue raised was the same: whether the requirement that the consumer is obliged to initiate proceedings in order to suspend or halt mortgage enforcement proceedings initiated by extrajudicial means goes against the effectiveness of consumer law. The Opinion of AG Wahl was in the negative. However, it stressed the necessity of the existence of a safety net of procedural guarantees that should be put in place in the course of mortgage enforcement proceedings:

> where the property concerned by the procedure at issue is the consumer's home, there must be specific guarantees. Failure to provide such guarantees may prove problematic from a fundamental rights perspective. Indeed, the loss of a family home is one of the most extreme forms of interference with the rights of the consumer. As respect for the home is a right guaranteed under Article 7 of the Charter of Fundamental Rights of the European Union, in the light of which Directive 93/13 must be interpreted, any person at risk of an interference of this magnitude should be able to have the proportionality of such a measure reviewed by an independent judicial body.[1284]

One of the decisive elements in *Aziz* that led to an interpretation of the Unfair Contract Terms Directive to the effect that the national court possesses the necessary powers to grant interim relief was the fact that the mortgaged property was the family home of the consumer and that any loss of his dwelling would be definitive and irreversible. This is an essential element for the consumer's

---

1280 ECtHR *McCann* v *United Kingdom* (n. 1275), para. 46.

1281 S. Nield (n. 1279), 105.

1282 Opinion AG Wahl in Case C-482/12 *Macinský* (n. 1271).

1283 The reference was removed from the register after a relevant request being made by the national court. The reason for the withdrawal is not mentioned in the Order, but it may be assumed that it related to the admissibility of the question. Indeed, in his Opinion, AG Wahl found the question inadmissible on the basis that the litigation in question had ended.

1284 Opinion AG Wahl in Case C-482/12 *Macinský* (n. 1271), point 82.

"personhood."[1285] Article 7 of the Charter, the Court stated, "must be taken into consideration" when implementing the Unfair Contract Terms Directive. This represents a case of indirect horizontal effect where a Union law instrument, the Unfair Contract Terms Directive, had to be interpreted *in the light* of fundamental rights. Constitutional values indirectly permeate the private law relationship.[1286] The mortgage relationship thus becomes subject to the dynamism of "humanization," being shaped indirectly by the consideration of the fundamental rights of the mortgagor. For the purposes of the specific cases, this meant that such procedures should be available that allow the courts the possibility to scrutinize repossession through the constitutional prism. With reference to *Aziz*, *Kušionová* makes the connection between the effectiveness of consumer protection under the Unfair Contract Terms Directive, the provision of interim measures and the protection of the principal family home of the consumer:

> with regard in particular to the consequences of the eviction of the consumer and his family from the accommodation forming their principal family home, the Court has already emphasized the importance, for the national court, to provide for interim measures by which unlawful mortgage enforcement proceedings may be suspended or terminated where the grant of such measures proves necessary in order to ensure the effectiveness of the protection intended by Directive 93/13.[1287]

In view of the above, it has to be made clear that in both cases there was no direct human rights challenge to the *right* of the mortgage creditor to repossess. The challenge concerned the capacity of procedural law to provide for adequate safeguards. When the Court requires that interim measures exist, it is the responsibility of the state to provide for effective judicial protection in light of its duty to *positively protect* the right to respect to home that is engaged. Article 7 of the Charter *informs* the application of the right to effective judicial protection of consumers against the use of unfair terms. The procedural protection of consumers requires that interim relief is available, enabling the courts to raise an unfair term of their own motion and order the suspension of the proceedings. This is a situation of vertical application of the right of the mortgagor against the state.

---

1285 M. J. Radin, "Property and Personhood" (1982) 34 *Stanford Law Review* 957–1015.

1286 For recent accounts on the highly complex issue of constitutionalization and horizontality of fundamental rights, see the contributions of distinctive scholars in the field in H.-W. Micklitz (ed.), *The Constitutionalisation of European Private Law* (Oxford, Oxford University Press, 2014); U. Bernitz et al. (eds.), *General Principles of EU law and European Private Law* (Dordrecht, Kluwer, 2013); S. de Vries et al. (eds.), *The Protection of Fundamental Rights in the EU After Lisbon* (Hart, 2013). Also, Opinion of AG Trstenjak in Case C-282/10 *Dominguez*, EU:C:2011:559 and Opinion of AG Cruz Villalón in Case C-176/12 *AMS*, EU:C:2013:491.

1287 Case C-34/13 *Kušionová* (n. 1274), para. 66.

Moving the reflection a step further, let us assume that the mortgagee has a lawful right to repossess and that there are no unfair terms in the contract that could invalidate his right. Can we infer from *Aziz* and *Kušionová* that courts should nevertheless have the power to balance the mortgagee's right to repossess with the mortgagor's right to respect of his home? It is true that in *Kušionová* reference is made to the relevant ECtHR case law on the requirement that the courts proceed with the judicial review of the proportionality of any measure which could result to the loss of the home.[1288] But this reference should arguably not be understood to mean that the Court endorses proportionality review in mortgage repossessions initiated by a private creditor. First of all, the issue in *Kušionová* did not concern proportionality review but the procedural protection of the consumer against the use of unfair terms in the context of extrajudicial enforcement proceedings. Then, it has to be stressed that *McCann v. United Kingdom*, as well as the subsequent Strasbourg cases on eviction, arose in the context of social-housing tenancy law, involving *public landlords* and tenants.[1289] Moreover, in *Vrzić v. Croatia*[1290] the ECtHR decided that proportionality review does not apply in eviction proceedings involving private interests, for as long as the judicial procedure offers the necessary procedural guarantees.[1291]

In any event, if the matter raised before a national court does not involve the existence of unfair terms of the enforcement instrument and the *ex officio* powers of the courts in that regard, it will necessarily fall outside the scope of the Unfair Contract Terms Directive. However, the exercise of creditor remedies in repossession proceedings does not fall outside Union law overall. Article 28(1) of the Mortgage Credit Directive[1292] provides that "Member States shall adopt measures to encourage creditors to exercise reasonable forbearance

1288 ECtHR *McCann* v *United Kingdom* (n. 1275), para. 50 and ECtHR *Rousk* v *Sweden* (n. 1274), para. 137.

1289 For an account of this case law *see* C. Schmid and J. Dinse, "Towards a Common Core of Residential Tenancy Law in Europe? The Impact of the European Court of Human Rights on Tenancy Law" in L. Nogler and U. Reifner (eds.), *Life Time Contracts, Social Long Term Contracts in Labour, Tenancy and Consumer Credit Law* (The Hague, Eleven International Publishing, 2014) 627–639; M. Thompson, "Possession Actions and Human Rights" (2011) *Conv.* 421–440.

1290 ECtHR *Vrzić v. Croatia*, judgment of 12 July 2016, App. No 43777/13. Cf. the judgment of the UK Supreme Court in *McDonald (by her litigation friend Duncan J McDonald) v McDonald and others* [2016] UKSC 28, analyzed by A. Dymond, "McDonald – Private Landlords and Article 8" (2016) 19 *Journal of Housing Law* 93–96; S. Pascoe, "The end of the road for human rights in private landowners' disputes?" (2017) *Conv.* 2017, 269–286; S. Nield, "Thumbs down to the horizontal effect of article 8" (2015) *Conv.* 77–88; S. Nield, "Shutting the Door on Horizontal Effect: McDonald v McDonald" (2017) *Conv.* 60–71.

1291 ECtHR *Vrzić v. Croatia* (n. 1290), para. 101.

1292 Directive 2014/17/EU of the European Parliament and of the Council of 4 February 2014 on credit agreements for consumers relating to residential immovable property and amending Directives 2008/48/EC and 2013/36/EU and Regulation (EU) No 1093/2010 [2014] OJ L60/34.

before foreclosure proceedings are initiated." The wording of this provision clearly implies that forbearance is not made obligatory under the Mortgage Credit Directive, even less a requirement of judicial review of proportionality. In former drafts the provision was worded in a more prescriptive way, which was finally regrettably "softened."[1293] It will be a matter of national law to determine if creditors will be simply *encouraged* or *required* to follow certain pre-action requirements and what the consequences will be if a creditor does not resort to repossession as a means of last resort.[1294] The level of intensity of forbearance and the normative force it will have in a given judicial system will depend on the balance that the legislator will draw between property rights and economic and financial interests on the one hand and considerations of social welfare on the other hand. This will also determine the extent to which courts will be allowed to invest what Susan Bright calls the "personal story" of the homeowner with legal relevance.[1295] To achieve due process and "humanity" in repossession procedures, the lines between property rights and social rights have to be redrawn within a broader perspective of the consideration of the citizenship dimension raised in residential mortgage relationships and in repossessions.

#### 3.2.2.3. The "Citizenship" Dimension of Residential Mortgage Contracts

The constitutional perspectives set out above open up a wider spectrum for considering residential mortgage repossession as apposite for "a new legal encounter with the 'citizen-consumer'."[1296] In the past, the concept of the European citizen-consumer has been explored mainly within a discourse of a new participation governance encompassing the phenomenon of "political consumerism," where the consumer "emerges as a political actor."[1297] The emphasis

---

1293 See the Parliamentary debate held in Strasbourg on 10 September 2013 and in particular the contributions of the members of the European Left political party.

1294 I have elaborated upon the question of forbearance and proportionality in A. Beka, "The Protection of the Primary Residence of Mortgage Debtors: Embedding the 'Basic Needs' Principle in Residential Mortgage Repossession Proceedings" (n. 1278), 258–266. For the relevant discussion in England and the Pre-Action Protocol see L. Whitehouse, "The Mortgage Arrears Pre-Action Protocol: An Opportunity Lost" (2009) (72) 5 *Modern Law Review* 783–814.

1295 S. Bright, "Dispossession for Arrears: The Weight of Home" in L. Fox O'Mahony and J. Sweeney (eds.), *Home: Displacement and Dispossession* (Farnham, Ashgate, 2010) 13–41.

1296 M. Everson and C. Joerges, "Consumer Citizenship in Postnational Constellations?" EUI Working Papers Law No 2006/47 (available at the European University Institute website and the Social Science Research Network Database). See G. Davies, "The Consumer, the Citizen, the Human Being" in D. Leczykiewicz and S. Weatherill (eds.), *The Images of the Consumer in EU Law* (Oxford and Portland – Oregon, Hart Publishing, 2016) 325–338.

1297 In particular see D. Stolle and M. Micheletti, *Political Consumerism: Global Responsibility in Action* (Cambridge, Cambridge University Press, 2013), 39, who define political consumerism as follows: "Political consumerism, formally defined as a

there is placed upon *political* citizenship. This is the second of the elements forming citizenship, following the classic triptych conceptual thread of citizenship pronounced in the work of Thomas Humphrey Marshall.[1298] The triptych includes an array of civil, political and social rights forming the elements of "substantive citizenship," as further re-examined through the perspective of Tim Bottomore.[1299] The entitlement to welfare rights is central to social citizenship. In the words of the famous passage from *Citizenship and Social Class*:

> by the social element I mean the whole range from the right to a modicum of economic welfare and security to the right to share to the full in the social heritage and to live the life of a civilized being according to the standards prevailing in the society.[1300]

One of the central premises in the theory of T.H. Marshall is that the social element is essential for the citizenship status.[1301] This premise is also reflected in the Rawlsian theory of political liberties.[1302] It is also endorsed in the work of Jürgen Habermas[1303] pertaining to human dignity. The philosopher explains how human dignity is the "key to the logical interconnections" between the various categories of fundamental rights: "Only in collaboration with each other can basic rights fulfill the moral promise to respect the human dignity of every person equally."[1304]

---

consumer's use of the market as an arena for politics in order to change institutional or market practices found to be ethically, environmentally, or politically objectionable is a specific form of participation that characterizes individualized responsibility taking"; M. Micheletti, *Political Virtue and Shopping: Individuals, Consumerism and Collective Action* (New York and Basingstoke, Palgrave, 2010); J. Davies, *The European Consumer Citizen in Law and Policy* (Palgrave, 2011), 4; C. Barnett et al., "The Political Ethics of Consumerism: Citizenship Between Individualization and participation" (2005) 2 15 *Consumer Policy Review* 45–51.

1298 The seminal study of T.H. Marshall, *Citizenship and Social Class* (Cambridge, Cambridge University Press, 1950). See L. Whitehouse, "The Home-Owner": Citizen or Consumer?" in S. Bright and J. Dewar, *Land Law Themes and Perspectives* (Oxford, Oxford University Press, 1998), 183–205, 200, discussing the rights of the mortgagor from the perspective of the social element of citizenship.

1299 T. Bottomore, "Citizenship and Social Class, Forty Years On" in T.H. Marshall and T. Bottomore, *Citizenship and Social Class* (Pluto Press, 1992).

1300 T.H. Marshall, *Citizenship and Social Class* (n. 1298), 11.

1301 For an account on the contemporary approaches of social citizenship and the challenges from both left and right in P. Dwyer, *Understanding Social Citizenship* (Bristol, The Policy Press and Social Policy Association, 2nd ed., 2010).

1302 J. Rawls, *A Theory of Justice, Revised Edition* (Cambridge – MA, Harvard University Press, 1999), 198.

1303 J. Habermas, *The Crisis of the European Union* (Cambridge, Polity Press, 2013); J. Habermas, *Between Facts and Norms* (MIT Press, 1996).

1304 J. Habermas, "The Concept of Human Dignity" in *The Crisis of the European Union* (n. 1303), 79.

The application of this logic in the field of consumer law would mean that political consumerism should also be complemented by "social" consumerism, comprising an array of social rights and welfare. Political consumer citizenship, to borrow a term used by Nick Bell, implies a "proactive engagement"[1305] on the part of the consumer, who becomes a "politicized market actor"[1306] influencing the market. Social consumer citizenship implies a "defensive engagement"[1307] of the citizen against the erosion of social rights and goods that have been commoditized as a result of market forces. In essence, the theory of *social consumer citizenship* is a specific application of the classic "substantive citizenship" concept[1308] in the context of those consumer transactions that are liable to engage with the fundamental rights of the individual. In the area of universal services, Hans Micklitz has seen a prime example of "consumerisation of the citizen-consumer/universal service provider relationship," process which has to be the infiltrated by human rights values. In its part, mortgage finance has brought about a "consumerization" of the acquisition of the first residence of the consumer without the social value of the commodity being necessarily reflected in the procedural part of repossession. The constitutional approach to those consumer relationships whose implications well exceed the momentary transactional aspect reinstates the social origin of the rights involved.

As far as the role of Union case law is concerned, it has to be pointed out the only legislative instrument that the Court had available to it in order to decide the cases discussed here was the Unfair Contract Terms Directive. An instrument that was more than 20 years old, adopted within an economic context bearing no similarities to the Great Recession and respecting the market integration logic of the Treaties, it would at first sight appear irrelevant in the context of mortgage repossession. Through the construction of the appropriate nexus with the Charter, the same instrument acquires a new dynamic for the protection of the consumer-*citizen*. The preamble to the Unfair Contract Terms Directive reads that the citizen *in his role as a consumer* has to be safeguarded. The new procedural twist developed under the Court's jurisprudence requires that the consumer *in his capacity as a citizen* is not subject to a repossession process that does not observe due process requirements and that does not take into account the fundamental right for respect for one's home. When the Court speaks in terms of an "essential need" of the consumer in obtaining lodging, it detaches consumer-citizens from "market citizenship,"[1309] so that they will no

1305 N. Bell, "Proactive and Defensive Engagement: Social Citizenship in a Changing Public Sphere" (2000) 5: 3 *Sociological Research Online*.

1306 J. Davies (n. 1297), 3.

1307 N. Bell (n. 1305).

1308 T. Bottomore (n. 1299).

1309 M. Everson, "The Legacy of the Market Citizen" in J. Shaw and G. More (eds.), *New Legal Dynamics of European Union* (Oxford, Clarendon Press, 1995), 73.

longer be what former AG Miguel Poiares Maduro has called "prisoners of the functional logic of the Treaties."[1310] Without adequate housing, the citizen can no longer lead "a decent existence" required under Article 34 of the Charter; even less, of course, participate in the market. The Unfair Contract Terms Directive, read in the light of the Charter, has an impact on the conceptualization of Union social citizenship.

Koen Lenaerts and Petra Foubert already demonstrated at the turn of the millennium that social rights thinking[1311] underpins the jurisprudence of the Court, in particular in relation to non-discrimination and Union citizenship. Recognizing the fundamental rights implications on mortgage repossession proceedings, the Court also demonstrates its sense of social sensitivity in this field. The Charter can become through proper interpretation the "plinth" of a new "social contract"[1312] for Europe. The social dimension of the economic crisis makes it more imperative than ever before in Europe's history that a definition be given to what Miguel Poiares Maduro has called "Europe's social self."[1313] In his contribution to the debate, the former AG underlines that if the citizenship of the constituents of an emerging European *demos* is narrowly defined and excludes the safety net of social rights, it will be a concept for an elite few, while the majority "will feel estranged from European citizenship." Inspired by Jürgen Habermas' pledge for the development of European "civil solidarity,"[1314] he deplores the fact that without a debate on "a criterion of distributive justice," there can be "no true social contract capable of legitimizing the emerging European polity."

Almost 15 years after the M. Poiares Maduro wrote those lines and in the aftermath of the worst crisis in modern economic history, the Commission is at the time of writing taking initiatives in the direction of establishing a "pillar of social rights."[1315] As for the Court, at the time that the mortgage crisis unfolded, it made a bold step forward in terms of the strengthening of the protection of consumer-citizens. Its case law in the field of mortgage repossession is exemplary of a court with social sensitivity.[1316] This is done by means of reintroducing the discourse of fundamental rights in the field of mortgage repossession

1310 M. Poiares Maduro, "Europe's Social Self: "The Sickness Unto Death" in J. Shaw (ed.), *Social Law and Policy in an Evolving European Union* (Oxford, Hart Publishing, 2000), 325–349.

1311 K. Lenaerts and P. Foubert, "Social Rights in the Case-Law of the European Court of Justice" (2001) 28: 3 *Legal Issues of Economic Integration* 267–296, 272.

1312 M. Poiares Maduro (n. 1310), 340.

1313 Ibid.

1314 J. Habermas, *The Postnational Constellation: Political Essays* (Cambridge – MA, MIT Press, 2001), 100.

1315 See the European Commission, *European Pillar of Social Rights* (April 2017).

1316 See the response to the critiques of the Court being "neoliberal' in J. Kokott, "Der EuGH, eine neoliberale Institution?" in *Grundrechte und Solidarität: Festschrift für Renate Jaeger* (Kehl am Rein, Engel Verlag, 2011) 115–134.

proceedings in circumstances where it has been insulated from such considerations. Norbert Reich and Hans Micklitz speak of "social engineering" and note that the Court, by placing the center of gravity on the weaker party:

> turns into a some sort of social manager which counterbalances the much harsher and market-oriented philosophy in particular of the European Commission, if not the European legislator.[1317]

In that regard, the reflection of Tim Koopmans and Pierre Pescatore always remain relevant:

> for the citizens, the judiciary has perhaps become, as Pierre Pescatore puts it, "the only independent interlocutor" ... Generally speaking, judicialisation is not inspired by some secret wish of the judiciary to decide as many issues as possible, but rather by the unresponsiveness of the political system to problems of society. If something is to be reformed, it should presumably be politics.[1318]

The nexus between consumer law and solidarity[1319] has been given new impetus since the inclusion of consumer protection within the realm of the solidarity principles under Article 38 of the Charter. Iris Benöhr undertakes a systematic theoretical enquiry of the "progressive convergence"[1320] between consumer rights and the protection of human rights. Mortgage repossession is a particularly apposite field for the discourse of rights. Even if Article 38 of the Charter is too vague to found a subjective right "by itself,"[1321] it is not deprived of a

---

1317 N. Reich and H.-W. Micklitz, "Economic Law, Consumer Interests and EU Integration" in N. Reich et al. (eds.), *European Consumer Law* (Cambridge, Intersentia, 2nd ed., 2014), 50.

1318 T. Koopmans, "Judicialisation" in N. Colneric, D. Edward, J.P. Puissochet and D. Ruiz-Jarabo Colomer (eds.) *Une communauté de droit Festschrift für Gil Carlos Rodríguez Iglesias* (Berlin, BWV, 2003), 51–57, 56; B. de Witte and E. Muir (eds.), *Judicial Activism at the European Court of Justice* (Cheltenham, Edward Elgar, 2013); H.-W. Micklitz and B. de Witte (eds.), *The European Court of Justice and the Autonomy of the Member States* (Cambridge, Intersentia, 2013); A. Stone Sweet, *The Judicial Construction of Europe* (Oxford, Oxford University Press, 2004); A. Stone Sweet, *Governing with Judges, Constitutional Politics in Europe* (Oxford, Oxford University Press, 2001); P. Syrpis (ed.), *The Judiciary, the Legislature and the EU Internal Market* (Cambridge, Cambridge University Press, 2012).

1319 See A. Sangiovanni, "Solidarity in the European Union" in J. Dickson and P. Eleftheriadis, *Philosophical Foundations of European Union Law* (Oxford, Oxford University Press, 2012), 384–411.

1320 I. Benöhr, *EU Consumer Law and Human Rights* (Oxford, Oxford University Press, 2013), 6; Also I. Benöhr and H.-W. Micklitz, Consumer Protection and Human Rights" in G. Howells et al. (eds.), *Handbook of Research on International Consumer Law* (Cheltenham, Edward Elgar, 2010); S. Deutch, "Are Consumer Rights Human Rights?" (1995) 32 *Osgoode Hall Law Journal* 537–578.

1321 Case C-470/12 *Pohotovost'*, EU:C:2014:101, para. 52. See above Chapter 4, Section 6.2.

normative value.[1322] Iris Benöhr and Hans Micklitz see its concretization "in combination with other rights of the Charter."[1323] In the case of mortgage repossession, those rights are Article 47 of the Charter and also Article 8 (on the right to family life and home) and Article 34(3) (on social exclusion and housing assistance). The status of the "principle" of Article 38 is not an obstacle in terms of its constitutional weight being placed in the balance of competing fundamental rights.[1324] The right of the mortgage creditor to repossess is an expression of the right to property, but this right has to be balanced against a high level of consumer protection, the right to effective judicial protection and the quality of the mortgaged property as the consumer's home. The residential mortgagor cannot be reduced to a debtor of any kind of debt. The mortgagee cannot be deprived of the right to repossess either. But the law can impose certain limitations on an absolute right of the mortgage creditor to evict and repossess for as long as those limitations serve a legitimate aim and are proportionate to the aim pursued. Considering mortgage repossession as an area isolated from its fundamental rights implications cannot validly stand, especially in times of severe economic crisis. The principle of *forbearance* introduced into the Mortgage Credit Directive should reflect those considerations.

The analysis of the constitutional perspectives of the mortgage repossession process demonstrates the evolution of the consumer individual litigation under the Unfair Contract Terms Directive, which could hardly have been envisaged by the legislator at that time. The Court has highlighted the vulnerability of the consumer in the residential mortgage relationship (*Aziz*,[1325] *Kušionová*[1326]), but also in the residential tenancy relationship (*Asbeek Brusse*[1327]). The object of a mortgage contract, the home of the consumer, is not a mere commodity; it fulfills an "essential need of the consumer."[1328] It is, as Lisa Whitehouse points out, the "precondition for citizenship."[1329] The normative pattern governing such a relationship cannot therefore be placed on the same level as any other type of consumer good. The protection based on enhanced information obligations, which lies in itself upon the assumption that the consumer will act as a reasonable "homo economicus" and will seize the best offer in a competitive market, relies upon the paradigm of autonomy at the pre-contractual and

---

1322 See introductory remarks under Part II, and Chapter 4, Section 1.

1323 Also, I. Benöhr and H.-W. Micklitz, "Consumer Protection and Human Rights" in G. Howells et al. (eds.), (n. 1320), 31.

1324 See to that effect, Case C-12/11 *McDonagh*, EU:C:2013:43.

1325 Case C-415/11 *Aziz* (n. 1201), para. 61.

1326 Case C-34/13 *Kušionová* (n. 1274), para. 63.

1327 Case C-488/11 *Asbeek Brusse*, EU:C:2013:341, para. 32.

1328 Ibid. and Case C-169/14 *Morcillo and García* (n. 1248), para. 38.

1329 L. Whitehouse, "The Home-Owner": Citizen or Consumer?" in S. Bright and J. Dewar (eds.), *Land Law Themes and Perspectives* (Oxford, Oxford University Press, 1998), 183–205, 200.

contractual stages.[1330] But such protection might prove to be insufficient for mortgage contracts, the "prototype" of consumer credit and one of the main examples of a "life-term"[1331] contract. The law should also provide for the "dark side"[1332] of the post-contractual phase. To this effect, it is encouraging that Article 28 of the Mortgage Credit Directive advances the requirement of forbearance to avoid foreclosure.

## 3.3. THE LEGACY OF *AZIZ* FOR PROCEDURAL GUARANTEES IN THE MORTGAGE REPOSSESSION PROCESS

The case law following the *Aziz* judgment builds upon the legacy it created for the standards of protection of the mortgage debtor from unfair terms. The first group of cases are references from Spain, either directly connected to the issue raised in the *Aziz* case or following the reform of Spanish civil procedural law in the aftermath of *Aziz*. The second group of cases concern the application of *Aziz reasoning* and procedural safeguards within the framework of extrajudicial or simplified proceedings.

### *3.3.1. Cases Building Upon the Constitutional Elements of* Aziz

After the pronouncement of the judgment in *Aziz*, the disputed provisions of the Spanish Civil Procedural Law (LEC) were amended by Law 1/2013. This was a broader legislative reform aiming at the reinforcement of protection of the mortgage debtors.[1333] Before this reform, two references for preliminary ruling from Spain had already been made to the Court, touching upon an issue closely connected to the one that arose in *Aziz*, concerning the powers of the enforcement court to consider the fairness of the underlying enforcement instrument. The Court decided on this issue by means of reasoned order in the Joined Cases *Banco Popular Español* and *Banco de Valencia*. This order has been discussed together with the *Aziz* judgment in view of their close connection. The case that directly concerned the new legislative regime was *Morcillo and García*.[1334] This raised the issue of equality of arms in enforcement proceedings. As was the case

1330 See H.-W. Micklitz, "The Expulsion of the Concept of Protection from the Consumer Law and the Return of Social Elements in the Civil Law: A Bittersweet Polemic" (2012) 35 *Journal of Consumer Policy* 283–296.

1331 L. Nogler and U. Reifner (eds.), *Life Time Contracts, Social Long-Term Contracts in Labour, Tenancy and Consumer Credit Law* (The Hague, Eleven, 2014).

1332 Ibid., Introduction, 44.

1333 Ley 1/2013 de medidas para reforzar la protección a los deudores hipotecarios, reestructuración de deuda y alquiler social (Law 1/2013 laying down measures for the strengthening of the protection of mortgagors, the restructuring of debt and social rent) of 14 May 2013 (BOE No 116 of 15 May 2013); analyzed below Chapter 6, Section 1.2.

1334 Case C-169/14 *Morcillo and García* (n. 1248).

in *Aziz*, the Spanish legislator intervened in the aftermath of *Morcillo and García* in order to render the law compliant with the requirements of effective judicial protection set out in that ruling. The transitional provisions of Law 1/2013 raised new issues which form the core of the judgment in *BBVA*.[1335] *Unicaja Banco*[1336] also concerned the transitional provisions of the new legislation. As that case mainly addressed the issue of the *ex officio* powers of the courts after finding a term unfair, it was discussed already above in Chapter 4.[1337] In *Barclays Bank*,[1338] the Court was given the occasion to set out the outer limits of the reach of the Unfair Contract Terms Directive on procedural law.

#### 3.3.1.1. Procedural Imbalance in Mortgage Repossession Proceedings and Effective Judicial Protection

Following the reform which was brought about by Law 1/2013, the new system of opposition to enforcement introduced a new ground which allows the defendant to challenge the enforcement on the basis of the unfairness of the contractual term in the enforcement instrument (Article 695(1), point 4 LEC). If the court upholds the objection based on the unfairness, it shall order that enforcement shall be discontinued where it is based on the unfair contractual term. Otherwise, the enforcement proceeds without application of the unfair term (Article 695(3), point 2 LEC). So far so good. However, as the law stood at the time of the reference in *Morcillo and García*, the right of appeal was made available only to the mortgage creditor. The mortgage creditor had the right to appeal against an order of the court that upheld the objection of the defendant and stopped the enforcement. By contrast, the mortgage debtor had no corresponding right to appeal against an order dismissing his objection and allowing the continuation of enforcement. This limitation of the right to appeal created "a difference of treatment between the consumer and the seller or supplier in their position as parties to the proceedings."[1339] In view of this, the referring court entertained doubts as to the compatibility of the disputed provision with the right to effective judicial protection enshrined in Article 47 of the Charter.

In order to assess the extent of compatibility of the national provisions with the requirements of the Unfair Contract Terms Directive, the Court

1335 Case C-8/14 *BBVA*, EU:C:2015:731. The case concerned the limitation of one month for the exercise of the right of defense of the mortgage debtor.

1336 Joined Cases C-482/13, C-484/13, C-485/13 and C-487/13 *Unicaja Banco and Caixabank*, EU:C:2015:21. Following publication of this case, the Court removed, from its register, Case C-548/13 *Caixabank v Jiménes* by Order of the President of the Court on 16 April 2015, EU:C:2015:281. See also Order of the Court in Case C-602/13 *Banco Bilbao Vizcaya Argentaria*, EU:C:2015:397.

1337 Above Chapter 4, Section 5.2.2.

1338 Case C-280/13 *Barclays Bank*, EU:C:2014:279.

1339 Case C-169/14 *Morcillo and García* (n. 1248), para. 30.

follows a sophisticated balancing path. The starting point in the reasoning is the principle of procedural autonomy. In the absence of harmonization of enforcement procedures, the detailed rules governing the right of appeal against a decision ruling on the legality of a contractual clause is a matter for domestic orders, subject however to the principle of equivalence and effectiveness. Assessing the compatibility with the principle of equivalence, the Court found no disparity between the regime governing objections based on the national rules of *public policy* and Article 6 of the Unfair Contract Terms Directive.[1340] With regard to the principle of effectiveness, the Court established for the first time in the context of consumer procedural protection an explicit connection with the principle of effective judicial protection.

In the analysis of the "constitutional" elements of the *Aziz* case, reference has already been made to this important feature of *Morcillo and García*,[1341] in that the principle of effectiveness is *infused* by considerations of effective judicial protection.[1342] There it has also been explained that although it was not the first time that Article 47 of the Charter was applied in the context of the procedural protection of consumers from unfair terms (the Court referred to that *effect* to *Banif Plus Bank*),[1343] in the present case the principle of effectiveness of the protection of the consumer from unfair terms is *tied* to and *implies* a requirement of effective judicial protection. This resembles another formulation of the Court according to which the requirements of equivalence and effectiveness were held to *embody* the obligation to ensure effective judicial protection.[1344]

The issue raised concerned a quintessential element of the right to fair trial: the equality of arms. The reasoning weaves considerations of contractual *inequality* into individual litigation, underscored by *social rights thinking* in mortgage repossession. The Court departed from the premise that "the principle of effective judicial protection does not afford a right of access to a second level of jurisdiction."[1345] Therefore:

> the fact that the only remedy available to the consumer, as a debtor against whom mortgage enforcement proceedings are brought, is to bring an action before a single

---

1340 With reference to the same statement regarding the assessment of parity with national rules of public policy Case C-415/11 *Aziz* (n. 1201), para. 52, Case C-618/10 *Banco Español de Crédito* (n. 1148), para. 48.

1341 Above, Section 3.2.2.1.

1342 This is a primary example of the "superposition" method of the Court, according to M. Safjan and D. Düsterhaus, "A Union of Effective Judicial Protection: Addressing a Multi-level Challenge through the Lens of Article 47 CFREU" (2014) 33 *Yearbook of European Law* 3–40, 12.

1343 Case C-472/11 *Banif Plus Bank* (n. 1265).

1344 Joined Cases C-317/08–C-320/08 *Alassini*, EU:C:2010:146, para. 49; Case C-268/06 *Impact*, EU:C:2008:223, para. 47; See above Chapter 1, Section 2.2.

1345 Case C-169/14 *Morcillo and García* (n. 1248), para. 36.

> jurisdictional level in order to protect the rights derived from Directive 93/13 is not, in itself, contrary to EU law.[1346]

But once the scheme of the mortgage enforcement procedure is taken into account as a whole and the importance of the asset involved is also taken into account, the outcome turns to be different. First of all, the mortgage enforcement proceedings relate to "an asset that meets an essential need of the consumer, namely provision of a dwelling."[1347] This becomes a recurrent consideration in the Court's appreciation of procedural safeguards in residential repossession proceedings (also taken into account in *Asbeek Brusse* and *Aziz*). The Court pointed out that the mortgage creditor may initiate enforcement *directly* against the mortgaged property (pursuant to Article 681 (1) LEC):

> on the basis of an enforceable notarial instrument, without the contents of that instrument having been subject to judicial scrutiny in order to determine whether one of more clauses is unfair.[1348]

It is true that after the reform of Spanish procedural law in the aftermath of *Aziz*, the courts have a power to consider the unfairness of the mortgage instrument in the course of enforcement proceedings (*procedimiento de ejecución*) (Article 552(1), point 2 LEC). However, the Court noted that there is *no obligation* of the enforcement court to examine the fairness of the contractual clauses, but only a *discretionary power* to do so.[1349] The right of the seller to proceed directly to enforcement against an asset which is of essential or existential importance for the mortgage debtor – consumer-citizen:

> renders it all the more necessary that the consumer, in the position of a debtor against whom mortgage enforcement proceedings are brought, can avail himself of effective judicial protection.[1350]

Particular attention needs to be paid to the position of the mortgage debtor as a consumer.[1351] The mortgage credit was brought relatively recently within the ambit of Union consumer protection with the coming into force of the Mortgage Credit Directive. The Court confirmed not only that the residential mortgage debtor is a consumer[1352] but also that the disputed procedure,

---

1346 Ibid.
1347 Ibid., para. 38.
1348 Ibid.
1349 Ibid., para. 39.
1350 Ibid., para. 38.
1351 Ibid.
1352 In an interview with the current author, Judge José María Fernández Seijo noted that in the pre-crisis period, there was the perception in the banking sector that the mortgage debtor did not qualify as a consumer but as an investor.

whereby the mortgagee may appeal against an order terminating enforcement without the consumer being equipped with a corresponding right against an order rejecting his objection:

> places the consumer as a debtor against whom enforcement proceedings are brought, in a weaker position compared with the seller or supplier, as a creditor bringing mortgage enforcement proceedings, as regards the judicial protection of the rights that he is entitled to rely on by virtue of [the Unfair Contract Terms Directive] against the use of unfair clauses.[1353]

The consumer-citizen is more vulnerable, taking into account the long-term character of the contract, the importance of the financial engagement, the significance of the asset for his family life and the risks of societal marginalization to which he is exposed if he loses his home and if he is faced with the perspective of overindebtedness.

With regard to the appreciation of the absence of a right to appeal within the context of the scheme of the enforcement, the Court noted that if the court responsible for issuing the enforcement order appreciates that the enforcement instrument might contain unfair terms, it has to receive the observations of the parties within 15 days and then decide within five days (Article 552(1), point 2 LEC). Thus, the timeframe for deciding on the unfairness is subject to strict constraints. Moreover, the separate procedure in declaratory proceedings that can run in parallel to the enforcement has not been affected by the legislative reform. This means that if the consumer brings the issue of contractual unfairness before the judge of the declaratory proceedings (*juez del declarativo*), the latter still has no *explicit* power to stay the pending enforcement proceedings, except in residual circumstances.[1354]

If the consumer's objection to the enforcement is dismissed, the Spanish civil procedural system:

> exposes consumers, and possibly, as in the case in the main proceedings, their family, to the risk of losing their dwelling in an enforced sale, while the enforcing court may have, at most, delivered a rapid assessment of the validity of the contractual clauses upon which the seller or supplier bases his application.[1355]

The protection offered under the separate declaratory proceedings "cannot offset that risk," since if a term would be found to be unfair, there would be no remedy of restitution in the prior situation, but at best an award of compensation which "would confer on him only incomplete and insufficient protection."[1356]

1353 Case C-169/14 *Morcillo and García* (n. 1248), para. 45.
1354 Ibid., para. 42.
1355 Ibid., para. 43.
1356 Ibid.

It follows that although the absence of an express provision on the powers of the courts in the course of declaratory proceedings to order interim relief under the new legislative regime has not been the object of the *Morcillo and García* case, any limitation on the powers of the courts in that regard would be incompatible with consumer protection. *Aziz* is good law even after the introduction of the new ground of objection based on unfair terms within the framework of the enforcement proceedings. This would mean that the introduction of the new powers of the courts within the framework of enforcement proceedings does not interfere with the necessity of recognition of the *ex officio* powers of the courts (and their power to order measures of interim relief) also within the framework of declaratory proceedings.

In the final part of the reasoning, the issue of this one-sided right to appeal is conceptualized in terms of *procedural imbalance*. The consumer is in a weaker position not only at the stage of formation of the contract, but also at the stage of enforcement of his rights. The crystallization of the procedural imbalance on the basis of contractual imbalance is given shape as follows:

> the imbalance between the procedural rights available to the consumer, on the one hand, and to the seller or supplier on the other hand, simply accentuates the imbalance existing between the parties to the agreement ... and which is also echoed in the context of an individual action involving a consumer and the seller or supplier who is his co-contractor.[1357]

In light of the above, the specific configuration of the proceedings for entering an objection under Spanish mortgage enforcement law was held to be:

> contrary to the principle of equality of arms or procedural equality ... integral element of the principle of effective judicial protection of the rights that individuals derive from EU law, such as that guaranteed by Article 47 of the Charter.[1358]

It was therefore liable to jeopardize the principle of effectiveness "read in conjunction" with Article 47 of the Charter, in that it "reinforces the inequality of arms" between the sellers as mortgage creditors and the consumers as mortgage debtors.[1359] The use of the term "reinforcement" indicates that the design of the procedure was such as to perpetuate and even accentuate the existing imbalance.

In sum, *Morcillo and García* consolidates more than a decade of settled case law on the procedural implications of the Unfair Contract Terms Directive in its function as a source not only of substantive rights for the consumer but also of a procedural framework for the correction of the imbalance perpetuated in

1357 Ibid., para. 46.
1358 Ibid., paras. 48–49.
1359 Ibid., para. 50.

the procedure. Meanwhile, it shows the way forward for a framework of fair process and procedural guarantees that need to exist when the litigation involving the consumer could affect his status as a citizen.

The Spanish legislator intervened quickly following the pronouncement of the judgment in order to amend the provision that was held to be in breach of the effective judicial protection of consumers.[1360] The preamble of the law amending the disputed provision makes explicit reference to the judgment in *Morcillo and García*.[1361] The new provision of Article 695(4) point 1 LEC addresses the former situation of inequality of arms by providing for the right of the mortgage debtor to introduce an appeal against the judgment ordering enforcement.[1362]

#### 3.3.1.2. Limitation Periods for Entering Grounds of Objection in Repossession Proceedings

One of the major improvements of the procedural protection of mortgage debtors brought about by Law 1/2013 was the recognition of their right to enter opposition on the basis of the existence of unfair terms in the enforcement instrument. The time limit to enter such opposition is set at 10 days of service of the enforcement order.[1363] The effect of objection is the suspension of the enforcement proceedings. With regard to pending enforcement proceedings that had not been concluded by the time of the publication of the law, one of the transitional provisions (the fourth) provided that the debtor could enter an objection within a time period of one month following the publication of the law. This was the legal background against

1360 Third final provision, Real Decreto Ley 11/2014 de medidas urgentes en materia concursal (Royal Decree Law 11/2014 on urgent measures in the area of bankruptcy) of 5 September 2014 (BOE No 217 of 6 September 2014).

1361 Ibid., Preamble VI: "La disposición final tercera modifica la Ley 1/2000, de 7 de enero, de Enjuiciamiento Civil, para adaptarla a la reciente Sentencia del Tribunal de Justicia de la Unión Europea de 17 de julio de 2014. Con ello, el deudor hipotecario podrá interponer recurso de apelación contra el auto que desestime su oposición a la ejecución, si ésta se fundaba en la existencia de una cláusula contractual abusiva que constituya el fundamento de la ejecución o la cantidad exigible". [The final third provision modifies Law 1/2000, of 7 January, of the Civil Procedure Code, in order to adapt to the recent judgment of the Court of Justice of 17 July 2014. With this judgment, the mortgage debtor may appeal against a judgment which rejects his opposition to enforcement, if this appeal is founded upon the existence of an unfair term that constitutes the foundation of the enforcement of the amount claimed] (translated by the author).

1362 The new provision reads as follows: "Contra el auto que ordene el sobreseimiento de la ejecución, la inaplicación de una cláusula abusiva o la desestimación de la oposición por la causa prevista en el apartado 1.4. anterior, podrá interponerse recurso de apelación". (Translation: "An appeal may lie against the order discontinuing enforcement, disapplying an unfair term or dismissing the opposition for the reason provided under the previous Art. 1(4) [i.e. objection based on unfair terms]").

1363 Arts. 556.1 and 695.1(2) and (4) LEC.

which *BBVA*[1364] was decided. The issue which arose was the compatibility of the limitation period set out by the transitional provision with Articles 6 and 7 of the Unfair Contract Terms Directive and in particular with the *ex officio* powers of the courts.

The limitation period had to be assessed in the specific context of mortgage repossession proceedings. In the abstract, a limitation period of a month to bring an objection did not appear to be insufficient for the preparation of an effective action. However, the reasoning goes beyond the length of the limitation period as such, extending to the circumstances triggering the period for entering an objection. The particularity of the case was that those consumers caught by the transitional provision had not been *personally informed* of the possibility of raising a new ground of objection on the basis of the potential existence of unfair terms. The notification that they had received before the publication of the new legislative provision referred to the 10-day limitation period to enter an objection, but not to the specific ground of objection with respect to unfair terms (as such a ground did not exist at that time). This meant that this category of consumers could miss the opportunity to benefit from the new protective provisions and that the limitation period for entering an objection could expire for them as they had not been specifically informed of the existence of this new ground of opposition. From this perspective, the Court concluded that the transitional provision infringed the principle of effectiveness to the extent that it deprived some consumer mortgage debtors of effectively and usefully exercising their right derived by the Unfair Contract Terms Directive.

#### 3.3.1.3. The Limits of the *Ex Officio* Doctrine in Influencing Reform of the National Repossession Procedure

It is unlikely that the impact that the Unfair Contract Terms Directive would have upon national procedures could have been foreseen when that instrument was adopted 20 years before the judgment in *Aziz*. The acknowledgment of the procedural difficulties faced by the consumer as a weaker party in litigation was reinforced in the new context of the financial crisis. This was one of a number of circumstances which signaled the transformation of the Unfair Contract Terms Directive into a flagship of effective judicial protection. This observation is particularly relevant in Spain, where the archaic mortgage enforcement law had to govern a galloping foreclosure rate of subprime borrowers or of borrowers whose economic situation has deteriorated due to the crisis. This type of situation and the legacy of *Aziz* led the Spanish judiciary to follow the case law of the Court very closely and to actively engage in a dialogue on those matters. In a constantly rising number of references originating from

[1364] Case C-8/14 *BBVA*, EU:C:2015:731.

Spain, the common theme was the challenge of aspects of national procedural law in the light of the procedural protection of the consumer against the use of unfair terms. The Court, as we have seen so far, has welcomed this wave of references proceeding toward an innovative, "constructive"[1365] and purposive interpretation of the Unfair Contract Terms Directive. However, this interpretation is circumscribed by the scope of the Union legislation determining the extent to which the principle of effectiveness can be used as a standard of compatibility of national legislation with Union law. A case that has shown the limits of the Unfair Contract Terms Directive upon the national procedural laws is *Barclays Bank*.[1366] At the same time, it has probably also exposed the limits of Union legislation overall, which lacked, until the adoption of the Mortgage Credit Directive, a regulatory framework on mortgages. It illustrates part of the problematic that has led finally the Union legislator to set certain parameters for mortgage repossessions.

The core issue in *Barclays Bank* was whether the Unfair Contract Terms Directive could form the basis for providing protection against the personal liability of the mortgage debtor where the property auctioned is obtained by the creditor at a significantly lower price compared to its original valuation. Moreover, the referring court brought forward the disparity in the obligations of the parties, reflected in a "draconian" provision which required the extension of the mortgage to other assets where the valuation of the property would decrease by 20% (for market reasons or as a result of any other circumstances) and which engaged the liability of the debtor if the extension would not be provided for. Before the reform brought about by Law 1/2013, the threshold at which the creditor could be awarded the property in the event of a lack of bidders was set at 50%. Since the reform, there is a special provision for the case when the foreclosed property is the residence of the debtor. The threshold is raised at 70% of the original value or, if the amount owed is lower than that, at 60%.[1367] At the time the reference was made, there was no anti-deficiency protection in the Spanish civil procedural law. The creditor had the right to pursue the shortfall when the proceeds from the property auctioned were proved to be insufficient to cover the outstanding debt.[1368] Anti-deficiency protection in the form of a deed in lieu of foreclosure (or *dación en pago* in Spanish) has been a major demand of Spanish homeowners since the beginning

---

1365 M. Safjan and D. Düsterhaus (n. 1342), 13.

1366 Case C-280/13 *Barclays Bank*, EU:C:2014:279.

1367 Art. 671 LEC.

1368 According to the former version of Art. 579 LEC and Art. 105 Ley Hipotecaria, which provided that the mortgage does not alter the unlimited personal liability of the debtor. Art. 140 Ley Hipotecaria allows the parties to agree that the mortgaged property limits the debtor's liability up to the amount of its value and that no personal liability is engaged further than that. Such agreement had not been made in the case of the debtors in *Barclays Bank* (and it was not common for mortgage contracts to provide for such term).

of the crisis.[1369] It has resulted in a limited right awarded in 2012 only to a very narrowly defined category of homeowner-debtors on the verge of social exclusion ("en el umbral de exclusion").[1370] For all other homeowners, no right of *dación en pago* exists as such, but there is limited anti-deficiency protection subject to the disbursement of a certain percentage of the outstanding debt after foreclosure.[1371] The Royal Decree Law 1/2015,[1372] as part of consumer debt restructuring, introduced a *limited possibility* for mortgage debtors to qualify for the discharge of their mortgage debt in lieu of the mortgaged property in certain circumstances.[1373]

The question put to the Court was in essence seeking to challenge legal rules that place the risk entirely on the consumer of a fall in the price of the mortgaged asset allowing for unlimited liability for the shortfall, on the basis of the principles of consumer protection and contractual balance deriving from the Unfair Contract Terms Directive. The Court pointed out two things. First of all, the Unfair Contract Terms Directive excludes from its scope contractual terms that reflect mandatory provisions of national law, applicable "between the contracting parties where no other arrangement has been agreed"[1374] where "it may legitimately be supposed that the national legislature struck a balance between all the rights and obligations of the parties to certain contracts."[1375]

---

1369 A citizen initiative (*Iniciativa legislative popular*) was submitted by the activist movement of *Plataforma de Afectados por la Hipoteca* urging the government to adopt a law regulating the right of *dación en pago*: Proposición de Ley de regulación de la dación en pago, de paralización de los desahucios y de alquiler social (Legislative Proposal for the regulation of payment in lieu of eviction, the moratorium on foreclosures and social rent) of December 21, 2012 (BOCG B No 102-1 p. 1). This proposal was aiming at a major reform of mortgage repossession when exercised against homeowners. It suggested the addition of a new provision in Art. 693 LEC to the effect that the mortgage debtor could request that the property offsets the debt ("la entrega del bien hipotecado en pago de la deuda"). Morover, according to this proposal the personal action (*ejecución dineraria*) following repossession should be prohibited. It was also proposed to prohibit the initiation of such a procedure against the homeowner who faces an impossibility to pay for reasons which are independent from his will. Finally, the debtor would maintain the right to remain in the residence as a tenant with a monthly rent which could not go beyond 30% of his or her total income. This proposal was not accepted. See also below Chapter 6, Section 1.2.

1370 Real Decreto-ley 6/2012 de medidas urgentes de protección de deudores hipotecarios sin recursos (Royal Decree Law 6/2012 on urgent measures to protect mortgage debtors without resources) of 9 March 2012 (BOE No 60 of 10 March 2012) amended by Chapter IV of Law 1/2013 (n.1333).

1371 Art. 579 LEC.

1372 Real Decreto-ley 1/2015 de mecanismo de segunda oportunidad, reducción de carga financiera y otras medidas de orden social (Royal Decree Law 1/2015 on a second chance mechanism, reduction of financial burden and other measures of social order) of 27 February 2015 (BOE No 51 of 28 February 2015).

1373 See in detail J.M. Fernández Seijo, *La tutela de los consumidores en los procedimientos judiciales, Especial referencia a las ejecuciones hipotecarias* (n. 1202).

1374 Case C-280/13 *Barclays Bank* (n. 1366), para. 42.

1375 Ibid., para. 41.

Second, its case law on the procedural protection of consumers deriving from the Unfair Contract Terms Directive covers situations of limitations on the powers of national courts to raise unfair terms of their own motion. In the main proceedings, none of the provisions at issue was contractual in nature and at the same time none of them related "to the extent of the powers of the national courts to determine whether a contractual term is unfair."[1376]

In view of those considerations, the Court held that the national provisions fell outside the ambit of the Unfair Contract Terms Directive. With regard to the principles of consumer protection to which the national court made reference, the Court clarified that the Unfair Contract Terms Directive is *lex specialis* and gives concrete form to the general principles. Provided that the *lex specialis* was not applicable, a different solution could not be established on the basis of general principles on consumer protection.

The reasoning of *Barclays Bank* was then applied in the Order of the Court in *Banco Popular Español*.[1377] In this case, the referring court entertained doubts as to the compatibility with the Unfair Contract Terms Directive and Articles 38 and 48 of the Charter of a national legislative provision setting out limitations on the right of the debtor to buy back its debt ceded to a third party (Article 1535 of the Civil Code). The Court found that such provision fell outside the scope of the Unfair Terms Directive as, on the one hand, it reflected mandatory legislation and, on the other hand, it did not attempt to govern the scope of the powers of the courts to assess the unfairness of a contractual clause.[1378]

*Barclays Bank* illustrates the limits of resorting to judicial interpretation in order to extrapolate procedural implications out of an instrument (the Unfair Contract Terms Directive) governing substantive contractual relations. It is also the first case to reach the Court dealing in essence with the issue of mortgage release. These are hard policy issues and it would probably go beyond the competences of the Court to strike out such legislation on the basis of the Unfair Contract Terms Directive. The Mortgage Credit Directive is the first legislative instrument which touches upon that subject by going beyond the mere information disclosure model. The fierce political debate in the European Parliament led to a "compromise,"[1379] according to which the deed in lieu of

---

1376 Ibid., para. 39.

1377 Case C-7/16 *Banco Popular Español and PL Salvador*, not published, EU:C:2016:523 (available in French and Spanish).

1378 Ibid., para. 26.

1379 As a Member of the European Parliament (EPP), Mr. Pallone submitted it during the debate in Parliament in the plenary session held in Strasbourg on 10 September 2013. A summary record of the submissions can be found in the Note of the Council of the European Union, 13507/13, Strasbourg, 10 September 2013.

foreclosure is not obligatory, but it is encouraged. According to Article 28(4) of the Mortgage Credit Directive:

> Member States shall not prevent the parties to a credit agreement from expressly agreeing that return or transfer to the creditor of the security or proceeds from the sale of the security is sufficient to repay the credit.

Member States are, however, required to put in place procedures to ensure that the *best efforts price* is obtained for the foreclosed property and that at least some form of anti-deficiency protection exists in the form of measures to facilitate repayment in order to protect consumers where outstanding debt remains.[1380]

Admittedly, the motion for resolution of the European Parliament contained much bolder statements than the final legislative text:

> in the case of mortgage contracts involving the principal home, any evictions or foreclosures arising from defaults in payments due to causes not attributable to the consumer, such as unemployment, should be suspended, applying a moratorium on monthly payments or replacing the mortgage payments with a lease-purchase option on that home, or setting a monthly rent.[1381]

### *3.3.2. Extrajudicial Proceedings and Consumer Protection: Building Upon* Aziz

*Aziz* cast its legacy far beyond the Spanish borders. Two new references, from Slovakia in *Kušionová*[1382] and from Hungary in *Erste Bank Hungary*,[1383] brought to light another aspect that could affect the effective judicial protection of consumers in mortgage repossession proceedings: the compatibility of the extrajudicial avenue of mortgage enforcement with the effective judicial protection of the consumer.[1384] References to *Kušionová* have already been made above[1385] in relation to the appropriate level of procedural guarantees when the mortgage enforcement proceedings are initiated against the principal home of the consumer. In this place, the emphasis is placed on the compatibility of extrajudicial enforcement with consumer law. The common feature in both *Kušionová* and *Erste Bank Hungary* is that the creditor had the possibility to proceed with the enforcement without prior judicial review of the contractual terms upon which the enforcement instrument is based. The difference is

1380 Art. 28 (5) of the Mortgage Credit Directive.

1381 V.M. Garcés Ramón (S&D) *Amendments, A new agenda for European Consumer Policy* (Draft report, 2012/2133 (INI)).

1382 Case C-34/13 *Kušionová*, EU:C:2014:2189.

1383 Case C-32/14 *ERSTE Bank Hungary*, EU:C:2015:637.

1384 See also my contribution on this subject in A. Beka (n. 1278), 255–258.

1385 Section 3.2.2.2.

that the Slovakian case concerned the direct sale of the mortgaged property by the creditor, whereas the Hungarian case concerned the enforcement of a notarial instrument. The possibility of enforcement on the basis of an authentic instrument raised, in turn, the question whether the *ex officio* doctrine extends to the notarial function. It should be noted that the first case where the issue of extrajudicial enforcement arose was *Macinksý*.[1386] This case was removed from the register of the Court at an advanced stage in the proceedings, after the delivery of the Opinion of AG Wahl.[1387] The reference for preliminary ruling in *Kušionová* concerned the same procedural issue. The Court decided without an Opinion, but given the identity of the legal issue, the Opinion in *Macinksý* lay in the background.

Extrajudicial enforcement vests the creditor with a particular procedural advantage to secure a swift and inexpensive realization of the asset pledged. Although in the abstract, such a process can be considered a legitimate means to serve the broader purpose of a healthy mortgage credit market, it could be questioned whether it is still appropriate and proportionate when it is directed against consumers – residential mortgage debtors. The issue becomes particularly pressing in the context of the depressed housing market following the financial crisis. The question that the Court had to answer more specifically was whether such a procedure is compatible with the effective judicial protection of the consumers against unfair terms.

Starting with the analysis of *Kušionová*, it is interesting to note, as a preliminary observation, that the German government had pleaded against the admissibility of the question. It argued that the Unfair Contract Terms Directive concerns only substantive approximation and not the conditions for the enforcement of mortgages. The Court by contrast, held from the outset that the issue raised in the case had all necessary elements to allow for a consideration in light of the right to effective judicial protection (Article 47 of the Charter), even if the relevant provision did not explicitly figure in the question of the national court. The fact that extrajudicial enforcement was based on a contractual clause reflecting mandatory law did not impede the Court in ruling upon its compatibility with Union law. That is so, as the referring court did not raise an issue of unfairness of the specific term (which, according to Article 1(2) of the Unfair Contract Terms Directive, lies outside its scope). The Court was actually asked whether the procedure in place excessively impeded the exercise of the rights that the consumer derives from the Unfair Contract Terms Directive and the judicial powers to ensure that unfair terms are not enforced.[1388]

---

1386 Case C-482/12 *Macinský* was removed from the Register of the Court [2014] OJ C184/22.

1387 The referring court decided to recall the reference, perhaps under the admissibility concerns which AG Wahl addressed in his Opinion in Case C-482/12 *Macinský* (n. 1282).

1388 Interestingly, the same argument on inadmissibility was made by the Spanish Government in Case C-598/15 *Banco Santander*, EU:C:2017:945, para 33. There, the Court distinguished between a question pertaining to the potential unfairness of a term reflecting mandatory

The Court confirmed the compatibility of an extrajudicial mechanism for initiating enforcement for as long as *procedural safeguards* are put in place. Far from giving an abstract "clearing" of all extrajudicial enforcement mechanisms, it considered whether in the particular context of Slovakian civil procedural law, the consumer was deprived of all means of effective judicial protection. The reasoning of the Court is construed around constitutional concepts, the right to effective judicial protection pursuant to Article 47 of the Charter, and the right to protection of the family home pursuant to Article 7 of the Charter. Those considerations of *Kušionová* have already been integrated into the analysis of *Aziz* case above. The decisive element for the Court, which had also been highlighted by AG Wahl, is that this particular procedure gave to the consumer the possibility of judicial protection before as well as after the conclusion of the enforcement. The law empowers the courts to order *interim relief* against ongoing enforcement allowing judicial examination of the question of unfairness of the underlying instrument. After enforcement, the consumer has the right to challenge the sale three months after it has taken place, claiming that the sale be declared void. This would allow full restitution and would not amount to a mere compensatory remedy, as was the case in *Aziz.*[1389]

The position of the Court is that the fact that the consumer has to enter an objection is not *as such* liable to affect judicial protection. In his Opinion in *Macinský*, AG Wahl viewed this as an expression of the minimum threshold of the "test" of effectiveness, as a limitation to procedural autonomy, which requires that national procedural laws do not make the exercise of Union rights impossible or excessively difficult, not that they make their exercise "easy."[1390] Moreover, he considered that "simply by dint of the fact that the property at issue is the consumer's home,"[1391] Member States should not be prevented from requiring that the consumer makes the first move, although the Opinion does stress the necessity of the existence of specific guarantees. The Court reached the same conclusion in *Kušionová*. The starting point is the "total inertia" argument originally spelled out in *Asturcom Telecomunicaciones*,[1392] in the sense that "the need to comply with the principle of effectiveness cannot be stretched so far as to make up fully for the total inertia on the part of the consumer concerned." However, this statement is accompanied by the important caveat that interim measures have to be available by virtue

---

provisions (excluded from the scope of the Unfair Contract Terms Directive) and a question pertaining to the impact of the design of a simplified extrajudicial enforcement procedure on the effectiveness of the protection conferred on consumers, a question on which the Court has certainly jurisdiction to decide.

1389 Case C-34/13 *Kušionová* (n. 1382), paras. 61 and 66.

1390 Opinion of AG Wahl in Case C-482/12 *Macinský* (n. 1282), point 77.

1391 Ibid., point 81.

1392 C-40/08 *Asturcom Telecomunicaciones*, EU:C:2009:615, referred to in Case C-34/13 *Kušionová* (n. 1382), para. 56.

of which unlawful mortgage enforcement proceedings may be suspended or terminated, in the light of the fundamental importance of the protection of one's family home.

The "total inertia" argument also underlies the reasoning of the Court in *Erste Bank Hungary*. This case concerned, more particularly, the compatibility of the simplified notarial enforcement procedure in Hungary with the *ex officio* doctrine due to the fact that the notaries are not vested with the power to review the legality of unfair terms. The referring court nurtured doubts, more particularly, as to the compatibility with Article 7(1) of the Unfair Contract Terms Directive of the national enforcement system, whereby the notary may affix an enforcement clause to an authentic instrument (in the present case the acknowledgment of the mortgaged debt by the debtor) without prior examination of the underlying contract. Drawing a parallel with the establishment of an *ex officio* obligation of the courts to rule *in limine litis* on the unfairness of contractual clauses in payment order proceedings, it asked whether the consumer should have the right to request the cancellation of the notarial enforcement clause on the basis of the absence of a similar examination by the notary. In essence, *Erste Bank Hungary* raised the issue of the extension of the *ex officio* obligation beyond the judicial authorities.

The Commission had taken the view that the similarity of the notarial procedure to the court procedure should imply the extension of the *ex officio* powers. Indeed, it could reasonably be argued that in those legal systems where notaries are afforded powers similar to judicial powers in the enforcement process,[1393] they should also be invested with the same powers in relation to the *ex officio* control of unfair terms. The Court did not share this point of view, following a more nuanced approach. The key reason for not making a pure transposition of its *ex officio* case law to the notaries lies with the fact that this case law "falls within the specific framework of the exercise of the judicial function" and that there are "fundamental differences between [the judicial function] and the notarial function."[1394] On the basis of the aforementioned "total inertia" argument, the Court considered that the fact that the consumer may benefit from the protection on unfair terms only if he brings

1393 The Hungarian law on judicial enforcement provided that a notarized instrument containing the enforcement clause produces the same effect as a judgment of a local court (Case C-32/14 *Erste Bank Hungary* (n. 1383), para. 36). It should be noted that in Hungary, in summary proceedings concerning orders to pay, the notary figures among the national authorities falling within the concept of "court", for the purposes of Regulation (EU) No 1215/2012 of the European Parliament and of the Council of 12 December 2012 on jurisdiction and the recognition and enforcement of judgments in civil and commercial matters [2012] OJ L351/1, to the extent that it has jurisdiction in matters falling within the scope of this Regulation, pursuant to its Art. 3. See Judgment of 9 March 2017, *Pula Parking*, C-551/15, EU:C:2017:193, para. 46.

1394 Case C-32/14 *ERSTE Bank Hungary* (n. 1177), para. 47.

court proceedings ("makes the first move") was not, in itself, contrary to the principle of effectiveness:

> therefore, the fact that the consumer may rely on the protection of legislative provisions on unfair terms only if he brings court proceedings cannot be regarded in itself, contrary to what the Commission argues, as contrary to the principle of effectiveness. The effective legal protection guaranteed by Directive 93/13 is based on the premise that one of the parties to the contract will bring an action before the national courts.[1395]

However, following the Opinion of AG Cruz Villalón, the Court added an important "caveat" to the compatibility with the protection from unfair terms (and with the active consumer court doctrine) of national legislation, which, like the Hungarian one, allows for summary notarial enforcement without prior judicial control. The "safety valve" is the "preventive role with respect to unfair terms" that the notary plays. According to the Hungarian legislation, the notary is required to verify the potential unfairness of a legal transaction and to inform the parties in writing if he entertains any doubt as to its conformity with the law. This is all the more important as "there is a substantial risk that consumers will be less vigilant" when the documents contained potentially unfair terms are drafted by notaries, in view of the particular confidence that they place, as a general rule, in their capacity as impartial advisors.[1396] The Court therefore confirmed the compatibility of the particular system of notarial enforcement with the requirements of effective judicial protection, duly taking into account the safeguards of the whole procedure: first, the notary had an advisory role; and, second, the consumer could initiate proceedings to exclude or limit the enforcement challenging the underlying enforcement instrument (the credit contract).

Following the Court's ruling, the Hungarian referring court[1397] confirmed the legality of the decision of the notary to refuse to cancel the enforcement clause on the basis that it is not the responsibility of the notary to review the potentially unfair character of the contractual clauses. Therefore, the notary was entitled to affix the enforcement clause without proceeding with such a review.

The Court then had the occasion to clarify in the subsequent case *Banco Santander*[1398] that the standards of effective procedural protection at the stage of extrajudicial enforcement proceedings laid out in case law, relate to

1395 Ibid., para. 63.
1396 Ibid., para. 54.
1397 Judgment of 21 October 2015, the summary of which is available in the "Dec.Nat" online database of the ACA Europe (Association of the Councils of State and Supreme Administrative Jurisdictions of the European Union).
1398 Case C-598/15 *Banco Santander*, EU:C:2017:945.

the enforcement of the instrument which potentially contains unfair terms. It does not apply to the stage of enforcement of an instrument of ownership by virtue of which the successful bidder seeks to protect the real rights derived from the title acquired in auction proceedings.

More particularly, in Spain from which the reference for preliminary ruling derived, the extrajudicial enforcement of mortgages was allowed provided that a power of sale was agreed in the enforcement instrument, that certain specific information was stipulated therein and that the relevant term appeared separately from the other terms of the instrument.[1399] Law 1/2013 brought about some modifications to this procedure which were applicable to the extrajudicial sales of mortgaged property beginning after the coming into force of the law.[1400] Two of the most important aspects of this amendment were the introduction of the requirement that the notary shall notify the debtor and the creditor of the existence of unfair terms in the enforcement instrument, and that, the notary shall suspend proceedings when the consumer has challenged the enforcement instrument before the court, alleging the existence of unfair terms.[1401] Another improvement in the direction of reinforcement of the protection of the mortgage debtor (in extrajudicial enforcement proceedings) is that the value of the immovable property, as estimated by the parties, for use as the auction value, cannot go below 75% of the value made in the original appraisal.[1402]

In the case of the main proceedings in *Banco Santander*, the extrajudicial enforcement was commenced and completed before the entry into force of Law 1/2013, by the award of the mortgaged property to the mortgagee (Banco Santander) for 59.7% of the value at which it had been assessed for the purposes

---

1399 Art. 129 (1) of the Decreto de 8 de Febrero 1946 por el que se aprueba la nueva redacción oficial de la Ley Hipotecaria (Decree of 8 February 1946 approving the new official version of the Law on Mortgages) (BOE No 58 of 27 February 1946) and Art. 234 of the Decreto de 14 de febrero de 1947 por el que se aprueba el Reglamento Hipotecario (Decree of 14 February 1947 approving the Mortgage Regulation) (BOE No 106 of 16 April 1947).

1400 See the fifth transitional provision of Ley 1/2013 de medidas para reforzar la protección a los deudores hipotecarios, reestructuración de deuda y alquiler social (Law 1/2013 laying down measures for the strengthening of the protection of mortgagors, the restructuring of debt and social rent (BOE No 116 of 15 May 2013). According to this provision, as far as concerns extrajudicial sales begun before the entry into force of Law 1/2013 and sales where the mortgaged property has not been auctioned, the notary was to suspend enforcement where, within a strict time limit of one month running from the day after the entry into force of Law 1/2013, one of the parties shows that he has brought an action before a competent court, in accordance with Art. 129 of the Law on Mortgages (n. 1399), alleging that one of the terms of the mortgage loan agreement on which the extrajudicial sale is based, or a term determining the amount payable, is unfair (Case C-598/15 *Banco Santander* (n. 1388), para. 12).

1401 Art. 129(2) point (f) of the Law on Mortgages (n. 1399), as modified by Art. 3 of Law 1/2013 (n. 1400).

1402 Art. 129(2) point (a) of the Law on Mortgages (n. 1399), as modified by Art. 3 of Law 1/2013 (n. 1400).

of mortgage enforcement. Moreover, the debtor continued to be personally liable for the outstanding amount. On the basis of the entry into the land register pursuant to the instrument of sale, the bank brought before the referring court a claim seeking an order for "possession" of the dwelling and the ejection of the former mortgage debtor. This court held doubts as to the effectiveness of the protection conferred on consumers under the Unfair Contract Terms Directive in the light of the fact that in the framework of the "possession" procedure, the consumer had no real possibility of successfully claiming that a term in the mortgage enforcement instrument was unfair.

The Court distinguished between the enforcement of the mortgage guarantee and the enforcement pertaining to the protection of real rights lawfully acquired following a sale by auction. Even if those rights were acquired by means of extrajudicial enforcement of a mortgage instrument which might have contained unfair terms and escaped judicial control, the present proceedings were no longer initiated on the basis of this instrument but on the basis of the instrument of ownership as entered in the land register.[1403] The judgment was sensible to the fact that the person acting in the capacity of the owner of the immovable property at issue was identical to the mortgage creditor. Nonetheless, following an extrajudicial enforcement procedure, any interested third party may become the owner of the property and, as a result, bring proceedings for possession. For the sake of legal certainty, the Court therefore found that:

> in such circumstances, to allow the debtor who has granted a mortgage over that property to set up defences founded on the mortgage loan agreement against the transferee of that property, an agreement to which that transferee may nevertheless be a third party, would be liable to affect legal certainty in pre-existing proprietary relationships.[1404]

Yet the Court stresses out the importance of procedural safeguards during the extrajudicial enforcement procedure, by observing that the mortgage debtor appeared to have had the opportunity, at the time of such procedure, to challenge the enforcement instrument or seek a suspension of the procedure on the ground that the mortgage loan contained unfair terms, and to apply for interim measures so as to suspend the sale of her dwelling.[1405] It was in the course of such procedure (which should have been, however, initiated by the debtor herself) that the court seised would have been in the position to carry out a review of the potential unfairness of the terms stipulated in the mortgage loan agreement.

---

1403 Case C-598/15 *Banco Santander* (n.1398), paras. 42–44 and 46.
1404 Ibid., para. 45.
1405 Ibid., para. 49.

The Court did not have to deal with the question of the powers of the courts in proceedings brought by a mortgage creditor to claim an outstanding mortgage amount after the sale of a property. Such proceedings would be based on the mortgage enforcement instrument. Therefore, it could reasonably be argued that when a creditor pursues a default judgment on that basis, the courts "regain" their power to review the enforcement instrument for the existence of unfair terms. National procedural provision which would restrict judicial powers in such proceedings would be liable to violate the effectiveness of the protection conferred by the Unfair Contract Terms Directive.

From the case law on extrajudicial enforcement proceedings, it follows that the compatibility of such proceedings with the effectiveness of consumer judicial protection under the Unfair Contract Terms Directive cannot be considered in the abstract, but must be considered in relation to the procedural guarantees with which they are accompanied. The issues addressed by the Court have not been, admittedly, easy ones. In its reasoning, it had to reach a balance which would be reasonable from both the perspective of the competence of Member States to organize their systems of enforcement and from the perspective of the effective protection of the consumer. However, the question of principle, whether it is appropriate and proportionate to repossess without an order of the court, remains open for the Member States to decide. The Opinion of AG Wahl in *Macinský* had pointed out the parameter of the costs that an *ex ante* judicial review would imply for the professionals "even where the contract at issue does not contain unfair terms."[1406] Even worse, the costs of the proceedings could be shifted by standard contractual clauses to the mortgage debtor.[1407]

On the other hand, dispossessing homeowners without prior review entails certain risks for the protection of the mortgage debtor. The consumer as a party in individual litigation is not considered to be a resourceful litigant and according to the case law of the Court, the imbalance has to be redressed through positive action by the national courts. As such, it should not be consistent to assume that the consumer will be aware of his rights in the course of extrajudicial proceedings and he will challenge the enforcement instrument in court. The "total inertia" argument in those cases seems to have a certain negative connotation of moral reproach and of indifference. However, the indifference assumption, particularly when enforcement concerns the family home, does not seem plausible and does not easily correspond to empirical evidence on the profile of overindebted consumers. Studies demonstrate that the causes of indebtedness

1406 Opinion of AG Wahl in Case C-482/12 *Macinský* (n. 1282), note 43.

1407 *See* L. Whitehouse, 'A Longitudinal Analysis of the Mortgage Repossession Process 1995–2010: Stability, Regulation And Reform', *in* S. Bright (Ed.), *Modern Studies in Property Law*, (Oxford, Hart Publishing, 2011), 151–174, p. 151, who explains that the practice of English banks in mortgage contracts is to shift the cost of the procedure to the mortgage, thus adding to the financial burden of the borrower.

have roots in shocks to household income such as unemployment, illness, loss of earnings or relationship breakdown.[1408] The sense of "defeat" and impotence due to the "debt-spiral" can lead the consumer to forego legal protection before even knowing that the instrument enforced against him contains unfair terms, a factor which can have actually contributed to his overindebtedness. The fact that the consumer faces financial difficulties might deter him to seek for advice so as not to pay further legal costs for a "lost case." The empirical study undertaken by Susan Bright and Lisa Whitehouse demonstrates that even where a prior court order is sought, there are barriers to borrower attendance in court.[1409] Maybe among the most "embarrassing" for the rule of law are the barriers that have been identified in this study as arising out of "fear or misunderstanding of the legal system" and out of the "acceptance of what is perceived as an unfair system." In such circumstances, it is more likely that the enforcement instrument will escape judicial control.

It is relevant in context to note that in England, although the lender has a power of sale without prior court order, it is a practice that lenders will not resort to.[1410] In 2009, a bill was proposed (which did not become an Act of Parliament), entitled the Home Repossession Protection Bill, which made it mandatory that eviction takes place only following an order of the court. Scotland offers an example of a more progressive stance on the issue. Under the Home Owner and Debtor Protection Act 2010 (Scotland), repossession is not possible without a warrant from the court, save for specified circumstances of voluntary surrender.[1411] Such voluntary surrender allows extrajudicial enforcement in circumstances in which the security subject is unoccupied and the debtor consents to the creditor's exercise of his enforcement rights upon the debtor's default. However, the creditor proceeding with a voluntary surrender has to certify that the consent was "given freely and without coercion of any kind."[1412] It would, therefore, probably appear that a standard contractual clause

---

1408 See the study of Citizens Advice Bureau, Advice UK, and Shelter, *Turning the Tide? Evidence from the free advice sector on mortgage and secured loan possession actions in England in July 2009*, December 2009; A. Wallace and J. Ford, "Limiting Possessions? Managing Mortgage Arrears in a New Era" (2010) 10:2 *International Journal of Housing Policy* 133–154; T. Wilhelmsson, "Social Force Majeure" – A New Concept in Nordic Consumer Law" (1990) 13 *Journal of Consumer Policy* 1–14.

1409 S. Bright and L. Whitehouse, *Information, Advice & Representation in Housing Possession Cases*, 25 April 2014, University of Oxford, University of Hull (available in the website of the University of Oxford <https://www.law.ox.ac.uk/sites/files/oxlaw/housing_possession_report_april2014.pdf>, last accessed 15 January 2018).

1410 *Horsham Properties Group Ltd v Clark and Others* [2008] EWHC 2327 (Ch), stirred a fierce debate as the lender repossessed without a court order. The case was quite exceptional, because it was a buy-to-let property but in which the mortgagors finally resided.

1411 Home Owner and Debtor Protection (Scotland) Act 2010, Part 1, para. 1 entitled "Residential standard securities: restriction of creditor's remedies".

1412 Ibid., Sec. 1(3)(1)(b)(iii).

in the mortgage contract, according to which the mortgage debtor consents to extrajudicial enforcement upon default, would not be sufficient alone to prove voluntary surrender. Instead of the borrower having to obtain suspension of possession, the burden is shifted to the lender to seek a court order justifying his compliance with the pre-action forbearance requirements.

This approach departs from a *new procedural ethos* that governs the field of residential repossession and that takes due account of the constitutional dimensions involved. Procedural advantages that were set in a different era of mortgage lending now have to pass strong tests of due process when they are employed within the context of residential mortgages.

## 3.4. SUBSTANTIVE GUIDELINES ON THE CONCEPT OF UNFAIRNESS

The second part of the reference for preliminary ruling in *Aziz* was seeking the Court's guidance on the application of the unfairness concept upon three types of contractual terms. To be more precise, the referring court employed the concept of "disproportion."[1413] The Court understood the question more broadly as seeking to flesh out the concepts of "significant imbalance" and "good faith" laid down in the Unfair Contract Terms Directive. In that regard, two yardsticks are identified. The first one lies upon a *comparative analysis* with the national law that would be applicable by default. The second one is what Hans Micklitz and Norbert Reich call the "reasonable supplier standard"[1414] based on a consideration of what the consumer would have agreed if he would have individually negotiated the contract. The standards of "significant imbalance" and "good faith" were examined separately.[1415]

It will be recalled that the landmark judgment setting the extent and degree of involvement of the Court in the concretization of the test of unfairness is

1413 The Opinion of AG Kokott in C-415/11 *Aziz* (n. 1232), point 59, observes that this term reflects the terminology of point 1(e) of the Annex. As this point refers to disproportion only with regard to the payment of sums in case of failure to fulfill obligations, it had to be understood as seeking an interpretation of the overall concept of "imbalance".

1414 H.-W. Micklitz and N. Reich, "The Court and Sleeping Beauty: The Revival of the Unfair Contract Terms Directive" (2014) 51 *CMLR* 771–808, 790.

1415 *Cf.* H. Collins, "Good Faith in European Contract Law" (1994) 14 *Oxford Journal of Legal Studies* 229–254, at 249, who discerns a "*substantive fairness*" yardstick under the concept of "good faith" and a "*procedural fairness*" yardstick under the concept of "significant imbalance". In *Director General of Fair Trading v First National Bank Plc* [2001] UKHL 52; [2002] 1 A.C. 481 per Lord Bingham of Cornhill, para. 17, it is stated that both standards seem to form a "*composite test covering both the making and the substance of the contract*". Lord Steyn recalls the classification of H. Collins (ibid.), while observing at para. 37 that: "It is however, also right to say that there is a large area of overlap between the concepts of good faith and significant imbalance".

*Freiburger Kommunalbauten.*[1416] In this judgment, the Court introduced the "theory of judicial restraint,"[1417] clarifying that it would interpret the "general criteria" of the legislation without proceeding with a concrete assessment of the unfairness of a given term. The national court is better placed to carry out this task. This position appeared to contradict with the categorical assessment of unfairness of the exclusive jurisdiction clause in *Océano Grupo*. However, the Court explained that the latter case concerned a situation where the term obviously undermined the effectiveness of the rights afforded to the consumer and that therefore it had been possible to decide on its unfairness without the need to consider all the circumstances of the contract. Subsequent case law would seem to follow a middle path[1418] in between *Freiburger Kommunalbauten* restraint and *Océano Grupo* exhaustiveness. The role of the Annex to the Unfair Contract Terms Directive has been an "essential element"[1419] in the case law of the Court for lighting this path. In *Aziz*, the Court provides for guidance in order to superimpose, on the balance between abstraction and precision, "common standards of control"[1420] that go beyond the individualized circumstances of the contract in question. In their analysis of the case law of the Court on the concept of unfairness, Hans Micklitz and Norbert Reich put forward the thesis of the advancement of an "autonomous definition" of the concept.[1421]

### *3.4.1. Significant Imbalance: The National Rule Benchmark*

An important criterion identified by the Court which could indicate a shift in the contractual balance is the content of the national rule that would be

---

1416 Case C-237/02 *Freiburger Kommunalbauten*, EU:C:2004:209.

1417 H.-W. Micklitz, "Unfair Terms in Consumer Contracts" in N. Reich et al. (eds.), *European Consumer Law* (Cambridge, Intersentia, 2nd ed., 2014), 150.

1418 S. Weatherill, *EU Consumer Law and Policy* (Cheltenham, Edward Elgar, 2013), 153, talks about a mix of both judgments.

1419 Case C-472/10 *Invitel*, EU:C:2012 242, para. 23: "If the content of the annex does not suffice in itself to establish automatically the unfair nature of a contested term, it is nevertheless an essential element on which the competent court may base its assessment as to the unfair nature of that term". In this way, according to H.-W. Micklitz, "Unfair Terms in Consumer Contracts" in N. Reich et al. (eds.) (n. 1417), 158–159 and H.-W. Micklitz and N. Reich, "The Court and Sleeping Beauty" (n. 1251), 789, the indicative list is "*gaining importance as an overall benchmark in consumer contracts*".

1420 Ibid.

1421 Ibid. See also G. Straetmans and C. Cauffmann, "Legislatures, courts and the Unfair Terms Directive" in P. Syrpis (ed.), *The Judiciary, the Legislature and the EU Internal Market* (Cambridge, 2012), arguing that the Court "should give more substantive guidance as to which terms, taking into account the specific legal and factual context, may be unfair in view of re-establishing the effective balance between the rights and obligations of the parties to the contract".

applicable by default, in the absence of an agreement by the parties in that regard.:

> such a comparative analysis will enable the national court to evaluate whether and, as the case may be, to what extent, the contract places the consumer in a legal situation less favourable than that provided for by the national law in force.[1422]

A deviation from the statutory provision will not automatically lead to unfairness, but it can be one of a number of other "circumstances attending the conclusion of the contract," which will, according to Article 4 of the Unfair Contract Terms Directive, lead to the conclusion that an unfair contractual balance has been tilted to the detriment of the consumer. According to the Opinion of AG Kokott in *Aziz*, this approach ensures the observance of the principle of contractual freedom, also allowing for derogations from the provision applicable by default.[1423] The Court added that in assessing the derogation from national law as a criterion of significant imbalance, it should also be considered what means the consumer has at his disposal under national legislation to prevent the continued use of unfair terms.[1424]

Further precisions on the use of the national statutory rule as a benchmark to assess the criterion of *significant imbalance* were given in *Constructora Principado.*[1425] In that case, the term in question concerned the transfer of a tax liability arising from the capital gains on the sale of a dwelling to the consumer, whereas under the applicable national legislation that liability would be allocated to the seller. According to the Court, the analysis of unfairness should concentrate upon:

> a sufficiently serious impairment of the legal situation in which the consumer, as a party to the contract in question, is placed by reason of the relevant national provisions, whether this be in the form of a restriction of the rights which, in accordance with those provisions, he enjoys under the contract, or a constraint on the exercise of those rights, or the imposition on him of an additional obligation not envisaged by the national rules.[1426]

---

1422 Case C-415/11 *Aziz* (n. 1201), para. 68. H.-W. Micklitz and N. Reich (n. 1251), 791 concur with this approach of the Court. They cite views that have been expressed in literature, namely that of K. Riesenhuber, *EU-Vertragsrecht* (Tubingen, Mohr, 2013), para. 10.23, who supports that comparison with default provisions of national law should be the primary criterion. M. Schmidt, *Konkretisierung von Generalklauseln im europäischen privatrecht* (Berlin, De Gruyter, 2009), 248, favors an autonomous concept of unfairness which can only exceptionally be modified by reference to national law.

1423 Opinion of AG Kokott in Case C-415/11 *Aziz* (n. 1232), point 73.

1424 Case C-415/11 *Aziz* (n. 1201), para. 68.

1425 Case C-226/12 *Constructora Principado*, EU:C:2014:10.

1426 Ibid., para. 22.

The extent of deviation from the national measure bringing along a "sufficiently serious impairment" to the legal situation of the consumer is an objective yardstick. However, it remains possible for the seller to bring forward proof to the effect that the structure of rights involved in the contract reveals behind the contractual deviation a genuine and fair bargain reflected in the total price. On the other hand, a simple statement from the seller to that effect in the contract "does not of itself constitute proof of consideration which the consumer would have benefited from."[1427]

The consideration of the extent of derogation from national law is presented in *Aziz* as one element among others that can have an impact on the appreciation of unfairness. It does not appear to be, as Sara Iglesias Sánchez notes, an "insurmountable"[1428] criterion in the sense of excluding the unfairness assessment where there would be *no derogation* from national law. This would require, in turn, a strict interpretation of the concept of "mandatory statutory or regulatory provisions," which when reflected in a contractual term are excluded from the scope of the Unfair Contract Terms Directive. The analysis of the concept of "mandatory statutory or regulatory provisions" made in *RWE Vertrieb*[1429] is also relevant in the context of *Aziz*. In *RWE Vertrieb*, it was clarified that the rules which are excluded from the assessment of unfairness are those which apply between the contracting parties "independently of their choice" or "by default in the absence of other arrangements established by the parties."[1430]

It is important to note in that regard that the first of the disputed contractual clauses, the acceleration clause in the case of default of one single installment, *reflected* the national provision applicable *at the time* (before amendment by Law 1/2013). This provision allowed the mortgage creditor to call in the totality of the debt in the event of the default of *any* installment for as long as it has been *so agreed* by the parties and this agreement had been recorded in the property register.[1431] This parameter was not submitted explicitly to the Court.[1432]

1427 Ibid., para. 29.

1428 S.I. Sánchez, "Unfair terms in mortgage loans and protection of housing in times of economic crisis: *Aziz v. Catalunyacaixa*" (2014) 51 *CMLR* 955–974, 969.

1429 Case C-92/11 *RWE Vertrieb*, EU:C:2013:180. There the Court ruled that a clause which reproduces a rule of national law but which is, however, applicable to another category of contracts not subject to the national legislation concerned, cannot be excluded from the scope of the Unfair Terms Directive. In Joined Cases C-359/11 and C-400/11 *Shulz and Ebringhoff*, EU:C:2014:2317, by contrast, where the contractual clause in question reflected the same mandatory national law provision as in *RWE* on the termination of an energy contract, the clause was held to be excluded by the scope of the Directive.

1430 Case C-92/11 *RWE Vertrieb* (n. 1429), para. 26.

1431 Former Art. 693(2) LEC (original text): "Podrá reclamarse la totalidad de lo adeudado por capital y por intereses si se hubiese convenido el vencimiento total en caso de falta de pago de alguno de los plazos diferentes y este convenio constase inscrito en el Registro."

1432 In Case C-280/13 *Barclays Bank* (n. 1366), the question was put in terms of an assessment of the unfairness of provisions of national law directly.

If it would have been, the question which would probably arise would be whether the clause reflected "mandatory provisions of national law" so as to escape from the scope of the Unfair Contract Terms Directive. On the basis of the explanations provided under the 13th recital, it could be considered that the clause on acceleration should not be excluded from the scope of unfairness review as the relevant provision of Spanish law could only apply *if the parties have so agreed*. Alignment with national law will thus not automatically mean that the respective term would have to be excluded from the scope of the Directive. The consideration of national law as a starting point but not an "insurmountable" criterion is exemplified in the question regarding the assessment of unfairness of the last disputed clause (referred to in the second question for preliminary reference in *Aziz*) pertaining to the unilateral quantification of the debt. There, the clause reflected the national law, but this legislation was not mandatory and the parties could derogate.

### 3.4.2. *Good Faith: Fair and Equitable Dealing as if There Would Have Been Negotiation*

The understanding of the criterion of *good faith* by the Court is a more concrete explanation of the preamble (no 16) of the Unfair Contract Terms Directive worded as follows: "the requirement of good faith may be satisfied by the seller or supplier where he deals fairly and equitably with the other party whose legitimate interests he has to take into account." In this vein, the Court held that: "the national court must assess for those purposes whether the seller or supplier, dealing fairly and equitably with the consumer, could reasonably assume that the consumer would have agreed to such a term in individual contractual negotiations." The seller is then obliged to take into account the weaker bargaining position of the consumer and not to impose terms which could not *reasonably* be expected as an outcome of negotiation between equals. Commenting on this criterion, Hans Micklitz and Norbert Reich observe that the seller "cannot simply pursue his own business interests of contractual efficiency against the legitimate expectations of the consumer."[1433]

[1433] H.W. Micklitz and N. Reich (n. 1419), 790. The guidance given in the famous banking litigation case of the House of Lords in *Director General of Fair Trading v First National Bank plc* [2001] UKHL 52, is very instructive for the concretisation of what should be expected from a supplier: "Fair dealing requires that a supplier should not, whether deliberately or unconsciously, take advantage of the consumer's necessity, indigence, lack of experience, unfamiliarity with the subject matter of the contract, [or] weak bargaining position … Good faith in this context is not an artificial or technical concept; nor, since Lord Mansfield was its champion, is it a concept wholly unfamiliar to British lawyers. It looks to good standards of commercial morality and practice."

### 3.4.3. *Application of the Criteria for Appreciation of Unfairness with Regard to the Disputed Contractual Terms*

The referring Spanish court was seeking the guidance of the Court in its assessment of unfairness with regard to three contractual stipulations: the acceleration clause (*vencimiento anticipado*),[1434] the default interest rate exceeding 18% and the unilateral determination of the unpaid debt.

The first term concerned the right of the mortgage lender to terminate the contract and to call in the totality of the loan in the case of default occurring within a limited period of time.[1435] It is interesting to mention the position of the Commission, which had argued that the term should be considered as "manifestly effective, since the non-payment of even one installment constitutes a breach of the borrower's main contractual obligation and the lender cannot reasonably be expected to adhere further to the agreement."[1436]

However, the Court (also following the Opinion of AG Kokott) adopted a balancing approach bearing in mind the long-term nature of the mortgage contract – or, better yet, its "life-time"[1437] nature – while "giving shape"[1438] to the content of the indicative "gray" list of the Annex.[1439] The national court should assess in particular the *seriousness of non-compliance* in light of the term and the amount of the loan, the extent of derogation from the national applicable rules so as to make it more difficult for the consumer, given the procedural means at his disposal, to take legal action and to exercise the rights of defense and the options available to him by law to remedy the effects of the unilateral cancellation of the loan.[1440] In her Opinion, AG Kokott adds one

1434 Further clarifications on the unfairness assessment of the acceleration clause were also the subject of a question in the second of the Joined Cases C-537/12 and C-116/13 *Banco Popular Español* and *Banco de Valencia*, EU:C:2013:164.

1435 The clause of the loan agreement provided that default of even *one* of the total 396 monthly installments gave the bank the right to call in the totality of the loan.

1436 The position of the Commission as reproduced in the Opinion of AG Kokott in Case C-415/11 *Aziz* (n. 1232), point 70.

1437 L. Nogler and U. Reifner, *Life Time Contracts, Social Longterm Contracts in Labour, Tenancy and Consumer Credit Law* (The Hague, Eleven International Publishing, 2014).

1438 H.-W. Micklitz, "Unfair Terms in Consumer Contracts" in N. Reich et al. (eds.) (n. 1417), para. 3.26.

1439 Point 1(g) deems unfair terms as those which have the object or effect of "enabling the seller or supplier to terminate a contract of indeterminate duration without reasonable notice except where there are serious grounds for doing so".

1440 Case C-415/11 *Aziz* (n. 1201), para. 73 and Order of the Court in Joined Cases C-537/12 and C-116/13*Banco Popular Español* (n. 1234), para. 70. With respect to the means the consumer has at his disposal to remedy the effects of the loan being called in, it is of particular relevance, according to the Opinion of AG Kokott in Case C-415/11 *Aziz* (n. 1232) para. 78, that the borrower had the possibility according to Art. 693(3) LEC to eliminate the effects of termination of the loan. It is important to note that for the adoption of this provision an important role was played by the judgment of the Tribunal Supremo de 27 de marzo 1999,

more element against the background of which the extent of seriousness of non-compliance has to be tested. This element is the importance of the loan for the *existence* of the borrower ("seine existenzielle Bedeutung"). This is a crucial reference to the underlying value of the asset in question, the home of the consumer, satisfying an "essential need"[1441] necessary for the "self-realization" of his personality in the society.[1442] Framing housing in terms of *existence* maybe also draws influence from the German Constitutional Court (*Bundesverfassungsgericht – BVerfG*) case law with respect to the necessity of ensuring the fundamental right to a minimum subsistence in line with human dignity ("das Grundrecht auf Gewährleistung eines menschenwürdigen Existenzminimums"). In one of its latest famous judgments which links the minimum subsistence guarantee to a fundamental right entitlement,[1443] the BVerfG highlighted the necessity of positive protection of human dignity, enshrined in Article 1.1 of the *Grundgesetz,* in conjunction with the principle of the social state under Article 20.1 of the *Grundgesetz.* The guarantee encompasses the material conditions indispensable for a person's physical existence, namely food, clothing, household goods, *housing*, heating, hygiene and health, which then further allow for a minimum level of participation in social, cultural and political life.

Following reform by Law 1/2013, the acceleration of the entire mortgage debt is still provided as a possibility to be agreed by the parties but the default has to amount to at least three monthly installments.[1444] In a judgment of the Plenary in 2015, the Spanish Supreme Court (*Tribunal Supremo*)[1445] ruled that once a term on acceleration in a mortgage contract due to failure to pay one single installment is declared unfair, the court may still allow the continuation of the mortgage enforcement proceedings and apply the supplementary provision of national law according to which the right of the creditor to call in the totality of the loan is subject to default of at least three monthly installments, provided that an express agreement of the parties exists. In this case, the continuation of the mortgage enforcement proceedings would, in particular, be allowed where the court, taking into account the criteria of appraisal of the unfairness of an acceleration clause as enounced in *Aziz*, would consider that the consumer would be better off than if the mortgage enforcement proceedings would be stayed and if the

---

for the discussion of which see J. M. Fernández Seijo, *La defensa de los Consumidores en las ejecuciones hipotecarias* (Dordrecht, Wolters Kluwer, 2013).

1441 Case C-488/11 *Asbeek Brusse*, EU:C:2013: 341.

1442 See L. Nogler and U. Reifner, "Introduction: the new dimension of life time in the law of contracts and obligations" in L. Nogler and U. Reifner (eds.) (n. 1437), 29–83, 34.

1443 BVerfG, 1 BvL 1/09 of 9 February 2010.

1444 Article 693 (2) LEC.

1445 Judgment No 705/2015 of 23 December 2015, STS 5618/2015, ES:TS:2015:5618, followed by judgment No 79/2016 of 18 February 2016, STS 626/2016 ES:TS:2016:626.

creditor would instead initiate ordinary civil law proceedings to terminate the contract.[1446]

The second term in question concerned the fixing of an annual default interest rate of 18.75% automatically applicable to sums not paid when due without the need for prior notice. The question of the unfairness of a clause on default interest (at an annual rate of 91.22% (!)) also arose in *Pohotovost*.[1447] In the latter case, the Court made reference to point 1(e) of the Annex of the Unfair Contract Terms Directive according to which a term is considered unfair when the consumer who fails to fulfill his obligations is required to pay a *disproportionately high sum* in compensation. Further precision was given in *Aziz*, which employed a method of comparison to the applicable national rule by default. The national court must therefore consider:

> the rate of default interest laid down compared with the statutory interest rate in order to determine whether it is appropriate for securing the attainment of the objectives pursued by it in the Member State concerned and does not go beyond what is necessary to achieve them.[1448]

In her Opinion, AG Kokott illustrated further the criterion of comparison to statutory interest rate. The fact that Spanish law limits default interest to 2.5 times the statutory interest rate in the case of other consumer loans could be an indication of a possible imbalance, also taking due account of the fact that the bank's refinancing costs for mortgage loans are generally much lower due to the security provided compared to other consumer loans.[1449] On the purpose of the default rate, AG Kokott observed that if it is intended merely as a flat-rate compensation for damage caused by default, then there is a situation of disproportionality as the actual damage is exceeded. If it has the purpose of deterrence of default, then it should be regarded as unfair if it is much higher than necessary to achieve that aim.[1450]

Following reform by Law 1/2013 a cap has been set on default interest rates applicable to residential mortgage credits. The amended Article 114 of the Law on Mortgages (Ley Hipotecaria) provides that:

> default interest on loans or credits for the purchase of a habitual dwelling, secured by mortgages charged on the dwelling in question, may not be more than three times the statutory rate of interest and may accrue only on the outstanding principal.

1446 The Tribunal Supremo has submitted a reference for preliminary ruling to the Court in the pending (at the time of writing) Case C-70/17 *Abanca Corporación Bancaria* [2017] OJ C 121/17, quering on the compatibility with the Unfair Contract Terms Directive of its own line of case law on the acceleration clause.

1447 Order of the Court in Case C-76/10 *Pohotovost'*, EU:C:2010:685.

1448 Case C-415/11 *Aziz* (n. 1201), para. 74.

1449 Opinion of AG Kokott in Case C-415/11 *Aziz* (n. 1232), point 85.

1450 Ibid., point 87.

Such default interest may not in any circumstances be capitalised, except in the case provided for in Article 579(2)(a) of the Law on Civil Procedure.

This provision is, however, without prejudice to the powers of the courts to rule on the unfairness of clauses setting the default interest rate below this threshold, as the Court clarified in *Unicaja Banco*.[1451] In order to ensure consistency of interpretation of default interest rate clauses by lower jurisdictions, the *Tribunal Supremo*, in a series of cases decided in 2015 and 2016,[1452] set up a threshold of twice the statutory interest as sufficient to establish the unfairness of a default interest rate stipulated in a consumer credit contract (unsecured or mortgage credit contract).[1453] In that regard, explicit reference was made to the criteria pronounced in *Aziz* with regard to the assessment of unfairness of a clause fixing a default interest rate.[1454]

The Mortgage Credit Directive would appear to reflect the considerations made in *Aziz* with regard to the issue of proportionality of default charges. Article 28(2) of the Directive departs from the logic of a *compensatory* function of default charges, with regard to which Member States may provide that they "are no greater than is necessary to compensate the creditor for costs it has incurred as a result of the default." Article 28(3) provides that in the event that Member States allow for default charges, a cap should be put in place.

The last term examined concerned the clause on unilateral determination by the lender of the amount owed (*liquidación unilateral*). On the basis of this term, the lender may initiate simplified mortgage enforcement proceedings and the debtor cannot challenge the quantification, unless he resorts to the declaratory

1451 Joined Cases C-482/13, C-484/13, C-485/13 and C-487/13 *Unicaja Banco and Caixabank*, EU:C:2015:21. The Court ruled that a national provision under which the national court hearing mortgage enforcement proceedings is required to adjust the amounts due under a term in a mortgage-loan contract providing for default interest at a rate more than three times greater than the statutory rate in order that the amount of that interest may not exceed that threshold, is compatible with the Unfair Contract Terms Directive provided that the application of that national provision a) is without prejudice to the assessment by that national court of the unfairness of such a term and b) does not prevent that court removing that term if it were to find the latter to be 'unfair', within the meaning of Article 3(1) of that Directive. *See* Chapter 4, Section 5.2.2.

1452 With regard to personal (unsecured) consumer credit contracts TS Judgment No 265/2015 of 22 April 2015, STS 1723/2015, ES:TS:2015:1723 (plenary); Judgment No 470/2015 of 7 September 2015, STS 3828/2015, ES:TS:2015:3828 and Judgment No 469/2015 of 8 September 2015, STS 3829/2015, ES:TS:2015:3829. With regard to mortgage consumer credit contracts Judgment No 705/2015 (n.1445); Judgment No 79/2016 (n.1445); Judgment No 364/2016 of 3 June 2016, STS 2401/2016, ES:TS:2016:2401 (plenary).

1453 In the second reference for preliminary ruling in the pending (at the time of writing) Joined Cases C-96/16 and C-94/17 *Banco Santander and Escobedo Cortés* [2016] OJ C 145/24, the *Tribunal Supremo* brought before the Court the question of compatibility of its own line of case law on default interest rates with Union law on consumer protection.

1454 See STS 1723/2015 and in particular point 3 of the the part pertaining to the unfair nature of default interest rates (*interés de demora*).

proceedings which have no suspending effect upon repossession. The lender is given a quick and easy way of realizing the security without, however, a counterbalance being reflected upon the provision of effective means for the borrower's defense. The Court provided its assessment in light of point 1(q) of the Annex of the Unfair Contract Terms Directive pertaining to clauses that hinder the consumer's right to take legal action. It guided the referring court in that it:

> must in particular assess whether and, if appropriate, to what extent, the term in question derogates from the rules applicable in the absence of agreement between the parties, so as to make it more difficult for the consumer, given the procedural means at his disposal, to take legal action and exercise [his] rights of the defense.

In the specific national procedural context, there was no derogation from the national provision as the Law on Mortgages provided that the parties could agree on unilateral quantification.[1455] However, this was not a provision applicable by default, since it required the agreement of the parties. The Court therefore implicitly confirmed that the derogation from a legal provision which is merely facilitative and requires the intervention of private autonomy does not exclude the assessment of unfairness.

### 3.4.4. *The Decision of the National Court*

Mr Aziz, the mortgage debtor, initiated the declaratory proceedings before the referring court after the auction of the dwelling had taken place, but shortly before his eviction. The national judgment rendered following the decision of the Court ruled on the impact of the existence of unfair terms in the enforcement instrument upon the legality of the enforcement procedure that was already closed, upon the personal action for the remaining debt and also upon the issue of damages. The decision was given by the *Jugzado de lo Mercantil 3 de Barcelona.*[1456] Some key points of this ruling will be summarized here.

The national court considered the subjective circumstances of the loan and the personal circumstances of the debtor. First of all, the property had been

---

1455 Art. 153bis Ley Hipotecaria (original text): "Podrá pactarse en el título que la cantidad exigible en caso de ejecución sea la resultante de la liquidación efectuada por la entidad financiera acreedora en la forma convenida por las partes en la escritura".

1456 Roj SJM B 21/2013, No de Recurso 13/2011 de 02/05/2011. See Consejo General del Poder Judicial, *Noticias Judiciales TSJ Cataluña*, jueves 16 de majo de 2013 (General Council of the Judiciary, *Judicial News TSJ Catalonia*, Thursday 16 March 2013), available from the CGPJ Portal <http://www.poderjudicial.es/cgpj/es/Poder-Judicial/Tribunal-Supremo/Portal-de-Transparencia/> accessed 02.10.2017.

valued at an excessive price.[1457] The bank granted the loan entirely aware of the precarious situation and the limited creditworthiness of the debtor, a worker who was the sole breadwinner of his family with an estimated income of approximately €1,100 net per month. As from the beginning of the mortgage crisis in 2008, the consumer had to disburse 70% (!) of the net family income in order to repay the mortgage. At the moment of enforcement of the mortgage loan, the consumer was unemployed. The property had been adjudicated at only 50% of its original valuation.

In his application, the consumer had challenged the validity of only one clause – the one referring to the unilateral determination of the debt by the credit institution. However, the referring court extended the control as to the validity of two more terms (the conditions for acceleration of payment of the loan and the default interest). The credit institution contested such an extension of the scope of the dispute. Recalling the settled Union case law on the *ex officio* doctrine, the national ruling confirmed its power to extend the scope of control to other terms closely connected to the contested term, pointing out that it had given the parties the opportunity to present their observations in that respect.[1458]

Taking due account of the guidelines of the Court and of the Opinion of AG Kokott on the assessment of the unfair nature of the clause regarding the default interest rate, the national ruling held the term to be unfair. The national court also noted that after the pronouncement of the judgment in *Aziz*, a legislative and judicial debate began in Spain so that a default interest rate exceeding two or three times the legal interest would have to be considered unfair.[1459] Therefore, the stipulated default interest of 18.75% had to be considered unfair, both from the compensatory function perspective and from the perspective of deterring "moral hazard." From the perspective of providing reasonable compensation to the creditor, the interest stipulated clearly exceeded the actual damage caused by the default. From the perspective of nurturing a culture of respect of payment, it went beyond the objective pursued. The debtor did not pay not because he was recalcitrant, but because he was *unable* to do so, with a net salary of €1,100 supporting an entire family. Mr Aziz then also lost this sole source of income as he was unemployed and he had no other assets apart from the family residence. As a result of this finding of the term to be unfair, the national court simply set aside the application of the contested term, pursuant to *Banco Español de Crédito*. Part of the debt claimed had then been incorrectly calculated and pursued.[1460]

---

1457 More than €194,000 for a small apartment of $50m^2$ in a residential neighbourhood few kilometers outside Barcelona.

1458 The judgment quotes passages from Case C-472/11 *Banif Plus Bank* (n. 1265).

1459 Law 1/2013 introduced a cap of default interest rate in the framework of mortgage enforcement proceedings to three times the statutory rate (n. 1451).

1460 For the reason also that the interest had been calculated upon the amount recapitalized.

The national court also held that the clause on the acceleration of payment of the loan (*vencimiento anticipado*) on account of a default on one sole installment was void in light of the financial circumstances of the consumer, for which he was not responsible and which the bank could have predicted when it decided to grant the loan. In abstract, default in the payment of four installments could be deemed to be an essential breach of contractual obligations.[1461] Moreover, the bank demonstrated a certain level of forbearance before repossession (as the default amounted to the four monthly installments and not one). However, the court stressed that default *should have been expected* by the bank in light of the information it had available on the creditworthiness of the debtor. The court recalled that the bank was aware that the consumer would have to disburse 70% of his salary on paying the mortgage. Measuring the breach of contractual obligations by the debtor against the means that the consumer had at his disposal to remedy the effects of the loan being called in, the court held that the right to reinstate the default loan (pursuant to Article 693(3) LEC) could not be considered to be an adequate or effective means of protection. The fact that the Spanish legislator, in view of the economic crisis, had already established a moratorium of two years for homeowners in a state of vulnerability (Real Decreto 6/2012) had to be taken into consideration. The repossession in the present case had been completed before adoption of the law, so Mr Aziz could not benefit from its protective scope. The national court took into account that, at that time, it was already debated whether a two-year moratorium would actually be sufficient to protect vulnerable homeowners or whether an extension would be required. In view of those developments, it would not be possible to hold the term of *vencimiento anticipado* to be fair. Therefore, the bank did not have the right to resort to repossession for the totality of the loan.

As the acceleration clause was considered to be void, the term on the unilateral quantification of the loan (*cláusula de liquidez)* also had to be considered unfair. The only amount that could validly be claimed corresponded to the outstanding installments (amounting to €3,153.46 plus interest as opposed to the totality of the loan that had been called in of €139,746.76). Although the *Tribunal Supremo* had confirmed in the past the validity of a term of unilateral quantification, under the circumstances of the main proceedings, that could not hold true as the result would be to enforce invalid clauses. Moreover, the mortgage debtor had limited possibilities of defense. At this point, reference was made to the ruling of the Court in *Aziz* on the incompatibility

1461 See the discussion on the unfairness assessment of the related clause before *Aziz* case in J.M. Fernández Seijo, *La defensa de los consumidores en las ejecuciones hipotecarias. Una aproximación desde el Derecho comunitario* (Dordrecht, Wolters Kluwer, 2013), 223–224 with reference to the ruling of Tribunal Supremo of 2nd of November 2000 that had ruled on the unfairness of such clause in view of the circumstances of the case.

of the procedural system with the Unfair Contract Terms Directive. The consumer had neither had the chance to advance grounds of opposition against enforcement on the basis of the unfairness of the terms, nor could he obtain interim relief in the ongoing declaratory proceedings in order to avoid repossession of his property.

The consequence of the finding of unfairness of the terms is that repossession could not have been pursued in the terms it did. The unfair terms had more specifically affected the *quantification* of the amount claimed with respect to the excessive default rate and the incorrect calling in of the entire debt. However, this decision does not call into question the debt due for the mortgage credit as such, or the possibility of the credit institution further pursuing its claims in ordinary proceedings, which would not present the situation of procedural imbalance that existed during the enforcement proceedings. The result of this finding was that the bank could not found a personal anti-deficiency action on the basis of the original quantification. However, such action could not be excluded on the basis of a new determination of the debt outstanding without application of the unfair terms. An important observation is made with respect to the fact that the debtor was unable to advance his defense at the stage of repossession. The incompatibility of the Spanish civil procedural system with the Unfair Contract Terms Directive could have provoked damages to the debtor. However, those damages have not been claimed within the framework of the present proceedings, although they could still be claimed in future proceedings.

It can be inferred from the national judgment that a damage claim for the breach of the right to effective judicial proceedings in the enforcement proceedings should be addressed not against the bank, *but against the Spanish state.* It also needs to be pointed out that the national court *did not hold* the enforcement proceedings to be null and void. According to that ruling, it would have been complex to decide on the matter of nullity, as the exact consequences of such a claim could not be appreciated on the basis of the elements of the case. Moreover, this would raise an issue of legal certainty in the event of possession by an "innocent" third party who acquired the property after foreclosure and who did not participate in the current proceedings, a reason which impeded the pronouncement of the court on damages.

# CHAPTER 6

# THE INFLUENCE AND EFFECTIVENESS OF THE ACTIVE CONSUMER COURT DOCTRINE ON NATIONAL LEGAL SYSTEMS

This chapter attempts to illustrate the influence of the active consumer court doctrine upon national legal orders, by giving examples where national legislation was modified to give effect to the doctrine. This influence is not restricted to instances where the Court has found a certain national provision incompatible with Union law. It suffices that the national legislator has taken into account the respective developments at the level of Union case law. The illustrations derive from three legal orders where a clear imprint of the case law of the Court could be identified. The first one is Spain, where certain legislative provisions had to be revamped in order to comply with the decisions of the Court. The second example is France. The case law of the Court had an "accelerating effect"[1462] on the decision of the French legislator to enshrine the duty of courts in the French Consumer Code (*Code de la Consommation*). The final example is from the UK and the express provision on the duty of courts in consumer litigation involving unfair terms in the Consumer Rights Act 2015.

This chapter demonstrates the recognition by national legislators of the distinctiveness of proceedings involving consumers. It depends on the Member States to identify the appropriate way to accommodate the active consumer court doctrine in national procedural laws. In France, for instance, the legislator chose to introduce a provision on the powers of the courts in the *Code de la Consommation* in view of the former position to the contrary of the *Cour de Cassation* which has given rise to uncertainty. Such legislative intervention would not be necessary only if it is already clear to the courts that they have to discharge their positive role in consumer law proceedings. The effect of this in some jurisdictions would be to recognize that in the field of consumer protection law, the theory that a relative nullity cannot be raised by a court of its own motion does not apply.[1463]

---

1462 This observation is owed to Professor Elise Poillot.

1463 *See* the Belgian law modernizing consumer sales which refers, in the preamble, to the *Océano Grupo* line of case law. The explanatory memorandum of Art. 1649octies of the Belgian

Moreover, the body of case law of national supreme courts, in which they interpret national law *in line* with the case law of the Court, dispels uncertainty. Such body of case law is a valuable source of guidance for national jurisdictions. The judgment of the *Hoge Raad* (the Supreme Court of the Netherlands) in *Heesakkers*[1464] is a good example in that respect. As appears from the references for a preliminary ruling by the Dutch lower courts to the Court,[1465] there has been quite a lot of uncertainty as to what the *ex officio* role in consumer law proceedings entails, and as to the possibility of extending to consumer rules the same procedural status as that afforded to national rules of public policy. The uncertainty was due in part to the fact that Dutch law (as Balázs Fekete and Anna Maria Mancaleoni point out)[1466] allows the *ex officio* application of public policy rules but not mandatory rules (which also explains the hesitation of lower courts to follow the case law of the Court). In its landmark judgment, the *Hoge Raad* proceeded with the *harmonious interpretation* of Article 6:233 of the Dutch Civil Code (*Burgerlijk Wetboek*), which provides for the voidability of unfair terms, to the effect that Dutch courts are obliged to assess of their own motion whether a contractual term falls within the scope of the Unfair Contract Terms Directive and whether it is unfair.

The examples in this chapter, particularly from Spain, demonstrate that the procedural law applicable in civil disputes might not be suitable for consumer litigation. This does not mean that a separate *forum* for consumer disputes must be available; what is meant is that the particularities of consumer litigation require special procedural rules and the adaptation of specific proceedings to

Civil Code (*Code Civil*), which provides for the nullity of clauses limiting the rights afforded to the consumer before the lack of conformity is discovered, refers to the power of the court to raise the respective nullity: "Contrairement à la règle généralement admise selon laquelle une nullité relative ne peut jamais être soulevée d'office par le juge, il y a lieu de tenir compte, en cette matière, de la jurisprudence résultant de l'arrêt dit *Océano* ... Cette jurisprudence semble applicable à la directive transposée par le présent projet et il faut donc en conclure que le juge pourra soulever d'office la nullité." (Translation: "Contrary to the generally applicable rule according to which a relative nullity may never be raised by the court of its own motion, it has to be taken into account, in this filed, the case law resulting from the judgment known as *Océano* .... This case law seems to be applicable to the [consumer sales] directive transposed by the present bill; as a result the court should be able to raise the nullity on its own motion"). See *Exposé des motifs de la loi du 1er septembre 2004* (explanatory memorandum of the law of 1 September 2004), Doc. parl., Ch. Repr., sess. Ord. 2003-2001, no 982/1, 22–23, cited by P. Wéry, *Droit des Obligations Vol. I* (Paris, Larcier, 2010), 320, note 52.

1464 Hoge Raad der Nederlanden, 13 September 2013, *Heesakkers v Voets*, NJ 2014, 274, NL:HR2013:691. The judgment is reported in English by B. Fekete and A.M. Mancaleoni, "Application of Primary and Secondary EU Law on the National Courts' Own Motion" in A. Hartkamp, C. Sieburgh and W. Devroe (eds.), *Cases, Materials and Text on European Law and Private Law* (Oxford, Hart Publishing, 2017), 421–461, 436.

1465 Case C-488/11 *Asbeek Brusse*, EU:C:2013:341; Case C-497/13 *Faber*, EU:C:2015:357.

1466 B. Fekete and A.M. Mancaleoni in A. Hartkamp, C. Sieburgh and W. Devroe (eds.) (n. 1464), 439–440.

the model of the "weaker party." The national examples given in this chapter can provide an inspiration for prospective reform in other jurisdictions and act as a *blueprint* for reform, where required. This would particularly be the case if in a given jurisdiction there is as yet not enough visibility of the *ex officio* doctrine, or if in a given jurisdiction courts would hesitate over their active role and explicit legislative recognition would facilitate the exercise of this role. But even where the *ex officio* doctrine is established by law, it has to gain ground among the judiciary as it entails an active role which they might not have been accustomed to exercise.[1467]

## 1. SPAIN: THE REFORM OF THE *LEY DE ENJUICIAMIENTO CIVIL*

The establishment of the *ex officio* doctrine owes a lot to the many references for a preliminary ruling from Spanish courts. The ruling in *Océano Grupo*, a reference originating from the industrious court in Barcelona, was the first breakthrough in terms of opening up the path for reform of the role of the courts in individual consumer litigation in Spain. More than 10 years later, this judgment was given a "second life"[1468] with *Aziz*.[1469] In *Aziz*, the same referring court "came back" with a new question, inviting a contemporary reading of the Unfair Contract Terms Directive in the context of the acute social crisis in Spain with respect to home repossessions. The implications of the strengthening of consumer judicial protection prompted by the *ex officio* doctrine would now involve consumer mortgage debtors, demonstrating the "social relevance"[1470] of this line of case law. In the aftermath of this case, the Spanish legislator reconsidered the role

1467 The extent to which national courts are aware of the *ex officio* doctrine and how they perceive their role requires empirical analysis. The first study carried out to that effect is "An evaluation study of national procedural laws and practices in terms of their impact on the free circulation of judgments and on the equivalence and effectiveness of the procedural protection of consumers under EU consumer law", study carried out by the Max Planck Institute – Luxembourg on behalf of the European Commission. The first strand of the study is available at <https://publications.europa.eu/en/publication-detail/-/publication/531ef49a-9768-11e7-b92d-01aa75ed71a1/language-en/format-PDF/source-61204569> accessed 02.10.2017. The second strand of the study concerning consumer procedural protection is available at <http://ec.europa.eu/newsroom/just/item-detail.cfm?item_id=612847> accessed 19/04/2018. The study identifies the *ex officio* question as one of its "most controversial issues" (para. 351). The author of the current work was the national rapporteur for Luxembourg together with Professor Gilles Cuniberti.

1468 F. Nicola and E. Tichadou, "Océano Grupo: A Transatlantic Victory for the Consumer and a Missed Opportunity for European Law" *in* F. Nicola and B. Davies (eds.), *EU Law Stories, Contextual and Critical Histories of European Jurisprudence* (Cambridge University Press, 2017), 369–390, 383.

1469 Case C-415/11 *Aziz*, EU:C:2013:164.

1470 F. Nicola and E. Tichadou, (n. 1468), 388.

of the courts in mortgage repossessions and had to redefine the standards of procedural fairness informing the process. *Aziz* contributed to the *forging* of a more rigorous framework in Spain to protect the principal family residence of mortgage debtors and, in essence, to protect consumers as citizens. The interest in the case goes beyond legal circles. It should be recalled that it made headlines not only in the Spanish press but also in the international press.[1471] The day after its pronouncement, the Prime Minister of Spain, Mariano Rajoy, announced that his government would take into consideration the ruling of the Court in the elaboration of a new law that was then being discussed in parliament. In the analysis of the case law in Chapter 5, references were made to the law which brought about the reform in Spain, namely Law 1/2013. This was due to the fact that following the promulgation of the new law, the Spanish courts returned with new references for a preliminary ruling challenging certain of its provisions. Section 1.1 refers to the changes following *Banco Español de Crédito*[1472] and section 1.2 will be devoted to the changes following *Aziz.*

## 1.1. THE REFORM FOLLOWING *BANCO ESPAÑOL DE CRÉDITO*

The judgment in *Banco Español de Crédito* triggered reform of Spanish law in the procedure applicable in order for payment proceedings involving consumers, as well as in the consequences of finding a term unfair.

In the immediate aftermath of the ruling, as has already been mentioned above in the analysis of the judgment of the Court,[1473] there has been a certain uncertainty as to the compatibility of the then existing order for payment proceedings (*proceso monitorio*) with Union law. A judgment of the Provincial Court of Madrid decided in Plenary (*Audiencia Provincial de Madrid*)[1474] found that the (at the time) existing framework of *proceso monitorio* had to be considered compatible with Union law requirements and that professionals could still resort to this procedure to pursue a consumer debt. However, an interpretation of national law in light of the wording and spirit of the Unfair Contract Terms Directive would require that the courts before which an application for an order for payment procedure is brought have to examine of their own motion the existence of an unfair term in the contract on the basis of the claim pursued and, if that is the case, to declare its nullity.

Finally, the Spanish legislator intervened so as to establish specific rules for the role of the courts within an order for payment procedure.

1471 See 15/03/2013 "European Court Strikes down Spain's Draconian Foreclosure Law" *Financial Times*, 15 March 2013.

1472 Case C-618/10 *Banco Español de Crédito*, EU:C:2012:349.

1473 Chapter 5, Section 1.1.

1474 Audiencia Provincial de Madrid (Sección 19), Monitorio 906/2012, (Recurso de Apelación 811/2012).

Before that, civil procedure had been amended in order to vest the judicial clerk (*Secretario judicial*) with specific powers within order for payment proceedings to enhance their expediency. However, there was no specific provision governing the procedure to be followed in cases where the claim was founded upon a consumer contract. It was in this legal framework that the Court found in *Finanmadrid EFC*,[1475] that the powers of the courts to raise of their own motion the unfairness of terms in an order for payment procedure may not be called into question by the previous decision of the *Secretario judicial* (which had been vested with the force of *res judicata*).

The reform bill of the Civil Procedure Code (*Anteproyecto de Ley de Reforma de la Ley de Enjuiciamiento Civil*)[1476] proposed the amendment of the respective section of the *proceso monitorio* to cover the situation of the initiation of the process by a professional against the consumer. In particular, the proposal concerned the addition of a new paragraph 4 in Article 815 LEC which would provide that once the *Secretario judicial* has perceived the possible existence of unfair terms in the instrument on the basis of which a claim is pursued, he would have to inform the court. After that, the court would have to hear the parties within five days and decide by issuing an order, again within five days. The Supreme Judicial Council had criticized the original proposal of reform.[1477] In its view, the proposed text did not comply with the judgment of the Court in *Banco Español de Crédito*. The reason for this is that it attributed the first level of judgment to the *Secretario judicial*, a power which would encroach upon the effective judicial protection of the consumer from unfair terms, which can only be afforded by the court.[1478]

The provision which finally became law creates, in essence, a separate regime for applications for an order of payment directed against a consumer. According to the new paragraph 4 added to Article 815 LEC, where a claim is founded upon a consumer contract, the *Secretario judicial* is required to notify the court that will be responsible for assessing the potential existence of

1475 Case C-49/14 *Finanmadrid EFC*, EU:C:2016:98.

1476 Of 3 March 2013.

1477 Consejo General del Poder Judicial, *Informe al Anteproyecto de Ley de Reforma de la Ley de Enjuciamiento Civil*, 3 July 2013 (Supreme Judicial Council, *Report on the preliminary draft Law for the reform of the Law of Civil Procedure*, 3 July 2013), available at <http://www.poderjudicial.es/cgpj/es/Poder-Judicial/Consejo-General-del-Poder-Judicial/Actividad-del-CGPJ/Informes/Informe-al-anteproyecto-de-Ley-de-reforma-de-la-Ley-de-Enjuiciamiento-Civil> accessed 02.10.2017.

1478 According to this criticism (ibid., 1477): "Se considera, en consecuencia, que la nueva regulación es una clara invasión de la función jurisdiccional y no cumple los términos de la sentencia del TJUE cuyo cumplimiento se pretende, por lo que desde este momento se recomienda su modificación." [It has to be considered, as a consequence, that the new provision is a clear invasion of the judicial function and does not correspond to the conditions set out by the judgment of the Court with which it is supposed to comply, so it is recommended that the provision be modified] (translated by the author).

unfair terms. This control will be conducted of the court's own motion. If the court appreciates that a term could qualify as unfair, it has to invite argument from the parties in five days and to decide within five days. There is no requirement for legal representation of the parties throughout this process. Upon the finding of unfairness of a clause, the court determines the consequences of such finding, being either to bring to an end the order for payment proceedings or to decide to continue with the process without the application of the unfair terms. If the court considers that there is no issue in terms of the potential existence of unfair terms, the procedure will continue as with any other claim. Such a finding can be challenged by appeal.

The reform of the Spanish law is a welcome development. It demonstrates the necessity of accommodating the particularities of consumer law into a specific type of proceeding. The Spanish legislator did not prohibit the creditor from having recourse to an order for payment procedure overall in order to recover consumer debt. That would unduly deprive creditors of a fast way of claiming unpaid, even uncontested, debt. It would involve unnecessary costs and use of judicial resources and would result in the protraction of proceedings. The choice made in the new law is to provide for sufficient safeguards in such types of proceedings in order to ensure that the court is vested with the power, *in limine litis*, to examine the contract upon which the debt is based and ensure that the decisional powers of other organs in the process will not render such a power nugatory.

With regard to the consequences of a finding of unfairness by the courts, the *Banco Español de Crédito* judgment resulted in the repeal of the power of moderation of unfair terms by the courts. Law 3/2014,[1479] which in its recital makes express reference to the need to comply with the ruling of the Court in *Banco Español de Crédito*, modifies Article 83 of the Law on Consumer Protection[1480] to the effect that the court, after having heard the parties, will declare the nullity of the unfair terms of the contract; the contract, however, remains binding among the parties if it is capable of continuing in existence without the unfair terms.

---

1479 Ley 3/2014 por la que se modifica el texto refundido de la Ley General para la Defensa de los Consumidores y Usuarios y otras leyes complementarias, aprobado por el Real Decreto Legislativo 1/2007 de 16 de noviembre (Law 3/2014 amending the revised text of the General Law for the Protection of Consumers and Users and other supplementary laws, approved by the Legislative Decree 1/2007 of 16 November) of 27 March 2014 (BOE No 76 of 28 March 2014), Preamble point III.

1480 Real Decreto Legislativo 1/2007 por el que se aprueba el texto refundido de la Ley General para la Defensa de los Consumidores y Usuarios y otras leyes complementarias (Royal Decree Law 1/2007 approving the revised text of the general law for the protection of consumers and users and other complementary laws) of 16 November 2007 (BOE No 287 of 30 November 2007).

## 1.2. THE "*AZIZ* EARTHQUAKE"

The judgment in *Aziz* has been very much awaited in Spain, by the government, the courts, the banks and mortgage debtors. On the day it was pronounced, the referring judge, José María Fernández Seijo, said in an interview that the judgment now had its own existence, and from the day onward, everything would change because the rules of the game of many mortgage actions had changed.[1481] In Chapter 5, the social and legal framework surrounding this judgment was discussed. In Spain foreclosures became "the image of the economic crisis" ("los desahucios son la imagen de la crisis económica").[1482] This situation had already prompted the legislator before *Aziz* to proceed with certain modifications to the "draconian" mortgage law that dated back more than a century.

The first attempt of reform of Spanish mortgage law came in 2011 with Royal Legislative Decree 8/2011.[1483] This law raised the threshold of the assets exempt from seizure. In particular, the threshold of the minimum wage that cannot be seized in the pursuit of the outstanding debt after foreclosure of the sole family residence was raised by 50%.[1484] It also modified the Civil Procedure Code (*Ley de Enjuiciamento Civil* - LEC)[1485] in order to raise the minimum price required for the adjudication of immovable property to 70% of the appraised value and never below 60% in the absence of bidders.[1486] The second reform came with Royal Legislative Decree 6/2012 on urgent measures for the

1481 Interview of the judge in *El Periódico Barcelona*, 15 March 2013: "Se lo que tienen que hacer los jueces, que es aplicar la sentencia. El Gobierno tiene la oportunidad de poder sintonizar las reformas de acuerdo con la resolución, pero la sentencia, por si misma, tiene vida propia. Aunque no haya reformas, la sentencia, a partir de mañana [hoy para el lector], va a cambiarlo todo, modifica las reglas del juego de muchas ejecuciones hipotecarias." [The judges now have to apply the ruling. The government has the opportunity to pass the reforms which will make the Spanish legal system compatible with the judgment, because this judgment now has its own life. Although, at the moment, no reform has yet taken place, the ruling as from tomorrow [today for the reader] will change everything, because it modifies the rules of the game for many foreclosures] (translated by the author).

1482 Interview with Judge José María Fernández Seijo in *El Periódico Barcelona*, 6 April 2013. The most unfortunate is the story of homeowners who committed suicide. There were many distressing reports at that time on that extremely sad situation in the Spanish, but also the international, press. See e.g. "Human Cost of Spain's Financial Disaster", *Financial Times*, 16 November 2012.

1483 Real Decreto-ley 8/2011 de medidas de apoyo a los deudores hipotecarios [...] (Royal Decree Law 8/2011 on means to support the mortgage debtors [...]) of 1 July 2011 (BOE No 161 of 7 July 2011).

1484 Ibid., Art. 1; an additional increase of 30% was provided for every family member who lacks income.

1485 Arts. 670–671 LEC.

1486 Art. 2 Royal Decree Law 8/2011 (n. 1483).

protection of mortgagors without resources.[1487] These measures responded to the strong social pressure resulting from the situation of mortgage debtors, reflected in the movement of the so-called "antidesahucios."[1488] This law approved a Code of Good Practice for Banks, providing *inter alia* for debt restructuring and a limited possibility of deed in lieu of foreclosure (*dación en pago*).[1489] These measures shielded a limited category of mortgagors from foreclosure, namely those whom the law identified as particularly vulnerable (*situados en el umbral de exclusion*).[1490] The "timid" approach of the legislator compared to the extent of the social problem of evictions has been criticized in academic and judicial circles,[1491] but also by citizens and political movements, who continued to press

---

1487 Real Decreto-ley 6/2012 de medidas urgentes de protección de deudores hipotecarios sin recursos (Royal Legislative Decree 6/2012 on urgent measures to protect mortgage debtors without resources) of 9 March 2012 (BOE No 60 of 10 March 2012).

1488 On the developments of the action of the *antidesahucios* movement, see the website of the Plataforma de Afectados *por la Hipoteca* (PAH) organized in various cities in Spain: <http://afectadosporlahipoteca.com/> accessed 02.10.2017. See also the scientific studies and action of the University of Cordoba with the establishment of a "legal laboratory" on the issue: Laboratorio Jurídico sobre Desahucios <http://www.uco.es/laboratoriojuridico/> accessed 02.10.2017.

1489 See also Chapter 5 Section 3.3.1.3.

1490 Art. 3 of Royal Decree Law 6/2012 (n. 1487) defines the circle of persons falling within this restrictive definition. In brief: all members of the family should lack income, the mortgage payment should be greater than 60% of the net income received by all the members of the family, all members should lack property and the credit should be secured by a mortgage upon the main residence of the debtor.

1491 See e.g. the approach of Judge Jose María Ferández Seijo, who in his interview in *El Pais*, 30 November 2012, said that the problem had already become so important that such a measure (in 2012) could be of little avail, because in fact the foreclosures that were taking place in 2012 had already been initiated three years ago in the beginning of the crisis: "Algunas entitades ya están asumiendo, al margen de ese código, el coste social de la situación y en algunos casos no ejecutan. Pero la hemorragia es tan grande, que este tipo de medidas no van a server para nada. De hecho, los lanzamientos que ahora se producen son casos que se inicaron hace tres anos, al comienzo de la crisis. Le peor, lo más gordo, está aún por venir." [Some financial institutions have assumed, outside the framework of the [civil procedure code], the social cost of the situation and in some cases they do not initiate proceedings. The financial "hemorrhage" is so important, that such type of measures will not serve anyone. In fact, the foreclosures that are currently taking place have been initiated already three years ago at the beginning of the crisis. The worst is still to come] (translated by the author). The judge regretted the interconnection of politics and finance that resulted in the compromise of the decree of 2012: "El sector financier es un lobby muy poderoso. Lo hemos visto en el real decreto sobre desahucios. Estoy seguro de que los técnicos de los dos partidos entraron a necogiar con el propósito de encontrar una solución y modificar a fondo las leyes, pero en esos tres días de reuniones, el lobby financiero mantuvo reuniones paralelas y presionó al Gobierno hasta conseguir sus propósitos ...". [The financial sector is a very powerful lobby. We saw this with the decree on the mortgage debtors against whom enforcement is being initiated. I am sure that the experts of both parties entered the negotiations with the purpose of reaching a solution and amending in detail the law, but during those three days of meetings, the financial lobby held parallel meetings and put pressure on Government in order to achieve its own purposes] (translated by the author).

for a genuine right of *dación en pago.*[1492] Royal Legislative Decree 27/2012[1493] imposed a temporary moratorium on evictions as an urgent measure which would benefit a very narrowly defined category of "vulnerable debtors" at high risk of social exclusion due to specific situations of hardship defined by this law.[1494] Royal Legislative Decree 5/2017 extended the category of persons which fall within the category of "vulnerable debtors" and extended the moratorium until 15 May 2020.[1495]

### *1.2.1. The Framework of Reform of Law 1/2013*

The Spanish government was contemplating reform in terms of measures to provide protection from foreclosures when the ruling in *Aziz* was rendered in March 2013. Therefore, it was the perfect occasion to integrate the lessons of *Aziz* into the new law,[1496] which was finally published two months after the publication of the judgment in *Aziz*. Law 1/2013[1497] covers a much wider

---

1492 Real Decreto-ley 1/2015 de mecanismo de segunda oportunidad, reducción de carga financiera y otras medidas de orden social (Royal Decree Law 1/2015 on a second chance mechanism) of 27 February 2015 (BOE No 51 of 28 February 2015) introduced a limited possibility for mortgage debtors to qualify for the discharge of their mortgage debt in lieu of the mortgaged property under certain circumstances. For a detailed account on this mechanism as part of the system of consumer debt discharge and more broadly on mortgage reform in Spain, see J.M. Fernández Seijo, *La tutela des los consumidores en los procedimientos judiciales, Especial referencia a las ejecuciones hipotecarias* (Dordrecht, Wolters Kluwer, 2017).

1493 Real Decreto-ley 27/2012 de medidas urgentes para reforzar la protección a los deudores hipotecarios (Royal Decree Law 27/2012 on urgent measures to strengthen the protection of mortgage debtors) of 15 November 2012 (BOE No 279 of 16 November 2012).

1494 See P. Gutierrez de Cabiedes and M. Cantero Gamito, "Country Report Spain" in H.-W. Micklitz and I. Domurath (eds.), *Consumer Debt and Social Exclusion in Europe* (Farnham, Ashgate, 2015), 67 *et seq*; S. Nasarre-Aznar, "A Legal Perspective of the Origin and the Globalisation of the Current Financial Crisis and the Resulting Reforms in Spain" and V. Valino, "Mortgage Foreclosure and Housing Rights in Spain: Crisis or General Deception?" both in P. Kenna (ed.), *Contemporary Housing Issues in a Globalised World* (Farnham, Ashgate, 2014); and my contribution on urgent measures aiming to protect the primary family residence in A. Beka, "The Protection of the Primary Residence of Mortgage Debtors: Embedding the 'Basic Needs' Principle in Residential Mortgage Repossession Proceedings" in L. Ratti (ed.), *Embedding the principles of Life Time Contracts, A Research Agenda for Contract Law* (The Hague, Eleven Publishing, 2018), 247–276, 267 et seq.

1495 Real Decreto-ley 5/2017, de 17 de marzo, por el que se modifica el Real Decreto-ley 6/2012, de 9 de marzo, de medidas urgentes de protección de deudores hipotecarios sin recursos, y la Ley 1/2013, de 14 de mayo, de medidas para reforzar la protección a los deudores hipotecarios, reestructuración de deuda y alquiler social (Royal Decree Law 5/2017 modifying Royal Decree Law 6/2012 [n. 1487] and Law 1/2013 of 14 May laying down measures for the strengthening of the protection of mortgagors, the restructuring of debt and social rent) of 17 March 2017 (BOE No 66 of 18 March 2017).

1496 See the declarations to that effect of the Spanish Prime Minister Mariano Rajoy in Brussels on the day *Aziz* was rendered (14 March 2013).

1497 Ley 1/2013 de medidas para reforzar la protección a los deudores hipotecarios, reestructuración de deuda y alquiler social (Law 1/2013 laying down measures for the

array of issues than those raised in *Aziz*. That being so, the modification of the provisions concerning the powers of the courts with regard to the finding of unfairness in mortgage repossession proceedings is a direct response to the case. Overall the law is the first legislative effort to address the dramatic situation ("drama social")[1498] of mortgage debtors in a more comprehensive way. This does not mean that it addressed all the issues surrounding the problem of evictions or that it satisfied all stakeholders. On the contrary, its publication launched a new round of references for a preliminary ruling concerning the compatibility of certain of its provisions (particularly the transitional provisions) with the *ex officio* doctrine. *Morcillo and García*,[1499] *Unicaja Banco*[1500] and *BBVA*,[1501] discussed in earlier chapters in the context of *Aziz*, were rendered against the background of the new law. Moreover, the problem of evictions in Spain led the local governments in Navarre and Andalusia to resort to more radical solutions, with the so-called laws "to fight evictions" (*antidesahucios*) for the protection of the social function of property.[1502] All this only goes to show that the problem of foreclosures in Spain has become a major political struggle that did not stop after the passing of the new law. For the purposes of this work, the discussion shall be limited to sketching some important features of Law 1/2013 that draw their immediate influence from *Aziz*.[1503]

Law 1/2013 is divided into four chapters. Chapter I provides for the suspension of evictions from the sole family residence of persons in a situation of special vulnerability (*especial vulnerabilididad*) under certain

---

strengthening of the protection of mortgagors, the restructuring of debt and social rent) of 14 May 2013 (BOE No 116 of 15 May 2013).

1498 Preamble Law 1/2013, para. 2.

1499 Case C-169/14 *Morcillo and García*, EU:C:2014:2099.

1500 Joined Cases C-482/13, C-484/13, C-485/13 and C-487/13 *Unicaja Banco and Caixabank*, EU:C:2015:21.

1501 Case C-8/14 *BBVA*, EU:C:2015:731.

1502 Decreto-Ley 6/2013 de medidas para asegurar el cumplimiento de la Función Social de la Vivienda (Decree Law 6/2013 on measures to ensure compliance with the Social Function of Housing) of 9 April 2013 (Official Gazette of the Government of Andalusia No 69 of 11 April 2013); Ley foral 24/2013 de medidas urgentes para garantizar el derecho a la vivienda en Navarra (Statutory Law 24/2013 on urgent measures to guarantee the right to accommodation in Navarra) of 2 July 2013. The laws would allow, under certain circumstances, the families that have been evicted from their homes to occupy vacant properties, paying a certain sum to the owner bank. These measures were held to be partially unconstitutional by the Spanish Constitutional Court on the ground that the regional government had overridden its competences in the adoption of certain provisions of the respective legislation, taking into account that the issue of the homeowners' protection had already been dealt with at the national level (TS Sentencia 93/2015 of 14 May 2015) (BOE No 146 of 19 June 2015).

1503 For a detailed account of the law, see D. Gutiérrez Alonso, "Magistrado del Juzgado de Primera Intancia No3 de Lleida 'La Reforma del Procedimiento de Ejecución Tras la Ley 1/2013 de 14 de Mayo'", presented on 4 March 2014 as part of the workshop organised by the Consejo General del Poder Judicial on *Reforma del Proceso de Ejecución Hipotecaria y Jurisprudencia del Tribunal de Justicia de la Unión Europea*, Madrid, 3–5 March 2014.

strict conditions.[1504] Chapters II and III cover the legal framework on the mortgage enforcement procedure, many provisions of which integrate the lessons from *Aziz*, bringing about particular modifications on the Law on Mortgages (*Ley Hipotecaria*) and the Civil Procedure Code (*Ley de Enjuiciamiento Civil* – LEC). Chapter IV modifies Royal Legislative Decree 6/2012 on urgent measures for the protection of mortgagors without resources. This chapter also modifies the Code of Good Practice for the sustainable debt restructuring of family residence mortgages. This Code of Good Practice also governs the right to *dación en pago* for those who fall within the restrictive personal ambit of social exclusion defined by Royal Legislative Decree 6/2012 ("umbral de exclusión"). Law 1/2013 has 10 transitional provisions, the first of which has already been the subject of litigation in *Unicaja Banco*.

#### *1.2.2. The Modifications in Relation to the Control of Unfair Terms in Mortgage Enforcement Proceedings*

The new law brings about modifications in the Law on Mortgages and the Civil Procedure Code that affect the content of the terms of the mortgage contract and their control within the framework of extrajudicial enforcement. There are also changes to the Civil Procedure Code which affect the *ex officio* control of unfair terms and the grounds of defense within the framework of judicial mortgage enforcement.

#### 1.2.2.1. The Content of Mortgage Terms and their Control in Extrajudicial Enforcement Proceedings

Law 1/2013 amends the Law on Mortgages[1505] by placing a cap on the default interest rate applicable in mortgage contracts for a habitual dwelling (*vivienda habitual*). The default interest cannot exceed the cap of three times

---

1504 From a comparative perspective, it could be noted that in Greece from 1 January 2012 until 31 December 2013, with two successive laws, there was a suspension of auctions for debts against financial institutions up to a ceiling of €200,000. This ban was relaxed with a law that provided further conditions of eligibility to benefit from the suspension for the period from 1 January 2014 until 31 December 2014 (Law 4224/2013, FEK A 288 of 31 December 2013, Art. 2); see N. Κατηφόρης, "Αναστολή πλειστηριασμού της κύριας κατοικίας, Ερμηνευτική προσέγγιση του άρθρου 2 του ν. 4224/2013" (Σάκκουλας, 2014) (translated as N. Katiforis, *Suspension of Auction of the First Residence, Analysis of Article 2 of Law 4224/2013* (Sakkoulas, 2014)). As of 1 January 2016, the horizontal suspension of enforcement has been lifted. However, debtors have the opportunity to apply to shield their family residence from foreclosure under the strict means-tested conditions of Law 3869/2010 on debt rescheduling of natural persons and other provisions (FEK A 130 of 3 August 2010), as it was subsequently amended (the so-called "Katseli Law" from the name of the minister who promoted the legislation). *See* A. Beka (n.1494), 267–269.

1505 Art. 114 Law on Mortgages (Ley Hipotecaria).

the statutory interest.[1506] The default interest cannot be capitalized, except under certain circumstances provided for by the Civil Procedure Code. This is a *mandatory* provision, which means that the notaries have to refuse to include a term in a mortgage contract which would exceed the ceiling.[1507] This provision should also be read together with the second transitional provision of Law 1/2013 which governs the application of the limitation of default interest in proceedings for enforcement or extrajudicial sale commenced and not concluded by the entry into force of this law. This provision provides the clerk or the notary with the possibility of allowing the party seeking enforcement a period of 10 days in order to recalculate the sum of default interest. This provision was the subject of the ruling in *Unicaja Banco*. As has already been explained, the Court examined the compatibility of the cap and the modification provision. It ruled that the provision does not in principle infringe upon the powers of the courts insofar as they are not impeded from proceeding to an unfairness assessment of a contractual term which sets the default interest at a rate other than the one provided for by the law and from setting the term aside if it is found to be unfair. The Court clarified that the setting of a statutory cap is beneficial for consumers as it extends to any mortgage loan and not only consumer loans. The related provisions of Law 1/2013 are therefore compatible with Union law, provided they do not impede the powers of the courts to proceed, if necessary, with an assessment of their own motion of the fairness of the default interest term.

It has already been explained in the analysis of *Aziz* that in Spain it is possible to initiate foreclosure either judicially or extrajudicially. For an extrajudicial sale to take place, there must be an explicit agreement. The Spanish Consumer Protection Law provided that notaries and public registrars shall refuse to insert in the deed they draw up a term that has been ruled to be unfair, where the respective decision has been inserted in the Register of General Contract Terms.[1508] In the new law, we note the reform of Article 129(2)(f) *Ley Hipotecaria*, which provides that once the notary entertains doubts as to the fairness of one of the clauses in the mortgage credit on the basis of which the extrajudicial sale is initiated, he shall bring it to the attention of the debtor and

---

[1506] On the case law of the Spanish Supreme Court on the default interest rate clause see Chapter 5, Section 3.4.3.

[1507] D. Gutiérrez Alonso (n. 1503), 6 citing the decision of *Dirección General de los Registros y del Notariado* of 18 November 2013.

[1508] Art. 84 Law 1/2007 (n.1480): "Los Notarios y los Registradores de la Propiedad y Mercantiles, en el ejercicio profesional de sus respectivas funciones públicas, no autorizarán ni inscribirán aquellos contratos o negocios jurídicos en los que se pretenda la inclusión de cláusulas declaradas nulas por abusivas en sentencia inscrita en el Registro de Condiciones Generales de la Contratación". [The Notaries and the Property and Commercial Registrars, in the exercise of their professional or public function accordingly, do not allow nor inscribe those contracts or legal negotiations in which there have been included terms that have been declared unfair by a judgment inserted into the Register of the Gereral Contract Terms] (translated by the author).

the creditor. The notary will suspend the extrajudicial sale when the parties confirm that the subject of unfairness has been submitted to the competent court. The issue of unfairness will then be decided on the basis of the provisions of the LEC. The new provision on the notarial duty has been criticized as being timid. The notary is obliged to suspend enforcement only insofar as the consumer has *challenged* the enforcement instrument, whereas the courts are obliged to suspend the enforcement of their own motion as soon as they consider that there might be an issue of unfairness. The extrajudicial sale would then seem to afford inferior protection compared to the one in the judicial sale.[1509]

One of the terms that was challenged in *Aziz* was the acceleration clause, which allowed the creditor to initiate enforcement proceedings for the entire debt in the absence of payment of one single installment. Law 1/2013 provides that the creditor may not proceed with enforcement unless at least three installments have not been paid. This limitation has to be set out in the notarial mortgage deed so that the creditor is entitled to proceed to debt acceleration.[1510] The limitation only concerns mortgage enforcement (*ejecución hipotecaria*), but does not impede the initiation of ordinary proceedings (*ejecución ordinaria*) for payment of the entire debt.[1511]

#### 1.2.2.2. Judicial Control of Unfair Terms and Grounds of Defense

Within the framework of ordinary or mortgage enforcement proceedings (*ejecución ordinaria/hipotecaria*), which are based upon non-judicial or arbitral enforcement title, the courts explicitly have the power to raise the issue of unfairness of contractual terms of their own motion.[1512] From the moment the court appreciates the eventual application of the law on unfair terms, it has to call the parties to a hearing within 15 days. The court has to make a decision within five days. If following the hearing the court is persuaded of the existence of unfair terms, it will determine the consequences of this appreciation: either the termination of the enforcement procedure or its continuation without the application of unfair terms.[1513] The law has not modified the applicable procedure within the framework of declaratory proceedings on the issue of nullity of the title, or the maturity, certainty, extinguishment or amount of the debt. However, read against the background of *Aziz* and *Banco Popular Espanol*, the new powers of the courts within the framework of enforcement proceedings

[1509] D. Gutiérrez Alonso (n. 1503), 20, referring to a communication by the Consejo General del Notariado in J.I. Navas Olóriz, "Venta extrajudicial de bienes hipotecados" (2014) 1(1) *Revista de Derecho Civil, Notarios y Registradores* 6.

[1510] Amendment of Art. 693(3) Spanish Civil Procedure Code (Ley de Enjuiciamiento Civil – LEC). On the case law of the Spanish Supreme Court regarding the clause of accelaration of payment see Chapter 5, Section 3.4.3.

[1511] D. Gutiérrez Alonso (n. 1503), 12.

[1512] Art. 552(1) LEC.

[1513] Art. 561(3) LEC.

should not be understood as impeding the *ex officio* powers of the courts and their power to take interim relief within the framework of declaratory proceedings.[1514]

Law 1/2013 adds a new ground for opposition to enforcement which consists of the existence of unfairness of a contractual term. The ground can first of all be presented in *ordinary* enforcement proceedings when the enforcement title contains unfair terms.[1515] Where the court finds the opposition to be well founded, it will decide upon the consequences of the finding of unfairness by deciding upon either the termination of the enforcement or its continuation without the application of the unfair terms.[1516] With regard to *mortgage* enforcement proceedings, the consumer may lodge an objection on the ground of unfairness when the unfair clause constitutes the foundation of the enforcement title or when it otherwise determines the amount due.[1517] If an objection is lodged under that provision, the clerk shall suspend the mortgage enforcement and shall summon the parties to appear before the court that issued the enforcement order no earlier than 15 days after the issue of the summons.[1518]

The court has to make a decision and issue an order within two days. The decision can be one of the following: i) the court declares the nullity of the term that serves as a foundation of the enforcement, in which case it orders that enforcement shall be discontinued; ii) it declares the nullity of the term that does not serve as a foundation of the enforcement, in which case it orders that the enforcement shall continue without application of the unfair term; or iii) it rejects the objection. An appeal may be lodged against the order discontinuing enforcement, or the order disapplying an unfair term or the order dismissing the objection of the mortgage debtor when the enforcement is based on the alleged unfair term or determines the amount due.[1519] The last ground of appeal was added following the ruling of the Court in *Morcillo and García.*[1520] Save in those

1514 See above in the analysis of the *Aziz* case and D. Gutiérrez Alonso (n. 1503), 13, 18.

1515 Art. 557(1) n. 7 LEC.

1516 Art. 561(1) n. 3 LEC.

1517 Art. 695(1) n. 4 LEC. However, the courts remain competent to raise of their own motion an unfair term, even if the enforcement is not based on that term.

1518 Art. 695(2) LEC.

1519 Art. 695(4) LEC.

1520 Third final provision, Real Decreto Ley 11/2014 de medidas urgentes en materia concursal (Royal Decree Law 11/2014 on urgent measures in matters of bankruptcy) of 5 September 2014 (BOE No 217 of 6 September 2014) (BOE No 217, of 6 September 2014). The Preamble (VI) makes an explicit reference to the judgment of the Court: "La disposición final tercera modifica la Ley 1/2000, de 7 de enero, de Enjuiciamiento Civil, para adaptarla a la reciente Sentencia del Tribunal de Justicia de la Unión Europea de 17 de julio de 2014. Con ello, el deudor hipotecario podrá interponer recurso de apelación contra el auto que desestime su oposición a la ejecución, si ésta se fundaba en la existencia de una cláusula contractual abusiva que constituya el fundamento de la ejecución o la cantidad exigible." [The final third provision, modifies Law 1/2000, of 7 January, of the Civil Procedure Code,

circumstances, no appeal shall lie against orders adjudicating upon the objection to enforcement and the effects of those orders shall be confined exclusively to the enforcement proceedings in which they are made.

### *1.2.3. Other Modifications of Civil Procedure Reinforcing the Protection of Mortgage Debtors*

It is worth noting two more modifications of the Civil Procedure Code which strengthen consumer protection within the framework of mortgage enforcement proceedings. These modifications concern in particular the minimum price at which the family residence can be auctioned and the personal liability of the debtor where outstanding debt remains after the auction has taken place. Before the reform, the provisions governing these issues were challenged in *Barclays Bank*[1521] on the basis of the Unfair Contract Terms Directive. As has been mentioned in the analysis of this case,[1522] the Court considered that these provisions were excluded from the scope of application of the Unfair Contract Terms Directive.

Specific provision is made for the situation in which there are no bidders in the auction, the creditor applies to have the property adjudicated and the property is the family residence of the debtor.[1523] The property cannot be adjudicated at a value of less than 70% of the initial estimation. If the amount owed is less, the threshold is set at 60%.

The principle set out in the Civil Procedure Code is that the creditor may pursue the debtor for the outstanding debt following the auction of the mortgaged property. However, the amendment following Law 1/2013 provides a possibility for debt discharge, under strictly circumscribed conditions when the property that has been enforced is the dwelling of the mortgage debtor.[1524]

---

in order to adapt to the recent judgment of the Court of 17 July 2014. With this judgment, the mortgage debtor has the right to lodge an appeal against a judgment dismissing his objection against enforcement, where this objection is founded upon the existence of an unfair contractual term which constitutes the basis of the enforcement of the amount claimed] (translation by the author).

1521 Case C-280/13 *Barclays Bank*, EU:C:2014:279.

1522 Chapter 5, Section 3.3.1.3.

1523 Art. 671 LEC. If the property is not the main residence, the threshold is set at 50%.

1524 Art. 579(2) LEC. The conditions set are the following: (i) the debtor repays in the five years following the coming into force of the law a percentage equal to 65% of the outstanding debt, accrued solely by the legal interest; or (ii) the debtor repays a percentage equal to 80% of the outstanding debt within a period of 10 years. The next possibility of debt discharge also has the objective of avoiding unjust enrichment of the creditor. In the situations where the property is adjudicated to the creditor or to a person to which the latter has assigned its rights or to any society of its group and within 10 years of this adjudication they proceed to a sale of the property, the outstanding debt is reduced to 50% of the capital gain obtained on such a sale.

## 2. FRANCE: ENSHRINING THE POWERS OF THE COURTS IN THE CONSUMER CODE

The example of France provides an important demonstration of the powerful influence of the active consumer court doctrine, particularly if account is taken of the fierce debate that preceded its establishment. The Consumer Code (*Code de la Consommation*) raises certain of its provisions to the status of ordre public[1525] and provides for the powers of the courts to raise of their own motion *all* the rules of the Consumer Code. Moreover, the courts bear an obligation (and not merely a faculty, an amendment directly inspired by the Union doctrine of the active court) to raise unfair terms, provided that the parties have been heard and that the unfair character of the term derives from the elements of the case file. This section traces the tormented history of adoption of this rule which brought about a "seismic change" ("seism")[1526] to the role of the courts.

In 2008 the French legislator introduced with the so-called *Loi Chatel*,[1527] a new provision in the *Code de la Consommation* with regard to the powers of the courts in proceedings involving its application. In 2014 a new law added one more sentence to this provision on the role of the courts with regard to the finding of unfairness of a contractual term.[1528] In its current version, as a result of the Decree of 29 June 2016, the provision of Article R632-1 reads as follows:

> le juge peut soulever d'office toutes les dispositions du présent code dans les litiges nés de son application. Il écarte d'office, après avoir recueilli les observations des parties, l'application d'une clause dont le caractère abusif ressort des éléments du débat.[1529]

These two sentences settle a long debate and give reason to the lower-tier courts which have opposed the vision of a "passive court" in proceedings involving

---

1525 Among which the provisions on unfair terms (Article L212-3).

1526 As it is qualified in the Report of the *Sénat* no 112 for the Loi no 2014-344 relative à la consommation (Law no 2014-344 in relation to consumer law) of 17 March 2014, under Art. 28.

1527 Loi no 2008-3 pour le développement de la concurrence au service des consommateurs (Law no 2008-3 for the development of competition in the service of consumers) of 3 January 2008, Art. 34 amending Art. L. 141-4 of the *Code de la Consommation*.

1528 Art. 81 Law 2014-344 (n. 1526).

1529 [The court may raise of its own motion all the provisions of the present code in the disputes which arise of its application. It sets aside of its own motion, after having heard the parties, the application of a clause the unfairness of which derives from the elements of the dispute] (translated by the author).

the consumer as the weaker party.[1530] As has been developed elsewhere,[1531] the French *Cour de Cassation* had in the past adopted a negative stance as to an eventual positive role of lower courts in the proceedings, on the ground that consumer law provisions belong to the category of rules of public policy of protection (*ordre public de protection*) which should not be raised by the courts of their own motion. The majority of the disputes which uncovered the unfair results of this approach arose in the field of consumer credit.[1532] The report of the Senate (*Sénat*)[1533] on the adoption of the new provision of the *Code de la Consommation* provides a very useful insight into the legal and social context that generated reform. In brief, the report states that the legislative body has been alerted by the Mediator of the French Republic on the important imbalances that were observed in consumer law disputes. The practice of litigation had demonstrated the perverse effect of the right of self-representation in consumer disputes. The lack of legal representation could actually work against the consumer when he lacks the legal sophistication to invoke the protective rules that support his case. By contrast, the professionals – in particular, the banks in the usual context of consumer credit litigation – possess the necessary expertise. In this way, powerful professionals would "come out ahead" in litigation, to use the famous statement of Marc Galanter.[1534] The report refers to the restrictive jurisprudential line of the *Cour de Cassation*. In many instances of a breach of the requirements on consumer credit, the sanction imposed by the legislator was the forfeiture of the contractual interest. The denial of an active role of the courts posed a great risk to the effectiveness of that law, as most consumers would not invoke nullity and courts would not be empowered to raise the issue. The intervention of the legislator was therefore deemed necessary in order to restore the powers that the courts should have and in order to ensure equality of the parties and fair process.

The French procedural provision devoted to the powers of the courts has the widest scope possible. It covers all the provisions of the *Code de la*

---

1530 The literature is abundant on this subject. See extensively with further references E. Poillot, "Le relevé d'office" in N. Sauphanor-Brouillaud et al. (eds.), *Les contrats de Consommation Règles Communes* (Paris, LGDJ, 2013), paras. 963 *et seq.*; G. Poissonier, "Office du juge en droit de la consommation: une clarification bienvenue" (2008) *Recueil Dalloz* 1285 ; G. Poissonier, "Mode d'emploi du relevé d'office en droit de la consommation" (2009) 5(5) *Contrats, concurrence, consommation*; B. Gorchs, "Le relevé d'office des moyens tirés du code de la consommation: une clarification inappropriée" (2010) *Recueil Dalloz* 1300.

1531 Chapter 3, Section 2.2.4.

1532 See G. Biardeaud and P.Florés, *Credit à la Consommation, Protection du consommateur* (Paris, Delmas Express, 2012).

1533 *Sénat Rapport no 111 au nom de la commission des Affaires économiques sur le projet de loi, pour le développement de la concurrence au service des consommateurs par M. Gérard Cornu*, Sénat de la session ordinaire de 2007–2008, 99–103.

1534 M. Galanter, "Why the 'Haves' Come out Ahead: Speculations on the Limits of Legal Change" (1974) 9 *Law & Society Review* 95–160.

*Consommation*, irrespective of whether they are of domestic or Union origin. This is the simplest and optimal solution to guarantee the highest level of consumer protection. In this way the legislator avoids a new round of uncertainty that would ensue from the use of an abstract criterion to single out rules which the courts would have the power to raise of their own motion and others for which they would not have the power to do so. The courts are empowered to exercise their role to ensure that all the rules of the *Code de la Consommation* have been observed. Moreover, the codification of consumer legislation renders the exercise of such role manageable. This wide scope of the *ex officio* powers is of great importance for the pronouncement of the civil sanctions, in particular the forfeiture of interest in consumer credit cases.[1535]

The report of the Senate makes reference to the fundamental judgments in *Océano Grupo, Cofidis* and *Rampion and Godard.* The last two cases particularly concerned the French legal order and demonstrated that the denial of a positive role for the French courts would prejudice the effectiveness of Union (consumer) law. Against this background, it became evident, according to the report, that the case law of the *Cour de Cassation* could no longer apply and that it had to evolve in order to respect the interpretation given by the Court. The report views the active role of the courts as an expression of fundamental rights protection. The positive action is necessary to ensure the right to a fair trial pursuant to Article 6 ECHR:

> en effet, seule la reconnaissance du pouvoir dont dispose le juge de soulever d'office l'application d'une disposition protectrice du consommateur permettrait de rétablir un équilibre dans le cadre d'un procès entre la partie faible et la partie dominante … le juge qui supplée, lorsque l'occasion lui parait propice, la faiblesse ou l'ignorance d'une partie, illustre et conditionne le droit à un procès équitable.[1536]

The report concludes that the exceptional character of the consumer legislation requires the establishment of an exceptional power.

The provision on the powers of the courts was completed in 2014 with an additional sentence stating the *obligation* of the courts to raise of their own

---

1535 Art. L. 341-47 of the *Code de la Consommation*. The forfeiture can be total or partial, up to a percentage defined by the Court. The borrower has to repay only the capital or the interest that has not been forfeited. The unduly paid interest has to be reimbursed or deducted from the capital due. See B. Bouloc, "La perte du droit aux intérêts", *in Mélanges Calais-Auloy* (Paris, Dalloz, 2004), 81. See C-565/12 *LCL Le Crédit Lyonnais*, EU:C:2014:190, discussed above Chapter 4, Section 5.5.

1536 [Indeed, only the recognition of a power for the court to raise of its own motion the application of a provision protective of the consumer would make it possible to establish a balance in the framework of a dispute between the weaker party and the dominant party … the court which compensates, once it considers it appropriate to do so, for the weakness of the ignorance of one of the parties, illustrates and conditions the right to a fair trial] (translated by the author).

motion the unfairness of a contractual term. In its report, the Senate points out that a mere faculty of the courts to raise the unfair term is not compatible with the ruling of the Court in *Pannon*.[1537] The former provision of a judicial faculty had raised criticism from within judicial circles[1538] and from scholars[1539] for being at variance with the principle of equality. The Report of the Senate points out the concern that a judicial faculty may give rise to arbitrariness and even partiality depending on a "consumer-friendly" or a "business-friendly" attitude.[1540] Moreover, according to Judge Ghislain Poissonier, the important advantage of providing that the court bears an obligation to raise an unfair term is the incitement of the courts to unify their practice and to ensure a systematic application of the law.[1541]

However, the obligation of the courts is circumscribed by two conditions: the court has to invite an opposing argument, and the issue of unfairness has to be based on elements which form part of the case file (*ressort des éléments du débat*). This requirement corresponds to the double "brake" that the jurisprudence of the Court also sets. Yet, this should be weighed against the *Pénzügyi Lízing*[1542] requirements with regard to the obligation to adopt investigative measures so that the court can ascertain whether a certain term falls within the *scope* of the Unfair Contract Terms Directive.[1543] The hearing of an opposing argument is essential in order to comply with the requirements of a fair trial.

The lesser formality in lower courts deciding on consumer disputes gives the courts the possibility to raise the plea pertaining to consumer law in a simple way, namely orally, and to invite argument from the parties.[1544] The court may

1537 Case C-243/08 *Pannon GSM*, EU:C:2009:350.

1538 See G. Poissonier, "La CJCE franchit une nouvelle étape vers une réelle protection du consommateur" (2009) *Recueil Dalloz* 2312.

1539 See E. Poillot (n. 1530), para. 965, 981 with further references; V. Telier, "L'office du juge en matière de crédit à la consommation: la Cour de cassation récidive" *Les Petites Affiches*, 30 June 2004.

1540 Report of the Senate no 112 (n. 1526).

1541 G. Poissonier (n. 1538), adding that the mandatory character of the judicial powers will contribute to ensuring a systematic application of the law by means of more reinforced scrutiny of contracts and equality of treatment among citizens thanks to a more uniform case law.

1542 Case C-137/08 *VB Pénzügyi Lízing*, EU:C:2010:659.

1543 E. Poillot (n. 1530), para. 1983, proposes *de lege ferenda* that a new article should be introduced into the *Code de la Consommation* which would read as follows: "En matière de clauses contractuelles, le juge, outre son obligation de relever d'office tout clause susceptible d'etre qualifiée d'abusive, est tenu d'ordonner les mesures d'instruction nécessaires à la reconnaissance d'une telle qualification." [In the field of contractual clauses, the court, in addition to its obligation to raise of its own motion the unfairness of any clause, is also obliged to take any measure of investigation necessary in order to proceed to such a qualification] (translated by the author).

1544 Provided that there is respective mention in the record of trial: G. Biardeaud and P.Florés (n. 1532), para. 2707.

also raise the issue during the deliberation phase, in which case it would of course have to invite argument from the parties before deciding. If necessary, the court might have to order the reopening of the debate.[1545]

It follows from the above that in the current state of play in French law, the courts have an *obligation* to raise a plea of consumer law only with regard to protection against unfair terms, but they have a faculty with regard to all other rules of consumer law. This distinction, at least with regard to the provisions of consumer law of Union law origin, would seem to be no longer in line with the case law of the Court, according to which the courts are required to examine compliance with the requirements which flow from the *entire body* of Union consumer law. Independently of the evolutions in Union case law, academia had already supported the establishment of an *ex officio* obligation with regard to all rules of consumer law, provided that the court has all the facts available to it.[1546] Elise Poillot proposes a flexible formulation that would make it possible to capture the possible evolutions in the case law of the Court.[1547]

That being said, it should be observed that the discretion insofar as other provisions of consumer law are concerned should not be understood as allowing arbitrariness, but merely for a wider margin of appreciation by the courts. The courts exercise their *judicial* discretion within the confines of the law.[1548] A reason that might support the framing of judicial powers in terms of *faculty* is to avoid unmeritorious complaints against a court for its not raising of any possible point based on facts that have not been pleaded by the parties, where those facts have not been brought to the attention of the court ("faits novices"). The French judges Gérard Biardeaud and Philippe Flores take the view that the current state of the law reflects a "realistic" and "pragmatic" position, because the existence of a faculty on behalf of the sitting judge:

> responsabilise le consommateur et prévient tout glissement du contentieux vers la question de savoir si le juge aurait dû voir ce qui avait échappé aux parties [stimulates the sense of personal responsibility of the consumer and prevents the litigation from

1545 Ibid.

1546 See Y. Picod and H. Davo, *Droit de la consommation* (Sirey, 2nd ed., 2010), no 295-1, who propose a broader formulation for the exercise of the *relevé d'office* so that "as from the moment that the court has available all the sufficient elements of fact, it has to raise of its own motion any provision of the Consumer Code in disputes arising from its application. (Original text: "dès lors qu'il dispose des éléments de faits suffisants, le juge doit soulever d'office toute disposition du Code de la consommation dans les litiges résultant de son application").

1547 E. Poillot (n. 1530), para. 983, suggesting a formulation according to which the court may raise of its own motion the provisions of the present code in disputes arising from its application, but when required by law, this faculty is transformed into an obligation. (Original text: "Le juge peut soulever d'office toutes les dispositions du présent code dans les litiges nés de son application. Lorsque les textes l'exigent cette faculté se transforme en obligation").

1548 On judicial discretion, see R. Dworkin, *Taking Rights Seriously* (Cambridge – MA, Harvard University Press, 1977), 90 *et seq.*

descending into an enquiry of whether the court should have taken notice of an issue which escaped the attention of the parties] (translated by the author).[1549]

Underlying this argument, we may discern the approach of Gérard Cornu on the *application* of points of law by the courts of their own motion. In his penetrating view, it is preferable to avoid establishing "straitjacket" rules for the courts in that regard:

> le juge ne méconnait son devoir que s'il ne relève pas ce qu'il devait raisonnablement voir, critère souple ... L'esprit des principes est la moderation. Un perfectionnisme absolutiste ne devrait pas faire du chapitre préliminaire le lieu d'inflexibilité droit [the court does not violate its duty if it does not raise what it could not reasonably notice, this is a flexible criterion ... The spirit of the principles is moderation. An absolute perfectionism should not render a preliminary chapter the place for the inflexibility of law] (translated by the author).[1550]

On the other hand, it should be pointed out the establishment of the *ex officio* doctrine in consumer litigation (and more broadly in disputes which involve the application of mandatory law intended to protect the weaker party) has the particularity that the effective application of that law does not rely upon that weaker party. Moreover, reliance upon the traditional mechanism of appeal for the correction of errors of law at the lower level does not apply in the same way as in other fields of litigation. If the consumer is deemed to lack sophistication at the level of the lower courts, this applies *a fortiori* with regard to his knowledge and determination to correct an error of law or even to claim on appeal that the lower court breached its *ex officio* obligation. The vague risk of unmeritorious claims from consumers on the ground of breach of the role of the courts would therefore seem quite distant. In any event, the effective application of the *ex officio* doctrine relies much more upon the combination of a high level of diligence, knowledge and sensitivity on the issue on behalf of the lower courts and upon an institutional framework that can offer certainty and support to the judges in discharging their duty.[1551]

The establishment of the *ex officio* doctrine in France is a synthesis of domestic considerations on consumer litigation and of Union considerations stemming from the developments in European law. It demonstrates the importance of recognizing the specific nature of individual consumer litigation and provides an example of a method of inclusion for the doctrine within a given legal order. This does not, of course, imply that all issues of application of the case law of the Court on the question of *ex officio* application

1549 G. Biardeaud and P.Florès (n. 1532), para. 2802.

1550 G. Cornu, "Les principes directeurs du procès civil par eux-mêmes (fragment d'un état des questions)" in *Etudes offertes à Pierre Bellet* (Paris, Litec, 1991), 83–100, 90.

1551 See the developments below in Section 4.

have been addressed.[1552] But the fact that the Consumer Code devotes a provision to the powers of the courts invites constant reflection on the compatibility of civil procedure with the effective judicial protection of consumers.

Finally, it should be noted that the 2016 reform of contract law in France does not affect the question of the powers of the courts in consumer law proceedings. Yet consumer law will be a source of inspiration for the concept of "significant imbalance" which has become now part of the general contract law theory.[1553] According to Article 1171 *Code Civil*, a clause which creates "significant imbalance" in the rights and obligations of the parties in a contract which contains general contract terms (*contrat d'adhésion*) is deemed to be non-existent (*non écrite*). This provision is of general application to all contracts containing general contract terms that have not been negotiated between the parties.[1554] The contractual consequence of use of a clause which causes *significant imbalance* is the same as the contractual consequence of use of an unfair term.[1555] Since the contractual consequence is the same, the power of the courts should also normally be the same, at least in those contractual relations where one of the parties is in weaker position. It falls upon case law to develop this aspect in the framework of general contract law.

## 3. THE UK: THE CONSUMER RIGHTS ACT 2015

The Consumer Rights Act 2015 (CRA) has been described as "arguably one of the most significant and important pieces of consolidating legislation in decades."[1556] The CRA, Simon Whittaker observes, "has a close relationship with EU law, but the nature of that relationship differs."[1557] This is so, the author explains, because sometimes "the law implements requirements of

1552 See E. Poillot, H. Aubry and N. Sauphanor-Brouillaud, "Panorama droit de la consommation Avril 2014–15" (2015) 10 *Recueil Dalloz* 588–599, pointing out the potential of conflict with French law, as it has been interpreted by a judgment of the *Cour de Cassation* (Cass. civ. 2ème, 11 mars 2010, no 09-13.312, Bull. civ. II, no 55), with *Morcillo and García* and the right of appeal against a judgment ordering repossession.

1553 See A. Bénabent, *Droit des Obligations* (LGDJ, 2016, 15th ed.), para. 197; P. Malaurie, L. Aynès and P. Stoffel-Munck, *Droit des Obligations* (Paris, LGDJ, 8th ed., 2016), para. 450; L. Gratton, "Les clauses abusives en droit commun des contrats" (2016) *Recueil Dalloz* 22.

1554 Art. 1110 of the *Code Civil* defines the *contrat d'adhésion* as a contract of which the general conditions, excluded from negotiation, are defined in advance by one of the parties.

1555 Art. L.241-1 of the *Code de la Consommation.*

1556 Editorial, "The Consumer Rights Act 2015" (2015) 125 *Civil Practice Bulletin* 1–2.

1557 S. Whittaker, "Distinctive Features of the New Consumer Contract Law" (2017) 133 *Law Quarterly Review* 47–72, 47.

EU secondary legislation," sometimes "the new law is tied directly to an EU legislative scheme implemented in UK law, even though it is not required by EU law," while some of the provisions are specific to English consumer contract law without being paralleled in EU legislation.[1558] The provision on the powers of the courts (section 71) derives from the case law of the Court, but it does not, strictly speaking, implement a specific requirement in that regard of the Unfair Contract Terms Directive. The introduction in the CRA of the doctrine of the active court aims, pursuant to its explanatory memorandum, to raise the awareness of the lower courts as to the obligatory character of the relevant power.

Back in 2002, a Law Commission and Scottish Law Commission Joint Consultation Paper made a first attempt to analyze the impact of the case law of the Court, which at that time consisted of only one (albeit landmark) case, *Océano Grupo*,[1559] on the power of the courts. According to the Paper, the obligation of the courts to raise the issue of fairness of their own motion when the consumer does not put forward the respective claim:

> presumably applies only when the unfairness of the clause is clear on the face of the documents or from the way that the case was presented to the court ... it may be argued that the business is still entitled to have its clause enforced unless the court has been convinced (by the consumer or otherwise) that the term is unfair.[1560]

At the time, Simon Whittaker had analyzed *Océano Grupo*, in terms of a "neutral judicial assessment"[1561] by the courts.

The new provision on the powers of the courts with regard to unfair terms is included in Part 2 of the CRA. This part clarifies and consolidates the existing consumer legislation on unfair terms which was included in two pieces of legislation, the Unfair Contract Terms Act 1977 (UCTA), on the one hand, and the Unfair Terms in Consumer Contracts Regulations 1999[1562] (UTCCR), on the other. Section 71, entitled "Duty of court to consider fairness of term," has a clear Union law influence, reiterating almost verbatim the settled case law

---

1558 For a detailed account of the act and the comparison of the new provisions with the ones that were repealed, see S. Whittaker, "Consumer Contracts" in H. Beale (ed.), *Chitty on Contracts* (London, Sweet & Maxwell, 32nd ed., 2015), Vol. II, 38-334 et seq.

1559 Joined Cases C-240/98 to C-244/98 *Océano Grupo*, EU:C:2000:346.

1560 Law Commission and Scottish Law Commission, *Unfair Terms in Contracts, A Joint Consultation Paper* (London, 2002), point 3.80, available at https://www.lawcom.gov.uk/project/unfair-terms-in-contracts/ (accessed at 15/01/2018).

1561 S. Whittaker, "Judicial Interventionism and Consumer Contracts" (2001) 117 *Law Quarterly Review* 215–220, 218; the author draws an analogy with unfair dismissal disputes where the tribunal will assess the question whether the employer "acted reasonably or unreasonably" as a "neutral" issue, although the parties may adduce facts or arguments in support of their positions (citing *Boys and Girls Welfare Society v. McDonald* [1996] IRLR 129, at 132).

1562 The Unfair Terms in Consumer Contracts Regulations 1999 implemented the Unfair Contract Terms Directive.

of the Court on the issue. Its first subsection provides its scope of application "to proceedings before a court which relate to a term of a consumer contract." According to the second subsection:

> the court must consider whether the term in the contract is fair even if none of the parties to the proceedings has raised the issue or indicated that it intends to raise it.

However, according to the third subsection, this obligation does not apply:

> unless the court considers that it has before it sufficient legal and factual material to enable it to consider the fairness of the term.

This influence is also reflected in the Explanatory Memorandum of the CRA:

> courts hear a wide variety of disputes between traders and consumers concerning contracts. However, courts are not always specifically asked to look at the fairness of a term in a consumer contract. This provision places a duty upon the courts to look at the fairness of terms even if the parties do not specifically ask the court to do so. This provision reflects the view of the ECJ in Case C-168/05 [*Mostaza Claro* (at para. 38)] … In fulfilling this duty, the courts would not have to look the fairness of the term if they do not have adequate information to do, as was emphasized by the Court of Justice in Case C-243/08 [*Pannon* (at para. 35)]. In addition the courts would only have to look at the term or terms in question, not the entire contract; this reflects the principle in Case C-137/08 [*Pénzügyi Lizing*].

The 2013 Law Commission Advice[1563] acknowledges that although the express statement of an obligation of the courts to raise of their own motion unfair terms "is already the law," it will be "particularly helpful in raising the awareness of the lower courts that this is in fact an obligation rather than just a power given to the courts."[1564] Moreover, this statement clarifies the issue of the burden of proof. In 2002, the Law Commission had considered that *Océano Grupo* would not necessarily change the general common law rule on the burden of proof that it is the party which claims unfairness that is required to prove it. By virtue of the new statement on the duty of the courts, it considered that it will be "sufficient to establish that the consumer does not have to prove the unfairness of a term"[1565] since the obligation of the courts brings about "a de facto reversal"[1566] of the burden of proof. At the same time, by not requiring

---

1563 Law Commission and Scottish Law Commission, *Unfair Terms in Consumer Contracts: Advice to the Department for Business, Innovation and Skills* (London, March 2013), available at <https://www.lawcom.gov.uk/project/unfair-terms-in-consumer-contracts/> (accessed at 15/01/2018).

1564 Ibid., para 7.90.

1565 Ibid., para 7.94.

1566 Ibid., para 7.74 quoting Professor Christian Twigg-Flesner.

that under all circumstances the trader has to prove the fairness of the term, the law avoids the obligation "to suggest that all contract terms are assumed to be unfair unless the contrary is shown."[1567] Besides, the Law Commission observes that the UTCCR experience has shown the burden of proof on the business is "a light one," because when the trader wishes to rely on a specific term, the only evidence that will usually be required is the contract. It is then up to the court to assess the fairness of the term.[1568]

It should be noted that section 72 of the CRA has a broader formulation than the 2013 Law Commission recommendation. While the recommendation made reference to the *ex officio* duties of the courts only in relation to proceedings brought by individual consumers, the current text uses the broader term "parties to the proceedings." Does that mean that the duty of the courts equally applies in the context of proceedings brought by enforcement bodies? A purposive approach probably leads to a response in the negative.[1569] The deviation from the common law rule on the burden of proof is justified by inequality in the parties' strength and representation. This justification is not present in the case of injunctive proceedings brought by the regulator.[1570] The restriction on the court's duty in individual consumer litigation is underpinned by considerations of protection of the "unrepresented consumers in low level litigation," intending to "make the law accessible."[1571]

The CRA makes no reference to the role of the courts with regard to other rights which consumer derives from other Union legislative instruments of consumer protection. However, Simon Whittaker observes that given the most recent case law broadening the scope of the own motion assessment obligation:

> it is clear that a court in England and Wales may have a duty to raise of its own motion the issue of whether a party to the proceedings is a "consumer" and, if so,

1567 Ibid., para 7.91.

1568 Ibid., para 7.92. See also the statement under the list of proposed changes to the unfair contracts legislation in BIS, *Consumer Rights Bill: Proposals on Unfair Contract Terms, Impact Assessment: Final* (June 2013) that: "the new consolidated legislation should retain the UCTA provision placing the burden of proof on the business to show that a term is fair. In addition, the legislation should codify the case law to make clear that the court is entitled to consider the fairness of a term, even if the consumer has not raised the issue."

1569 There is also one contextual argument. The rules on enforcement of the law on unfair terms are set out in Schedules 3 and 5. No reference is made therein to reversal of the burden of proof or the duty of the courts to consider unfairness. On the contrary, the enforcer requiring the production of information in order to apply for injunction must have a "reasonable cause to suspect" that the trader is using an unfair contractual term (Schedule 5, Part 3, para. 13(8) Consumer Rights Act).

1570 Cf. Case C-413/12 *Asociación de Consumidores Independientes de Castilla y León*, EU:C:2013:800; Case C-470/12, *Pohotovosť*, EU:C:2014:101.

1571 2013 Law Commission Advice (n.1563), para. 7.94.

> what rights he or she may enjoy under the legislation implementing EU consumer contract law subject principally to the condition that the right is important for the effectiveness of the particular consumer protection which is foreseen by the EU directive and a court may even be required to request a party to clarify the facts to do so.[1572]

The force of the above statement will have to be relativized in view of the forthcoming exit of the UK from the European Union. Nonetheless, the new provision of the CRA on the powers of the courts with regard to unfair terms might at least incite the English courts to more easily apply the logic of the active consumer court doctrine in other fields of consumer contract law.

## 4. THE "EFFECTIVENESS" OF THE DOCTRINE OF THE ACTIVE CONSUMER COURT

The doctrine of the active court in consumer litigation is a very powerful instrument of effective judicial protection, provided that the judiciary actually makes use of it. There are perhaps two factors which are liable to affect the "effectiveness" of implementation by national judges. Where the doctrine is not incorporated into national law, the district judge might find it difficult to accommodate it within his own national legal system, or the judge might not even be aware yet of its existence and scope. The second factor relates to the doctrine's observance. As the doctrine relies upon the premise of lack of legal sophistication of the weaker party, it cannot be expected that this party will ensure observance of the doctrine. On the other hand, judges might not yet be familiar with the modalities of discharging their "new" role, particularly if they had previously managed only adversarial types of proceedings. Moreover, being a nascent doctrine, developed in the case law of the Court of Justice, its boundaries are not yet perfectly clear. This is liable to create a sentiment of uncertainty for the bench, which will be cautious not to overstep the mark in the "arena." The assessment of the level of effective application of the *ex officio* doctrine by the judiciary would require rigorous empirical analysis which goes beyond the scope of this work. This question has recently attracted the interest of the Commission, which has funded a comparative study undertaken by the Max Planck Institute - Luxembourg, comprising a strand on the enforcement of consumer rights derived from EU law.[1573] Any future initiative at that

---

1572 S. Whittaker (n.1558), 38-019.

1573 N. 1467. Among the most important problems the study identifies is the clarification of the active role of the national judge. It proposes the enactment of a provision in an EU directive which could state explicitly the active role of the judge "as a common procedural standard in all EU Member States" (p. 250).

level will be expected to take into account the findings resulting from the comprehensive data that were collected across the Union, particularly the interviews with the judiciary. Some observations can still be made in this place.

## 4.1. VISIBILITY OF THE DOCTRINE BEFORE NATIONAL COURTS

With regard first to the visibility of the doctrine, the most obvious way to ensure the awareness of the bench and its application of the doctrine is an explicit provision in national legislation. The examples of the English CRA or of the French *Code de la Consommation*, analyzed in sections 2 and 3 above are instructive in that sense. Even if the judiciary is deemed to know the respective case law of the court, it is important to have the doctrine enshrined in national legislation. This would allow the courts to discharge their role with certainty and confidence and remove any doubt as to whether such an active role bodes well in relation to the domestic civil procedure rules.[1574] For the time being, there is no explicit legal obligation stemming from secondary law for Member States to implement the doctrine of an active consumer court. However, the settled case law makes it clear that national legislation which would not allow the courts to exercise such a role would not be compatible with Union law, jeopardizing the practical effect of the protective consumer legislation.

It could also be argued that the time is ripe for the doctrine to be formalized as a standard clause of consumer directives so as to ensure its uniform application across the Union. Such a proposal would have as its objective the proper establishment and functioning of the internal market, in accordance with the harmonization clause of Article 114 TFEU. The case law of the Court already provides for the justification of such a clause. In view of the particularities of individual consumer litigation, if the courts would not take positive action, there would be a high risk that the consumer legislation would remain inapplicable. On the other hand, such legislation could go no further than to attach the active role of courts to the substantive mandatory provisions on consumer protection. The impact of the active bench upon the effectiveness of specific proceedings will still be examined in the framework of the *Van Schijndel* balancing test, on a case by case basis, taking into account the particular context of national legislation.

That being said, the incorporation of the doctrine into national law would not be necessarily sufficient to ensure its effective application. If the courts

[1574] Almost all the judges with whom the author had the chance to discuss expressed the same view. See in more detail the empirical study of the Max Planck Institute (n. 1467, para. 467) suggesting that "those member states that do not already provide for an explicit role in their procedural codes change their legislative framework in order to ensure that the power of the judge is both visible and explicit."

are not accustomed to playing an active role in the proceedings, they will probably not be at ease with its modalities. The specificities attached to an active role of the courts are not new ones. Within the framework of English small claims proceedings, for instance, where judges are called on to play a more interventionist role, Lord Woolf[1575] insisted on the need for more guidance and training. The interventionist role is an admittedly "highly skilled task ... more demanding than the traditional judicial role, because controlling fluid procedures is more difficult."[1576] It is demanding because above all it rests upon a judge's "sensitivity and tact, and this human dimension can prove more challenging than most forms of adjudication."[1577]

Moreover, irrespective of the "managerial" dimension, the application of the doctrine of the active court relies upon the availability of all the legal and factual elements. Where national proceedings provide for self-representation, the unrepresented party, either as a plaintiff or as a defendant, might not know how to prepare for the case, and this will have an impact upon the elements (and in particular the evidence) that the court will have before it in order to assess the legality of a given term. However informal the procedural setting might be, the courts will apply the law.[1578]

---

1575 Lord Woolf, *Access to Justice: Interim Report to the Lord Chancellor on the Civil Justice System in England and Wales* (London: HMSO, 1995), paras. 27–35.

1576 Ibid., para. 32.

1577 N. Andrews, *English Civil Procedure, Fundamentals of the New Civil Justice System* (Oxford, Oxford University Press, 2003), 535, para. 22.23. The author of the current work had the chance to attend small claims proceedings in the County Court of Kingston Upon Hull on November 2013 and to appreciate personally this dimension in the role of district judges. Here are some of the passages noted, which are representative of how the court conducted the hearing: "This setting is informal, I won't ask you for an oath but I expect everyone to tell me the truth; what that means in plain English is [...] I should not use Latin terms in these days ... I will not use legal terms but if anybody has questions please do ask ... please respond on the specific question that I ask you, anything else is peripheral and is not going to help me to decide ... let me ask you a question on behalf of the defendant ... I know it is difficult because you are not a lawyer ... If you want I can put the questions instead of you to the other party ... Is there anything you want to tell me on why you think you have to succeed or why should the claimant not win on their claims?".

1578 As one judge put it in response to the empirical study carried out by J. Baldwin with regard to English small claim proceedings, "the procedure and protocol have changed and the formality of the court has been removed, but nobody has altered the law": J. Baldwin, "Litigants' Experiences of Adjudication in the County Courts" (1999) 18 *CJQ* 12–40, 33. While the author of the current work attended small claim proceedings in the County Court of Kingston Upon Hull, one district judge stressed the limits of the judicial role in flexible proceedings: "We cannot give legal advice. For instance you saw during the hearing that I explained to one of the parties the implications of the judgment of the bailiff ... I could not tell him what is best for him. Only what his options are. Was it being otherwise then the party would say 'the judge told me I should do this or do that.'" Another judge in Luxembourg (*justice de paix*), discussed with the author the difficulties related to the role of an active court, particularly when the consumer is present and the judge entertains doubts over the legality of a certain contractual term. The judge provokes a debate on the question of legality of the term, but as the consumer does not know what to answer, the judge has to insist

Therefore, it is important that the design of a procedural system that takes into account a power imbalance is combined with investment in consumer education. Information technology (IT) infrastructure and legal advice are important tools that combined can effectively even out the power imbalance between the parties. Evidential issues become more pressing when higher monetary values are at stake. The judges cannot be expected to do the work of a solicitor. There must be available enough trained court staff to ensure that litigants have received prior free legal advice or that they are directed to organizations that offer such advice.[1579] Guidance on the essential elements of preparing a case is also important and must go beyond explanatory leaflets, especially with respect to the required evidence that needs to be submitted at the hearing. Preliminary hearings could exceptionally be held where the judge deems it appropriate to do so.[1580] IT can contribute to a great extent to "procedural" education. Videos of mock hearings in representative disputes that frequently arise, also focusing on the evidential aspects, may help the lay litigant to familiarize himself with the hearing experience.

In view of the above, it is suggested that the effectiveness of the doctrine may be enhanced by means of both its entrenchment in the law as a legal obligation and by the proper training of the judiciary. The added value of having an explicit positive obligation is not only that the courts will be confident in their role, but also that it will be made clear to the parties (particularly the professionals) that this is the path the courts are going to follow; it will be transparent and applicable across all jurisdictions.

The different perceptions of the role of the judiciary might exercise an important influence in how the doctrine materializes across the Union jurisdictions. In order to fully embrace the doctrine, it is necessary to deflect any incorrect perceptions of the judiciary that the doctrine obliges them to overstep their role and meddle in private affairs and business policy.[1581] Moreover, considerations of proportionality of the value of the case with regard to the time allocation and the overall workload and time pressures on the district

with more questions that go in a certain direction. From this point onwards, the judge might start to have the troubling sentiment of becoming counsel for the consumer.

1579 Such as the Citizens Advice Bureau in the UK.

1580 Discussing the issue of preliminary hearings, however, Baldwin warns that "over-elaboration of procedures at an early stage rapidly comes to defeat the object of the exercise" and that therefore "striking the right balance between attaining an adequacy of legal and evidential refinement and encouraging the effective participation of lay people lies at the heart of the small claims dilemma". J. Baldwin, *Small Claims in the County Courts in England and Wales: The Bargain Basement of Civil Justice* (Oxford, Clarendon Press, 1997).

1581 One district judge said to the author of the current work: "I agree that the judges have to ensure that the law is not ignored and if there is a manifest unfairness the judge must act and be given the positive power to do so; it is something that would be appreciated by the district bench. The question that I raise is to the fact how does that play out and the mechanics ... we have to see how a positive obligation cascades down to the judge across the jurisdictions."

bench have to be taken into account. In that regard, a system of preliminary reference to an independent consultation committee, such as that which exists in France with the Unfair Terms Commission (*Comité des Clauses Abusives*), could be a good means of assisting the courts. That Commission provides for recommendations and it is responsible for keeping a register of judgments declaring terms unfair but can also be seised by judges to give an opinion on the issue of unfairness of a certain clause. This is very important if we consider that judges do not have infinite resources and time to carry out an assessment of terms where complex issues might be raised. The establishment of an independent consultation committee composed of judges and professors of law, for instance, and a database that is regularly updated with all terms that have been ruled unfair could assist the courts while ensuring more consistency[1582] across jurisdictions.[1583] The judiciary should be supported by a broader institutional framework.

## 4.2. EFFECTIVE APPLICATION OF THE DOCTRINE AND CONSEQUENCES FOR THE COURTS NOT APPLYING THE DOCTRINE

The second element of effectiveness of the doctrine relates to the legal means of ensuring its observance. A court which does not raise of its own motion a rule of consumer law, despite being required to do so, commits an error of law. Such an error may be corrected by the conventional means of appeal. The ultimate

---

[1582] On a procedural mechanism to ensure the consistency of case law in a single jurisdiction, see Case C-567/13 *Baczó and Vizsnyiczai*, EU:C:2015:88. According to the Hungarian legislation, a local court which has jurisdiction to hear an action brought by a consumer on the *invalidity* of a standard contract does not have jurisdiction to hear an application from that consumer for a declaration that a contractual term is *unfair*, this jurisdiction being given to a higher county court. The Court did not find such a procedural rule incompatible with the Unfair Contract Terms Directive. It recognized that the designation of higher courts to rule on the unfairness of contractual terms "which are less numerous and hierarchically superior to the local courts, may facilitate a more homogeneous and specialized administration of justice in cases concerning the rules arising from Directive 93/13", at para. 46. The purpose of such procedural rule is "to assign disputes relating to unfair contract terms to the judges of the county courts who have more extensive professional experience and, thereby, to ensure uniform practice and a more effective protection of consumer rights."

[1583] The need for consideration of all the parameters around a positive obligation is apparent in the words of one district judge: "You may find that you have one judge in Hull saying 'I think that is an unfair term' and another district judge in Newcastle saying 'I think it is not unfair'. But if we take the example of an unfair rate, if other courts have considered that one term is unfair, realistically, the judge couldn't ignore that and the discretion would not play. I think that for a humble district judge trying to deal with people not having the equality of arms, it is preferable that he is allowed the manoeuver so as to correct injustice, because otherwise what is the nature of that job supposed to be?".

consequence can theoretically be state liability deriving from the well-known *Köbler* case law.[1584] In this fundamental judgment, the Court laid down the strict conditions under which state liability may arise for breach of Union law from a decision of a court adjudicating at last instance. Particularly with regard to the condition of a "sufficiently serious breach of the law," the Court clarified that the liability of national jurisdictions may be incurred "only in the exceptional case where the court has manifestly infringed the applicable law," taking into account a set of factors.[1585] This would in any event be the case where the infringement of Union law "was made in manifest breach of the case-law of the Court in the matter."[1586]

In the field of the duty of the courts to raise of their own motion the Union consumer protection legislation, for the time being, there has not been a case concerning the obligations of courts of cassation in that regard. But the Court has found rules of Union consumer protection law to be of equal standing to the rules which rank in the national legal order as rules of public policy. On the basis of the *public policy equivalence principle*, the Court decided that if a court of appeal has the power to raise of its own motion a rule of *public policy*, it is obliged to afford the same procedural treatment to mandatory rules of Union consumer protection law (whether that be a rule affecting the validity of a legal act[1587] or another provision of Union consumer protection law).[1588] Logically, the same rule should then apply for the courts of cassation. So if a court of last instance does not raise a mandatory rule of consumer law of its own motion in the same way that it would do for rules of public policy, even though it has all the legal and factual elements available to it, this may result to state liability if all *Köbler* conditions are met. Admittedly, such a situation is hard to envisage. Consumer litigation proceedings are marked by a lack of legal sophistication. It is unlikely that a consumer would take the case to cassation and bring the complaint that the lower court erred in law by not raising a plea in relation to consumer law. It is also unlikely that the consumer would bring proceedings against the state for the reason that the cassation court did not raise the matter of its own motion.

The possibility that the Commission will initiate an infringement procedure against the state because of failure of national courts to raise an issue of Union consumer law is hard to envisage for obvious reasons. Judge Christian Timmermans wrote that bringing infringement proceedings in such a form of presumed violation "would put the relationship between national courts and the

1584 Case C-224/01 *Köbler*, EU:C:2003:513; Case C-173/03 *Traghetti del Mediterraneo*, EU:C:2006:391.

1585 Case C-224/01 *Köbler* (ibid.), para. 56.

1586 Ibid. See also Case C-446/04 *Test Claimants in the FII Group Litigation*, EU:C:2006:774, para. 214; Case C-429/09 *Fuß*, EU:C:2010:717, para. 52.

1587 Case C-488/11 *Asbeek Brusse* (n. 1465), para. 45.

1588 C-497/13 *Faber* (n. 1465), para. 56.

ECJ under severe strain."[1589] In his view, when it comes to judicial dialogue, it all comes down not to "coercion," but to a gentle persuading of the judges of their double roles as national judges and judges of the Union.

The question which arises is whether the effective application of the doctrine of an active court in consumer litigation would require the "relaxation" of the criteria of liability, particularly with regard to the requirement that the manifest breach of EU law be attributed to a court of last instance. The consumer *ex officio* doctrine relies upon the premise of imbalance between the parties and the need for positive action on behalf of the courts in order to restore that balance. If the consumer is supposed to be unaware of the legal means to defend himself at the trial level and to lack legal sophistication, he should even less be expected to be aware that the trial judge committed an error in law and to lodge an appeal. In *Tomášová*,[1590] the Court confirmed the application of the *Köbler* line of case law within the framework of the active consumer court doctrine. However, it is true that in that case the Court did not find it necessary to elaborate on whether the effectiveness of the consumer judicial protection would actually require a different approach with regard to the judicial instance at the level of which the breach of EU law will have to be assessed. Instead, the Court departed from the assumption that the national court, whose decision was alleged to have infringed Union law, ruled as a court of last instance and concentrated on the condition of the "sufficiently serious breach of Union law." In that regard, it found that at the time when the national court had allegedly infringed its obligation to raise of its own motion the unfairness of a contractual term and allowed the enforcement of an arbitration award upheld on the basis of such an unfair term, the case law of the Court had not clearly established the obligation of the courts to raise of their own motion issues pertaining to the breach of consumer law. The clarification of the role of the courts, according to that same judgment, was brought about only as from the judgment of the Court of 4 June 2009 in *Pannon GSM*.[1591] Therefore, the Court ruled that:

> it cannot be concluded that a national court which prior to [this] judgment, failed, in the context of proceedings for enforcement of an arbitral award upholding a claim for payment of debts under a contractual term which must be regarded as unfair ..., to assess of its own motion whether that term is unfair, although it has available to it all the legal and factual elements necessary for that purpose, manifestly disregarded the Court's case-law on the matter, and therefore committed a sufficiently serious breach of EU law.[1592]

---

1589 C. Timmermans, "Multilevel Judicial Co-operation" in P. Cardonnel, A. Rosas and N. Wahl (eds.), *Constitutionalising the EU Judicial System: Essays in Honour of Pernilla Lindh* (Oxford and Portland – Oregon, Hart Publishing, 2012), 15–23, 16.

1590 Case C-168/15 *Tomášová*, EU:C:2016:602.

1591 Case C-243/08 *Pannon GSM*, EU:C:2009:350.

1592 Case C-168/15 *Tomášová* (n. 1590), para. 36 and operative part of the judgment, point 1.

A particular feature of the *Tomášová* case was that the enforcement proceedings were still ongoing and the consumer introduced a claim for damages without having exhausted all the available remedies, namely the claim for recovery of unjustified enrichment. However, in the absence of one of the main conditions of state liability, the Court did not deem it necessary to examine the effect on the incurrence of liability, of the passivity of the consumer in the proceedings, of the fact that the enforcement proceedings were still ongoing or of the fact that the available remedies were not exhausted.[1593] With the consumer *ex officio* doctrine now being established in the case law of the Court, the question of the exhaustion of remedies may arise in the future. It could be argued that the claim for damages for state liability is the ultimate remedy and that it presupposes that the legal system has failed to protect the rights of the plaintiff. But where a given legal system still provides for the opportunity to seek damages from the person who is directly liable (the professional for using unfair terms), there is no good reason why a claim for damages against the state should supersede it.

It could be argued that the recognition of an exception to the rule of liability for manifest breach of Union law attributed to a court of last instance within the framework of individual consumer litigation could be justified from the perspective of the weaker party. As the weaker party in litigation, the consumer is not supposed to know the legal rules intended for his protection and *a fortiori* he is not supposed to know of the existence of an obligation on behalf of the courts to raise these rules of their own motion. As mentioned earlier, the chances that the consumer would enter an appeal against the judgment on the basis of an error in law therefore appear to be rather theoretical and thin. Therefore, so the argument goes, the recognition of state liability at the level of lower instance courts could compensate for the lack of legal sophistication in the employment of the means of judicial review and could create a further incentive for the courts to exercise their new role.

On the other hand, the recognition of state liability as a result of a ruling of a lower instance court seems to be contrary to the very same *exceptional* character of that liability. As the Court stated in its seminal judgment in *Köbler*,[1594] the infringement of Union rights by a final decision "cannot thereafter normally be corrected," a situation which justifies the notion that the *genesis* of liability lies only at the last instance level. Moreover, the application of the doctrine of the active court is subject to the condition that the national court has all the legal and factual elements available to it. The courts cannot be held liable if their attention has not been drawn, "either by the consumer himself of by any other means of information"[1595] to those elements which point to the application of a certain rule of consumer legislation.

1593 Ibid., para. 35.

1594 Case C-224/01 *Köbler* (n. 1584), para. 34.

1595 Opinion of AG Wahl in Case C-168/15 *Tomášová*, EU:C:2016:260, point 79.

Another element which should not be ignored is the effect that the establishment of liability at the level of the lower instance courts would have upon the judiciary. It is more probable that it would *backfire* against the intended goal of the effectiveness of the doctrine. The success of the doctrine cannot be achieved if it takes the form of a *Sword of Damocles* for the courts, but it relies to a great extent upon an evolving judicial mindset. "Penalising" lower courts for not exercising their *ex officio* duty is not, as Elise Poillot rightly observes[1596] either an appropriate or an effective remedy. Besides, the case law that formed the backbone of the doctrine demonstrates that if the courts hesitated to raise of their own motion the mandatory rules of consumer protection, the reason was that they did not feel confident to do so with regard to their own procedural rules. The courts themselves raised the issue of procedural protection for consumers and resorted to the Court for a constructive interpretation of Union law. Now it is for the Member States to ensure that the procedural framework exists which allows the courts to comply with their jurisdictional role in relation to individual consumer litigation. Judicial training and institutional support play very important roles in this. The *ex officio* doctrine will be effective only if it is *tuned* into an activist national judicial mindset.

Another dimension of the effectiveness of the *ex officio* doctrine relates to the question whether it should entail such a shift to the principle of party autonomy to the effect that the withdrawal of one of the parties from the action would not end litigation. In other words, should the effectiveness of the doctrine require that the courts maintain a reference for preliminary ruling despite there being no object of litigation because of withdrawal? It is true that in the field of consumer law the professional might be more easily incited to withdraw his action once a question for preliminary ruling is made in order to avoid the creation of a potentially unfavorable precedent. The result is that litigation ends and the court may no longer exercise its *ex officio* duty. However, ensuring effective consumer judicial protection presupposes the existence of an individual dispute. If this is no longer the case, it falls upon the regulator to enforce consumer law and not upon the courts to advance consumer protection policy in abstract. Particularly in case of withdrawal as the result of a settlement between the professional and the consumer, an eventual intervention of the court would go against the will of the consumer and would risk, as AG Wahl observed in *Gavrilescu*, "frustrating rather than achieving the goal of protecting the weaker party."[1597] As far as the reference for preliminary ruling is concerned (Article 267 TFEU), this is a mechanism of judicial dialogue which presupposes

[1596] E. Poillot (n. 1441), paras. 977–979.

[1597] Opinion of AG Wahl in Case C-627/15 *Gavrilescu*, EU:C:2017:690, point 52. The case was withdrawn from the register by Order of the Court on 4 October 2017 (EU:C:2017:749) following the decision of the referring court to withdraw the reference for preliminary ruling.

the existence of a *genuine* case *pending* before the referring court.[1598] An exception to this important condition for the Court to be seised of a case, would probably require explicit reference in the Treaty. In any event, the Court in its "Recommendations to national courts and tribunals in relation to the initiation of preliminary ruling proceedings"[1599] encourages the national jurisdictions to join the cases in circumstances "where the outcome of a number of cases pending before the referring court or tribunal depends on the reply to be given by the Court to the questions submitted by that court or tribunal" so as "to enable the Court to reply to the questions referred *notwithstanding any withdrawal* of one or more cases."

## 4.3. THE TRANSPOSABILITY OF THE DOCTRINE OF THE ACTIVE CONSUMER COURT

At present, there have not yet been cases before the Court which would consider the application by analogy of the *Océano Grupo* logic in other fields of litigation, outside of consumer law. The question arises as to whether the doctrine is "consumer-specific" or whether the underlying reasons that have underpinned its establishment could be applicable in similar situations. Despite the absence of case law, some preliminary reflections can be advanced in that regard.

It could be argued that the reasons for which a court must apply EU consumer protection law of its own motion are equally applicable with regard to other provisions of EU law which can be qualified as a *mandatory law of protection of structurally weaker parties*. Essentially, we may speak of a Union *ordre public de protection*, where the rule is intended to protect one of the parties that is considered to be weaker, but also serves a wider purpose of *general interest*. The Union general interest encompasses not only the good functioning of the internal market but also the broader objective of social protection and the well-being of the citizens of the Union.[1600] The doctrine of the active consumer court is an illustration of the rise of a "*Union public policy of protection*" on a par with the economic order of the market. It transforms procedural law in the same way that consumer protection law transforms private law by mitigating the effects of unrestrained contractual autonomy. The positive intervention by the courts can ensure the effective protection of the party that the legislator

1598 It follows from settled case-law of the Court that the "justification for a reference for a preliminary ruling is not that it enables advisory opinions or general or hypothetical questions to be delivered but rather that it is necessary for the effective resolution of a dispute": Case C-470/12 *Pohotovost'*, EU:2014:101, para 29 and the case-law cited.

1599 [2016] OJ C 439/1, point 25 [emphasis added]. This possibility is also underlined in the Opinion of AG Wahl in Case C-627/15 *Gavrilescu* (n. 1597), point 40.

1600 In Case C-201/15 *AGET Iraklis*, EU:C:2016:972, para. 77, the Court states that the EU "has not only an economic but also a social purpose".

intends to protect and redress the procedural inequality which results from the underlying "disparity in the power structure."[1601]

The core of the active consumer court doctrine is the connection between the *weaker position* of the consumer and the *procedural intervention* of the court to restore equality. This link can be established in other fields of litigation where one of the parties is structurally weaker than the other. Union employment law is, together with consumer law, the most prominent field of Union law with strong elements of protection and "corrective" function. It is settled case law that "the worker must be regarded as the weaker party in the employment contract."[1602] The legislation on Union employment law is not particularly extensive, given the limited competence that the Union enjoys in that field.[1603] Among the existing instruments, there are provisions which could qualify for consideration by the courts of their own motion. This could, for instance, be the case for the recognition of abusive recourse to successive fixed-term contracts and the application of the sanctions provided under national law or with regard to the application of the principle of non-discrimination between fixed-term workers and comparable permanent workers.[1604] The court should also be able to raise of its own motion the breach of the prohibition of dismissal of a pregnant worker for a reason related to her pregnancy.[1605]

The above instances of non-discrimination of fixed-term workers or of pregnant women are specific manifestations of the principle of equality which has a constitutional status in the Union legal order, pursuant to Article 21 of the Charter of Fundamental Rights of the European Union.[1606] The secondary legislation which implements this principle in the field of employment law[1607] is

1601 N. Reich, "Balancing in Private Law and the Imperatives of the Public Interest: National Experiences and (Missed?) European Opportunities" in R. Brownsword et al. (eds.), *The Foundations of European Private Law* (Oxford and Portland – Oregon, Hart Publishing, 2011), 221–248, 230.

1602 Joined Cases C-397/01–C-403/01 *Pfeiffer and Others*, EU:C:2004:584, para. 82; Case C-429/09 *Fuß* (n. 1586), para. 80.

1603 Art. 153 TFEU.

1604 Council Directive 1999/70/EC of 28 June 1999 concerning the framework agreement on fixed-term work concluded by ETUC, UNICE and CEEP, [1999] OJ L 175/43. According to its Art. 1, that directive puts into effect the framework agreement on fixed-term work (also 'the Framework Agreement'). The measures to prevent abuse are laid down in clause 5 of the Framework Agreement. The principle of non-discrimination is laid down in clause 4 of the Framework Agreement.

1605 Council Directive 92/85/EEC of 19 October 1992 on the introduction of measures to encourage improvements in the safety and health at work of pregnant workers and workers who have recently given birth or are breastfeeding (tenth individual Directive within the meaning of Art. 16 (1) of Directive 89/391/EEC) [1992] OJ L348/1.

1606 On the general principle of non-discrimination on grounds of age *see* Case C-441/14 *DI*, EU:C:2016:278, para. 22 and case-law cited.

1607 Council Directive 2000/43/EC of 29 June 2000 implementing the principle of equal treatment between persons irrespective of racial or ethnic origin [2000] OJ L180/22; Council Directive 2000/78/EC of 27 November 2000 establishing a general framework for equal treatment

applicable both against the state and the private employer. If, therefore, the court has before it all the legal and factual elements, it should be empowered to raise of its own motion the violation of the principle of equality in an employment contract as concretised in secondary law and to draw the appropriate consequences according to national law.

Within the limits of the powers conferred upon the Union, the principle of equality, as an overarching principle, is also applicable to consumer law relations.[1608] More particularly, the prohibition of discrimination on grounds of racial or ethnic origin applies in relation to "access to and supply of goods and services which are available to the public, including housing."[1609] The courts should also be able to consider of their own motion the application of the national provisions which implement sex equality in the field of access and supply of goods and services.[1610] The same goes with contractual relations covered by the Services of General Economic Interest (SGEI) law, in the fields of energy[1611] and electronic communications.[1612] In this field of law, the principle of equality translates, as Hans Micklitz has famously demonstrated,

---

in employment and occupation [2000] OJ L303/16; Directive 2006/54/EC of the European Parliament and of the Council of 5 July 2006 on the implementation of the principle of equal opportunities and equal treatment of men and women in matters of employment and occupation [2006] OJ L 204/23.

1608 See N.Reich, "The Social, Political and Cultural Dimension of EU Private Law" in R. Schulze and H. Schulte-Nölke (eds.), *European Private Law - Current Status and Perspectives* (Munich, Sellier, European Law Publishers, 2011), 57–88.

1609 Council Directive 2000/43/EC (n. 1607), Art. 3(1)(h).

1610 Council Directive 2004/113/EC of 13 December 2004 implementing the principle of equal treatment between men and women in the access to and supply of goods and services [2004] OJ L373/37.

1611 Directive 2009/72/EC of the European Parliament and of the Council of 13 July 2009 concerning common rules for the internal market in electricity and repealing Directive 2003/54/EC [2009] OJ L 211/55 (Internal Market in Electricity Directive); Directive 2009/73/EC of the European Parliament and of the Council of 13 July 2009 concerning common rules for the internal market in natural gas and repealing Directive 2003/55/EC [2009] OJ L 211/94 (Internal Market in Natural Gas Directive).

1612 Directive 2002/22/EC of the European Parliament and of the Council of 7 March 2002 on universal service and users' rights relating to electronic communications networks and services (Universal Service Directive) [2002] OJ L 108/51, as amended by Directive 2009/136/EC of the European Parliament and of the Council of 25 November 2009 amending Directive 2002/22/EC on universal service and users' rights relating to electronic communications networks and services, Directive 2002/58/EC concerning the processing of personal data and the protection of privacy in the electronic communications sector and Regulation (EC) No 2006/2004 on cooperation between national authorities responsible for the enforcement of consumer protection laws [2009] OJ L 337/11 and by Regulation (EU) 2015/2120 of the European Parliament and of the Council of 25 November 2015 laying down measures concerning open internet access and amending Directive 2002/22/EC on universal service and users' rights relating to electronic communications networks and services and Regulation (EU) No 531/2012 on roaming on public mobile communications networks within the Union [2015] OJ L 310/1.

into a general principle of "access-justice."[1613] The secondary law which liberalises the market for services, formerly provided by the state, makes specific provision for the "vulnerable customers," most particularly for the disabled end-users.[1614] The courts should be able to raise of their own motion the provisions of contract law which implement the protective provisions set out in this framework. A characteristic example in that regard could be the prohibition of disconnection of electricity of vulnerable customers.[1615] The courts should have the power to examine of their own motion the quality of a customer as "vulnerable" and the applicability of the relevant protective framework. It must, however, be admitted, that equality law raises complex issues of law and fact which in practice minimizes the potential for an *ex officio* intervention.

It can be validly argued that the presence of structural imbalance should not necessarily be a condition *sine qua non* for the *ex officio role* of the courts. Where the breach of Union mandatory law may affect the validity of the contract, the courts must raise the respective ground even in the absence of a submission by the parties. As Arthur Hartkamp explains, the obligation for the courts to raise the nullity of a contract covers not only contracts in breach of competition law provisions, but also "contracts that are contrary to comparable mandatory provisions of EU law, if these produce direct effects in the national legal system and have direct horizontal effect, and therefore imply a requirement imposed on individuals."[1616]

That being so, the difficulties experienced at national level with the establishment of the active consumer court doctrine (to the extent that legislation or national case law would not admit the *ex officio* powers of the courts) demonstrate that in order to establish a Union active court doctrine in another field of Union law, the rules in question may be required to have certain characteristics. The mere existence of a mandatory rule of Union law might not be enough to justify the imposition of a Union active court doctrine upon national courts, where these courts would not have raised of their own motion the comparable mandatory provision of national law. In these circumstances, the justification for such a limitation of national procedural autonomy would likely need to be the criterion of the *general interest*, as well as the element of *protection* intended by the legislator, in order to ensure genuine effective protection of Union rights.

---

1613 H.-W. Micklitz, "From Social Justice to Access Justice in Private Law, the European Challenge" (2009) *EUI Working Papers/Law* 60.

1614 Art. 7 of the Universal Service Directive (n. 1612); Art. 3, paras. 7–8 of the Internal Market in Electricity Directive (n. 1611); Art. 3 paras. 3–4 of the Internal Market in Natural Gas Directive (n. 1611). See N. Reich, "Vulnerable Consumers in EU Law" in D. Leczykiewicz and S. Weatherill (eds.), *The Images of the Consumer in EU Law* (Oxford, Hart Publishing, 2016), 139–158.

1615 Art. 3, paragraph 7 of the Internal Market in Electricity Directive (n. 1611).

1616 A. Hartkamp, *European Law and National Private Law* (Deventer, Kluwer, 2012), para. 128.

On the other hand, it could also be observed that the doctrine of the active court has developed to such an extent over the past fifteen years that it has occupied the terrain and somewhat "monopolized" the issue of the *ex officio* application of Union law. At first sight, there could be an impression that consumer law is disproportionately advantaged compared to other fields of Union law. Why consumer law and not every plea involving Union law? Why the consumer and not every citizen? In that connection, we should not lose sight of the fact that the general position on the *ex officio* application of Union law relies already heavily on the effectiveness of Union law. The courts must raise the pleas of mandatory Union law in the same way as they would raise of their own motion pleas of domestic public policy. But this applies only insofar as the courts would not be obliged to go outside the ambit of the dispute. *Kraaijeveld* (Case C-72/95), for instance, concerned a mandatory provision of environmental protection. The national court was obliged to raise it as a result of the principle of public policy equivalence. Moreover, the general position on the *ex officio* application requires that the party has a genuine opportunity to raise the argument of Union law. Normally, these requirements are sufficient to ensure the effective application of mandatory Union law in national legal orders without interfering with the role of the courts. In litigation involving Union consumer law, the effectiveness argument has been drawn even further because the *status* of consumer law in national legal orders significantly varies, and this has an impact upon the definition of a uniform role of the courts. Moreover, it is a field of extensive substantive harmonization. The effective application of the uniform Union consumer law could not be allowed to vary depending on the status that each legal order would confer on the national legislation implementing it. The difficulties consumers face in the enforcement of their rights derived from Union law corroborate the need to create a uniform role for their effective judicial protection. But, this distinctiveness of consumer law is not amenable to a broad generalization in such a way that the effectiveness of Union law would overcome domestic judicial traditions and allow an unrestricted presentation by the parties.[1617] The *Van Schjindel* line of case law remains therefore good law with regard to the general position on the *ex officio* application of Union law.

To conclude, the *ex officio* doctrine in consumer litigation may more broadly signal the recognition of the "redistributive function"[1618] of procedure in alignment with the function of the underlying substantive instrument. The

[1617] This statement was analyzed in Chapter 2 on the *ex officio* application of Union law and its differences with respect to the *ex officio* application of consumer law.

[1618] M. Galanter (n. 1534). See S. Ménétrey, "La procédure est-elle un outil de rééquilibrage des intérêts?" Conference Paper, *Déséquilibres économiques et droit économique* (Economic imbalances and economic law), 7 and 8 February 2013, Nice.

powers of the courts to intervene of their own motion in circumstances of structural weakness are intended to redress "equipage disparity."[1619] The model of the weaker party trickles down to all levels of civil procedure, permeates their structure and redefines the constituent elements of a fair trial within such type of proceedings.

[1619] W. Rubenstein, "The Concept of Equality in Civil Procedure" (2002) 23 *Cardozo Law Review* 1865–1915 with further references to legal theory.

# FINAL CONCLUSIONS: CHANGING THE NARRATIVE AND MOVING FORWARD

This book has attempted to follow at least fifteen years of evolution on an issue which lies at the heart of civil justice, the role of courts in civil proceedings. However technical it might appear, the establishment of the active consumer court signaled an intellectual "revolution." By infusing a common high standard of judicial protection into proceedings involving consumers, the doctrine marks an evolution in the role of the courts and reforms the ethos of litigation, moving towards a more "humanized" vision of law and procedure. The numerous references for a preliminary ruling uncover the change that has taken place in the mindset of the judges. Industrious courts view procedural laws from a new perspective, through the prism of the *ex officio* doctrine. The active consumer court doctrine invites us to rethink fairness in the proceedings by "reestablish[ing] social justice in contract law."[1620] The active court doctrine is a major expression of a Europeanized consumer procedural law, imbued by the considerations of weaker party protection. From this perspective it signals the emergence of a "Union public policy of protection". The rationale underlying the doctrine – the addressing of power imbalances – trickles down through various domestic procedural systems and contexts. The doctrine's implementation requires national procedural law to be interpreted in such a way that embraces the specific nature of consumer litigation. The example of Spain is instructive in this respect. An archaic mortgage repossession law which did not take into account the specificities of residential property has been profoundly reshaped by the doctrine.

The *ex officio* doctrine has started to gain pace. Already it has been a driver for reform of civil procedural laws in multiple jurisdictions, and it could be a source of inspiration for other national legal systems in the future. It invites reflection on the necessity of procedural clauses related to the exercise of substantive consumer rights. The doctrine reshapes proceedings, requiring that high standards of effective judicial consumer protection be safeguarded. The *ex officio* doctrine changes the narrative of consumer litigation, and this can become a springboard for reform of any procedural setting characterized by a

1620 F. Nicola and E. Tichadou, "Océano Grupo: A Transatlantic Victory for the Consumer and a Missed Opportunity for European Law" *in* F. Nicola and B. Davies (eds.), *EU Law Stories, Contextual and Critical Histories of European Jurisprudence* (Cambridge University Press, 2017), 369–390, 390.

power imbalance. Through procedural reform, there comes along an evolution of the values underlying a certain system. Beyond the strict confines of procedure, the active consumer court doctrine envisages a better standard of protection of the consumer-debtor-citizen. From this perspective, rethinking procedure goes along with rethinking the consumer concept.

The story of the active consumer court doctrine will continue to be told by the Union courts (namely the Court of Justice and the national courts in their function as Union courts) and legislators because its potential is still unfolding. The next few sections will summarize the main findings of this work.

## 1. AN AUTONOMOUS UNION DOCTRINE ON THE BASIS OF A UNION PUBLIC POLICY OF PROTECTION

The specific nature of individual consumer litigation has to accommodate a specific role for the courts. The doctrine of the active consumer court has to be embraced within a broader framework of flexible and accessible proceedings. The exact positioning of such an active court in the scale of the relative role of the courts and the parties in civil proceedings seems to be somewhere in the middle, between adversarial and inquisitorial. The courts have the duty to assess the unfairness of contractual terms and the duty to raise of their own motion other protective provisions of consumer law without waiting for the submissions of the parties. However, the courts will do so without introducing new facts. Their obligation to investigate is limited only to the extent necessary to identify whether a case falls within the scope of application of the Unfair Contract Terms Directive. The court has to provide the parties with the opportunity to present their observations on points it raises of its own motion. Moreover, consumers may renounce the protection afforded to them. These limitations on the judicial role categorically *exclude* three features of the "consumer court": it is not an inquisitorial court, it is not a partial court and it is not a "paternalist" court. The "consumer court" therefore operates within the boundaries of civil justice, albeit adapted to the specificities of litigation involving consumers. The consumer court ensures that the law is observed and that economic or structural disadvantages will not transform into a procedural "handicap" for the consumer. Assuming an active role in consumer disputes, the courts apply, in essence, the intention of the legislator to end contractual asymmetries.

This perception of the particular role for courts in consumer litigation does not reinvent the role of the courts overall. It draws upon links that exist in many national legal systems between the mandatory laws of public interest and the powers of the courts to raise them of their own motion. Union law necessitates a conceptual broadening of national mandatory rules so that they can include the core of consumer protection legislation. This legislation aims at protecting the weaker party, but it also serves a broader objective of public interest. It forms the core of a "Union public policy of protection." The effective protection of the rights forming this core necessitates that a link be established between the Union mandatory law of protection and an active role for national courts. The Court is inspired in the construction of its active court doctrine by various national contractual legal theories. However, at the end of this process, the Court rises "over and above"[1621] the national legal constructions and classifications, "autonomising" the doctrine. In this sense, the national concepts are immersed into an autonomous Union consumer *ex officio* doctrine, itself part of the Union "autonomous legal order."[1622]

## 2. THE WEAKER PARTY AND THE ACTIVE ROLE OF THE COURTS

The doctrine of the active consumer court is not the same as the general application of Union law by national courts of their own motion. With regard to the latter, no change in the role of the courts is required, provided that the principle of "public policy equivalence" is observed (the provisions of Union law that are of fundamental importance for the Union legal order rank equally to the provisions of national public policy which have to be raised by the courts of their own motion) and that the parties are given a genuine opportunity to present their case. With regard to the application of mandatory consumer law by the courts of their own motion, the European Court, in most cases, has gone beyond the principle of "public policy equivalence" and has established the active role of the courts as an intrinsic feature of consumer litigation independent of domestic conceptual categorizations. To achieve this, it has relied upon the weaker party "image"[1623] of the consumer, transposed in proceedings. The specific context of consumer litigation assigns a particular meaning to what a genuine opportunity for the consumer to raise his case as the weaker party should be. It sustains the proposition that even if in theory the procedure does not impede the consumer from putting forward a legal submission, the consumer will in practice not raise the law that is enacted for his protection. The procedural omission should not be equated to a voluntary renouncement of his rights. In principle, the consumer will be either self-represented or absent. Absence of legal representation, lack of sophistication and ignorance of the law beg for positive action by the courts to correct the imbalance and restore equality.

---

1621 Opinion of AG Mengozzi in Case C-429/05 *Rampion and Godard*, EU:C:2007:199, point 82.

1622 See Opinion 2/13 (Accession of the EU to the ECHR), EU:C:2014:2454.

1623 *See* D. Leczykiewicz and S. Weatherill (eds.), *The Images of the Consumer in EU Law, Legislation, Free Movement and Competition Law* (Oxford and Portland, Oregon, Hart Publishing, 2016).

## 3. A BENCHMARK OF EFFECTIVENESS: STRENGTHENING CONSUMER PROCEDURAL PROTECTION IN A WIDE ARRAY OF PROCEEDINGS

Two interlinked stages can be discerned in the evolution of the consumer *ex officio* doctrine. The first stage comprises the genesis of the doctrine and the progressive refinement of its mode of operation. The national courts have an obligation to raise of their own motion the provisions of Union consumer protection law, provided that they have available the all relevant legal and factual materials. In the absence of the doctrine, at least for certain legal systems, the exercise of comparable powers would lead to the judgment being quashed on the ground of a breach of the principle of party presentation. In the second stage of the evolution of the doctrine, the doctrine of the active consumer court becomes the benchmark of effectiveness of the procedural framework within which it is applied. This is particularly evident in the procedure for an order for payment or in mortgage repossession proceedings. The question in such proceedings is as follows: does the specific procedural setting impede the application of the *ex officio* doctrine? As the doctrine acquires a transprocedural character, new "fine margins"[1624] of balancing of interests will have to be drawn on the basis of the *Van Schijndel* "procedural rule of reason."[1625] By becoming the gauge of effectiveness, the doctrine of the active consumer court can question procedural "orthodoxies" or require their adaptation within the consumer litigation context. For example, creditors should have recourse to a quick way of enforcing settled debts. But when an order is addressed against consumers, the courts should have the power to reject the order on the ground of the existence of unfair terms. In another example, a mortgage creditor should have the power to quickly enforce the mortgaged asset in the case of arrears. But when the enforcement is based on a residential mortgage contract, the courts should have the power to intervene at the stage of initiation of the proceedings.

## 4. A CONTEMPORARY READING OF CONSUMER LEGISLATION

The doctrine of the active consumer court results from a contemporary reading of the Unfair Contract Terms Directive and of other protective instruments of consumer law. This requires judicial intelligence, the capacity for teleological

1624 S. Weatherill, "Art. 38 – Consumer Protection" in S. Peers et al. (eds.), *The EU Charter of Fundamental Rights: A Commentary* (Hart Publishing, 2014), para. 38.57.

1625 S. Prechal, "Community Law in National Courts: The Lessons from *Van Schijndel*" (1998) 35 *CMLR* 681, 690.

reasoning and social sensitivity. In a few lines the Court combined two elements: the *telos* of the law and the empirical reality of consumer litigation. It is not difficult to envisage the outcome of a different reasoning that does not take into account these considerations. In France, for instance, the *Cour de Cassation* refused for years to recognize the powers of the courts to raise of their own motion unfair terms on the basis of the established perception of the role of the courts with regard to relative nullities. In Spain, the Constitutional Court (in its judgment of 19 July 2011) considered that there was no reason to depart from the line it had established some 20 years ago and to recognize that the lack of suspensive effect in mortgage enforcement proceedings raises an issue of effective judicial protection. But the dissenting opinion had suggested that the findings of former judgments should be read in light of the new economic and social context. To a certain extent, it is normal that the arguments of a more purposive and pragmatic line of thinking originated in the lower courts and not the higher courts. It will mainly be those courts that will encounter the difficulties that the consumer faces in his defense against a sophisticated party. The Court lent an attentive ear to the concerns of "procedural crystallization" of the market imbalance raised by national courts and gave them the form of the active consumer court doctrine.

## 5. FUNDAMENTAL RIGHTS CONSIDERATIONS

The establishment of the active consumer court doctrine can be traced back to the reading of consumer legislation in light of fundamental rights, in particular the right to effective judicial protection and respect for home and family life. This is in line with the growing constitutionalization of consumer law, a thesis demonstrated by Norbert Reich.[1626] The principle of equality of arms and procedural equality guided the assessment of compatibility with Union law of a Spanish civil procedural provision that disadvantaged the mortgage debtor with regard to the exercise of appeal. But even outside the context of this case, the doctrine of the active consumer court is informed by broader considerations of effective judicial protection and fair trial. From the statement of the Court that the imbalance may only be corrected by "positive action unconnected with the actual parties to the dispute," it can be deduced that there would be a situation of denial of justice for those consumers for whom the imbalance will not be compensated for by the positive action. In the field of mortgage enforcement proceedings, the right to effective judicial protection

[1626] N. Reich, *Individueller und kollektiver Rechtschutz im EU Verbraucherrech, Von der "Nationalisierung" zur "Kosntitutionalisierung" von Rechtsbehelfen* (Baden-Baden, Nomos, 2012).

and the right to one's home and respect for family life are the guiding values to ensure that procedural safeguards are in place, so that the courts can examine the potential unfairness of the underlying instrument. Following that line of reasoning, the object of the mortgage is not just a pledged property, it is the consumer's family home, and the consumer is not a market operator, he is a citizen who has to be protected. As Hans-Wolfgang Micklitz observed, the "constitutionalized" consumer may enable the EU to turn a new page in the history of private law.[1627] The doctrine therefore has a "permeable" (*perméabilité*)[1628] nature perfused with fundamental and social rights thinking.

## 6. THE VARIABLE DEGREE OF INFLUENCE OF THE DOCTRINE ON NATIONAL LEGAL ORDERS

The influence that the active consumer court doctrine will exercise upon Member States may vary. It might be that in certain jurisdictions, the doctrine can be received without the need for a specific provision or modification. But, in the UK, the choice was made to devote a specific provision to the duty of court to assess unfairness, so that it will be clear to the courts that this is an obligation. The French legislator also devotes a specific provision to the powers of the courts to raise of their own motion the provisions of the consumer code. The Spanish legislator proceeded with reform in part to restore the features which rendered the procedural law applicable to mortgage debtors incompatible with the effective exercise by consumers of their rights according to the Unfair Contract Terms Directive. The most important wave of reform of the Spanish civil procedure in 2013 did not come down only to the question of raising unfair terms in the course of mortgage enforcement proceedings. This issue was accommodated within a wider agenda of reform of the respective procedure and of new measures for strengthening the protection of mortgage debtors in times of crisis.

## 7. THE DOCTRINE IN TIMES OF CRISIS

The cases pertaining to the influence exercised by the active consumer court doctrine on the strengthening of procedural safeguards for mortgage debtors were generated within the context of the social impact of the crisis. During the

1627 H.-W. Micklitz, 'The Consumer: Marketised, Fragmentised, Constitutionalised' *in* D. Leczykiewicz and S. Weatherill (n. 1623), 21–42.

1628 An expression borrowed from F. Sudre, "La perméabilité de la Convention européenne des droits de l'homme aux droits sociaux" in *Mélanges J. Mourgeon* (Bruylant, 1998), 467 *et seq.*

property boom, the impact of the existence of unfair terms in the mortgage enforcement instrument would have been felt less because the mortgage debtor would at least have had the possibility to sell and repay. This was no longer the case when the property market crashed. In such circumstances, the detrimental effect of unfair terms is multiplied. When combined with a procedural system which does not afford consumers a high standard of effective judicial protection, the consequences can be harsh.

Some key cases are symbolic of the cause of an entire group of consumers. *Aziz* represents the cause of mortgage debtors, *Radlinger* the cause of overindebted consumers and *Kásler* the cause of mortgage debtors in foreign currency. But the people behind such cases did not choose to be activists or heroes. They were brought to court because their goods were seized or because they were unable to pay excessive debts created due to the excesses of unfair lending practices. Behind the cases lie the true sad stories of fellow citizens that needed protection. It is at times like these that the responsibility of the legislator to afford protection is higher than ever. As the former President of the ECtHR, Sir Nicolas Bratza, has said: "it is in times like these that democratic society is tested." In this climate we must remember that human rights are not a luxury."[1629]

Unfortunately, during the Great Recession, social rights were the first to be undermined and not the first to be protected. The European Union Agency for Fundamental Rights noted that "the socio-economic downturn is the most enduring crisis facing the EU."[1630]

At the level of the Union and in particular with regard to mortgage repossessions, the Mortgage Credit Directive aims to strengthen procedural standards, but it was only adopted in 2014 and entered into force in 2016. The responses of the Court in addressing procedural imbalances have been considerably faster thanks to industrious national courts that would raise the issue of compatibility of national legislation with the effectiveness of Union law and the Charter. The courts cannot procrastinate; within their jurisdiction, they have to decide. The following passage by Judge Tim Koopmans remains relevant:

> generally speaking, judicialisation is not inspired by some secret wish of the judiciary to decide as many issues as possible, but rather by the unresponsiveness of the political system to problems of society. If something is to be reformed, it should presumably be politics.[1631]

---

1629 Sir Nicolas Bratza, Solemn hearing of the European Court of Human Rights on the occasion of the opening of the judicial year, 27 January 2012.

1630 FRA, *The European Union as a Community of Values* (Vienna, FRA, 2013), 5.

1631 T. Koopmans, "Judicialization" in N. Colneric et al. (eds.), *Une communauté de droit, Festschrift für Carlos Rodríguez Iglesias* (BWV, 2003), 51–57, 57.

## 8. CHANGING THE NARRATIVE IN INDIVIDUAL CONSUMER LITIGATION WITH THE RECOGNITION OF DISTINCT PROCEDURAL RULES

The final conclusion of this work is that probably the most important contribution of the doctrine of the active consumer court is that it changed the narrative of civil justice in the field of individual consumer litigation by "tuning" the judicial mindset to an activist bench for the protection of the weaker party. The doctrine has brought about an indirect Europeanization of procedural law applicable in consumer law disputes, to the effect that higher standards are afforded to the consumer as the weaker party in proceedings. Member States have to ensure that their procedural laws can accommodate the doctrine and, where necessary, have to adjust proceedings so as to embrace the specific nature of litigation involving the application of the mandatory law of protection. Certain Member States have already started to transform the doctrine into specific procedural clauses inserted into consumer legislation in order to give visibility to the doctrine and legal certainty for the judiciary in discharging its role.

Certainly, the doctrine alone cannot revolutionize procedure. It has to be integrated within a wider context of accessible justice. But it should be recognized that the doctrine is not a mere technical rule. It touches upon a fundamental aspect of civil procedural law governing the role of the lower courts in proceedings and, under certain circumstances, courts of appeal. It incorporates a philosophy of litigation that pleads for the protection of the weaker party. The same philosophy can be applicable to legislation which embodies special rules intended to address structural imbalance. The doctrine extends to different kinds of proceedings and tests them for the capacity to embrace the specific nature of consumer law. The doctrine *is* the incorporation of a distinct procedural law for consumers.

The exact content of the doctrine has to be carefully reflected upon according to the characteristics of each procedural context. We have seen its effect up to now in ordinary proceedings, judicial review of an arbitration award, payment order proceedings, mortgage repossessions and consumer insolvency. It will probably continue to evolve across various levels and rules. But the crucial idea has already been revealed: the specific nature of consumer law as a mandatory law of protection has to be matched with procedure and, where appropriate, in the form of distinct rules.

This work will end here with a passage from the novel of Emmanuel Carrère, *D'autres vies que la mienne*. This passage is a tribute to the judges of national jurisdictions, who, like, José María Fernández Seijo, Etienne Rigal, Gérard Biardeaud, Philippe Florès, Diego Guitiérrez Alonso, Françoise Hilger or

Andràs Osztovitz had the intellectual strength to advance litigation toward this "brave new world" of effective judicial protection:

> as a result of their campaign, the law on the statute of limitations provision was changed, the duties of a judge were expanded, and the debts of tens of thousands of poor people were alleviated, entirely legally. That's not as spectacular as, say, abolishing the death penalty but is enough for Etienne and Juliette to tell themselves that they did some good, and even that they were great judges.[1632]

---

[1632] E. Carrère, *Other lives but mine* (tr. Linda Coverdale) (London, Serpent's Tail, 2012).

# BIBLIOGRAPHY


Amrani Mekki, S., "Les catégories de Common Law et de Civil Law à l'épreuve de l'office du juge et des parties" in *Mélanges en l'Honneur de Serge Guinchard, Justices et droit du procès, Du légalisme procédural à l'humanisme processuel* (Paris, Dalloz, 2010), 157–173

Andrews, N., "A New Civil Procedural Code for England: Party-Control 'Going, Going, Gone'" (2000) 19 *Civil Justice Quarterly* 19–38

——, *Andrews on Civil Processes, Court Proceedings*, vol. I (Cambridge, Intersentia, 2013)

——, *English Civil Procedure, Fundamentals of the New Civil Justice System* (Oxford, Oxford University Press, 2003)

Arnull, A., "The Principle of Effective Judicial Protection in EU Law: An Unruly Horse?" (2011) 36 *EL Rev* 51–70

Balate, E., "Le contrôle des clauses abusives : premier bilan" (1997) 37 *Droit de la consommation* 321–361

Baldwin, J., "Litigants' Experiences of Adjudication in the County Courts" (1999) 18 *Civil Justice Quarterly* 12–40

——, *Evaluating the Effectiveness of Enforcement Procedures in Undefended Claims in the Civil Courts* (Lord Chancellor's Department Research Series 3/03, 2003)

——, "Small Claims Hearings: The 'Interventionist' Role Played by District Judges" (1998) 17 *Civil Justice Quarterly* 20–34

——, *Small Claims in the County Courts in England and Wales: The Bargain Basement of Civil Justice* (Oxford, Clarendon Press, 1997)

Barnard, C. and Peers, S. (eds.), *European Union Law* (Oxford, Oxford University Press, 2014)

Beale, H. (ed.), *Chitty on Contracts Vol. I* (London, Sweet & Maxwell, 32nd ed., 2015)

Beka, A., "The Protection of the Principal Residence of Mortgage Debtors: Embedding the 'Basic Needs' Principle in Residential Mortgage Repossession Proceedings" in L. Ratti (ed.), *Embedding the Principles of Life Time Contracts* (The Hague, Eleven Publishing, 2018)

——, "Commentary Note on Case C-618/10 *Banco Español de Crédito*, judgment of 14 June 2012" (2012) 6 *Zeitschrift für Gemeinschaftsprivatrech* 326–328

Bénabent, A., *Droit des Obligations* (Paris, LGDJ, 15th ed., 2016)

Bernitz U. et al. (eds.), *General Principles of EU Law and European Private Law* (Dordrecht, Kluwer, 2013)

Biardeaud, G. and Florès P., *Credit à la Consommation, Protection du Consommateur* (Paris, Delmas Express, 2012)

——, "L'office du juge et le crédit à la consommation" (2009) *Recueil Dalloz*, 2312

——, *Le Contentieux du droit de la consommation Vol. I, Le crédit aux consommateurs* (Bordeaux, École Nationale de la Magistrature, 2005)

Bolard, V., "La Cour de Cassation consacre l'obligation de requalifier. A propos de l'arrêt de la Cour de Cassation du 10 mars 2011" (2012) (1) 19 *Journal des Tribunaux Luxembourg*, 8–22

Bright, S., "Dispossession for Arrears: The Weight of Home" in L. Fox O'Mahony and J. Sweeney (eds.), *Home: Displacement and Dispossession* (Farnham, Ashgate, 2010), 13–41

——, "Dispossession for Arrears: The Weight of Home", in L. Fox O'Mahony and J.A. Sweeney (eds.), *The Idea of Home in Law: Displacement and Dispossession* (Farnham, Ashgate, 2010), 13–41

Bright, S., Hopkins, N. and Macklam, N., "Owning Part But Losing All: Using Human Rights to Protect Home-Ownership" in N. Hopkins (ed.), *Modern Studies in Property Law* (Oxford, Hart Publishing, 2013), 15–39

Brownsword, R., Micklitz, H.-W., Niglia, L. and Weatherill, S. (eds.), *The Foundations of European Private Law* (Oxford, Hart Publishing, 2011)

Cadiet, L. and Jeuland E., *Droit Judiciaire Privé* (London, LexisNexis, 8th ed., 2013)

Cadiet, L., Normand, J. and Mekki S.A., *Théorie générale du procés* (Paris, PUF, 2nd ed., 2013)

Cafaggi, F. and Micklitz, H.-W. (eds.), *New Frontiers of Consumer Protection: The Interplay between Private and Public Enforcement* (Cambridge, Intersentia, 2009)

Cafaggi, F. and Iamiceli, P., "The Principles of Effectiveness, Proportionality and Disuassiveness in the Enforcement of EU Consumer Law: The Impact of a Triad on the Choice of Civil Remedies and Administrative Sanctions" (2017) 3 *ERPL* 575–618

Cahn, A., "Gemeinschaftsrecht und nationales Verfahrensrecht" (1998) 6 *Zeitschrift für europäisches Privatrecht* 969–980

——, "Prozessuale Dispositionsfreiheit und zwindgendes materielles Recht" (1998) 198 *Archiv für die civilistische Praxis* 35–71

Cappelletti, M., *The Judicial Process in Comparative Perspective* (Oxford, Clarendon Press, 1989)

Cardonnel, P., Rosas, A. and Wahl, N. (eds.), *Constitutionalising the EU Judicial System: Essays in Honour of Pernilla Lindh* (Oxford, Hart Publishing, 2012)

Castillo de la Torre, F., "Le relevé d'office par la juridiction communautaire" (2005) *Cahiers de Droit Européen* 395–463

Clausen, F., "Invocation tardive et relevé d'office du droit de l'Union européenne devant le juge national" (2012) *Annuaire de droit de l'Union européenne* 215–242

Collins, H., "Good Faith in European Contract Law" (1994) 14 *Oxford Journal of Legal Studies* 229–254

Collins, H. (ed.), *European Contract Law and the Charter of Fundamental Rights* (Cambridge, Intersentia, 2017)

Cornu, G., "Les principes directeurs du procès civil par eux-mêmes (fragment d'un état des questions)" in *Etudes offertes à Pierre Bellet* (Paris, Litec, 1991), 83–100

Corthaut, T., *EU Ordre Public* (Dordrecht, Wolters Kluwer, 2012)

Couchez, G. and Lagarde, X., *Procédure Civile* (Paris, Sirey, 17th ed., 2014)

Croze, H., "Le juge doit-il dire le droit?" in *Mélanges en l'Honneur de Serge Guinchard, Justices et droit du procès, Du légalisme procédural à l'humanisme processuel* (Paris, Dalloz, 2010), 225–232

Damaska, M.R., *The Faces of Justice and State Authority: A Comparative Approach to the Legal Process* (New Haven, Yale University Press, 1986)

Davies, J., *The European Consumer Citizen in Law and Policy* (Basingstoke, Palgrave Macmillan, 2011)

De Vries, S. et al. (eds.), *The Protection of Fundamental Rights in the EU after Lisbon* (Oxford, Hart Publishing, 2013)

De Witte B. and Muir, E. (eds.), *Judicial Activism at the European Court of Justice* (Cheltenham, Edward Elgar, 2013)

Delforge, C., "Clauses abusives, office du juge et renonciation" (2008) 3 *Jurisprudence de Liège, Mons et Bruxelles*, 93–100

Deshayes, O., "L'office du juge à la recherche de sens. A propos de l'arrêt d'assémblée plénière du 21 décembre 2007" (2008) *Recueil Dalloz* 1102 *et seq*

Devenney, J. and Kenny, M., *Consumer Credit, Debt and Investment in Europe* (Cambridge, Cambridge University Press, 2012)

——, *European Consumer Protection: Theory and Practice* (Cambridge, Cambridge University Press, 2013)

Dolny, T., "Procedural Treatment of Consumer Organisations in the Judicial Proceedings Concerning the Use of Unfair Terms" (2014) 1 *Revue Européenne de Droit de la Consommation*, 31–51

Domurath, I., "The Case for Vulnerability as the Normative Standard in European Consumer Credit and Mortgage Law: An Inquiry into the Paradigms of Consumer Law" (2013) 2 *Zeitschrift für europäisches Unternehmens- und Verbraucherrechti*, 124–137

Dougan, M., "The Vicissitudes of Life at the Coalface Remedies and Procedures for Enforcing Union Law" in P. Craig and G. de Burca (eds.), *The Evolution of EU Law* (Oxford, Oxford University Press, 2nd ed., 2011), 412–424

Dworkin. R., *Taking Rights Seriously* (London, Bloomsbury, 1997)

Dwyer, D. (ed.), *The Civil Procedure Rules Ten Years On* (Oxford, Oxford University Press, 2009)

Dwyer, P., *Understanding Social Citizenship* (Bristol, Policy Press and Social Policy Association, 2nd ed., 2010)

Everson, M., "The Legacy of the Market Citizen" in J. Shaw and G. More (eds.), *New Legal Dynamics of European Union* (Oxford, Oxford University Press, 1995), 73–90

Fazekas, J., "The Consumer Credit Crisis and Unfair Contract Terms Regulation" (2017) 6 *EuCML* 120–124

Fekete, B. and Mancaleoni, A.M., "Application of Primary and Secondary EU Law on the National Courts' Own Motion" in A. Hartkamp, C. Sieburgh and W. Devroe (eds.), *Cases, Materials and Text on European Law and Private Law* (Oxford, Hart Publishing, 2017), 421–461

Fernández Seijo, J.M., "La audacia del derecho" (2013) 2 *Revista Aranzadi Doctrinal* 195–203

——, *La defensa de los consumidores en las ejecuciones hipotecarias. Una aproximación desde el Derecho comunitario* (Dordrecht, Wolters Kluwer, 2013)

——, *La tutela de los consumidores en los procedimientos judiciales, Especial referencia a las ejecuciones hipotecarias* (Dordrecht, Wolters Kluwer, 2017)

FRA, European Union Agency for Fundamental Rights, *The European Union as a Community of Values: Safeguarding Fundamental Rights in Times of Crisis* (Vienna, FRA, 2013)

Galanter, M., "Why the "Haves" Come out Ahead": Speculations on the Limits of Legal Change" (1974) 9 *Law & Society Review* 95–160

Ghestin, J., "L'annulation d'office d'un contrat" in *Mélanges offerts à Pierre Drai : Le juge entre deux millénaires* (Paris, Dalloz, 2000), 593–607

Ghestin, J., Loiseau, G. and Serinet, Y.M., *La formation du contrat, Vol. II : L'objet et la cause - Les nullités* (Paris, LGDJ, 4th ed., 2013)

Guinchard, S., "Les métamorphoses de la procédure à l'aube du troisième millénaire" in *Clés pour le siècle* (Paris, Dalloz/Université Panthéon-Assas, 2000), 1134–1211

——, "Quels principes directeurs pour les procès de demain?" in *Mélanges Jacques van Compernolle* (Brussels, Bruylant, 2004), 201–248

Guinchard, S. et al., *Droit processuel, Droits fondamentaux du procès* (Paris, Dalloz, 7th ed., 2013)

Guinchard, S., Ferrand, F. and Chainais, C., *Procédure Civile* (Paris, Dalloz, 3rd ed., 2012)

Habermas, J., *The Crisis of the European Union* (Cambridge, Polity Press, 2013)

Hartkamp, A, "*Ex Officio* Application in Case of Unenforceable Contracts or Contract Clauses: EU Law and National Laws Confronted" in L. Gullifer and S. Vogenauer (eds.), *English and European Perspectives on Contract and Commercial Law: Essays in Honour of Hugh Beale* (Oxford, Hart Publishing, 2014), 467–484

——, *European Law and National Private Law* (Deventer, Kluwer, 2012)

——, *European Law and National Private Law: Effect of EU Law and European Human Rights Law on Legal Relationships between Individuals* (Cambridge, Intersentia, 2016)

Herb, A., *Europäisches Gemeinschaftsrecht und nationaler Zivilprozess* (Tubingen, Mohr Siebeck, 2007)

Hess, B. et al., *An Evaluation Study of National Procedural Laws and Practices in Terms of their Impact on the Free Circulation of Judgments and on the Equivalence and Effectiveness of the Procedural Protection of Consumers Under EU Consumer law* (Max Planck Institute, June 2017/European Commission, January 2018).

HERON, J. and LE BARS, T., *Droit Judiciaire Privé* (Paris, Lextenso, 5th ed.)
HODGES, C., *The Reform of Class and Representative Actions in European Legal Systems* (Oxford, Hart Publishing, 2008)
HODGES, C. et al., *Consumer ADR in Europe* (Oxford, Hart Publishing, 2012)
HOUYET, Y., "L'application d'office du droit de l'Union européenne par les juges nationaux" (2010) 167 (3) *Journal de droit européen* 69–76
——, *Access to Justice: Final Report to the Lord Chancellor on the Civil Justice System in England and Wales* (London, HMSO, 1996)
JACOB, J.I., *The Fabric of English Civil Justice* (London, Stevens, 1987)
JANS, J.H., DE LANGE, R., PRECHAL, S. and WIDDERSHOVEN, R.G.J.M., *The Europeanisation of Public Law* (Groningen, Europa Law Publishing, 2007)
JANS, J.H. and MARSEILLE, A.T., "Case Analysis in Joined Cases C-222 and 05, *Van der Weerd and Others v. Minister van Landbouw, Natuur en Voedselkwaliteit*, Judgment of the Court (Fourth Chamber) of 7 June 2007, [2007] ECR I-4233" (2008) 48 *CMLR* 853–862
JEULAND, E., "Remarks on the Power of French Judges in a European Perspective" in *Festschrift für Rolf Stürner zum 70. Geburstag* (Tubingen, Mohr Siebeck, 2013), 1545–1553
——, *Droit processuel général* (Paris, Lextenso, 2nd ed., 2012)
JOERGES C., "Le droit et la politique dans la crise en Europe: L'impact d'une malencontreuse configuration" in N. THIRION (ed.), *Crise et droit économique* (Paris, Larcier, 2014), 11–25
JOLOWICZ, J.A., "Adversarial and Inquisitorial Models of Civil Procedure" (2003) 52 *International & Comparative Law Quarterly* 281–295
——, "ADR and the Role of Civil Litigation" in L. CADIET ET AL. (eds.), *Mélanges dédiés à la mémoire du Doyen Jacques Héron* (Paris, LGDJ, 2009), 271–281
——, "*Da Mihi Factum Dabo Tibi Jus*: A Problem of Demarcation in English and French Law" in *On Civil Procedure* (Cambridge, Cambridge University Press, 2000), 79–99
——, "On the Nature and Purposes of Civil Procedural Law" in *Essays in Honor of Sir Jack I. H. Jacob, QC* (Toronto, Carswell Legal Publications, 1990), 27–45
——, "On the Nature and Purposes of Civil Procedural Law" in *Essays in Honor of Sir Jack I.H. Jacob QC* (London, Sweet & Maxwell, 1990)
——, "Substantive and Procedural Justice in Civil Litigation: A Measure of the Role of Civil Litigation" in *De Tous Horizons, Mélanges Xavier Blanc-Jouvan* (Paris, LGDJ, 2005), 549–566
——, "The Woolf Report and the Adversary System" (1996) 15 *Civil Justice Quarterly* 198–210
JÓZON, M., "Unfair Contract Terms Law in Europe in Times of Crisis: Substantive Justice Lost in the Paradise of Proceduralisation of Contract Fairness" (2017) 6 *EuCML* 157–166
JUDT, T., *Ill Fares the Land: A Treatise on Our Present Discontents* (London, Allen Lane, 2010)
KAKOURIS, C.N., "Do the Member States Possess Judicial Procedural Autonomy?" (1997) 6 *CMLR* 1389–1412
KARASIS, M., "Σκέψεις για μία Ευρωπαική Μεθοδολογία του Δικαίου" (2011) *ΧρΙΔ* 401–407 (in Greek)
KENNY, M., DEVENNEY, J. and O'MAHONY, L.F., *Unconsionability in European Private Financial Transactions: Protecting the Vulnerable* (Cambridge, Cambridge University Press, 2010)
KILPATRICK, C., NOVITZ, T. and SKIDMORE, P., *The Future of Remedies in Europe* (Oxford, Hart Publishing, 2000)
KOCH, H., *Verbraucherprozessrecht, Verfahrensrechtliche Gewährleistung des Verbraucherschutzes* (Karlsruhe, C.F. Müller, 1990)
KOKOTT, J., "Der EuGH, eine neoliberale Institution?" in *Grundrechte und Solidarität: Festschrift für Renate Jaeger* (Kehl am Rein, Engel Verlag, 2011), 115–134

KOOPMANS, T., "Judicialisation" in N. COLNERIC, D. EDWARD, J.P. PUISSOCHET and D. RUIZ-JARABO COLOMER (eds.), *Une communauté de droit, Festschrift für Gil Carlos Rodríguez Iglesias* (Berlin, Berliner Wissenschafts-Verlag - BWV, 2003), 51–57
KOVAR, R., "L'incidence du droit communautaire sur l'intangibilité des décisions nationales définitives" *in Mélanges en hommage à Georges Vandersanden, Promenades au sein du droit européen* (Brussels, Bruylant, 2008), 203–243
KRANS B., "EU Law and National Civil Procedure Law: An Invisible Pillar" (2015) 4 *ERPL*, 567–588
KRONENBERGER, V., D'ALESSIO, M.T. and PLACCO, V. (eds.), *De Rome à Lisbonne: Les jurisdictions de l'Union européenne à la croisée des chemins, Mélanges en l'honneur de Paolo Mengozzi* (Brussels, Bruylant, 2013)
KRUGER W. and RAUSCHER T. (eds.), *Münchener Kommentar zur ZPO (MünchKomm-ZPO)* (Beck, 4th ed., 2013)
KRUGMAN, P., *End This Depression Now!* (New York, Norton, 2013)
LECZYKIEWICZ, D. and WEATHERILL, S. (eds.), *The Images of the Consumer in EU Law, Legislation, Free Movement and Competition Law* (Oxford, Hart Publishing, 2016)
—— (eds.), *The Involvement of EU Law in Private Law Relationships* (Oxford, Hart Publishing, 2013)
LEMPERT, R., "A Classic at 25: Reflections on Galanter's 'Haves' Article and Work it Has Inspired" (1999) 33 *Law & Society Review* 1099–1112
LENAERTS, K., "Exploring the Limits of the EU Charter of Fundamental Rights" (2012) 8 *European Constitutional Law Review* 375–403
——, "Le Traité de Lisbonne et la Protection Juridictionnelle des Particuliers en Droit de l'Union" (2009) *Cahiers de Droit Européen* 711–745
——, "Social Rights in the Case-Law of the European Court of Justice" (2001) 28(3) *Legal Issues of Economic Integration* 267–296
——, "The Rule of Law and the Coherence of the Judicial System of the European Union" (2007) 44 *CMLR* 1625–1659
LENAERTS, K., MASELIS, I. and GUTMAN, K., *EU Procedural Law* (Oxford, Oxford University Press, 2014)
LENAERTS, K. and VAN NUFFEL, P., *European Union Law* (London, Sweet & Maxwell, 2nd ed., 2011)
LEWIS, P., "The Consumer's Court? Revisiting the Theory of the Small Claims Procedure" (2006) 25 *Civil Justice Quarterly* 52–69
LIGHTMAN, G., "Civil Litigation in the 21st Century" (1998) 17 *Civil Justice Quarterly* 373–394
LORD WALKER OF GESTINGTHORPE, "The Saga of Strasbourg and Social Housing" in N. HOPKINS (ed.), *Modern Studies in Property Law Vol. 7* (Oxford, Hart Publishing, 2013), 3–14
LORD WOOLF, *Access to Justice: Interim Report to the Lord Chancellor on the Civil Justice System in England and Wales* (London, HMSO, 1995)
LUZAK, J., "You Too Will Be Judged: *Erga Omnes* Effect of Registered Unfair Contract Terms in Poland" (2017) 6 *EuCML* 120–124
MAK, V., "The Myth of the 'Empowered Consumer': Lessons from Financial Literacy Studies" (2012) 4 *Journal of European Consumer and Market Law* 254–263
MALAURIE P., AYNES, L. and STOFFEL-MUNCK, P., *Les Obligations* (Paris, LGDJ, 8th ed., 2016)
MANCALEONI, A.M., "The Obligation of Dutch and Italian Courts to Apply EU Law of Their Own Motion" (2016) 3–4 *ERPL* 553–578
MANN, F.A., "Fusion of the Legal Professions?" (1977) 93 *Law Quarterly Review* 367–390
MARSHALL, T.H. and BOTTOMORE, T., *Citizenship and Social Class* (London, Pluto Press, 1992)
MEEÙS, A., "Note: La notion de loi impérative et son incidence sur la procédure en cassation et sur l'office du juge" (1988) 4 *Revue Critique de Jurisprudence Belge* 495–527

Mekki, M., *L'intérêt général et le contrat. Contribution à une étude de la hiérarchie des intérêts en droit privé, thése* (Paris, LGDJ, 2004)

Menetrey, S., "La procédure est-elle un outil de rééquilibrage des intérets?" in L. Boy (ed.), *Les déséquilibres économiques et le droit économique* (Paris, Larcier, 2014)

Menetrey S. and Bolard V., "Le plein office du juge et le rôle des parties" (2013) 2(3–4) *JurisNews* 21–28

Micklitz, H.-W., "The Consumer: Marketised, Fragmented, Constitutionalised" in D. Leczykiewicz and S. Weatherill(eds.), *The Images of the Consumer in EU Law: Legislation, Free Movement and Competition Law* (Oxford, Hart Publishing, 2016), 21–41

——, "The Regulation of Over-indebtedness of Consumer in Europe" (2012) 35 *Journal of Consumer Policy* 417–419

——, "The Transformation of Enforcement in European Private Law: Preliminary Considerations" (2015) 4 *ERPL* 491–524

——, *Universal Services: Nucleus for a Social European Private Law* (EUI Working Paper 2009/12)

Micklitz, H.-W. (ed.), *Constitutionalisation of European Private Law* (Oxford, Oxford University Press, 2014)

Micklitz H.-W. and De Witte, B. (eds.), *The European Court of Justice and the Autonomy of Member States* (Cambridge, Intersentia, 2014)

Micklitz, H.-W. and Domurath, I. (eds.), *Consumer Debt and Social Exclusion in Europe* (Farnham, Ashgate, 2015)

Micklitz, H.-W. and Reich, N., "The Court and Sleeping Beauty: The Revival of the Unfair Contract Terms Directive" (2014) 51 *CMLR* 771–808

Micklitz H.-W., Reich, N. and Rott, P., *Understanding EU Consumer Law* (Cambridge, Intersentia, 2009)

Micklitz H.-W., Stuyck J. and Terryn E. (eds.), *Cases, Materials and Text on Consumer Law* (Oxford, Hart Publishing, 2010)

Möslein, F., "Richtlinienkonforme Auslegung im Zivilverfahrensrecht? - Uberlegungen zur Auswirking der EuGH - Urteile Océano Grupo und Cofidis, aufgezeigt am Beispiel des §281 Abs. 2 S. 4 ZPO" (2004) *Zeitschrift für Gemeinschaftsprivatrecht-GPR* 59–66

Motulsky, H., *Ecrits, Études et notes de procédure civile* (Paris, Dalloz, 2010)

Murray, P. and Sturner, R., *German Civil Justice* (Durham, NC, Carolina Academic Press, 2004)

Musielak, H.-J. (ed.), *Zivilprozessordnung* (Munich, Beck, 11th ed., 2014)

Neframi, E., "Quelques réflexions sur l'article 19, para. 1, alinéa 2, TEU et l'obligation de l'État Membre d'assurer la protection juridictionnelle effective dans les domaines couverts par le droit de l'Union" in *La Constitution, l'Europe et le droit, Mélanges en l'honneur de Jean-Claude Masclet* (Paris, LGDJ, 2013), 807–816

Nicola, F. and Tichadou, E., "Océano Grupo: A Transatlantic Victory for the Consumer and a Missed Opportunity for European Law" *in* Nicola, F. and Davies, B. (eds.), *EU Law Stories, Contextual and Critical Histories of European Jurisprudence* (Cambridge, Cambridge University Press, 2017), 369–390

Nield, S., "Clash of the Titans: Article 8, Occupiers and their Home" in S. Bright (ed.), *Modern Studies in Property Law* (Oxford, Hart Publishing, 2011), 101–129

Nogler, L. and Reifner, U., *Life Time Contracts, Social Longterm Contracts in Labour, Tenancy and Consumer Credit Law* (The Hague, Eleven International Publishing, 2014)

Normand, J., "Principes directeurs du procès" in L. Cadiet (ed.), *Dictionnaire de la justice* (Paris, PUF, 2004)

Ostlund, A., "Effectiveness of European Union Law versus Procedural Protection: Tracing the Tension throughout the Case-Law of the Court of Justice on the *Ex Officio* Review by the National Judge" (Dissertation, University of Luxembourg, 2017)

Osztovits, A. and Nemessányi, Z., "Missbräuchliche Zuständigkeitsklauseln in der Ungarischen Rechtssprechung im Licht der Urteile des EuGH" (2010) 1 *Zeitschrift für Internationales Privat- und Zivilverfarhrensrecht* 22–26

Podimata E., "Standard Contract Terms and Rules of Procedure" in *Essays in Honour of Konstantinos D. Kerameus* (Brussels, Bruylant, 2009) 1079–1105

——, "Η δικονομική μεταχείριση του ισχυρισμού από το άρθρ. ΑΚ 281. Αποτίμηση ορισμένων νομολογιακών θέσεων ιδίως σε αναφορά με τον έλεγχο καταχρηστικότητας ΓΟΣ κατ' άρθρ. 2 παρ. 6 ν. 2251/1994" (2008) *ΧρΙΔ* 673–679 (in Greek)

Poiares Maduro M., "Europe's Social Self: 'The Sickness unto Death'" in J. Shaw (ed.), *Social Law and Policy in an Evolving European Union* (Oxford, Hart Publishing, 2000), 325–389

Poillot, E. "Chroniques Droit de la Consommation" (2014) *Journal de droit européen* 297–305

——, "Chroniques Droit de la Consommation" (2013) *Journal de droit européen* 26–32

——, "Chroniques Droit de la Consommation" (2014) *Journal de droit européen* 20–28

——, "Les Litiges Relatifs au Contrat de la Consommation" in N. Sauphanor-Brouillaud et al., *Les Contrats de Consommation Règles Communes* (Paris, LGDJ, 2013), 915–1094

Poissonier, G., "Mode d'emploi du relevé d'office en droit de la consommation", (2009) 5 *Contrats Concurrence Consommation*, étude 5 (study No 5)

——, "Office du juge en droit de la consommation : une clarification bienvenue" (2008) *Recueil Dalloz* 1285 *et seq.*

Polanyi, K., *The Great Transformation, The Political and Economic Origins of Our Time* (Boston, Beacon Press, 2nd ed., 2002)

Posner, R., *A Failure of Capitalism, The Crisis of '08 and the Descent into Depression* (Cambridge–MA, Harvard University Press, 2011)

Prechal, S., "Community Law in National Courts: The Lessons from Van Schijndel" (1998) 35 *CMLR* 681–706

Prechal, S. and Cath, K., "The European Acquis of Civil Procedure: Constitutional Aspects" (2014) 19 *Uniform Law Review* 179–198

Prechal, S. and Widdershoven, R., "Redefining the Relationship between '*Rewe*-Effectiveness' and Effective Judicial Protection" (2011) 4 *Review of European Administrative Law* 31–50

Prütting H. and Gehrlein M., *Kommentar ZPO* (Munich, Luctherhand Verlag, 5th ed., 2013)

Ramsay, I., *Consumer Law and Policy* (Oxford, Oxford University Press, 3rd ed., 2012)

Ratti, L. (ed.), *Embedding the Principles of Life Time Contracts, A Research Agenda for Contract Law* (The Hague, Eleven Publishing, 2018)

Reich, N., *General Principles of EU Civil Law* (Cambridge, Intersentia, 2014)

——, *Individueller und kollektiver Rechtschutz im EU-Verbraucherrecht, Von der "Nationaliesierung" zur "Kostitutionalisierung" von Rechtsbehelfen* (Baden-Baden, Nomos, 2012)

——, "The Social, Political and Cultural Dimension of EU Private Law" in R. Schulze and H. Schulte-Nölke (eds.), *European Private Law-Current Status and Perspectives* (Munich, Sellier, European Law Publishers, 2011), 57–88

Reich, N., Micklitz, H.-W., Rott, P. and Tonner, K., *European Consumer Law* (Cambridge, Intersentia, 2nd ed., 2014)

Rosas, A., Levits, E. and Bot, Y. (eds.), *The Court of Justice and the Construction of Europe: Analyses and Perspectives on Sixty Years of Case-Law* (The Hague, TMC Asser Press, 2013)

Rosenberg L. and Shwab L.H. and Gottwald P., *Zivilprozessrecht* (Munich, Beck, 2010)

Rott, P., "Case Note on *Banco Español de Credito v Joaquín Calderón Camino*" (2012) 8(4) *ERCL* 470–480

——, "Improving Consumers' Enforcement of their Rights under EU Consumer Sales Law: *Froukje Faber*" (2016) 53 *CMLR* 509–526

Rühl, G., "The Unfairness of Choice-of-Law Clauses, or: The (Unclear) Relationship Between Article 6 Rome I Regulation and the Unfair Terms in Consumer Contracts Directive: *VKI v. Amazon*"(2018) 55 *CMLR* 201–224

SACHPEKIDOU, E., «Επίδραση της Νομολογίας του ΔΕΚ στη διαμόρφωση των θεμελιωδών δικονομικών αρχών» *εις* N. NIKAS, *Η πολιτική δίκη υπο το φως της νομολογίας του ΔΕΚ και του ΕΔΑΑ, Ακαδημαικό Συμπόσιο προς τιμήν του Κωνσταντίνου Κεραμέως* (Σάκκουλας, 2008) (in Greek)
SÄCKER, F.J. (ed.), *Münchener Kommentar zum Bürgerlichen Gesetzbuch: BGB – MünchKomm BGB* (Munich, Beck, 7th ed., 2015)
SAFJAN, M. and DÜSTERHAUS, D., "A Union of Effective Judicial Protection: Addressing a Multi-level Challenge through the Lens of Article 47 CFREU" (2014) 33 *Yearbook of European Law* 3–40
SÁNCHEZ, S.I., "Unfair Terms in Mortgage Loans and Protection of Housing in Times of Economic Crisis: *Aziz v. Catalunyacaixa*" (2014) 51 *CMLR* 955–974
SCHULTE-NÖLKE, H., TWIGG-FLESNER, C. and EBERS, M. (eds.), *European Consumer Law Compendium* (Munich, Sellier, 2008)
SKOURIS, V, "The Principle of Procedural Autonomy and the Duty of Loyal Cooperation of National Judges under Article 10 EC" in M. ANDENAS and D. FAIRGRIEVE (eds.), *Tom Bingham and the Transformation of the Law: A Liber Amicorum* (Oxford, Oxford University Press, 2009), 493–507
——, "Der Einfluss des nationalen Rechts und der Rechtsprechung der mitgliedstaatlichen Gerichte auf die Auslegung des Europarechts" (2014) 3 *Zeitschrift der Verwaltungsgerichtsbarkeit* 203–208
SORABJI, J., *English Civil Justice after the Woolf and Jackson Reforms, A Critical Analysis* (Cambridge, Cambridge University Press, 2014)
SØRENSEN, M J., "In the Name of Effective Consumer Protection and Public Policy" (2016) 5 *ERPL* 791–822
SPIGELMAN, J.J., "Judicial Accountability and Performance Indicators" (2002) 21 *Civil Justice Quarterly* 18–28
STEENOT, R., "Public and Private Enforcement in the Field of Unfair Contract Terms" (2015) 4 *ERPL* 589–620
STEIN F. and JONAS M., *Kommentar zur Zivilprozessordnung* (Tubingen, Mohr Siebeck, 2005)
STORME, M., "Le juge et son panier" *in Mélanges J. Héron* (Paris, LGDJ, 2009), 474–476
—— (ed.), *Rapprochement du Droit Judiciaire de l'Union européenne* (Kluwer, 1993)
STORSKRUBB, E., *Civil Procedure and EU Law: A Policy Area Uncovered* (Oxford, Oxford University Press, 2008)
STRAETMANS, G. and CAUFFMANN, C., "Legislatures, Courts and the Unfair Terms Directive" in P. SYRPIS (ed.), *The Judiciary, the Legislature and the EU Internal Market* (Cambridge, Cambridge University Press, 2012), 92–117
STUYCK, J., *Landmark Cases of EU Consumer Law: In Honour of Jules Stuyck* (Cambridge, Intersentia, 2014)
SUPIOT, A., *L'Esprit de Philadelphie, La crise sociale face au marché totale* (Paris, Seuil, 2010)
TAELMANN, P., "Some European Challenges for Belgian Civil Procedure" in NYLUND, A. and KRANS, B. (eds.), *The European Union and National Civil Procedure* (Antwerp, Intersentia, 2016) 5–17
TEMPLE LANG, J., "The Duties of National Courts under Community Constitutional Law" (1997) 22(1) *European Law Review* 3–18
TERRYN, E., STRAETMANS, G. and COLAERT, V. (eds.), *Landmark Cases of EU Consumer Law* (Cambridge, Intersentia, 2014)
TOURAIN, A., *Après la crise* (Paris, Seuil, 2010)
TREITEL, G., *The Law of Contract* (London, Sweet & Maxwell, 13th ed., 2011)
TRIDIMAS, T., *The General Principles of EU Law* (Oxford, Oxford Law Library, 2nd ed., 2006)
TROCKER, N. and VARANO, V. (eds.), *The Reforms of Civil Procedure in Comparative Perspective* (Turin, Giappichelli, 2005)
TRSTENJAK, V., "Procedural Aspects of European Consumer Protection Law and the Case Law of the CJUE" (2013) 2 *ERPL* 451–477

TRSTENJAK, V. and BEYSEN, E., "European Consumer Protection Law: *Curia Semper Dabit Remedium?*" (2011) 48 *CMLR* 95–124
TWIGG-FLESNER, C., "Time to Do the Job Properly – The Case for a New Approach to EU Consumer Legislation" (2010) 33 *Journal of Consumer Policy* 355–375
——, *The Europeanisation of Contract Law: Current Controversies in Law* (Abingdon, Routledge, 2nd ed., 2013)
TWIGG-FLENSER, C. and VILLATA PUIG, G. (eds.) *Boundaries of Commercial and Trade Law* (Munich, Sellier, 2011)
VAN COMPERNOLLE, J., "Le rôle actif du juge dans l'application de la règle de droit: la consécration par la jurisprudence belge de la conception factuelle de la cause de la demande" in *Mélanges Dédiés à la Mémoire du Doyen Jacques Héron* (Paris, LGDJ, 2009), 477–485
VAN DER WALT, J., *The Horizontal Effect Revolution and the Question of Sovereignty* (Berlin, De Gruyter, 2014)
VAN DROOGHENBROECK, J.F., "La loyauté procédurale au-dessus de l'ordre public" in *Mélanges en l'honneur de Serge Guinchard* (Paris, Dalloz, 2010) 425–436
VAN DUIN, A., "Metamorphosis? The Role of Article 47 of the EU Charter of Fundamental Rights in Cases Concerning National Remedies and Procedures Under Directive 93/13" (2017) 6 *EuCML* 190–198
VAN GERVEN, W., "Of Rights, Remedies and Procedures" (2000) 37 *CMLR* 501–536
VON STAUDINGER J. (ed.), *Kommentar BGB* (Munich, Sellier/De Gruyter, 2009)
WASSERMANN, R., *Des soziale Zivilprozess, Zur Theorie und Praxis des Zivilprozesses im sozialen Rechtstaat* (Munich, Luchterhand, 1978)
WEATHERILL, S., *EU Consumer Law and Policy* (Cheltenham, Edward Elgar, 2nd ed., 2014)
WÉRY, P., "Les clauses abusives relatives à l'inexécution des obligations contractuelles dans les lois de protection des consommateurs du 14 juillet 1991 et du 2 aout 2002" (2003) *Journal des Tribunaux* 797–810
——, *Droit des Obligations, Vol. I, Théorie générale du contrat* (Paris, Larcier, 2010)
WHELAN, C.J. (ed.), *Small Claims Court: A Comparative Study* (Oxford, Oxford University Press, 1990)
WHITEHOUSE, L., "A Longitudinal Analysis of the Mortgage Repossession Process 1995–2010: Stability, Regulation and Reform" in S. BRIGHT (ed.) *Modern Studies in Property Law* (Oxford, Hart Publishing, 2011), 151–174
——, "The Home Owner: Citizen or Consumer?" in S. BRIGHT and J. DEWAR (eds.), *Land Law: Themes and Perspectives* (Oxford, Oxford University Press, 1998), 183–206
——, "The Mortgage Arrears Pre-Action Protocol: An Opportunity Lost" (2009) 72(5) *Modern Law Review* 783–814
WHITTAKER, S., "Distinctive Features of the New Consumer Contract Law" (2017) 133 *Law Quarterly Review* 47–72
——, "Consumer Contracts" in H. BEALE (ed.), *Chitty on Contracts* (London, Sweet & Maxwell, 32nd ed., 2015), Vol. II
——, "Who Determines What Civil Courts Decide? Private Rights, Public Policy and EU Law" in D. LECZYKIEWICZ and S. WEATHERILL (eds.), *The Involvement of EU Law in Private Law Relationships* (Oxford, Hart Publishing, 2013), 89–129
——, "Judicial Interventionism and Consumer Contracts" (2001) 117 *Law Quarterly Review* 215–220
WILHELMSSON, T., "Varieties of Welfarism in European Contract Law" (2004) 10(6) *European Law Journal* 712–733
ZUCKERMAN, A., *Civil Procedure* (London, LexisNexis, 2003)
——, *Zuckerman on Civil Procedure: Principles of Practice* (London, Sweet & Maxwell, 3rd ed., 2013)

# INDEX

# ABOUT THE AUTHOR

Dr. Anthi Beka works as legal administrator with the chambers of Judge M. Vilaras at the Court of Justice of the European Union. She obtained her doctoral degree with honors from the Faculty of Law, Economics and Finance (Research Unit in Law) of the University of Luxembourg, where she worked as a research and teaching assistant in European Private Law. She undertook graduate studies in European Law at the College of Europe in Bruges, Belgium, as well as in Civil Law, Civil Procedural and Labor Law at the Aristotle University of Thessaloniki, Greece.

www.ingramcontent.com/pod-product-compliance
Ingram Content Group UK Ltd.
Pitfield, Milton Keynes, MK11 3LW, UK
UKHW051919100926
8556IPUK00021B/1260

9 781780 686172